Paris

Maps

About the authors

Andrew Gumbel was born in a distant corner of that great anonymous expanse, the London suburbs. He first decided he loved London at the age of 10, and has been trying to make sense of it ever since. A journalist as well as a travel writer, he has returned to London periodically between lengthy periods abroad as a foreign correspondent for *The Guardian* and *The Independent*. He currently lives in Los Angeles.

Dana Facaros and Michael Pauls have now written over 30 Cadogan Guides. For three years they and their two children Jackson and Lily lived in a tiny Umbrian hilltop village, then an equally remote French village in the Lot valley, where they have now returned after a brief spell on the southern Irish coast. Their Paris guide was written while staying in Andrew Gumbel's flat on Boulevard Sébastopol.

Updated 2005 by Lily Delancey Pauls (Paris) and Joss Waterfall (London). Thanks too to David Winch, Paul Jessop, Jacqueline Chnéour and Diane Calvet.

Cadogan Guides
Network House, 1 Ariel Way,
London W12 7SL
info@cadoganguides.co.uk
www.cadoganguides.com

The Globe Pequot Press
246 Goose Lane, PO Box 480, Guilford,
Connecticut 06437–0480

Cover design by Kicca Tommasi
Book design by Andrew Barker
Art Director: Sarah Rianhard-Gardner
Cover photographs © front: ImageState / Alamy and Beth Evans, back: FAN & MROSS Travelstock / Alamy
Maps © Cadogan Guides, drawn by Maidenhead Cartographic Services Ltd
Managing Editor: Natalie Pomier
Editorial Assistant: Nicola Jessop
Editors: Antonia Cunningham and Dominique Shead, with assistance from David Winch
Proofreading: Catherine Bradley and Dominique Shead
Indexing: Isobel McLean

Printed in Italy by Legoprint
A catalogue record for this book is available from the British Library
ISBN 1-86011-194-7

Please help us to keep this guide up to date. We have done our best to ensure that the information in this guide is correct at the time of going to press, but places and facilities are constantly changing, and standards and prices in hotels and restaurants fluctuate. We would be delighted to receive any comments concerning existing entries or omissions. Authors of the best letters will receive a copy of the Cadogan Guide of their choice.

Introduction

Empress of townes, exalt in honour;
In beawtie beryng the crone imperiall;
Swete paradise precelling in pleasure;
London, thou art the flour of Cities all.

William Dunbar

The man who is tired of London is tired of life.

Dr Johnson

Prince, aux dames Parisiennes
De beau parler donne le pris;
Quoy qu'on die d'Italiennes,
Il n'est bon bec que de Paris.

François Villon

The universe does nothing but pick up the cigar butts of Paris.

Théophile Gautier

These two cities have been at it since the Middle Ages, and if anything, the passing centuries have only amplified the boasting. One thing is certain: each of these two Imperial, imperious urban personalities dominates the country it leads. Each of them, today, contains a solid fifth of its country's population; each jealously draws all the talent, all the money, all the glitter, to itself, leaving only crumbs for a Bordeaux or a Birmingham.

Politically, economically and culturally, London and Paris today are closer than they have been for 700 years. William Dunbar and François Villon wrote their tributes shortly after the Hundred Years War, the big commotion that helped spin these two cities into very different orbits. Even before that their political destinies had been cast. London's merchants kept their fists firmly clenched around the strings of their King's purse, and helped force him to sign the Magna Carta. Paris's merchants overplayed their hand in 1358, under Etienne Marcel, and their king squashed them once and for all. So Paris became a city that looks the way kings and dukes, and their mistresses, and their favoured architects, wanted it to look, while London's plan, like a tree trunk, shows only rings of helter-skelter property speculation. Paris grew up tightly packed behind a wall; London had all the room in the world to sprawl. That's why it has so many more trees. In manners too, Paris took its cues from a court and aristocracy that liked to fool around, while London, except for a refreshing Hogarthian interlude in the 18th century, stayed generally under the influence of its serious and respectable merchants; instead of sexual tolerance, duels and the occasional revolution, it settled for Protestantism, tea and early closing hours.

When these cities had their differences, London nearly always won. A Londoner founded Paris's first fashion house, and when Baron Haussmann started building little residential parks around Paris they were called *les squares* – even though London's first squares were inspired by the Place des Vosges. Throughout it all, naturally, the Londoners were jealous of Paris, and the Parisians looked across the Channel with disdain.

But long before the Channel Tunnel and the Eurostar, fate has been slowly knitting these two surly twins back together. A major landmark in the process, an event that convinced many on both sides that the British and French were meant to be friends after all, was Queen Victoria's trip to Paris for the World Fair in 1855. Another landmark of a sort came in 1977, when London closed down the old market in Covent Garden at the same time Paris was knocking down the last iron arches of Les Halles – a perfect symbol for the near-total yuppification that has overtaken both central cities in recent years. Convergence has been on the march ever since. In these days when London is filled with ersatz bistros and Parisians study the financial papers over a pint in their Irish pubs, getting to know the real cities underneath the Euro-bland veneer can be difficult; if they have anything in common, these former Imperial capitals are equal masters at keeping up appearances. A good, steady, cold-eyed guidebook might come in handy, above all for having fun with the stereotypes...

A Parisian, on average, is more likely to be seen carrying an umbrella; a Londoner much, much more likely to read his wine label in a restaurant. Londoners, like the Chinese, are still fond of bright colours for their city – shiny pub fronts and red buses; Parisians find a quieter elegance in the serene unbroken grey of their building stone, covered by the red tile and bluish-tinted metal roofs, occasionally highlighted by a spot of gilding that brings a streetscape together. Ride the bus. Go down the back streets. Ask some difficult questions; stick your nose in. Take some mental notes about these towns, and tell us how you liked them.

A Guide to the Guide

This guide is aimed at those of you who haven't much time to spend in these two great capitals of Europe. Getting from one to the other couldn't be easier, and each can be rewarding for a week, a weekend or even just a day trip. The **Travel** chapter will tell you how to get to London and to Paris, move between the two, orientate yourself when you arrive, and get around efficiently.

Each half of the book launches with a few **practical tips**, then gets right to the heart of the matter with an alphabetical list of **Essential Sights** – the big places you've heard about, and seen in a thousand photos, the places your friends will ask you about when you get home. This is followed with a chapter (or two) describing the city's key areas, or **Neighbourhoods**, or ***Quartiers*** – places which may not be full of museums but which have a distinct atmosphere of their own, where just walking round the streets is a pleasure in itself (to plan your day, look at the box at the very end of each neighbourhood for suggestions for sights or things to do nearby). If museums are your passion, though, you can find just what you want, from the imposing to the quirky, in the comprehensive **Museums and Galleries** chapter.

Shopping gives you clues about which areas to head for to stock up on gifts to take home or treats for yourself, from department stores to bookshops to buzzing markets; and if you wake up and the sun is shining, **Green Spaces** covers both the famous and the lesser known parks to help you decide where to take the air. **Children and Sports** makes plenty of suggestions for active toddlers, trendy teens or sports fanatics, and **Food and Drink**, **Where to Stay** and bang-up-to-date **Entertainment and Nightlife** listings ensure you get the best out of London and Paris whatever your budget.

Travel

Getting to Europe from North America

By Air to London

London has five airports, with flights landing frequently from practically every major city in the USA and Canada. Shop around and consider the less obvious airlines as well as major carriers like British Airways. Travel time for direct flights from New York or Montreal is 6 hours, from Los Angeles 9 hours. Flights from New York start at around $350, from LA at $450, from Montreal or Toronto at $450 and from Vancouver at $500.

The best place to find value flights is the **Internet**: in the USA, *www.expedia.com*, *www.flights. com*, *www.priceline.com*, *www.travelocity.com*, *www.hotwire.com*; in Canada, *www.flightcentre.ca*, *www.last minuteclub.ca*, *www.exitnow. ca*.

London's Airports

Heathrow, **t** 0870 000 0123, *www.baa.co.uk*. The largest of London's airports, with four passenger terminals, is about 15 miles west of the centre.

Gatwick, **t** 0870 000 2468, *www.baa.co.uk*. Two terminals, about 20 miles south of London. Handles a lot of charter flights and the less prestigious airlines.

Stansted, **t** 0870 000 0303, *www.baa.co.uk*. The furthest from London, about 35 miles to the northeast, but in compensation is far and away the most pleasant. Only a few airlines, mostly arriving from continental Europe, use it for now, but it is likely to expand as pressure on Heathrow and Gatwick increases.

London City Airport, **t** (020) 7646 0088, *www.londoncityairport.com*. About 6 miles east of the centre, serves mainly business passengers arriving from Europe.

Luton, **t** (01582) 405100, *www.london-luton.com*. Has had a complete overhaul and new modern design, but can still be overcrowded. Mostly charter flights for British tourists heading for the sun.

Paris's Airports

Charles de Gaulle, **t** 01 48 62 22 80, also known as **Roissy** from the suburb in which it is located. North of Paris.

Orly, **t** 01 49 75 52 52. South, but a little nearer the centre.

Major Carriers

Air Canada, **t** 888 247 2262, *www.aircanada.ca*.

American Airlines, **t** 800 433 7300, *www.aa.com*.

British Airways, **t** 800 247 9297, *www.ba.com*.

Continental Airlines, **t** 800 231 0856, *www.continental.com*.

Delta, **t** 800 241 4141, *www.delta.com*.

United Airlines, **t** 800 538 2929, *www.ual.com*.

Virgin Atlantic, **t** 800 862 8621, *www.virgin-atlantic.com*.

By Air to Paris

Paris, as a major transatlantic destination, often benefits in the airline price wars, though direct flights can still be over $1,000. There are many discount options; check the travel section of your Sunday paper. Agencies that have long had cheap flight options to Paris are: **CTS Travel**, **t** 877 287 6665, *www.cts travelusa.com*; **STA Travel**, **t** 800 781 4040, *www.statravel.com*.

From Canada, there are decidedly fewer juicy options: **Travel Cuts** is a good place to start hunting: branches throughout Canada, **t** 866 246 9762, *www.travelcuts.com*.

Also try the websites listed above.

Between the Two Cities: London–Paris–London

By Air

For getting between Paris and London, few air fares can match the Eurostar for price and convenience. For best prices by air keep an eye peeled for special deals in the Sunday papers, *Time Out*, and in the window of your local travel agent. A cheaper option is to travel with one of the low-cost **no-frills airlines** such as **easyJet**, **t** 0871 750 0100, *www.easyjet.com*, or **Ryanair**, **t** 0818 30 30 30, *www.ryanair.com*. **BA** and **Air France** offer competitive packages with a selection of hotels.

Travellers under 26 or students under 32 can pick up discounts at branches of **STA**, **t** (020) 7361 6161, *www.statravel.co.uk*, or branches of **Trailfinders**, **t** (020) 7938 3939, *www.trailfinders.com*.

By Rail

Through the Channel Tunnel, it's under 3hrs on the high-speed **Eurostar** train directly between Paris Gare du Nord and London Waterloo. Fares are generally lower than planes, at about £79 standard class APEX return (though ask about special offers), there are about 20 trains a day in each direction, and the stations are much more convenient than the airport. You keep your baggage with you so check-in is only 20mins and there's no weight limit. The terminal is clean and modern. If you want to travel in comfort, First Class offers wider seats and a meal, and Premium First adds an executive car to whisk you to and from the station in style. Eurostar also offers **city break packages**.

Eurostar, **t** 08705 186186, *www.eurostar.com*, or book in person at Waterloo station.

By Bus

The cheapest way to get between the cities is by bus or coach; from Victoria Coach Station in London to Paris takes about 8hrs.

Eurolines, Victoria Coach Station, **t** 08705 143219, *www.eurolines.co.uk*.

By Car

You can take your car on a train through the Channel Tunnel with **Eurotunnel** (what used to be called 'Le Shuttle'), between Folkestone and Calais. The crossing under the Channel should only take 35mins, during which time you can stay in the car or get out and stretch your legs and use the facilities, but in busy periods you may have to queue. Prices fluctuate according to the season.

Eurotunnel, **t** 08705 353535, *www.eurotunnel.com*.

Any car entering France must have its registration and insurance papers. If you're coming from the UK, the dip of the headlights must be adjusted to the right. Carrying a warning triangle is mandatory. Drivers with a valid licence from an EU country, Canada, the USA or Australia don't need an international licence.

Arrivals

Arriving by Air in London

Heathrow: There is an excellent new direct train link from Heathrow to Paddington, the **Heathrow Express**, costing £13 one-way and taking a mere 15mins.

All Heathrow terminals link up with the **London Underground** system, which runs from 5.30am to midnight. The frequent Piccadilly Line service gets you into the centre in about an hour for about £3.80. If you have a lot of luggage and your destination is not on the Piccadilly Line, it may be worth getting off at ⊖ *Earls Court* or ⊖ *South Kensington* and proceeding by taxi.

There is also an **Airbus A2** service, **t** 08705 757747, which provides far more space for luggage but is also less frequent, slower (depending on traffic), quite a bit more expensive (about £8) and only runs until 7pm. It goes to King's Cross with stops at the Kensington Hilton in Holland Park Avenue, Notting Hill Gate, Queensway, Paddington, Marble Arch and Russell Square.

If all this sounds like too much hassle, you can take a **taxi**, but it will set you back £35–50 and, if you arrive during the rush hour, could take as long as 90mins.

Gatwick: The most practical way into town is by the **Gatwick Express** train, **t** 0870 530 1530; this non-stop service to Victoria station (£12) leaves every 15mins from 5am until 1.35am. Look out for the signs in your terminal. **National Express**, t 0870 575 7747, runs 18 coaches a day (service 025) direct to Victoria Coach Station (£6 single). Don't even think about a taxi.

Stansted: The **Stansted Express**, **t** 0845 950 5000, runs every 30mins (every 15mins at peak times) between 6am and midnight to and from Liverpool Street Station, taking 45mins. Tickets cost £13.50 single. **Airbus A6** runs every 20mins to Victoria Coach Station, Marble Arch and Hyde Park Corner, taking 1hr 40mins.

There are less frequent services all night. Tickets cost £10 single.

London City: A regular **Airbus** shuttles between the airport and Liverpool Street every 10 mins. Shuttle buses also connect the airport with Canning Town, Canary Wharf and Liverpool St stations. A taxi ride into the City of London costs around £15.

Luton: Between 8am and 10pm, **Thameslink**, **t** 0845 330 6333, runs frequent trains from King's Cross Thameslink Station (10mins' walk from the King's Cross Station), via Blackfriars, London Bridge and Farringdon, to Luton Airport Parkway. Tickets cost £10 single. At Luton a free shuttle bus takes you to and from the airport. **Greenline bus 757**, **t** 0870 608 7261, runs roughly every half-hour between Luton Airport and Victoria Coach Station, via the West End. Tickets cost £8.50 single.

Arriving by Air in Paris

You won't need to take a **taxi** from either **Roissy/Charles de Gaulle** or **Orly** unless you have tons of baggage. However, they aren't the airport rip-off they are in some cities (about €40 to central Paris from Roissy and €25 from Orly depending on traffic).

Roissy: Terminal 2 at Roissy is directly on the **RER B** line to central Paris, Gare du Nord (around €7.50); Terminal 1 is linked to the RER B by airport shuttle bus (so for travelling to or from this terminal a direct bus service to Paris is probably preferable). All airport RER tickets allow you to transfer on to the Métro to complete your journey.

Air France buses (€10–11.50) run from both terminals to Porte Maillot and the Arc de Triomphe and to Gare de Lyon and Gare Montparnasse; or take the slightly cheaper RATP (city) **Roissybus** (€8) to the American Express Offices on Rue Scribe. Buses depart every 15 mins, 5.45am–11pm; 1hr journey.

Orly: Orly is linked every 4–8mins by an automatic métro, Orlyval (€9), to the **RER B** line to central Paris, Gare du Nord. All airport RER tickets allow you to transfer on to the Métro to complete your journey.

Air France buses (€7.60) to the Air France terminal at the Invalides and Gare Montparnasse (36 Av du Maine, until 11pm); the **Orlybus** (€5.50) goes to the RER station at Place Denfert-Rochereau. Buses depart every 15–20mins, 6am–11pm; 45mins journey.

Arriving by Train in London

Waterloo station is just south of the Thames and is on the **Underground**'s Northern line, Bakerloo line and Jubilee Line, any of which will take you straight into the centre in a matter of 10mins. There is a direct link from the international terminal and it's about a 5min walk inside the station; just follow the signs.

If you've got a lot of baggage it might be better to take a **taxi**, which will cost you from £10–15; there's a taxi rank just as you exit the Eurostar gate.

Bus 211 goes from Waterloo to Westminster, Victoria and Sloane Square.

Arriving by Train in Paris

Gare du Nord is just as central as Waterloo and is on two RER lines and two Métro lines. The station is large and on several levels: **taxis** are down a level and not expensive.

If you're going straight on to the **Métro** from the Eurostar, a good tip is to send someone off the train fast to start queuing at the Métro *guichet* before the whole train gets there! If it's too late, and you're only in Paris for the day, **buses** from the front of the station will sell you a ticket on board and get you to another Métro station away from the crowds.

Passports, Visas and Customs

London: Britain has opted not to join the eight-strong group of European countries (the Schengen Group) practising an open-border policy, so EU citizens will still have to bring their passports or identity cards. That means a few delays and detours, but basically they can expect to breeze through Customs in a separate queue to avoid hold-ups. Anyone else can expect a fair grilling, particularly at airports. If you are a national of the United States, Canada, Australia, New Zealand, South Africa, Japan, Mexico or Switzerland, you won't need a visa to get into the country if you are just on holiday or on a business trip.

Paris: Visitors from the EU, USA or Canada can enter France for up to 90 days without a visa. If you plan to stay longer than 90 days, you're officially supposed to have the proper visa in your passport to apply for a *carte de séjour*. Other nationals must apply for a visa just to get in.

Duty-free allowances have been abolished within the EU. For travellers from outside the EU, the duty-free limits are 1 litre of spirits or 2 litres of liquors (port, sherry or champagne), plus 2 litres of wine and 200 cigarettes.

Much larger quantities – up to 10 litres of spirits, 90 litres of wine, 110 litres of beer and 3,200 cigarettes – bought locally, can be taken through Customs provided that you are travelling between EU countries, and can prove that they are for private consumption only.

Getting Around London

London Transport*, t *(020) 722 1234. Transport for London's website, www.tfl.gov.uk, has information on the Tube, bus, DLR, river transport, rail and taxis.

By Underground and DLR

London's **Underground** system (also known as the Tube) is 100 years old, and it shows. It's creaky and unpunctual, and the most expensive city transport system in Europe, a single adult ticket costing from £2, compared with less than 95p in Paris. For better or worse, though, it is still by far the quickest way to cross London, especially during office hours; very useful lines for the main sights include the Central Line and the speedy Piccadilly Line. Trains run from around 5.30am (7am on Sundays) until at least 11.30pm and as late as 1am on some lines (no service on Xmas Day).

The East End, Docklands and Greenwich are served by the **Docklands Light Railway**, or DLR, an overground monorail which links up with the Tube at Bank and Tower Hill (call the DLR travel hotline, **t** (020) 7363 9700, or visit *www.tfl.gov.uk/dlr*). DLR trains run daily till 11.30pm.

By Bus

London's buses are much cheaper than the Underground, and at least you can see trees and sky, as well as the life of the city zipping by. Since the bus system was deregulated, many different private companies have been running services all over town, but all are integrated into the London Transport network. Prices are simple: £1.20 for the whole of London. On some routes you pay before you board the bus (ticket machines are located at the bus stops). If you plan to use the bus a lot, you should pick up a bus map, available from major Underground stations. After midnight a large network of N-prefixed **night buses** takes over; the hub is Trafalgar Square.

There is a vast range of **tourist buses**, with stops all over central London – for example the **Hop-on Hop-off**, which takes you round all the main sights and allows you to get on and off as many times as you like.

By Train

Overground trains around London are integrated into the London Transport system and can be useful for crossing large chunks of town, or else for accessing certain parts which the Underground neglects. Two useful services are the **Thameslink**, which starts at Luton Airport and snakes through West Hampstead, Kentish Town, King's Cross and Blackfriars and the south London suburbs including Wimbledon; and the north London **Silverlink**, which starts in Richmond and goes through Kew Gardens, Hampstead and Highbury on its way through to the East End.

The rail lines are all marked on the larger Underground maps (called *Journey Planners*), and you don't have to pay extra if you have a Travelcard (*see* p.10). Also look out for the quick and efficient **Waterloo and City** line (on the Underground) between Waterloo and Bank.

By Taxi

Taxis are part of the mythology of London, perhaps because their drivers are the only people who can make sense of the great metropolitan labyrinth. Cabbies have to train for 3 years to take their qualifying exam, known as The Knowledge. For years taxis conformed to a single sleek black design, but recently there have been some changes, notably the advent of advertising and different body colours. You can still recognize them, however, by the distinctive For Hire

Tube and Bus Tickets and Passes

The Underground fare system is organized in concentric zones, Zone 1 being the centre, and Zone 6 being the outermost ring including, among other places, Heathrow Airport. Pick up a map from any station and you will see that the lines are colour-coded to make them easier to follow.

The most practical kind of ticket is an **Off-Peak One Day Travelcard**, from £4.70, which you can buy to cover as few zones as you need and which is valid on buses and overground trains as well. One-Day Travelcards are available after 9.30am; weekly and monthly passes are available any time, although you'll need a passport photo to get these. Zone 1 tickets are now sold in useful **carnets** which cost £17 for 10 tickets (saving you £3).

You can also buy a **Weekend Travelcard** for less than the price of two One-Day Travelcards and valid for night buses on the first night.

If you can plan your day using only buses, by far your best bet is to buy a **One Day Bus Pass** for just £3, which covers all of London. You can now also buy a book of six bus tickets for £6 from newsagents.

Never ever travel beyond the zone or bus stop you have bought a ticket for. Even if you present yourself openly to the excess fares window, you may be liable for an instant £10 'penalty fare' (£5 on buses).

signs on the roof which light up in orange when the cab is free.

During the day it is easy to hail a taxi off the street, unless it's raining when they all disappear. All licensed cabs are metered. They are more expensive than in most cities, but you can be confident of getting to your destination by the quickest route. For lost property call **t** (020) 7833 0996. If you want to order a taxi, contact **Dial-A-Cab**, **t** (020) 7253 5000.

Black cabs are harder to find at night, and more expensive after 8pm, and you may choose to call a **minicab**. These tend to be cheaper, less reliable and occasionally a little hazardous. Some good ones are:

Atlas Cars, **t** (020) 7602 1234.

Lady Cabs, **t** (020) 7254 3501, a specialist service run by women for women.

Town and Country Cabs, **t** (020) 7622 6222. For South and Central London.

By Car

Traffic in London moves at an average of 8 miles an hour during the day, so you will be much better off forgetting about a car. Parking is also a huge problem. Car parks and meters are very expensive and can prove ruinous if you outstay your welcome – at least £40 for a parking fine (or £80 if you leave it for longer than two weeks). Restrictions on parking, both on meters and on single yellow lines, vary wildly from borough to borough and catch out even switched-on Londoners by changing with no notice. If you're very unlucky you will have a nasty yellow clamp placed around one of your wheels. There is one even worse horror that could befall you, which is having your car towed away altogether. Call **t** (020) 7747 4747 to find out where your vehicle is and bring at least £150 in cash to the vehicle pound.

To add to these miseries, in February 2003 a £5 daily 'congestion charge' was introduced for driving within a designated central zone, marked on the streets of entry. You need to pay by 10pm on the day of travel; see *www.cclondon.com*, **t** 0845 900 1234.

A car can nevertheless be useful in London, particularly for trips out of town. You don't need to carry your driving papers with you, but if you are stopped you can be asked to show them at a police station within five days.

If you are hiring a car, you need to be over 21 and have at least one year's experience.

Avis, central booking **t** 0870 010 0287, *www.avis.com*.

easyCar, **t** 0906 333 3333, *www.easyCar.com*.

Hertz, central booking **t** 0870 844 8844, *www.hertz.com*.

By Bicycle

The bicycle is a good mode of transport in London, if you can cope with the danger and bear the pollution. It is faster than going by car, at least during the day, and more pleasant than the Tube, especially if you make use of London's extensive parkland.

You could also contact **The London Cycling Campaign**, **t** (020) 7928 7220, *www.lcc.org.uk*, for advice and maps of safe routes.

Dial-a-Bike, 51 Marsham St, **t** (020) 7233 4224.

On Your Bike, 52–4 Tooley St (by London Bridge), **t** (020) 7378 6669. Bike hire.

By River

There is a plethora of commercial companies that run services from Westminster Pier or Charing Cross Pier, both just south of Trafalgar Square. Services downriver to Greenwich and the Thames Barrier – the most attractive destinations – run every half-hour and take about 45–50mins. In the other direction, services upriver to Kew, Richmond and Hampton Court are more erratic and may not run more than four times a day. You buy your ticket at the pier or on the boat. Call London Transport on **t** (020) 7222 1234 for further info, or visit the Transport for London website, *www.tfl.gov.uk*.

Getting Around Paris

The RATP is the authority controlling the buses and the Métro. For recorded information call **t** 01 43 46 14 14; for information in French call **t** 08 36 68 77 14 (*35¢ a minute*), *www.ratp.fr*.

Lost property, **t** 01 40 06 75 27.

By Métro and RER

The **Métro** is a godsend to disorientated visitors; not only is it quick and convenient for travelling, but its stations serve as easy reference points for finding addresses. Contrasts with the London Underground are unavoidable. A ride in Paris costs less than half as much, and for that you get cleaner stations and faster service. A minor complaint would be about the *direction* system, which is harder to read than the simple coloured maps in London, where each line has a name. To find the right train, it isn't simply a matter of looking for 'northbound' or 'eastbound'; you'll need to look at the map and remember the name of the station at the *end of the line*, in the direction you wish to travel.

The *Réseau Express Régional* (**RER**) is Paris's suburban commuter train system, run jointly by the SNCF (Société Nationale des Chemins de Fer Français) and RATP, so it's separate, but part of the system, and you can use Métro tickets on it within the Paris boundaries. It can come in handy for getting across town fast or for visiting places like the Musée d'Orsay or the Jardin du Luxembourg, where it has the closest station. From almost all the other stations, you can easily change on to the Métro. The RER can also take you to Versailles, Disneyland, or out to the airports.

By Bus

Bus routes are more of a challenge than the Métro, but much more fun. An unused Métro ticket is equally valid for the bus, but you'll need two separate tickets if you travel by both Métro and bus. Also note that you can change Métro lines as often as you want on the same journey for the same ticket, but the bus requires a fresh ticket with each bus you catch. Enter from the front of the bus and leave from the middle or the rear; press the *arrêt demandé* button just before your stop; you'll need to stamp your ticket (*oblitérer*) in the machine next to the driver as you enter.

The *Noctambus*, Paris's **night bus** network, can be useful; there are 18 lines, many converging at Place du Châtelet from points around the edge of the city.

Route 29, through the Marais (from Gare St-Lazare to Gare de Lyon), features a modern version of the old Paris buses with open-back platforms from which to view the city.

Sightseeing: *Paris L'Open Tour*, *www.paris-opentour.com*, a system of tourist buses with an open upper deck, follows a circular route of the principal sites with further loops out to Montmartre and to Bercy, €25.15 for two days, get on and off anywhere.

Balabus (operated by RATP) runs from the Grande Arche along the river to the Gare de Lyon and back (*from 1pm to 8pm Sundays and holidays 15 April–15 Sept*); needs three tickets for the full one-way journey.

Montmartrobus, another circular route, runs up, down and around Montmartre; get on or off anywhere, one ticket per journey; or ride the *Funiculaire de Montmartre* instead of climbing all the steps up to the Sacré-Cœur.

Tickets and Passes

Buying single tickets (€1.40) is crazy – always get a ***carnet*** of 10 from any Métro window or machine for €10.50, good for buses too. Most Parisians carry the basic pass, valid for buses, Métro, RER and SNCF suburban trains.

A ***carte orange*** weekly pass is €15.40; a month is €50.40. These are valid for two zones only; for more zones the fee is higher; bring a passport photo when you buy and be sure to write the number of your carrying pouch on your ticket, or you could end up with a fine.

Note – these passes expire at the end of the week or month, so purchase them at the beginning of the period. There is also a special tourist travel card, ***Paris Visite***, starting at €8.35 for 1 day and €18.25 for 3 days. This is a rotten deal – you'll need to ride seven or eight times a day just to break even in comparison with a *carnet*.

Always keep your ticket until the end of the journey, not only for spot checks, but because some of the bigger stations have automatic exit gates that require it to let you out.

By Taxi

There are 14,900 taxis in Paris and on the whole they're competent, and a pleasure to ride. They'll get you to the station on time if it kills you both. Radio taxis (**Taxis Bleus**, **t** 01 49 36 10 10, and **G7**, **t** 01 47 39 47 39, credit cards accepted, charge from time of call) can be especially helpful in rush hours.

By Car

This is, of course, absurd. Parking is almost impossible in Paris, and battalions of the world's most elegant meter maids cheerfully await your every indiscretion. None of the smaller hotels and few even of the luxury variety have a garage. Underground car parks are fairly common, though (shown on the Michelin map with a blue P). Remember the golden rule of driving in France: at intersections without signals, *the car on your right has right of way*.

Hire Car Firms

City Loc, 4 Av de la Porte de Villiers, 17e, **t** 01 40 68 96 96, Ⓜ *Porte de Champeret*.

Rual, 78 Bd Soult, 12e, **t** 01 43 45 52 20, Ⓜ *Porte de Vincennes*.

SNAC, 118 Rue de la Croix-Nivert, 15e, **t** 01 48 56 11 11, Ⓜ *Félix-Faure*.

By Bicycle

Fearless, experienced urban cyclists can hire bikes by the half-day, day or week from:

La Maison du Vélo, 11 Rue Fénelon, 10e, **t** 01 42 81 24 72, Ⓜ *Gare du Nord*.

Paris à Vélo C'est Sympa!, 37 Bd Bourdon, 4e, **t** 01 48 87 60 01, Ⓜ *Bastille*.

Paris-Vélo, 4 Rue du Fer-à-Moulin, 5e, **t** 01 43 37 59 22, Ⓜ *Censier-Daubenton*.

By Boat

The famous *bateaux-mouches* got their name (literally, fly boats), because the first ones were built in Lyon, on the Quai des Mouches. Most charge €8–10 for a 1hr tour, and may offer lunch/dinner cruises.

Bateaux-Mouches de Paris, **t** 01 42 25 96 10, *www.bateaux-mouches.fr*. From Pont de l'Alma, RER *Pont de l'Alma* (north side, 8e); this one has night tours in summer and a fancy dinner cruise for €77. Lunch is available Sats, €46, and on public holidays, €54.

Bateaux Parisiens, **t** 01 44 11 33 44, *www.bateauxparisiens.com*. From the Port de La Bourdonnais, 7e, Ⓜ *Bir-Hakeim/Iéna*.

Canauxrama, **t** 01 42 39 15 00, *www.location-bateaux.info*. Reserve for 3hr tours of Canal St-Martin (€12).

Paris Canal, **t** 01 42 40 96 97, *www.canauxrama.com*. From the Musée d'Orsay up the Canal St-Martin to La Villette, through old locks and under tunnels.

Vedettes de Paris, **t** 01 47 05 71 29, *www.vedettesdeparis.com*. From the Port de Suffren, 7e, Ⓜ *Bir-Hakeim*. Dinner cruises €88.50; book ahead.

Vedettes du Pont Neuf, **t** 01 53 00 98 98. From Square du Vert-Galant, Ile de la Cité, 1er, Ⓜ *Pont-Neuf*.

London: Introduction

Oh thou, resort and mart of all the earth
Chequer'd with all complexions of mankind
And spotted with all crimes, in whom I see
Much that I love and more that I admire,
And all that I abhor...

William Cowper, *The Task*, Book III (1785)

London, like all great cities, has a habit of going through drastic mood swings: grey, worthy and dull one minute, hip and ultra-modern the next. Down its long history it has been accused of everything from provincialism to irredeemable sinfulness;

The Pick of London in a Weekend

There's nothing more dreary than spending a week in London going round museum after museum. Variety should be the watchword, whether this is your first time in the city or your 50th. Treat the following not as a list of must-sees to check off one by one, but rather a rich menu from which to pick the items that suit you best.

First-time visitors

National Gallery, Westminster Abbey, Tate Britain/Tate Modern, Soho, British Museum, St Paul's, the South Bank, Victoria and Albert Museum, Portobello Market, Greenwich (including a boat ride down there) and the London Eye for the views.

Occasional visitors

Banqueting House and Houses of Parliament, the Sir John Soane Museum, the Clink and the Old Operating Theatre, the Wallace Collection, Holland Park, Hampstead, Kew Gardens, Hampton Court.

Residents

Spencer House and the Queen's Chapel, Westminster Hall and, if you can, the Foreign Office, Jeremy Bentham's corpse, St Etheldreda, Kensington Palace, Leighton House, Carlyle's House, Highgate Cemetery, Rotherhithe.

Not been back lately

To catch a whiff of the extraordinary changes in London, all you really have to do is stand in the middle of Soho in mid-evening and marvel at the variety, exuberance and sheer numbers of the people around you. Eat at one of the Moroccan or stylish hip hotel restaurants such as One Aldwych or the Metropolitan, or grab some conveyor-belt sushi served by robots on Poland Street. Further afield, there is the irrepressible trendiness of Notting Hill. For sightseeing, the South Bank is a must, particularly the London Eye, Oxo Tower, the rebuilt Globe Theatre, the Millennium Bridge and the developments at Butler's Wharf. Look out, too, for quirky new places such as Tate Modern or the Aquarium and Saatchi Gallery at County Hall, and ones that have had a major overhaul such as the British Museum and the Wallace Collection.

at times it has positively creaked under the weight of its own impossible size and complexity. At others, it has been hailed as everything a city could ever hope to be: a beacon of wealth, liberty, cosmopolitanism and artistic flair. And so, just when it was being written off as the crumbling capital of a dead empire, London has come roaring back to life. Freed from the shackles of empire and the bitter ideological divisions of the Thatcher years, it is enjoying a renaissance of extraordinary dimensions. In Covent Garden or Notting Hill or Islington, you can barely move for people thronging to the latest designer shop, the newest art opening, or the hottest ethnic restaurant. The capital is being redefined by a new, highly creative generation of artists and designers iconoclastic enough to break down the fusty London of the past and rebuild it in their

Not been back in years

In addition to the above, you'll probably want to have a sniff round Docklands, not just the monster towers at Canary Wharf, but also less obvious novelties, such as the riverfront at Rotherhithe. Go to the action-packed Science Museum which has changed beyond recognition. If you remember the strict old licensing laws, you'll get a buzz just sitting in a pub mid-afternoon and ordering a drink. As for eating, just about anywhere should come as a pleasant surprise; try a riverside location.

Can't stand all this new-fangled stuff

If what you want is good, old-fashioned London, St James's and Mayfair are the places to start. No doubt you'll stay in a favourite quiet hotel in South Kensington, or even one of the posher establishments in Mayfair, but that shouldn't stop you dropping in on Brown's or the Ritz for tea – ideal stopping-off points during shopping sprees on Jermyn Street (bespoke clothes, as well as marmalade and Earl Grey at Fortnum's). Once you've exhausted sights such as Buckingham Palace and the Wallace Collection, you might want to stroll around Chelsea, meet the eccentric pensioners at the Royal Hospital, or even venture out to the fine Adam houses at Syon Park and Osterley. Back in town, there are cocktails at the Café Royal and enticing dinner options around Covent Garden at Simpson's, The Ivy and Rules.

Romantic London

Okay, this isn't Paris or Venice, but London is more romantic than you might think. Anthony Minghella's film *Truly, Madly, Deeply* highlighted the heart-wrenching pleasures of Kenwood (those great views of the metropolis over the Heath) and the pavement cafés on the South Bank. For dreamy walks, Holland Park or the riverside at Richmond and Twickenham are perfect. Hampstead is London's dinkiest neighbourhood – visit Keats' house to relive the poet's romance with Fanny Brawne, and find yourselves a quiet nook in the atmospheric Holly Bush pub. Otherwise try kite-flying on Parliament Hill (more good views as well as bracing air), or the canal walks and Georgian rows of Canonbury (plus the romantic association of penniless Lord Compton and the rich local merchant's daughter), while Byron's or Lindsey House make fine settings for a romantic dinner.

own image. Suddenly, everything seems possible and Londoners are embracing the changes with barely a whiff of scepticism or critical distance.

The city invents and discards fads at an astonishing rate. Old definitions no longer fit the new trends: sculpture and painting have given way to new media such as video art; the erstwhile household design guru Terence Conran, meanwhile, has moved beyond the restaurant business into gastrodomes, veritable palaces of food consumption in custom-made settings such as an old tyre factory, say, or a sports car showroom. This new London has even contrived to pretend that the weather is better: pavement cafés and al fresco dining are the new watchwords, along with Italian or American coffee and Mediterranean clothes. No city in Europe is so desired, or so desirable.

Be warned, however. Amidst this creative frenzy, the old caveats about London still apply. It may be the most exciting city in Europe, but it is not the most beautiful, nor the easiest to get around. Indeed, there are times when it seems like one of those eccentric English aristocrats who deliberately dress in rags and forget to wash for weeks at a stretch. This is not a city that shouts its beauties from the rooftops, and many visitors who expect too much too quickly come away with a sense of bewildered disappointment.

There is an art to exploring London; you cannot only do the rounds of its celebrated sights and museums and say you have seen it all. You have to engage on a personal level, ferreting out neighbourhoods you feel at home in, finding little back streets you can admire without necessarily looking for them in a guidebook, discovering the museums and theatres and pubs that give you a sense of personal satisfaction. Two visitors meeting after a week in London might discover that one had hung around wine bars in Kensington, taken a river trip to Hampton Court and shopped at Harrods, while the other had sought out Freud's house, done some sketching in the National Gallery and sat in pub theatres at lunchtime. They would not have visited the same city at all, but they would both have been to London.

Once you have got over the sheer vastness and inconvenience, once you have traced out your route around the labyrinth, the sense of diversity and discovery can be immensely liberating. Nobody can know all of London – not poets, not politicians, not even guidebook writers. You have to make up your own version of it. Out of the chaos you produce a personalized sense of order, your own map of the city.

The centre is, of course, the part with most history, but that does not mean that it is necessarily the most interesting or most enjoyable to visit. What is central geographically may be only peripheral in terms of interest, and vice versa. As in Dante's *Inferno*, appearances can be deceptive. Certainly you should make sure you get to the National Gallery and St Paul's, but it would be a mistake to skip Hampstead, Greenwich or Kew just because they are not slap bang in the centre of town. In the same way, it would be foolish to spend too long in Mayfair or the City just because they happen to be where they are.

London: Practical A–Z

04

Calendar of Events

Actual dates for nearly all the events listed below change every year. Numbers for checking are given where possible.

January

1 Jan *New Year's Day Parade*.

Early Jan Harrods' after-Christmas sale.

Mid-Jan to early Feb *Chinese New Year* celebrations around Gerrard St in Soho. Lots of food and colourful floats.

February

Shrove Tues *Soho* and *Great Spitalfields Pancake Day Races*. Sprints down Carnaby Street and Spitalfields, with participants tossing pancakes in a pan; **t** (020) 7375 0441.

April

1 April Check newspapers for April Fool's Day hoaxes.

Sun before Easter *Oxford and Cambridge Boat Race*; *www.theboatrace.org*. Teams from the rival universities row their hearts out from Putney to Mortlake.

Easter Sun *Easter Day Parade* in Battersea Park, complete with funfair and sideshows.

Mid-April *London Marathon* from Blackheath to The Mall; *www.london-marathon.co.uk*.

May

Late May *Chelsea Flower Show* at the Royal Hospital Gardens, **t** 0870 906 3781. Funfairs on Hampstead Heath, Blackheath and Alexandra Park on Spring Bank Holiday Mon.

June

Throughout June *Spitalfields Festival*. Classical music in Christ Church, plus guided walks of the area; **t** (020) 7377 1362.

First Sat *Derby* horse race at Epsom racecourse, Surrey.

Early June *Greenwich Festival*: concerts, theatre and children's events, plus fireworks on the opening night. Also, *Hampton Court Festival*, opera music and dance; **t** 0870 752 7777 (*see* pp.33–4). Also, *Beating the Retreat*, floodlit evening display by the Queen's Household Division outside Buckingham Palace.

Second Sat *Trooping the Colour*. The Queen's Guards in a birthday parade for Ma'am. The date is chosen by the palace and is usually the second Saturday, but it does vary. It's difficult to get a ticket, but people line the Mall to watch.

Mid-June *Royal Ascot*. Society horse races at Ascot in Berkshire.

Late June/early July *Henley Royal Regatta*. Rowers row on the Thames while very posh spectators get sozzled in their champagne tents.

Late June to July *Wimbledon* tennis; **t** (020) 8944 1066, *www.wimbledon.org*.

June to Aug *Summer Exhibition* at the Royal Academy (*see* p.141).

June to Sept *Kenwood Lakeside Concerts*. Open-air concerts at the top of Hampstead Heath every Saturday. Magical if the weather's good; tickets **t** 0870 333 6206, *www. picnicconcerts.com*.

Consulates in London

You can always find the number of your consulate by calling directory enquiries.

Australian High Commission, Australia House, The Strand, **t** (020) 7379 4334, *www.australia.org.uk*; *open Mon–Fri 9–5*.

Canadian High Commission, 38 Grosvenor St, W1, **t** (020) 7258 6506, *www.canada.org.uk*; *open Mon–Fri 8–11am*.

US Embassy, 24 Grosvenor Square, W1, **t** (020) 7499 9000, *www.usembassy.org.uk*; *opening hours vary according to service required; see website*. There is a 24hr helpline for US citizens.

Crime and the Police

Serious crime in London has been stable for several decades. You won't be at greater risk in London than in any other biggish city in Europe; the greatest hazard is petty theft and pickpocketing, for which the usual precautions apply. Although drug use is on the increase, drugs have not become the kind of overwhelming crime problem they are in the United States or parts of southern Europe; firearms are extremely uncommon and even police officers do not carry them. Don't hang around lonely neighbourhoods late at night – Hackney or Tottenham spring to mind – and

July

First week *Gay Pride Day*; *www.pridelondon.org.uk*. Procession followed by pop concert.

Early July *Hampton Court Flower Show*; **t** 0870 906 3791 (*see* pp.33–4). The world's largest flower show in a beautiful setting.

July *City of London Festival*: classical concerts around the City; **t** (020) 7377 0540.

July to Sept *The Proms* in the Albert Hall; **t** (020) 7589 8212 (*see* p.178).

August

Aug to Sept Buckingham Palace open to the public (*see* p.31), while the usual royal inhabitants are on holiday in Scotland.

Last Sun and Mon *Notting Hill Carnival*. Steel bands, dancing and general Caribbean fun (*see* p.98).

September

Mid-Sept *Chelsea Antiques Fair*, Chelsea Old Town Hall, Kings Road.

Third week *Open House Weekend*, *www.londonopenhouse.org*. Houses and buildings which are normally closed to the public open up for free; also walking tours. Details on what's open from August.

Late Sept *Clog and Apron Race*. A sprint through Kew by gardening students in strange attire; **t** (020) 8332 5655.

October

First Sun *Pearly Harvest Festival* at St Martin-in-the-Fields (*see* p.69). Lots of folklore cockneys in their button-splashed coats playing ukeleles.

November

Late Oct/early Nov *London Film Festival*. Two weeks of national and international feature films and shorts; based at the NFT on the South Bank (*see* p.182), but with showings all over town.

5 Nov *Bonfire Night*. Fireworks and bonfires, plus plenty of booze, in parks all over London (Highbury Fields and Battersea Park are good venues, but contact Visit London on **t** 0871 566 3666, *www.visitlondon.com*, or check *Time Out* for details) to commemorate Guy Fawkes's attempt to blow up parliament in 1605.

First Sun *London to Brighton Veteran Car Run*. Starts in Hyde Park; **t** (01753) 765100 for details.

Early Nov *Lord Mayor's Show*. The new Lord Mayor goes on a grand procession through the City in his 18th-century gilded coach. Most people stand around St Paul's to watch, but you can sit down if you ask the Pageant Master: **t** (020) 7332 1456, *www.lordmayorsshow.org.uk*.

Sun nearest 11 Nov *Remembrance Day Service* to commemorate war dead at the Cenotaph in Whitehall.

Nov to Dec Christmas lights go on in Oxford Street, Regent Street, Bond Street and Trafalgar Square.

December

31 Dec New Year's celebrations beneath the Christmas tree in Trafalgar Square (*see* pp.46–7).

don't leave valuables in your hotel room. Women have a far more hassle-free time in London than in Rome or Madrid, and it is accepted as normal for a woman to be out on her own. They should watch out on the Underground, however, late at night.

You'll find the authorities sometimes jumpy about the risk of terrorist attack, particularly in the City: waste-bins have been removed from the Underground, automatic luggage lockers have been taken out of railway stations, many buildings bristle with security guards, and there are more police officers on the beat. All this may make you feel more nervous, but in fact increases your safety.

The police are usually friendly enough, although you might encounter suspicion or idle prejudice if you are Irish or black. If you need to go to the police to report a theft or other crime, simply visit your nearest station and you should receive a civil hearing – though you probably won't get your stolen goods back. In case of emergency, dial either **t** 999 or **t** 112. If you yourself get picked up by the police, you must insist, if you feel it necessary, on calling your embassy or consulate, or a lawyer if you know one. Keep your cool and remain polite at all times. Be particularly careful how you drive around Christmas time.

Lost Property

Black Cab Lost Property Office, 15 Penton St, Islington, **t** (020) 7833 0996, Mon–Fri 9–4.

London Transport Lost Property Office, 200 Baker St, Mon–Fri 9–2, **t** (020) 7486 2496.

Disabled Travellers

London is reasonably wheelchair-conscious, and most of the major sights have proper access and help on hand if necessary. There are still problems, however, with the transport system and many theatres and cinemas. The London Tourist Board has a leaflet which you can find in tourist offices called ***Information for Wheelchair Users Visiting London*** which covers hotels, tourists sights and transport.

London Transport publishes ***Access to the Underground*** and ***Tube Access Guide*** with information on lift access to Tubes, available free from Tube stations or by post from **Access and Mobility**, Transport for London, Windsor House, 42–50 Victoria Street, W1, **t** (020) 7941 4600.

Transport For All, **t** (020) 7737 2339, *www.transportforall.com*, gives information on door-to-door transport services and accessible buses and Underground stations in London.

Useful Addresses

Artsline, **t** (020) 7388 2227, *www.artsline.org.uk*. Information on access to arts venues.

Holiday Care Service, **t** 0845 124 9971. Advice on hotels, transport, tour operators.

RADAR (**Royal Association for Disability & Rehabilitation**), 12 City Forum, 250 City Road, London EC1V 8AF, **t** (020) 7250 3222, **t** (020) 7250 4119 (minicom), *www. radar.org.uk*.

SATH (Society for Accessible Travel and Hospitality), 347 5th Avenue, Suite 610, New York NY 10016, **t** (212) 447 7284, **f** (212) 725 8253, *www.sath.org*.

Tripscope, **t** 0845 758 5641, *www.tripscope.org.uk*. Help for people visiting London.

Electricity

Britain uses three-prong square-pin plugs quite unlike anything else in Europe or North America. All British plugs have detachable fuses of three, five or 13 amps, so you will need an adaptor for any electrical device you bring in from abroad. The airport is as good a place as any to find one. Note also that the electricity supply is 240 volts AC.

Health

Citizens of the European Union and some Commonwealth countries enjoy free medical care in Britain under the state National Health Service. The days when you could get free treatment on production of just a passport are probably over, so you'll need to fill out the appropriate paperwork before you leave home (in the EU the form is called an E111). Thus armed, the only things you will have to pay for are prescriptions and visits to the optician or dentist, although these should not cost more than a few pounds.

Anyone else, and that includes Americans, Africans, Indians and Canadians, should take out **medical insurance**, and in fact it would be advisable for everyone.

If you need urgent medical treatment, you should head for one of the casualty (accident and emergency) departments (in the United States known as ERs) of the major hospitals. These include St Thomas's on the South Bank, University College Hospital on Gower St in Bloomsbury and the Charing Cross Hospital on Fulham Palace Rd. You can call an ambulance by dialling **t** 999 or **t** 112.

Useful Addresses

Bliss Chemist, 5 Marble Arch. Stays open until midnight every day. Details of other late-opening chemists are available from police stations.

Dental Emergency Care Service, **t** (020) 7937 3951. An advisory service open 24 hours which will direct you to the nearest clinic for emergency dental care.

NHS Direct, **t** 0845 4647. The National Health Service helpline, offering medical advice.

Internet

London has a variety of Internet centres, ranging from cosy cafés to large warehouse-style venues. The big department stores on Oxford St often provide Internet access, too.

Cyberia, 39 Whitfield St, **t** (020) 7681 4123, *www.cyberiacafe.net*.

easyEverything, 358 Oxford St, **t** (020) 7436 0459, *www.easyeverything.com. Opening hours vary from branch to branch, but usually 8am–midnight*. Large branch of the famous Internet café chain, with 350 PCs. There are 32 other branches including Kensington High St, Tottenham Court Rd, the Strand, Wilton Rd and King's Rd.

London for Free

You'll hear plenty of moans about the high cost of living in London, so here as an antidote is a list of things to do without spending a single penny.

Museums and galleries: Most of London's best museums are now free thanks to new government subsidies (although you usually have to pay a charge for special exhibitions). These include the National Gallery, National Portrait Gallery, Tate Britain, Tate Modern, British Museum, Museum of London, Victoria and Albert Museum, Museum of London, Natural History Museum, Science Museum, Wallace Collection, National Maritime Museum, Bethnal Green Museum of Childhood,Theatre Museum, Whitechapel Art Gallery, Crafts Council Gallery, Geffrye Museum, Bank of England Museum and Imperial War Museum.

Other sights: Churches, with the exception of Westminster Abbey and St Paul's Cathedral, are all free. So, too, are the Guildhall, the Changing of the Guard outside Buckingham Palace, court cases at The Old Bailey or The Royal Courts of Justice on the Strand, the Sunday afternoon haranguing sessions at Speakers' Corner and the more frequent haranguing sessions at the Houses of Parliament. London's wonderful riverside walks and parks – St James's, Battersea Park, the 19th-century dinosaurs in Crystal Palace Park, Hampstead Heath, Hyde Park and Regent's Park – are always free. So also are the beautiful cemeteries in Kensal Green, Highgate and Brompton.

Shopping: Some of the fancier delicatessens in Soho and St James's (for example, the cheese sellers Paxton and Whitfield in Jermyn Street) will give away free nibbles, although you are under some pressure to purchase something in return. Food markets (try Berwick Street for starters) sometimes knock down the price of fruit and vegetables at the end of the day.

Entertainment: There are free foyer concerts at the National Theatre and Barbican in the early evening. Covent Garden boasts plenty of street theatre and music, although you should offer something as the hat comes round. If you turn up to concert or theatre venues at the interval, you will often find people leaving and if you ask nicely they will give you their tickets. Another option in the summer is to go up to Kenwood on Hampstead Heath on a Saturday evening. You can sit on the rolling hills and listen to the outdoor concerts there without actually paying to get in.

Maps

London is one city where wandering around clutching a map will not automatically mark you out as a visitor; few Londoners venture out of familiar territory without a copy of the *London A–Z Street Atlas*, an inch-thick book of maps with an index of street names to help you find your destination. Bus and Tube maps are available from most main Underground stations; the large *Journey Planner* maps show both Tube and British Rail links. Cyclists will find the *Central London Cyclists' Map* a helpful guide to the quickest, safest and most pleasant routes through London's traffic mayhem. Published by the London Cycling Campaign, it can be bought from their office at Unit 228, Great Guildford St, London SE1 0HS, *www.lcc.org.uk*, and from some book-shops and cycle shops.

Money and Banks

The currency in Britain is the pound sterling, divided into 100 pence. You'll come across notes worth £5, £10, £20 and £50, and coins worth 1, 2, 5, 10, 20, 50 pence, £1 and £2. London is also fully up to speed on credit card technology, and many shops, restaurants and hotels will accept Visa, Mastercard or American Express for all but the smallest purchases. Britain has not yet subscribed to the euro (single European currency), but many Oxford Street stores accept euros.

Minimum **banking hours** are Mon–Fri 9.30am–3.30pm, although many banks in central London stay open later and, in some cases, on Saturday morning too. Most branches have automatic cash dispensers (**ATMs**) open 24 hours a day; check the stickers to see if your card and PIN number will be accepted, although if you don't have a British card you can expect your bank to charge a commission fee for any transaction.

You can change **travellers' cheques** at any bank or *bureau de change*, but remember to bring a passport or similar ID along with you. By and large, the big banks offer a better rate and lower commission fees, but shop around. If you need non-British currency, *bureaux de change* will be more likely to stock it. Try:

American Express, 30–1 Haymarket, **t** (020) 7484 9600.

Chequepoint, 550 Oxford St, and other branches, **t** 0800 699799.

Thomas Cook, Victoria Station, Marble Arch and other branches, **t** (020) 7302 8600.

National Holidays

With the exception of Christmas and New Year's Day, Britain's national holidays, known as **bank holidays**, shift slightly every year to ensure they fall on a Monday. This avoids being 'cheated' out of holidays, as happens in continental Europe when they fall at the weekend, but it also leads to the absurdity of May Day being celebrated as late as 7 May. Banks and many businesses close down on bank holidays, but quite a few shops and most tourist attractions stay open. Public transport theoretically runs a Sunday service, but in practice tends to be very threadbare.

1 Jan New Year's Day (plus the following Monday if it falls on a weekend)
Mar/April Good Friday
Mar/April Easter Monday
1st Mon in May May Day
last Mon in May Spring Bank Holiday
last Mon in Aug Summer Bank Holiday
25 Dec Christmas Day
26 Dec Boxing Day (plus 27 December if one of them falls on a weekend)

Opening Hours

Traditionally, shops and offices stay open from around 9 to 5.30 or 6 – significantly earlier than the rest of Europe. Pubs and bars still have fairly strict licensing rules and many of them will not serve alcohol after 11pm. Late opening for shops is becoming more and more common, however (*see* p.130).

Post Offices

Post offices are generally open Mon–Fri 9–5.30 and Sat 9–12.20pm; avoid going at lunchtime as they can get very crowded. They are marked on most London maps (in the *A–Z*, for example, by a black star). You will be able to buy books of stamps at many newsagents.

Two of the biggest **post offices** are at 24 King William IV St next to Trafalgar Square (*open Mon–Sat 8–8*) and at King Edward St near St Paul's Cathedral. Both have stamp shops and a *poste restante* service, as well as a very useful mail collection on Sunday eves.

Postcodes: London postcodes are fairly confusing, and rely on an intimate knowledge of city geography to be intelligible. Postcodes begin with a direction (W for West, WC for West Central, N for North, NW for Northwest, and so on) and a number from 1 to 28. The full postcode then adds a letter immediately after the number, followed by a space, a number and two more letters. So a postcode might read EC1R 3ER – gobbledygook to anyone but a post office computer. This book uses postcodes sparingly, preferring to indicate the geographical district.

Pronunciation

Modern English spelling was standardized at the end of the 18th century by a small group of educationalists who evidently thought it would be hilarious to make pronunciation as difficult as possible for the uninitiated. Foreign tourists are forever inviting ridicule by asking for Glaw-sister Road or South-walk; it is hardly their fault if they are merely following the written word. Here is a survival guide to some of London's more common spelling anomalies:

Written	Spoken
Balham	Bal'm
Berkeley Square	Barkly Square
Berwick St	**Ber**rick Street
Cadogan	Caduggan
Charing Cross	Charring Cross
Cheyne Walk	Chainy Walk
Chiswick	Chizzick
Cholmondeley Walk	Chumly Walk
Clapham	Clap'm
Dulwich	Dull Itch
Gloucester Road	Gloster Road
Greenwich	Gren Itch
Grosvenor Place	Grove-ner Place
Holborn	Hoe Burn
Leicester Square	Lester Square
Southwark	Suth'k
Thames	Tems
Wapping	Wopping
Woolwich	Wool Itch

Religion

The state religion in Britain is Anglicanism, a peculiar hybrid of Protestant theology and Catholic ritual that developed after Henry VIII broke with the Roman Church to divorce his first wife, Catherine of Aragon. The biggest **Anglican** churches are St Paul's Cathedral, which has the finest organ in London, and Westminster Abbey. If you want to attend a service, a smaller church may be more to your liking. Leaf through some of the churches in the index for ideas. The biggest **Catholic churches** are Westminster Cathedral (off Victoria St) and the Brompton Oratory near the South Kensington museums. A more intimate place is St Etheldreda's in Ely Place off Holborn Circus.

London also has a sizeable **Jewish community**, concentrated around Golders Green and Stamford Hill in north London. For information about services and activities contact the Liberal Jewish Synagogue, 28 St John's Wood Road, NW8, **t** (020) 7286 5181; West London Synagogue (Reform), 33 Seymour Place, W1, **t** (020) 7723 4404; or the United Synagogue (Orthodox), Adler House, 735 High Road, N12, **t** (020) 8343 8989.

The Pakistani immigrants of the 1950s, supplemented by Bengalis, Indians and Arabs from many countries, form the backbone of the **Islamic community**. The London Central Mosque at 146 Park Road near Regent's Park, **t** (020) 7725 2212, is a magnificent building which also contains a library and nursery school. Another popular place for Friday prayers is the East London Mosque at 84–98 Whitechapel Road, **t** (020) 7247 1357.

Smoking

Britain has caught on to the anti-smoking craze in a big way, and you will find total bans in theatres, cinemas, museums, buses and Underground stations. Most restaurants have non-smoking areas, and some bars and pubs are introducing a similar partition. If you are invited to someone's home, ask in advance if smoking will be tolerated. It is considered quite normal to send guests wanting a puff into the garden or street.

Telephones

The biggest company is British Telecom, the former national monopoly. A few of their famous red telephone boxes remain; however, since mobile phones have become commonplace, booths are now seldom used. If you need to use one, coins of course are accepted (minimum charge 20p), or you can use credit or debit cards. If you are making lots of calls abroad it's worth getting an international phone card for cheap rates. For prices and information, check with any post office (the rates are constantly changing). Evening and weekend calls are always cheaper, particularly for international calls.

You can hire a phone for your stay, or if you already own a mobile phone handset you can hire a SIM card so that you pay local rates and are not charged for each incoming call.

London phone numbers differ by area. They begin with the **London code**, 020, followed by an 8-digit number. For inner London these numbers begin with 7, for outer London with 8 (so a number in the City will be **t** (020) 7xxx xxxx). Within London, you need only dial the 8-digit number; from a mobile phone or from outside London you must also dial 020. Anyone calling from abroad must dial the international prefix 00 44, then 20, then the rest of the number.

Directory enquiries are on **t** 118500. There is a charge. The telephone directory lists private numbers and businesses in separate volumes. There's also the **Yellow Pages** (*www.yell.com*), ordering businesses by activity.

Operator services: **t** 100.

International operator: **t** 155.

International directory enquiries: **t** 118505.

The **international dialling code** is 00, followed by the country code (1 for the United States and Canada, 61 for Australia, 64 for New Zealand).

Finally, Britain has peculiar **telephone jacks** that are wider than the US variety. If you need to plug in a telephone or computer, make sure you buy an adaptor, available at decent-sized general stores.

Time

Britain is one hour behind the rest of western Europe (except Portugal), just to be difficult. During the winter (roughly the end of October to the third week of March) it follows Greenwich Mean Time; in the summer it follows British Summer Time which is one hour ahead of GMT. New York is 5 hours behind London time, San Francisco 8 hours behind, while Tokyo and Sydney are 10 hours ahead.

Tipping

Britain does not have the United States' established tipping code, but 10–15 per cent is considered polite in restaurants, hairdressers, hotels and in taxis. Watch out for restaurant bills which already include a gratuity but leave space for another – a common occurrence.

Toilets

The old-fashioned underground public toilets are disappearing fast – and with good reason, given their dubious hygiene record and reputation for attracting gay men on the prowl for casual sex.

In their stead you will find free-standing automatic 'Super-Loos' which are coin-operated (20p) and smell of cheap detergent (there is one, for example, in Leicester Square).

Generally speaking, you'll have a more salubrious experience in pubs, bars and restaurants. If you don't want to buy anything, just pop in to the toilets discreetly and nobody should give you a hard time.

Tourist Information

London is one of the tourist brochure capitals of the world; show one faint sign of interest and you will be inundated with glossy paper. The main tourist offices, which can also help you find accommodation, are:

Britain and London Visitor Centre, 1 Regent St, Piccadilly Circus, SW1Y 4XT, *www.visitbritain.com*. *Open Mon 9.30am–6.30pm, Tues–Fri 9am–6.30pm, Sat and Sun 10am–4pm (June–Sept Sat 9am–5pm).*

Heathrow Underground Station (Terminals 1, 2 and 3). *Open daily 8am–6pm.*

Liverpool St Underground Station. *Open daily 8am–6pm.*

Victoria Station. *Open Mon–Sat 8am–7pm, Sun 8am–6pm.*

Waterloo Station, Arrivals Hall, International Terminal. *Open daily 8.30am–10.30pm.*

Many districts also have local tourist information offices, which can be excellent and provide guides to show you round for the appropriate fee. The centres at **Greenwich**, **t** 0870 608 2000, and **Richmond**, **t** (020)8940 9125, also have accommodation services, but often don't even try to help you in high season. You'll have to visit their offices, as none of them takes phone bookings.

The **London Tourist Board** operates a 'Visit London' website, *www.visitlondon.com*, and gives recorded information on **t** 0871 566 3666.

London: Essential Sights

05

Albert Hall and Albert Memorial

Albert Hall

Kensington Gore; ⊖ South Kensington, High Street Kensington; bus 9, 10, 52; www.royalalberthall.com. Call **t** *(020) 7589 8212 for details of concert programmes and other events.*

As a concert venue the Albert Hall has one unforgivable flaw: an echo that has been the butt of jokes ever since the Bishop of London heard his prayers of blessing reverberate around the red-brick rotunda at the opening ceremony in 1871. The irascible conductor Sir Thomas Beecham remarked that the hall was fit for many things, but playing music was not one of them. But the Albert Hall is still well loved. Visually, it is one of the more successful Victorian buildings in London, and the high frieze around the outside depicts the Triumph of Arts and Sciences – a most Albertian theme. The hall is huge (capacity 7,000 or more) and remarkably versatile; through the year it hosts symphony orchestras, rock bands, conferences, boxing matches and tennis tournaments. Every summer it becomes the headquarters of the Proms, a series of cheap concerts widely broadcast on radio and television, the last night of which, in early September, is a national institution, *see* p.178.

Albert Memorial

Kensington Gore, opposite the Albert Hall.

A year after her beloved husband's death, the widowed Queen Victoria launched a competition for a memorial and picked George Gilbert Scott, nabob of neo-Gothic excess. The 175ft-high monument he built is a bloated, over-decorated stone canopy housing an indifferent likeness of Albert reading a catalogue from the Great Exhibition by John Foley: a ponderous pickle of allegorical statuary and religious imagery decked out in far too much marble, mosaic panelling, enamel and polished stone, and now, after recent restoration, clad in startling resplendent gold to boot. It was a big hit with the Victorians and remained popular well into the 20th century. Osbert Sitwell described it in 1928 as 'that wistful, unique monument of widowhood'. It took a writer as cynical as Norman Douglas to puncture the myth. 'Is this the reward of conjugal virtue?' he wrote in 1945. 'Ye husbands, be unfaithful!'

London Aquarium

County Hall, Westminster Bridge Rd; ⊖ Waterloo, Westminster; bus 12, 53, 148, 159, 211; **t** *(020) 7967 8000, www.londonaquarium.co.uk. Open daily 10–6, last adm 5pm; adm exp.*

To the left of Westminster Bridge, directly across the river from the Houses of Parliament, is **County Hall**, a grand, grey, stone public building in the pompous Edwardian 'Wrenaissance' style. Until 1986 it was the headquarters of the Greater

London Council, the elected city government that proved such a threat to Margaret Thatcher in the 1980s that she abolished it.

County Hall has now been converted into a multipurpose centre for housing and conferences, and is home to the Saatchi Gallery (*see* p.141). The basement accommodates one of London's newer attractions, one of the largest **aquaria** in Europe, with three subterranean levels of tanks filled with every fish imaginable. The tanks are arranged according to native habitats, taking you on a journey through freshwater streams, rivers and ponds, coral reefs, mangroves and rainforests, and introducing you to such characters as the Picasso triggerfish, the tongueless albino African clawed frog and the electrical Peter's elephantnose, as well as the more familiar starfish, seahorses, octopi and crabs. The highlights are the Pacific tank, where sharks weave their lazy way past a backdrop of Easter Island head statues, and a pool where you can stroke an array of rays, who genuinely seem to enjoy the attention. Touch-screen quizzes and information points are dotted around for children, and there's a strong emphasis throughout the aquarium on environmental issues, although inquisitive adults are largely uncatered-for, having to source their information predominantly from animated cartoon fish introducing themselves in funny voices. Take a drink with you: the aquarium can get fairly sticky.

British Museum

Great Russell Street; ⊖ Tottenham Court Road; bus 7, 10, 24, 29, 134; ***t*** *(020) 7636 1555, recorded information* ***t*** *(020) 7323 8783; www.thebritishmuseum.ac.uk.*

Museum: open Sat–Wed 10–5.30, Thurs and Fri 10–8.30; free; guided tours available. Reading Room: open daily 10–5.30, first Thurs of month until 10pm.

Back in the 1770s, the grumpy novelist Tobias Smollett complained that the fledgling British Museum was too empty and lacked a decent book collection. The museum has certainly made up for both deficiencies since. Stuffed with treasures gathered from the farthest reaches of the British empire, and until recently boasting one of the finest and fullest libraries in the world, it became an irresistible magnet for visitors and scholars of every temperament and interest. With its stunning new Great Court, it is by far the most popular tourist attraction in London – triumphant proof that real quality beats the tackiness of the Tower or Madame Tussaud's any day.

There is more in the museum than can possibly be described below; what follows is a guide to its most famous and appealing artefacts. Your best strategy is to pick up a floor plan and make up your own mind what to see.

Ground Floor and Lower Level

The Great Court and Reading Room

On entering the museum, unsuspecting visitors stroll through the dim Victorian cavern of the South Portal and out into the luminous **Great Court**. All eyes rise at once to the latticework glass roof, which makes a mosaic of the sky and sends cloud shadows scudding across the marble floors. It's like stumbling across a magnificent landscape. Norman Foster's ingenious design, based on geometry and light, has attracted wide-ranging praise: it is London's Louvre pyramid, but with more dramatic effect. In the centre of the Court is the Reading Room revealed, wrapped in grand curving staircases and linked with the courtyard's outer walls by a doughnut of glass (from above, the whole resembles a fried egg). You may find the futuristic roofing and neoclassical façades a little out of sync, but it hardly matters. Drawn by the open space and the dazzling light, you'll find yourself returning time and again from the relative gloom of the galleries, which lead off the court in all directions.

For the first time in its history, the **Reading Room** is open to the public. For over a hundred years this was one of the best loved rooms in the world, with a beautiful cavernous dome bigger in diameter than St Paul's or St Peter's in Rome. Although designed by Sydney Smirke, it was the brainchild of Sir Antonio Panizzi, an Italian exile who invented the systems for labelling and cataloguing that are used in libraries to this day. A steady stream of the world's political thinkers and revolutionaries came to this wonderfully spacious domed circular room, among them Marx (who wrote *Das Kapital* in Row G), Mazzini and Lenin. Other writers who found inspiration, consolation and even, occasionally, love among its 18 million tomes include Macaulay, Thackeray, Hardy, Dickens and Yeats.

Sainsbury African Galleries

As part of the British Museum's 250th Anniversary programme, the ethnography collections of the Museum of Mankind are being returned to their original home. The new Sainsbury Galleries on the north side of the Great Court house the African collections – among the finest in the world and unusual in that they combine archaeological and contemporary material.

Western Asia

Western Asian treasures are spread throughout the British Museum, but the most accessible, the **Assyrian relics** of Nineveh, Balawat and Nimrud, are here on the ground floor. The Assyrians, occupying an exposed area in what is now northern Iraq, constructed a civilization essentially built on war with their neighbours, especially the Babylonians, between the 9th and 7th centuries BC. Their palaces are decorated with figures of wild animals, mythical creatures and magic symbols as well as depictions of conical-helmeted soldiers at arms with their chariots, battering rams and pontoons. The most extraordinary artwork depicts a royal lion hunt; the dying animals, shot through with arrows, are sculpted with great emotional force.

Egypt

There are more lions here in the Egyptian sculpture gallery, this time red and black ones carved in granite and limestone for the tombs of Pharaohs; Ruskin described them as 'the noblest and truest carved lions I have ever seen'. Among the huge Pharaohs' heads and ornate sarcophagi, look for the likeness of Amenophis III, an

18th Dynasty ruler, and the gilded coffin containing Henutmehit, the Chantress of Amen-Re, from around 1290 BC. Many of the riddles of the ancient Egyptian world were deciphered through the **Rosetta Stone**, a slab of black basalt discovered by Napoleon's army in the Nile Delta in 1799, which by extraordinary good fortune reproduces the same text in three languages: Greek, demotic and Egyptian.

Greece

Two monuments overshadow the Greek collections: the Nereid Monument and the Elgin Marbles. The **Nereid Monument** is a reconstruction of a vast tomb found at the Greek colony of Xanthos in Asia Minor. Built like a temple with a pediment supported by Ionic columns, it is a stunning tribute to the Lycian chieftains who are buried there; it also features remarkable frieze sculptures.

As for the **Elgin Marbles**, they have aroused so much controversy for being in Britain rather than Greece that their artistic merit is sometimes entirely overlooked. The Elgin Marbles are the frieze reliefs from the Parthenon, the temple to Athena on top of the Acropolis, and are considered some of the finest sculptures of antiquity. Depicting a Panathenaic festival to commemorate Athena's birthday, they reveal a remarkable mastery of detail and human feeling. Lord Elgin, the British Ambassador to the Ottoman Empire, discovered the stones when he visited Athens in 1800. The Parthenon, from which the marbles came, had been half wrecked in a skirmish between the Turks and a Venetian fleet besieging them in 1687, when a supply of gunpowder kept in the building exploded and brought many of the colonnades crashing to the ground. Elgin obtained a licence from the Turkish Sultan in 1802 and proceeded to transport the treasures back home. The British Museum has them displayed in a vast room that gives an idea of the scale of the Parthenon itself.

Oriental Collections (halfway between Ground and Upper Floors)

These rooms cover a huge amount of ground, from Chinese Tang dynasty glazed tomb figures to Turkish and Syrian ceramic work, by way of Thai banner painting and religious monuments from India and Nepal. Perhaps the most impressive section for the non-specialist is the room devoted to South and Southeast Asia.

Upper Floor

Egypt (*continued*)

The display of **Egyptian mummies and sarcophagi** is the most popular section of the British Museum, no doubt for its gruesomeness. Here is the Egyptian way of death in all its bizarre splendour: rows and rows of spongy bodies wrapped in bandages and surrounded by the prized belongings and favourite food of the deceased.

Western Asia (*continued*)

The collection is more eclectic here than downstairs: Bronze Age tools from Syria, a mosaic column from Tell-al-Ubaid, reliefs from Kapara's palace in Tell Halaf (now in northeastern Syria) as well as further relics from Nimrud (ivory carvings) and Nineveh (tablets from the royal library). The two highlights are a collection of magnificently preserved funerary busts from Palmyra dating from the 1st and 2nd centuries AD, and the extraordinary sculpture ***The Ram in the Thicket*** from Ur, birthplace of Abraham.

The Italy of the Greeks, Etruscans and Romans

Have a look down the western staircase, which is adorned with a Roman mosaic. On the walls are more mosaic fragments, this time from Greek palaces in Halicarnassus, Ephesus and Carthage. The collections themselves are a bit of a mixed bag: Greek red-figure vases found in Lucania and Apulia in southern Italy (1400–1200 BC), a carved stone Etruscan sarcophagus found at Bomarzo north of Rome (3rd century BC) and plenty of bronze heads of Roman emperors. The highlight of the Roman collection, though, is the **Portland Vase**, so called because the Barberini family sold it to the Dukes of Portland. The vase, made around the time of the birth of Christ, is of cobalt-blue glass and coated in an opaque white glaze depicting the reclining figures of Peleus and Thetis, with Cupid and his love arrows hovering overhead.

Romano-British Section

The oldest and most gruesome exhibit here is **Lindow Man**, the shrivelled remains of an ancient Briton preserved down the centuries in a peat bog. The body, which has been dated between 300 BC and AD 100, shows evidence of extreme violence. All you see here is his torso and crushed head, freeze-dried like instant coffee, with a hologram giving you a better idea of what he originally looked like. Excavations in Britain have provided more pleasant surprises, notably the **Mildenhall Treasure**, 34 remarkably well-preserved pieces of 4th-century silver tableware dug up from a field in Suffolk in 1942. There are some beautiful mosaics, the largest of them a 4th-century floor from Hinton St Mary in Dorset which appears to be Christian in inspiration.

Medieval Antiquities

Here you will find more extraordinary finds from digs around the British Isles. You should not miss the **Lewis chessmen**, a collection of 78 pieces in walrus ivory discovered in the remote Outer Hebrides in 1831. The farmer who first came across them fled thinking they were elves and fairies, and it was only the fortitude of his wife that persuaded him to go back for another look. The figures do not make up complete chess sets and are thought to have been left by a travelling salesman, possibly from Scandinavia, some time in the 12th century.

Prints and Drawings

The museum's vast collection is displayed in rotation. On a good day you can find Michelangelo's sketches for the roof of the Sistine chapel, etchings and sketches by Rembrandt and a large selection of anatomical studies by Albrecht Dürer. Look out, too, for William Hogarth's satirical engravings, notably *Gin Lane*, which castigates the corrupting influence of drink on 18th-century London, and his series on cruelty.

Buckingham Palace

Buckingham Palace Road; ⊖ Green Park, Victoria; bus (closest stop Royal Mews) 2, 8, 16, 36, 38, 52, 73, 82; info **t** *(020) 7799 2331,* **t** *(020) 7766 7300 to book in advance, www.royal.gov.uk; buckinghampalace@royalcollection.org.uk.*

Open Aug and Sept daily 9.30–4.15; last adm 45mins before closing; adm exp. The ticket office, an elegant tent structure designed by architect Michael Hopkins, is at the western end of St James's Park just off the Mall, and the entrance is at Ambassadors' Court on the south side of the building. The opening hours are subject to change at short notice; check the website or send them an email.

On 7 August 1993, miracle of miracles, Buckingham Palace opened its doors to the public for the first time. For generations, royalists had invoked the need to preserve the mystery of the monarchy and refused, in the words of Walter Bagehot, to 'let daylight in upon its magic'. But by the early 1990s the British monarchy was in a crisis of quite astonishing proportions. Two royal marriages had broken up in quick succession, and half of Windsor Castle had burned down. Little knowing the revelations and tragedies that were still to come, the Queen herself dubbed 1992, the year of most of these misfortunes, her '*annus horribilis*'. To rally public opinion back behind the monarchy she made two unprecedented concessions. The first was to agree to pay income tax for the first time. The second was to unveil some of the mysteries of Buckingham Palace for two months of the year. As a public relations coup, opening the doors of the queen's official residence proved less than spectacular. Quite a few newspaper critics, their knives already well sharpened by the preceding flurry of royal scandals, complained that the tour was impersonal, poorly put together and even boring. The public seemed more forgiving, fawning happily over every precious object listed in the official catalogue.

So what exactly is all the fuss about? What do you get to see? Certainly not a glimpse of the 'working palace' constantly alluded to by the Queen's public relations flaks. The tour takes in just 18 of Buckingham Palace's 661 rooms, and even these feel as though they have been stripped down to the bare minimum to ensure they are not sullied by the savage hordes. The original carpets are rolled away each summer and replaced with industrial-strength red Axminster rugs that clash awkwardly with the fake marble columns, greens, pinks and blues of the flock wallpapers and gold and cream ornamental ceilings. The place feels hollow and spookily empty; in fact it is hard to imagine that anybody lives or works in such soulless surroundings. There is not so much as a photograph of the royal family on the whole tour, let alone a flesh-and-blood prince or princess to welcome the guests.

The Grand Staircase, with its elegant wrought-iron banister, leads up to the first of the state rooms, the Green Drawing Room. All the rooms are filled with ostentatious chandeliers, somewhat chintzy furniture and ornate gilt and painted plaster ceilings. Whether you are in the Green, Blue or White Drawing Room you can't help feeling as though you are trapped in a Dairy Milk chocolate box. The real highlight is the 155ft-long **Picture Gallery** which is crammed from floor to ceiling with the cream of the royal collection of some 10,000 paintings. The walls are a bit crowded for comfort, but the gems stand out easily enough: Van Dyck's idealized portraits of Charles I, Rembrandt's *Lady with a Fan*, *Agatha Bas* and *The Shipbuilder and His Wife*, landscapes by Ruisdael, Poussin and Claude Lorrain, portraits by Frans Hals, Rubens' underwhelming *St George and the Dragon*, Albert Cuyp's *Landscape with a Negro Page*, and much more besides. Apart from Charles I, the only royal to receive anything like pictorial justice in Buckingham Palace is Victoria, whose family is cosily captured in Franz Winterhalter's 1846 portrait in the East Gallery.

In the **garden** you may linger and enjoy some fine views, before moving on to the highlight of the visit which is the souvenir shop. In many ways this is the most telling part of the trip, with mugs and videos and other royal memorabilia displayed to the public in glass cabinets, Buckingham Palace Belgian chocolates moulded into the shape of the crown, or the attractive-looking Buckingham Palace gold tooth-mug, an ideal Christmas present for regally inclined mothers-in-law.

Globe Theatre

New Globe Walk; ⊖ Southwark; London Bridge; bus to Southwark Bridge or London Bridge, 17, 21, 35, 40, 43, 47, 48, 133, 141, 149; **t** *(020) 7902 1400; box office* **t** *(020) 7401 9919; book tours on* **t** *(020) 7901 1500, www.shakespeares-globe.org.*

The season runs from April to October; exhibition and theatre tour daily Oct–April 10–5; May–Sept 9–12, and exhibition and virtual tour daily 12.30–5; no access to the theatre during matinee performances; adm.

The original Globe was in fact a few hundred feet away from this site, on the corner of present-day Park Street and Southwark Bridge Road. When London's first playhouse, The Theatre, was forced to move off its premises in Finsbury Fields, just north of the City, in 1598, its manager Richard Burbage had it dismantled and reassembled here on Bankside where the Rose Theatre had taken root 12 years earlier. Shakespeare helped finance Burbage's enterprise and had many of his plays, including *Romeo and Juliet*, *King Lear*, *Othello*, *Macbeth* and *The Taming of the Shrew*, performed in its famous O-shaped auditorium for the first time. Bankside was the perfect location for theatrical entertainment; all manner of pursuits not deemed proper across the river in the stiff-collared City had moved here, and the area was already notorious, among other things, for its taverns and its whorehouses.

The Globe never properly recovered from a fire in 1613 and was finally demolished during the Civil War. This reconstruction was the brainchild of the late American actor Sam Wanamaker, who devoted most of his retirement to realizing the scheme, which remained unfinished when he died in December 1993 at the age of 72. The theatre finally opened four years later, following an extraordinary fund-raising effort.

The construction is remarkably faithful to the original, from the distinctive red of its brickwork to its all-wooden interior and thatched roof (the first of its kind to appear in London since the Great Fire of 1666). If you are in London during the summer you should try to see a performance to appreciate the peculiarities of Elizabethan theatre. The huge stage, with its vast oak pillars holding up a canopy roof, juts out into the open area holding up to 500 standing members of the audience. The rest of the public is seated on wooden benches in the circular galleries, giving a peculiar sense of intimacy and audience involvement. Again, there are a few concessions to modern sensibilities: the seating is more spacious and comfortable than in Shakespeare's day, and performances take place in the evening as well as the traditional afternoon slot.

Whether or not you come for a play, you can visit the **Shakespeare Globe Exhibition** which charts the building of both the original and the reconstructed theatre and offers a guided tour around the auditorium itself. Wanamaker's Globe is more than just a venue for authentic performances of Shakespeare, however: there is also a study centre and library, open to scholars and theatre performers.

Hampton Court

East Molesey, Surrey. If you don't travel by river (by far the most pleasant but slowest means), go by train from Waterloo to ⇌ Hampton Court, or else catch bus R68 from Richmond; **t** *0870 752 7777, www.hrp.org.uk.*

Open Nov–March Mon 10.15–4.30, Tues–Sun 9.30–4.30; April–Oct Mon 10.15–6, Tues–Sun 9.30–6; adm.

Hampton Court Palace is one of the finest Tudor buildings in England, a place that magnificently evokes the haphazard pleasures and cruel intrigues of Henry VIII's court. We are lucky to have it. Oliver Cromwell meant to sell off its treasures and let it go to pieces, but then fell in love with it and decided to live there himself. A generation later, Christopher Wren had every intention of razing it to the ground to build a new palace; only money problems and the death of Queen Mary prevented him from wreaking more damage than he did.

Hampton Court started as the power base of Henry VIII's most influential minister. Cardinal Thomas Wolsey bought the property from the Knights of St John in 1514, one year before he became Lord Chancellor of England. As his influence grew, so did the palace: at its zenith it contained 280 rooms and kept a staff of 500 busy, constantly entertaining dignitaries from around Europe. Seeing the grandeur to which his chief minister was rapidly allowing himself to become accustomed, Henry VIII grew nervous and threatened to knock Wolsey off his high perch. Wolsey responded in panic by offering Hampton Court to the monarch; Henry was unimpressed and at first snubbed him by refusing to take up residence there. Wolsey was then given the impossible task of asking the Pope to grant Henry a divorce from his wife, Catherine of Aragon. When he failed, his possessions were seized by the crown, he was arrested for high treason and eventually died as he was escorted from York to London.

Henry first got interested in Hampton Court as a love nest for himself and his new flame, Anne Boleyn. The two of them moved here even before Henry had annulled his first marriage, and set about effacing every possible trace of Wolsey. They removed his coat of arms, since restored, from the main entrance arch and renamed it **Anne Boleyn's Gateway** – a magnificent red brick structure with octagonal towers at either end. In 1540, Henry added a remarkable astronomical clock, and renamed the main courtyard within Clock Court.

The mid-1530s were Hampton Court's heyday. Henry built the **Great Hall**, with its 60ft-high hammerbeam roof and its stained-glass windows, amended right up to the end of his life to include the crests of each of his wives, even the ones he repudiated or executed. The king also established the gardens, planting trees and shrubs, notably in the Pond Garden, and built a **real tennis court** which still survives in the outhouses at the northeastern end of the palace. Hampton Court began to turn sour for him after Jane Seymour died in 1538 while giving birth to his much anticipated son and heir, Edward. For a century after Henry's death, Hampton Court continued to thrive. The Great Hall became a popular theatrical venue, and the state rooms filled with fine paintings, tapestries, musical instruments and ornaments. Charles I built the gardens' fountains and lakes as well as the long waterway, originally cut to provide the palace with water at the expense of neighbouring communities. Charles also accumulated a vast collection of art including the wonderfully restored *Triumph of Caesar* series by Mantegna which hangs in its own gallery at the south end of the palace.

By the time William and Mary came to the throne, appreciation of Tudor architecture had waned considerably. The apartments at Hampton Court were considered old-fashioned and uncomfortable, and Christopher Wren was drafted in to build an entirely new palace to rival Louis XIV's extravaganza at Versailles – a project that, perhaps fortunately, never saw the light of day. The bulk of Wren's work is at the eastern end of the palace and centres around the cloisters of **Fountain Court**. The new apartments were decorated by the likes of Antonio Verrio, James Thornhill, Grinling Gibbons and Jean Tijou in sumptuous but stilted fashion; the **Chapel Royal** was also rebuilt, with only the Tudor vaulted ceiling surviving from the original. The best work carried out under William III was in the **gardens**, notably the lines of yew trees along the narrow strips of water, the herb garden and the famous **maze**. Originally the maze was a religious penance to impress upon ordinary mortals the labyrinthine complications of a life in the service of Christ. Now it is a popular diversion, particularly for children too small to peer over the hedges to see what is coming next.

Houses of Parliament and Big Ben

Parliament Square; ⊖ Westminster; buses 3, 11, 12, 24, 53, 77A, 88, 159, 453 all go to Parliament Square; www.parliament.uk.

*To visit the **Houses of Parliament**, you should head for St Stephen's entrance, which is roughly halfway along the complex of buildings. Visiting arrangements for parliament are phenomenally complicated, change all the time and vary according to whether you are a UK resident or not (overseas visitors may currently tour only in the summer recess; check on the website above); telephoning in advance (**t** (020) 7219 4272 for information on what is being debated) will avoid wasting time.*

If you turn up on spec, you must queue outside St Stephen's entrance; don't expect to sit down before 5pm. Note that both houses have long recesses, particularly in the summer, and that debates of particular public interest are likely to be very crowded.

To see the rest of the Palace of Westminster (notably Westminster Hall) you need to apply for a permit about two months in advance from your MP or embassy. It's a good idea whatever your arrangements to bring your passport and leave behind any large bags or cameras. You should also dress reasonably formally. The one bit of good news is that the Houses of Parliament, once you get in, come free.

The best way to approach the Palace of Westminster is to imagine it as a multi-layered onion. Most of today's building is the dizzy virtuoso work of Charles Barry and Augustus Pugin, two Victorian architects working at the height of their powers to replace the old parliament destroyed by fire in 1834.

The story of the palace begins with **Westminster Hall**, which has survived the centuries more or less intact. The hall was originally a banqueting chamber built by King William Rufus, the son of William the Conqueror, in 1097. The Hall was the meeting-place of the Grand Council, a committee of barons which discussed policy with the monarch in an early incarnation of parliament. Westminster Hall also became the nation's main law court. From about 1550, the lower house of parliament, known as the House of Commons, began meeting in St Stephen's Chapel in the main body of the palace. It may seem odd to convene parliament in a religious setting, but the juxtaposition is curiously appropriate: ever since the Reformation, parliament has been a symbol of the primacy of Protestantism in English politics. Pugin and Barry recognized this, and incorporated the chapel into their design. It was only when St Stephen's was destroyed in the Blitz that the House of Commons became an entirely secular chamber.

The inadequacies of the old Palace of Westminster were recognized as early as the 1820s. A new building might have been proposed there and then, but it took a calamity to spring them into action. On 16 October 1834 the Clerk of Works, a Mr Richard Wibley, was asked to destroy several bundles of old talley-sticks in a cellar furnace. The fire raged out of control, and the whole palace was soon engulfed in flames. Augustus Pugin had been an eye-witness to the 1834 fire and revelled in every minute of it. He hated neoclassical architects and was only too happy to see their various improvements to the old parliament go up in smoke. Fearing that a neo-classical architect would be asked to design the new parliament, Pugin put his name forward and, although he was only 24 at the time, was named assistant to the older, more experienced Charles Barry. Theirs was a near perfect partnership. Barry sketched out the broad lines of the design, while Pugin attended to the details of ornamentation. Some of Pugin's work was lost in the bombing of the Second World War; you can nevertheless admire the sheer fervour of his imagination in the sculpted wood and stone, stained glass, tiled floors, wallpaper and painted ceilings. Despite Pugin's rantings against the classicists, he was happy to go along with Barry's classical design and

Gothicize it to his heart's content. The Palace of Westminster's blend of architectural restraint (Barry) and decorative frenzy (Pugin) is one of its most appealing aspects.

Pugin went mad and died in 1852, and so never lived to work on the most famous feature of the new building, the clock tower at the eastern end known universally by the name of its giant bell, **Big Ben** (*visits to the clock must be arranged through an MP or serving member of the House of Lords or, for horologists with a specific interest in the clock, directly through Mike McGann on* **t** *(020) 7219 3767*). Nowadays the clock is renowned for its accuracy and its resounding tolling of the hour, but the story of its construction is one of incredible incompetence and bungling. The 320ft-high clock tower was finished in 1854, but because of a bitter disagreement between the two clockmakers, Frederick Dent and Edmund Beckett Denison, there was nothing to put inside it for another three years. Finally a great bell made up according to Denison's instructions was dragged across Westminster Bridge by a cart and 16 horses. But, as it was being laid out ready for hoisting into position, a 4ft crack suddenly appeared. Similar embarrassments ensued over the next two years, until a functioning but still cracked bell was at last erected at the top of the tower. It remains defective to this day. As for the name, the most common explanation is that the bell was named after Sir Benjamin Hall, the unpopular Chief Commissioner of Works who had to explain all the muddles in his project to the House of Commons. Another theory has it that Big Ben was in fact Benjamin Caunt, a corpulent boxer who owned a pub a couple of hundred yards away in St Martin's Lane. The chimes are a bastardized version of the aria 'I Know That My Redeemer Liveth' from Handel's *Messiah*.

From the moment that Barry and Pugin's building opened in 1852, it set an entirely new tone to proceedings in parliament. It was no longer just a legislative assembly, it was a *club*. Like so many British institutions, parliament is a place of deeply embedded rituals, established by a ruling order intent on protecting itself and its idiosyncratic ways; even if the institution has changed, many of the rituals have survived out of a quirky fondness for the past.

Kensington Palace

Kensington Palace Gardens; ⊖ Queensway, High Street Kensington; bus 94, 148, 390 stopping to the north of the palace on Bayswater Road, and 9, 10, 52 stopping to the south on Kensington Road; **t** *0870 751 5170, www.hrp.org.uk.*

Open Nov–Feb daily 10–5, Mar–Oct daily 10–6, last adm 1hr before closing; adm; includes small café.

Since the death of Princess Diana, Kensington Palace has become something of a shrine to her memory; this was where she, along with that other well-known royal divorcee Princess Margaret, lived after the failure of her marriage to Prince Charles. You won't be able to visit her private apartments, but the Palace offers other delights in their place. The tour is divided into two sections: the historic apartments, and an exhibition of royal clothes including the coronation robes worn by monarchs from George II onwards. The most interesting aspect of the apartments is the decoration work by William Kent: a beautifully patterned ceiling in the Presence Chamber, some fine *trompe l'œil* murals of court scenes on the King's Staircase and painted episodes from the *Odyssey* on the ceiling of the King's Gallery. The Cupola Room plays clever optical tricks to make you believe the ceiling is taller and more rounded than it is; from the King's Drawing Room there is a fine view over Kensington Gardens, the Serpentine and Hyde Park.

The fashions in coronation garb charted by the special exhibition give a good reading of the changing status of the monarchy itself. The over-confident Georges wore ermine galore, particularly the profligate George IV, who sported a ludicrously flamboyant white feather hat and a train as thick as a shag-pile carpet. William IV and Victoria, whose coronations went almost unnoticed by a populace more interested in democratic reform than regal pomp, were sober almost to the point of blandness. Edward VII, who helped restore the monarchy's image, showed renewed confidence with his bright military uniform and ermine mantle braided with gold.

London Eye

Jubilee Gardens; ⊖ Waterloo, Embankment, Westminster; **t** *0870 5000 600, www.ba-londoneye.com.*

Open May–Sept 9.30am–10pm; Oct–April daily 9.30–8; adm; tickets may be booked in advance; ticket office in County Hall.

The world's biggest observation wheel and the fourth tallest structure in London, the Eye provided almost as much entertainment during its construction as it has since it began operating; too big to be made in one place, the various components were built in different European countries and then towed up the Thames and assembled horizontally on a river platform. London watched in awe as the enormous wheel began to be slowly hoisted into position, and in disbelief as industrial-strength winches began snapping under the strain of raising the mighty load. Finally upright, following a hasty redesign of the lifting equipment, the wheel had its opening ceremony postponed following the discovery of technical problems.

Despite these difficulties, the Eye has, since its maiden turn in February 2000, proved a resounding success, attracting rave reviews for its architecture and the striking impact the structure has had on the city's skyline – as well as for its stunning views: you can see for over 25 miles in almost every direction. Passengers board 32 slow-moving glass-sided capsules (they can be stopped briefly for the less-than-sprightly) and are taken 450ft up into the city sky on a smooth 30-minute journey. It takes a while to orientate yourself, but there are geographical markers in the pods. A breathtaking panorama unfolds as familiar landmarks gradually reveal themselves. Some buildings are obscured, such as Tower Bridge and the Tower of London, and the Millennium Dome can't be spotted until the very top, but the Eye is handily positioned for most of the key sights. It doesn't have to be a clear and sunny day for you to enjoy the views; even grey mists give the city a romantic hue.

National Gallery

Trafalgar Square; ⊖ Charing Cross, Leicester Square; bus: very nearly all of London's day and night bus services go around Trafalgar Square; ***t*** *(020) 7747 2885, www.nationalgallery.org.uk.*

Open daily 10–6, Wed 10–9; free.

The National Gallery is an astonishing collection of West European painting from the 13th to the early 20th centuries, including masterpieces from virtually every major school. Its great names include Leonardo da Vinci, Piero della Francesca, Van Eyck, Raphael, Titian, Veronese, Rubens, Poussin, Rembrandt, Velázquez, Caravaggio, Turner, Constable, Delacroix, Monet, Van Gogh, Cézanne and Picasso.

The National Gallery is very much a 19th-century phenomenon: a catalogue of paintings from the Grand Tradition reflecting the pride and power of the collector nation. Many of the gallery's masterpieces were bought in the Victorian era, particularly under its first director Charles Eastlake. The picture-buying has continued ever since; and although money has grown tighter in recent years the annual budget remains well over £2 million.

The first work of art, which most visitors miss, is a mosaic of Greta Garbo's head by Boris Anrep (1933) on the floor of the main entrance hall. Pick up a floor plan from the information desk and you'll see that the gallery's four wings each concentrate on a different historical period, starting with early medieval Italian painting in the new Sainsbury Wing and moving gradually eastwards towards the 20th century.

Rooms devoted to individual painters are clearly marked. At the entrance to each wing, you are given the names of the major paintings to look out for. The gallery is magnificently lit, with intelligent explanations displayed alongside each picture. There is a computer database in the Micro Gallery in the Sainsbury Wing, where you can look up and print out detailed information on pictures or artists. There are also organized lectures on individual pictures, as well as a changing special exhibition in the Sunley Room to the left of the central hall, where paintings from the collection are grouped to illustrate a specific theme. And if that is not enough for you, there are hundreds of minor paintings stored on lower floors available for public view.

Natural History Museum

Cromwell Road; ⊖ South Kensington; bus C1 from Victoria, 74 from Baker St, 14 from Tottenham Court Road; ***t*** *(020) 7942 5000, www.nhm.ac.uk.*

Open Mon–Sat 10–5.50, Sun 11–5.50; free.

This place looks for all the world like a cathedral, but you are soon jolted out of any notion that this is a place of worship by the giant dinosaur in the central hall. This skeletal creature, a 150-million-year-old plant-eating beast called a diplodocus that warded off predators with its giant tusks and whiplash tail, really sums up what is best and worst about the Natural History Museum. Our prehistoric friend *looks* very impressive; the trouble is, he's a fake, just a cast. Ever since *Jurassic Park*, the **dinosaurs** have been the museum's main attraction. The special section devoted to them is long on history but short on real skeletons, though one display gives an intriguing list of theories on why prehistoric monsters died out.

Much of this museum resembles a science classroom. There are games explaining human perception and memory, interactive displays on creepy-crawlies and a politically correct **Ecology Gallery** explaining the importance of the rainforests in the world's ecosystem. All of this is fine for children, but not so great for adults. For grown-ups, the museum only really gets going with the **Bird Gallery**, featuring a remarkable collection of stuffed birds and wild animals from the 18th century onwards, and a geological section known as the **Earth Galleries**, which are filled with beautiful stones and gems, and where there's a chance to step inside the 'Earthquake Experience'. A newer part of the museum is the **Earth Lab Datasite**, an educational resource where you can investigate UK geology using an extensive online database. And at the end of 2002, the museum opened the first phase of its **Darwin Centre**: 22 million zoological specimens including fish, reptiles, crustaceans and amphibians, all stored in alcohol, displayed with all the newest interactive computer technology.

St Paul's Cathedral

St Paul's Churchyard; ⊖ St Paul's; bus 8, 25, 242 from Oxford Street, 11, 15, 23, 26, 76 from the Strand; **t** *(020) 7236 6883, www.stpaulscathedral.co.uk.*

Open Mon–Sat 8.30–4; adm.

St Paul's is more than just a cathedral or famous landmark. It is an icon for a whole city. Get to know St Paul's and you understand many of the ambitions and failings of London itself. For nearly 1,400 years, succeeding buildings on this site have sought to express the material confidence of a powerful capital while at the same time delineating its spiritual aspirations. Back in the 7th century, St Paul's was England's first major Christian temple; in its medieval incarnation it was the largest single building in the land. In the hands of Christopher Wren, who rebuilt it from scratch after the Great Fire, it was hailed as an architectural masterpiece. Since then St Paul's has dutifully propped up all the myths of the nation: as the burial place for heroes during the glory days of empire; as a symbol of British endurance during the Second World War when it miraculously survived the Blitz; or as the fairytale setting for Prince Charles's marriage to Lady Diana Spencer in 1981.

And yet St Paul's has often shared more with the commercial world outside its doors than with the spiritual world celebrated within. Back in the Middle Ages the cathedral was itself a kind of market, with horses parading down the nave and stallholders selling beer and vegetables to all-comers. Even today, the first thing confronting the swarms of tourists who come here is a cash register, a sign of the cathedral's peculiar ease in reconciling religious faith with the handling of money. It is a cool, cerebral place. While we admire Wren's pure lines and lofty vision, we feel little warmth or sense of a living church community. St Paul's is a monument to wealth first, and God second.

By the time of the Great Fire of London, old St Paul's was so dilapidated that several architects wanted to pull it down and rebuild it from scratch. Christopher Wren, commissioned to consider the cathedral's future in 1663, called it 'defective both in beauty and firmness ... a heap of deformities that no judicious architect will think corrigible by any expense that can be laid out upon it.' He did not have to lobby long for the merits of demolition. On 4 September 1666, the first flames of the Great Fire of London reached St Paul's and proceeded to engulf it entirely.

Nothing was easy about the rebuilding. Wren initially used gunpowder to clear the wreck of old St Paul's, but had to resort to battering rams instead after terrified locals complained of rogue pieces of stonework flying through their living-room windows. As for the design, Wren set his heart on building a dome in the manner of the great Italian Baroque churches. That idea, too, met stiff resistance – it was considered excessively Popish in those religiously sensitive times. You can see his magnificent 20ft oak replica of the Great Model on display in the crypt. Eventually the dome problem was solved through a mixture of guile and compromise. Wren submitted a third plan dispensing with a dome in favour of a steeple, and had it approved in 1675; in return the royal warrant giving him the go-ahead granted him the liberty 'to make some variations rather ornamental than essential, as from time to time he should see proper'. By the time the cathedral opened 35 years later, the dome was back, as were many of the architect's other rejected ideas.

The sheer imposing scale of St Paul's is apparent as soon as you approach the entrance at the west front. The broad **staircase** leads up to a two-tiered portico upheld by vast stone columns and flanked by two clocktowers. Dominating the high pediment in the centre is a statue of St Paul, with St Peter to his left and St James to his right. It is surely no coincidence that these three figures look down on the sovereign of the day, Queen Anne, whose statue stands on the ground outside the entrance. The ensemble, the work of a single artist, Francis Bird, forges a clear mystical link between the City, the crown and the church.

The **nave** is vast but remarkably simple in its symmetries; concentrate on the harmony of the architecture and try to blank out the largely hideous statuary and incidental decoration added well after Wren's time. As you walk beneath the dome, look down at the marble floor and you'll see the famous epitaph to Wren, added by his son after his death in 1723, '*Lector, si monumentam requiris, circumspice*' (Reader, if you seek a memorial, look around you). Look, in particular, up towards the magnificent **dome**. This is something of an optical illusion, nowhere near as big on the inside as it is on the outside. In fact, Wren built a smaller second dome inside the first to keep the interior on a manageable scale. The story goes that the first stone used to construct the dome was a relic from the old St Paul's which by coincidence bore the Latin word *resurgam* (rise up). Wren took it as a good portent and had the word inscribed in the pediment above the south door, adorning it with an image of a phoenix rising from the ashes. You can climb up into the dome, or domes, from a staircase on the south side of the cathedral, in exchange for another cash contribution.

The first stopping-off point is the **Whispering Gallery** 100ft up, so called because you can murmur with your face turned towards the wall and be heard with crystal clarity on the other side of the dome, 107ft away. You can also admire James Thornhill's series of frescoes on the life of St Paul which stretch all the way around the gallery. Vertigo permitting, you can continue on up to the Stone Gallery, the Inner Golden Gallery and the Outer Golden Gallery, offering panoramic views over London from just below the ball and cross at a height of 365ft.

And so down to the **crypt** (entrance near the south door), whose highlight is undoubtedly Wren's Great Model and the fine exhibition that accompanies it. Most of the space, though, is taken up with tombs commemorating Britain's military leaders. Among the rows and rows of nonentities you can find the Duke of Wellington in his pompous porphyry casket and, directly beneath the dome, the black marble sarcophagus honouring Horatio Nelson. The Florentine sarcophagus, by Pietro Torrigiano, was originally commissioned by Cardinal Wolsey back in the 16th century, but was deemed too good for him and spent three centuries unused and neglected in Windsor Castle until Nelson's mourners unearthed it for his funeral in 1805.

Science Museum

Exhibition Road; ⊖ *South Kensington; bus C1, 14, 74;* ***t*** *(020) 7942 4455, disabled persons' enquiry line* ***t*** *(020) 7942 4446, sleepovers* ***t*** *(020) 7942 4747, www.sciencemuseum.org.uk.*

Open daily 10–6; free, but adm to special exhibitions.

The Science Museum has done perhaps more than any other institution in London to make itself accessible and popular, undergoing constant updating and improvement. Children have always loved it; one of the latest gimmicks is to allow them to sleep at the museum overnight. Anyone aged 8–11 who brings a sleeping bag will be treated to an after-hours tour of the building, a choice of workshops and bedtime stories before lights out (children may also bring an adult).

For less privileged visitors, the best place to start is with the synopsis on the mezzanine above the **Ground Floor**, giving an overview of industrial and technological progress from Neolithic tools to the first aircraft. Here you can disabuse yourself of a few basic misconceptions: Jethro Tull was not just a bad 1970s heavy metal band, but also an 18th-century agricultural pioneer who introduced rowcrop farming. Beneath the mezzanine, the **Power** section gives a brief history of engines including models by Boulton and Watt from the 1780s. Then comes a **Space** section, complete with Second World War V2 rocket, satellites and a replica lunar lander module. Beyond, **Making the Modern World** traces the history of the modern industrial world, with Stephenson's Rocket at one end of the hall and the scorched Apollo 10 module at the other.

Moving down to the basement, you come to one of the highlights for children, a gallery full of interactive games called the **Launch Pad**. Here children are taught the rudiments of such diverse phenomena as bicycle gears and hangovers. Two further hands-on exhibits in the basement are **Garden** and **Things**.

On the first floor is **Challenge of Materials**, where a prototype pod from the London Eye dangles threateningly above a spectacular glass bridge supported by almost-invisible steel wires. **Time Measurement** traces the technology of clocks from the first Egyptian timepieces, based on water, to modern quartz and atomic clocks. Next to the tickers is **Food for Thought**, which explains everything you wanted to know about nutrition (and a few things you didn't – a group of see-through plastic vats, for example, demonstrating all too graphically how much urine, faeces and sweat a 10-year-old boy produces in a month).

The highlight of the second floor is the **Chemistry of Everyday Life**, exploring the history of the science through the discoveries of such pioneers as Priestley, Dalton, Davy and Faraday. Under **Living Molecules** you'll find Crick and Watson's metal-plate model of the structure of DNA. Further along the floor are displays on the development of computers and an overview of nuclear physics, as well as a beautiful collection of model ships.

On the third floor most children head for the **Flight Lab**, featuring simulators, a wind tunnel and a mini hot air balloon. The main **Flight** section is a display of more than 20 historic aircraft, plus a collection of models and an ingenious air traffic control display. Equally intriguing is **Optics**, a collection of spectacles, telescopes, microscopes and the like, leading up to such modern developments as lasers and holograms. The fourth and fifth floors are devoted to **medicine**.

The five floors of the new open-plan **Wellcome Wing** are terraced, somewhat like a shopping centre, though bathed in otherworldly blue light so that it feels more like a space station. This is in keeping with the wing's aim to remain up to date with the latest in computer technology. The scanty exhibits, designed to shock and stimulate, include the very computer on which the World Wide Web was conceived, a genuine £2 million Formula 1 McLaren and a human heart whose owner still walks the streets.

Tate Britain

Millbank; ⊖ Pimlico; bus 77A from Strand; **t** *(020) 7887 8000, www.tate.org.uk.*

Open daily 10–5.50; free; free tours, each covering different periods of art, Mon–Fri at 11, 12, 2, 3, Sat 12, 3.

Founded at the end of the 19th century by the sugar baron Sir Henry Tate of Tate & Lyle fame, this is the second great London art collection after the National Gallery. In spring 2000 the collection was divided into two: 20th-century international art moved across the river to the massive new **Tate Modern** at Bankside (*see* below); the gallery here was renamed **Tate Britain** and the entire building devoted to a survey of home-grown works from the Renaissance until the present day.

As well as the original building, James Stirling's attractive **Clore Gallery** extension opened in 1987 and contains an outstanding collection of paintings by the great 19th-century artist J. M. W. Turner.

The collection includes British landscapes by Stubbs, Gainsborough, Nash and Constable as well as Turner. There are key works by William Blake, Hogarth and Joshua Reynolds, and the Tate is well known for its Pre-Raphaelites, who strove to reject the ideal style symbolized by Raphael in favour of a more naturalistic approach.

Tate Modern

Bankside; ⊖ Southwark; ***t*** *(020) 7401 5120, www.tate.org.uk.*

Open Sun–Thurs 10–6, Fri and Sat 10–10; free (charge for special exhibitions); free guided tours daily at 11, 12, 2, 3.

Hailed as the cultural phenomenon of the Millennium, Tate Modern surpassed all visitor-figure estimates within the first few months of its grand opening. Wide critical acclaim has been lavished on Swiss architects Herzog and de Meuron's sensitive but spectacular transformation of the former power station, which has played as big a part in drawing the crowds as the internationally renowned Tate Collection itself.

The building is flooded with natural light via a glass canopy that spans its entire length, adding two floors to its height and giving visitors excellent views across the City. More light shines down courtesy of illuminated balconies overlooking the Turbine Hall, the cavernous main entrance that also serves as a temporary exhibition space.

There are seven floors in all, with the majority of the works spread out over six gallery suites on the three middle floors. The exhibitions comprise rotating works from the Tate modern art collection, one of the most important in the world, with significant works by the 20th century's most influential artists including Picasso, Matisse, Brancusi, Dalí, Pollock, Giacometti, Warhol and Hockney; and loan exhibitions. The rooms are arranged thematically rather than chronologically and combine painting and sculpture with video and photography, the idea being to interweave movements and traditions and draw out unexpected resonances and relationships. Thus, despite being born a century apart, you will find Claude Monet's *Water Lilies* next to Richard Long's mud wall paintings, the juxtaposition highlighting both artists' sense of immersion in landscape. Some cynical voices have suggested that this unusual decision may have sprung from a failure to procure certain works for the gallery, thereby serving the useful purpose of smudging any gaps in the collection. Whatever the reason, the liberation of the works from their historical constraints is a refreshing experience. Only around half the permanent collection is on show at any one time, and the themes change every few months, but it's a rich mix, with plenty of controversial art works on show, the kind which the general public loves to hate, including Carl André's *Equivalent Viii* (a pile of bricks) and Marcel Duchamp's hugely influential *Fountain* (a urinal), and well-represented movements such as German Expressionism, Abstract Expressionism and Pop Art.

The gallery's facilities are superb, with cafés, sensitively designed reading points, excellent bookshops and, best of all, lots of easy-to-find loos.

10 Downing Street

Off Whitehall; ⊖ Westminster; bus 3, 11, 12, 24, 53, 77A, 88, 159, 453.

Downing Street has been home to British prime ministers on and off since 1735. Unfortunately, you won't be able to sidle up to the famous Georgian front door at No.10 without a security pass; the best you can hope for is a glimpse through the heavy iron gates installed in 1990. Next door at No.11 is house of the Chancellor of the Exchequer, the British equivalent of treasury secretary or finance minister, and next door to him, at No.12, is the government whips' office, where the party in power keeps tabs on its members in parliament.

It is rather pleasing to think that this street, the scene of many a heated cabinet meeting and ministerial bollocking, was once an open venue for cock-fighting. A theatre dedicated to the proposition that encouraging animals to tear each other apart with spurs is just as entertaining as watching politicians doing the same thing in the Palace of Westminster stayed in business on this site alongside the Axe brew-house until about 1675. It was only then that a rather modest building development, later to become the powerhouse of the British establishment, was undertaken by one George Downing, a slippery fellow who managed to spy for both Oliver Cromwell and Charles II during the Civil War and come out of it not only alive but stinking rich into the bargain. It was more accident than design that led to Downing Street's lasting fame. When the prime minister, Robert Walpole, succeeded a certain Mr Chicken as tenant in 1735 he never meant to establish No.10 as an official residence, and indeed many of his successors preferred to conduct the business of government from their more lavish homes elsewhere in London. Only in the early 19th century was 10 Downing Street kitted out with proper facilities, such as Sir John Soane's sumptuous dining room; only in 1902 did it become the prime minister's home as well as office. The shortcomings of the place have never gone away, though; when Tony Blair became prime minister in 1997, he installed his family in the more spacious No.11 next door, swapping places with his then unmarried Chancellor, Gordon Brown.

Tower Bridge

⊖ Tower Hill; bus 42, 78 from the City, or 15 to the Tower of London; www.towerbridge.org.uk.

Tower Bridge Exhibition, ***t*** *(020) 7403 3761. Open daily April–Sept 10–6.30, Oct–Mar 9.30–6, last entry 1hr before closing; adm.*

Tower Bridge is one of the great feats of late Victorian engineering, half suspension-bridge and half drawbridge, linked to two neo-Gothic towers. Designed by an engineer, John Wolfe-Barry, and an architect, Horace Jones, working in tandem, it has become one of London's most recognizable landmarks. Its fame was not exactly instant; indeed, at its opening in 1894, the critics found its evocation of medieval style crude. *The Builder* called it 'the most monstrous and preposterous architectural sham that we have ever known...an elaborate and costly make-believe.' There is still a reasonable case to be made that Tower Bridge is a kind of Victorian Disneyland, but time has mellowed its vulgarity and made it both awe-inspiring and loveable. Its two bascules, the arms that rise up to let tall ships through, weigh an astonishing 1,000 tonnes each. Despite the decline of river freight traffic, the bridge still opens at least once a day on average; phone ahead (**t** (020) 7403 3761) to find out the times.

At the southern tower you can join the **Tower Bridge Experience**, a hi-tech retelling of the history of the bridge, plus a chance to enjoy the view from the overhead walkways and admire the giant Victorian hydraulic engines that once operated the bridge (it is now done with electric power).

Tower of London

⊖ Tower Hill, bus 15; ***t*** *0870 756 6060, www.hrp.org.uk.*

Open March–Oct Tues–Sat 9–6, Sun and Mon 10–6; Nov–Feb Tues–Sat 9–5, Sun and Mon 10–5; last adm all year round 1hr before closing; adm exp.

The Tower is one London sight that everyone knows but nobody particularly likes. Ever since the monarchy moved out in the early 17th century, the Tower has existed principally as a stronghold of historical nostalgia, a place that owes its appeal more to romantic notions of the past than to real past events. Modern Americans might want to compare it to the fantasy castles of Disneyland, especially if they follow the **Tower Hill Pageant** (entrance near All Hallows' Church), a 15-minute underground ghost train ride, complete with commentary and nasty smells and sounds, past tableaux of famous episodes in London's history.

So what is the big attraction? First of all the site, which is one of the best preserved medieval castles in the world. The **White Tower**, the keep at the centre of the complex, dates back to William the Conqueror and includes the magnificent heavy round arches and groin vaults of the 13th-century **St John's Chapel**. More importantly, the Tower corresponds to every myth ever invented about England. Its history is packed with tales of royal pageantry, dastardly baronial plots, ghoulish tortures and gruesome executions. The Tower is still guarded by quaint liveried figures, the Beefeaters, who obligingly conduct their Ceremony of the Keys at 9.45 each evening. And, of course, the Tower contains the Crown Jewels.

Under Henry III the Tower expanded considerably and included for the first time a menagerie, complete with lions, leopards, a polar bear and an elephant. Prisoners were brought in from the river through **Traitor's Gate**, which you can still see today.

Inevitably, you also will be drawn towards the **Crown Jewels** (no longer the real thing but very good reproductions). You'll probably have to share the spectacle with the entire adult population of Cleveland, Ohio, not to mention several thousand Euro-teenagers, but at least there is a decent attempt at crowd control, thanks to a relatively new conveyor-belt system. There are two main crowns: St Edward's Crown, a heavy, somewhat unwieldy piece used only during the coronation ceremony itself; and the golden Crown of State, encrusted with 3,000 gems, which was originally made for Queen Victoria and is still used for grand occasions such as the state opening of parliament. Next are the jewelled sword and spurs, also used to anoint the new monarch, followed by the orb, bracelets and two sceptres which symbolize the sovereign's secular and divine mission. The orb represents the spread of Christianity around the world, the sceptres forge the link between the monarch and his or her subjects, while the bracelets are an emblem of Britain's link to the Commonwealth. The Ring of Kingly Dignity is a sapphire mounted with rubies, while the Great Sword of State, the sovereign's symbolic personal weapon, is decorated with a lion and unicorn as well as the royal arms.

Trafalgar Square

Back in the 1810s and 1820s, when Britannia really did rule the waves and London was the capital of a burgeoning empire, a hitherto taboo concept suddenly came into fashion: urban planning. Previously it had been considered perfectly proper for London to develop organically according to the whims of private landowners. But then industrialization arrived, threatening to stifle the capital in factory smoke if the *laissez-faire* planning policy persisted. At the same time, Britain's victory in the Napoleonic Wars unleashed a broad desire for some decent monumental architecture. The Prince Regent, an ardent patron of grand building schemes, was only too happy to sponsor major projects, and soon architects were putting forward proposals for the wildest and most outlandish schemes.

It was in such an atmosphere that Trafalgar Square was first conceived. The Prince Regent (later crowned George IV) and his chosen architect, John Nash, wanted to create a vast open space glorifying the country's naval power which would also provide a focal point from which other urban projects could spread. It was a fine idea, but one that was destined to be cruelly truncated by the vagaries of history. George developed a reputation as a spendthrift and a philanderer, and as economic crisis gripped the nation in the mid-1820s all his dreams were brought to a halt by a hostile parliament. Nash was dismissed as soon as George died in 1830, and from then on Trafalgar Square was left at the mercy of successive parliamentary committees who argued for the best part of a generation over its final form.

Modern Trafalgar Square evolved partly out of a desire to raise the tone of the Charing Cross area. Nash pulled down the old King's Mews (incidentally, a fine Georgian building by William Kent) to make room for his planned ensemble of grand classical buildings. But he never got to build them before his fall from grace. The whole Trafalgar Square project might have been abandoned had it not been for a lingering determination to bestow grand honours on Horatio Nelson, the country's legendary naval commander who had died at sea during the Battle of Trafalgar in 1805. In 1808, the essayist William Wood wrote a rousing eulogy of England 'proudly stemming the torrent of revolutionary frenzy', and proposed erecting a giant pyramid to his hero. Over the years 120 official proposals were submitted, including myriad columns, pyramids and even a Coliseum. In the absence of a co-ordinating architect, however, the scheme made painfully slow progress. Where Nash was extravagant, the special select committee of the House of Commons proved downright stingy. The new planners were not interested in producing monumental architecture unless it could be done on the cheap.

As for **Nelson's Column**, it did not see the light of day until 1843. The Corinthian column, topped by an unremarkable and scarcely visible likeness of Nelson in his admiral's three-cornered hat, by E. H. Baily, was erected on a sloping concrete basin prepared by the neoclassical architect Charles Barry. Railton based his design on a triumphalist precedent from ancient Rome, the Temple of Mars in the Forum of Augustus. The bronze bas-reliefs at the base of the column represent Nelson's four greatest victories, at Cape St Vincent, the Nile, Copenhagen and Trafalgar, while the surrounding statuary is of Nelson's generals. The two granite fountains at the base arrived in 1845, while the bronze lions, the most appealing feature of the ensemble, appeared a quarter of a century later.

As if the project were not truncated enough already, the plinth at the northwest corner of the square – described by some as a testimony to British inertia – remained empty for over 150 years, while successive authorities bickered over who should be honoured by a statue. In 1999 the Royal Society for the encouragement of Arts (RSA) stepped in to unveil the Fourth Plinth Exhibition, a temporary display of contemporary sculpture. Mark Wallinger's *Ecce Homo* and Bill Woodrow's *Regardless of History* were followed by Rachel Whiteread's *Monument*, a direct-take on the plinth itself. Since its dismantling in May 2002, no decision has been made about what will follow.

Trafalgar Square, still an active venue for political demonstrations and victory parades, is the point from which all measurements in London are drawn; there is a plaque indicating this on the corner of Charing Cross Road. On the eastern side of the square is South Africa House, where anti-apartheid protesters maintained a constant vigil through the latter part of Nelson Mandela's 26-year imprisonment. Next door is James Gibbs's church of St Martin-in-the-Fields (*see* p.69). In the southeastern corner stands a lamp-post known as the smallest police station in the world, which contains a telephone linked up to police headquarters at Scotland Yard. On the western side, in a building designed by Robert Smirke, builder of the British Museum, is Canada House, home to the Canadian High Commission. The northern side, in front of the National Gallery, was pedestrianized in 2004.

Victoria and Albert Museum

Cromwell Road and second entrance on Exhibition Road; ⊖ South Kensington; bus C1, 74, 14, 414; ***t*** *(020) 7942 2000, www.vam.ac.uk.*

Open Thurs–Tues 10–5.45, Wed and last Fri of every month 10–10; free; guided tours throughout the day.

This huge, sprawling museum is nominally dedicated to applied art and design, but in fact even such a broad definition does not sufficiently cover the sheer vastness of its collections. Over the years it has become the nation's treasure trove. You could liken it to a magical chest in some long-forgotten attic; but the V&A has also kept bang up to date, displaying everything from Donatello to Dalí, from medieval reliquaries to Reebok sneakers. Its former director, Sir Roy Strong, once defined it as an 'extremely capacious handbag'. Unlike most large museums, you would be ill-advised to pick and choose your way around the V&A on a first visit. To get a proper feel of it, you should aim to get hopelessly lost along its seven miles of corridors.

Pick up a free **museum plan** at the reception desk.

Level A

The Dress Gallery and Musical Instruments

An enthralling starting point is the room dedicated to European fashion across history. Watch how the flamboyant clothes of the 17th and 18th century gradually grow more restricted by corsets and bodices, then become blander and fussier in the 19th century, turn morose in the 1930s and 1940s before exploding in new-found freedom and colour in the 1960s and beyond. Up a spiral staircase from the dress section are musical instruments, a range of music boxes, virginals and a Dutch giraffe piano with six percussion pedals, as well as the usual strings, wind and brass.

Italy 1400–1500

The V&A calls this the greatest collection of Renaissance sculpture outside Italy. The pieces here are so disparate they could have come from some glorified car boot sale held by the great churches of Tuscany and northern Italy. There are rood sculptures and reliefs, beautifully decorated cassones in gilt and gesso, a *Neptune and Triton* by Giovanni Bernini and *Samson Slaying a Philistine* by Giovanni Bologna. The greatest treasures are two delicate reliefs by Donatello, the *Ascension With Christ Giving The Keys To St Peter*, which may have been commissioned for the Brancacci chapel in Santa Maria del Carmine in Florence, and *Dead Christ Tended by Angels*.

Poynter, Gamble and Morris Rooms

On your way through the Italian section you pass the world's first museum café-restaurant. Each of the three rooms is a rich, highly decorated example of Victorian design. The Poynter Room, originally the grill room, is decked out in blue tiles depicting idyllic country harvest scenes in between allegories of the seasons and the months of the year. The Gamble Room, used for the cold buffet, is a throwback to the Renaissance with its gold and blue tiles, enamelled metal ceiling and apt quotation from Ecclesiasticus around the walls: 'There is nothing better for a man than to eat and drink.' The last room is the work of William Morris.

Raphael Gallery

On the other side of the Dress Gallery, this vast room houses a hugely important Renaissance collection – the series of cartoons painted by Raphael in 1514–15 as designs for tapestries to be hung in the Sistine Chapel.

Plaster Casts

Two rooms, straddling the altogether disappointing collection of fakes and forgeries, are devoted to near-perfect copies of some of the most famous sculptures and monuments in the world. The effect is altogether surreal: how can you get your mind around seeing Michelangelo's *David and Moses*, Ghiberti's *Gates of Paradise*, Trajan's Column from Rome, the *Puerta de la Gloria* from Santiago de Compostela and chunks of Bordeaux, Aix-en-Provence, Amiens, York and Nuremberg cathedrals all in one place?

Asian Art

The central section of Level A is devoted to art from the Islamic world, India, China, Japan and Korea. The most famous piece is **Tipu's Tiger** in the Nehru Gallery of Indian Art. This is an adjustable wooden sculpture dating from 1790 in which a tiger can be seen mauling the neck of an English soldier. There are Indian sculptures of deities dating back to the 1st century BC, and paintings and artefacts giving an overview of two millennia of Indian decoration.

The Toshiba Gallery of **Japanese Art** boasts some particularly fine lacquer work: tables, trays and some amazing playing-card boxes. There are also some interesting ceramics, including a huge porcelain disc originally shown in Europe at the 1878 Paris Exhibition.

The **Chinese Art** section focuses principally on fine objects used in everyday life, particularly ceramics and a collection of ornaments and figurines used in burial ceremonies. Grander pieces include a large Ming dynasty canopied bed and a Qing dynasty embroidered hanging for a Buddhist temple. The **Korean Art** gallery also focuses on everyday objects, including some ancient metalwork, and ceramics from the Koryo and Choson dynasties that go back to the 9th century. Finally the section on **Art in the Islamic World** contains a potpourri of carpets and prayer mats from Egypt and Turkey and finely decorated bowls and earthenware from Persia.

Medieval Treasury

Sandwiched in the middle of the oriental art sections is the **Medieval Treasury**, a beautiful collection of mainly religious artefacts from the 5th to the 15th century.

Level B

20th Century Gallery and Silver Gallery

This series of altogether enthralling rooms is a far more engaging history of 20th-century design than the Design Museum at Butler's Wharf. The focus is on household furniture, but within that remit is everything from Marcel Breuer's pioneering Bauhaus chair to Salvador Dalí's totally frivolous lipstick-pink sofa in the shape of one of Mae West's kisses. There is also a high-tech gallery with 500 years of British silver.

Tapestries

Beyond the 20th Century Gallery you have to walk through yards and yards of unexciting silver pots, metalwork and armour before reaching the tapestry collection and, in particular, the medieval series known as the **Devonshire Hunt**. Famed for their beauty, wealth of detail and high standard of preservation, these tapestries were commissioned in the 15th century for Hardwick Hall, a country mansion in southwestern England.

Henry Cole Wing

On the light and airy 6th floor is the world's largest collection of **Constable paintings**, a clutch of Turners and a series of **Rodin sculptures** . Otherwise this wing, named after the museum's founding director, comes closest to the chest-in-the-attic analogy: much of what is in here is junk, particularly the painting section on the fourth floor, but a bit of patient burrowing will be well rewarded.

On the second floor is the **Frank Lloyd Wright Gallery**, a series of rooms dedicated to the great 20th-century American architect and figurehead of the modern movement. Floor three is reserved for special exhibitions of prints.

The glittering **glass gallery** at Room 131 shouldn't be missed, either, with its staircase made entirely of green glass blocks.

British Galleries

In November 2001, the V&A finally opened the doors of the new British Galleries, its most ambitious project for half a century. The 15 galleries contain the most comprehensive collection of British design and art (from 1500 to 1900) anywhere in the world. There are more than 3,000 objects on display, but the highlights are Henry VIII's writing desk, James II's wedding suit and the famous vast **Great Bed of Ware**, which was made for an inn and became instantly famous – Shakespeare and Ben Jonson both mentioned it in their plays. All of the top British designers are featured here – Morris, Gibbon, Macintosh and Adam – as well as famous manufacturers such as Chippendale, Morris, Mackintosh, Wedgwood and Liberty. One of the most elaborate pieces is an elegant 18th-century tea table, carved in the days when tea-drinking was an expensive hobby enjoyed only by the very wealthy. As well as individual objects, there are also some handsomely re-created rooms. In 2005 a new architecture gallery opened. The galleries have interactive computer terminals to learn more about the displays.

Westminster Abbey

Parliament Square; ⊖ Westminster; bus 3, 11, 12, 24, 53, 77A, 88, 159, 453; ***t*** *(020) 7222 5152, www.westminster-abbey.org.*

Admission to the abbey is free for services or prayers. For visitors the Chapter House, Nave and Royal Chapels are open Mon–Tues and Thurs–Fri 9.30–3.45, Wed 9.30–7, Sat 9.30–1.45; adm. The Abbey Museum is open Mon–Sat 10.30–4. Last entry 1hr before closing. Guided tours conducted by the vergers are also available, call ***t*** *(020) 7654 4900 to book.*

It is impossible to overestimate the symbolic importance of Westminster Abbey in English culture. This is where monarchs are crowned and buried, where the Anglican Church derives its deepest inspiration and where the nation as a whole lionizes its artistic and political heroes. No other country invests so much importance in a single building.

Architecturally the abbey derives its inspiration from the great cathedrals at Reims and Amiens and the Sainte-Chapelle in Paris. 'A great French thought expressed in excellent English,' one epigram has it. The abbey's origins go back to the mists of the Dark Ages; it found a mystical patron in Edward the Confessor, saint and monarch. It was rebuilt from scratch in the finest Gothic traditions from the 13th until the 16th century, and completed in 1745. Thus the abbey spans virtually the whole of modern English history. To be buried there, or at least to have a plaque erected, is still the highest state honour for an English citizen. The tombs of the medieval kings and other relics bestow much of the legitimacy to which the modern monarchy can still lay claim. If St Paul's is a monument to the secular wealth of London, Westminster Abbey enshrines the mystical power of the crown.

It was Westminster's association with the crown that saved the abbey during the dissolution of the monasteries in the late 1530s, when it escaped with just a few smashed windows and broken ornaments. The royal connection made it a target during the Civil War, when Cromwell's army used it as a dormitory and smashed the altar rails. Cromwell succumbed to its lure once he was Lord Protector, however, and had himself buried in the abbey after his death in 1658. His body was dug up at the Restoration and eventually reburied at the foot of the gallows at Tyburn. After the Civil War, the abbey was once again given over to burials and coronations. Aside from royals, the place is stuffed with memorials to politicians (in the Statesman's Aisle), poets (in Poets' Corner), actors, scientists and engineers.

The coronation ceremony has become familiar around the world thanks to television re-runs of the investiture of Elizabeth II in 1953, the first coronation to be televised. But ceremonies have not always gone as smoothly as the establishment might have liked. Richard I had a bat swooping around his head during his ceremony, a sign perhaps of bad luck to come. Richard II lost a shoe in the abbey, while James II's crown wobbled and nearly fell off during his parade down Whitehall. George IV was so weighed down by his outrageously extravagant coronation garb that he nearly fainted and had to be revived with smelling salts.

Pick up a floor plan at the entrance. Everything west of the choir screen is free; beyond is the old east end, now St Edward's Chapel; and beyond that the late Gothic extension including the Henry VII Chapel. The Cloisters and Chapter House are off the end of the south transept.

The Nave

Measuring 103ft from floor to ceiling, the nave of Westminster Abbey is by far the tallest in England. But the nave is very long as well as high, giving an impression of general grandeur but not necessarily of loftiness. The columns, made of Purbeck marble, grow darker towards the ceiling, thus further deadening the effect of height. And the ceiling decorations push the eye not upwards, but along towards the altar. Overall, ornamentation is just as important as effects of perspective. As you come in, there is a 14th-century gilded painting of Richard II. The north aisle of the nave has become crowded with memorials and stones to politicians, earning the nickname **Statesman's Aisle**. Plenty of other walks of life are celebrated in this part of the abbey, notably scientists and engineers including Michael Faraday (a memorial tablet) and Sir Isaac Newton (a splendid monument against the choir screen by William Kent).

The Choir and St Edward's Chapel

The first attraction beyond the ticket counters, the choir screen, is a 19th-century reworking by Edward Blore of the gilded 13th-century original. Note the elegant black and white marble floor, and the heraldic shields commemorating the families who gave money to construct the abbey in the 13th century. Behind the High Altar is St Edward's Chapel, the epicentre of the abbey with its memorials to medieval kings around the Coronation Chair. Until November 1996, when it was finally removed to Edinburgh Castle, the simple gilded wooden chair contained the Stone of Scone, the most sacred symbol of the kings of Scotland, which was stolen by Edward I in 1279 and arrogantly kept for five and a bit centuries here in England.

Henry VII Chapel

The penny-pinching Henry VII managed one great feat of artistic patronage during his reign, this extraordinary fan-vaulted chapel which is nominally dedicated to the Virgin Mary but is in fact a glorification of the Tudor line of monarchs. Henrys VII and VIII, Edward VI, Mary and Elizabeth I are all buried here in style, along with a healthy sprinkling of their contemporaries and successors. Elizabeth shares her huge tomb with her embittered half-sister Mary in a curious after-death gesture of reconciliation. The bodies believed to be the two princes murdered in the Tower of London in 1483 also have a resting place here. The highlight of the chapel, though, is the decoration. The wondrous ceiling looks like an intricate mesh of finely spun cobwebs, while the wooden choirstalls are carved with exotic creatures and adorned with brilliantly colourful heraldic flags.

Poets' Corner

The south transept and the adjoining St Faith's Chapel are part of the original 13th-century abbey structure, and boast a series of wall paintings and some superbly sculpted figures of angels. Geoffrey Chaucer was buried in the south transept in 1400, and ever since other poets and writers have vied to have a place next to him after their deaths. When Edmund Spenser, author of *The Faerie Queen*, was buried in 1599, several writers tossed their unpublished manuscripts into the grave with him. His contemporary, the playwright Ben Jonson, asked modestly for a grave 'two feet by two feet' and consequently was buried upright. Few of the writers commemorated in Poets' Corner are actually interred here; among the 'genuine' ones are Dryden, Samuel Johnson, Sheridan, Browning and Tennyson. To free up more space in the increasingly crowded corner, the abbey authorities have recently installed a stained-glass window with new memorials to parvenus such as Pope, Robert Herrick and Oscar Wilde.

London: Central Neighbourhoods

06

Bloomsbury

⊖ Holborn, Euston, Russell Square, Goodge Street, Warren Street.

Bloomsbury, according to William the Conqueror's survey *Domesday Book*, started life as a breeding ground for pigs, but it has acquired a rather more refined pedigree since. Home to London University, the British Museum, the new British Library and countless bookshops and cafés, it is the intellectual heart of the capital. George Bernard Shaw, Giuseppe Mazzini, Marx and Lenin all found inspiration among the tomes of the Reading Room in the British Library. Bertrand Russell and Virginia Woolf helped form an intellectual movement here, the Bloomsbury Group, whose members invited each other for tea and gossip in the area's Georgian townhouses. More recently, Bloomsbury has become a favoured location for advertising companies, the book trade and a new wave of independent television production companies. It is a quiet, slightly shabby but youthful quarter of London.

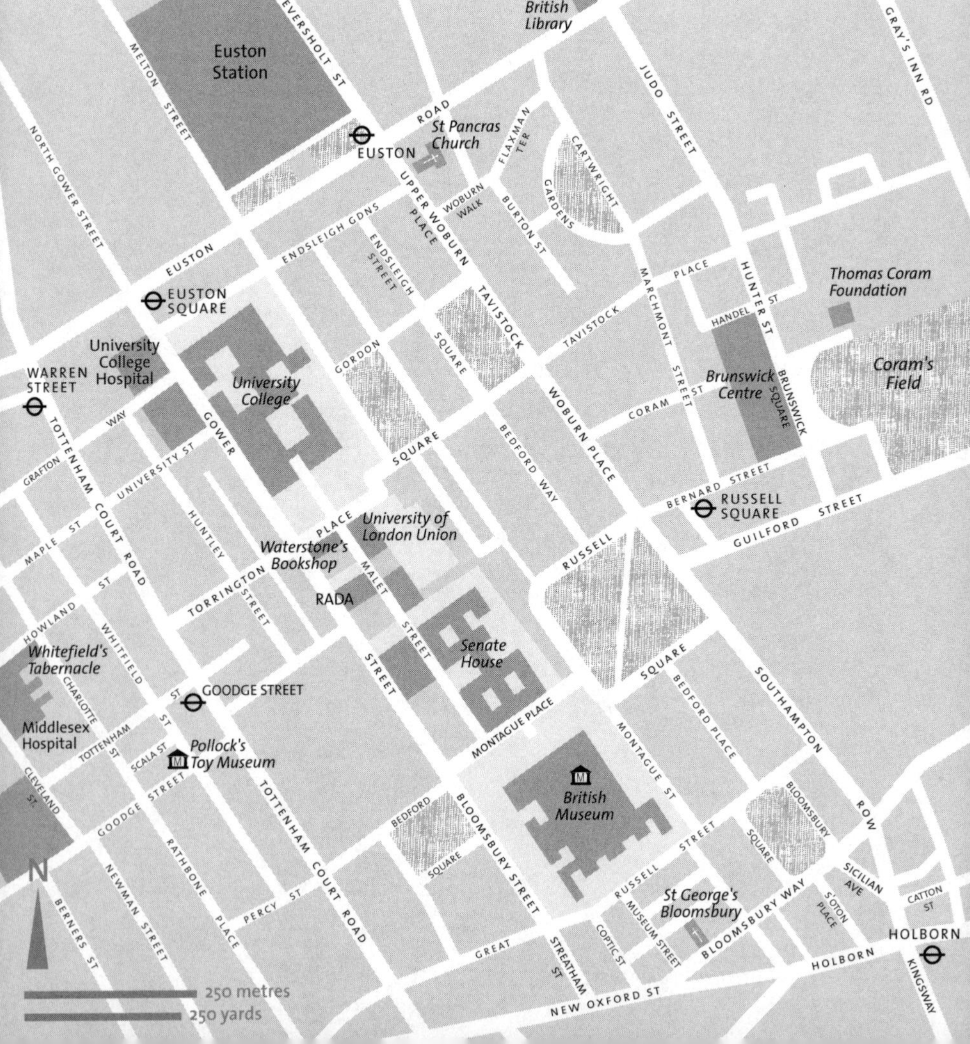

Bloomsbury Square

This was the original London housing development based on the leasehold system, and the model for the city's phenomenally rapid growth throughout the 18th and 19th centuries. Nowadays it is one of the more elegant squares in central London, with a ring of stately Georgian homes surrounding a flourishing garden. The square also has a plaque commemorating the **Bloomsbury Group**, a movement most often associated with its brightest member, the novelist Virginia Woolf, but which also included Woolf's husband Leonard, the novelist E. M. Forster, the economist John Maynard Keynes, the philosopher Bertrand Russell and the essayist Lytton Strachey. The group had no manifesto or specific aim; it was a loose association of like-minded intellectuals (most of them politically soft left) who met to exchange ideas. Following the teachings of the philosopher G. E. Moore, they believed that the appreciation of beautiful objects and the art of fine conversation were the keys to social progress.

Russell Square and the University of London

On the western side of the square looms **Senate House**, one of the spookiest buildings in London, which stands at the heart of the schools and colleges of the **University of London**. The School of Oriental and African Studies (SOAS) sits in the northwest corner of Russell Square. On the corner of Malet Street is the students' union (ULU). If you happen to be a student yourself, you can use its good, cheap bar. Halfway down Malet Street is **Birkbeck College**, which in 1823 became the first college in England to run evening courses for the working classes. It joined London University in 1920. Continuing down Torrington Place, you come to **Gower Street**, the blackened brick terraces of which sum up everything the Victorians disapproved of in Georgian building. Ruskin called it 'the *ne plus ultra* of ugliness in street architecture'. You can see what he meant: the sameness of the houses, relieved only by the occasional splash of paint on the lower storey, and the arrow-like straightness of the street.

Along on the right, **University College** is a fine, if rather heavy, example of the Greek Revival style by William Wilkins, the architect of the National Gallery. Many Victorians hated the place. Visitors should head straight for the South Cloister in the far right-hand corner. Near the door is the glass cabinet with the stuffed body of **Jeremy Bentham**, the utilitarian philosopher and political reformer who died in 1832.

Cafés and Pubs

The Coffee Gallery, 23 Museum Street. Mediterranean and organic food: grilled aubergines, fishcakes with rocket, and scrumptious Sicilian salads.

Bar Centrale, 4 Bernard Street. A typical London 1970s-style Italian coffee shop, of the kind that are fast dying out.

Wagamama, 4 Streatham St. Cheap, popular, delicious Japanese noodle ('ramen') restaurant, part of a chain but fast and delicious. Shared long tables are the norm. £6–12.

Hakkasan, 8 Hanway Place. Cutting edge Chinese cuisine and amazing cocktails in chic and sleek surroundings. It's not cheap, but the food has won awards.

Malabar Junction, 107 Great Russell Street. Set lunch £13 in smart but laid-back restaurant close to the British Museum.

Fitzroy Tavern, 16 Charlotte St. Drinking hole for Dylan Thomas, George Orwell and 1940s Fitzrovia; now serving traditional pub grub – chicken tikka masala, Sunday roasts, baked potatoes, etc.

The British Library

96 Euston Rd; **t** *(020) 7412 7332. Open Mon and Wed–Fri 9.30–6, Tues 9.30–8, Sat 9.30–5, Sun 11–5; guided tours certain days; bookshops and restaurant.*

The history of this new building has been such a shambles that it came as a shock to most people when it finally opened, a decade late, in November 1997. Construction work on Colin St John Wilson's building began back in 1978 and took longer than the building of St Paul's Cathedral. By the time it was completed, Wilson had overspent by £350 million, his practice had dissolved and the building itself had been exposed to that peculiarly violent brand of venom that the British reserve for new architectural projects. Ironically, some of the building's most vicious critics have been stunned and delighted by the spectacular interior, with its vast scale, open tracts of Travertine marble, and complex and fascinating spaces flooded with light.

The big attraction is the library's vast number of **manuscripts**: from the sacred to the profane; from the delicate beauty of illuminated Bibles to the frenzied scrawl of Joyce's first draft of *Finnegan's Wake*; from musical scores to political documents to private letters. Among the greatest treasures are the **Lindisfarne Gospels**, the work of a monk named Eadfrith who wrote and illuminated them on the island of Lindisfarne (also called Holy Island), off the northeastern coast of England. The other star exhibit is the **Magna Carta**. The British Library has two of the four surviving copies of this document, one of the founding texts of the modern democratic system signed by King John at Runnymede under pressure from his barons in 1215. Among the other manuscripts are Lenin's reapplication for a reader's ticket under the pseudonym Jacob Richter. There is an extensive collection of literary manuscripts, including an illuminated version of Chaucer's *Canterbury Tales*, and Lewis Carroll's notebook version of *Alice in Wonderland*. Stamp-lovers should head for the **Philatelic Collections** which include first issues of nearly every stamp in the world from 1840 to 1890.

Also here is the **British Library National Sound Archive** (*open to reader's pass holders only*). This wonderful collection includes early gramophones and record sleeves, and a series of priceless historical, literary and musical recordings: Florence Nightingale, Paul Robeson in a live performance of *Othello*, James Joyce reading from *Ulysses*, the Beatles interviewed by Jenny Everett, and Charlie Parker's club performances.

Pollock's Toy Museum

41 Whitfield St; **t** *(020) 7636 3452, www.pollocksmuseum.co.uk. Open Mon–Sat 10–5; cheap adm.*

Benjamin Pollock was the leading Victorian manufacturer of toy theatres, and this small but very attractive museum is based on the collection that he left. It's an atmospheric place, the four narrow floors connected by creaky staircases. The theatres are on the top floor, and exhibits also include board games, tin toys, puppets, wax dolls, teddy bears and dolls' houses.

***Also see*: The British Museum, p.27.**

***Onwards to*: Covent Garden, p.66; Tottenham Court Road shopping, p.132.**

The City of London

⊖ *Bank, St Paul's, Tower Hill, Mansion House, Monument, Barbican;*
⇌ *City Thameslink, Barbican, Fenchurch Street.*

The City is the heart of London, the place where the whole heaving metropolis began, and yet there is something so strange about it that it scarcely seems to be part of London at all. Tens of thousands of commuters stream in each morning, the bankers, brokers and clerks that oil the wheels of this great centre of world finance, spilling out of Liverpool Street or crossing over London Bridge towards their jumble of gleaming, high-rise offices. During the lunch hour, you can see them scurrying from office building to sandwich bar to post office, a look of studied intensity stamped on their harried faces. By early evening they have all vanished again, back to their town-houses and dormitory communities, leaving the streets and once-monumental buildings to slumber eerily in the silent gloom of the London night.

This is T. S. Eliot's 'Unreal City', a metropolis without inhabitants, a place of frenzied, seemingly mindless mechanical activity that the poet, back in the apocalyptic early 1920s, thought worthy of the lost souls of limbo. And yet it remains oddly fascinating, full of echoes of the time when it *was* London. Its streets still largely follow the medieval plan. Its fine churches and ceremonial buildings express all the contradictory emotions of a nation that built, and then lost, an entire empire. Its business is still trade, as it was in the 14th century, even if it is trade of a most abstract and arcane sort.

Wren's churches, and St Paul's Cathedral in particular, grace the skyline, but the area is also characterized by the bloody carcasses of Smithfield meat market and the grim legacy of Newgate prison, now converted into the Central Criminal Court.

Cafés and Pubs

Dirty Dick's, 202 Bishopsgate. Dirty Dick was a dandy called Nathaniel Bentley. His fiancée died on the eve of their wedding in 1787, and he never washed again. When he died in 1809, the house was in ruins. Rebuilt in 1870, it's now a jolly cellar bar; lunch is well-cooked bar food (sausage and mash, roast chicken, steaks and chips) from £7–10.

Punch Tavern, 99 Fleet St. A huge variety of food, soft drinks and ales, the food served as an imaginative all-you-can-eat buffet for £6.50, in an ex-journalists' pub where the satirical magazine *Punch* was invented.

Ye Old Mitre Tavern, 1 Ely Court, off Ely Place. A 260-year-old warren of a pub located up a narrow alley next to St Etheldreda's, where there has been a pub since 1546. Snacks from £3; real ales. *Open 11–11 Mon–Fri.*

Obertelli's, 60 Leadenhall Market. Sandwiches and café-style food. £5–9.

The Eagle, 159 Farringdon Road. Trailblazing pub that kickstarted the quality pub-grub revolution. Food £7.50–12; *open daily.*

The Place Below, St Mary-le-Bow, Cheapside. Award-winning, popular and nutritious breakfasts, lunches and snacks in the undercroft of this beautiful City church. £5–8.

Simpson's Tavern, 38 Cornhill. Traditional English food in a much-loved, excellent value eaterie off Cornhill: grills, bubble and squeak, steamed jam roll. £3–4 for starters, £7–10 for main courses.

Royal Exchange Grand Café and Bar. In the atrium of the old Royal Exchange, serving simple food like grilled asparagus in a grand city setting.

Carluccio's Caffè, 12 West Smithfield. Branch of this unmatchable small chain, with excellent coffee and Italian food.

Caravaggio, 107 Leadenhall St. A big brasserie in an old bank, serving Italian food.

At the other end of the Square Mile, the Tower of London is a striking relic of medieval London and a reminder of the constant historical struggle between wealth creation on the one hand and the jealous encroachment of political interests on the other. The City is a weekday place only, although you won't have any difficulty getting into the Tower or Guildhall on Saturday.

In keeping with London's new-found passion for all things big and tall, there are plans to construct a 728ft-high, 43-storey office block with a 128ft spire in Bishopsgate. The Heron Tower, as it will be called, will be the tallest building in the Square Mile and, for a brief while (until the Piano skyscraper at London Bridge enters the war of the behemoths), the second tallest building in London after Canary Wharf. Norman Foster has recently created a 180ft tapered glass building for the Swiss-Re company, located on the site of the former Baltic Exchange which was destroyed by an IRA bomb in 1992. The state-of-the-art structure has become a modern London icon and has been generally well received – a little too well, perhaps, for it has inspired the affectionate nickname 'the gherkin'.

Temple Bar

In the Middle Ages this monument in Fleet Street was a barrier to control comings and goings into the City. So powerful were the City fathers that any unwelcome visitors were simply slung into the jail that stood on the site. The unlucky ones had their heads and pickled body parts displayed on spikes. Even the sovereign had to ask permission to pass this way, a tradition that has lasted in ritualistic form into the modern era. For 200 years an arched gateway designed by Wren marked this spot, but in 1878 it was removed because of traffic congestion and replaced with the present, rather modest monument by Horace Jones. The bronze **griffin** on top is one of the City's emblems, introduced by the Victorians who remembered that the griffins of mythology guarded over a hidden treasure of gold. They presumably forgot, however, that griffins also tore approaching humans to pieces as a punishment for their greed.

Dr Johnson's House

17 Gough Square, EC4; **t** *(020) 7353 3745, www.drjh.dircon.co.uk. Open May–Sept Mon–Sat 11–5.30; Oct–April Mon–Sat 11–5; cheap adm.*

This is the elegant 17th-century house where the Doctor lived from 1748 to 1759. For many of those years he was busy compiling his famous dictionary, the first of its kind in the English language. He worked in the attic, sitting in a rickety three-legged chair and ordering about his six clerks, who must have had a tough time coping with his boundless energies and inexhaustible wit. Boswell said the attic looked like a counting house. The chief legacy of the dictionary to modern lexicographers is its scrupulous references to literary texts. But it is also full of jokey definitions that poke fun at anyone and everyone, including Johnson himself: a lexicographer is defined as 'a writer of dictionaries, a harmless drudge'. The dictionary, published in 1755, made Johnson's reputation as both a serious academic and a great wit. The house is of interest more for its atmosphere than its contents.

St Mary-le-Bow

Cheapside; **t** *(020) 7248 5139. Open Mon–Thurs 6.30–6, Fri 6.30–4.*

Wren almost certainly left the bulk of his church renovations to subordinates; it is hard to imagine that he had time to redesign all 52 himself. This church, however, bears all the signs of his own imprint. It is famous for two reasons, first for its massive, distinctive steeple, which soars 217ft into the sky, and secondly for its **Bow Bells**, which have formed part of the mythology of London for centuries. It was their resounding peal that persuaded the fairytale Dick Whittington to turn again and return to London in search of fame and fortune. Ever since, the tradition has been that anyone born within earshot of the bells can call himself a true Londoner. There is a third, less well-known, reason why you should visit St Mary-le-Bow: its magnificently preserved Norman **crypt.** Along with the Guildhall's, it is one of the few left in London.

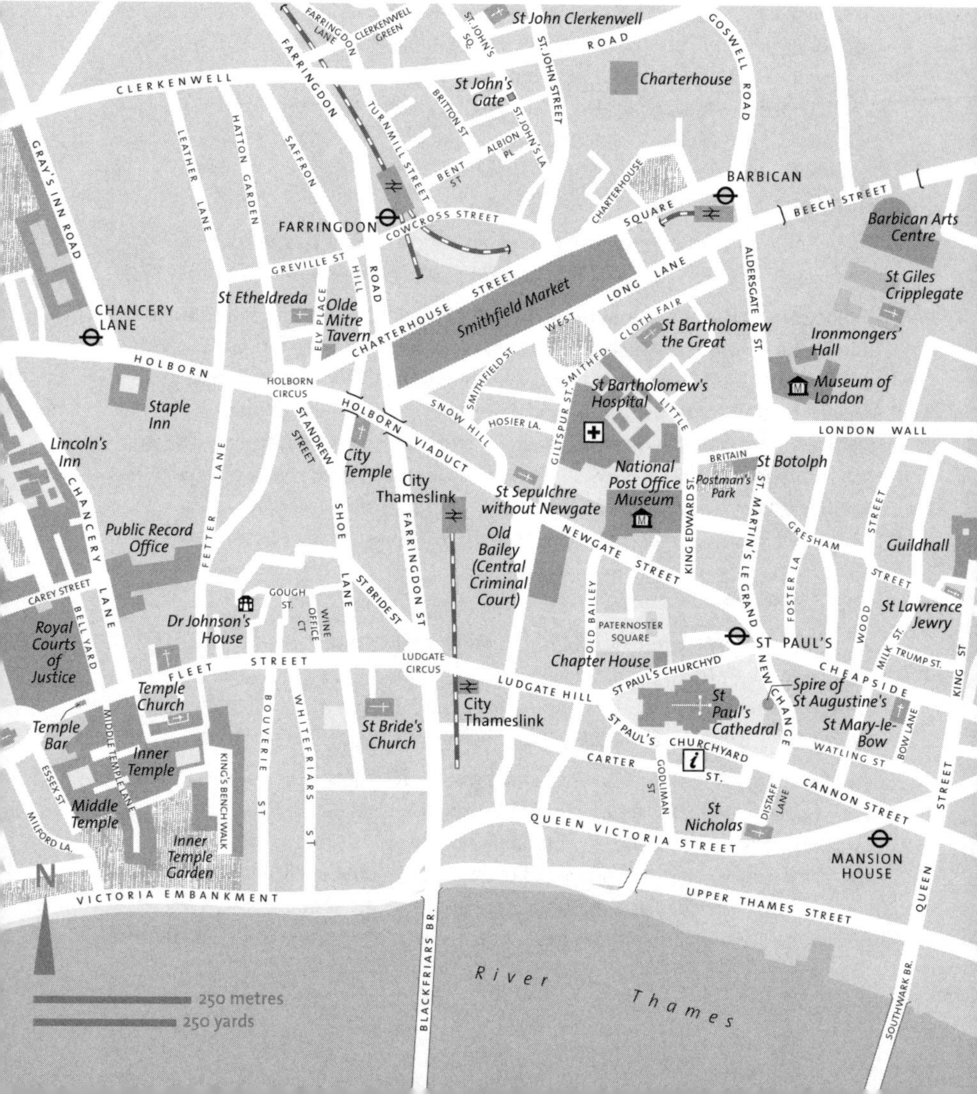

Guildhall

Gresham Street; **t** *(020) 7606 3030, www.cityoflondon.gov.uk. Open Mon–Fri 10–4; often closed for special occasions; free.*

The Guildhall is the seat of the City's government, headed by the Lord Mayor and his sheriffs and aldermen and composed principally of the 12 Great Livery Companies, or guilds, that nominally represent the City's trading interests. Nowadays the governing body, known as the Corporation of London, is little more than a borough council for the City, but back in the Middle Ages it wielded near-absolute power over the whole of London. Even kings could not touch it, since the guilds generated much of the nation's wealth and made sure everyone knew it. Henry III tried to impose direct rule on London in the 13th century but eventually gave up, describing the City fathers as 'nauseously rich'. First built in the 15th century, architecturally the Guildhall has also retained much from the medieval era, despite the calamities of the Great Fire and the Blitz. The building nevertheless bears the marks of countless renovations. The pinnacled façade looking on to Guildhall Yard is a bizarre 18th-century concoction of classical, Gothic and even Indian styles.

You'll need to make an advance booking for a group to see the **crypt**, the most extensive of its kind left in London.

Guildhall Art Gallery

Guildhall Yard, off Gresham St; **t** *(020) 7332 3700, www.guildhall-art-gallery.org.uk. Open Mon–Sat 10–5, Sun 12–4 (last adm 30mins before closing); adm.*

Reopened to the public in summer 1999 for the first time since it was burnt down during the Blitz, the gallery houses works collected by the Corporation of London since the 17th century. Much of the collection is of historical rather than aesthetic appeal: portraits of kings, queens and dignitaries, depictions of important battles, and views of London from the 17th century to the present. There are some artistic highlights, including works by Constable and Millais, and a specially built, double-height wall has been installed for the gallery's star turn: John Singleton Copley's *The Defeat of the Floating Batteries at Gibraltar*, the largest oil painting in Britain.

The Old Bailey

Old Bailey and Newgate Street, public galleries accessible via flights of steps only; **t** *(020) 7248 3277. Open Mon–Fri 10.30–1 and 2–5; free; no children under 14; visitors subject to search on entry, no cameras, large bags, drink, food, mobile phones, pagers, radios, etc; no cloakroom.*

The soaring gilt statue of Justice rising from the **roof** of the Old Bailey has become such a potent symbol of temperance in the English legal system that it has eradicated virtually all memory of the barbarity once associated with this site. Until 1902 this place was Newgate Prison, one of the most gruesome of all jails, which Henry Fielding once described as a prototype for hell. Generations of prisoners were left here, quite literally, to rot; to this day judges wear posies of sweet-smelling flowers on special occasions as a grim reminder of the stench that used to emanate from the cold, filthy cells. The mood now could not be more different. The nickname 'Old Bailey', referring to the alley running off Newgate Street, conveniently avoids all reference to the old prison. Ask about the place's history and you will be given a list, not of the horrors of incarceration, but of the names of the famous people whose trials took place here: Oscar Wilde; the Edwardian wife-murderer Dr Crippen; and William Joyce, known as Lord Haw-Haw, who broadcast enemy propaganda from Nazi Germany.

You are welcome to attend a **court hearing** in one of the public galleries, although the tightly arranged wooden benches are not exactly designed for comfort. The rituals are similar to those of the civil courts, although the mood is more sombre.

St Etheldreda's

*14 Ely Place; **t** (020) 7405 1061. Open daily 8–6.*

Etheldreda was a 7th-century Anglo-Saxon princess who had the distressing habit of marrying and then refusing to sleep with her husbands. When husband number two, Prince Egfrith of Northumbria, finally lost patience with her and made unseemly advances, she withdrew into holy orders and founded a double monastery at Ely in Cambridgeshire. Seven years later, in 679, she was stricken with a tumour on her neck and died. None mourned Etheldreda more than her sister, the unfortunately named Sexburga, who campaigned ardently to have her sanctity recognized. In 695, Sexburga had Etheldreda's coffin opened and found that the tumour had vanished. Her skin was now quite unblemished. A miracle!

Etheldreda became Ely's special saint and was the obvious choice of patron for this double-storeyed church, built in the 13th century as part of the Bishop of Ely's palace. The Gothic **upper church** is a warm, lofty room with a fine wooden-beamed ceiling and huge stained-glass windows at each end. The east window, behind the altar, is particularly striking with its depiction of the Holy Trinity surrounded by the apostles and Anglo-Saxon and Celtic saints, including Etheldreda herself. The west window is much starker, portraying the martyrdom of three Carthusian priors at Tyburn in 1535 with Christ hovering over them. Both windows date from after the Second World War; their predecessors were shattered by German bombs. Downstairs, the lower church or **crypt** is much simpler, no more than a room with a plain altar and little decoration.

Barbican Centre

*Silk Street; box office **t** (020) 7638 8891, general information **t** (020) 7638 4141, www.barbican.org.uk.*

The Brave New World architecture of the Barbican comes straight out of the 1950s, all high-rise concrete and labyrinthine walkways. The City's only residential area worthy of the name, rebuilt after wartime bombing, would not be out of place in a 1960s television escape drama, though there are some advantages to living here: the leafy balconies, the forecourts and the fountains.

The main reason for coming, apart from the dubious pleasure of gaping and shuddering, is a trip to the **Arts Centre**, home to the London Symphony Orchestra, as well as two theatres, three cinemas, two art galleries, two exhibition halls and a concert hall (*all opening times and adm charges vary, call for details*). The centre also houses a sculpture court and a semitropical conservatory (*on Level 3; open Sun 10–5.30*), restaurants and visual arts and literature-related shops. Visible from the centre is **St Giles Cripplegate** (***t*** *(020) 7638 1997, www.stgilescripplegate.com; open Mon–Fri 9.30–5.30*), where John Milton was buried in 1674. The church itself, mostly built in the 16th century, escaped the 1666 fire but was destroyed by wartime bombs and faithfully rebuilt in the 1950s. A stretch of the Roman city wall can be seen just behind it.

Museum of London

150 London Wall, EC2; ***t*** *(020) 7600 3699, www.museumoflondon.org.uk. Open Mon–Sat 10–5.50, Sun 12–5.50; free.*

This ambitious and fast-changing museum sets out to tell the story of London from prehistoric times to the present, drawing on a vast collection of documents and historical relics. It is an ideal place to come if you want to familiarize yourself with the basic facts about the city. It is also a tremendous resource for students and researchers. The museum is very strong on early history, particularly the Roman era, and gives a rich impression of life in the 19th century. It also has an imaginative section on contemporary London. In other areas, perhaps inevitably, the museum is a bit patchy, since the quality of the displays varies according to the illustrative material available. The main problem, in the end, is that the museum's archive of documents is far richer than its collection of artefacts. That said, the museum is never boring. It is beautifully laid out over three descending levels. There are lucid explanations of the historical evidence yielded by lumps of Roman paving stone and recovered coinage. One angled window cleverly gives you a view down on to a piece of Roman wall (AD 200) on the ground outside. Many of the best displays in the rest of the museum are reconstructions of contemporary buildings: a 16th-century grocer's shop, a cell at Newgate Prison, a Victorian pub, a Second World War bedroom kitted out with a protective cage called a Morrison shelter. The museum also has a magnificent range of clothing, giving an insight into changing fashions since the 17th century. The undisputed centrepiece, though, is the Lord Mayor's Coach. Built in 1757 in blazing red and burnished gold, the coach is still used every November for the investiture of the new Lord Mayor. It looks the sort of thing Prince Charming might have used to drive Cinderella home; it is covered in allegorical paintings depicting both the virtues of modesty and the glories of wealth.

Smithfield Market

Smithfield has come a long way since the 14th century, when cattle was slaughtered in front of the customers and witches boiled alive for the entertainment of the populace. This is still where Londoners come to buy their meat, but nowadays it is a civil, sanitized sort of place. The carcasses arrive ready-slaughtered and are stored in giant fridges so you'll barely see a speck of dirt or blood. The covered market halls have been refurbished and are surrounded by restaurants and pubs.

Clerkenwell

By turns a centre for monks, clockmakers, gin-manufacturers and Italian labourers, Clerkenwell has the feel of a cosy village with its squares, winding streets and pretty churches. Its proximity to the City made it an ideal headquarters for the knights of the Order of St John, who stayed here until the dissolution of the monasteries in the 1530s. Then in the early 17th century the digging of the New River put Clerkenwell on the main freshwater route into London and so attracted brewers and distillers. In the 19th century much of Clerkenwell was slumland, and the Victorians built forbidding prisons there to cope with the overflow from the city jails. After decades of neglect, it is now undergoing a revival, its grimy backstreets filling with offices, converted lofts and attractive cafés.

The sites of Clerkenwell are all within easy reach from the **Green**, which was often used in the 19th century as a starting point for protest marches. The **Marx Memorial Library** at No.37a (***t** (020) 7523 1485, www.marxlibrary.net; open to visitors Mon–Thurs 1–2pm only; closed Aug and 24 Dec–2 Jan*) has the best private collection of radical literature in the city; Lenin wrote pamphlets here in 1902–3. Clerkenwell Close (off to the left) leads to the attractive yellow brick **St James's Church**, once part of a Benedictine nunnery but rebuilt many times. The steeple, the latest addition, dates from 1849.

Mansion House

Mansion House, the official residence of the Lord Mayor of London, was intended to be something of a trend-setter, the first project of the Georgian era to be designed in Palladian style. There is a story that a design by Palladio himself was proposed, but rejected because the 16th-century Italian master was a foreigner and a Papist. In the end George Dance's building, erected on the site of the old Stocks Market, was completed in 1752, nearly 40 years after the project was first put forward. The end result is not a tremendous success; the awkward shape of the surrounding square does not allow the eye to be drawn towards its grandiose portico, which in any case is top-heavy and unwieldy with its six Corinthian columns.

Unfortunately Mansion House is now almost always shut and more or less the only way to get in is to apply in writing for parties of 15–40 people six months in advance (*call **t** (020) 7626 2500 for details*).

Royal Exchange

The eight huge Corinthian pillars give this building a sense of importance to which it can no longer lay claim. The Royal Exchange was once the trading centre of the City *par excellence*, home to all of London's stock and commodity exchanges, but it lost this crucial role in 1939 when it was bought by the Guardian Royal Exchange insurance company. It now houses a number of company offices. This is the third Royal Exchange building to occupy the site. The present building, designed by Sir William Tite, dates from 1844, a rare example of neoclassical architecture from the Victorian era. Tite's Exchange comes complete with an equestrian **statue of the Duke of**

Wellington, made in suitably triumphalist fashion from the melted-down metal of French guns. There is also a memorial to the war dead of London.

Bank of England Museum

Follow the Bank of England building round into Bartholomew Lane; ***t*** *(020) 7601 5545, www.bankofengland.co.uk. Open Mon–Fri 10–5; free.*

The playwright Richard Sheridan described the Bank of England as 'an elderly lady in the City of great credit and long standing'. Its record as prudent guardian of the nation's finances is well known; it rescued London from bankruptcy at the end of the 17th century, resisted the temptations of the South Sea Bubble and kept the country's economy buoyant throughout the trauma of the Revolutionary wars against France. As the bank of last resort it played a crucial role in the development of Britain's capitalist system during the 18th and 19th centuries.

But the Bank has had a tough time of it in recent years, particularly since the abandonment of worldwide currency controls in the 1970s. The rise of virtually unfettered currency speculation has severely limited its control over the value of sterling. At the same time, the changing nature of international capital has made it increasingly hard for the Bank to monitor the activities of the commercial houses. In compensation, it has won independence from the Treasury and is now free to set interest rates

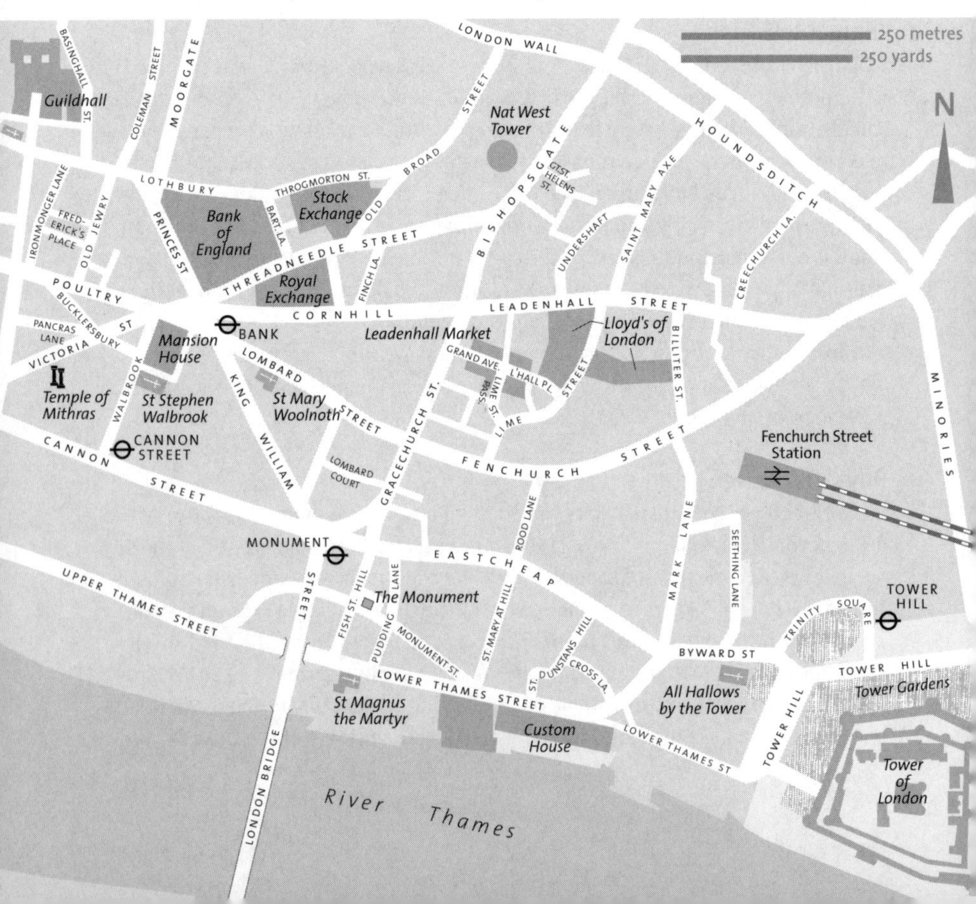

as it sees fit. But even this role is under threat from the single European currency and the establishment of a pan-European central bank in Frankfurt.

Architecturally, the Bank has a distinctly mixed record. At the end of the 18th century Sir John Soane, that most quirky and original of English architects, came up with a magnificently intricate neoclassical design, a veritable treasure trove of interconnecting rooms each with its own peculiarities of light and decoration. In 1925 the Bank governors decided they needed more space, and instead of considering an extension or a new building they simply demolished Soane's work and replaced it with an unimaginative multistorey patchwork by Sir Herbert Baker.

All that remains of Soane's original work is the secure curtain wall on the outer rim of the building and, thanks to a postwar reconstruction, the first room in the museum, the **Bank Stock Office**. Beneath Soane's vaulted roof, illuminated naturally through a series of skylights, the museum's displays recount the architectural fortunes of the Bank and show off some of the original mahogany counter-tops and oak ledger-rests. You are then led through a series of rooms, culminating in Herbert ker's Rotunda, that give an account of the Bank's history. The museum is surprisly entertaining, offering insights into the intricacies of bank-note design and duction, a simulated market trading game where you can try your hand at being a tual City whizz-kid and, most absorbing of all, a large transparent pyramid full of ld bars.

Lloyd's Building

The City's most innovative and challenging building is Richard Rogers' design for **Lloyd's of London**, the world's biggest insurance market. On Leadenhall St itself, to the right, you can see a fine façade from the 1925 incarnation of Lloyd's. The entrance to the Richard Rogers building is on Lime St, the continuation of St Mary Axe, although since the IRA bombs of 1992 and 1993 the building has been closed to the public.

Leadenhall Market

Leadenhall Market is a pleasant surprise: a whiff of real life among the office blocks. It has considerable charm, plenty of bustle, often live music and excellent food, particularly meat, fish and cheese. The prices match the clientèle, many of them businessmen doing some inexpert and usually extravagant housekeeping on behalf of their wives stranded in suburbia; hence the popularity of game and exotic fish.

Monument

***t** (020) 7626 2717; viewing platform (spiral staircase).*
Open 10–6, last adm 5.30; adm.

The Monument commemorates the Great Fire of London. On its completion in 1677 it was the tallest free-standing column in the world; now it is so obscured by office buildings it is easy to miss. The view from the top is limited, but still enjoyable.

***Also see*: St Paul's Cathedral, p.39; Sir John Soane's Museum, p.142.**

***Onwards to*: Tower of London, p.45; the South Bank and Southwark, p.85.**

Covent Garden

⊖ Leicester Square, Covent Garden, Charing Cross, Tottenham Court Road.

Covent Garden, home to the Royal Opera House and the converted fruit and vegetable market, is teeming with restaurants, natty boutiques and street performers. Sundays are rather quiet as the theatres are dark, but the market and shops are open. The London Theatre Museum is shut on Mondays.

There are those who find modern Covent Garden too ritzy and spoiled with its boutiques, upmarket jewellery stalls and prettified pubs; too much of an easy crowd-pleaser with its mime artists and bands belting out yet another rendition of 'I'm a Believer' or 'The Boxer'; too much – heaven forbid – of a *tourist attraction*. Looking into the past, however, one should perhaps be relieved it is even half as pleasant as it is. When the wholesale fruit and vegetable market moved out to the south London suburbs in the 1970s, the London authorities initially wanted to build office blocks and a major roadway through here. Wouldn't that have been fun? It was the local traders and residents who saved Covent Garden with protests and petitions; it is also the locals who, by and large, have the run of the place today. Dig a little, and behind the tourist draws are plenty of quieter, more discreet spots. If Covent Garden seems a little derivative, it is because it deliberately and self-consciously echoes its own past – a dash of Inigo Jones's original piazza with its street life and sideshows, several measures of Charles Fowler's covered market, plus plenty of the eating, drinking and general revelry that have always characterized this neighbourhood.

Covent Garden Market

With the loss of the original fruit and vegetable market, Covent Garden has undoubtedly lost its rough edges. The main hall, once littered with crates and stray vegetables, is now spick and span, while the Flower Market houses museums devoted

Cafés and Pubs

Café in the Crypt, church of St Martin-in-the-Fields. Wholesome hot and cold food in an atmospheric vaulted crypt: welcoming, well located and extremely tasty.

World Food Café, 14 Neal's Yard, 1st fl. Cheap, tasty and delicious home-made vegetarian 'worldfood', from Mexican to Indian and African street food. £6–10 for a full meal.

Food for Thought, 31 Neal Street. One of London's pioneering vegetarian canteen-style cafés: still setting the highest standards. £5–7.50.

Lamb & Flag, 33 Rose Street. Built in 1623 but with Georgian décor, serving real ales.

Livebait, 21 Wellington Street. Tucked away behind the Strand, a fish chain with high standards and £5 set lunches as well as a more costly menu.

Joe Allen, 13 Exeter Street. Great burgers (but not on the menu; you have to know to ask!), American-style food and monster puddings. Theatrically 'luvvie' in the evenings.

Belgo, 50 Earlham Street. *Frites*, mussels and Belgian beer, high-tech interior décor.

Calabash, downstairs in the Africa Centre, 38 King St. Come here for unusual and excellent dishes from all over Africa (grillled plantain, groundnut stew, sambusas, fried fish, etc.).

Punch & Judy, 40 The Market. This large pub has cellar, ground floor and first floor bars, with a balcony overlooking the Piazza. A busy but great spot for watching the street performers. Hot food and jacket potatoes.

Paul, 29 Bedford Street. Genuine French café and bakery/*pâtisserie* with filled baguettes, delicious omelettes and mouthwatering pastries and a vast variety of breads.

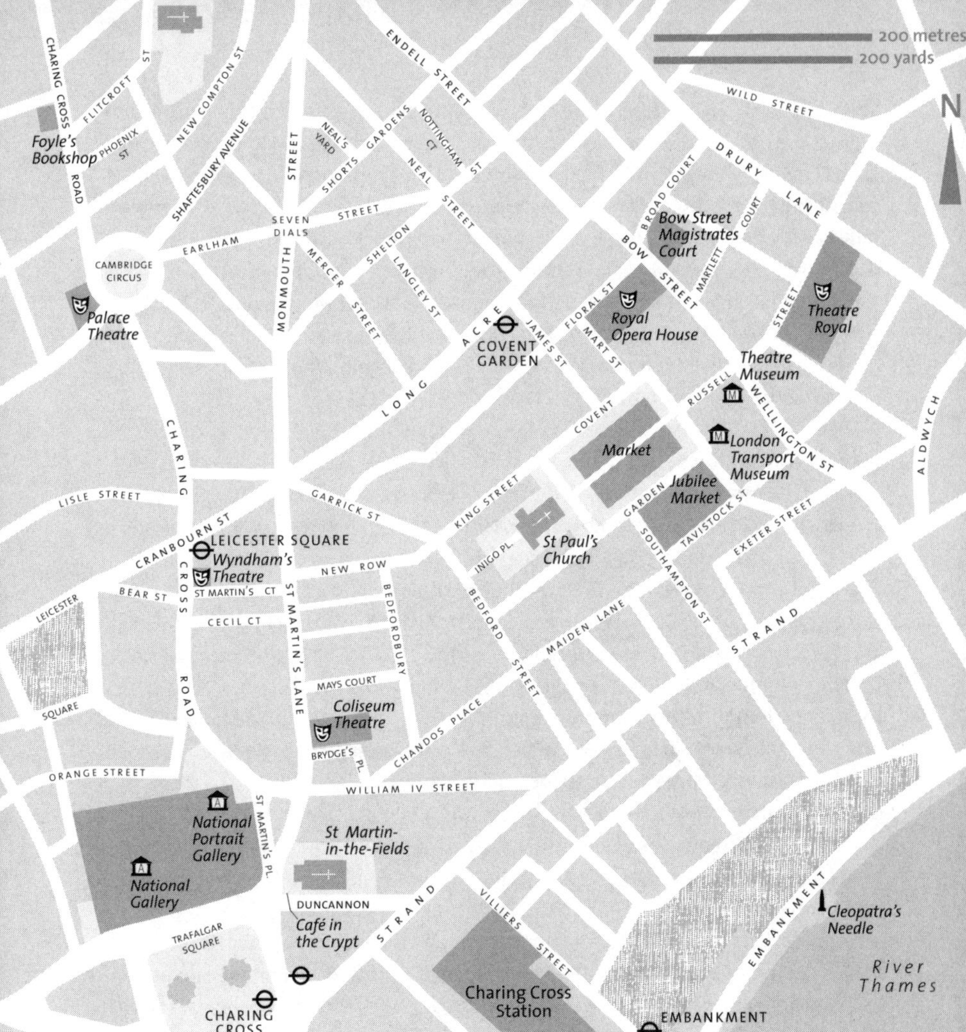

to transport and the theatre. Unlike the disastrous redevelopment of Les Halles in Paris, however (*see* p.223), the place has not lost its soul. You can still buy roast chestnuts or a greasy baked potato from a street vendor as Dickens did, or watch clowns and jugglers performing in front of St Paul's where Punch and Judy shows first caught the public imagination in the 17th century.

Neal Street

This pedestrian alley is a pleasant throwback to the hippy era, all beads, home-made earrings and wholefood shops vying for custom alongside designer boutiques. While Carnaby Street, the in-place in the 1960s, has faltered and died, Neal Street, a development from the late 1970s, has survived. Turn left down Shorts Gardens and you come to distinctly New Age **Neal's Yard**, a tranquil triangular oasis planted with trees and an excellent place to sit, away from the traffic fumes and confusion. There are plentiful cheap vegetarian eats here, a world food café, a beach café, an East-West herb shop, a groovy hairdresser's, a walk-in backrub parlour, an excellent bakery, a natural cosmetics shop, and the famous Neal's Yard Therapy Rooms, offering the gamut of complementary therapies, from acupuncture to lymphatic drainage, from past-life counselling to 'rolfing'. As a last resort, there's a host of New Age shops stuffed with rainbow crystals, candles, incense and books on mystical healing. On your way in, don't miss the Heath Robinson clock above the wholefood shop.

On the other side of Shorts Gardens is **Thomas Neal's Arcade**, filled with designer shops. With its wrought iron lamps and glass roof, this is another derivative piece of modern London architecture, this time a throwback to the arcaded emporia of the 19th century.

Royal Opera House

Two of the most famous London theatres are a mere stone's throw away: the **Theatre Royal Drury Lane**, which is not in Drury Lane but on the corner of Russell Street and Catherine Street (you can see it as you come out of the Theatre Museum to your right); and the **Royal Opera House**, better known simply as Covent Garden, which is off to the left down Bow St. Both buildings have been scourged by fire in their lives, and the Royal Opera House was razed to the ground in 1856, except for its portico.

A long-overdue redevelopment of the 1858 building that took its place was finally completed in 1999, integrating the Opera House with Covent Garden Market for the first time. The Georgian houses on the north side of Russell Street were replaced with elegant glass and wrought-iron shopping arcades with a loggia walkway above, a design based on Inigo Jones' original Piazza. The political rows and financial problems that dogged the redevelopment project still haunt the House, however. Prior pledges to open up opera to the masses by reducing seat prices have yet to materialize fully (top tickets for some productions cost £175, although you can sit in the slips for £4), and accusations of unimaginative productions and pervasive snobbery have not helped. Despite these thorny issues, the building itself has been hailed a success, with its beautifully revamped Floral Hall; the Link, a new arcade connecting Bow St to the Piazza; and excellent views across Covent Garden from the Amphitheatre restaurant. And the odd concession has been made to *hoi polloi* – some productions are broadcast live during the summer on a giant screen in Covent Garden or in Trafalgar Square.

Bow Street Magistrates' Court

Opposite the entrance to the Opera House is the old Bow Street Magistrates' Court where the Fieldings, Henry and John, held court in the 18th century. Henry, who was a trained barrister as well as the author of *Tom Jones*, used his tenure here to set up the Bow Street Runners, an informal plain clothes police force that worked to crack down on underworld gangs and challenge the infamous official marshals, or 'thief-takers', who were usually in cahoots with the thieves themselves. The Runners proved remarkably effective and soon became famous throughout the land, particularly for their role in thwarting the Cato Street conspiracy in 1820. Until Robert Peel's uniformed 'bobbies' appeared in the 1830s, they were the closest thing to a police force that London had.

St Paul's Church

*Inigo Place; **t** (020) 7836 5221, www.actorschurch.org. Church and gardens open Tues–Fri 9.30–4.30, services Sun 11am.*

Don't be surprised if you feel you are sneaking up on this church from behind. That is exactly what you are doing. Properly speaking, St Paul's is part of the original Covent Garden piazza which Inigo Jones built in mock-Italian style in the 1630s. Jones made one crucial oversight, however. He and his low-church patron, the Earl of Bedford, thought they could get away with putting the altar of their church at the western end, so breaking with convention which insists it should be in the east. The Bishop of London, William Laud, ordered Jones to put the altar where it traditionally belongs, in this case flush against the planned main entrance. The interior is of disarming simplicity: a double square, 100ft by 50ft. St Paul's quickly won the affections of the theatre folk of Covent Garden, who preached here as well as attending services. They nicknamed it the Actors' Church, and several luminaries of the stage are buried here, including Ellen Terry, the *grande dame* of the late-Victorian theatre (plaque in the south wall). St Paul's is one of the few pre-Great Fire buildings still left in London.

St Martin-in-the-Fields

***t** (020) 7766 1100, www.stmartin-in-the-fields.org. Open Mon–Sat 10–8, Sun 12–6; free concerts Mon, Tues, Fri 1pm.*

The church of St Martin-in-the-Fields is the oldest building on Trafalgar Square, and the only one truly to benefit from the exposure the square affords; its curious combination of Greek temple façade and Baroque steeple catches the eye, even if the mix is a little awkward. Its churchyard, now a daytime junk market (*open daily 10–5.30*), contains the graves of Charles II's mistress Nell Gwynne and the 18th-century painters Reynolds and Hogarth. The church has become popular for its concerts and resident orchestra, the Academy of St Martin-in-the-Fields. There is a café in the crypt.

St Martin's Lane

Already you have stepped into London's theatreland, as the black strip at the bottom of the street signs says. The theatres along St Martin's Lane – the Albery and Duke of York's as well as the Coliseum – all date from the turn of the century and so were among the last great playhouses to be built in London. But as early as the 18th century the street was attracting such artistic residents as Joshua Reynolds, first president of the Royal Academy, and Thomas Chippendale, the furniture maker.

One of the main sites in St Martin's Lane is the globe of the **Coliseum** (*tickets and information, **t** (020) 7632 8300, www.eno.org*), home to the English National Opera. Built in 1904, this was the first theatre in England with a revolving stage.

***Also see*: National Gallery, p.38; National Portrait Gallery, p.140; Trafalgar Square, p.46; London Transport Museum, p.145; Theatre Museum, p.148.**

***Onwards to*: The City of London, p.57; Soho and Chinatown, p.77; Covent Garden shopping, p.137.**

Mayfair

⊖ *Bond Street, Green Park, Piccadilly Circus.*

The May Fair was once exactly that: an annual festival of eating, drinking, entertainments and (usually) debauchery that took place in the first two weeks of May. The custom began in 1686 when the area was in its infancy; by the middle of the 18th century, the neighbourhood had gone so far upmarket that the residents described the fair as 'that most pestilent nursery of impiety and vice' and made sure it was shut down for good. Mayfair has been pretty staid ever since, the preserve of London's *beau monde* who want nothing more than to be left alone. You will nevertheless notice, particularly around Curzon Street, some fine 18th-century houses and a few oddities. If you have ever played the London version of *Monopoly*, you will know that Oxford Street, Bond Street, Regent Street, Park Lane and Mayfair itself are the most desirable properties on the board. But Mayfair has not lived up to its early promise. It is cosmopolitan and expensive, but not really fashionable; elegant and well maintained, but not sophisticated; central and self-important, but at the same time strangely quiet.

Bond Street

Two kinds of shopkeeper dominate Bond Street: jewellers and art dealers, whose gaudy if not always particularly attractive shop fronts make for a diverting stroll. **Old Bond Street**, the lower part of the thoroughfare, concentrates mainly on jewellery and includes all the well-known international names including Tiffany's at No.25 (note the distinctive gold-trimmed clock hanging above the entrance). Evidently these establishments have kept going through fallow times thanks to the patronage of the Russian mafia, which has made London its main foreign outpost. Old Bond Street brought a rare piece of good luck to the inveterate 18th-century rake and gambler, Charles James Fox, who once made a bet with the Prince of Wales on the number of cats appearing on each side of the street. No fewer than 13 cats appeared on Fox's side, and none on the Prince of Wales's. Maybe, though, Fox should have taken his inauspicious number of cats as an omen and steered clear of the gambling dens of St James's, since he later went bankrupt and had to be bailed out by his father.

Cafés and Pubs

Boudin Blanc, 5 Trebeck St. Good French bistro food. Popular, atmospheric and good value with a two-course set lunch £26.

Al Hamra, 31–3 Shepherd Market. Upmarket Lebanese fare. Delicious but expensive. £30.

Sofra Bistro, 18 Shepherd Market. Attractive, more relaxed Middle Eastern alternative to the above, this time Turkish. Set lunch £8.95.

Mô, 23 Heddon St. Fantastic-value Moroccan delicacies in stylishly decadent tearooms. Near the Royal Academy (and next door to a more upmarket and expensive sibling, trendy Momo). Try the *meze* (£7.50).

Veeraswamy, 99–101 Regent St. Excellent Indian set lunch in elegant but very welcoming upstairs dining rooms.

Mirabelle, 56 Curzon St, **t** (020) 7499 4636. Glamorous Art Deco French restaurant, popular with the smart set. *Reserve.*

Sotheby's Café, 34–5 New Bond St. Genteel, very English café for afternoon tea and lunch, in the famous auction house.

Victory Café and Milk Bar, basement, Gray's Antiques Market, South Molton Lane. Old-school English all-day breakfasts and soups and sandwiches, with generous helpings, in a charming nostalgic setting.

The turning on the left just after Stafford Street is the **Royal Arcade**. Built in 1879, it is one of the kitschier examples of the genre with caryatids painted orange and white above the entrance. Walk through the arcade to emerge on Albermarle Street. Across the road on the right is one of the entrances to **Brown's Hotel**. This old-fashioned hotel remains one of the quintessential addresses of aristocratic London. Founded by a former manservant in 1837, it retains the kind of service one imagines to have been quite commonplace in the houses of gentlemen of quality. Franklin and Eleanor Roosevelt spent their honeymoon here, while in room 36 the Dutch government declared war on Japan during the Second World War. Nowadays, the time to come is for tea when, for a slightly cheaper rate than the Ritz, you can fill up on scones and cucumber sandwiches and enjoy the attentions of demure waiters in tails. Dress smart or they won't let you in (*see* p.165).

New Bond Street, the top half towards Oxford Street, is the province of high-class designer clothes and accessory shops, plus the showrooms of art dealers such as Bernard Jacobson and Le Fevre (or Waddington on Cork Street). Sotheby's, the famous auctioneer, is at Nos.34–5 New Bond Street; above the front door is the oldest outdoor sculpture in London, an ancient Egyptian figure made of igneous rock dating back to 1600 BC.

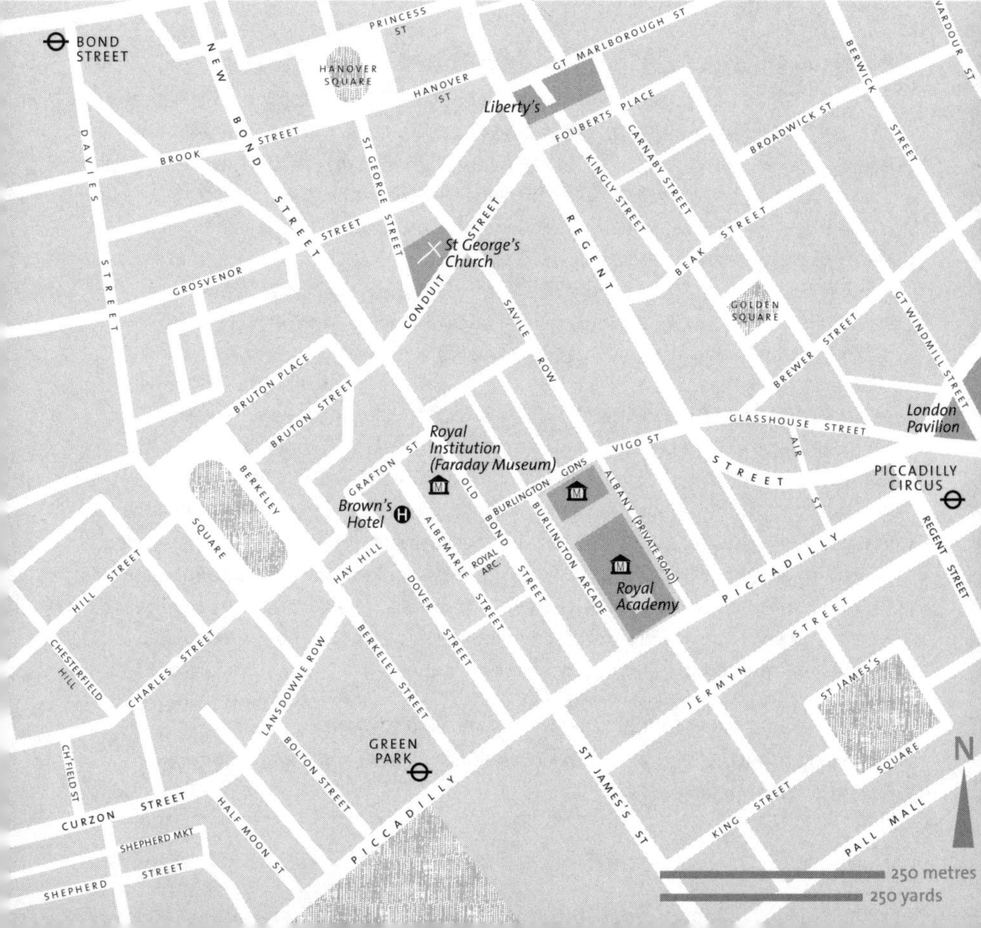

Royal Institution/Faraday Museum

21 Albermarle St; **t** *(020) 7409 2992. Open Mon–Fri, 10–5; museum adm.*

This large, grand building, with its pompous façade based on the Temple of Antoninus in Rome, is to science what the Royal Academy is to the arts: the most prestigious association of professionals in the land. Founded in 1799, the Institution built up a formidable reputation thanks to early members such as Humphrey Davy (inventor of the Davy Lamp for detecting methane down mines) and his pupil, Michael Faraday. The small museum (the only part of the building open to the public) is in fact Faraday's old laboratory where he carried out his pioneering experiments with electricity in the 1830s; his work is explained with the help of his original instruments and lab notes. The Royal Institution also organizes excellent lectures.

Shepherd Market

There may not be any more May Fairs in Mayfair, but this enchanting warren of cafés, restaurants and small shops nevertheless comes as a nice surprise after all the stuffiness of its surroundings. Back in the 17th century, this was where the fire-eaters, jugglers, dwarves and boxers would entertain the crowds in early spring. The entrepreneur Edward Shepherd then turned the area into a market in 1735 (notice the attractive low Georgian buildings).

Berkeley Square

This is a key address for débutantes and aristocratic young bucks, who come for the annual Berkeley Square Charity Ball and vie to join the square's exclusive clubs and gaming houses. The chief interest to the visitor is the elegant row of Georgian houses on the west side. No.44, described by Nikolaus Pevsner as 'the finest terraced house in London', was built in 1742–4 for one of the royal household's maids of honour. Unfortunately the house is now a private casino called the Clermont Club, and its stunning interior, including a magnificent double staircase designed by William Kent, is out of bounds to the public. They say the house is haunted by the ghost of its first major-domo, who can be heard coming down the stairs with his slight limp.

St George's Hanover Square

A neoclassical church with a striking Corinthian portico, St George's was built in 1721–4 as part of the Fifty New Churches Act. It is the parish church of Mayfair and has proved enduringly popular as a venue for society weddings, including the match between Shelley and Mary Godwin. The interior, restored at the end of the Victorian era, has some fine 16th-century Flemish glass in the east window and a painting of the Last Supper above the altar attributed to William Kent. Notice also the cast-iron dogs in the porch; these once belonged to a shop in Conduit St and were brought here in 1940 after their original premises were bombed.

***Also see*: Bond Street shopping, p.132; Royal Academy, p.141.**

***Onwards to*: Piccadilly, p.76; Green Park, p.120; St James's and Royal London, p.81; Oxford Street shopping, p.130.**

Piccadilly and Leicester Square

⊖ Leicester Square, Piccadilly Circus, Green Park.

The Piccadilly area has long been considered rather vulgar. The strange name derives from the fortunes of Robert Baker, a 17th-century tailor who made a fortune and built himself a mansion here on the proceeds in 1612. At the time, the land was totally undeveloped apart from a windmill (which inspired the name of the street leading off to the north of Piccadilly Circus, Great Windmill Street). Baker's peers thought his ostentation ridiculous and nicknamed his house Pickadilly Hall to remind him of his humble origins, a *pickadil* being a contemporary term for a shirt cuff or hem.

The development of St James's and Mayfair in the 18th century made Piccadilly one of the busiest thoroughfares in London. The area grew more crowded still in the late 19th century with the construction of Shaftesbury Avenue and a flurry of new theatres. Bus routes multiplied and an Underground station was constructed, followed by vast advertising hoardings on the side of the London Pavilion music hall. Virginia Woolf and others thought it was all marvellous, describing Piccadilly Circus as 'the heart of life...where everything desirable meets'. After the Second World War the ads went international – Coca Cola rather than Bovril – and electric, giving a touch of modernity to the 'swinging' city of Europe.

Leicester Square

Towards the end of the 19th century, Leicester Square was *the* place to be seen of an evening, especially for middle-class men looking to let their hair down and flirt with

Cafés and Tearooms

Photographers' Gallery Café, 5 Great Newport Street. Well-informed creative types make a beeline for the wholesome sandwiches, salads, home-made cakes and cappuccinos at this tranquil, friendly café.

The Criterion, 224 Piccadilly (at Piccadilly Circus). Quality cuisine in a glittering (and high decibel) 1920s neo-Byzantine basilica; worth visiting for the stunning mosaic interior alone. 2-course lunch £14.95.

Waterstones, Piccadilly. In this big bookshop are the Studio Lounge on the 5th floor, with great views over London, cocktails and snacks (10–5); and, in the basement, a café and a more expensive restaurant.

Royal Academy Restaurant, Burlington House, Piccadilly. Assisted-service lunch in an airy room, and a small separate café. *Open 10–5.30, till 10 on Fridays.*

Fortnum & Mason, 181 Piccadilly. The luxury food shop has two smart restaurants: the posh Fountain (open till 7.45pm), serving breakfast, lunch, tea and dinner, is renowned for its ice-cream sundaes; and the St James's on the fourth offers a 2-course set lunch for £23 plus afternoon tea.

Caffè Nero, St James' Church, Piccadilly. A chain coffee bar, but the joy is in the setting – outdoor seats in the courtyard of this old church (*see* p.76), facing the market.

La Maison du Chocolat, 46 Piccadilly. Enter and breathe in deeply – this is a chocolate shop straight out of a Joanne Harris novel. Tiny cups of thick hot chocolate are a real pick-me-up in the middle of the afternoon.

Ritz Hotel, 150 Piccadilly. Tea at the Ritz (£31 a head) is a London institution: a steeply priced indulgence but worth it for immersion in this quintessentially Edwardian paradise of gilded statues, filigree ironwork, plashing waterfalls and palms. The food isn't bad either: cucumber or salmon sandwiches, plus scones with clotted cream and jam.

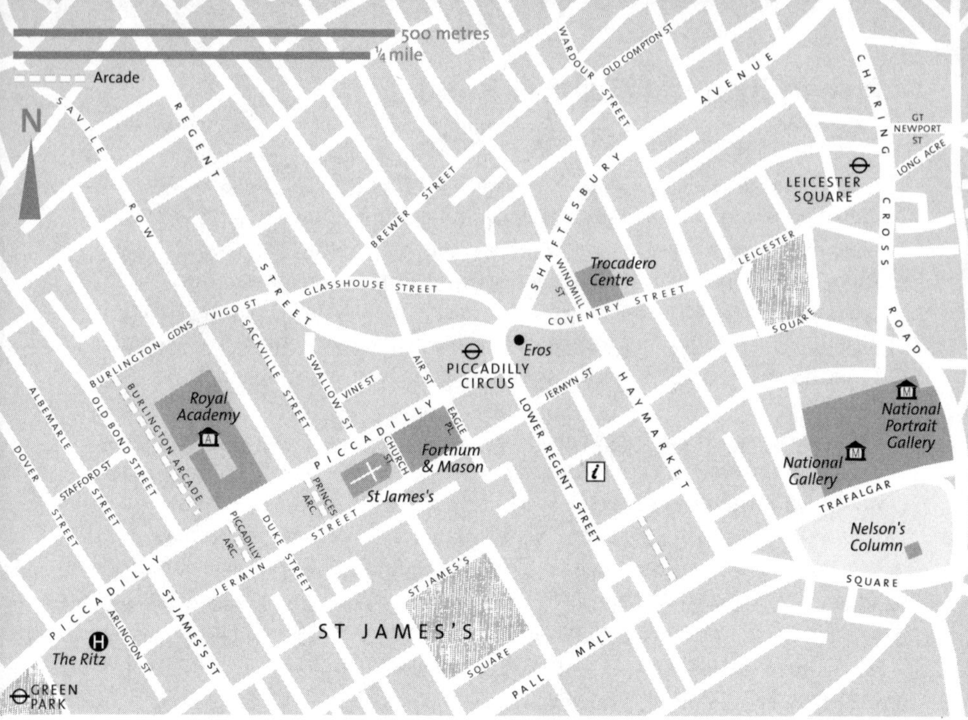

'unrespectable' women. Attractions included the gaudily decorated Alhambra Music Hall (now replaced by the Odeon cinema), Turkish baths, oyster rooms and dance halls. But all the fine buildings of the past, including the 17th-century Leicester House which gave its name to the square, are long gone. The Blitz was largely responsible for destroying the buildings and spirit of the place.

Leicester Square has nowadays recovered some of its happy-go-lucky spirit; the square has been pedestrianized and the central garden tidied up. Come here at more or less any time of the day or night and you will find a rough and ready crowd of cinema-goers, student tourists, buskers, street performers, portrait painters and pick-pockets blocking up the ever-steady stream of people making their way between Piccadilly and Covent Garden. For the dedicated sightseer, the only historical curiosity is a bronze statue of Charlie Chaplin with his bowler hat and walking stick. For the dedicated star-spotter, however, it's the place to catch A-list celebs treading the red carpet whenever there's a glitzy première at the Odeon.

Piccadilly Circus

The car horns and neon advertising hoardings of Piccadilly Circus have become synonymous with London, along with red double-decker buses and the Queen. Quite why is something of a mystery. For some inexplicable reason, hordes of European teenagers are prepared to spend whole afternoons trudging across Piccadilly Circus's crowded traffic islands, from burger bar to music megastore to the Trocadero Centre, in search of the ultimate cheap thrill. The best thing about Piccadilly Circus is the view down Lower Regent Street towards St James's Park.

Two curiosities are nevertheless worth a moment's attention. The first is the **Criterion Brasserie** on the south side of the Circus, which has a long dining room sumptuously adorned in neo-Byzantine style (*see* p.154). The second attraction of Piccadilly Circus is the **Eros statue** at its centre, a winged aluminium figure fashioned by Sir Alfred Gilbert in memory of the Victorian philanthropist Lord Shaftesbury and unveiled in 1893. The figure is not in fact supposed to be Eros, the cherubic god of love, at all; Gilbert intended it to be an Angel of Christian Charity, in memory of Lord Shaftesbury's work with destitute children.

Walking towards Leicester Square, on the north side of Coventry Street is the **London Pavilion**. This was once a music hall, but has now been tarted up a bit and revamped as the **Rock Circus** (*open Mon–Tues 11–5.30, Wed–Sun 10–5.30; adm exp*). This can be quite fun in a tacky sort of way – a sanitized history of rock'n'roll told with the help of wax figures from Madame Tussaud's and a vast array of lighting tricks, and a revolving theatre featuring an automaton of the Beatles. Right opposite the London Pavilion, with entrances on Great Windmill St, Coventry St and, round the back, on Shaftesbury Avenue, is the **Trocadero Centre** (*open daily 10–midnight; free, separate charges for attractions*), a mélange of overpriced theme-u-rants, screaming kids and intimidating teenagers. Amidst the horrors, there are some thrilling and expensive virtual reality simulators, and a dodgem ride (also thrilling and expensive).

Regent Street

Regent Street was once the finest street in London, although you might not think so to look at it now. In fact, all it boasts are a few fine shops (particularly men's clothes stores) and some rather stuffy, impersonal buildings livened up just once a year by the overhead display of electric Christmas decorations. The street could scarcely be further from the original plan, drawn up in 1813 by John Nash for the Prince Regent, which intended to bring revolutionary changes to the way London was organized. Nash's idea was to make Regent Street the main north-south artery linking the prince's residence at Carlton House on The Mall to the newly landscaped expanse of Regent's Park; as such it would have been the centrepiece of a carefully planned ensemble of squares, palaces and public thoroughfares.

One address that has not changed too much on the outside is the **Café Royal** (***t** (020) 7437 9090; open Mon–Sat 10–11, lunch served in the Grill Room 12–2.45; 2 courses £15, 3 courses £20*) at No.68 on the right-hand side of The Quadrant. A liveried doorman stands guard over what was one of the most fashionable addresses of the decadent years leading up to the First World War. Its extravagant mirrors, velvet seats and caryatid sculptures have remained more or less as they were when Oscar Wilde, Aubrey Beardsley and Edward, Prince of Wales, held court here in the naughty 1890s, albeit rather more spruced-up since the Café's redecoration in spring 2001, but its incarnation as a conference centre, with boards listing companies due in, tarnishes the glamour somewhat – pop in if you're passing, but don't make a special trip.

Piccadilly

From Piccadilly Circus to Green Park, this wide, straight, busy thoroughfare is the southern edge of Mayfair (*see* p.70) and it shows. Here you can find **Fortnum & Mason**, the ultimate old-fashioned luxury English food shop (***t*** *(020) 7734 8040, www.fortnumandmason.com; open Mon–Sat 10–6.30, Sun 12–6, afternoon tea on the 4th floor 3–5.30pm*), and the **Ritz Hotel**, where afternoon tea is an institution (***t*** *(020) 7493 8181; served 12–5 daily*). Small high-class shops can be found in the streets to either side: Jermyn Street and Savile Row (*see* p.133), and small, elegant shopping arcades. Piccadilly is also home to the Royal Academy (*see* p.141).

St James's Piccadilly

Open daily, with lunchtime recitals and evening concerts; call ahead on ***t*** *(020) 7734 4511/0441 for details.*

St James's (1684) seems curiously at odds with the rest of the neighbourhood, being totally unmarked by either pretension or exclusivity. Nowhere here do you see the trappings of wealth or snobbery; instead there is an arts and crafts market in the churchyard (*Wed–Sat, with an antiques market on Tues*), a café (*open till 7, later if there's a concert*) in the annexe, a Centre for Healing, and a message of warm welcome on the noticeboard in the porch. Nevertheless, from an architectural point of view, St James's is an object lesson in effortless grace and charm. It is the only church that Christopher Wren built from scratch in London (the others were all renovations or rebuildings on medieval sites), and as such most clearly expresses his vision of the church as a place where the relationship between the priest and his congregation should be demystified. St James's is airy and spacious, with the altar and pulpit in full view and accessible to all. An elegant gilded wooden gallery with rounded corners runs around the western end, supported by Corinthian pillars in plaster adorned with intricate decorations. There are beautiful carvings by Grinling Gibbons, notably on the limewood reredos behind the altar (fruit and nature motifs) and on the stone font.

Burlington Arcade

London never really went in for shopping arcades the way that Paris did at the beginning of the 19th century; nowhere in this city will you find the graceful iron and glasswork of the Parisian *passages* (*see* p.260), the precursors of the modern department store. Arcades nevertheless enjoyed a brief popularity in the final decade of George IV's life. The most famous is Burlington Arcade (1819), no doubt because of its top-hatted beadles who enforce the arcade's quaint rules: no whistling, no singing and no running. Originally it had a magnificent triple-arched entrance, but in 1931 the shopkeepers of the arcade demanded more girth to take deliveries, and the arches were destroyed. Nowadays it remains elegant enough, its high-ceilinged halls decorated in green and white, and home to upmarket shops.

***Also see*: Royal Academy, p.141; Jermyn Street and Savile Row shopping, p.133; Green Park, p.120; Faraday Museum, p.72.**

***Onwards to*: Mayfair, p.70; Covent Garden, p.66.**

Soho and Chinatown

⊖ *Leicester Square, Piccadilly Circus, Tottenham Court Road, Oxford Circus.*

Here, halfway between the clubbish pomp of Westminster and the venal frenzy of the City, is where Londoners come to enjoy themselves. Soho still thrives off its reputation as a seedy but alluring hang-out for exotic freaks and sozzled eccentrics who made the place famous after the Second World War. The establishment has always been suspicious of this area; the artistic community has never shown such squeamishness – indeed, this is the heart of London theatreland. Nowadays the sleaze is slowly disappearing, supplanted by the flashy cars and modish whims of the advertising and media darlings.

Low life and aristocrats have always dwelt side by side in Soho. In the 18th century it was fashionable with salon hostesses as well as artists and whores. In Victorian times it was full of cowsheds and slaughterhouses. For polite society, the area became a byword for depravity and lack of hygiene. In 1931 the Lord Chamberlain authorised nudity on stage for the first time at a revue at the Windmill Theatre, although he stipulated that the lighting had to remain low and the showgirls were not allowed to move, rules which remained unchanged until the Second World War.

It was after the war that Soho really came into its own. In the 1950s it became the centre of the avant-garde in jazz, new writing, experimental theatre and cinema. In many ways Soho prefigured the social upheavals of the 1960s, creating a youth subculture based on rebellion, permissiveness, *joie de vivre*, booze and drugs. Above all, Soho developed its own community of intellectuals and eccentrics, people of all classes mingling, borrowing money off each other and getting pleasantly tippled in pubs or illicit 'near-beer' bars that stayed open outside the stringent licensing hours.

Like all golden ages, 1950s Soho and its low life came to a somewhat sorry end. The liberalizations of the 1960s and 1970s brought peepshows and strip joints galore that nearly caused the destruction of the neighbourhood. The planning authorities, outraged by prostitutes openly soliciting on every street, threatened to bulldoze the whole district to make way for office blocks. It wasn't until the mid-1980s that new laws regulated the pornography business and Soho regained some of its spirit. The number of peepshows is strictly controlled, and most of the prostitutes now solicit illegally via cards left in telephone booths. So attractive has Soho become that the trendies have inevitably moved in to join the fun. Not a week goes by without a new bar, a new restaurant, a new fad. Today it might be sushi served by robots, or caramelized onions; next week these will be passé and the new obsession will be pine-scrubbed noodle bars, or cafés that look like middle-class living rooms.

Soho Square

This was where Scott built his mansion, Monmouth House (long ago destroyed). A contemporary statue of Charles II by Caius Gabriel Cibber still stands in the square gardens, looking somewhat worse for wear behind a mock-Tudor toolshed which covers an underground air vent. On the north side of the square is the **French Protestant Church**, originally built for the Huguenots and then reworked by the

Victorians in flamboyant neo-Gothic style. To the east is the red-brick tower of **St Patrick's Roman Catholic Church**, which holds weekly services for the local Spanish and Cantonese communities in their own languages.

Greek Street

On the corner of Greek Street is a stern Victorian establishment, the **House of St Barnabas**. Founded in 1846, the House set out to improve the lot of the poor through Christian teaching. This was where William Gladstone, that pillar of Victorian politics, would take prostitutes during his extraordinary night-time walks through the area in the early 1850s. His declared aim was to talk them out of their sinful ways, but inevitably cynical tongues began wagging.

Frith Street and Dean Street

The Frith Street Gallery at No.60 specializes in works on paper. In Frith Street you will also see **Ronnie Scott's** famous jazz club (*see* p.179) at No.47 (Scott, a jazz saxophonist, died in 1996, but his dingy basement club still gets high-profile bookings) and a plethora of restaurants including **Jimmy's** at No.23 (*open Mon–Sat 12–3 and 5.30–11.30*), a basement Greek café serving cheap moussaka and chips that has changed little since the Rolling Stones ate there in the 1960s.

Many phantoms also haunt Dean Street. No.49 is the **French House**, which became the official HQ of the Free French forces under De Gaulle during the Second World War. Now it's a lively pub-cum-wine bar. Two clubs further down the street illustrate the changes in Soho since the 1950s. **The Colony**, at No.41, was once described as 'a place where the villains look like artists and the artists look like villains'. The **Groucho** – so called because of Groucho Marx's one-liner that he never wanted to join a club that would have him as a member – opened at No.44 in 1985 and has been a hit with the world of television, music, comedy, publishing and film ever since.

Cafés and Pubs

Bar Chocolate, 28 D'Arblay St. A wide range of food – bangers and mash, *nachos*, *bruscetta*, *meze*, in a trendy dark brown bar, £6.50–£10.

Movie Café, 132 Wardour St. Fresh squeezed juices, cappuccino and toasted sandwiches.

Randall & Aubin, 16 Brewer Street. A bustling seafood brasserie in an atmospheric old tiled fishmonger's shop.

Soho Spice, 124–6 Wardour St. High quality Indian food, with a great-value set lunch £7.

Pizza Maletti, 26 Noel Street. Real Roman pizza by the oblong slice, incredibly fresh. Mainly takeaway, but there are a few stools.

Pâtisserie Valerie, 44 Old Compton St. More delicious croissants, cakes and *vol-au-vents*. Very crowded and self-consciously arty.

Bar Italia, 22 Frith St. Open 24 hours, a Soho institution catering to everyone from after-hours clubbers to gaggles of tourists: arguably the best espresso and cappuccino in town. Some snacks.

Maison Bertaux, 28 Greek St. Mouthwatering French pastries, the perfect place for excellent-value tea, gâteaux and pastries.

Mildred's, 45 Lexington Street. Classy vegetarian fare, including enormous *tostadas*, ale pies, stir-fries and delectable desserts. Very popular. Under £10.

Wagamama, 10A Lexington St. Perenially popular Japanese noodle restaurant, where you sit at long communal canteen-style tables. Excellent value at £10.95–14.95.

For a Chinese feast, walk along Lisle Street and Gerrard Street and take your pick – look for Chinese customers inside.

Fung Shing, 15 Lisle Street. Not cheap, but Chinese cuisine at its best.

Quo Vadis (***t*** *(020) 7437 9585; open Mon–Sat, closed Sun*), the restaurant at No.28, became instantly trendworthy in 1996 after it was bought from its original Italian owners by Marco Pierre White (famous London superchef) and Damien Hirst (Britpack conceptual artist-cum-restaurateur) and refurbished. Downstairs are works by Hirst and Marcus Harvey. The rooms upstairs are on the site where Karl Marx lived with his family in 1851–6 in a two-room attic flat in conditions of abject penury.

Old Compton Street and Wardour Street

In many ways Old Compton Street is the archetypal Soho street, as well as the heart of gay London. Here you'll find cafés such as **Pâtisserie Valerie** at No.44, restaurants, delicatessens, gay clubs and bars, and modest-looking newsagents stocking every conceivable title on the planet. Wardour Street, once known for its furniture and antique stores, is now occupied by film companies who advertise their forthcoming productions in the high glass windows on the left-hand side of the street.

Berwick Street Market and Brewer Street

Berwick Street Market (*open Mon–Sat 9–4*) always has beautifully fresh produce at incredibly low prices for central London. Ever since Jack Smith introduced the pineapple to London here in 1890, the market has also had a reputation for stocking unusual and exotic fruit and veg. The houses behind the stalls, like the market itself, date back to the 18th century. There's a couple of old pubs (The Blue Posts is the most salubrious), a scattering of noisy independent record stores and several excellent old-fashioned theatrical fabric shops specializing in unusual silks, satins, velvets, Chinese printed silks and printed cottons, sold by the metre and the place to go if you're looking for something exotic for yourself or your sofa.

At the southern end of Berwick St is a poky passage called **Walker's Court**, dominated by peepshows and the London equivalent of the Moulin Rouge, Raymond's Revue Bar. Turn right into **Brewer Street**, the ultimate Soho mixture of sex-joints and eclectic shops, with discreetly signposted peep-shows, an excellent fishmonger's, a well-stocked poster shop and, at No.67, the shop Anything Left-Handed.

Chinatown

London's Chinese population came mostly from Hong Kong in the 1950s and 1960s, victims not so much of the political upheavals in the region as the cruel fluctuations of the Asian rice market. Back then Gerrard Street, like the rest of Soho, was cheap and run-down and welcoming to foreigners. It took more than a generation for the new community to be fully accepted, however, and it was not until the 1970s that this street was pedestrianized and kitted out with decorative lamps and telephone boxes styled like pagodas – a spectacular backdrop to the Chinese New Year celebrations which take place here at the end of January or early February. Many of the older generation have only a rudimentary grip of English, and remain suspicious of their adoptive environment. The younger generation has integrated rather better; those born here are mockingly nicknamed BBCs (British-born children).

London's Chinatown is still very small – just Gerrard Street and Lisle Street really – and the trade is overwhelmingly in food. There are a few craft shops, and there's always been a discreet business in gambling – underground dens for mah-jong, pai-kau and fan tan. The eastern end of Gerrard St and Newport Place are crowded with supermarkets and craft shops, which are well worth poking around for a bargain.

***Onwards to*: Covent Garden, p.66; Bloomsbury, p.54; Charing Cross Road shopping, p.133; Oxford Street shopping, p.130.**

St James's and Royal London

⊖ *Green Park, Charing Cross, Victoria.*

St James's is the fairyland of London, a peculiarly British kind of looking-glass world where everyone eats thickly cut marmalade sandwiches and drinks tea from Fortnum & Mason, where the inhabitants are for the most part kindly middle-aged gentlemen with bespoke tailored suits and ruddy complexions, where shopkeepers are called purveyors and underlings wear livery coats. What's more, this fairytale comes with its very own queen, who lives in a palace surrounded by broad lush parks and guarded by toy soldiers in busby hats and red, blue and black uniforms. Everything is clean and beautiful in fairyland, even the roads, some of which have been coloured pink to add to the general feeling of well-being. St James's is the preserve of the establishment, not the vulgar money-making classes of the City but an older, rarefied pedigree which whiles away the hours in the drawing-rooms of fine houses and private clubs. It is a world that has been endlessly depicted and lampooned on film and on television.

The Mall

A sense of place, and occasion, is immediately invoked by the grand concave triple entrance of **Admiralty Arch**, the gateway to St James's and start of the long straight drive along The Mall up to Buckingham Palace. Passing through the arch, you'll appreciate the full splendour of St James's Park (*see* p.127) ahead to your left; notice, too, the white stone frontings to your right. These are part of **Carlton House Terrace**, the remnants of one of London's more lavish – and ultimately futile – building projects. In the early 18th century this site was home to Henry Boyle, Baron Carlton. The Prince of Wales (later George IV) decided he rather liked the place and hired the architect, Henry Holland, to spruce up the house to the standards of a royal palace. For 30 years Holland and his associates toiled away, adding Corinthian porticoes here, brown Siena marble columns there. One contemporary critic said the end result stood comparison with Versailles; that did not stop the extravagant George from declaring himself bored with the new palace and having most of it demolished. It was left to John Nash to salvage what he could from the wreckage of Carlton House and construct these elegant terraces in their place. They have housed many a club and eminent society in their time; now the most interesting address is No.12, the **Institute of Contemporary Arts**. Perhaps surprisingly given the setting, the ICA is a mecca for the 'Britpack' school of art, the pre-post-avant-garde and the obscure. There is a modest day membership fee (*£1.50 weekdays, £2.50 weekends*) to get into the main shows and the excellent café; otherwise you are restricted to the foyer and bookshop.

Horse Guards Parade (the Changing of the Guard)

The Horse Guards in question are the queen's very own knights in shining armour, properly known as the Household Division. Altogether, seven regiments are allocated the task of dressing up in chocolate-soldier costumes and parading in front of Buckingham Palace. Housed both here and at Wellington Barracks on the south side of the park are the Household Cavalry (look out for the horses), the Life Guards, the

Blues and Royals, the Grenadiers, the Coldstream Guards and the Scots, Irish and Welsh guards. The best time to see them is on the first weekend in June, when they all take part in a grand parade in front of the Queen known as **Trooping the Colour**. Otherwise you can make do with the **Changing of the Guard** (*outside the Horse Guards Mon–Sat 11am, Sun 10am; or outside Buckingham Palace at 11.15am daily April–Aug, and every other day the rest of the year*).

Pall Mall and Clubland

The street's curious name derives from an ancient Italian ball game called *palla a maglio*, literally ball and mallet. Charles II liked it so much that he built this pall mall alley. If you enjoyed birdwatching in St James's Park, maybe you should pull your binoculars back out for some ornithological study of a different kind here in Pall Mall, the high street of London's **clubland**. The rare bird you are after is male, 50-ish and well-dressed; he tends to stagger somewhat, especially after lunch, and looks rather like one of those old salt-of-the-earth types that Jack Hawkins or Trevor Howard used to play. The author and former club *maître d'* Anthony O'Connor has defined the London club as a place 'where a well-born buck can get away from worries, women and anything that even faintly smacks of business in a genteel atmosphere of good cigars, mulled claret and obsequious servants'. The end of the empire and the emancipation of domestic servants brought about a sharp decline in clubland: before the Second World War there were 120 clubs in London; now there are fewer than 40.

The **Athenaeum** on Waterloo Place, designed by Decimus Burton, is one of the best Greek Revival buildings in London, its frieze inspired by the relief sculptures from the

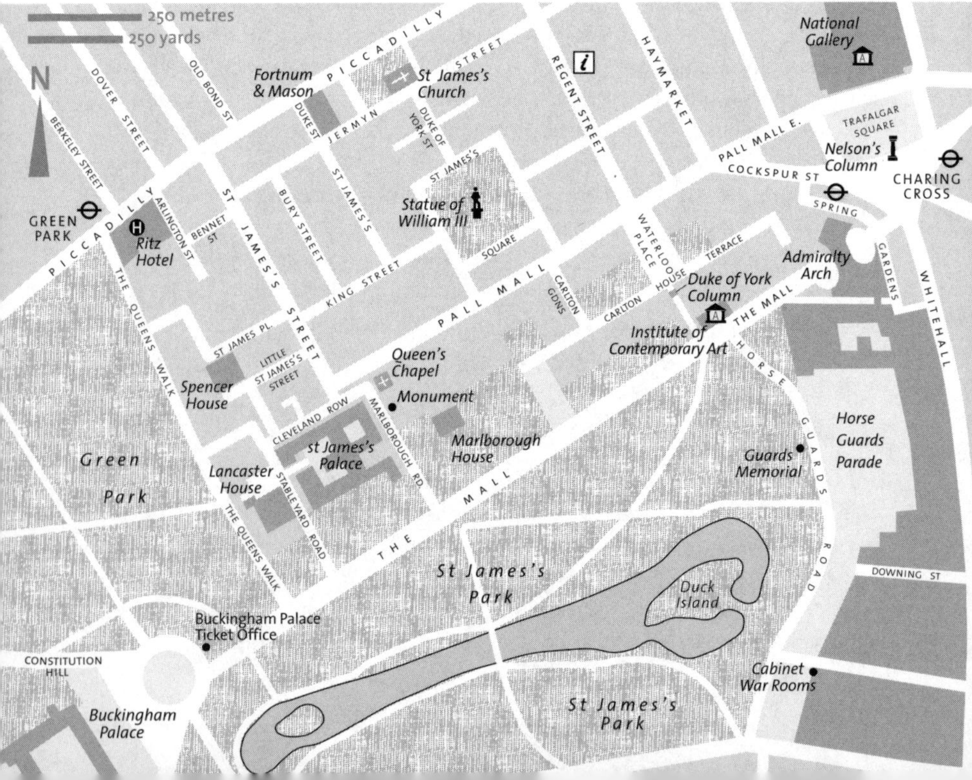

Cafés and Pubs

Wiltons, 55 Jermyn St, best to reserve in advance on **t** (020) 7629 9955. Archetypally English, strong on fish, in an urbane gentleman's club setting. £30–40.

Quaglino's, 16 Bury St, **t** (020) 7930 6767. Ferociously expensive, complicated Modern European cuisine in a pillared dining room. £25 or more for lunch.

Just St James's, 19 King St, **t** (020) 7930 9292. Sleek English food such as duck breasts, seared scallops, Aberdeen Angus beef in a modern dining room. 2 courses £16.50.

ICAfé, The Mall. The trendy arts centre café does delicious fresh Italian brasserie food, though you'll have to pay day-membership (£1.50, includes entrance to exhibitions) to get in. £5–£14.

Fuzzy's Grub,6 Crown Passage, off Pall Mall. This little passageway (go down St James's Street, turn left into Pall Mall and it's just on the left) has all the cheaper establishments in the area and is where the workers go. This place is great – choose a roast meat, choose whether you want it in a sandwich or a meal, choose the veg and the relish, and your meal is ready instantly for £5–6.

Chubby's, Crown Passage. An English fry-up.

Il Vicolo, 3–4 Crown Passage. Pleasant Italian, with pasta from £9.

Parthenon housed in the British Museum. The club was known in the 19th century as the haunt of the intellectual élite, which explains the gilt statue of Athena, goddess of wisdom, above the entrance and the Greek letters of Athena's name in the mosaic above the porch.

As you walk past the Athenaeum down Pall Mall, look out for the brass plates announcing a host of other clubs, including the Travellers', the Reform, the Royal Automobile, the United Oxford and Cambridge, and the Army and Navy Club. The **Reform Club**, at Nos.104–5, is where Jules Verne's fictional hero Phileas Fogg made his wager and set out to travel around the world in 80 days.

St James's Street

Along with Pall Mall, St James's Street is clubland *par excellence*, although in the past it has enjoyed a less than irreproachable reputation because of its gambling dens. **White's**, the oldest London club, may well have instituted the national mania for bets and betting in the mid-18th century when it ran books on everything from births and marriages to politics and death. White's was soon eclipsed, however, by **Brooks** down the road. One particularly obsessional gambler, Charles James Fox, ran up debts of £140,000 and was seen cadging money off the waiters at Brooks before his father, Lord Holland, stepped in to bail him out in 1781.

St James's Street has changed quite a bit in the 20th and 21st centuries. The bottom end, at the junction with Pall Mall, is dominated by two early 1900s office buildings by Norman Shaw. There is an astonishing office block that resembles a bronze space-ship. More striking still is the **Economist Building** at Nos.25–7, a series of three concrete hexagonal towers designed in 1964 by Peter and Alison Smithson for the weekly news magazine *The Economist*. Much praised at the time, the building is certainly one of the more successful of London's experiments in 1960s modernism.

St James's Palace

For more than 300 years this was the official residence of England's kings and queens; indeed, foreign ambassadors are still formally accredited to the Court of St James even though they are received, like every other official on royal business, at

Buckingham Palace. Although endowed with fine buildings (of which only the octagonal towers of the gatehouse survive), St James's Palace became known as a raucous place of ill manners and debauchery, particularly under Queen Anne and the early Hanoverians who used it to hold drunken banquets. Anne was well known for her unseemly appetite for food and drink, particularly brandy, and for the bodily noises she frequently emitted at table. Not suprisingly, the place soon came to be described as 'crazy, smoky and dirty'. The Prince Regent celebrated his disastrous marriage with Caroline of Brunswick here in 1795, spending his wedding night fully dressed in a drunken slumber in the fireplace of the bridal chamber. Soon afterwards he moved into Carlton House, and the palace's somewhat tarnished glory days were over. A fire destroyed most of the original buildings in 1809; the rebuilt courtyards now house offices for members of the royal household. The palace is closed to the public.

Spencer House

27 St James's Place (off St James's St); www.spencerhouse.co.uk. Open Feb–July and Sept–Dec Sun 10.30–5.45, last adm 4.45; adm; visit by guided tour only.

This gracious Palladian mansion was born in sorrow: its original backer, Henry Bromley, ran out of money and shot himself moments after reading his will over with his lawyer. The site was then taken over by the Spencer family (ancestors of Princess Diana) who hired a bevy of architects including John Vardy and Robert Adam to produce one of the finest private houses in London. Completed in 1766, Spencer House boasts magnificent parquet floors, ornate plaster ceilings and a welter of gilded statues and furniture. The highlight is Vardy's Palm Room, in which the pillars are decorated as gilt palm trees with fronds stretching over the tops of the arched window bays. James Stuart's Painted Room features classical murals, graceful chandeliers and a fine, highly polished wooden floor. The whole house was renovated by its current owners, RIT Capital Partners, in 1990 and looks magnificent. Unfortunately only eight rooms are open to the public; the rest are kept for the pleasure of the financial executives who occupy it during the week.

St James's Square

This square was where St James's turned from a mere adjunct to the royal palaces into a fashionable residential district in its own right. Just before the Great Fire of 1666, Charles II had granted a lease to Henry Jermyn, Earl of St Albans, charging him to build 'palaces fit for the dwelling of noblemen and persons of quality'. The result was to set the tone for nearly all of London's squares, creating a haven of privacy and seclusion. The equestrian statue in the middle is of William III; his horse has one hoof atop the molehill which caused the king's fatal riding accident in 1702. Nowadays there are no more private residences in the square's spacious, mainly Georgian houses; they have been replaced by a succession of clubs, libraries and offices.

Also see: **Buckingham Palace, p.31; St James's Park, p.127; Jermyn Street and Savile Row shopping, p.133; Green Park, p.120.**

Onwards to: **Piccadilly, p.76; Mayfair, p.70.**

The South Bank and Southwark

⊖ *Waterloo, Embankment, London Bridge, Southwark.*

Southwark, the London borough stretching from Waterloo Bridge to the other side of Tower Bridge, has seen it all: butchers, leather-makers, whores, corrupt bishops, coach drivers, actors, bear-baiters, railwaymen and dockers. Shakespeare's Globe Theatre was here, and so was the notorious Marshalsea debtors' prison. It is one of the most atmospheric and historic parts of London, used over and over by the city's novelists, particularly Dickens.

In the 17th century, Bankside and the whole borough of Southwark were bywords for a raucous good time. The boisterous character of the area is easily explained by history. When the Romans first built London Bridge in AD 43, Southwark naturally developed as a small colony and market town opposite the City of London. As the City grew in wealth and importance, Southwark attracted some of the dirtier, more unpleasant trades that might have offended the rich merchants across the river. In 1556 Southwark came directly under the City's jurisdiction and cleaned up its act somewhat. The theatres made the available entertainment a little more thought-provoking, if only for a brief period. And then local industries sprang up: Bankside was bustling with wharves, breweries, foundries and glassworks.

Southwark remained a promising, if still raucous area until the mid-18th century, when the construction of Westminster Bridge and the first Blackfriars Bridge diminished its importance as the most accessible of London's southern satellites. The arrival of the railways in the Victorian era made it even more isolated, reducing it to no more than a row of warehouses stuck between the noisy train tracks. Further

Cafés and Pubs

Gourmet Pizza Company, Gabriel's Wharf. Pizza with nice views of the Thames from a riverside terrace. From £8.95; choose from the spectrum of exotic toppings.

Blueprint Café, Design Museum, Butler's Wharf, **t** (020) 7378 7031. Inventive, tasty, trendy Mediterranean cuisine in the excellent Design Museum; good views of the river. Worth booking. £20–25.

Fina Estampa, 150 Tooley Street. London's only Peruvian restaurant.

The Fire Station, 150 Waterloo Rd. Renovated fire station opposite the Old Vic Theatre, serving fashionable modern European cuisine and Sunday roasts.

Le Pont de la Tour, Butler's Wharf. Jewel in the crown of Conran's restaurant empire: sophisticated brasserie food with stunning views of the river and the City. Weekday set lunch from £31.

Oxo Tower Restaurant, Bar & Brasserie, 8th Floor, Oxo Tower Wharf, Barge House St. A magnet for fashionable London as well as visitors, the Oxo Tower combines London's most exclusive cutting edge designer crafted shopping (check out the award-winning Studio Fusion Gallery) with this sleek and very stylish restaurant/brasserie owned and run by Harvey Nichols. High decibel and packed out at night (book ahead, **t** (020) 7803 3888) but worth it for the ambience and views.

Tate Modern. A touch overpriced (like most museum cafés), but worth it, especially if you're visiting late night Friday or Saturday. There is also a more expensive restaurant on the upper floors.

George Inn, 77 Borough High St. An old coaching inn dating back to the days of Shakespeare. Basic pub grub.

Anchor & Hope, 36 The Cut. Unusual, imaginative food in a smart gastropub.

The Archduke, Concert Hall Approach. By Hungerford Bridge and the Royal Festival Hall, a two-floor wine bar serving good food.

decline came after the Second World War, as the London docks became more obsolete and the area's warehouses closed. For a long time, like so many neglected areas of London, it had only its past to turn to as a source of income, and could only devote itself to the heritage industry.

Nowadays, the atmosphere is very much intact, but in a wholly new form. The South Bank has become one of the most vibrant, fastest-changing parts of the city. Museums and arts venues have flourished where industrial life curled up and died. Art galleries and restaurants have moved into the derelict wharves, and trendy new housing developments have livened up the old railway sidings. Even the **Globe Theatre** is back, not quite where it was in Shakespeare's day, but almost. Best of all, these attractions are now linked by a wonderful river walkway stretching from Westminster Bridge to London Bridge and beyond – so you encounter little more than the distant rumble of traffic along the way.

The South Bank was where it was all happening in the run-up to the millennium, and Britain's newest, biggest and brightest landmarks continue to draw excited crowds to areas rarely set foot in just a couple of years ago. In marked contrast to the cynical reception accorded to the poor doomed Dome, the **London Eye** (*see* p.37) received a rapturous welcome and has quickly established itself as a leading London attraction, as has the glorious **Tate Modern** (*see* p.43) – even the **Millennium Bridge**, beset upon opening by engineering problems, has worked its way into the public's affections. It seems South Bank projects can do no wrong at the moment, and that, after years of waiting in the wings, the area has finally burst into the limelight, all glammed up and ready to party.

The South Bank Centre

From the outside, the buildings lying at the heart of the South Bank Centre look rather forbidding – lumps of dirty grey concrete streaked with rain, and proof if ever it were needed that concrete does not suit the English climate. Aesthetics apart, though, the South Bank works remarkably well as a cultural complex. The Royal

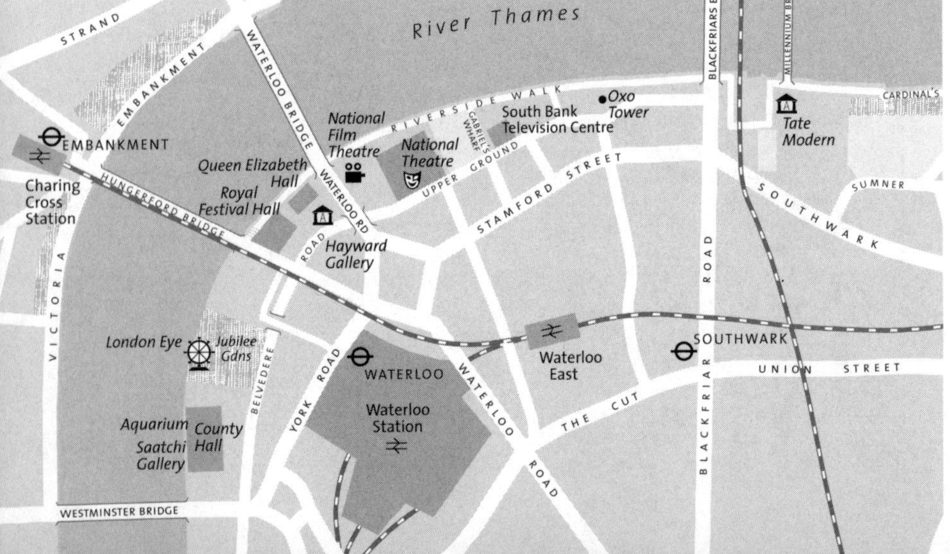

Festival Hall is the South Bank's main concert venue; there are also the National Film Theatre, the Hayward Gallery (for major international exhibitions), Queen Elizabeth Hall and Purcell Room (also for concerts), and the three-stage Royal National Theatre. Everything is subsidised and tickets relatively cheap. People enjoy coming not just for the scheduled events, but also to hang out in the spacious halls with their plentiful cafés, occasional musicians, elegant bookstalls, piers and river views. The merits of the various venues are dealt with in 'Entertainment and Nightlife'. The National Theatre foyers have excellent bookshops, particularly for drama, as well as free live concerts in the early evening. The Festival Hall has free lunchtime concerts.

A Lottery-funded Millennium Project is planning to make great changes for the South Bank Centre. The concrete will, with any luck, be obscured by a giant master-plan affecting each of the centre's venues, except the Royal National Theatre, which has gone solo and spent a £32 million Lottery grant on a refurbishment all of its own.

County Hall

Westminster Bridge Road; ⊖ Waterloo, Westminster.

Begun in 1911, but not completed until 1958, County Hall's construction had to take into account interruptions caused by two world wars and the discovery on-site of a 3rd-century Roman ship. The imposing home of the Greater London Council until the mid 1980s, the grand old building sat neglected and empty for years after the council's abolition. Its apparent uselessness provoked the odd threat of demolition until it was bought by a Japanese company, whereupon it was whipped into shape as a gleaming new leisure complex. The Hall now houses the **Namco Station**, a 35,000 sq ft hi-tech amusement arcade (***t** (020) 7967 1067, www.namcostation.co.uk; open daily 10am–midnight; free adm, charge per ride*); the **Dalí Universe**, a new permanent exhibition which includes the surrealist's famous Mae West Lips sofa and the 'Spellbound' backdrop (***t** (020) 7620 2720, www.daliuniverse.com; open daily 10–5.30; adm exp*); the **London Eye ticket office** (*see* p.37), the **London Aquarium** (*see* p.26), and the new **Saatchi Gallery** (*see* p.141).

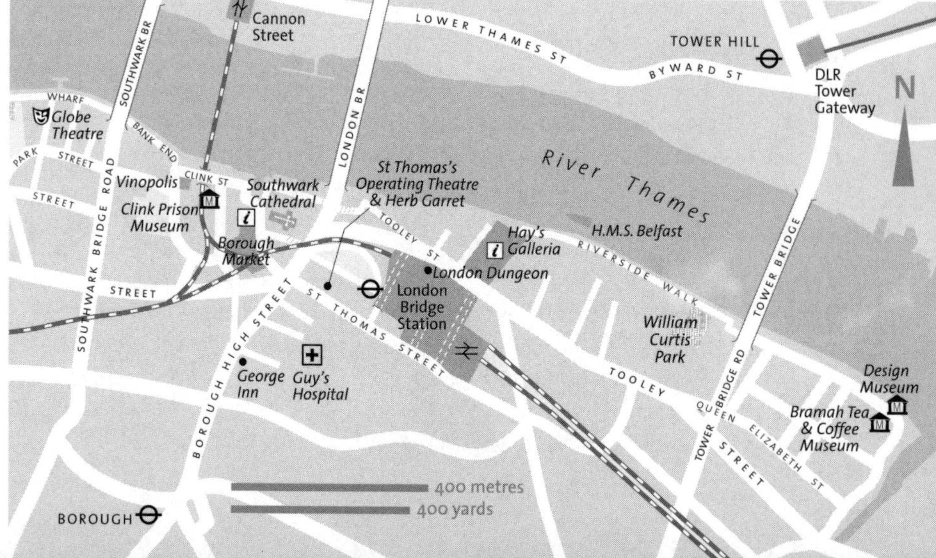

IMAX Theatre

1 Charlie Chaplin Walk, South Bank; ⊖ Waterloo; **t** *(020) 7902 1234, www.bfi.org.uk/imax. Box office open daily 10.30–7.30; adm.*

Rising phoenix-like from a depressing roundabout outside Waterloo Station, this shiny £20m glass drum is the biggest, newest, most technically advanced IMAX in Europe. Inside the 500-seat theatre, 2D and 3D films are shown on a 10-storey screen via a projector the size of two small cars. For the time being the library consists of 130 films, including the stupendous documentary *Into the Deep*, exploring the underwater coast of Southern California. The theatre also screens 2D mainstream films that lend themselves to the grand-scale experience, such as *Gladiator*.

Gabriel's Wharf

This is an attractive square set back from the river, a little way east from the National Theatre. Formed by the backs of warehouses painted in *trompe l'œil* fashion to resemble house-fronts, it is occupied by speciality shops, sculpture, ceramics, fashion and jewellery workshops. There are some good cafés, bars and restaurants.

Oxo Tower

Bargehouse Street; **t** *(020) 7401 2255, www.oxotower.co.uk. Bars, restaurants and ground floor shops and galleries open daily, design shops open Tues–Sun 11–6.*

Oxo, the stock cube people, neatly sidestepped the strict advertising regulations of the 1930s by working the letters 'OXO' into the design of the tower itself. In 1996 the Art Deco warehouse was magnificently restored by the Coin Street Community Builders, and it now contains over 30 designer and jewellery workshops, as well as a couple of restaurants and bars. In the tower you can buy work from the highest-quality designers and craftsmen at prices that are significantly cheaper than in galleries and shops in central London. At the very top is a free public viewing gallery with glitzy views of the London skyline.

Millennium Bridge

Connecting the historic to the brand spanking new, this Norman Foster creation links St Paul's Cathedral to the southeast corner of the Tate Modern. The 330m-long, 4m-wide 'blade of light', rising 13m above the Thames, is central London's first new bridge since 1894. Around 150,000 people gathered on its opening weekend in the summer of 2000, hoping to be among the first to sashay across the river. All seemed well at first, until the sashaying turned to staggering as the suspension bridge began to sway alarmingly from side to side. Nicknamed 'The Wobbly Bridge' by the press, the bridge was promptly closed three days after opening to allow engineers to examine the problem. Scientific explanations were proffered – something to do with excessive parallel kinetics, apparently – and although there was never any danger to the public, action clearly needed to be taken. In early 2002 – after 2,000 volunteers and a host of computers agreed that the 'wobble' had been corrected – it was reopened.

The Rose Theatre

56 Park St; ***t*** *(020) 7902 1500, www.rosetheatre.org.uk. Contact Globe Theatre (see p.32), which offers tours to pre-booked groups; adm.*

Until all the millennium redevelopments you could look through the ground-floor windows of this office block on the corner of Rose Alley to see the ruined foundations of the Rose Theatre, the first Bankside playhouse (1587), which was rediscovered here in 1989. Now you can see them from inside, along with a multimedia presentation.

Southwark Cathedral

Montague Close; ***t*** *(020) 7367 6700, www.southwark.anglican.org. Open Mon–Fri 7.30–6, Sat–Sun 8.30–6; free, but £4 donation requested.*

You can enter through the modern annexe slightly to your left. Once inside, there is a café to the left and the cathedral entrance to the right.

Southwark Cathedral has a past almost as chequered as the neighbourhood, suffering fire, neglect and patchwork reconstruction over a history stretching back to the 7th century. It started life as the parish church of St Mary Overie (which despite the weird name merely means 'St Mary over the river'), built according to legend by the first boatman of Southwark to ferry gentlemen to and from the City. It burned down at least twice before being incorporated into a priory belonging to the Bishop of Winchester sometime around 1220. In the Civil War it was a bastion of Puritanism where preachers denounced the Bankside playhouses as offences to the Almighty. By the 19th century it had largely fallen to pieces, and the nave was rebuilt – twice as it turned out, since the first attempt was considered an appalling travesty. By the 20th century, with a little help from the restorers, Southwark was elevated to the rank of cathedral for the whole of south London. The architecture is still predominantly Gothic, particularly the choir, fine retro-choir and altar, making it something of a rarity in London. The tower is 15th-century, although the battlements and pinnacles weren't completed until 1689. The nave is the only significant portion from a later era, although you will also notice Victorian statues atop the reredos behind the altar. An imaginative Lottery-funded permanent exhibition entitled 'The Long View of London' opened in 2001 within the cathedral's restored chapterhouses. The hi-tech exhibition examines the changing views of the city from the cathedral's tower since Wenceslas Holler drew his famous 'Long View' from here in 1638.

Clink Prison Museum

1 Clink Street; ⊖ London Bridge; ***t*** *(020) 7403 0900, www.clink.co.uk. Open Sept–mid-June daily 10–6; mid-June–Aug daily 10–9; adm.*

The Clink was the Bishop of Winchester's private prison, where anyone who dared to challenge the extortion rackets he ran on Bankside would be locked up in gruesome conditions. For 400 years successive bishops acted as pimp to the local whores, known as Winchester Geese, and used the prison as dire punishment for any who tried to conceal their earnings, or work for somebody else. The name 'Clink' is familiar enough nowadays as a synonym for jail; it derives from a Latin expression meaning, roughly speaking, 'kick the bucket', which gives a good indication of the fate a prisoner could expect inside.

The exhibition in this macabre museum highlights the cruelty of life in medieval Bankside, particularly the barbaric treatment of women both in prison and outside. Wives deemed too talkative would wear a scold's bridle, an iron gag shoved into their mouth and left there for days; sometimes the gag would be spiked. Crusaders off to the Holy Land would lock their womenfolk in chastity belts which prevented not only sexual contact but all genital hygiene. Women often died of infections or, if the belt was fitted while they were teenagers and still growing, of constriction of the pelvis. In 1537 Henry VIII ruled that women who murdered their husbands were to be boiled in a vat of oil; it was up to the executioner whether or not to boil the oil in advance.

George Inn

George Inn Yard, off Borough High Street; ⊖ London Bridge.

The coaching inns were like the railway stations that eventually superseded them, each one providing a transport service to a specific group of destinations. Unlike railway stations, however, the inns had no fixed timetable but functioned according to demand. As a result there was often a great deal of waiting to do, and the inns made up for this by ensuring a ready supply of draught ale for waiting passengers. The George Inn goes back to the 16th century, although the present buildings date from shortly after the Great Fire. It is an elegant terrace of small interconnecting wooden bars looking out on a quiet courtyard, where during the summer you can see morris dancing (an old English ritual which involves wearing folklore costumes festooned with bells) and open-air productions of Shakespeare's plays.

Old Operating Theatre, Museum and Herb Garret

9a St Thomas's Street; ⊖ London Bridge; **t** *(020) 7188 2679, www.thegarret.org.uk. Open daily 10.30–5; adm.*

The old church tower you enter used to be attached to the chapel of St Thomas's, one of the biggest hospitals in London, founded on this site back in the 12th century. The hospital moved to Lambeth in the 1860s to make way for London Bridge railway station, and all the old buildings except this one were destroyed. For a century the chapel was considered a mere curiosity, an unspectacular relic from a bygone age. Then, in 1956, a historian named Raymond Russell noticed a curious hole above the tower belfry. He squeezed through and discovered a garret containing a 19th-century operating theatre, the only one of its kind to have survived in the country. It was restored and in 1968 turned into a museum charting the tower's history, first as a medieval garret devoted to herbal remedies, then as an operating room attached to a women's ward in the next building. Nowhere else in London will you get such a graphic insight into the horrors of medicine before the modern age. The museum also gives a lightning account of the history of apothecaries , accompanied by a display of gynaecological instruments that would not look out of place in a torture chamber.

The most famous woman in the hospital's history was Florence Nightingale, the legendary nurse of the Crimean War who set up London's first nursing school at St Thomas's in 1858.

London Bridge

'London Bridge is falling down' goes the old nursery rhyme. Too right. London Bridge has fallen down so often that there's nothing left to see. No, it's not the one on all the postcards that opens in the middle (that's Tower Bridge), although God knows there are enough tourists who haven't realized this yet (and one American who, back in the 1960s, bought the previous incarnation of London Bridge and had it reconstructed stone for stone back home in Lake Havasu, Arizona – how disappointed his friends must have been). London Bridge stopped being interesting some time around 1661, when the spikes that used to display the severed heads of criminals were finally removed. It ceased to be London's one and only river crossing about a century later with the construction of Westminster and Blackfriars bridges. Now London Bridge is nothing more than a cantilevered lump of concrete with four busy lanes of traffic on top. And it hasn't fallen down for centuries. The only striking feature of London Bridge at the moment is the building at the Southwark End, **One London Bridge**, a 1980s office complex in shining chrome and glass that links up with Hays Galleria (*see* below). Things are about to get exciting around here, however. The Italian architect Renzo Piano has designed 'The Shard', a 1,016ft spire-shaped skyscraper right next to London Bridge. At twice the height of the London Eye, this would be the tallest building in Europe.

London Dungeon

28–34 Tooley Street; ⊖ London Bridge; ***t*** *(020) 7403 7221, www.thedungeons.com. Open summer 9.30–7.30, winter 10.30–5; adm.*

'Enter at your peril', says the sign above the door. It's an appropriate warning for a museum that strives to make a spectator sport out of medieval torture, but can only manage the ketchup-splattered inauthenticity of a 1950s Hammer horror movie. In the first place, this is not a dungeon at all, but in fact a converted warehouse underneath the arches of London Bridge station. And secondly, there is scarcely a genuine historical artefact to be found in the place. That said, younger children may not view the exhibits with such a cynical eye, so it's not really suitable for under 7s.

Hay's Galleria

London's oldest wharf dates back to 1651, but the present structure is dominated by the tall yellow brick façades of the Victorian dock buildings, covered with a barrel-vaulted glass roof to form a pleasant arcade of shops, cafés and restaurants. The best feature is the central fountain sculpture, *The Navigators* by David Kemp, a fantasy in which a Viking galley is overtaken by naval commanders, astronomers and modern sailors with half-umbrellas for hats.

Butler's Wharf and the Design Museum

t 0870 833 9955 for details of temporary exhibitions, www.designmuseum.org. Museum open daily 10–5.45, last adm 5.15; adm. Museum houses a Conran restaurant (the Blueprint Café).

Created by Terence Conran and Stephen Bayley, the Design Museum is the only museum in the world devoted to industrial design and the cult of consumerism. A bower bird's shrine on the second floor showcases such mass production classics as the car (including designs by Le Corbusier from 1928), the vacuum (Dyson *et al*), early televisions and radios, telephones, tableware (by Enzo Mari) and chairs (by Charles and Ray Eames), while the ground floor is devoted to a diverse and diverting range of temporary exhibitions, from Porsche cars to Bosch washing machines. The museum is based in a disused warehouse which Conran and his partners rebuilt and – in a somewhat wistful homage to the International Style – painted white. Upstairs there are stunning views of Tower Bridge from the pricey Blueprint Café terrace.

The complex of buildings around the Design Museum is known as **Butler's Wharf**. As recently as the 1950s it was a hive of trade in commodities from tea and coffee to rubber, spices, wines and spirits. The rise of container shipping sounded the wharf's death knell; now only tourism and service industries can save it.

Vinopolis

*1 Bank End; **t** 0870 241 4040 (24hrs), www.vinopolis.co.uk. Open Tues–Thurs and Sun 12–6, Mon, Fri and Sat 12–9; adm exp.*

This two-and-a-half-acre complex under rumbling railway arches is the brainchild of a former wine merchant whose declared mission it is to educate and entertain 'anyone who enjoys a glass of wine'. This democratic principle, borne of a canny business eye, has resulted in a distinctly unpretentious, if a little banal, experience: part-museum, part-gallery (a separate section displays works from the Hess Collection) and part-wine-tasting class. Atmospheric, cellar-like rooms explore the world of wine and its regions via historical artefacts, video screens and interactive exhibits including virtual tours through Chianti on a Vespa, simulated flights over vast Australian vineyards, and touch-screen computers imparting such nuggets as Oz Clarke's top tips for finding just the right wine simile, which appropriately comes just before the highlight of the tour: the tasting tables. Five free tastings come with each ticket (which may bear some relation to the hefty admission price), from a limited but interesting choice. After the tour, there's a luxury gift shop, a well-stocked branch of Majestic Wine Warehouse, the award-winning Cantina Vinopolis and a bar, Wine Wharf, which is also directly accessible from Stoney Street, if you wanted to skip the tour and head straight for the booze.

***Also see*: London Aquarium, p.26; Globe Theatre, p.32; Saatchi Gallery, p.141; *Golden Hinde*, p.143; Bramah Museum of Tea and Coffee Museum, p.147.**

***Onwards to*: Docklands, p.102; The City of London, p.57.**

London: Villages

07

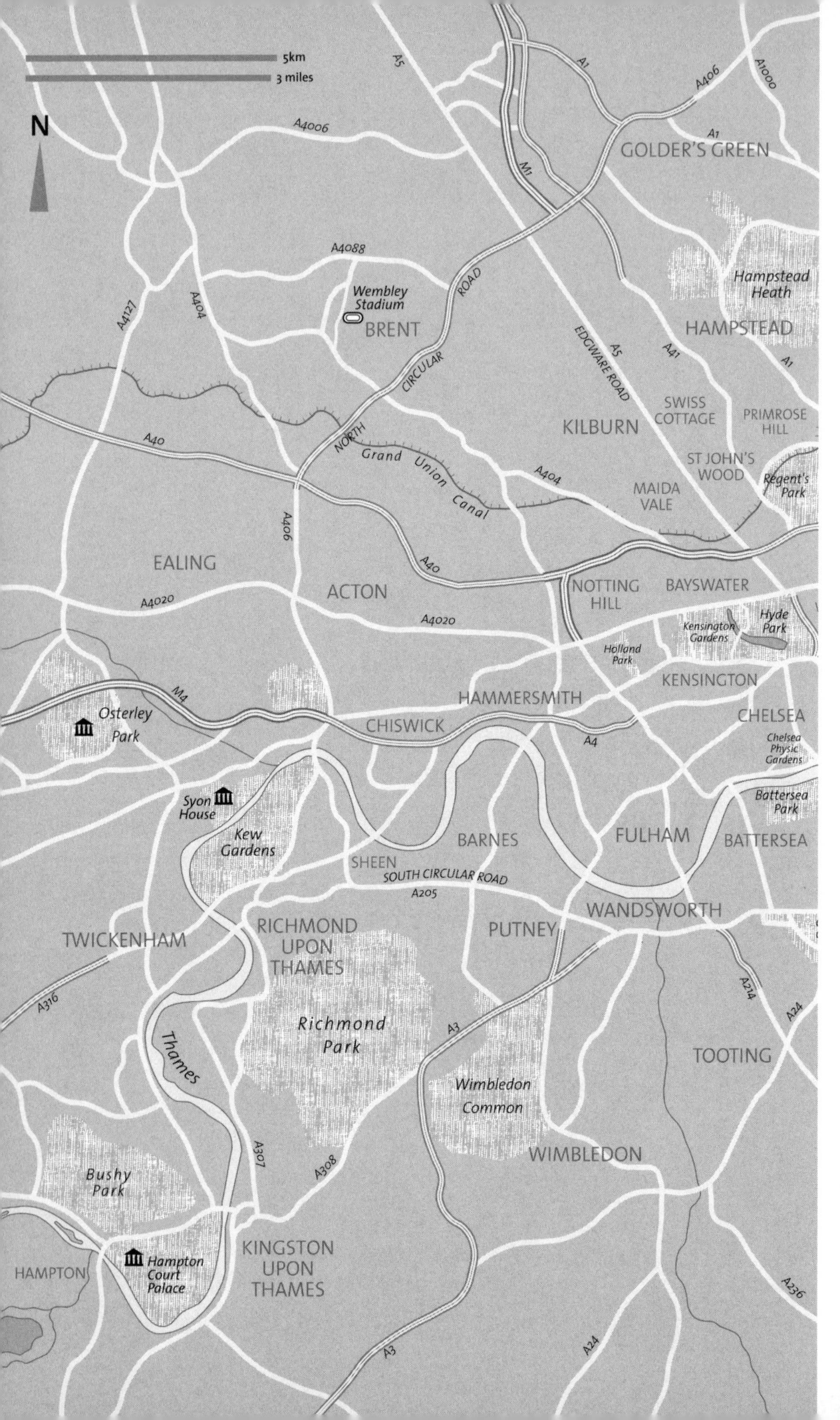
5km
3 miles
N
A5
A1
A406
A1000
A4006
A1
GOLDER'S GREEN
M1
A4088
Wembley Stadium
ROAD
Hampstead Heath
A4127
A404
BRENT
HAMPSTEAD
CIRCULAR
EDGWARE ROAD
A5
A41
A1
SWISS COTTAGE
PRIMROSE HILL
KILBURN
A40
NORTH
Grand Union Canal
ST JOHN'S WOOD
A404
Regent's Park
MAIDA VALE
A406
EALING
A40
NOTTING HILL
BAYSWATER
A4020
ACTON
A4020
Kensington Gardens
Hyde Park
Holland Park
KENSINGTON
M4
HAMMERSMITH
Osterley Park
CHISWICK
CHELSEA
A4
Chelsea Physic Gardens
Syon House
Battersea Park
Kew Gardens
BARNES
FULHAM
BATTERSEA
SHEEN
SOUTH CIRCULAR ROAD
A205
WANDSWORTH
RICHMOND UPON THAMES
PUTNEY
TWICKENHAM
A214
A316
A24
A3
Richmond Park
Thames
TOOTING
Wimbledon Common
WIMBLEDON
A307
A308
Bushy Park
KINGSTON UPON THAMES
Hampton Court Palace
HAMPTON
A236
A24
A3

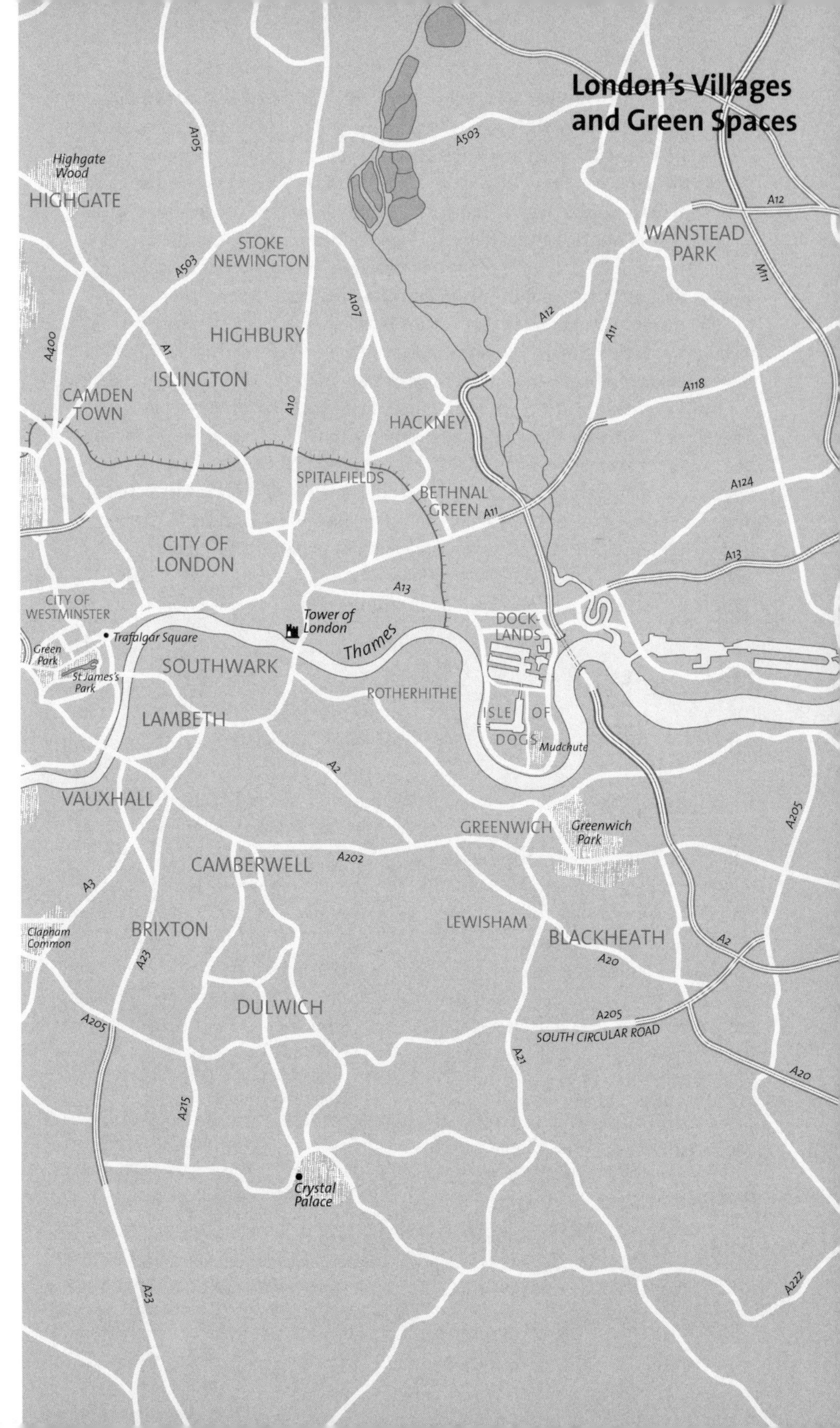
London's Villages and Green Spaces
Highgate Wood
HIGHGATE
STOKE NEWINGTON
WANSTEAD PARK
HIGHBURY
ISLINGTON
CAMDEN TOWN
HACKNEY
SPITALFIELDS
BETHNAL GREEN
CITY OF LONDON
CITY OF WESTMINSTER
Trafalgar Square
Tower of London
Thames
DOCK-LANDS
Green Park
St James's Park
SOUTHWARK
ROTHERHITHE
ISLE OF DOGS
Mudchute
LAMBETH
VAUXHALL
GREENWICH
Greenwich Park
CAMBERWELL
LEWISHAM
BLACKHEATH
Clapham Common
BRIXTON
DULWICH
SOUTH CIRCULAR ROAD
Crystal Palace
A105
A503
A12
M11
A107
A11
A400
A1
A10
A118
A124
A13
A2
A205
A202
A3
A23
A20
A215
A21
A222

The London that stretches away beyond the centre is often described as a series of villages. Indeed, some of the geographical terms used to describe the various districts – Highgate Village, Camden Town, and so on – encourage this way of thinking, as though the outskirts of the city were a patchwork of truly autonomous communities separated by fields and trees. To compare anything within the London urban area to village life is, of course, wishful thinking; there is little of a real village's close-knit sense of community, only hints of the unbroken greenery of the countryside, and none of the gossiping about the neighbours. It is important when visiting outer London, therefore, not to think that you are heading off into the sticks, as you might if you strayed 10 or 12 miles out of the centre of Paris or New York. Rather you should think of yourself as exploring another side of a multifaceted city. Each outer satellite has a distinct identity of its own and a sense of integration with the whole.

Partly for this reason, the point at which central London ends and outer London begins is not easy to define. You might justifiably feel that Camden, Notting Hill and Chelsea are really part of the centre and do not belong in this section at all. The difference is that the wealth of history and culture is less focused. What you find instead is a sense of identity and atmosphere that can be described more usefully than an exhaustive list of tourist attractions.

The 'villages' below are arranged roughly in order of their distance from the centre.

Notting Hill

⊖ Notting Hill Gate, Ladbroke Grove, Westbourne Park; buses 12, 23, 27, 31, 52, 94, 148.

Notting Hill conjures up many images: of imposing, pastel-stuccoed or gleaming white terraced houses; of antiques dealers on the southern end of Portobello Road pulling a fast one on unsuspecting tourists; of young Caribbeans dancing in the streets during the annual carnival; of arty types standing in line outside the Gate cinema; of young people riffling through second-hand records and cheap jewellery underneath the A40 flyover; of Moroccans and Portuguese chatting away in the ethnic cafés of Golborne Road; of affluent professional families relaxing in their large gardens in Stanley Crescent or Lansdowne Rise. To say Notting Hill is a melting pot is both a cliché and an understatement. It has been an emblem of multicultural London

Cafés and Pubs

Sausage and Mash Café, 268 Portobello Rd. Sausage and mash joy: delicious with gravy.

Market Bar, 240a Portobello Rd. Atmospheric bar; excellent Thai restaurant on first floor.

Books for Cooks, 4 Blenheim Crescent. Test out their recipe books in the delicious café.

Eat and Two Veg, corner of Westbourne Grove and Monmouth St. Good vegetarian food all day – pastas, salads and soups, but quite expensive, from £6.

Mike's Café, 12 Blenheim Crescent. Resolutely un-trendy English staples: cottage pie for £6.

Coffee Plant, 180 Portobello Rd. For just a quick coffee, grab one at this little shop.

Tom's deli'café, 226 Westbourne Grove. Tom Conran's great *traiteur* with a popular café.

Café Grove, 253a Portobello Rd. Popular terrace overlooking the market: rather expensive breakfasts and snacks but full of locals.

Geales, 2 Farmer St. Superb gourmet fish and chip restaurant; one of the best in London.

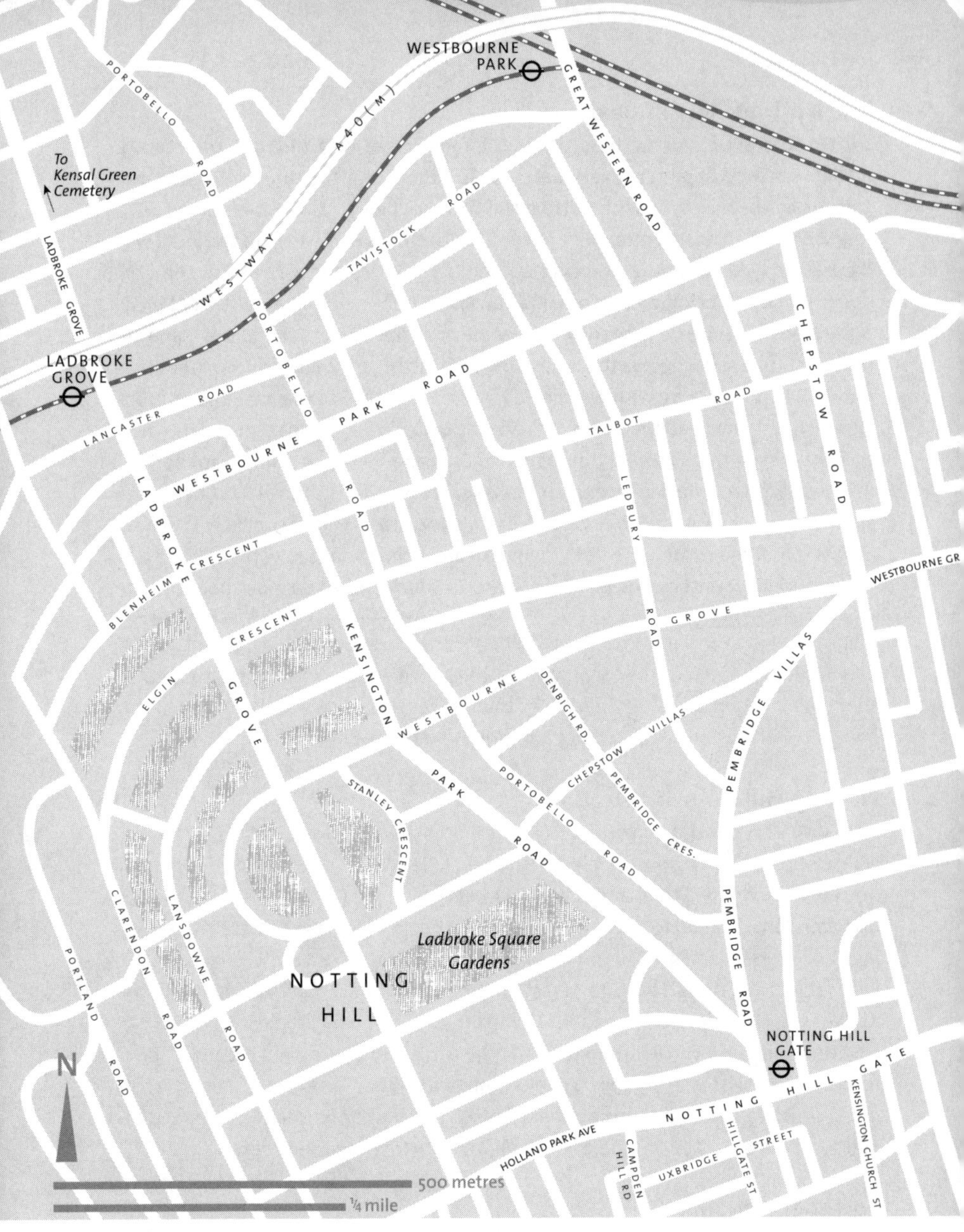

ever since the big immigrant waves from the Caribbean in the 1950s. Once considered irredeemably out of fashion, Notting Hill is now so hip with the liberal middle classes that it risks becoming as exclusive as the posh villas on Campden Hill on the south side of the main road. A rapid period of gentrification in the 1980s smartened things up, but it has also created barriers of class and status. The motorway flyover has created a neat divide between the spruced-up pastel-painted Victorian houses to the south (Notting Hill proper), and the high-rise 1960s council estates to the north (dismissively described as North Kensington).

The Notting Hill Carnival

After an explosion of racial tension in the summers of 1957 and 1958, community leaders resolved to put on an annual show to vaunt the attractions of Caribbean culture; by the mid-1960s the Notting Hill Carnival, held on the last weekend of August, had become a permanent fixture. For two days each year, on the Sunday and Bank Holiday Monday, the streets throb with steel bands and soca music. The crowds dance while balancing glasses of Jamaican Red Stripe – and some people get pleasantly high on choice Caribbean weed. People of all ages and nationalities come along for the party. Everywhere is the tangy smell of saltfish, goat curry, fried plantain and patties. Floats cruise by with dancers in fantastical outfits. In the past, the tension between residents and the police occasionally boiled over; but in recent years the police have got things just about right, and are generally to be photographed limboing with revellers in an embarrassed sort of way. The Carnival has been occasionally marked by gang violence, but, as a visitor, you are highly unlikely to see this at first hand. You're far more likely to have a great time, make new friends, get a patty stuck to your shoe and go home with a headache from too much beer and sun.

Most recently, the success of the 1999 film *Notting Hill* led to huge rent increases and has really undercut the very nature of the area it sought to eulogize on celluloid; the small independent shops and cafés that made the area fun and different are being pushed out and replaced by chain shops and coffee bars.

Notting Hill Gate and Around

Most visitors pile out of Notting Hill Gate station and head straight for Portobello Market. It's worth dallying for a while, though, to look at the pretty mews-style houses on **Uxbridge Street** and **Hillgate Street** behind the Gate cinema, and to head up **Campden Hill Road** to peek through the box hedges at the grandiose properties overlooking Holland Park. This is one of the most attractive residential areas in London. It is also dotted with good restaurants and pubs like the Uxbridge Arms and Malabar on Uxbridge Street, and the Windsor Castle pub on Campden Hill Road.

Notting Hill Gate and **Pembridge Road** have a mixture of excellent second-hand record and book stores, cheap chain restaurants and, towards Holland Park, sofabed stores and beauty salons. Look out for Mimi Fifi (27 Pembridge Rd) for quirky '50s toys and paraphernalia, and Frontiers (37 Pembridge Rd) for ethnic jewellery.

Portobello Road

Antiques market Sat (7am–5.30pm); fruit and vegetable market Mon–Sat till 5pm with early closing at 1pm on Thurs.

The antiques stalls start at the southern end of Portobello Road towards Notting Hill, and the rather shabbier furniture, food, jewellery, cheap records, books, postcards and funky bric-a-brac are at the north end, towards the A40 flyover. In between is a stretch of fruit and vegetable market popular with the whole community. The street is also lined with quirky, individual shops, some cheap, some expensive, such as Justin Kara (No.253) for trendy fashion, or The Cloth Shop (No.290) for expensive old linen sheets from France. Mingling among these counter-culture vultures are smarter, more self-conscious types on their way to the Travel Bookshop, Books for Cooks, Graham and Green, Ceramica Blue, Neal's Yard Apothecary, the Spice Shop, the delis Mr Christian and Felicitous or restaurants like Osteria Basilico, Mediterraneo and Essenza on **Blenheim Crescent**, **Elgin Crescent** and **Kensington Park Road**. At this level too is the restored Electric Cinema, showing arthouse films, with a café next door.

Broadly speaking, the crowd gets more unorthodox and eclectic the further north you go. Under the flyover is a bric-a-brac and cheap clothes market, as well as vegetarian cafés and an indoor arcade called Portobello Green packed with young designers (grab a falafel from Pitta the Great opposite the entrance). Further north still, among the ugly modern brick housing estates, you stumble across small art dealers, the excellent jazz shop Honest Jon's, and Spanish restaurant Galicia, good for cakes and coffee. Finally, off to the right is **Golborne Road**, a bustling short street divided between Portuguese and Moroccan communities, and the restaurant Lisboa.

Westbourne Grove and Ledbury Road

The Portobello Road end of **Westbourne Grove** is home to Agnès B, Whistles, Joseph, Tom's deli'café, jewellery designer Dinny Hall, L.K. Bennet, Diptyque, and scores of antiques shops; in a traffic island you can't miss the award-winning eau-de-Nil public toilet designed by Piers Gough, with one of London's best flower stalls attached. The Oxfam shop is one of London's best, with designer cast-offs. Further east towards Queensway are swanky shops like Space NK Apothecary (No.131), and Planet Organic, a wholefood emporium serving juices by the glass. Also, in Needham Road, make a detour for Miller Harris perfumes. **Ledbury Road** is also packed with fashion and accessory designers, including Ghost (No.36), Emma Hope (61a), Diane von Furstenberg (83), Brora for cashmere, and Anya Hindmarch (63a).

Kensal Green Cemetery

Walk right up Ladbroke Grove and turn left after the canal into Harrow Rd. The cemetery entrance, an imposing Doric arch, is opposite the William IV pub. Open April–Sept 8–6, Oct–Mar 9–5; guided tours Sun 2pm (£5), plus visit to catacombs (bring a torch) on Sundays.

The large entrance arch frames an avenue leading to the Anglican Chapel, itself adorned with Doric pillars and colonnades. The chapel stands atop a layered cake of underground burial chambers, some of which used to be served by a hydraulic lift. Around the rest of the cemetery are extraordinary testimonies to 19th-century delusions of grandeur: vast ornate tombs worthy of the Pharaohs, decorated with statues, incidental pillars and arches. What made Kensal Green such a hit was a decision by the Duke of Sussex, youngest brother of George IV, to eschew royal protocol and have himself buried among the people, so to speak. Eminent occupants include Thackeray, Trollope, Wilkie Collins, Leigh Hunt and Marc and Isambard Kingdom Brunel.

***Onwards to*: Kensington Gardens, p.124; High Street Kensington shopping, p.134; Holland Park, p.122.**

Chelsea and the King's Road

⊖ Sloane Square, South Kensington; bus 11, 19, 22, 211, 319.

Chelsea was an attractive riverside community long before it was ever integrated into greater London. The humanist and martyr Thomas More made the district fashionable by moving here in the 1520s, and soon every courtier worth his salt, even Henry VIII himself, was building a house near his. By the mid-19th century, Chelsea had turned into a bustling little village of intellectuals, artists, aesthetes and writers as well as war veterans – the so-called Chelsea pensioners who lived in the Royal Hospital built by Christopher Wren for Charles II.

Chelsea in the first half of the 20th century turned into little more than an annexe of South Kensington – a little more classy perhaps, a little more established, but just as snobbish and sterile. In the 1950s and 1960s, it became the refuge of the dying aristocracy. In the 1980s, the sons and daughters of these last-ditch aristos mutated into a particularly underwhelming social animal known as the Sloane Ranger – a special kind of upper-class twit with deeply misguided delusions about being trendy.

Chelsea's artistic streak never entirely disappeared, however, and in the 1960s and early 1970s it flourished with a vengeance along the King's Road. Like Carnaby Street in Soho, the King's Road let its hair down and filled with cafés and fashion shops selling mini-skirts and cheap jewellery. The Royal Court Theatre, in Sloane Square, came into its own as a venue for avant-garde writers such as John Osborne (the original Angry Young Man), Edward Bond and Arnold Wesker. Mods, later replaced by punks, set the fashion tone for whole generations of young people.

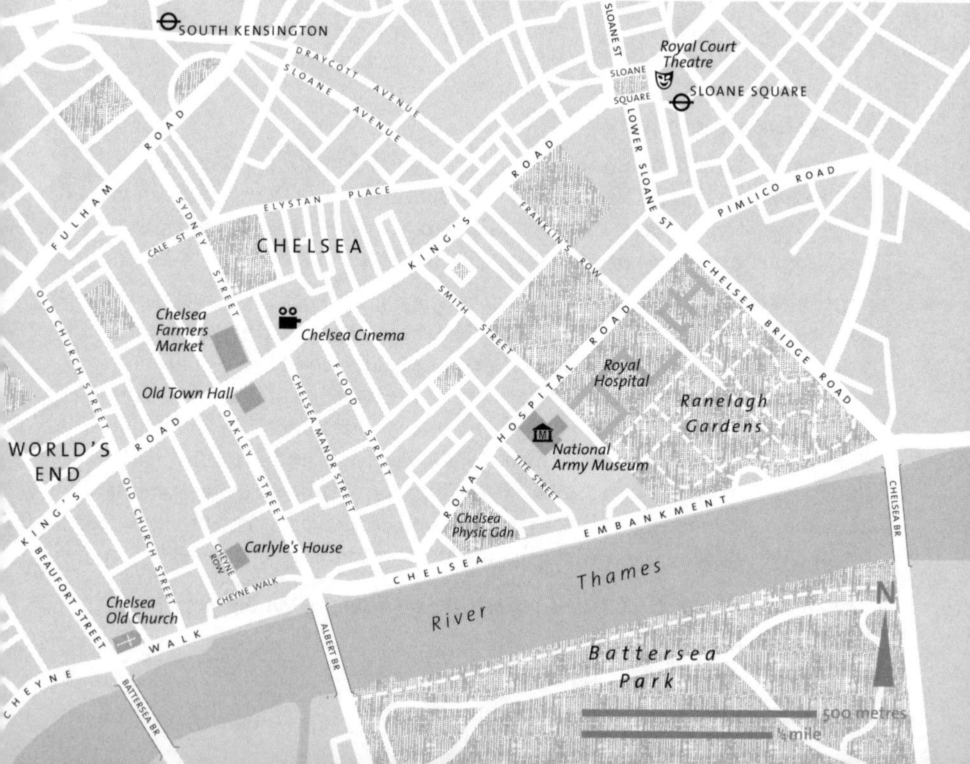

Cafés and Pubs

Habitat Café, King's Road. Airy, colourful room on the top floor of the shop with scrubbed wooden tables and an authentically Italian menu of pasta and risotto. Good cakes too.

Gordon Ramsay, 68–9 Royal Hospital Rd, **t** (020) 7352 4441. Former football player Gordon Ramsay is one of the best chefs in London. A truly memorable gastronomic experience (book ahead).

Phene Arms, 9 Phene St, off Oakley St. Small, resolutely authentic Chelsea pub with a courtyard garden in a quiet residential street; creative pub food.

Chelsea Kitchen, 98 King's Rd/**Stockpot**, 273 King's Rd. Food and wine for less than £10.

Bluebird, 350 King's Rd. Converted 1930s garage: food, flowers and Conran restaurant.

Ed's Easy Diner, 362 King's Road. American diner – burgers and enormous malt shakes.

The King's Road

During the 1960s, old-fashioned shops were superseded by the likes of Terence Conran, who opened his first household store **Habitat** on the King's Road as a direct challenge to the fusty, old-fashioned goods then on sale at **Peter Jones** department store by Sloane Square. Meanwhile most of the boutiques have either gone upmarket or been replaced by generic highstreet chainstores. Some of the 1960s spirit lives on, however, in the delightfully sprawling **antiques markets** on the south side of the road. You might also want to take a look at the **Chelsea Farmer's Market**, on Sydney Street.

Chelsea Riverside

The heart of old Chelsea is down by the river. Either take the bus to Battersea Bridge, or walk down Old Church Street until you reach the water. Just to the left of the bridge is **Chelsea Old Church**, which preserves the memory of Sir Thomas More, author of the humanist tract *Utopia*. The church's history goes back to Norman times, but most of it was rebuilt in classical style in the 17th century. The churchyard has been converted into a small park.

Stretching to the east, just behind the Chelsea Embankment, are the delightful 18th-century brick houses of **Cheyne Walk**, one of London's most fashionable addresses for the past 200 years. Amongst the famous residents have been George Eliot, who died at No.4; Henry James, who spent the latter years of his life in Carlyle Mansions, a Victorian house standing just beyond the King's Head and Eight Bells pub; Whistler, who was living at No.101 when he produced some of his most extraordinary paintings of the Thames; and Turner, himself no mean painter of the Thames, who used No.119 as a retreat. The Queen's House at No.16 was shared during the 1860s by a trio of poets, Dante Gabriel Rossetti, Algernon Swinburne and George Meredith, who kept a whole bestiary of animals including some noisy peacocks.

The most interesting address, however, is 24 Cheyne Row, just around the corner: **Carlyle's House** (*open April–Oct Wed, Thurs, Fri 2–5, Sat, Sun 11–5, last adm 4.30; adm*). Few houses in London evoke such a strong sense of period or personality as this redbrick Queen Anne building, where the historian Thomas Carlyle, author of *The French Revolution* and *Frederick the Great*, lived with his wife from 1834 until his death in 1881. It has been kept almost exactly as the Carlyles left it.

***Also see*: Chelsea Physic Garden, p.120; King's Road shopping, p.135.**

***Onwards to*: Knightsbridge shopping, p.135; Battersea Park, p.120.**

Docklands

⊖ Tower Hill, Wapping, Rotherhithe, Canary Wharf; ***DLR*** *Tower Gateway, Shadwell, Canary Wharf, Mudchute, Island Gardens;* ***t*** *(020) 7363 9700 (office hours),* ***t*** *(020) 7918 4000 (out of hours), www.dlr.co.uk;* ***buses****: 100 from Liverpool Street for Wapping and Shadwell, D3 from Shadwell for the Isle of Dogs.*

Boats *from Charing Cross or Westminster Pier every half-hour (less often in winter) 11am–5pm, stopping at London Bridge, St Katharine's Dock, Canary Wharf, Greenland Dock (Surrey Quays), Greenwich and the Thames Barrier. Westminster Passenger Services:* ***t*** *(020) 7930 2062, www.wpsa.co.uk; Thames Cruises:* ***t*** *(020) 7930 3373, www.thamescruises.com.*

Travelcards are valid on the DLR. A ***Sail and Rail*** *Ticket entitles you to a day's unlimited travel on the DLR plus a riverboat trip from Westminster or Greenwich Piers, and discounted entry to the London Aquarium at Westminster, the National Maritime Museum at Greenwich, the Royal Observatory and the Queen's House* *(see Greenwich, p.115)**.*

Free ***street map*** *of the area and other tourist information from the Tourist Board Centre at DLR Canary Wharf, or the potentially helpful roving Tourist Assistants employed by DLR.*

To head downriver from the Tower is to enter a different world – more in tune with the Emerald City in *The Wizard of Oz*. The converted Docklands show the face of a city of the future: a vision of shimmering high-rise glass and steel reflected in the lapping tides of the River Thames, a Phoenix risen from the ashes of the derelict wharves and warehouses of a bygone age. It's disorientating, endlessly surprising, pock-marked by building sites and cranes, and – in terms of sheer visual impact – extraordinarily impressive.

The Docklands were built in the 1980s without a shred of planning or civic sense, resulting in what was, at the time, a spectacular financial flop. The development

Cafés and Pubs

Dickens Inn, St Katharine's Way. In an 18th-century spice warehouse. The pub food in the restaurant is good, if a little expensive.

The Prospect of Whitby, 57 Wapping Wall. Charming historical pub dating from 1543, with a hangman's noose to remind you of the executions once held nearby. Marvellous bar food (fish and chips, steak, etc.).

The Grapes, 76 Narrow Street. Immortalized by Dickens in *Our Mutual Friend* and renowned for its high quality fresh fish dishes.

Canary Wharf restaurants and takeaways, within the complex, include **Pizza Express** and **Itsu** (conveyor belt 'Euro-sushi').

Moshi Moshi Sushi, 2nd floor, Canada Place. Tasty Japanese sushi and other specialities ride a snaking conveyorbelt as speedily and cheaply as you wish.

Royal China, 30 Westferry Circus. One of the best Chinese restaurants in London, overlooking the Thames. £25.

Plateau, Canada Place, Canada Square. Terence Conran's latest bar and grill – 'design' interior and modern European food. For a treat.

Carluccio's Caffè, 2 Nash Court, Canary Wharf. A small Italian-run chain with excellent coffee and well-priced Italian food. Breakfast is a good time to come, as well, with baskets of different breads on offer.

The Docklands Light Railway

You can see a great deal of the Docklands by taking the overland Docklands Light Railway (DLR) from Bank or Tower Gateway to Island Gardens on the Isle of Dogs or Beckton. This elevated railway is like the futuristic monorail in Truffaut's *Fahrenheit 451*: the trains are computerized and sometimes quite eerily driverless. A ride on it – sitting at the front where you get panoramic views as you go, and getting on and off to explore – makes for an entertaining day out in itself. If you board at Tower Gateway on the hour between 10am and 4pm you are treated to a commentary on your trip all the way to Crossharbour.

failed to respect its environment and the wishes of local people, many of whom were pushed out of their modest homes to make way for a higher-class breed of resident. Furthermore, nobody thought to provide proper services or adequate transport links, so the gleaming palaces were almost impossible to get to or live in. When recession struck at the end of the 1980s, hundreds of speculators went bust because they simply could not attract tenants. The place became a ghost town. However, with the opening of the Jubilee Line extension in 2000, which connected the Canary Wharf complex with Waterloo and London Bridge stations, City businesses have slowly begun to move in. If London is successful in its bid to host the 2012 Olympics, this area will receive further redevelopment.

Ultimately, for the visitor the area consists mainly of office blocks with bland reflective façades, the impersonal shopping centres you will find in any New Town suburbia, and luxury housing estates where the main luxury is a near-total absence of an identity. It's a sad irony, too, that even today, amongst the shiny skyscrapers and flashy apartment pads, there still exists one of the poorest and most socially deprived areas in the country.

Wapping

Until the 16th century, when the land around it was drained, Wapping was little more than a sliver of land hemmed in by swamps to the north and the river on the south. It has almost always been poor: John Stow described Wapping High Street in his *Survey of London* (1598) as 'a filthy strait passage, with alleys of small tenements or cottages'. Sailors made up the bulk of its modest population, later replaced by dockers. Nowadays it's rather more appealing, a quiet, leafy and residential area, with a sprinkling of traditional pubs and smart restaurants. It was where some of the first failed luxury flats of the 1980s were built. Some of the newer architecture is rather soulless, but among the developments original features from Wapping's past still stand, such as the old Customs House on the High Street and the more successful warehouse conversions. The waterfront near **Wapping Wall**, known as **Execution Dock**, earned its name because pirates and smugglers were hanged there and displayed in chains for as long as it took for three tides to wash over them, by which time the bodies had swelled to a 'whopping' size. The dock is now marked with a large 'E' on the building at Swan Wharf, opposite Brewhouse Lane. It's a few minutes' walk from the **Prospect of Whitby** pub, once named 'The Devil's Tavern' and a haunt of the bloodthirsty Judge Jeffries, who would watch the hanging of felons over a meal.

St Katharine's Dock, over near the Tower of London, looks benign enough now with its yachts, trees and cafés, but it was once one of the most callous of riverside developments. To build the docks and commodity warehouses here in the 1820s, the authorities knocked down 1,250 houses and made more than 11,000 people homeless. For all that, the dock was not a great financial success and lost money until its closure in 1968. Now prettified with boats and bright paint, its walkways are linked with a series of attractive iron bridges. It is an obvious lunch spot, along a signposted walkway, after a hard morning's sightseeing at the Tower of London. At the Dickens

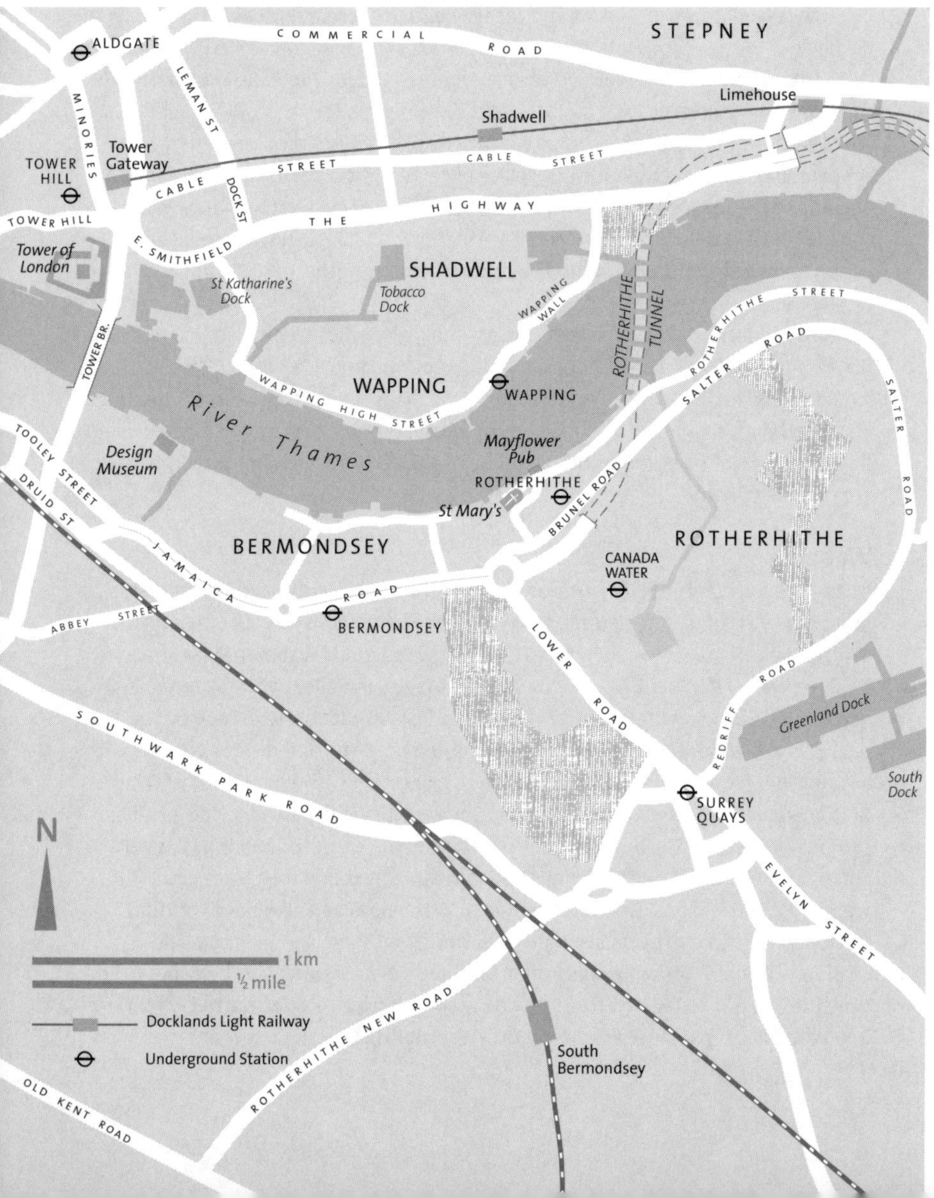

Inn and other local watering holes, sightseers make stange drinking companions for the brokers who work in Commodity Quay.

Opposite the Murdoch empire is Nicholas Hawksmoor's church **St George in the East** (1714–29), with its broad, tall tower with pepperpot turrets. The church was the site of an unholy row in the 19th century between a High Church rector and the Low Church Bishop of London, who disagreed about the liturgy. The congregation joined in the mayhem by blowing horns, whistling and bringing dogs into the Sunday service, forcing the rector to resign. The docks were heavily bombed during the Blitz, when the interior of St George was destroyed. It has now been redesigned as an intriguing hybrid – part church, part block of flats, part courtyard.

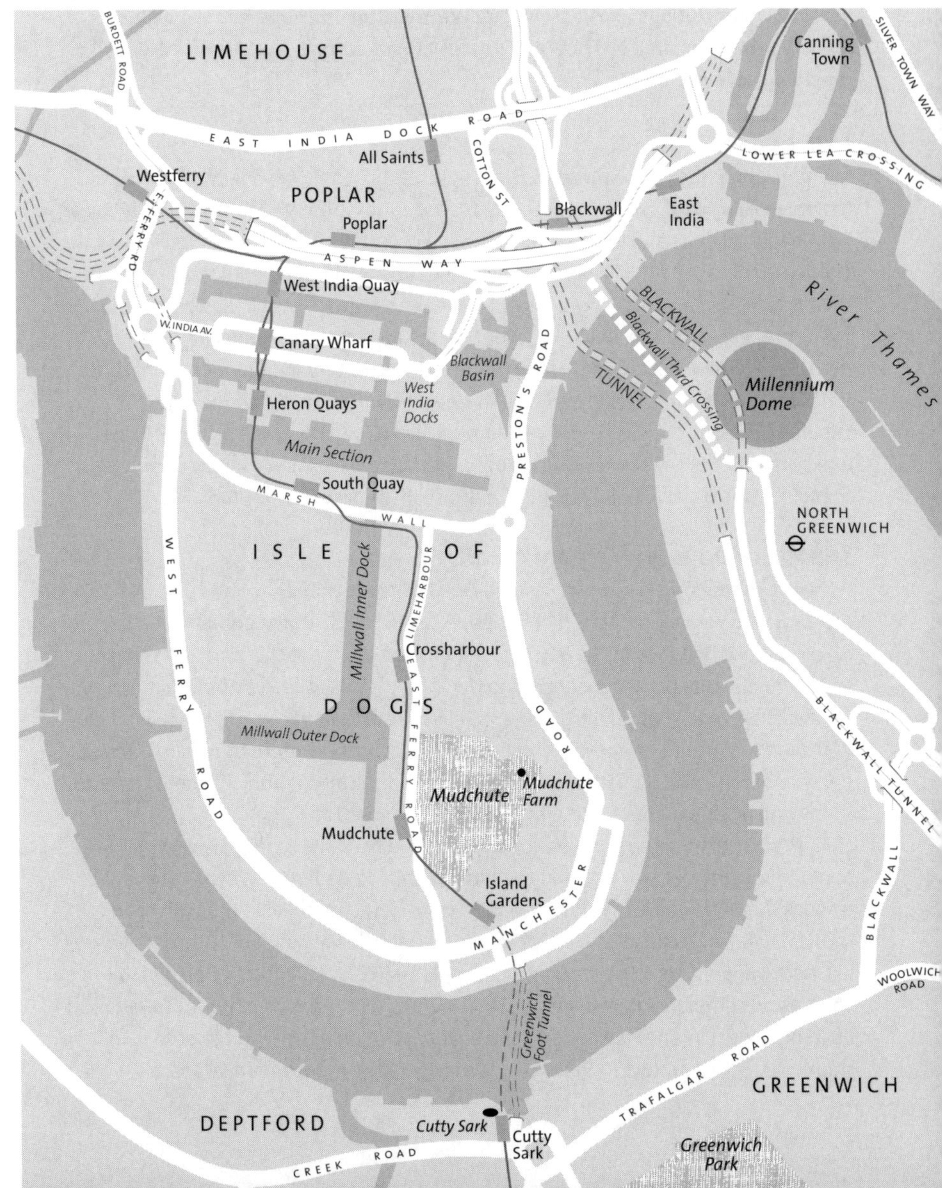

The Jubilee Line

The extension to the Jubilee Line, running from Bond Street in central London to Stratford in the east, is truly a millennium showpiece for London. Eminent architects and designers such as Richard Rogers, Norman Foster and Will Alsop have put a 21st-century twist on the Tube with station buildings that come straight from the cutting edge of architectural design. In each station the importance placed by individual architects on space, natural light and surface texture can be seen. At Southwark, for example, you emerge from the escalator to a breathtaking curved wall of triangular panels. North Greenwich station, with its beautiful blue tiles and glass wall, is large enough to hold 3,000 double-decker buses, or even the Canary Wharf tower laid on its side. Other stations worth seeing are Westminster, the huge hooded halls of Canary Wharf, inspired by Fritz Lang's 1920s film *Metropolis*, and Stratford, with its rippling, wave-like profile.

Limehouse

A more complete Hawksmoor church can be found a mile or so to the east, past Limehouse Basin off the Commercial Road. The chunky tower of **St Anne's Limehouse** has been a guide to ships coming into London ever since it was completed in 1724. Named after the lime kilns which used to operate here in the manufacture of quick-lime, Limehouse bears few vestiges of the mini-Chinatown that it was before the 1980s property bonanza. In the 19th century the area was considered an iniquitous den of vice, where people came to watch as well as partake in opium-smoking. Oscar Wilde set the opium-smoking scene in his novel *The Picture of Dorian Gray* in Limehouse. Along Narrow Street you'll find a terrace of early Georgian houses, among which stands **The Grapes**, a 16th-century pub said to have been used by Dickens as a model for the 'Six Jolly Fellowship-Porters' pub in his novel *Our Mutual Friend*.

The Isle of Dogs and Canary Wharf

The **Isle of Dogs** is a peninsula defined by a tight loop in the river and crisscrossed by artificial waterways. There are many theories as to how the area got its name – there is no evidence that it ever had any association with dogs, but there are tales that the royal kennels were once sited here. One theory is that 'dogs' is a corruption of 'docks'; after all, that was what provided the area's livelihood from 1802 until the second half of the 20th century. But another suggestion is that, since cargoes of bananas and tomatoes were once unloaded on to the wharfs from the Canaries, it comes from the islands' Spanish name, *Las Islas Canarias* – The Islands of the Dogs.

There's no mistaking the main attraction around here: the 812ft glass and steel tower block at the centre of **Canary Wharf**. Along with its two new sister towers at 8 and 15 Canada Square (689ft and 653ft respectively), Cesar Pelli's monster tower (*closed to visitors*) soars over the Docklands skyline, the flashing light atop its pyramidal apex winking 40 times a minute. Officially known by its address One Canada Square and completed in 1991 after just 18 months under construction, it is the tallest building in Britain. The Pelli tower is the first skyscraper in the world to be clad in stainless steel, 50 storeys high, with 32 passenger lifts, 3,960 windows and 4,388 steps in its four fire stairways. Building materials included 27,500 tonnes of steel, 500,000 bolts and a staggering 90,000 sq ft of marble in the lobby alone. Every feature is state-of-the-art. There are so many faxes and photocopiers in the building that heating is quite unnecessary, even in the dead of winter. Canary Wharf is Europe's largest single property development and clustered around the towers are a series of lower-lying buildings (mostly hi-tech reworkings by American architects of Edwardian styles), courtyards, shopping plazas, waterside footpaths, a car park, a fountain, incidental artworks and sculpted metal railings. Continuity with the past is not its strong point; it bears no resemblance to the Canary Wharf of the 19th century. The fountain in Cabot Square is computer-controlled, adjusting the jet intensity according to wind strength so that passers-by never get splashed.

Hop back on to the DLR to go further south, past the ongoing development, until you reach **Island Gardens** (across the road from the station), a small riverside park with an outstanding view across the river to Greenwich and the Old Royal Naval College (*see* p.116). You can walk over to Greenwich through the **foot tunnel** built in 1902 beneath the river, its two onion-domed brick towers marking the entrances at either end. If you prefer, the DLR continues under the river to Greenwich and beyond.

Rotherhithe

Rotherhithe was where the Pilgrim Fathers set out for America in their ship *The Mayflower* in 1620. You might think hordes of American tourists come to pay homage to their forefathers, but in fact Rotherhithe is a delightfully unspoiled, unknown part of riverside London. The old warehouses have been repaired, but not tarted up, and the streets have been kept narrow. The green in front of St Mary's church lends an air of village-like cosiness, attracting a modest number of artists and artisans.

The departure of the Pilgrim Fathers is commemorated in **The Mayflower** pub, which is partly built out of the broken-up segments of the original ship and has a model of the vessel hanging outside its front door. Because of its tourist clientele, the pub is allowed to sell postage stamps, including American ones. This was probably the tavern where Captain Christopher Jones and his crew spent the night before their departure for the Americas. Within two years, the ship came back from its expedition, and Jones was eventually buried, along with the three co-owners of the *Mayflower*, in the churchyard of **St Mary's** opposite. The church itself, which was attractively rebuilt in the 18th century, contains a plaque to Jones as well as remains of the *Fighting Temeraire*, the battleship whose demise was so poignantly captured by Turner in his famous painting in the National Gallery. Next to the church you'll see **Brunel's Engine House**, built to house the boilers which provided the power to drain the Thames Tunnel. This underwater tunnel, the first in the world, was doggedly built between 1825 and 1843, costing lives as well as money. Today the tunnel is used by London Underground's East London Line, taking trains between Rotherhithe and Wapping.

***Also see*: Tower of London, p.45.**

***Onwards to*: Greenwich, p.115; the South Bank and Southwark, p.85; the City of London, p.57.**

Camden

⊖ Camden Town, Chalk Farm; bus 24, 29, 31, 253.

Visit at the weekend to see the area at its liveliest.

Camden's modern identity as a haven for artists and small shopkeepers was established in the 1970s, when the market started and the old Victorian warehouses were slowly converted into artists' studios, music venues and restaurants. Camden now is above all its buzzing open-air market, or rather series of markets, that have sprung up around the canal and the surrounding streets. There is something for everyone: cheap clothes, pianos, herbal cures, tarot card readings, off-beat bookshops, furniture stores, pubs and lots and lots of restaurants. At the weekends, traffic comes to a standstill. The atmosphere is very relaxed, young but not overly self-conscious. You can easily spend hours sorting through the leather and second-hand records, stopping for a drink or snack from a street stall; later, you can head off for a meal or a spot of dancing; or you can easily escape the crowds by strolling away along Regent's Canal.

Markets and Shops

The nerve centre of the market is at **Camden Lock**, just next to the canal off Chalk Farm Road (the extension of Camden High Street). Some but not all of the stalls and shops stay open all week. In the middle of the market is a covered three-storey building with narrow staircases and passages selling jewellery and crafts; in the immediate vicinity are stalls selling clothes, antiques, books and records. The stalls then continue for about 500 yards up the Chalk Farm Road, in an area known as **The Stables**. **Chalk Farm Road** itself has interiors shops with an ethnic slant. Some of the most interesting shops are on **Camden High Street**, which is really a market unto itself; the Electric Ballroom nightclub doubles on Sundays as a bazaar for cheap designer fashions and jewellery. Finally, there is a fruit and veg market on **Inverness Street**, between the High Street and Gloucester Crescent, which is open Mon–Sat.

Jewish Museum

*129–31 Albert St; **t** (020) 7284 1997, www.jewishmuseum.org.uk.*
Open Mon–Thurs 10–4, Sun 10–5; adm.

This celebration of Jewish life in England from the Middle Ages, formerly in Woburn House on Tavistock Square, is notable mostly for its collection of old ritual objects from London synagogues. The centrepiece is an elaborately carved 16th-century Venetian Synagogue Ark. There are also illuminated marriage contracts and some Torah bells fashioned by the 18th-century silversmith Abraham Lopes de Oliveira.

Cafés and Pubs

Silks and Spice, 28 Chalk Farm Rd. Hugely popular Thai and Malaysian café-restaurant.

Marine Ices, 8 Haverstock Hill, near ⊖ Chalk Farm. Traditional old-fashioned Italian ice cream parlour, one of the best in London.

Café Delancey, 3 Delancey St. Camden stalwart: tasty and dependable brasserie food.

Mango Rooms, 10 Kentish Town Rd. Sensational Caribbean/West Indian cuisine.

Camden Arms, 1 Randolph St. Fine if quirky gastropub, with game and grilled prawns.

Islington

⊖ Angel, ⊖/⇌ Highbury and Islington; bus 19, 38, 73.

In the 1950s you wouldn't have found much in Islington apart from a clapped-out old music hall, a few eel and pie shops and an extended series of slummy terraced houses. How times have changed. Now it is one of the liveliest and trendiest districts in the capital, a Mecca for liberal-minded arty professionals, particularly writers and broadcasters, who live in attractively refurbished Georgian townhouses and eat out in expensive ethnic restaurants. The place is packed with pubs, cafés, designer bars and shops, and alternative theatres.

During the 1980s Islington was associated with a certain kind of earnest, occasionally radical left-wing politics that jarred completely with the prevailing Thatcherite ideology of free markets and individual responsibility. More recently, Islington has been taken to task in the right-wing press for spawning a more comfortable breed of liberal lefty who likes to discuss the meaning of socialism over a fancy plate of rocket and shaved parmesan. The occasion of this new wave of Islington-bashing has been the rise of Prime Minister Tony Blair, an Islingtonian of long standing.

In fact, the pleasures of Islington have been well known for centuries and were only seriously interrupted by the industrial revolution. In the 16th century it was popular as a royal hunting ground and noted for its pure spring water and good dairy farms. The open fields were dotted with well-appointed mansions, gardens and orchards. Elizabeth I used to meet her favourites here, and people from all walks of life came to enjoy the bowling greens, dance floors and taverns. The extension of Regent's Canal (here called the Grand Union Canal) and the advent of the railways in the 19th century did similar damage in Islington as it had in Camden: the attractive Georgian terraces which had sprung up in the district became dilapidated and dirty, as the local population, mostly made up of labourers, swelled uncontrollably. Soon Islington became a byword for everything that was *un*fashionable in London.

Just 20 years later, though, there was nothing marginal about Islington at all. The Camden Passage antiques market arrived in 1964, and pub theatres led by the King's Head on Upper Street began to flourish soon after. The old Collins Music Hall burned down and was replaced with the Screen on the Green cinema. The area retains a certain self-conscious shabbiness, but that is part of its charm. Islington doesn't have any tourist attractions in the traditional sense of the word, just bags of atmosphere. The best way to visit is to start at the Angel and work your way slowly northwards.

Camden Passage

Best visited Wed 10–2, Sat 10–5 for antiques. Bookstalls Thurs 10–2. Farmers' market on Sun mornings.

This is a cobbled row of elegant antiques shops and stalls, most of which open their doors on Wednesday mornings and Saturdays only. The market is ideal for browsing, since everything looks perfect and the prices of the furniture, prints, silverware and jewellery are probably too high to consider seriously for purchase.

Cafés and Pubs

Santa Fe, 75 Upper St. South American cuisine (pot roast with garlic mash, *quesadillas*, lots of lime and chile, great desserts) in large, bright, trendy bar/restaurant. Lunch £6–12.

King's Head, 115 Upper St. Great theatre pub: plush seats and bags of atmosphere.

Almeida Theatre Café, 7a Almeida St. Soup, baguettes, pastries, pasta, etc.

Strada, 105–6 Upper St. Delicious and authentic wood-oven cooked pizzas.

Pasha, 301 Upper St. Spicy Turkish food, with lots of choice including vegetarian dishes.

Almeida, 30 Almeida St, **t** (020) 7354 4777. This refreshingly unfussy Conran restaurant offers simple French *nouvelle* cooking; good-value set lunch £14.50, otherwise pricey.

Nam Bistro, 326 Upper St. Down to earth but very cheap and tasty Vietnamese-Chinese food: chicken satay, crispy duck, etc.

Angel Mangal, 139 Upper St. Great-value, delicious Turkish set lunch for £5.50.

Upper Street

All the streets around here, from Upper Street across to St Peter's Street and down to City Road, are a delight for strollers – small, relatively traffic-free and packed with elegant houses, cafés and restaurants. The area to the east, along the Grand Union Canal, is particularly charming and dotted with pretty Georgian houses. In the 1950s and 1960s this was the distinctly unfashionable home of the playwright Joe Orton and his lover Kenneth Halliwell. Just to the north, back on Upper Street, is the lumbering hulk of the **Business Design Centre**. This rather clumsy building is a redevelopment of the old Royal Agricultural Hall, a fine Victorian hangar made of iron and glass used for agricultural shows and industrial exhibitions. The Design Centre now hosts conferences, the Islington Art Fair and other odd art shows. On either side of the Design Centre, Upper St is packed with the restaurants and offbeat shops that characterize Islington, including several shops selling a variety of old furniture (try Castle Gibson, No.106a) and others even more miscellaneous, like After Noah (No.121), with its array of old and new lamps, clocks, soaps and old comics. Behind, on Liverpool Road, is **Chapel Market**, a lively fruit, veg and clothes market, open every day but Monday.

Triangular **Islington Green**, where Upper Street meets Essex Road, is more of a meeting place than a spot of any great beauty. Heading north on Upper St, you come to the **King's Head** theatre pub, which as a gimmick still counts money in the predecimal currency of pounds, shillings and pence (12 pence to a shilling, 20 shillings to a pound). The streets to the left of here, forming the beginning of the area known as Barnsbury, contain some fine Georgian townhouses. Theberton Street, not far from the pub, leads to the pale brick splendour of Gibson Square. One block further up is Almeida Street, home to the highly successful fringe theatre of the same name. The crowds and the trendiness factor gradually ebb away the further north you walk up Upper St. It is worth continuing for five minutes – past the town hall and right on to Canonbury Lane – to explore one of the most unspoiled areas of Georgian housing in north London. The most imposing building in the neighbourhood is **Canonbury Tower** on Canonbury Place, a building of mythical reputation whose history goes back to pre-Roman times; no fewer than 24 ley lines meet at the point where the central pillar of its main staircase stands.

***Onwards to*: Camden, p.108; the City of London, p.57.**

Hampstead

⊖ Hampstead, Belsize Park, ⇌ Hampstead Heath (Silverlink); bus 24, 46, 210, C11, C12.

Hampstead is a pretty hilltop village of Georgian rows and Victorian mansions, surrounded by the vast expanse of the Heath. Throughout its history, it has provided a refuge when life in the city has become too much. John Constable came here and painted some distant cityscapes that were barely distinguishable in tone from his great rural idylls. No wonder: the air is so pure and the Heath so big and wild that you can feel you are lost in the heart of the English countryside. Nowadays Hampstead has an unmistakable air of *established* comfort. More cosmopolitan than Camden and Islington, it is full of lively restaurants, bars and theatres frequented by its well-off, generally New Labour residents. But in contrast to its north London neighbours, Hampstead, for all its liberal credentials, is a staid and remarkably conservative place.

Hampstead Village

The real pleasure of Hampstead village is in getting lost in the winding back streets. Up near Whitestone Pond, Lower Terrace takes you past the entrance to **Judges Walk**, the legendary 'substitute' law court of the Great Plague which is now just a driveway to a couple of tumbledown houses. A little further down to the left is **Admiral's Walk**, which contains a splendid Georgian house with multilevelled rooms and balconies. At the other end of Admiral's Walk, Hampstead Grove takes you down to **Fenton House**, a splendid brick mansion dating from 1693 (***t** (020) 7435 3471; open April–Oct Wed–Fri 2–5, Sat and Sun 11–5; adm*). Aside from the elegant rooms and fine garden, the house has early keyboard instruments and porcelain. At the bottom of Hampstead Grove, the narrow road up to the left is **Hollybush Hill**, a cul-de-sac lined with beautiful small houses including the 17th-century Hollybush pub. Just after the pub is a steep staircase plunging down towards Heath Street. Better, however, to retrace your steps and head down **Holly Walk**, a cobbled path flanked by fine houses and a small flower-filled cemetery. At the bottom of the hill is **St John's**, an attractive 18th-century church with a tall tower and, inside, a gallery and a bust of Keats. Constable is buried in the churchyard. **Church Row**, from the church back to Heath Street, has some of the most elegant Georgian housing in London.

Heath Street is one of two Hampstead thoroughfares lined with fine shops, delicatessens, cafés and restaurants. The other, the **High Street**, can be reached through

Cafés and Pubs

Simply Scrumptious, 9 Flask Walk. Bright and friendly café with seats outside; British and European snacks.

The Flask, 14 Flask Walk. Rambling traditional pub behind flower-bedecked façade: fish and chips, steak and kidney pies, curries.

Maison Blanc, 62 Hampstead High St. Chic pâtisserie; beautiful cakes, imaginative sandwiches and tarts.

Base, 71 Hampstead High St. Mediterranean bistro: breakfast/brunch, sandwiches and light meals; £5–15.

Giraffe, 46 Rosslyn Hill. Funky restaurant and café: food and music from around the world. Main courses £8–11.

Jin Kichi, 73 Heath St, **t** (020) 7794 6158. Superb *robatayaki* cooking: meat and vegetables grilled in front of you on skewers; book ahead for evenings.

Oriel Place, which has an old plane tree growing in a minuscule patch of ground halfway along. Cross the High Street and you come into **Flask Walk** with its second-hand bookshops, galleries, children's boutiques, and a posh tea and coffee merchant. Along with its continuation **Well Walk**, this is where fashionable folk came to take the Hampstead spa waters in the 18th century.

The Spaniards Inn

The 16th-century **Spaniards Inn** at the junction of Hampstead Lane and Spaniards Road, named after two Spanish proprietors who killed each other in a duel, owes its fame to the 18th-century highwayman Dick Turpin who used to stop for drinks here in between coach hold-ups. During the Gordon Riots of 1780, a group of mobsters dropped by on their way to Kenwood House, which they intended to destroy. The publican offered the rioters pint after pint of free beer and soon the men weren't in a fit state to walk to Kenwood, let alone burn it down.

Keats' House

Wentworth Place, Keats Grove (walk down Hampstead High St and its continuation Rosslyn Hill, then turn left on to Downshire Hill and take the first right); **t** *(020) 7435 2062. Closed for renovation in 2005/6; call for details; usually open Mar–Oct Tues–Sun 12–5; adm, free for children.*

The main attraction is the plum tree in the garden, under which Keats wrote *Ode to a Nightingale* in 1819 (if you think the tree looks a bit young, you're right; it is a replacement). In all, Keats spent only two years here as a lodger of Charles Armitage Brown, a literary critic specializing in Shakespeare's sonnets. It was nevertheless an eventful time. He produced some of his best and most famous work, fell in love with Fanny Brawne who lived in the other half of the house, and contracted the consumption that was to kill him two years later at the age of 25.

Kenwood House

Hampstead Lane; entrance opposite Bishops Avenue; **t** *(020) 8348 1286. Open April–Sept daily 10–5, Oct–Mar 10–4; free. For Hampstead Heath, see p.121.*

The unpretentious atmosphere at Kenwood is a breath of fresh air. The expanse of the Heath rolls away to the south with breathtaking views over Highgate and central London. Kenwood is famous for its summer concerts held by the lake at the bottom of the garden; the orchestra sits under a white awning and the audience watches from across the water. The house itself dates back to 1616, but was given a facelift by Robert Adam in the 1760s. He stuck on the white neoclassical façade, and reworked most of the interiors. The pictures, bequeathed by Lord Iveagh, include works by Rembrandt (a remarkable self-portrait), Vermeer (*The Guitar Player*), Van Dyck, Gainsborough, Guardi, Reynolds, Landseer and Turner.

Also see: **Hampstead Heath, p.121; the Freud Museum, p.146.**

Onwards to: **Highgate Cemetery, p.122.**

Richmond

⊖/⇌ Richmond; bus 65, 391.

Richmond is a tranquil, affluent riverside community of attractive Georgian and neo-Georgian houses, flanked on all sides by wide expanses of greenery. On a sunny day it is an ideal place to walk along the river; the compact town centre beside Richmond Green has a pleasant villagey feel and there are plenty of cafés and riverside pubs. Richmond's sense of community is such that it boasts not one but two theatres: the Richmond Theatre on the Green, and the Orange Tree near the station.

Richmond Palace and the Green

In medieval times, the focal point of the district was Shene Palace, a relatively modest manor house used as a lodge for the excellent hunting in the surrounding hills. The village green (today's **Richmond Green**) became a popular venue for pageants and jousting tournaments. Henry VII was so attached to the place that he changed its name from Shene to Richmond, after his earldom in Yorkshire, and entirely rebuilt the palace after a fire in 1497. The new Richmond Palace must have been quite something, a riot of spires and turrets which you can see reconstructed as a model in the Richmond Town Hall's small **museum** (*entrance on Red Lion Street,* ***t*** *(020) 8332 1141; open Tues–Sat 11–5; free*). Sadly, almost nothing survives of medieval Richmond in real life. All that remains is a stone **gateway** off Richmond Green, bearing Henry VII's coat of arms, and the **palace wardrobe**, or household office, to the left just inside Old Palace Yard.

In Old Palace Yard is **Trumpeters' House**, an elegant mansion built by a pupil of Christopher Wren and subsequently used as a refuge for Prince Metternich after the upheavals in Vienna of 1848. Further fine Georgian houses are to be found in neighbouring streets, such as Old Palace Terrace and Maids of Honour Row.

The Riverside

Today, as ever, the biggest attraction of Richmond is the riverside, which boasts, among other things, the elegant five-arched **Richmond Bridge** dating from the 1770s. The houses on the north side have been extensively redeveloped as a neo-Georgian terrace of shops, restaurants and offices called **The Riverside**, opened in 1988. The architect responsible was Quinlan Terry, a chum of Prince Charles much in sympathy with the Prince's traditionalist leanings. On summer days its layered terraces descending towards the water are crowded with strollers and sunbathers. At the top of the bridge, Richmond Hill leads to wild **Richmond Park**, famous for its deer.

Ham House

Ham St, off Sandy Lane and Petersham Rd; ***t*** *(020) 8940 1950; bus 65, 371 from Richmond. Grounds open Sat–Wed 11–6; house open April–Oct Sat–Wed 1–5; adm.*

Ham House is one of the grandest surviving Jacobean mansions in London, a magnificent three-storey redbrick house that has been restored to something

Cafés and Pubs

White Swan, 26 Old Palace Lane. Unassuming upmarket pub in a lane running between the riverside and the Green. Gastro-style food, up to £30 per head.

Chez Lindsey, 11 Hill Rise, **t** (020) 8948 7473. Relaxed Breton restaurant serving high quality fish and traditional crêpes.

Terracotta, 9 Paved Court. This cosy, intimate little restaurant serves a great selection of pasta and traditional Italian dishes.

The Prince's Head, 28 The Green. Overlooks Richmond's picture-postcard green. Good pub grub and more interesting options.

Don Fernandos, 27F The Quadrant. Lively family-run *tapas* restaurant just near the station. Around £5.

White Cross Hotel, Water Lane, Riverside. Crowded in summer, but a delightful spot.

Tide Tables Café, under one of the arches beneath Richmond Bridge. Outdoor seating by the river, under shady trees.

approaching its original splendour. Built in 1610 and nicknamed the 'sleeping beauty' for its tranquil position, it became the home of William Murray, a friend of Charles I, who as a child had acted as the future king's whipping boy. In gratitude, Charles offered the adult Murray a peerage (he became the Earl of Dysart) and all the property around Ham and Petersham including this house.

The highlight is the **Great Hall**, a wonderfully airy room decorated in blue, with a gallery overlooking the black and white checked floor. The rest of the house, some of which is still under reconstruction, boasts a profusion of tapestries, velvet drapes and plaster ornamentation on the staircases and ceilings. The gardens have retained their original 17th-century formal layout; the hedges and rows of trees intriguingly conceal the house from the river, lending an air of mystery and anticipated pleasure as you approach from the ferry stop.

Marble Hill House

Richmond Road, Twickenham; **t** *(020) 8892 5115; ⇌ St Margaret's; bus 33, 90, 290, R68 from Richmond. Open April–Oct daily 10–2; Nov–Mar pre-booked guided tours only; adm.*

From the Twickenham side of Richmond Bridge you can enjoy a delightful mile-long walk along a stretch of the Thames that seems almost entirely rural. Marble Hill House is a simple white Palladian villa built in 1729 for Henrietta Howard, the 'exceedingly respectable and respected' mistress of George II. Henrietta could not stand the pressure of life at court, where she had to negotiate a tricky path between her lover and her influential husband, and so with a little help from the royal purse she set up home here, some 10 miles out of central London.

The house is rather empty, having been neglected for 200 years and depleted of most of its furniture. But the park is open and very green, affording the broadest possible view of the river. A series of annual open-air concerts is staged here every summer; it is a delightful venue when the weather holds.

Also see: **Richmond Park, p.127.**

Onwards to: **Hampton Court, p.33; Kew Gardens, p.124; Syon Park, p.128.**

Greenwich

DLR to Cutty Sark for Maritime Greenwich.

⇌ Greenwich (a bit off to the west) or Maze Hill (a bit off to the east) from Charing Cross, Cannon St and London Bridge.

***Bus** 188 from Waterloo and Bermondsey.*

*By **boat** from Charing Cross (Embankment), Tower and Westminster Piers daily.*

Greenwich has been a place of pleasure since the 15th century, when Henry V's brother, Duke Humphrey of Gloucester, built the first royal palace. While neighbouring districts such as Deptford and Woolwich have always had to live by their wits and the hard graft of building and unloading ships, Greenwich has concentrated on idle pleasures such as hunting and jousting, or rarefied pursuits like astronomy. Thanks to the contributions of Jones, Wren, Hawksmoor and Vanbrugh, it also boasts a remarkable architectural heritage, evident from the moment you look up from the ferry pier. It is an ensemble of great grace and proportion, which in recent years has spawned an affluent community of middle-class Londoners in fine Georgian houses up Crooms Hill or on the grassy verges of Greenwich Park and Blackheath.

Duke Humphrey's palace was replaced by a fine red-brick construction named Placentia in 1427, still popular with the royal family. Henry VIII was born at Greenwich and, after a boyhood spent jousting, hunting and attending balls, never lost affection for the place. Henry married his first wife, Catherine of Aragon, in the palace's private chapel and watched in frustration and rage as six of their seven children – four of them the boys he so desired – died here within a few weeks of their birth. The latter half of Henry's reign, when Hampton Court took over as the 'in' palace, saw a decline at Greenwich. Edward VI was sent here to convalesce in 1553. Queen Elizabeth came here occasionally, and it was here that Sir Walter Raleigh magnanimously threw his cloak on a 'plashy place' (i.e. a puddle) so Her Majesty would not get her feet muddy. But it was the Stuarts who breathed new life into Greenwich with the fine buildings we see today. As well as all the historical, riverside and maritime sights, you can also find the world's only Fan Museum, in a delightful Georgian townhouse in one of London's oldest streets.

Cafés and Pubs

Gambardella, 47–8 Vanbrugh Park. 70-year--old typical English fry-up café with Formica-topped tables and solid English comfort food: pie and mash, mugs of tea, apple pie and custard.

Trafalgar Tavern, Park Row. Traditional riverside pub for a warm day, with a dining room.

Goddard's Ye Old Pie House, 45 Greenwich Church St. Local haunt, open daily, 113 years old and serving pie and mash with liquor (a delicious thick green parsley gravy).

Bar du Musée, 17 Nelson Road. Gentleman's club-style brasserie, with comfortable leather seating and a garden for warm days.

High Chapparal, 35 Greenwich Church St. *Fajitas* and fun: noisy but extremely jolly.

Inside, 19 Greenwich South St, **t** (020) 8265 5060. Innovative contemporary cuisine using the freshest ingredients available: with a mouthwatering Sat brunch (11am–2.30pm) and top notch daily set lunch (from £14.95).

The Gipsy Moth, 60 Greenwich Church St. Substantial pub food and garden by the river.

Today, the village is mobbed at weekends by bargain-hunters coming for the markets: crafts in the covered market off Nelson Road, and antiques, bric-a-brac and vintage clothing around Stockwell Street.

The *Cutty Sark* and the *Gipsy Moth IV*

On the quay by the ferry pier; **t** *(020) 8858 3445, www.cuttysark.org.uk. Open daily 10–5; adm. Combined tickets for major attractions available.*

Much is made of the *Cutty Sark* as the last of the great tea clippers that plied the route from England to the Far East. Built in 1869, it was certainly one of the fastest sailboats of its time, winning the annual clippers' race in 1871. Its commercial usefulness was rather limited, however, since steamships soon took over the bulk of maritime trade, and the opening of the Suez Canal took a lot of the time pressure off merchant vessels. The greatest pleasure afforded by the *Cutty Sark* now is its magnificent gilded teak fittings, the rigging on its three masts and its fine collection of figureheads and other maritime memorabilia. The name, by the way, comes from Robert Burns's poem *Tam O'Shanter*, in which a witch called Nellie is described as wearing only a *cutty sark*, a corruption of the French *courte chemise*, or short shirt. You'll notice the female figurehead on the prow is dressed in this manner.

Next to the *Cutty Sark*, the *Gipsy Moth IV* was the ketch in which the British mariner Sir Francis Chichester made his solo round-the-world voyage in 1966–7, completing the trip in nine months and one day.

The Old Royal Naval College

King William Walk, on the site of the old Palace of Placentia; recorded information on **t** *(020) 8269 4747. Open Mon–Sat 10–5, Sun 12.30–5; free.*

The Pepys Building inside the college is home to the Greenwich Visitors' Centre, www.greenwichfoundation.org.uk (open daily 10–5), with all the usual tourist information plus gift shop, wall-sized 3D maps, historical timeline and café.

Charles II's first thought when he restored the monarchy was to rebuild Placentia, but he didn't have the money and gave up soon after the foundation stone was laid. Queen Mary had another idea after she witnessed the terrible wounds inflicted on British sailors at the battle of La Hogue in 1692: she commissioned Christopher Wren to clear the ruins of the old palace and build a naval hospital. Mary and Wren did not enjoy an altogether happy collaboration, since Mary insisted that the Queen's House should be visible from the river (something that was never the case when Placentia was still standing), and that the path of the Deptford to Woolwich road, which at the time ran through the middle of the building site, should be undisturbed. As a result, Wren and his successors, Hawksmoor and Vanbrugh, were obliged rather against their will to come up with a design based on four entirely separate buildings, with its majestic neoclassical façades overlooking the river and pepper-pot towers at the back. The hospital was eventually closed, and the Royal Naval College moved here in 1873, until 1998 when the site was taken over by the Greenwich Foundation, which leased some of the buildings to Greenwich University and some to Trinity College of Music.

Only the Chapel and Painted Hall are open to the public, plus a café with an impressive exhibition of reproductions of Crown Jewels from around the world. The **Chapel** is based on a design by Wren, but was entirely refurbished by James Stuart after a fire in 1789, in full-on Georgian style. It has an intricate, plaster-moulded ceiling, and a fine painting, *St Paul at Melitu*, by Benjamin West, above the altar. The **Painted Hall** is a magnificent ensemble of three rooms painted in opulent style by James Thornhill, the man who also decorated the cupola of St Paul's. Greenwich is the overall theme, whether expressed in allegorical depictions of battleships, or in portraits of the great astronomers.

National Maritime Museum and Queen's House

Romney Road; **t** *(020) 8858 4422, www.nmm.ac.uk. Open winter daily 10–5, summer daily 10–6; free. Combined ticket for attractions available.*

The **National Maritime Museum** reopened in 1999 after a £40 million overhaul and is now one of the most up-to date museums in the UK. A whole floor is devoted to interactive learning, ostensibly for kids, but everyone seems to enjoy shooting water pistols or blowing hair-dryers at model ships. The courtyard has been glassed over to airily accommodate the larger exhibits: an enormous propellor, a container, even a yacht. Historical memorabilia, particularly that of Napoleon's era, still features but the focus has shifted from history to an engagingly energetic portrayal of the high-tech world of modern shipping and cruise liner travel.

The **Queen's House**, now part of the museum, was Inigo Jones's first experiment in Palladian architecture after his return from Italy in 1615. James I's wife Anne of Denmark was the queen in question, who wanted her own private villa as an extension to the Palace of Placentia. For years after Anne's death in 1619 the house languished unfinished, but the project was taken up again by Queen Henrietta Maria in 1629. So happy was she with the final result, completed in 1640, that she nicknamed it her 'house of delights' and returned to live in it as the Queen Mother after the Restoration. The building is a textbook exercise in Palladian classicism – simple and sober on the outside, and full of 'licentious imaginacy', as Jones put it, on the inside. Much of the decay which the Queen's House suffered in the 18th and 19th centuries has been reversed, thanks to a recent restoration bringing the building back to something close to its 1660s state. The centrepiece is the **Great Hall**, a perfect 40ft cube immediately inside the main entrance with an elegant gallery at first floor level. Note the **Tulip Staircase** at the eastern end of the hall, a wrought-iron helix staircase which twists its way up to the Queen's Bedroom. This was the first open-well staircase to be built in England or, as Jones put it, with 'a vacuum in the middle'. The floral decorations on its banister are not tulips at all, but fleurs-de-lys in honour of Henrietta Maria, daughter of King Henry IV of France. The building houses the Maritime Museum's art collection.

Old Royal Observatory

Greenwich Park; recorded information on **t** *(020) 8312 6565, www.rog.nmm.ac.uk. Open daily 10–5; adm. Combined tickets for major attractions available. For the park itself, see p.121.*

Greenwich is, of course, a time as well as a place. Greenwich Mean Time, as measured at this observatory, has synchronized the world's watches and guided the world's ships since 1884. The first two things you see on approaching the museum entrance are the metal plaque marking 0° longitude and, next to it, a large red ball on a stick that lowers every day at 1pm precisely as a symbol of the accuracy and universality of GMT.

Why Greenwich? First, because this was where England's first Astronomer Royal, John Flamsteed, decided to build his home and observatory in 1675. And secondly, because Flamsteed and his successors did more than anyone to solve the oldest navigational problem in the book: how to measure longitude. Measuring latitude was relatively easy, as it could be ascertained from the angle of the Pole Star to the horizon. But longitude was something else. Scientists knew what they needed: a dependable and portable watch or clock with which to work it out. But for anything other than the shortest journeys no such timepiece existed. In 1754, parliament issued a Longitude Act, offering a reward of £20,000 to the person who could crack the problem. The first proposals ranged from the sublime to the ridiculous. It was a Yorkshire clockmaker called John Harrison who eventually broke the impasse. He constructed his first marine clock in 1730 and continued perfecting it all his life; by the time he came up with the prize-winning model in 1772 he was 79 years old. Captain Cook took Harrison's clock to Australia and called it his 'trusty friend'. The museum takes the history of navigation and time up to the present, including the 1884 Washington conference that selected Greenwich as the Prime Meridian, and the invention of atomic clocks based on the nine billion vibrations per second of a caesium atom. The observatory itself is also worthy of note, particularly Flamsteed's original observatory, the **Octagon Room**, designed by Christopher Wren.

Fan Museum

12 Croom's Hill, SE10; **t** *(020) 8305 1441, www.fan-museum.org. Open Tues–Sat 11–5 and Sun 12–5; adm.*

This Georgian house in one of London's oldest streets houses a delightful collection of 2,000 fans from the 17th century to the present.

Blackheath

A pleasant stroll across Greenwich Park is Blackheath village, dominated by the Victorian Gothic spire of All Saints church. Blackheath's high street has a few small local shops and a lot of estate agents, but the heath itself is very attractive.

***Also see*: Greenwich Park, p.121.**

***Onwards to*: Docklands, p.102.**

London: Green Spaces

08

Battersea Park

⇌ Battersea Park (from Victoria), Queenstown Road (from Waterloo); ⊖ Vauxhall and then bus 44, 137 or 344; ⊖ Sloane Square and then bus 19, 49 or 137; bus 137 from Marble Arch or Bond Street.

Right on the river, Battersea Park is an all-action activity centre with a café, children's zoo, tennis courts, a bowling green and a running track. Although opened by Queen Victoria in 1853, the park really came into its own in 1951 when it was one of the centrepieces of the Festival of Britain. Near the boating lake at the southern end is a Henry Moore statue entitled ***Three Standing Figures***. Near the river, about two-thirds of the way towards Albert Bridge, is the **Peace Pagoda**, built by a group of Japanese Buddhist monks in 1985. There's a small zoo, and art exhibitions at the Pump Room.

Chelsea Physic Garden

Swan Walk (off Royal Hospital Rd); ⊖ Sloane Square then a long walk: Lower Sloane St, and left to the end of Royal Hospital Rd, or buses 11, 19, 22, 211, 319 along King's Road, then walk. Alternatively, bus 329 to Royal Hospital Rd from ⊖ Victoria.

***t** (020) 7352 5646, www.chelseaphysicgarden.co.uk. Open April–Oct Wed 12–5 and Sun 2–6; adm.*

This wonderfully unusual garden of rare trees, plants, herbs and seeds has a history stretching back to 1676 when it was founded by the Apothecaries' Company. Some of England's first cedar trees were cultivated here in the 1680s and the hardiest of them lasted until 1903. In the 1730s the Physic Garden sent out the seeds that allowed James Oglethorpe, the colonist of Georgia, to sow the southern United States' first cotton fields. Among the wonders still visible today are the world's first rock garden, built in 1772 with old bits of stone from the Tower of London, a Chinese willow pattern tree, and a 30ft-high olive tree that once produced seven pounds of olives in a season (something of a miracle in rainy old England). The statue in the garden is of Sir Hans Sloane, the physician and philanthropist who saved the gardens from bankruptcy in 1722. Sir Hans owned large tracts of Chelsea (hence the number of streets named after him) and built up a huge collection of art and antiquities that were bequeathed to the nation after his death and provided the foundation of the **British Museum**.

Also *see*: **Chelsea and the King's Road**, p.100; **King's Road shopping**, p.135.

Green Park

⊖ Green Park, Hyde Park Corner; bus 8, 9, 14, 19, 22, 38.

This pleasant expanse, which is green all year round, has much the same history as St James's Park (*see* p.127). It was originally a burial ground for Queen Matilda's lepers (and, in deference to the dead beneath it, has never been planted with flowers). Henry VIII made it a royal park, and Charles II laid out its walkways. Green Park, like its neighbour, was a haunt of trouble-makers and duellists in the 18th century. On one occasion, Count Alfieri returned to the nearby Haymarket Theatre for the last act of a play after sustaining a duelling wound to his arm from Lord Ligonier, his mistress's husband. Deckchairs can be hired and you can pop to tea at the Ritz (*see* p.165).

Also *see* **Buckingham Palace**, p.31.

Greenwich Park

⇌ *Greenwich, Maze Hill;* ***DLR*** *Cutty Sark for Maritime Greenwich.*

The park, along with Blackheath beyond, was the hunting ground that attracted Duke Humphrey to Greenwich back in the 15th century. It has been tamed considerably since then, particularly under Charles II who hired the great French landscape gardener André Le Nôtre, of Versailles fame, to help lay it out anew in the 1660s. There is no evidence Le Nôtre ever visited the site for himself; indeed to judge from the way the park falls away abruptly at the bottom it looks as though he didn't even realize it was on a hill. It is nevertheless an elegant place, unusually continental in its formality. Sadly, the deer that used to roam freely are confined to The Wilderness on the south-eastern edge. On Chesterfield Walk, just beyond Croomshill Gate, is **Ranger's House** (*open Mar–June Sun 10–5, June–Aug Wed–Sun 10–5, Sept–Oct Sat–Sun 10–5; adm*), an elegant mansion dating from 1699 which is no longer the residence of the park ranger but instead holds a collection of musical instruments and 17th-century portraits. On the opposite side of the park, at 121 Maze Hill, is the eccentric **Vanbrugh Castle** (*not open to the public*) where the eponymous architect lived for six years until his death in 1725.

Right in the centre of the park is a **statue of General Wolfe**, who died fighting the French in Quebec in 1759 and is buried at St Alfege's. Note the shrapnel scars, and then look out across the Thames: you quickly appreciate what a perfect bombing route towards the Docklands this was for German aircraft during the Blitz. The **Old Royal Observatory** (*see* p.118) is next to the statue.

Also *see*: **Greenwich**, p.115.

Hampstead Heath

⇌ *Hampstead Heath, Gospel Oak;* ⊖ *Hampstead; bus 24 from Trafalgar Square, C11.*

Hampstead Heath is so big and wild you can easily feel you are lost in the deep heart of the English countryside, yet there are amazing views over London. At the top (north) end is the superbly located, unpretentious white neoclassical **Kenwood House** (*see* p.112), famous for its idyllic summer concerts held by the lake at the bottom of the garden; the orchestra sits under a white awning and the audience watches from across the water. The hill down from Kenwood leads to **Highgate Ponds**, a series of open-air pools segregated by sex to encourage nude bathing. The ladies' pool, discreetly hidden behind some thick bushes, is nearest the top just off Millfield Lane;

the men's pools are alongside the path nearer Highgate Road. Right down at the bottom of the Heath, should you stray that far, is **Parliament Hill**, site of an ancient barrow where the rebel queen Boudicca (Boadicea) is rumoured to have been buried. The view from the hill, no more than a bump compared to the heights of Kenwood, is rather disappointing, but the wind the site attracts is ideal for kite-flying.

Also *see*: **Hampstead**, p.111.

Highgate Cemetery

⊖ Archway, Highgate; bus 271.

To reach the entrance, start in Highgate High Street and turn right down the steep narrow hill called Swains Lane. At the bottom there are patches of gravel on either side of the road. To the right is the arched entrance to the ***western cemetery*** *(open for guided tours only, Mar–Nov Mon–Fri 2pm, Sat and Sun 11–4 hourly;* ***t*** *(020) 8340 1834; adm), and to the left is the more mundane iron grille leading to the* ***eastern cemetery*** *(open April–Oct daily 10–5; Nov–Mar daily 10–4; adm). Highgate is an 'active' cemetery, so people should be tactful about sightseeing when there's a funeral in progress.*

Highgate Cemetery has been a tourist attraction ever since it opened in 1839, both for its magnificent funereal Victorian architecture and for its views. 'In such a place the aspect of death is softened,' wrote the *Lady's Newspaper* in 1850. The **western side** is the older and more splendid of the two halves, a maze of winding paths leading to an avenue of mock-Egyptian columns and obelisks, and a hemicycle of tombs around a cedar of Lebanon. Winding roads and footpaths lead up to the so-called Egyptian Avenue, which you enter through an arch flanked with obelisks and mock-Egyptian columns. The avenue leads beneath a bridge to the Circle of Lebanon, a complex of tombs constructed on each side of a circular path with a magnificent cedar tree in the middle. The spire of St Michael's parish church looms above at the top of Swain's Lane. The guide will point out the eminent dead occupying these hallowed tombs; they include the physicist/engineer Michael Faraday and the poet Christina Rossetti.

The **eastern cemetery**, which opened in 1857 to cope with the overload of coffins from across the road, is altogether wilder and spookier (it features in Bram Stoker's *Dracula*). Here the cracked tombstones are covered in creepers and ivy, and you can roam around at will. Most people head straight for the large black bust of Karl Marx marking the place where the much-maligned philosopher was buried in 1883. The eastern cemetery contains a sprinkling of other left-wing revolutionaries, plus the remains of novelist Mary Ann Evans (aka George Eliot).

Holland Park

⊖ Holland Park, High Street Kensington; bus 94, 148 (north side) from Oxford Street, 9, 10, 49, 27 (south side).

Open daily 7.30am until half an hour before sunset. The best way to enter is through the wooded northern end. Take Holland Walk, a path opposite Holland Park Underground station, and look out for the first turning into the park, which is on the right after about 300 yards.

Holland Park turns reality on its head: it seems much bigger, much wilder, much more remote than it really is. Covering only about 40 acres (a fraction of the size of Kensington Gardens, for example), it feels like something out of a magical children's story – a maze of winding paths, wooded hideaways, rolling fields and formal gardens, wild flowers and birds. The park is what remains of the estate of **Holland House**, a grand Jacobean mansion devastated during the Second World War, which survives only in truncated form. You can see some of the ground-floor stonework of the original building, but little else. The east wing has been rebuilt as a **youth hostel** (a wonderful place to stay), while part of the ruined main house has been converted into an open-air theatre with a summer season of opera (*see* p.178).

Around the house to the north is a series of formal gardens, all different in style, including the peaceful **Kyoto Garden** with its still lake, lawns lined with gentle blooms and square, Elizabethan-style herb garden. On the south side is a calm terrace **café** overlooking a cricket pitch and tennis courts. Wild woodland areas surround the park on its outer edges. Wherever you walk, you will be startled by wild rabbits and peacocks and begged at by almost tame squirrels used to tourists and their sandwiches. Take nuts if you don't want to feel guilty.

Also *see*: **Leighton House**, p.142.

Hyde Park

⊖ *Hyde Park Corner, Marble Arch, Lancaster Gate, Knightsbridge; bus 94, 148 390 (north side), 9, 10, 52 (south side), 2, 10, 16, 36, 73, 74, 82, 137, 138, 414 (east side).*

Hyde Park is a remarkably large expanse of greenery for the centre of a big city. The east side of the park is rather hilly and open, giving views of the hotels along Park Lane up to Marble Arch. There are more trees towards Kensington Gardens, as the stretch beyond the Serpentine lake is known. **Rotten Row** is the sandy horse path running along the southern edge. Its name is a corruption of the French *route du roi* (royal road).

Hyde Park started out as part of the Westminster Abbey estate, a breeding ground for deer, boar and wild bulls. When Henry VIII dissolved the monasteries, he decided to keep it as a private hunting ground; it was not opened to the public until the beginning of the 17th century. William III hung lamps along Rotten Row to deter highwaymen while he made his way from Kensington Palace to St James's, instituting the idea of street-lighting in London. The park was a favourite hang-out for crooks of all kinds, and even George II was once robbed of his purse, watch and buckles while out walking. In the 18th century it also became London's most popular duelling ground.

In 1730 Queen Caroline created the **Serpentine** by having the underground Westbourne river dammed. The L-shaped lake is still the park's most prominent feature, famous for its New Year's Day swims which are open to anyone foolhardy enough to jump into the freezing winter water (some years the swimmers have to break the ice before they start). The Serpentine has provided the focus for many other events, from funfairs to political demonstrations. On its southwest side is the Princess Diana Memorial Fountain, opened in 2004. The northeastern end of Hyde Park remains the only place in Britain where demonstrators can assemble without police permission, a concession made in 1872 in a truce between the Metropolitan Police and a succession of angry demonstrators. The spot is known as **Speaker's Corner**, and every Sunday afternoon you can hear impassioned crackpots droning on for hours about the moral turpitude of the world. Despite the fame of Speaker's Corner, it is hardly an impressive symbol of free speech. Microphones are banned, and most of the words are drowned out by the traffic on Park Lane.

Kensington Gardens

⊖ *Queensway, Bayswater, Lancaster Gate, High Street Kensington; bus 94, 148, 390 (north side) 9, 10, 52 (south side).*

The Serpentine divides Hyde Park from the westerly Kensington Gardens, originally the grounds of Kensington Palace (*see* p.36) with its **Round Pond** where you can play with model boats. George Frampton's famous statue of **Peter Pan** is by the lakeside towards the Bayswater Road. On the south side of the park, just behind the Albert Memorial (*see* p.26), is an attractive area of bushes and flowering plants known as the **Flower Walk**, and near the Serpentine is the **Serpentine Gallery**, famous for its shows of modern art. The **Diana, Princess of Wales Memorial Playground** (*free*) is in the north-west corner, near Black Lion Gate. On summer weekends the park throngs with locals.

Kew Gardens

⊖ *Kew Gardens;* ⇌ *Kew Bridge (from Waterloo); bus 65, 391 from Richmond or Hammersmith, 190 from West Brompton.*

t *(020) 8332 5655, www.kew.org. Gardens open 9.30–dusk; adm. Glasshouses open 9.30–5.30. Guided tours at 11am and 2pm. There are several entrances to Kew Gardens, the most useful being the Victoria Gate on Kew Road, where you can pick up a free map and leaflets. Take sturdy shoes.*

For the visitor, Kew is a place of many wonders: 38,000 different plant species, some of them entirely extinct in the wild; vast glasshouses, historic houses and buildings and, above all, 300 acres of beautifully tended parkland, some of it wonderfully wild and remote. All year round, Kew provides a glorious array of colours: flowering cherries and crocuses in spring; roses and tulip trees in summer; belladonna lilies and heather in autumn; strawberry trees and witch hazels in winter.

The Royal Botanical Gardens at Kew have always been more than a collection of trees, flowers and plants; they are more like a giant vegetable laboratory, sucking up new information about the botanical world and, through the power of their research, influencing the course of human history in all sorts of unexpected ways. In the 19th century, Kew's laboratories first isolated quinine and, realizing it was an efficient natural antidote to malaria, recommended putting it in the tonic water with which the colonial administrators of India and Malaya diluted their gin. Kew was also involved in the development of commercial rubber and helped produce artificial fibres such as rayon and acetate. It is now actively researching plant substances for the treatment of AIDS. In these days of receding rainforests and dwindling numbers of species of all kinds, Kew also does vital work in cataloguing and preserving plant types and developing new, genetically engineered hybrids.

In the 18th century, Kew was part of the royal estates that stretched down as far as Richmond. Princess Augusta, the mother of George III, first had the idea of laying a botanical garden in the grounds of **Kew Palace** where she lived. This elegantly gabled two-storey Jacobean mansion (*closed for renovation until 2006*) so endeared itself to George II and his wife Queen Caroline a generation before Augusta that they leased it for 99 years, for 'the rent of £100 and a fat doe'. The botanical garden was at first of only incidental importance to Kew; George III spent his energies commissioning a series of follies and outhouses from the architect William Chambers. These included three pseudo-classical temples, a ruined Roman arch, the handsome Wren-like Orangery and – most striking of all – the **Pagoda**. Chambers took his inspiration for this 10-storey octagonal tower from a visit to China in his youth. When finished in 1762, it was the most accurate rendering of Chinese architecture in Europe – although to be truly accurate it should have had an odd number of storeys.

The botanical garden began to grow thanks to the enthusiasm of its keeper, Sir Joseph Banks, who organized Kew's first foreign plant-hunting expeditions and set about cultivating rare species. Banks's was nevertheless a small-scale enterprise, and Kew did not really take off until 1840 when it was handed over from the royal family to the state, opened to the public and expanded to more than 200 acres. The first director of the new public gardens, Sir William Hooker, put Kew on a firm scientific and research footing. Hooker's most lasting architectural influence was to commission two great glasshouses from Decimus Burton. The **Palm House** (1844–8) is a wondrous structure of curvilinear iron and glass, with a two-storey dome as its centrepiece. The **Temperate House**, built in the early 1860s and modified right up to 1898, is far bigger but more conventional in structure, using straight panes and iron rods to achieve its great height and width. William Hooker's son Joseph took over as director in 1865 and established the **Jodrell Laboratory** to enhance Kew's research credentials. He also encouraged a young artist called Marianne North to set up a special gallery to display her collection of 832 botanical paintings based on her travels around the globe between 1871 and 1885 (left of Victoria Gate).

In this century, a number of new glasshouses have been added to the park, including the **Princess of Wales Conservatory**, containing Kew's collection of tropical herbaceous plants not least of which the incredible Titan Arum, which at two metres high is one of the largest flowers in the world. **Museum No.1** contains Kew's fascinating 'Plants + People' exhibition of wood and plant materials which have been made into useful materials for man – a 200-year-old shirt made out of pineapple fibres, from the Caribbean, and an incredible collection of Japanese lacquer boxes.

Regent's Park and London Zoo

⊖ Baker St (for the boating lake and theatre), Regent's Park (for the theatre), Great Portland St (for theatre), Mornington Crescent, Camden Town (for zoo); bus C2 from Oxford Circus (for east side), 13, 82, 113 and 274 (for west side).

Regent's Park is the most ornate of London's open spaces, a delightful mixture of icing-sugar terraces, wildlife, lakes and broad expanses of greenery. It is the most rigorously planned of London's parks, the brainchild of George IV's favourite architect, John Nash, who conceived it as a landscaped estate on which to build several dozen pleasure palaces for the aristocracy. It was meant to be the culmination of a vast city rebuilding project, of which the centrepiece was Regent Street. Nash's dreams of a new London, endowing the city with a full sense of aristocratic majesty, were tempered by a succession of objections and financial problems; Regent's Park, however, perhaps comes closest to embodying the spirit of his plans. His stuccoed terraces around the perimeter of the park are at once imposing and playful; the handful of grand mansions inside the park exude the same air of nonchalant, summery elegance as the hunting villas and parks on the outskirts of central Rome; the park itself is beautifully manicured, giving it a curious air of exclusivity even though it is open to all; most delightfully, for the visitor, it is remarkably empty.

Within the Inner Circle of the park is **Queen Mary's Rose Garden**, a magnificent array of flowers and plants of all kinds. At the north end is the **Open Air Theatre** (***t** 08700 601811; www.openairtheatre.org.uk; open May–Sept*), a magical sylvan setting for summer productions of *A Midsummer Night's Dream* and *As You Like It*. On the west side of the Inner Circle (find the path next to the open air theatre) is the **Boating Lake**, a wonderfully romantic stretch of water where you can rent boats of all kinds.

London Zoo

*London Zoo, **t** (020) 7722 3333, www.londonzoo.co.uk. Open daily 10–5.30 (last adm 4.30); adm exp.*

The Zoological Gardens in Regent's Park were where the term 'zoo' originated. The abbreviation, which first surfaced in the late 1860s, was immortalized in a music-hall song of the time beginning: 'Walking in the zoo is the OK thing to do.' In these post-colonial, animally correct times, zoos are not quite as OK as they used to be. But London Zoo has responded to debate about its role with some energy. The **Bear Mountain**, once horribly overcrowded and a place of abject misery, has been redeveloped, and houses just two bears. The delightful new **Children's Zoo** is built entirely out of sustainable materials, with a Camel House whose roof is planted with wild flowers and grass seed, a wonderful touch paddock, barn and pet care centre. A new Lottery-funded **Conservation Centre**, with exhibitions explaining ecosystems and animal diversity, opened in mid-1998.

One of the attractions of visiting the zoo now is the fine array of well-designed animal houses – the penguin pool by Lubetkin and Tecton (1936), Lord Snowdon's spectacular polygonal aviary (1964), Hugh Casson's elephant and rhino pavilion (1965) or the recently built Macaw Aviary. On your way round you will be invited to 'adopt' *any* animal that takes your particular fancy. Pay £20 for an exotic breed of cockroach, £6,000 for an elephant, or £30 for a part-share in any animal, and you are assured the beast will be fed and nurtured for a year. Your name will also go on a plaque beside the animal's enclosure – you'll see plenty of these already in place.

Richmond Park

⊖ *Richmond; bus 190 and 391.*

Open summer 7–dusk; winter 7.30–dusk.

At 2,470 acres, Richmond is the largest urban park in Britain and one of the least spoiled in London. A few medieval oaks survive, as do many of the varieties of wildlife that medieval royal parties would have hunted. The deer are what make Richmond Park famous – around 350 fallow deer and 250 red deer, which do so well in the heart of London that there is an annual cull – but there are also hares, rabbits and weasels. Richmond Park also has two ponds for anglers, five cricket pitches, two golf courses, no fewer than 24 football grounds and numerous cycle paths.

At the top of Richmond Hill near the park entrance is the **Star and Garter Home**, once a humble tavern which rose to be one of the most fashionable addresses in outer London. Its Assembly Room was the setting for many a 19th-century wedding reception, and its modest bedrooms housed everyone from common wayfarers to continental royalty. In the 1860s the tavern was revamped as an imitation French Renaissance chateau, a project as unpopular as it was extravagant, and one that led to the establishment's demise at the turn of the 20th century. Used as a hostel for disabled soldiers after the First World War, it is now an old people's home. Few can enjoy its enviable views over Richmond and the river; it, however, is all too visible for a mile or more in each direction along the Thames towpath.

Also *see*: **Richmond**, p.113.

St James's Park

⊖ *St James's Park; bus (to Whitehall) 3, 11, 12, 24, 53, 77A, 88, 159, 453.*

The dreamy expanse of St James's Park explains much about the spirit of the neighbourhood. Certainly it seems perfectly spruce nowadays, even rather romantic in a restrained sort of way, with its tree-lined pond and proliferation of city wildlife; but its elegance is a cunning artifice created to overcome centuries of squalor. Back in the early 12th century, Queen Matilda founded a women's leper colony on the site of what is now St James's Palace. By the mid-15th century leprosy had subsided and the hospital was turned into a special kind of nunnery; special because its young occupants were better known for administering to the flesh rather than to the spirit of the eminent men who called on them. These so-called *bordels du roi* were closed by Henry VIII, who built St James's Palace in their place and drained the marsh to create a nursery for his deer. The first formal gardens were laid out under James I, who installed, among other things, an aviary (hence the name of the street on the south side, Birdcage Walk) and a menagerie of wild beasts including two crocodiles. The setting was romantic enough for Charles II to use it as a rendezvous with his mistress, Nell Gwynne; unfortunately it also attracted upper-class hooligans in search of both trouble and rumpy-pumpy with the local whores.

In 1672 Lord Rochester described the park as a place of 'buggeries, rapes and incest', a state of affairs not improved even after a decree issued by Queen Anne banning dogs, hogs, menials, beggars and 'rude boys' from the premises. James Boswell lost his virginity to a whore in St James's Park on 20 March 1763, an experience which brought him 'but a dull satisfaction'. It was only under George IV that the park developed its present dignity. George landscaped the lake as we see it today and added gas lighting to deter the ladies of the night. The sex-crazed aristocrat gave way to an altogether gentler breed, the birdwatcher, as St James's filled with more than 30 ornithological species. Look out for the pelicans, ducks, geese and gulls on the lake.

Also *see*: **St James's and Royal London**, p.81.

Syon Park

London Road, Isleworth, with another entrance off Park Road near the river.
⊖ Gunnersbury, then bus 237 or 267.

***t** (020) 8560 0881, www.syonpark.co.uk. House open end March–Oct Wed, Thurs, Sun and bank holidays 11–5; gardens open daily 10–5; adm.*

Across the river from Kew Gardens, officially in Isleworth, is Syon Park, not so much a stately home as a kind of theme park *à l'anglaise*. Here in the large if rather empty park stretching down to the river are a butterfly house, a vintage car museum and a gardening centre housed beneath an impressive Victorian domed conservatory.

Syon House itself, built in crenellated stone around a quadrangle, was once part of a monastery, but was seized by Henry VIII for his own private use after his break with the Roman church. He locked up his fifth wife, Catherine Howard, in Syon House before her execution on adultery charges. Since 1594 Syon Park has belonged to the Percy family, holders of the Duchy of Northumberland. At first they let it slowly decline, but then in 1762 Robert Adam was commissioned to rework the interior, and the landscape architect Capability Brown was set to work on the grounds.

The house is particularly successful, using only the bare bones of the original structure to create a sumptuous classical atmosphere. The highlights are the Great Hall, which makes up for the unevenness of the floor with a series of small steps embellished with Doric columns, and the ante-room, which has a lavishly gilded plasterwork ceiling and a multicoloured marble floor. Osbert Sitwell once said this room was 'as superb as any Roman interior in the palaces of the Caesars'.

London: Shopping

09

London…a kind of emporium for the whole earth.

Joseph Addison

London has been a cosmopolitan place to shop since the Romans traded their pottery and olive oil for cloth, furs and gold back in the 1st century AD. Until comparatively recently the best shopping was for the rich, channelled through prestigious department stores such as Harrods, or smaller establishments in St James's and South Kensington offering exceptional service. The Carnaby Street spirit of the 1960s changed that, and now you can find cheap clothes and jewellery, unusual music and exotic food all over town in flea markets and gaily coloured shops. Carnaby Street itself, regrettably, has long since sold its soul to the cause of tourist kitsch, but you will find its successors in Covent Garden, down the King's Road, around Notting Hill and at Camden Lock market.

Oxford Street

Oxford Street is forever packed with shoppers and tourists, for whom its wide pavements and large department stores symbolize the very essence of the big city. This rather puzzling mystique is not really borne out by the reality, which is impersonal, uniform and unremittingly grey. In 1825 John Wilson Croker called Oxford Street 'thou lengthy street of ceaseless din', and the description still applies; even if cars have been banned during the daytime, there is still noise from the zillions of buses and taxis.

The most prestigious address, a few blocks off to the right beyond Duke Street, is **Selfridge's**, which for sheer size and range of goods is the closest rival in London to Harrods. The other department stores such as Debenhams, House of Fraser and **John Lewis**, and outsize outlets of high street regulars like **Marks & Spencer**, H&M and Gap, are not as much fun (or as cheap) as the specialist shops dotted around more intimate parts of London, but they do offer a one-stop shopping day. Most are open on Sundays, except John Lewis.

Off and behind Oxford Street are a few side streets with interesting small stores: at the Selfridge's/Bond Street end try walking down **South Molton Street**, **Davies Street**, **St Christopher's Place**, **James Street**, **Duke Street** and **Wigmore Street**, and on up to **Marylebone High Street** north of Wigmore Street; and past Oxford Circus there's **Great Portland Street** and **Argyll Street**, and pedestrianized **Carnaby Street**, which bears no traces of its 60s heyday but still has some odd little one-offs and its own array of even tinier side alleys.

Selfridge's, 400 Oxford St. Classic department store. There are also perfume and make-up demonstrations and a travel agent's in the basement.

Marks & Spencer, 458 Oxford St and branches all over London. Suppliers of cheap, comfortable clothes and underwear to the nation – and the world. Don't overlook the food section, either, with excellent pre-prepared dishes and stunningly good ice-cream that beats Häagen Dazs for both quality and price.

John Lewis, 278–306 Oxford Street. With its slogan 'Never knowingly undersold', this cheerful and efficient department store promises to refund the difference if you find anything cheaper elsewhere. Well-stocked departments of household goods and accessories, and for decades one of London's

VAT

If you leave Britain for a non-EU country within six months of arriving, you are entitled to a refund on the Value Added Tax, or VAT, that you have paid on any goods you have bought from shops displaying a 'tax free for tourists' sign. You must pick up a form in the shop where you make your purchase, and then hand it in at the airport when you leave the country. Since the rate of VAT is 17.5 per cent, this is well worth the hassle with larger items.

Opening Hours

Traditionally, shops stay open from around 9 to 5.30 or 6 – significantly earlier than the rest of Europe. Late opening for shops is becoming more and more common, however, particularly on Thursdays and Fridays, and Sunday trading is much more flexible than in the past: areas like Queensway and the Edgware Road, Hampstead, Greenwich, Tottenham Court Road and most of the Oxford Street department stores are open on Sunday.

largest retailers of fabrics and haberdashery. *Not open Sundays*.

H.R. Higgins, 79 Duke St. Purveyor of fine coffee to Her Majesty the Queen. The atmosphere of the old Jacobean coffee houses.

Electrum Gallery, 21 South Molton St. Classic jewellery from around the world – at a price.

Browns, 23–7 South Molton St. Centre of a burgeoning empire of fashion shops along this bijou pedestrian street off Oxford Street. Lots of famous labels.

Vivienne Westwood, 6 Davies St. The punk queen of British fashion offers real clothes as well as eccentric pieces of tailoring art.

Gray's Antique Markets, 58 Davies St. An enclosed antiques market with over 200 dealers in a large Victorian building. Mainly silverware, glassware, jewellery, toys, ancient artefacts and china. Some odder stalls, such as Wheels of Steel model train sets stall or Pete McAskie's Dinky toys. The Thimble Society of London is a stall dedicated to antique and modern thimbles.

TopShop, Oxford Circus. A vast haven of cheap trendy gear for style-obsessed but cash-poor teenage girls.

Borders, 197 Oxford St. Huge branch of the US book and music shop, with readings, performances and a coffee shop. *Open till 11pm and Sun 12–6.*

Forbidden Planet, 71–5 New Oxford St. The best sci-fi bookshop around.

James Smith and Sons, 53 New Oxford St. Fend off the British weather with a trip to this Victorian shop dedicated to umbrellas. Also stocks walking sticks, often with carved handles.

Muji, 26 Carnaby St and 187 Oxford St. Minimalist Japanese paper, fabric, fashion and edible goods.

Lush, 40 Carnaby St. You can smell this shop from yards away! Handmade soaps and toiletries using only natural ingredients.

Storm, 21 Carnaby St and 6 Gees Court. Unusual modern watches as well as fashion, sunglasses, lava lamps and so on.

Mikey, 24 Carnaby St. Funky, young, modern jewellery and accessories.

Octopus, 28 Carnaby Street St. All kinds of gifts and gimmicks: lamps made of brightly coloured rubber, bags with holograms on, glasses mounted on toy cars. Great fun.

Regent Street

Regent Street was once the finest street in London, although you might not think so to look at it now. In fact, all it boasts are a few fine shops (particularly men's clothes stores), the new *Cheers* theme-u-rant (at 72 Regent Street, overpriced and depressingly anonymous) and some rather stuffy, impersonal buildings livened up just once a year by the overhead display of colourful electric Christmas decorations.

One address that has not changed too much is the **Café Royal** at No.68. If you're feeling tired, this is a good stopping off point for lunch in the Grill Room.

Liberty, 210–20 Regent St. A labyrinth of a store with warm wooden interiors. Famous for print scarves, also good for fashion, china, rugs and glass.

Dickins and Jones, 224–44 Regent St. Department store for counties matrons. Very strong on cosmetics.

Aquascutum, 100 Regent St. Raincoats, cashmere scarves and endless sober suits. Clothes to last, not look hip in.

Boosey and Hawkes, 295 Regent St. Classical music.

Shelleys, 266–70 Regent St. The latest looks in shoes without spending a fortune. Branches in Kings Road and Neal St, Covent Garden.

Apple Store, 235 Regent St. Double-fronted concrete and glass techno-barn full of desirable white and silver Apple consumables; Mac-savvy staff on hand to solve problems.

Crabtree and Evelyn, 151 Regent St. Herb and fruit scents, all beautifully packaged. Ideal for gift-hunting.

L'Occitane, 149 Regent St. Provençal herb and fruit scents, also all beautifully packaged. Also ideal for gift-hunting.

Past Times, 155 Regent St. Gift shop trading on nostalgia for the British past in all its incarnations. Not as tacky as it sounds.

Swarovski, 137–41 Regent St. Famous crystal specialists, from little animals to huge fruit bowls.

The Pen Shop, 199 Regent St. The world's leading brands of writing implement, and good specialist advice.

Hamley's, 188–96 Regent St. London's biggest toy emporium.

The English Teddy Bear Company, 153 Regent St, W1. Sells handmade (English) teddy bears. Traditional ones as well as more modern.

Zara, 118 Regent St. Stylish Spanish fashion.

Grant & Cutler, 55–7 Great Marlborough St, off Regent Street. Uneven, but nevertheless the best bookshop in London for obscure and not so obscure foreign-language books.

The European Bookshop, 5 Warwick St, off Regent St. Makes up for Grant and Cutler's deficiencies, especially in French literature in which it excels.

Agent Provocateur, 6 Broadwick St, Soho. The most talked-about lingerie shop in London, with saucy window displays and staff in nurses' uniforms.

Bond Street

Three kinds of shopkeeper dominate Bond Street: high fashion designers, jewellers and art dealers, whose gaudy if not always particularly attractive shop fronts make for a diverting stroll. **Old Bond Street**, the lower part of the thoroughfare, concentrates mainly on jewellery and includes all the well-known names including **Tiffany's** at No.25.

At the top of Albermarle St is the ultimate shop for country gents, **Asprey's**, whose windows are packed with rifles, shooting-sticks and waders. If you walk through the shop to the Bond Street side you can also enjoy its extraordinary collection of military jewellery, including tanks and fighter jets made of gold and silver.

Check out **Bruton Street** and **Conduit Street** for the latest high fashion such as Stella McCartney (30 Bruton St), Vivienne Westwood (44 Conduit St), Dolce and Gabbana (6–8 Old Bond St) and Alexander McQueen (4–5 Old Bond St).

New Bond Street is famous for the showrooms of art dealers like Richard Green and Agnew's (or, round the corner on Cork Street, Waddington).

Sotheby's, 34–35 New Bond Street The famous auctioneers .

Fenwick's, New Bond St. A fashion department store, strong on women's clothes (many labels), accessories, cosmetics.

Church's, 133 New Bond St. Solid, sober shoes to last half a lifetime.

Yves Saint Laurent, 32–3 Old Bond St.

Miu Miu, 123 New Bond St. The funkier offspring of Prada.

Calvin Klein, 55 New Bond St. Famous for jeans, underwear and scents.

Hermès, 155 New Bond St. Source of the famous scarves and accessories.

Donna Karan, 19 New Bond St, and **DKNY**, 27 Old Bond St. Trendy streetwear for women. DKNY includes a café.

Mulberry, 41 New Bond St. Traditional high-quality bags and leather goods, stamped with the recognizable mulberry tree symbol.

Louis Vuitton, 17 New Bond St. The famous monogrammed bags are back in trend.

Smythson, 40 New Bond St. Stylish stationery for the swish set; uninspired designs but good quality paper, and fountain pens that will last a lifetime.

Bulgari, 172 New Bond St. Top Italian jewellery.

Chanel, 173 New Bond St for jewellery and 26 Old Bond Street for everything else.

Voyage, 50–51 Conduit St. Bouncers decide whether you're elegant or trendy enough to be let in.

Tottenham Court Road

As late as the 1870s, cows grazed along this road which is now all too crowded with traffic. Its main attractions are its furniture stores – **Heal's** (very classy and upmarket), **Habitat** (cheaper but duller) and shop after anonymous shop specializing in sofa-beds and futons – and **discount computer and hi-fi** shops. Visit plenty of shops, ask to see write-ups in the trade magazines to back up the recommendations and haggle the price down as far as you can. North Americans will find prices rather high, but Europeans will be astounded at how cheap everything is.

Most shops open Sundays. There are only a few specific addresses to recommend:

Habitat, 196 Tottenham Court Rd. Everything for the house, from glasses and corkscrews to fitted cabinets. Cheap and practical.

Heal's, 196 Tottenham Court Rd. Upmarket sister to Habitat, with innovative designs.

Crime in Store, 32 Store St. Specialist crime and mystery bookshop, including many US titles unavailable elsewhere in Britain.

Paperchase, 213–15 Tottenham Court Rd. Stationery-lover's paradise: pens, notebooks, cards and wrapping paper, plus a good selection of art materials.

Computer Exchange, 70 Tottenham Court Road. A wide variety of secondhand PCs, monitors, etc. Staff know their stuff and there are lots of good bargains.

Charing Cross Road

Charing Cross Road is the traditional centre of the London **book** trade, although the pressure of high rents is pushing many original establishments out into other areas. The once-gentlemanly publishing and book trade has become something of a cut-throat environment. Stores no longer stock the eclectic range of titles that they once did, preferring to focus on titles they know will sell in large numbers. On the plus side, many assistants still give expert advice on titles and subjects. Browsing is not only tolerated, it is welcomed.

The most famous bookshop on the street is **Foyle's**, at No.113–9. Once maze-like and chaotic, it had a makeover a few years ago and is now a bit more organized. Part of one floor is devoted to the famous Ray's Jazz Shop.

The modern bookselling chains just down the road, **Borders** and **Waterstone's**, are efficient general stores. Charing Cross Road's charm, however, lies in higgledy-piggledy secondhand bookshops such as **Quinto** (think *84 Charing Cross Road*) or its specialist shops. Collet's, the celebrated left-wing bookshop at No.66 where radicals lectured on revolution in the 1930s, sadly went bankrupt in 1993, and Silver Moon women's bookshop closed in the late 1990s. Look down side alleys like **Cecil Court** for some real old-fashioned one-offs.

Waterstone's, 121–5 Charing Cross Rd and many branches. Probably the best chain overall, with an outstanding selection at every branch.

Borders, 120 Charing Cross Rd. A strong line-up of titles, including a lot of American imports that don't make it on to the shelves of other stores.

Zwemmer, 80 Charing Cross Rd. London's leading art bookshop.

Murder One, 71–3 Charing Cross Rd. New and secondhand genre fiction, mainly science fiction and crime.

Henry Pordes, 58–60 Charing Cross Rd. One of many secondhand and antiquarian booksellers on the Charing Cross Rd and its offshoot, Cecil Court.

Jermyn Street and Savile Row

Jermyn Street boasts some of the fanciest shopping in town. Royal and aristocratic patronage has showered down over the years on the old-fashioned emporia lining it. The names of the establishments hark back to another era: Turnbull and Asser the shirtmakers, George Trumper, barber and perfumer, or Bates the hatter (the full spectrum, from flat caps to bowlers). The shop assistants more closely resemble manservants from the great aristocratic houses of the past than paid employees of ongoing business concerns. Deference and attention to detail are the watchwords, sometimes pushed to rather absurd extremes. At Trumpers clients are still asked, at the end of a haircut, if Sir would like 'anything for the weekend' (a wonderfully euphemistic way of avoiding any mention of the dread word 'condom'). Anyone buying a shirt is in for a treat of careful measuring, discreet compliments and nonchalant chitchat about the fluctuating quality of modern cloth (try Harvie and Hudson at No.97, with its attractive mid-Victorian fronting).

Jermyn Street also has several galleries selling old prints, silverware and antiques. Another fine establishment is **Paxton and Whitfield** the cheese-seller at No.93, where the freshest cuts of the day are advertised on a blackboard behind the counter and samples of unusual cheese types are offered for tasting with water biscuits.

Along Jermyn St you pass two arcades lined with more purveyors of quality goods: first **Princes Arcade**, with its brown and white décor and then, after Duke St, the lower-ceilinged, green and white **Piccadilly Arcade**. Halfway between them is the back entrance to **Fortnum & Mason**, the ultimate old-fashioned English food shop (*open till 6.30pm with afternoon tea from £18.50 3–5.30pm*).

North of Piccadilly is the quintessential address for men's bespoke tailoring, **Savile Row**. Classic menswear like **Hardy Amies** can still be found here, although the styles on offer are beginning to look impossibly old-fashioned. The street has hit hard times recently, although you'll still find some atmospherically traditional establishments, and you can see tailors working away in the basements as you pass.

Also north of Piccadilly is **Burlington Arcade**, which contains a host of little shops selling Irish linens, old pens, leather, pashmina shawls, antique and modern costume jewellery, perfumes and accessories.

Gieves and Hawkes, 1 Savile Row. One of the last gentlemen's outfitters in Savile Row. Unwavering attention to detail, atmospherically traditional.

Turnbull and Asser, 71 Jermyn St. One of many old-fashioned clothing boutiques on Jermyn Street, with lots of shirts and ties.

Paxton and Whitfield, 93 Jermyn St. Impeccable, old-fashioned cheese shop with specials of the day and nibbles at the counter.

Floris, 89 Jermyn St. Old-fashioned, long established perfume shop.

Taylor of Old Bond Street, 74 Jermyn St. Old-fashioned barber paraphernalia: shaving brushes and so on.

Davidoff, 35 St James's St and 65 Jermyn St. Fine cigars.

Bates, 21a Jermyn St. Men's hatter, with straw Panamas and other traditional styles.

Immaculate House, Burlington Arcade. All manner of strange and wonderful objects for the home.

Prestat, 14 Princess Arcade (off Jermyn St). Delicious handmade chocolates and truffles.

High Street Kensington

This is a really fun place to shop, and not that expensive either; it's really a mini Oxford Street, more compact and less busy. It's got its very own department store, **Barker's**, recently completely redesigned and especially good for cosmetics and furniture and Christmas goods.

There are big branches of **Marks & Spencer** and **Boots**. At the western end of the High Street are all the women's fashion chains (**H&M**, **Kookaï**, **Karen Millen**, **Jigsaw**, **Warehouse**, **Hobbs**, **Monsoon**, **French Connection**) and a selection of shoe shops, but also a large branch of the chain booksellers **Waterstone's**. The street also has a collection of stores specializing in outdoor wear and sporting equipment.

For antiques, look around the lower end of **Kensington Church Street** and the cobbled passage, **Church Walk**, that snakes behind the Victorian-era St Mary Abbot's church.

Late-night shopping day is Thursday.

Crabtree and Evelyn, 6 Kensington Church St and branches. Herbs and fruit scents, all beautifully packaged.

Cologne & Cotton, 39 Kensington Church St. Luxury linen for the stylish bedroom, mostly in tasteful white, cream and blues.

Portmeirion, 13 Kensington Church St. Co-ordinated bakeware, tableware and kitchenware.

Sweaty Betty, Kensington Church St. Young sporty fashion.

Muji, 157 Kensington High Street and branches. Minimalist Japanese store selling clothes, kitchen equipment and stationery.

Urban Outfitters, 36 Kensington High St. Kitsch, young and fun, but you have to be fit to climb the stairs to the cool café.

Claire's Accessories, 169 Kensington High St. Pink ribbons, plastic earrings and hairslides: a little girl's paradise.

Snow and Rock, 188 Kensington High St. Everything necessary for skiing and mountaineering.

YHA Adventure, 174 Kensington High St. Outdoor wear, boots, tents and camping equipment, hiking gear.

Trotters, 127 Kensington High St. Children's clothes and toys (next to Boots).

East, 143 Kensington High St. Smart clothes shop.

Children's Book Centre, 237 Kensington High St. Books, CDs, story-telling and now jewellery and chocolate, too.

Diesel, 38A Kensington High St. Streetwear by the ultra-trendy Italian designers.

Habitat, 26–40 Kensington High St. Newest branch of the interior-design emporium.

King's Road

Like Carnaby Street in Soho, the King's Road let its hair down and filled up with cafés and fashion shops selling mini-skirts and cheap jewellery. Old-fashioned shops, including the delightfully named toilet-maker Thomas Crapper, were superseded by the likes of Sir Terence Conran, who opened his first household store **Habitat** on the King's Road as a direct challenge to the fusty, old-fashioned goods then on sale at **Peter Jones** (a branch of John Lewis) on Sloane Square.

Nowadays, most of the boutiques have either gone upmarket or been replaced by generic high street chainstores, and a brand new shopping centre on the site of the old military barracks. Some of the 1960s spirit lives on, however, in the delightfully sprawling antiques markets on the south side of the road: **Antiquarius** at No.137, **Chenil Galleries** at No.181–3 and the **Chelsea Antiques Market** at No.245–53. You might also want to take a look at the **Chelsea Farmer's Market**, with its cafés and craft shops just off the King's Road on Sydney Street. Behind the King's Road to the north, **Cale Street** and **Elystan Place** have nice little shops.

For a map of the area, *see* p.100.

Chelsea Antiques Market, 245–53 King's Rd. All sorts of antiques.

Rococo, 321 King's Rd. Zany chocolate shop; an Aladdin's cave of edible delights.

Habitat, 206 King's Rd. Everything for the house, from glasses and corkscrews to fitted cabinets. Cheap and practical. Good café for people-watching.

Heal's, 234 King's Rd. Upmarket sister to Habitat, with innovative designs for furniture, beds, lighting, etc.

Daisy and Tom's, 181–3 King's Rd. Children's emporium, complete with hairdressing salon, carousel, toys, clothes and shoes.

Designers Guild, 277 King's Rd. Bright and colourful textiles, linens, furniture and pottery.

Steinberg & Tolkein, 193 King's Rd. Vintage clothing and accessories.

Brora, 344 King's Rd. Scottish cashmere, tweed and wool with a modern twist.

The Holding Company, 241 King's Rd. A wealth of storage solutions for every room in the home or office.

Bluebird, 350 King's Rd. Part of the Conran empire, a converted 1930s garage containing a luxury food store, cookware shop, flower stall, restaurant and café.

Peter Jones, Sloane Square. A West London institution; a branch of John Lewis renowned for wedding lists and Chelsea 'ladies who lunch'. Recently refurbished.

Manolo Blahnik, 49–51 Old Church St. Shoes from £300 upwards in an exclusive salon (ring bell to be admitted).

Chelsea Town Hall, corner of Manor Street and King's Rd. Venue for antique sales and craft fairs.

Jimmy Choo, 169 Draycott Avenue. Spectacular shoes for upwards of £290.

The Chelsea Courtyard, Sydney Street. Pleasant haven from the main drag, with Bikepark, a bike shop where you can buy, hire and park bikes and get them repaired; an antiques centre; and the only authentic Vietnamese street barrow in London.

John Sandoe Books, 10–11 Blacklands Terrace, just off the King's Rd. An old-fashioned, higgledy-piggledy bookshop with knowledgeable staff.

American Classics, 398 King's Rd. All you need for that authentic 'street' look.

R. Soles, 109a King's Rd. Cowboy boot heaven.

L'Artisan Parfumeur, 17 Cale St. Beautifully gift-wrapped, elegant scents and colognes.

V.V. Rouleaux, 54 Sloane Square, just behind Peter Jones. An irresistible shop filled to the ceiling with rolls of ribbon and brocade.

Knightsbridge and Brompton Cross

It was the Great Exhibition that turned Knightsbridge into the birthplace of the late Victorian department store. **Harvey Nichols**, the most stylish (and the absolute favourite of Patsy and Edina in *Absolutely Fabulous*), is on the corner of Sloane Street and Knightsbridge. Harvey Nicks is justly famous for its weird and wonderful window displays, and fifth floor food halls, where swishly packaged exotica of every description are sold under an equally exotic steel panelled corrugated canopy with views of the Knightsbridge skyline. (If you need a break, coffee or even a drink, it's well worth making a short detour from here to the food hall's glamorous café and bar.)

The most famous department store of all, **Harrods**, is on the Brompton Road. Nowadays it is often mentioned in the same breath as the name of its owner, Mohammed al-Fayed – Egyptian tycoon, failed candidate for British citizenship and father of the ill-fated Dodi, last companion of Princess Diana. But its pedigree stretches back much further to the glory days of the 19th century. The vast, terracotta-fronted palace that Harrods now occupies was built in the first five years of the 20th century, at much the same time as the first modern luxury hotels like the Savoy and the Ritz. Indeed Harrods is itself in some ways more like a five-star hotel than a mere shop; service and indulgence towards the customer are paramount, and no request is ever too much trouble. The place is kitted out to provide a fitting welcome to the noblest of princes; particularly striking are the Food Halls with their beautiful food displays and Edwardian Art Nouveau tiles in the Meat Hall depicting hunting scenes. As you wander around, you are serenaded alternately by a harpist and a piano player. You'll find just about anything on its six floors, as long as money is no object.

Both **Brompton Road** and **Sloane Street** parade classy designer shops, some of them too scary to enter. Nicole Farhi, Dior, Christian Lacroix, Chanel, Gucci, Kenzo and a clutch of others stretch down Sloane Street, while beyond Harrods in the Brompton Road you will find Emporio Armani and Issey Miyake. The streets behind Harrods have hidden treasures, and halfway down Brompton Road to the left is **Beauchamp Place**, lined with tiny exclusive shops selling anything from underwear to jewellery to designer cast-offs. Yet around the many exits of Knightsbridge tube are branches of Monsoon and Miss Selfridge, Jigsaw and Laura Ashley as well.

Harrods, Brompton Rd. A shopping institution of such proportions that it demands to be seen. Whether you want to buy anything is another matter. Exotic foods, kitchenware, silverware and toys are all excellent, clothes rather less so. Look out for bargains on mundane things like CDs during the sales.

Harvey Nichols, 109–25 Knightsbridge. High-class fashionwear, plus an excellent food hall and café on the fifth floor.

Burberry, 2 Brompton Rd. Classic designs with familiar patterns. Branches in Regent Street and Bond Street.

Space NK Apothecary, 305 Brompton Rd. Make-up and beauty products not available elsewhere: Nars, Kiehl's, Stila.

Gant, 17 Brompton Rd. American sportswear.

Emporio Armani, 191 Brompton Rd. Elegant cuts from the king of classic Italian tailoring.

Mulberry, 171-5 Brompton Road. Classic English leather bags and luggage with the distinctive logo.

Descamps, 197 Sloane St. Fine French linen.

Marni, 26 Sloane St. Light, floaty Italian fashion.

Graff, Sloane Ave. Very expensive jewellery.

Joseph Menswear, 74 Sloane Ave. Sharply tailored men's fashion.

Rigby and Peller, 2 Hans Road. Sublime underwear.

La Bottega del San Lorenzo, 23 Beauchamp Place. Divine Italian deli.

Isabell Kristensen, 33 Beauchamp Place. Ballgowns.

Brompton Cross

Further along the Brompton Road is a small enclave of shops and restaurants at the start of the Fulham Road known as Brompton Cross. The most striking building at its centre is Terence Conran's remarkable Art Nouveau **Michelin Building** (at No.81), which he renovated in the 1980s complete with glass cupolas and car-themed mosaics to create offices, a Conran Shop and the Bibendum Restaurant and Oyster Bar.

Behind and parallel to the Brompton Road, first left off Draycott Avenue, **Walton Street**, like Beauchamp Place, is a quiet enclave of unmissable classy little shops and pleasant places to eat or have a coffee.

Conran Shop, Michelin House, 81 Fulham Road. Baskets, chairs, lighting, even notebooks are all beautifully designed and presented in this tremendous Art Deco building.

The Ringmaker, 191–3 Fulham Road. Huge jeweller's with stylish designs.

Divertimenti, 139 Fulham Road. Pots and pans of the highest quality and inventiveness.

Agnès B, 111 Fulham Road. One branch of the women's design shop: clothes and make-up.

Formes, 313 Brompton Road. Fashion for pregnant women.

Cox and Power, 95 Walton St. Flamboyant modern jewellery.

Farmacia Santa Maria Novella, 117 Walton St. Italian hand-milled soaps and fragrances.

Bertie Wooster, 284 Fulham Road. Second-hand clothes of excellent quality for men; evening wear too.

Covent Garden

Apart from the market, there are many shops that make this a rewarding area to take your credit card. Neal Street, Seven Dials and the streets radiating from it, Thomas Neal's Arcade, Long Acre, New Row and the streets around the market are the places to head for.

Oasis, 13 James St and branches. Stylish, fashionable womenswear at reasonable prices.

Stanfords, 12–14 Long Acre. Map specialist, indispensable if you are travelling to the Third World where maps are virtually non-existent. Also travel guides, travel literature and walking guides.

Ordning & Reda, 22 New Row. Stylish, colourful, Swedish-designed stationery and office accessories.

Natural Shoe Store, 21 Neal Street. A haven of hippiedom, with designs from Arche, Birkenstock and Ecco.

The Astrology Shop, 78 Neal St. Have your personal horoscope done; also books, CDs and astrological objects.

The Tea House, 15 Neal St. All kinds of teas from around the world: herbal, green, organic and fruit.

Sam Walker, 33 Neal St. Vintage clothing.

Neal's Yard Dairy, 17 Shorts Gardens. More than 70 varieties of cheese, matured and served with love.

Duffer of St George, 29 and 34 Shorts Gardens. Very trendy menswear store, selling street-/clubwear.

Neal's Yard Remedies, 15 Neal's Yard. Lots of oils and homeopathic remedies, all very natural.

Cybercandy, 11 Shelton St. Sweet shop selling all the foreign goodies that you can't get in the UK.

Nicole Farhi, 11 Floral St and 15 The Piazza. Stylish, elegant clothes for women.

Jones, 13 Floral St. At the cutting edge of fashion; Gaultier and Galliano are old hat.

Paul Smith, 40–44 Floral St. High-class gloss on the bovver-boy look. Mostly for men, but there is now a women's collection too.

The Tintin Shop, 34 Floral St. Books, videos and T-shirts.

Culpeper Herbalists, 8 The Market. Herbs, spices, bath salts and pot-pourri, mostly taken from homegrown sources.

Segar & Snuff Parlour, 27a The Market. A tiny shop selling pipes, lighters, and hand-rolled cigars from Cuba.

Vertigo Galleries, 22 Wellington St. Vintage movie posters.

The Africa Centre, 38 King St. African crafts; also a restaurant/café.

Dr Martens Department Store, 1–4 King St. Four floors of DMs for men, women and children; also sells clothing.

Penhaligon's, 41 Wellington St. Own-brand *eau de toilette* and other fragrances. Also delicious air freshener sprays.

Screen Face, Monmouth St. Professional media make-up for personal use.

Mysteries, Monmouth St. New age, self-help, crystals and tarot, with readings.

Monmouth Coffee Co., 27 Monmouth St. A huge selection of good coffees.

Dress Circle, 57 Monmouth St. 'The greatest showbiz shop in the world', they claim, with sheet music, scores, books, posters and CDs.

Koh Samui, 65 Monmouth St. This is a wonderful boutique which stocks colourful, feminine clothes from a range of labels.

Gold Kiosk, St Martin's Lane Hotel, 48 St Martin's Lane. A Philippe Starck-designed frosted-glass box, this gift shop has everything from sweets and mags (all very stylish, of course) to designer clothing and jewellery.

Markets

Street markets are one of the best things about London. They are where the city comes alive, showing off the vitality and variety of the neighbourhoods lucky enough to have them. Some, such as Covent Garden and Portobello, are described in the main sections of this book; what follows is a list of what to expect and details of opening hours.

Berwick Street, Soho. Outstanding fruit and veg (*open Mon–Sat 9am–4pm*). *See* p.80. ⊖ *Oxford Circus, Tottenham Court Road.*

Brick Lane, Whitechapel (*open Sun 6am–noon*). Very popular market where East End barrows try to offload their junk, especially furniture and old books. Keep a hard nose and you can haggle a real bargain. ⊖ *Aldgate East, Shoreditch.*

Brixton, Electric Avenue (*open Mon–Sat, 8–6*). London's biggest Caribbean market, with music, exotic vegetables, goats' meat and wafting spices. ⊖ *Brixton.*

Camden Lock, between Camden High St and Chalk Farm Rd (*open Sat and Sun 10–6*). A weekend institution, with an array of books, clothes, records and assorted antiques by the canal. Huge crowds guarantee a festive atmosphere, and there are lots of excellent refreshments on hand. ⊖ *Camden Town, Chalk Farm.*

Camden Passage, Islington (*open Wed and Sat only*). High-class antiques market in a quiet street next to the bustle of Upper Street. Books on Thurs. ⊖ *Angel.*

Chapel Market, Islington (*open Tues–Sun*). An exuberant north London food market, with excellent fish and, as a sideline, lots of household goods and cheap clothes. ⊖ *Angel.*

Columbia Road (*off the Hackney Road about three-quarters of a mile north of Liverpool St Station; open 8am–1pm Sun morning*). Columbia market was set up in 1869 as a covered food market set in a vast neo-Gothic palace. The traders preferred to do their business on the street, however, and the venture failed. The shortlived market building was knocked down in 1958 to make room for the lively, modern, highly successful flower market. As well as a wide range of cut flowers and pot plants, you can buy home-made bread and farmhouse cheeses and enjoy the small cafés that line the street. ⊖ *Old Street, Liverpool St.*

Earlham St, Earlham St, between Shaftesbury Ave and Seven Dials (*open Mon–Sat 10–4*). Extraordinary flowers, and secondhand clothes. ⊖ *Covent Garden, Leicester Square.*

Greenwich, College Approach, Greenwich (*open Sat and Sun 9–5*). Lots of crafts, books, furniture and coins and medals. Worth a detour. **DLR** *Cutty Sark, Greenwich.*

Petticoat Lane, Middlesex St, Whitechapel (*open Sun 9–2*). Leather, cheap fashion and household goods at London's most famous Sunday market. Look out for the jellied eel and whelk sellers on the fringes. ⊖ *Aldgate, Aldgate East, Liverpool Street.*

Portobello Road, Notting Hill (*open food Mon–Sat 9–5, with lunchtime closing Thurs; antiques Sat only 7–5.30; clothes, crafts and bric-a-brac Fri 7–4, Sat 8–5, Sun 9–4*). Perhaps the most atmospheric market in London. The southern end is stuffed with antique dealers, while the northern end is a mixed bag of design shops, cafés, food stalls, jewellery stands, record stores and more. Has a real neighbourhood feel, culminating in the wonderful half-Portuguese, half-Moroccan Golborne Road. *See* p.98. ⊖ *Notting Hill Gate, Ladbroke Grove.*

St James's, St James's Churchyard, Piccadilly (*Tues antiques, Wed–Sun 10–6*). Lots of books, old prints, coins and medals on a Tuesday, and ethnic crafts the rest of the time. ⊖ *Piccadilly Circus, Green Park.*

South Bank, Riverside Walk, in front of the NFT (*Sat and Sun*). Secondhand books and prints along the riverside, open rain or shine. ⊖ *Waterloo.*

London: Museums and Galleries

10

Art Collections

Courtauld Institute

Somerset House, The Strand, WC2; **t** *(020) 7848 2526, www.courtauld.ac.uk;* ⊖ *Covent Gdn, Temple. Open daily 10–6; adm, free Mon; full disabled access, café, entrance is to the right on the way in to Somerset House.*

Somerset House was the first Renaissance palace in England, built for one of the biggest thugs in the country's history. In 1547 the Duke of Somerset was named Lord Protector for the new king, nine-year-old Edward VI, and set about building a home grand enough to match his overweening ambitions. Somerset was executed in 1552 but his palace lived on, at least for a while, as a residence for royalty and a venue for peace conferences. It fell out of fashion in the 17th and 18th centuries and, despite boasting a chapel by Inigo Jones and Europe's first example of parquet flooring, was demolished in the 1770s. The replacement is a fine Georgian building by William Chambers.

Somerset House's chief attraction is the Courtauld Institute, with its exquisite collection of paintings, particularly Impressionists and postimpressionists. Most of the paintings were a bequest by the philanthropist Samuel Courtauld, who also set up a school of fine art affiliated to London University. An elegant staircase leads to 11 smallish rooms spread over two floors. There is a magnificent *Adam and Eve* by Lucas Cranach the Elder, some fine Rubens including his early masterpiece *The Descent from the Cross*, and a roomful of unusual 18th-century Italian art including a series of Tiepolos. The Impressionists include a copy by the artist of Manet's *Le Déjeuner sur l'Herbe*, some wonderful Degas studies of dancers and moody Cézanne landscapes.

Somerset House also hosts occasional rock concerts and, in winter, an outdoor ice rink.

Estorick Collection of Modern Italian Art

Northampton Lodge, 39a Canonbury Square, N1; **t** *(020) 7704 9522, www.estorickcollection.com;* ⊖ *Highbury & Islington. Open Wed–Sat 11–6, Sun 12–5; cheap adm.*

Fascinating private collection of Italian art, mainly futurists including Balla, Boccioni and Carra. With a library, café and shop.

Kenwood House

Hampstead Lane, NW3; **t** *(020) 8348 1286;* ⊖ *Hampstead, Highgate. Open April–Sept daily 10–5, Oct–Mar daily 10–4.* *See p.112.*

National Gallery

Trafalgar Square, WC2; **t** *(020) 7747 2885, www.nationalgallery.org.uk;* ⊖ *Charing Cross, Leicester Square. Open Thurs–Tues 10–6, Wed 10–9; free.* *See p.38.*

National Portrait Gallery

St Martin's Lane, WC2; **t** *(020) 7306 0055, www.npg.org.uk;* ⊖ *Charing Cross, Leicester Square. Open Sat–Wed 10–6, Thurs and Fri 10–9; free.*

This gallery is unique, and a true oddity. Unique, because no other Western country has ever assembled a similar collection of portraits of the glorious names populating its history. Odd, because the kings, generals, ministers, pioneers, inventors and artists on display here have not been chosen according to the quality of the painting. They are here because the Victorian aristocrats who originally founded the gallery believed that it would serve as a stern kind of history lesson. In here you will see no revolutionaries, few union leaders, few true dissidents.

The gallery has far more pictures than space: over 9,000 portraits with only five narrow floors to exhibit them. Chronologically, the collection starts at the top with the Tudor age and works its way down towards the present day, with a magnificent new 20th-century wing designed by Piers Gough. The best paintings, technically speaking, are probably Holbein's vividly life-like versions of Henrys VII and VIII and Sir Thomas More. There are also magnificent renditions of the 19th-century prime ministers Disraeli and Gladstone by Millais, self-portraits by Hogarth and Reynolds, an ambivalent Churchill by Sickert and a Cubist T. S. Eliot by Jacob Epstein.

Percival David Foundation of Chinese Art

53 Gordon Square, WC1; **t** *(020) 7387 3909, www.pdfmuseum.org.uk;* ⊖ *Euston Sq, Russell Sq. Open Mon–Fri 10.30–5; free.*

This fine collection of imperial porcelain is named after the philanthropic collector who acquired its treasures. With its extensive library and superb ceramics, this is a vital stopping-off point for China scholars.

Royal Academy of Arts

Burlington House, Piccadilly, W1; **t** *(020) 7300 8000, www.royalacademy.org.uk; ⊖ Green Park, Piccadilly Circus. Open 10–6 daily, till 10pm on Fridays; adm charges vary.*

In 1714, the third Earl of Burlington took a trip to Italy and, rather like Inigo Jones exactly one century earlier, came back an ardent convert to Palladian architecture. But where Jones failed to start a general trend, Lord Burlington succeeded triumphantly; Palladian buildings were soon sprouting all over London. One of the first was the earl's private residence here in Piccadilly, completed in 1720 to the designs of James Gibbs, Colen Campbell and the earl himself.

Burlington House was lived in for more than a century, until the government bought it in 1854 to house the Royal Academy of Arts. It has been one of London's most important exhibition venues ever since, staging major retrospectives as well as the famed **Summer Exhibition**, a traditional but fairly underwhelming showcase for over a thousand amateur British artists. The RA also has a permanent collection with works from each of its prestigious members (Reynolds, Gainsborough, Constable and Turner for starters), as well as a marble relief sculpture by Michelangelo. You won't get much sense of the original Palladian mansion, however, because the building was radically altered by the Victorian architect Sydney Smirke in 1872. The bronze statue in the centre of the courtyard is of Sir Joshua Reynolds, the founder.

Saatchi Gallery at County Hall

Westminster Bridge Rd, SE1; **t** *(020) 7823 2363; ⊖ Westminster, Waterloo. Open Sun–Thurs 10–8, Fri–Sat 10–10.*

The advertising mogul's notorious collection of the most controversial modern art: Damien Hirst, the Chapman Brothers and Tracey Emin.

Tate Britain

Millbank, SW1, **t** *(020) 7887 8000, www.tate.org.uk; ⊖ Pimlico. Open daily 10–5.50; free.* *See p.42.*

Tate Modern

Bankside, SE1; **t** *(020) 7401 5120, www.tate.org.uk; ⊖ Southwark. Open Sun–Thurs 10–6, Fri and Sat 10–10; free (charge for special exhibitions).* *See p.43.*

The Wallace Collection

Hertford House, Manchester Square, behind Oxford St, W1; **t** *(020) 7593 9500, www.wallacecollection.org.uk; ⊖ Marble Arch, Bond Street. Open Mon–Sat 10–5, Sun 12–5; free, donations welcome.*

One could not hope for a more perfect monument to 18th-century aristocratic life than the Wallace Collection, a sumptuous array of painting, porcelain and furniture housed in a period mansion called Hertford House. It is the location that makes it, the wonderfully uplifting feeling as you glide up the staircases with their gilded wrought-iron banisters and wander from one elegant, well-lit room to another. The collection is the result of several generations of accumulation by the Hertford family, whose link with the art world had already begun in the mid-18th century, when the first Marquess of Hertford patronized Joshua Reynolds. Richard Wallace, who gave his name to the collection, was the bastard son of the fourth Marquess and acted as agent for his father in all his transactions. He bequeathed the whole lot to the state, on condition that it remain on public view.

Highlights include works by Frans Hals (*The Laughing Cavalier*), Rembrandt (*Titus*), Rubens (*Christ's Charge to Peter* and *The Holy Family*), Poussin (*Dance to the Music of Time*) and Titian (*Perseus and Andromeda*).

Whitechapel Art Gallery

Whitechapel High St, E1; **t** *(020) 7522 7888, www. whitechapel.org; ⊖ Aldgate East. Open Tues–Sun 11–6, Thurs 11–9; free.*

A lively gallery focusing on contemporary and avant-garde work, housed in an interesting Art Nouveau building designed by Charles Harrison Townsend at the turn of the 20th century. It was the brainchild of Samuel Barnett, a local vicar who believed education could help eradicate the appalling poverty in the East End. Jackson Pollock and David Hockney both held exhibitions here early in their careers.

Design and the Decorative Arts

Clockmakers' Museum

Guildhall Library, Aldermanbury, EC2; **t** *(020) 7332 1868/1870, www.clockmakers.org;* ⊖ *Bank, Mansion House. Open Mon–Fri 9.30–4.45.*

Here you'll find more than 700 timepieces of all shapes and sizes belonging to the Worshipful Company of Clockmakers. Look out for the silver skull watch said to have belonged to Mary, Queen of Scots, and the wrist watch worn by Edmund Hillary during the first recorded ascent of Mount Everest.

Commonwealth Institute

Kensington High Street, W8; **t** *(020) 7603 4535, www.commonwealth.org.uk;* ⊖ *High Street Kensington, bus 9, 10, 27, 28, 49, 328, C1. Open Mon–Sat 10–4; adm.*

The shimmering green hyperboloid roof, made of Zambian copper, is only the first of many surprises at this highly imaginative cultural centre celebrating the diversity and imagination of Britain's former colonies, now grouped together as the Commonwealth. There are three floors of galleries, each dealing with a different country, where you can pluck a sitar, sit on a snowmobile or watch a model demonstrating the digestive system of a New Zealand cow. The Institute also has a lively programme of lectures, concerts and art exhibitions; a shop jam-packed with craft work; and a restaurant offering indigenous dishes from around the Commonwealth. A new 'interactive' attraction called The Commonwealth Experience is a vertiginous and quite scary simulated helicopter ride over a rather more visible Malaysia than in real life.

Crafts Council Gallery

44a Pentonville Rd, N1; **t** *(020) 7278 7700, www.craftscouncil.org.uk;* ⊖ *Angel, bus 19, 38, 73. Open Tues–Sat 11–5.45, Sun 2–5.45; free.*
Excellent exhibition of modern British crafts.

Design Museum

Shad Thames, Butler's Wharf, SE1; **t** *0870 833 9955, www.designmuseum.org;* ⊖ *Tower Hill. Open daily 10–5.45; adm.* *See p.92.*

Geffrye Museum

Kingsland Rd, E2; **t** *(020) 7739 9893, www.geffrye-museum.org.uk;* ⊖ *Old Street then bus 243. Open Tues–Sat 10–5, Sun 12–5; free.*

A thoroughly absorbing series of reconstructions of British living rooms from Tudor times to the present, housed in a row of former almshouses, with a new extension focusing on design.

Leighton House

12 Holland Park Rd, W14; **t** *(020) 7602 3316, www.rbkc.gov.uk;* ⊖ *Holland Park, High Street Kensington, bus 9, 10, 27, 28, 49. Open Wed–Mon 11–5.30; adm cheap.*

This apparently straightforward red-brick house opens into a grand extravaganza of escapist late Victorian interior design. Lord Leighton, one of the Pre-Raphaelite painters, used his imagination, his not inconsiderable funds and the inspiration of a number of friends to create an astonishing Oriental palace here in his London home. The highlight is undoubtedly the Arab Hall, which has a stained-glass cupola, a fountain spurting out of the decorated mosaic floor and glorious floral tiles which Leighton and his friends picked up in Rhodes, Cairo and Damascus. Dotted around the downstairs reception rooms, among the paintings of Leighton and his contemporaries Millais and Burne-Jones, are highly ornate details including Cairene lattice-work alcoves and marble columns decorated in burnished gold.

Sir John Soane's Museum

13 Lincoln's Inn Fields, WC2; **t** *(020) 7405 2107, www.soane.org;* ⊖ *Holborn. Open Tues–Sat 10–5, with a £3 guided tour (free to students) on Saturdays at 2.30 and with visits by candlelight on the first Tuesday of each month 6–9pm; free, but any donations are gratefully accepted.*

John Soane (1753–1837) was a great English eccentric and also one of the great architects of his age. He was a fanatical student of antiquity, and one of the towering figures of the neoclassical movement in Britain. One contemporary described him as 'personal to the point of perversity'. Soane did not seem unduly bothered by the relative paucity of high-profile commissions; he stayed busy throughout his professional life and won a formidable reputation as a lecturer. In later life he bought up and converted three adjacent houses here in Lincoln's Inn Fields, adapting each room to his quirky style and filling them with objects from his remarkable art collection. In 1833 (four years before his death in 1837), Soane saw through a private Act of Parliament in which he bequeathed the whole collection to the public, with the stipulation that the museum should be maintained forever as it was on the day of Soane's death.

One of the highlights is the Picture Room on the ground floor, containing two great satirical series of paintings by Hogarth: *The Rake's Progress*. The Picture Room also includes studies by Piranesi and architectural drawings by Soane himself. Soane's other prized exhibit is the sarcophagus of the Egyptian Pharaoh Seti I (1303–1290 BC) in the Sepulchral Chamber in the basement. This is the finest example of a sarcophagus you can see outside Egypt, beautifully preserved and covered in hieroglyphics honouring Osiris and Ra.

It would be a mistake, however, to visit this museum merely for its artistic highlights. Every room yields surprises, whether it is the enormous collection of plaster casts Soane made from classical models, or the classical colonnade running along the upstairs corridor, or simply the ambiguities of light, which Soane manipulated so intriguingly in every area of the house with the aid of mirrors.

Victoria and Albert Museum

Cromwell Rd, SW7, **t** *(020) 7942 2000, www.vam.ac.uk; ⊖ South Kensington. Open Thurs–Tues 10–5.45, Wed and last Fri of month 10–10; free.* *See p.47.*

William Morris Gallery

Lloyd Park, Forest Rd, E17, **t** *(020) 8527 3782, www.lbwf.gov.uk; ⊖ Walthamstow Central. Open Tues–Sat plus first Sun in the month 10–1 and 2–5; free.*

A long way to go to see William Morris's childhood home and its fascinating exhibition on his life and work. Lots of Arts and Crafts wallpaper, stained glass, tiles and carpets. There is also a collection of Pre-Raphaelite paintings and drawings by Burne-Jones and Rossetti, plus a few Rodin sculptures.

Historical, Political and Military

Bank of England Museum

Bartholomew Lane, Threadneedle St, EC2; **t** *(020) 7601 5545, www.bankofengland.co.uk; ⊖ Bank. Open Mon–Fri 10–5; free.* *See p.64.*

Cabinet War Rooms

Clive Steps, King Charles St, SW1 (Horse Guards Rd), **t** *(020) 7766 0120, www.iwm.org.uk/cabinet; ⊖ Westminster. Open daily 9.30–6; adm.*

Winston Churchill had the basement of a number of government buildings converted in preparation for war in 1938, and he, his cabinet and 500 civil servants worked here throughout the conflict, protected from the bombing by several layers of thick concrete. The floor below the present exhibition contained a canteen, hospital, shooting range and sleeping quarters. Churchill, whose office was a converted broom cupboard, kept a direct line open to President Roosevelt in Washington; all other telephone connections were operated from an unwieldy old-fashioned switchboard and scrambled, for perverse reasons of security, via Selfridge's department store. The War Rooms, with their Spartan period furniture and maps marking the British Empire in red, are a magnificent evocation of the wartime atmosphere.

Clink Prison Museum

1 Clink St, SE1; **t** *(020) 7378 1558, www.clink.co.uk; ⊖ London Bridge, bus 40, 133, 149. Open Sept– mid-June daily 10–6, mid-June–Aug daily 10–9; adm.* *See p.89.*

The *Golden Hinde*

St Mary Overie's Dock, Cathedral Street, **t** *(020) 7403 0123, www.goldenhinde.co.uk; ⊖ London Bridge, bus 40, 133, 149. Open daily May–Sept 10–6, Oct–April 10–5; adm cheap.*

A perfect replica of the galleon used by Sir Francis Drake to circumnavigate the world in 1580. The original rotted away in a berth in Deptford, and the reconstruction you see here is a working galleon which has sailed many more miles across the world than its progenitor. A crew of 15 lives aboard the ship.

Imperial War Museum

Lambeth Rd, SE1; **t** *(020) 7416 5320, www.iwm.org.uk;* ⊖ *Lambeth North, Elephant & Castle. Open daily 10–6; free.*

Until the First World War this was the site of the notorious Bethlehem Royal Hospital for the insane, better known as Bedlam, where inmates were kept like zoo animals in cages and cells. The building is now used to illustrate Britain's wartime experiences from 1914 to the present day. Despite the intimidating pair of artillery cannon at the entrance, this museum does everything it can to illustrate the human side of war, not just the military hardware. Certainly, there are plenty of Zeppelins, Lancaster bombers, Cruise missile launchers – there is even a distasteful flight simulator for which visitors cough up extra money to 'experience' a Second World War bombing mission. Fortunately there are also exhibits on rationing and air raids, sound and light shows illustrating the terrors and privations of life in a First World War trench, artworks including Henry Moore's drawings of London during the Blitz, and a permanent Holocaust exhibition.

Kensington Palace

Kensington Gardens, W8; **t** *0870 751 5170, www.hrp.org.uk;* ⊖ *High Street Kensington, Queensway. Open Mar–Oct daily 10–6; Nov–Feb daily 10–5; adm.* *See p.36.*

Museum of London

150 London Wall, EC2; **t** *(020) 7600 3699, www.museumoflondon.org.uk;* ⊖ *St Paul's. Open Mon–Sat 10–5.50, Sun 12–5.50; free.* *See p.62.*

National Maritime Museum

Romney Rd, Greenwich, SE10; **t** *(020) 8858 4422;* ⇌ *Maze Hill (from Charing Cross). Open daily 10–5, summer 10–6; free.* *See p.117.*

Royal Naval College

King William Walk, SE10; **t** *(020) 8269 4747, www.greenwichfoundation.org.uk;* ⇌ *Greenwich;* ***DLR*** *to Greenwich. Open Mon–Sat 10–5, Sun 10–12.30; free.* *See p.116.*

Winston Churchill's Britain at War Experience

64–6 Tooley Street, SE1; **t** *(020) 7403 3171, www.britainatwar.co.uk;* ⊖ *London Bridge, bus 47, P11. Open Oct–Mar daily 10–4.30, April–Sept daily 10–5.50; adm exp.*

This is the kind of museum you could cook up out of a recipe book. Take a popular subject (the Second World War), add plenty of period memorabilia (books, clothes, newspaper cuttings, radio broadcasts), mix in a couple of set-piece reconstructions (an Underground station during an air raid) and top with lashings of patriotism (Vera Lynn). There is not a drop of originality about the place. You'll see all of it, and more, at the Cabinet War Rooms.

Science, Medicine and Technology

Brunel Engine House

St Marychurch St, SE16; **t** *(020) 7231 3840, www.museumweb.freeserve.co.uk/brunel.htm;* ⊖ *Rotherhithe, bus 47, P11, 188. Open April–Oct Sat and Sun 1–5; Nov–Mar first Sun in the month 1–5; adm.*

Rotherhithe acquired a new cause for celebrity in the early 19th century, when Marc Isambard Brunel made it the starting point for the first tunnel to run beneath the Thames. Brunel was born in France and fled the Revolution with a forged passport. Although a talented engineer – he invented a system of pulley blocks still remembered today – he had no financial sense and spent far too much of his own money on his work. The Duke of Wellington had to haul him out of debtors' prison to start the tunnel from Rotherhithe to Wapping. The job took 18 years, from 1825 to 1843, and nearly ended in disaster on five separate occasions when the roof caved in.

Faraday Museum

Albemarle St, W1; **t** *(020) 7409 2992, www.rigb.org/heritage/faradaypage.html;* ⊖ *Green Park. Open Mon–Fri 10–5; adm.* *See p.72.*

Florence Nightingale Museum

2 Lambeth Palace Rd, SE1; **t** *(020) 7620 0374, www.florence-nightingale.co.uk;* ⊖ *Lambeth*

North, Waterloo, Westminster, bus 507. Open Mon–Fri 10–5, Sat and Sun 10–4.30; adm.

You won't learn much more about the founder of modern nursing here than at the Old Operating Theatre Museum (*see* p.90), but the museum nevertheless builds up a vivid image of her life and times. Here are the letters, childhood books and personal trophies that the 'Lady with the Lamp' brought back from the Crimean War. You can also see a reconstructed ward from the Crimea, contemporary nurses' uniforms and some of the equipment they used.

London Planetarium

Marylebone Rd, NW1; **t** *(0870) 400 3000, www.london-planetarium.com; ⊖ Baker Street. Open Mon–Fri 9.30–5.30, Sat–Sun 9–6; adm exp.*

A joint ticket buys admission to this and to Madame Tussaud's. If you have children, you might enjoy the Planetarium, with its exciting and informative laser, sound and light show projected over a vast dome-shaped auditorium via a high-tech Digistar Mark 2 projector. The show explains how the solar system works, what the galaxy and the Milky Way are (apart from the chocolate bars you chomped in the queue), how earthquakes and volcanoes happen, and more.

London Transport Museum

The Piazza, WC2; **t** *(020) 7565 7299, www.ltmuseum.co.uk; ⊖ Covent Garden. Open Sat–Thurs 10–6, Fri 11–6; adm, full disabled access.*

Londoners like to grumble about London Transport, but in their heart of hearts they are really rather fascinated by it. This cheerful museum celebrates everything that is excellent about the system, from the red London Routemaster bus to the London Underground map, designed in 1931 by Harry Beck, and never surpassed. In the main gallery, a glass walkway takes you past a series of historic buses, trams and steam locomotives. In adjoining galleries you can see an original watercolour of Beck's Underground map, and a superb collection of Art Deco period posters. The museum also organizes a programme of talks and events (including a regular tour, call for details, and lectures on London's disused Tube stations).

National Postal Museum

King Edward St, EC1, in the post office in King Edward Building on the left-hand side of the road; **t** *(020) 7239 5420; ⊖ St Paul's. Open Mon–Fri 9.30–4.30; free.*

This is a stamp collector's dream: three floors of postal memorabilia, from rare stamps to uniforms, Bantams (the motorbikes used for delivering telegrams) and red and green post boxes dating back to the 1850s.

Natural History Museum

Cromwell Rd, SW7; **t** *(020) 7942 5000, www.nhm.ac.uk; ⊖ South Kensington. Open Mon–Sat 10–5.50, Sun 11–5.50; free. See p.38.*

Old Royal Observatory

Greenwich Park, SE10; **t** *(020) 8312 6565, www.rog.nmm.ac.uk;* ***DLR*** *Greenwich, ⇌ Maze Hill (from Charing Cross), bus 188. Open daily 10–5. See p.118.*

Old Operating Theatre Museum

9a St Thomas St, SE1; **t** *(020) 7188 2679, www.thegarret.org.uk; ⊖ London Bridge. Open daily 10.30–5; adm. See p.90.*

Science Museum

Exhibition Rd, SW7; **t** *(020) 7942 4455, www.sciencemuseum.org.uk; ⊖ South Kensington. Open daily 10–6; free. See p.41.*

Thames Barrier Visitor Centre

Unity Way, SE18; **t** *(020) 8305 4188; ⊖ North Greenwich, ⇌ Charlton; bus 161, 177, 180. Open daily April–Sept 10.30–4.30, Oct–Mar 1–3.30; adm.*

A brief history of flooding in London, and an explanation on how the barrier works.

Famous Homes

Apsley House

Hyde Park Corner, W1; **t** *(020) 7499 5676, www.apsleyhouse.org.uk; ⊖ Hyde Park Corner. Open April–Oct Tues–Sun 10–5; Nov–Mar Tues–Sun 10–4; adm.*

Wellington was given this house as a reward for his victories against the French, and he modestly dubbed it No.1 London (its real address being the more prosaic 149 Piccadilly).

Robert Adam had built it half a century earlier for Henry Bathurst, a man generally reckoned to be the most incompetent Lord Chancellor of the 18th century. The Iron Duke succeeded in defacing Adam's original work, covering the brick walls with Bath stone, adding the awkward Corinthian portico at the front and ripping out much of the interior with the help of the architects Benjamin and Philip Wyatt. You feel the coldness of a man who terrified most who met him and who, according to legend, once defused a riot in Hyde Park with a single crack of his whip. Sadly the museum does not own a pair of Wellington boots, the man's greatest legacy to the 20th century. The highlight is indubitably Canova's double-life-size sculpture of Napoleon, which Wellington stole from the Louvre after its megalomaniac subject rejected it.

Carlyle's House

24 Cheyne Row, SW3; **t** *(020) 7352 7087; ⊖ Sloane Square then bus 11, 19, 22, 211, 319. Open April–Oct Wed–Fri 2–5, Sun 11–5, last adm 4.30; adm.* *See p.101.*

Dickens's House

48 Doughty St, WC1; **t** *(020) 7405 2127, www.dickensmuseum.com; ⊖ Russell Square. Open Mon–Sat 10–5, Sun 11–5; adm.*

The only one of Dickens's many London homes to survive. The furnishings have been drafted in from other Dickens homes; really just a collection of hallowed objects.

Dr Johnson's House

17 Gough Square, EC4; **t** *(020) 7353 3745; ⊖ Blackfriars, Temple. Open May–Sept Mon–Sat 11–5.30, Oct–April Mon–Sat 11–5; cheap adm.* *See p.58.*

The Freud Museum

20 Maresfield Gardens, NW3; **t** *(020) 7435 2002; ⊖ Finchley Road, bus 13, 46, 82, 113. Open Wed–Sun 12–5; adm.*

This is the house where Freud set up his last home after fleeing the Nazis in Vienna in 1938. Six rooms have been left untouched since the founder of psychoanalysis died of throat cancer on the eve of the Second World War. Of greatest interest is the couch where his patients lay during sessions – if, that is, it is not on loan to another museum. You can also see Freud's collections of furniture and artefacts, including some extraordinary phalluses, and watch the home movies he made of his family and dog at home in Vienna in the increasingly dark days of the 1930s.

Hogarth's House

Hogarth Lane, Chiswick, W4; **t** *(020) 8994 6757, www.hiddenlondon.com; ⊖ Turnham Green. Open April–Oct Tues–Fri 1–5, Sat and Sun 1–6; Nov–Mar closed 1hr earlier; closed Jan; free.*

This was where the great 18th-century painter and satirist, in the last 15 years of his life, came to get away from it all – hard to believe, given the current traffic level. It is no more than a curiosity, since the house itself is unspectacular and contains only prints of his most famous works.

Keats's House

Wentworth Place, Keats Grove, NW3; **t** *(020) 7435 2062; ⊖ Hampstead. Closed for renovation in 2005/6; call for details.* *See p.112.*

Religion

Freemasons' Hall

60 Great Queen St, WC2; **t** *(020) 7831 9811, www.grand-lodge.org; ⊖ Covent Garden, Holborn. Open Mon–Fri 10–5 and Sat 1pm, guided tour only, which must be pre-booked for Sats; free.*

An intriguing PR exercise stressing Freemasonry's principles of truth and brotherly love. Lots of regalia but no elucidation of those handshakes. 'It is not a secret society,' explains a leaflet. Right, and the Pope's not Catholic.

Jewish Museum

129–31 Albert Street, NW1; **t** *(020) 7284 1997, www.jewishmuseum.org.uk; ⊖ Camden Town. Open Mon–Thurs 10–4, Sun 10–5; adm.* *See p.108.*

Wesley's House

Wesley's Chapel, 49 City Road, EC1; **t** *(020) 7253 2262, www.wesleyschapel.org.uk; ⊖ Old Street/Moorgate. Open Mon–Sat 10–4; free.*

John Wesley's house, and the nonconformist chapel he built next door in 1778, with columns made from the masts of ships donated by George III. Lots of missionary paraphernalia, and the world's first electric chair.

One-offs

Bethnal Green Museum of Childhood

Cambridge Heath Road, E2; **t** *(020) 8980 2415; ⊖ Bethnal Green. Open Sat–Thurs 10–5.50, closed Fri; free.*

This extension of the V &A is housed in the building once known as the Brompton Boilers where the decorative arts collections were kept during the 1850s (you'll notice the very Victorian mosaic frieze on the outside depicting Agriculture, Art and Science). Inside are some intricate children's toys, notably dolls' houses, train sets, puppet theatres and board games; a shame, however, that they are displayed in such gloomy cabinets. (Cambridge Heath Road, incidentally, leads up to the East End extension of the Grand Union Canal and the western end of Victoria Park, the biggest piece of greenery in east London.)

Bramah Museum of Tea and Coffee

40 Southwark St, SE1; **t** *(020) 7403 5650, www.bramah-museum.co.uk; ⊖ London Bridge. Open daily 10–6; adm cheap.*

Coffee arrived in London in the 1640s and quickly became popular among the traders and brokers of the City. 'It is a very good help to digestion, quickens the spirit and is good against sore eyes,' remarked one contemporary quaffer. Coffee was very much a man's drink; indeed for a long time women were not admitted to coffee houses at all. They were expected to drink tea, which arrived in Europe at roughly the same time. This full fresh-flavoured museum was set up by a commodity broker, Edward Bramah, with his amazing collection of over 1,000 tea and coffee pots which tell the intricate history of the commodities, from the 17th and 18th century coffeehouses which spawned the Stock Exchange and Lloyds Insurance, to that most elegiac of 20th-century inventions, the mass-produced tea bag. A more authentic brew is made in the two cafés.

Dennis Severs' House

18 Folgate St, E1; **t** *(020) 7247 4013 for times and booking, www.dennisseversħouse.co.uk; ⊖ Liverpool Street. Open first and third Sun in the month 2–5pm, then at lunchtime the following Monday and on the evening of the same day by candlelight, then from January onward every Mon eve; adm; and also for evening performances three times a week with a special Silent Night on the first Monday of each month when the house is lit by candles and no one speaks, so that a 'silent poetry' is created; adm exp.*

This is not so much a house as a theatre, a place which offers a glimpse back into the past not by showing off well-preserved artefacts and objects in the way that National Trust homes do, but by forcing you to feel your way into the atmosphere of bygone eras, from neoclassical to romantic. Inside, each room is a living tableau, a lovingly constructed still-life time machine, where sheets are rumpled, candle wax is congealed on the floor and last week's vegetables sit half-eaten on the tables. The master of ceremonies is Dennis Severs himself, a mildly eccentric ex-pat American lawyer who dropped out of the southern Californian rat race in the late 1970s and bought this house as a way of getting back in touch with himself and with the past. In his startlingly original evening performances (for which you should book several weeks in advance since only eight people can attend), Mr Severs evokes the lives of five generations of occupants of the house, the fictional Jervis family, through a mixture of sound effects, light, still-life décor and sheer acting bravado. Emma Thompson came here to prepare for *Sense and Sensibility*. The effect is almost that of a seance. Mr Severs calls this 'perceiving the space between the eye and what you see'.

Fan Museum

12 Croom's Hill, SE10; **t** *(020) 8305 1441, www.fan-museum.org; ⇌ Greenwich,* ***DLR*** *Cutty Sark. Open Tues–Sat 11–5 and Sun 12–5; adm. See p.118.*

London Aquarium

County Hall, Waterloo, SE1, **t** *(020) 7967 8000, www.londonaquarium.co.uk; ⊖ Waterloo, Westminster. Open daily 10–6; adm. See p.26.*

Madame Tussaud's

*Marylebone Rd, NW1; **t** (0870) 400 3000, www.madame-tussauds.co.uk; ⊖ Baker Street. Open Mon–Fri 9.30–5.30, Sat and Sun 9–6 (longer hours in school holidays); joint adm with London Planetarium, exp; book for timed entry on website.*

There is no escaping the horrendous queues, which are little shorter in the winter. Nearly three million people put themselves through the crush each year, although it is hard to see why – the only thing you can say in the end about a waxwork is whether it is lifelike or not – and most of the film stars, politicians and famous villains here fare pretty indifferently. Back in the 19th century, of course, waxworks made more sense as they provided the only opportunity for ordinary people to catch a glimpse of the rich and famous, albeit in effigy. Marie Tussaud was a Swiss model-maker who trained with her uncle by making death masks of the victims of the revolutionary Terror in France. Her hallmarks were her attention to detail, particularly in the costumes, and her efforts to keep the exhibition bang up to date with the latest celebrities and figures in the news. One of Madame Tussaud's most inspired ideas, the Chamber of Horrors, survives to this day. The final section of Madame Tussaud's is called the Spirit of London, a funfair-type ride in a modified black cab featuring illustrations of London's history from the Great Fire to the swinging 1960s.

Museum of Garden History

*St Mary's, Lambeth Palace Rd, SE1; **t** (020) 7401 8865; ⊖ Lambeth North, Westminster, bus C10, 3, 344, 77, 507. Open Mar–mid-Dec daily 10.30–5; free (donations welcome).*

The plants on display were first gathered by Charles I's gardener John Tradescant, who is buried in the church with his son. You can also see gardening tools dating back to the ancient world. The church, largely rebuilt in 1852 but still based on its 14th-century precedent, is curious for other reasons too. It contains the only full-immersion font in London. It is the last resting place of Captain Bligh, of Mutiny on the Bounty fame. And in the south chapel is a stained-glass window commemorating a medieval pedlar who grew rich when his dog unearthed great treasure while scratching around one day on a piece of waste land in the area. The pedlar left an acre of land to the parish when he died, but asked for the window for him and his dog in return.

Sherlock Holmes Museum

*239 Baker St, NW1; **t** (020) 7935 8866, www.sherlock-holmes.co.uk; ⊖ Baker Street. Open daily 9.30–6; adm.*

The museum says its address is 221b Baker St, and certainly looks convincing enough to be the supersleuth's consulting rooms. Unfortunately, though, it is really No.239; the building encompassing No.221b (which never actually existed as a self-contained address) is the glass-and-concrete headquarters of the Abbey National Building Society. The museum is a lot of fun, if you enter into its spirit of artifice. You are greeted at the door by either a housekeeper or a policeman. Most entertaining of all is the folder containing Sherlock Holmes's fan mail.

Theatre Museum

*Russell St, Covent Garden, WC2; **t** (020) 7943 4700, www.theatremuseum.org; ⊖ Covent Garden. Open Tues–Sun 10–6; phone to check time of tours; free.*

This museum is confusingly laid out; by far the best way to see it is to join one of the very informative guided tours led by actors three times a day and free with the price of admission. A vast number of exhibits cover the history of the English stage from the Elizabethan public playhouses to the rise of the National Theatre, illustrated by period costumes and plenty of model theatres. Unfortunately all this wonderful stuff – from Edmund Kean's death mask to the psychedelic hand-printed costumes used by the Diaghilev Ballets Russes to premiere 'The Rite of Spring' in Paris in 1913 – is displayed behind the smudged glass of dully lit fish tanks. Rather more engaging fun is to be had by submitting yourself to the free make-up displays; you may have noticed some eccentric-looking people with werewolf faces or Mr Hyde expressions on your way in.

Vinopolis

*1 Bank End, Clink Street, SE1; **t** 0870 241 4040, www.vinopolis.co.uk; ⊖ Borough, London Bridge, bus 40, 133, 149. Open Tues–Thurs and Sun 12–6, Mon, Fri and Sat 12–9; adm. See p.92.*

London: Children and Sports

11

Children's London

Though noisy and crowded, London is a welcoming and exciting place for kids. It certainly has more child-orientated attractions than any other city in Britain, with treasure trails, puzzle books and kids' audio tours springing up in such seemingly stuffy places as the National Gallery and the British Museum. Cadogan Guides' *Take the Kids: London* provides a comprehensive guide to the child-friendly delights of the city.

Check *www.kidslovelondon.com*, a family entertainment website produced by the tourist board.

Sightseeing

The **Science Museum**, with its whirring gadgets and interactive displays, has long been a firm favourite with children (on its regular Science Nights, they can even come and stay the night). Kids can encounter dinosaurs at the **Natural History Museum,** Egyptian mummies at the **British Museum** and listen to Beefeaters' gruesome tales at the **Tower of London**. If you find that this whets their appetite for the macabre, you could also try the **London Dungeon** and the **Clink Museum**. For rather sweeter and more wholesome entertainment (and smaller queues), the **Bethnal Green Museum of Childhood** and **Pollock's Toy Museum** display historic toys and puppets, and the **London Transport Museum** offers the chance to drive a tube simulator.

Museums aren't the only family-friendly entertainment the city has to offer – children can join in an Artmix workshop at **Tate Modern**, spot landmarks from on high in a **London Eye** pod, take a **Duck Tour** (DUKW) around London via road and river in a bright yellow amphibious vehicle (*70min tours start at 10am year round, 4 times an hour at peak times; embarkation adjacent to London Eye, South Bank*) or explore the narrow, clunking decks of **HMS *Belfast***.

The **London Aquarium** is absorbing for everyone, and children can stroke the rays. As a guaranteed fall-back, there are, of course, the perennial attractions of **London Zoo** for animal-mad kids, especially its excellent Web of Life exhibition.

London's **parks** are great all-rounders. **Regent's Park** has plenty to offer kids, including playgrounds, a children's pool and the Open Air Theatre. In **Hyde Park** you can hire a rowing boat on the Serpentine and there's a collection of spanking new climbing equipment to clamber over in the **Princess Diana playground**. There are also many **funfairs** in the parks during the summer.

Entertainment

There's no shortage of entertainment for kids, with Punch and Judy shows at **Covent Garden** and children's films at the **National Film Theatre**, the **Barbican** and the **ICA**, and big-screen and 3-D films at the **IMAX** on the South Bank. At Christmas time there are **pantomimes** galore all over London.

Little Angel Theatre, 14 Dagmar Passage, Islington, N1, **t** (020) 7226 1787. A delightful puppet theatre. Weekend performances at 11am and 4pm, plus holiday features. Over-4s only. ⊖ *Angel*.

Polka Adventure Theatre, 240 The Broadway, Wimbledon, SW19, **t** (020) 8543 4888, *www.polkatheatre.com*. A popular and busy children's theatre, which has been staging top-quality shows for over 20 years, with a main theatre for over-fives (and now teens too), and a stage downstairs for pre-schoolers. ⊖ *Wimbledon*.

Puppet Theatre Barge, Blomfield Road, W9, **t** (020) 7249 6876, *www.movingstage.co.uk*. An enjoyable and bawdy introduction to the art of puppetry on an old working barge moored at Henley, Marlow and Richmond June–Oct, and Little Venice in winter. ⊖ *Warwick Avenue*.

Restaurants

Most of the city's restaurant chains, such as **Café Rouge**, **Pizza Express**, **Bella Pasta** and **TGI Fridays**, welcome children and often provide special menus, high chairs, activity packs and balloons.

Rainforest Café, 20 Shaftesbury Avenue, W1, **t** (020) 7434 3111, *www.therainforestcafe.co.uk*. Eat amongst dense tropical foliage in the company of mechanical squawking parrots, lumbering elephants and steely-eyed cheetahs. ⊖ *Piccadilly Circus*.

Child-minding Services

Childminders, 6 Nottingham St, W1, **t** (020) 7935 3000, *www.babysitter.co.uk*. An agency with a network of babysitters, nurses and infant teachers.

Pippa Pop-Ins, 430 Fulham Rd, SW6, **t** (020) 7385 2458. Crêche, nursery school and babysitting services.

Simply Childcare, **t** (020) 7701 6111. Offers childcare listings.

Universal Aunts, **t** (020) 7738 8937 (day)/7386 5900 (eve). Provides babysitters, entertainers, people to meet children off trains, and guides to take children round London.

Smollensky's, 105 The Strand, WC2, **t** (020) 7497 2101, *www.smollenskys.co.uk*. Weekend lunchtimes are dedicated to kids, with puppet shows, magic, and activity packs. Book. ⊖ *Covent Garden, Charing Cross*.

Shopping

No lack of outlets to shop *for* kids: for most emergency toy or clothing needs you should be satisfied by the many branches of the **Early Learning Centre**, **Mothercare**, **Toys R Us**, **Next**, **Baby Gap** or **Gap for Kids**. As for shopping *with* kids, here are a few key destinations:

Borders, 197 Oxford St, W1, *www.borders.co.uk*. American bookstore on five floors; excellent children's section with places to sit and read, and storytelling sessions. ⊖ *Oxford Circus*.

Daisy & Tom's, 181–3 King's Rd, **t** 0870 145 5050. A complete department store for kids: toys, books, even a hairdressers. Founded by Tim Waterstone, of bookshop fame. ⊖ *Sloane Square*.

Disney Store, 360–66 Oxford St, **t** (020) 8748 8886, *www.disney.store.go.com*. Anything Disney your kids could possibly desire. ⊖ *Oxford Circus, Piccadilly Circus*.

Hamleys, 188 Regent St, W1, **t** 0870 333 2450, *www.hamleys.co.uk*. One of the world's greatest toyshops. ⊖ *Oxford Circus*.

Harrods, Old Brompton Road, **t** (020) 7730 1234, *www.harrods.com*. The Christmas window displays and the huge toy department on the fourth floor are both big draws. ⊖ *Knightsbridge*.

Sports

London is rich in sports facilities and venues thanks to its extensive parkland and plentiful supply of ponds, reservoirs and lakes.

The city boasts several first-rate sports venues including Twickenham for rugby, Crystal Palace for athletics, Lord's and the Oval for cricket, and the legendary lawns of Wimbledon for tennis. The most famous venue of all, however, Wembley Stadium, the 'church of football' and host to a plethora of major concerts and sporting finals, is currently undergoing redevelopment.

Taking Part

For health fanatics in need of a workout, the **public sports centres** run by all London boroughs usually have good facilities.

There are some superb outdoor venues for **swimming**, notably the Highgate and Hampstead Ponds on Hampstead Heath. The Hampstead Pond, which is mixed-sex, is best reached from East Heath Road. The single-sex Highgate Ponds are accessible from Millfield Lane. Other council-run lidos worth trying are Bankside, Tooting, Brixton and Parliament Hill (lidos are large, unheated open-air pools, usually built in the 1930s). For the less hardy, the Covent Garden branch of Holmes Places has a heated outdoor swimming pool.

There are **tennis** courts in virtually every London park. Battersea Park has some of the cheapest courts, while Holland Park has the trendiest.

Hyde Park Riding Stables, 63 Bathurst Mews, W2, **t** (020) 7723 2813,*www. hydeparkstables.com*. Pay hourly for a ride around the park or a lesson in the arena. ⊖ *Lancaster Gate*.

Queens Ice Skating Club, 17 Queensway, W2, **t** (020) 7229 0172. Lessons, ice discos and more. Also tenpin bowling. ⊖ *Queensway*.

Regent's Park Boating Lake, **t** (020) 7724 4069. Rent a boat during the summer and idle away a few hours on either the large adult or the tiny children's lake between the Inner and the Outer Circle of Regent's Park. Cheap and wonderful. ⊖ *Baker Street*.

Wimbledon Village Stables, 24a/b High Street, Wimbledon, SW19, **t** (020) 8946 8579. Good for beginners, with the whole of Wimbledon

Common and Richmond Park in which to roam free. ⊖ *Wimbledon*.

Rowans Ten Pin Bowling, 10 Stroud Green Road, Finsbury Park, N4, **t** (020) 8800 1950. ⊖ *Finsbury Park*.

Spectator Sports

Football (soccer) is the nation's favourite game, second only to the weather as a pub conversation topic. Domestic games are safe and enjoyable, with large sections of the attendant crowds made up of families. London's biggest football teams are Chelsea, Tottenham Hotspur (Spurs) and Arsenal.

A game surely invented to be incomprehensible to the uninitiated, **cricket** incites great passions in its most ardent fans and sheer tedium in nearly everyone else. It would be foolhardy to attempt an explanation of the rules, which defy description, at least on paper. Atmosphere's the thing, and a visit to Lord's or the Oval usually provides plenty of good drink and conversation.

Rougher and more complex than football, **rugby** football involves hand as well as foot contact and is played with an ovoid ball.

Still an essential part of the summer season, the Wimbledon lawn **tennis** championships take place in the last week of June and the first week of July.

Lord's Cricket Ground, St John's Wood Road, NW8, **t** (020) 7289 1611, *www.lords.org*. The most famous cricket venue in the world, and home to the original governing body of the sport, the Marylebone Cricket Club. ⊖ *St John's Wood*.

The Oval, Kennington, SE11, **t** (020) 7582 6660. This vast pitch usually hosts the last Test match of the summer. ⊖ *Oval*.

Crystal Palace National Sports Centre, Ledrington Road, SE19, **t** (020) 8778 0131. Venue for national and international athletics and swimming. ⇌ *Crystal Palace*.

Stamford Bridge, Fulham Road, SW6, **t** 0870 300 1212, *www. chelseafc.co.uk*. Home to Chelsea FC. ⊖ *Fulham Broadway*.

Highbury Stadium, Avenell Road, N5, **t** (020) 7704 4040, *www.arsenal.com*. Home to Arsenal FC. ⊖ *Arsenal*.

White Hart Lane, 748 High Road, N17, **t** 0870 420 5000, *www.spurs.co.uk*. Home to Tottenham Hotspur FC. ⇌ *White Hart Lane*, ⊖ *Tottenham Hale, Seven Sisters*.

Twickenham Stadium, Rugby Road, Twickenham, TW1, **t** (020) 8892 2000, *www.rfu.co.uk*, tours (*adm*) Tues–Sat at 10.30, 12, 1.30,3, Sun at 1, 3. Headquarters of the Rugby Football Union (RFU) and host to international rugby fixtures and cup finals. ⇌ *Twickenham*.

Rangers Stadium, South Africa Road, W12, **t** (020) 8740 2575, *www.qpr.co.uk*. Home to Queens Park Rangers FC. ⊖ *White City, Shepherd's Bush*.

Annual Sporting Events

London Marathon, t (020) 7902 0200, *www.london-marathon.co.uk*. Sunday in late April. The 26-mile 385-yard course attracts over 30,000 participants each year, starting at 9 in the morning and ending when the last *papier mâché* rhinoceros staggers home. For the start: ⇌ *Blackheath*. For the finish: ⊖ *Westminster*.

Oxford v Cambridge Boat Race, *www.theboatrace.org*. Takes place on the Sunday before Easter (or Easter Sunday). The famous boat race can be viewed anywhere along the Thames between Putney Bridge and Mortlake, although the most popular spots are Putney and Chiswick Bridges. ⊖ *Putney Bridge, Ravenscourt Park*, ⇌ *Mortlake*.

Queens, Queens Club, 14 Palliser Road, W14, **t** (020) 7385 3421. One-week men's competition just before Wimbledon gives a good idea of who's on form to win the big one. Some tickets on the day. ⊖ *Baron's Court*.

Wimbledon, All England Lawn Tennis Club, Church Road, Wimbledon, SW19, **t** (020) 8944 1066, *www.wimbledon.org*. You'll need to apply nine months in advance for a seat on Centre or Number One Court during the late June championships – they're allocated by ballot. However, if you turn up early in the competition you'll see plenty of action on the outside courts. ⊖ *Southfields*.

London: Food and Drink

12

Food, Glorious Food

Nice manners, shame about the food: nothing about the English has traditionally left foreigners so aghast as their dining habits. The horror stories are legion: of wobbly, green-tinged custard, of vegetables boiled until they are blue, of white bread so vile you can roll it into little balls and use it as schoolroom ammunition, of rice pudding so sickly and overcooked it makes you gag. No wonder visitors from abroad have often contemplated packing a few home goodies to keep the wolf from the door.

In fact, you can put away your prejudices; London is now one of the great gastronomic centres on the planet. Never in its history has the city been so cosmopolitan, and never has there been such a wide variety of cuisines to sample. Its cutting-edge chefs are treated like superstars as they vie to reproduce, and improve on, the best that world cooking can offer. London boasts the best Indian food outside of India, and the best Chinese food in Europe. There are excellent Thai restaurants, Lebanese restaurants, Italian, Greek and Spanish restaurants, Polish, North African and Russian restaurants. Even the British restaurants aren't bad, and some of them may be outstanding.

Restaurants

London restaurants tend to take lunch orders between 12.30 and 2pm and dinner orders between 7 and 10pm, although you'll find cafés and brasseries that stay open all afternoon and accept orders until 11pm or even later. Listed restaurants are open every day for lunch and dinner unless indicated otherwise. Soho and Covent Garden are undoubtedly the most fertile areas, although there are excellent possibilities in Notting Hill, Kensington, Fulham, Chelsea, Camden Town and Islington, and on the south bank of the River Thames.

The one drawback is money – eating out in London is an expensive pleasure. There are some incredible bargains to be had, but overall you are lucky to get away with much less than £25–35 per head for a decent evening meal, roughly half as much again as you would in Paris, Rome or a number of North American cities. One reason for this is the wine, which can be cripplingly expensive without being especially reliable: watch out.

Meal prices will be inclusive of tax (VAT), but an extra cover charge (of no more than £3) may be added in swankier places. Look carefully to see if service is included. If not, leave an extra 10–15 per cent of the total, preferably in cash.

As for prices, we divide restaurants into five categories, according to the **price of a full meal with wine and service** (*see* box above).

All but the cheapest establishments will take cheques or credit cards. If you are paying with plastic, the total box will inevitably be left for you to fill, in anticipation of a fat tip. Don't feel under any pressure, especially if service is already included.

Restaurant Prices

luxury more than £60
expensive £40–60
moderate £25–40
inexpensive £15–25
cheap under £15

Soho/West End

Richard Corrigan at Lindsay House, 21 Romilly Street, W1, **t** (020) 7439 0450 (*luxury*). In a suite of elegantly ramshackle 18th-century rooms, the expertly executed modern Irish menu is exciting and rewarding. Cosy, eccentric atmosphere with entry by doorbell. *Closed Sat lunch and all day Sun.* ⊖ *Leicester Square, Piccadilly Circus.*

Alastair Little, 49 Frith St, W1, **t** (020) 7734 5183 (*expensive*). One of the first and also the best of modern British cuisine restaurants. The simplicity of the ingredients is echoed by the positively bare-essentialist décor. The menu changes according to what's fresh in the market. *Closed Sun evening.* ⊖ *Leicester Square, Tottenham Court Road.*

Criterion, 224 Piccadilly, W1, **t** (020) 7930 0488 (*expensive*). A magnificent Art Deco, gold mosaic interior, opened in 1870, Marco Pierre White's expensive brasserie draws big crowds. The place has seen much drama – suffragettes met here in the 1910s when women were not allowed into pubs. While the service is sometimes impatient and the room crowded, the food is exquisite without being exotic. *Closed Sun lunch.* ⊖ *Piccadilly Circus.*

The Portrait Restaurant, National Portrait Gallery, 2 St Martin's Place, WC2, **t** (020) 7312 2490 (*expensive*). Right at the top of the new extension to the National Portrait Gallery, with a glass wall giving heart-stopping views down Whitehall. Excellent, ungimmicky food, too – modern European dishes like salt cod fishcake with artichoke, or goat's cheese fritter, all served in generous portions. ⊖ *Leicester Square, Charing Cross.*

Quo Vadis, 26–9 Dean St, W1, **t** (020) 7437 9585 (*expensive*). Lime green airy interiors with meticulous table decoration. Positively serene compared with the new, trendy bustling bistros. Marco Pierre White's fine modern French food with Mediterranean influences is meticulously served. *Closed Sat lunch and all day Sun.* ⊖ *Leicester Square, Tottenham Court Road.*

J. Sheekey, St Martin's Court, WC2, **t** (020) 7240 2565 (*expensive*). This elegant suite of wood-panelled rooms is now the youngest sibling of The Ivy, with all the trendy elegance that that implies. The emphasis is still on fish (beautifully executed, from Dover sole to blue-fin tuna with Italian barley and herb salsa), plus particularly fine desserts. You can also eat at the bar. ⊖ *Leicester Square.*

The Sugar Club, 21 Warwick St, W1, **t** (020) 7437 7776 (*expensive*). Spectacularly innovative fusion fare in a cool, creamy ambience. Most weird and wonderful combinations – roast kangaroo with beetroot, duck with vanilla-scented flageolets – delight even the most discerning tastebuds. Particularly good contrasting textures and tastes, e.g. grilled scallops with sweet chilli sauce and *crème fraîche*. Expensive, but not over-priced. ⊖ *Oxford Circus, Piccadilly Circus.*

Zilli Fish, 36–40 Brewer St, W1, **t** (020) 7734 8649 (*expensive*). Fashionable haunt with comfy chairs, slow service and mostly superb fish (and prices to match). *Closed Sun.* ⊖ *Piccadilly Circus, Leicester Square.*

L'Escargot Marco Pierre White, 48 Greek St, W1, **t** (020) 7437 2679 (*expensive–moderate*). This one-time bulwark of the Soho scene serves high quality, classic French food under the gaze of high modern art (Picassos, Mirós, Chagalls). The first-floor dining room is more formal and expensive than the magnolia room below, but both serve ambitious dishes in daring sauces. A speciality is *feuilleté* of snails served with bacon. *Closed Sat lunch, all day Sun.* ⊖ *Leicester Square, Tottenham Court Rd.*

Fung Shing, 15 Lisle St, WC2, **t** (020) 7437 1539 (*expensive–moderate*). Beautiful, delicate, mainly Cantonese Chinese food, served with style in a bright lemon, blond-wood-panelled dining room; there is also an airy veranda at the back. The menu includes some more traditional Chinese dishes. One of the classic dishes is braised suckling pig. ⊖ *Leicester Square, Piccadilly Circus.*

Little Italy, 21 Frith St, W1, **t** (020) 7734 4737 (*expensive–moderate*). An offshoot of the famous Bar Italia, which was for many years the only place selling real espresso in London. The restaurant has a comparable authenticity that some of the more fashionable places may lack. Photographs of boxers adorn the walls. Friendly but can get too crowded. ⊖ *Leicester Square.*

Randall & Aubin, 16 Brewer St, W1, **t** (020) 7287 4447 (*expensive–moderate*). An old Victorian butcher's shop converted into an oyster and champagne bar, with a rôtisserie; the original tiled interior has been preserved. Specializes in seafood and spit-roasts, also langoustines, crabs, whelks – any of the ingredients can also be made into sandwiches to order. *Open from noon Mon–Sat, from 4pm Sun.* ⊖ *Piccadilly Circus, Leicester Sq.*

Spiga, 84 Wardour Street, W1, **t** (020) 7734 3444 (*expensive–moderate*). A chic and relaxed modern Italian restaurant with a wood-fire oven producing top quality pizzas. There are also tasty pasta options making the best of fresh traditional produce. ⊖ *Tottenham Court Road, Leicester Square.*

Vasco and Piero's Pavilion, 15 Poland St, W1, **t** (020) 7437 8774 (*expensive–moderate*). Loved by the media crowd, this nevertheless remains a friendly and cosy Italian restaurant serving immaculately presented dishes, such as grilled breast of guinea fowl with juniper berries. Cheaper two- or three-course set menus. Truffles from Umbria available in season. *Closed Sat lunch and all day Sun.* ⊖ *Oxford Circus.*

Andrew Edmunds, 46 Lexington St, W1, **t** (020) 7437 5708 (*inexpensive*). Simple dishes at low prices and excellent-value wine. Queues at the door, which makes the service understandably frenzied. Old-fashioned frontage, hard benches and restless sawdust effect belie the modern ethos and originality of the cooking. Menus change daily. *Closed Sat eve and Sun eve.* ⊖ *Oxford Circus, Piccadilly Circus.*

Aurora, 49 Lexington St, W1, **t** (020) 7494 0514 (*inexpensive*). This bijou café remains a joyous refuge from the clamour of Soho: easy Mediterranean food and a relaxed, cosy atmosphere. ⊖ *Oxford Circus, Piccadilly Circus.*

French House Dining Rooms, 49 Dean St, W1, **t** (020) 7437 2477 (*inexpensive*). Dark, worn wooden rooms above a pub of the same name. Atmospheric, 1920s ambience, much frequented by literati. Excellent modern European food, e.g. smoked eel salad, ox tongue, guinea fowl, duck. *Closed Sun.* ⊖ *Leicester Square.*

Livebait Café Fish, 36–40 Rupert St, W1, **t** (020) 7287 8989 (*inexpensive*). Although there is an underlying old French character to both the first-floor restaurant and the ground-floor canteen, the accent is fish, obviously. And you can order fish and shellfish in most cooked forms, be it chargrilled, steamed, *meunière* or fried, or sometimes even marinated. Come here for the bustling atmosphere, as well as the fish. ⊖ *Leicester Square.*

Melati, 21 Great Windmill Street, W1, **t** (020) 7437 2745 (*inexpensive*). Lively and authentic Indonesian restaurant with a cosy wooden interior. Good portions and a reliable menu including soups, satays, coconut desserts and exotica such as *cumi cumi istimewa* (stuffed squid in dark red, sweet soy sauce). ⊖ *Piccadilly Circus.*

Satsuma, 56 Wardour St, W1, **t** (020) 7437 8338 (*inexpensive*). Slick and trendy Japanese diner with bench seating, good sushi and a range of luxurious bento boxes. Friendly service. ⊖ *Piccadilly Circus, Leicester Square, Tottenham Court Road.*

Sri Siam, 16 Old Compton St, W1, **t** (020) 7434 3544 (*inexpensive*). Modern, minimalist and hip, a combination unusual in a Thai restaurant. The sleek cream walls, adorned here and there by banana and palm leaf themes, host throngs of diners in the evening, although it can be empty at lunch. *Closed Sun lunch.* ⊖ *Leicester Square.*

Bali Bali, 150 Shaftesbury Avenue, W1, **t** (020) 7836 2644 (*cheap*). A reasonable Indonesian place with a varied menu of light and well-spiced food. Incredibly cheap set lunches and dinners, too. ⊖ *Leicester Square.*

Beatroot, 92 Berwick St, W1 (*cheap*). Cheerful, down-to-earth vegetarian eat-in/takeaway café where you choose your size of food box and have it filled with any selection of hot dishes and salads from the food bar. Great puddings too. *Closed Sun. Open 9–6.30.* ⊖ *Oxford Street, Piccadilly Circus, Leicester Square.*

Café España, 63 Old Compton St, W1, **t** (020) 7494 1271 (*cheap*). Plain, authentic little Spanish restaurant – a far cry from self-conscious, un-Spanish *tapas* bars that have cropped up all over London. Good, generous portions of Galician and Castilian dishes, emphasizing fish. Deservedly popular. ⊖ *Leicester Square.*

Kulu Kulu, 76 Brewer St, W1, **t** (020) 7734 7316 (*cheap*). The handmade sushi is fresh and of high quality at this busy Japanese eating spot. A long, narrow conveyor belt runs along the counter and the food is served on colour-coded plates. *Closed Sun.* ⊖ *Piccadilly Circus.*

Mildred's, 45 Lexington St, W1, **t** (020) 7494 1634 (*cheap*). Eclectic wholesome vegetarian fare from Brazilian casserole to Chinese black bean vegetables and vegetarian sausages. Vegan daily specials. Also seasonal organic produce and even organic wines. Good Sunday brunch. Arrive early as bookings are not accepted. ⊖ *Oxford Circus.*

Photographer's Gallery Café, 5 Great Newport St, WC2, **t** (020) 7831 1772 (*cheap*). A real oasis, this relaxing café is right in the middle of the gallery. Entrance is free and the cakes and light snacks are home-made and delicious. *Closed from early eve.* ⊖ *Leicester Sq.*

Poon's & Co., 26–7 Lisle St, W1, and branches, **t** (020) 7437 4549 (*cheap*). Recently expanded, this has lost some of its chaotic caffness (it was one of the first Chinese restaurants in Chinatown). Famous for high-quality 'wind-dried' meats – especially the duck. ⊖ *Leicester Square.*

Soho Spice, 124–6 Wardour St, W1, **t** (020) 7434 0808 (*cheap*). One of the few Indian restaurants in Soho. Radiant blue, orange and magenta colour scheme makes for a modern Indian look. Genial service and very generous set menus; also a bar. ⊖ *Tottenham Court Road.*

Tokyo Diner, 2 Newport Place, W1, **t** (020) 7287 8777 (*cheap*). Japanese fast food – sushi and Japanese curries. One of the cheapest Japanese eateries in London. Noodles (about £6), *donburi* – rice and various toppings (£4–6). Ingredients are fresh and crisply cooked. Good service, authentic décor, no tips. *Open from 12 every day – all year.* ⊖ *Leicester Square.*

Wagamama, 10A Lexington St, W1, **t** (020) 7292 0990 (*cheap*). Wagamama, now an institution in Bloomsbury, has opened a new branch in Soho. The philosophy of this Japanese noodle bar is 'positive eating, positive living'. Hi-tech, efficient, fast service on long communal tables. Long queues do not diminish the experience. ⊖ *Oxford Circus, Piccadilly Circus.*

Covent Garden

The Admiralty, Somerset House, The Strand, WC2, **t** (020) 7845 4646 (*luxury*). Set in the newly refurbished Somerset House, this beautiful newcomer to London's restaurant scene has been snapping up awards left, right and centre. And justly too: the views and the elegant décor are more than matched by the exquisitely prepared French cuisine. Unusually, the restaurant also offers a spectacular five-course vegetarian set menu. *Closed Sun evening.* ⊖ *Charing Cross, Holborn.*

The Ivy, 1 West St, WC2, **t** (020) 7836 4751 (*luxury*). The moody oak panels and stained glass dating from the 1920s are offset by vibrant modern paintings. The menu caters for elaborate as well as tamer tastes. Salmon fishcakes on a bed of leaf spinach is a signature dish. Takes orders from 12–3 and 5.30–12, which ensures a diverse clientèle. A word of warning: book well in advance as many of the tables are kept free for celebrities. ⊖ *Leicester Square.*

Christopher's, 18 Wellington St, WC2, **t** (020) 7240 4222 (*expensive*). The opulent curved stone staircase in the foyer recalls a 19th-century pleasure dome – reinforced when one realizes that this was once London's first licensed casino (and later a high-class brothel). Up the stairs, in the dining hall, a more restrained elegance pervades. As an American restaurant, the menu emphasizes steaks and grills, but there are also seafood inspirations. ⊖ *Covent Garden.*

Orso, 27 Wellington St, WC2, **t** (020) 7240 5269 (*expensive*). High-quality Italian fare, served in a graceful terracotta Venetian dining room. Mainly Tuscan food, daringly interpreted, like pizza with goat's cheese and roasted garlic and oregano, or *puntarelle* with anchovy dressing. ⊖ *Covent Garden, Charing Cross.*

Rules, 35 Maiden Lane, WC2, **t** (020) 7836 5314 (*expensive*). The oldest restaurant in London (established 1798), with a long history of serving aristocrats as well as actors. Formal and determinedly old-fashioned, panelled in dark wood and decorated with hunting regalia. Specializes in game of the season: even rarities such as snipe, ptarmigan and woodcock. Dress smart. ⊖ *Covent Garden, Charing Cross.*

Mon Plaisir, 21 Monmouth St, WC2, **t** (020) 7836 7243 (*expensive–moderate*). Some of its ramshackle, bohemian charm has been lost, but it's still a safe bet for appetizing, well-presented French provincial dishes, especially seafood. Signature dishes include *coquilles St-Jacques meunière, gratinée à l'oignon, steak tartare, crème brûlée*, and also home-made *foie gras. Closed Sat lunch and all day Sun.* ⊖ *Covent Garden, Leicester Square.*

Bertorelli's, 44a Floral St, WC2, **t** (020) 7836 3969 (*inexpensive*). Conveniently located for opera-goers, 'Bert's' serves a broad range of proven Italian favourites, but also a more radical catalogue of Italian dishes, like *maltagliati* served with pumpkin, cream, chorizo, or *antipasti* of fried mozzarella. *Closed Sun.* ⊖ *Covent Gdn, Leicester Square.*

Café des Amis du Vin, 11–14 Hanover Place, WC2, **t** (020) 7379 3444 (*expensive–moderate*). A French brasserie, favoured by theatregoers. Caters for all tastes, from omelettes to stuffed trout. More formal upstairs dining room. Service can be slow. *Closed Sun.* ⊖ *Covent Garden.*

Joe Allen, 13 Exeter St, WC2, **t** (020) 7836 0651 (*inexpensive*). Started out as an American restaurant, serving hamburgers and steaks, but now embraces modern British and European too. The result is a long menu, lacking character – but there are some delights, particularly if you're into monster puddings. Joe Allen's is traditionally a venue to be seen in and also for star-gazers. Rollicking atmosphere with last orders at 12.45am (*except Sun: 11.30pm*). ⊖ *Covent Garden, Charing Cross.*

Calabash, Africa Centre, 38 King St, WC2, **t** (020) 7836 1976 (*cheap*). Dishes from all over Africa are served at this basement restaurant under the Africa Centre. A surprisingly institutional feel pervades the dining room, partly because of the collegey canteen. *Egusi* (stew of beef, melon, shrimps cooked in palm oil) from Nigeria, couscous from the Maghreb, *dioumbre* (okra stew) from Ivory Coast, with lots of fried plantain. *Closed Sat lunch, all day Sun.* ⊖ *Covent Garden, Leicester Square.*

Paul, 29 Bedford St, WC2, **t** (020) 7836 3304 (*cheap*). Part of the plush French chain, this elegant café offers superb bread, cakes and pastries to eat in or take away. ⊖ *Covent Garden, Charing Cross, Leicester Square.*

Holborn/Fleet Street/Strand

Bank Aldwych, 1 Kingsway, WC2, **t** (020) 7379 9797 (*expensive*). Set in a converted bank, this is a big, cheerful, stylish restaurant serving assured modern European cuisine. It's difficult when the food is this good, but try to leave room for dessert. ⊖ *Holborn.*

Indigo, One Aldwych Hotel, 1 Aldwych, WC2, **t** (020) 7300 0400 (*expensive*). This is the very stylish coffee shop, breakfast bar and restaurant for the glossy One Aldwych hotel. It's pricey, but very elegant, and the food (fashionable modern European) is generally of a high standard. ⊖ *Charing Cross, Embankment, Covent Garden.*

Bloomsbury/Fitzrovia

Pied à Terre, 34 Charlotte Street, W1, **t** (020) 7636 1178 (*luxury*). The neutral setting is a fine foil for Tom Aiken's virtuoso modern French cuisine. The food is just as magnificent at lunchtime, with the added bonus of generous set menus. *Closed Sat lunch and all day Sun.* ⊖ *Tottenham Court Rd, Goodge St.*

Townhouse Brasserie, 24 Coptic St, WC1, **t** (020) 7636 2731 (*expensive*). A fusion of modern French and international cooking, e.g. seafood tempura in French batter. Somewhat cramped quarters even though there is plenty of space. Friendly atmosphere, and huge portions. The three-course set menu is great value. ⊖ *Tottenham Court Road, Holborn.*

Archipelago, 110 Whitfield St, W1, **t** (020) 7323 9655 (*expensive–moderate*). This weird and wonderful Oriental fantasy restaurant (the menu an origami snake in a basket, the bill delivered in a birdcage) is rescued by the food from being a load of pretentious nonsense. The tone is playful and the innovative and spicy fusion fare is as dreamy as the surroundings. *Closed Sun.* ⊖ *Warren St.*

Camerino, 16 Percy St, W1, **t** (020) 7637 9900 (*expensive–moderate*). Classic but creative Italian food, with home made pastas and bread. Try the veal tower with tuna sauce, deep fried sardines with raspberry sauce, ravioli of beetroot and bufala ricotta cheese, sea bream with olive paste... Its name points to the decor (*camerino* translates as 'theatre dressing room'): red velvet curtains and wall paintings adorn the interior, giving it a warm feel. *Closed Sun.* ⊖ *Tottenham Court Road.*

Elena's L'Etoile, 30 Charlotte St, W1, **t** (020) 7636 7189 (*expensive–moderate*). This historic Fitzrovian locale has appropriated Elena Salvoni's name to its title in tribute to her personal contribution to the Etoile. Faded grandeur and old photographs of fêted regulars serve as the backdrop. But the menu is no longer only traditional French fare: some modern touches especially in the Eastern influence of some recipes. *Closed Sat lunch, all day Sun.* ⊖ *Tottenham Court Road, Goodge Street.*

Alfred, 245 Shaftsbury Ave, WC2, **t** (020) 7240 2566 (*inexpensive*). A modern angle on old

British favourites. Stark, no-nonsense décor which serves to underline the delicacy of the cooking. Straightforward dishes like roast pork combine with imaginative accompaniments. *Closed Sat, Sun.* ⊖ *Tottenham Court Road.*

October Gallery Café, 24 Old Gloucester St, WC1, **t** (020) 7242 7367 (*cheap*). Eclectic inspiration from around the world; busy, cosy and friendly. Two- or three-course meals for highly reasonable prices. A limited choice – but usually a vegetarian option. A courtyard to skulk in in summertime. *Open lunchtimes Tues–Fri.* ⊖ *Holborn, Russell Square.*

Wagamama, 4 Streatham St, WC1, **t** (020) 7323 9223 (*cheap*). *See* under Soho, p.157. ⊖ *Holborn, Tottenham Court Road.*

Marylebone

Blandford St Restaurant, 5–7 Blandford St, W1, **t** (020) 7486 9696 (*expensive*). Beautifully presented, inventive modern European cuisine at this low-key restaurant. Excellent service and an unusually good range of vegetarian options. *Closed Sat lunch and Sun.* ⊖ *Baker Street, Bond St, Marble Arch.*

Levant, Jason Court, 76 Wigmore St, W1, **t** (020) 7224 1111 (*expensive*). An exotic, candle-lit Lebanese bar-restaurant with long tables and little nooks with silky cushions scattered around low tables. Very tasty food and a good selection of Lebanese wines. There's even a belly-dancer at weekends. ⊖ *Bond Street.*

Maroush, 21 Edgware Rd, W2, **t** (020) 7723 0773 (*expensive*). The best of the Middle Eastern restaurants on Edgware Road. A fun atmosphere with lively décor. Wonderfully spiced dishes and excellent *meze*. Stuffed lamb is a favourite off the lengthy menu. Beware though: if you arrive to eat after 10pm the minimum charge is a startling £48 per person. There are now four restaurants in the Maroush chain, but this remains the best. ⊖ *Marble Arch.*

Giraffe, 6–8 Blandford St, W1, **t** (020) 7935 2333 (*inexpensive*). Bright colours, cheery staff and a lively modern global menu with a Middle Eastern slant make this all-day place a pleasant option. ⊖ *Baker Street, Bond Street, Marble Arch.*

The Quiet Revolution, 62–4 Weymouth St, W1, **t** (020) 7487 5683 (*inexpensive*). Wonderful organic café next to the Aveda shop; big chunky shared wooden tables. Great soups, sandwiches and light snacks. Very chic. *Open 9–6, closed Sun.* ⊖ *Baker Street, Bond Street.*

Seashell, 49–51 Lisson Grove, NW1, **t** (020) 7724 9000 (*inexpensive*). Arguably the best fish and chips in town. Fresh and crisp. Fine home-made fish cakes and, more's the rarity, home-made tartare sauce. Clean and attractive. Café-style eating as well as takeaway. *Closed Sun.* ⊖ *Marylebone.*

Mayfair/St James's

Le Gavroche, 43 Upper Brook St, W1, **t** (020) 7408 0881 (*luxury*). Albert Roux is one of the most revered cooks in Britain. He has now delegated the cuisine to his son, Michel, but standards are still de luxe. Extraordinary creativity, from the sautéed scallops to the coffee cup desert. A jacket is required. *Closed Sat, Sun.* ⊖ *Marble Arch.*

The Square, 6–10 Bruton St, W1, **t** (020) 7495 7100 (*luxury–expensive*). Constantly changing modern French menu, with strong emphasis on fish. Try the delicious seared tuna with niçoise dressing. *Closed Sat, Sun.* ⊖ *Green Park, Bond Street.*

Al Hamra, 31–3 Shepherd Market, W1, **t** (020) 7493 1954 (*expensive*). Sophisticated if rather overpriced Middle Eastern restaurant in the heart of the cosmopolitan chic of Shepherd Market, where you can sit 'out' in the summer months. Select a *meze* of different dishes from the 48 delicacies. ⊖ *Green Park.*

Le Caprice, Arlington House, Arlington St, SW1, **t** (020) 7629 2239 (*expensive*). Eternally fashionable (despite the slightly dated décor) with impressively high standards of cuisine and exceptional service. Essentially 'modern British' food with some imaginative Middle Eastern twists. A pianist tinkles away nightly from 7pm. ⊖ *Green Park.*

The Greenhouse, 27a Hay's Mews, W1, **t** (020) 7499 3331 (*expensive*). The principal idea behind this restaurant was to resurrect stale old English recipes into new categories. Liver and bacon or sponge pudding may sound dull, but they come to life here. Signature dishes include fillet of smoked haddock with

Welsh rarebit. *Closed Sat lunch and Sun lunch.* ⊖ *Green Park.*

Momo, 25 Heddon Street, W1, **t** (020) 7434 4040 (*expensive*). Top fashionable and popular Moroccan restaurant with plenty of noise and ambiance. Eye-catching geometric designs. Fusion cooking takes it beyond couscous and tagine, though these are done well. ⊖ *Piccadilly Circus.*

Nobu, Metropolitan Hotel, 19 Old Park Lane, W1, **t** (020) 7447 4747 (*expensive*). Dark glasses and a fat wallet are *de rigueur* at this glamorously minimalist New Wave Japanese restaurant. Exquisite menu, from meltingly delicious sushi and crisp tempura to unique Japanese dishes with South American touches. The excellent cocktails and saké list should not be missed. *Closed Sat lunch and Sun lunch.* ⊖ *Hyde Park Corner.*

Quilon, St James's Crowne Plaza, 41 Buckingham Gate, SW1, **t** (020) 7281 1899 (*expensive–moderate*). Upmarket Indian restaurant near Buckingham Palace; focuses on 'coastal food', mainly from Kerala. Expect exquisitely spiced fish and seafood. *Closed Sat lunch and all day Sun.* ⊖ *St James's Park.*

Mulligan's, 13–14 Cork St, W1, **t** (020) 7409 1370 (*expensive–moderate*). Hearty Irish cooking, but a new management has incorporated lighter dishes (such as smoked fish, or blue cashel cheese and artichoke and spinach salad), especially at lunchtime. But you can still find beef cooked in Guinness. Wicked puddings. *Closed all day Sat and Sun.* ⊖ *Green Park, Piccadilly Circus.*

Ozer, 4–5 Langham Place, **t** (020) 7323 0505 (*inexpensive*). Turkish and North African dishes with a French twist, in atmospheric surroundings: deep-red walls, candlelight and velvet. Try the red lentil soup, roast lamb shoulder in kumquat and limequat marmalade, or the baklava. ⊖ *Oxford Circus.*

Zinc Bar and Grill, 21 Heddon St, W1, **t** (020) 7255 8899 (*inexpensive*). Just off Regent St, this is yet another outpost of the Conran empire. Still, it's not too pretentious, the staff are friendly and helpful, and the food (modern European) is good. There are also tables outside in summer. *Closed Sun.* ⊖ *Piccadilly Circus.*

Strada, 15–15 New Burlington St, W1, **t** (020) 7287 5967 (*cheap*). Excellent, simple Italian pizza, pasta, salads and *secondi*. The pizza is thin, crispy and cooked in a wood-fired oven; the *linguine alla pescatora* is divine. Their own water is provided free of charge. Other branches all over London. ⊖ *Oxford Circus.*

Chelsea/Fulham

Gordon Ramsay, 68 Royal Hospital Road, SW3, **t** (020) 7352 4441 (*luxury*). It's very hard to get a table here but if you can, you can expect almost perfect modern French cooking from this temperamental footballer-turned-chef. *Closed Sat and Sun eves.* ⊖ *Sloane Square* and then a long walk or taxi.

Bibendum, Michelin House, 81 Fulham Rd, SW3, **t** (020) 7581 5817 (*luxury–expensive*). Excelling in ultra-rich French regional food, set in the sumptuously restored Art Deco Michelin building (ex-headquarters of the tyre manufacturers, designed by an untrained architect in 1905, and restored by Conran in 1987). The oyster bar downstairs, with a shorter fish-orientated menu, is cheaper though less grand. *Closed Sun lunch.* ⊖ *South Kensington.*

Bombay Brasserie, Courtfield Close, Courtfield Rd, SW7, **t** (020) 7370 4040 (*expensive*). Unlike most Indian restaurants in London, this is posh, in sumptuous colonial décor, and gastronomically flawless. Largely north Indian menu, including some unusual tandoori dishes. Beautiful veranda. ⊖ *Gloucester Road.*

River Café, Thames Wharf, Rainville Road, W6, **t** (020) 7386 4200 (*expensive*). Simple, very tasty Italian food in a splendid riverside setting designed by Richard Rogers – and then redesigned by him. Rogers' wife, Ruthie, and her friend Rose Gray, are the chief chefs – and they have written a series of influential cookbooks. *Closed Sun.* ⊖ *Hammersmith.*

Ken Lo's Memories of China, 67–9 Ebury St, SW1, **t** (020) 7730 7734 (*expensive–moderate*). Minimalist décor, but maximalist cooking. Ken Lo, one of Britain's best-known Chinese restaurateurs, who died a few years ago, founded this esteemed establishment which offers a stunning gastronomic tour of China to delight your eyes and satisfy every stomach. *Closed Sun.* His daughter, Jenny Lo, has opened a cheaper informal Chinese eatery, building on her father's inspiration, at **Jenny Lo's Tea House**, 14 Eccleston St, SW1, **t** (020) 7259 0399. *Closed Sun.* ⊖ *Sloane Square, Victoria.*

Chutney Mary, 535 King's Rd, SW10, **t** (020) 7351 3113 (*moderate*). Anglo-Indian 'Raj' décor complements a terrific menu of unusual specialities. Good service and wine list. ⊖ *Fulham Broadway*, then walk; bus 11, 22.

Chelsea Bun Diner, 9A Lamont Road, SW10, **t** (020) 7352 3635 (*cheap*). American-style all-day breakfasts, plus burgers and pasta from the 200-item menu. They have a selection of wine and beer, but you can bring your own wine if you prefer. Excellent value. ⊖ *Sloane Square, Fulham Broadway.*

Chelsea Kitchen, 98 King's Rd, SW3, **t** (020) 7589 1330 (*cheap*). Continental food and wine for less than £10. Known since the 1960s as a jostling, studenty joint for knock-down prices. ⊖ *Sloane Square.*

Stockpot, 6 Basil St, SW3, **t** (020) 7589 8627 (*cheap*). Three-course meals for not much more than a fiver. Strains of school dinner. Hardly makes pretensions at culinary art, but the quality isn't actually bad. ⊖ *Knightsbridge.*

Kensington/Hammersmith

Clarke's, 124 Kensington Church St, W8, **t** (020) 7221 9225 (*luxury–expensive*). A Californian restaurant to the extent that there is an emphasis on fresh produce. The set menu changes nightly, including salad of roasted pigeon with watercress, blood orange and black truffle dressing, and chargrilled turbot with chilli and roasted garlic mayonnaise. Small, intimate, nearly prissy room, but cooking is precise and professional. *Closed Sat eve and Sun eve.* ⊖ *Notting Hill Gate.*

Kensington Place, 201 Kensington Church St, W8, **t** (020) 7727 3184 (*expensive*). Sleek, airy, noisy, modern dining room with bold garden frescoes and 'eclectic European' cuisine. The highest quality ingredients; venison, sirloin steak, wild sea trout, sorrel omelette. Full of publishers lunching out with their favoured writers and journalists. ⊖ *Notting Hill Gate, Kensington High St.*

Phoenicia, 11–13 Abingdon Rd, W8, **t** (020) 7937 0120 (*expensive*). Swish, carpeted Lebanese restaurant attracting smartly dressed customers. Delicious *meze* selections – excellent *basturma* (smoked, cured Lebanese beef) and falafel – but portions can be modest. Makes much of pudding too: a variety of fresh cream and pastry dishes are given a dousing in aromatic syrups. ⊖ *High Street Kensington.*

San Lorenzo, 22 Beauchamp Place, SW3, **t** (020) 7584 1074 (*expensive*). Fashionable celeb hangout since the 1960s. Good, if over-priced, Italian food with mouthwatering desserts and perfect espresso. *Closed Sun eve.* ⊖ *Knightsbridge, South Kensington.*

Wódka, 12 St. Alban's Grove, W8, **t** (020) 7937 6513 (*expensive*). This site has been a Polish restaurant since the 1950s – but the current proprietor of this newish venture is intent on modernizing the image of Eastern European food in London. Plain interior with jazz backdrop. A list of 30 different vodkas and *eaux de vie*; also a daily changing set lunch at low prices. The result is both classy and professional. *Closed Sat lunch and Sun lunch.* ⊖ *High Street Kensington, Gloucester Road.*

Cambio de Tercio, 163 Old Brompton Rd, SW5, **t** (020) 7244 8970 (*moderate*). Exuberant contemporary Spanish cooking: delicate paella, skate wings, salt cod, octopus. Intensely popular; best to book ahead. Strong references to the bullring in the decorative theme. Some real *tapas* too to start with – *jamón serrano* with *fino* or *manzanilla*. ⊖ *Gloucester Road.*

The Gate, 51 Queen Caroline St, W6, **t** (020) 8748 6932 (*moderate*). It is worth heading west of Kensington for some of the most inventive vegetarian offerings in London. First-rate restaurant with mouth-watering fennel mousse, wild mushroom cannelloni and *teriyaki* aubergine. Sunflower walls and a leafy courtyard make an attractive ambience. Look out for the church, as the restaurant is not easy to find. *Closed Sat and Sun.* ⊖ *Hammersmith.*

Notting Hill/Bayswater

Bali Sugar, 33a All Saints Road, W11, **t** (020) 7221 4477 (*expensive*). First-rate experimental fusion food combines Latin and Asian flavours in a minimalist but cool setting. ⊖ *Westbourne Park.*

Notting Grill, 123A Clarendon Road, W11, **t** (020) 7229 1500 (*expensive*). Celeb-chef Anthony Worrall Thompson has transformed his tapas restaurant into this new steak house, serving British-sourced meats – 'well bred, well fed and well hung' – that are also organic where possible. ⊖ *Holland Park, Ladbroke Grove.*

40° at Veronica's, 3 Hereford Rd, W2, **t** (020) 7229 5079 (*expensive*). A restaurant that has unearthed historical and regional British dishes – spring lamb with crabmeat or calf's liver and beetroot – and even relaunched recipes that date from the 14th century, sometimes adapting them to more modern tastes. Elizabethan puddings. *Closed Sat lunch.* ⊖ *Bayswater, Notting Hill Gate.*

Al San Vincenco, 30 Connaught St, W2, **t** (020) 7262 9623 (*expensive–moderate*). Spicy southern Italian food prevails at this efficient and friendly establishment. Simple cooking, but some eccentric components are added to unlikely subjects, such as parmesan with lamb. Tiny, intimate room. Good wine list. *Closed Sun.* ⊖ *Marble Arch.*

Mandarin Kitchen, 14–16 Queensway, W2, **t** (020) 7727 9012 (*expensive–moderate*). Massively popular Chinese restaurant, with fish you can pick out of the fishtank. Mainly Cantonese food, in spite of its name. One of the best Chinese places outside Chinatown, hence the huge queues. ⊖ *Bayswater, Queensway.*

The Cow Dining Room, 89 Westbourne Park Road, W2, **t** (020) 7221 0021 (*moderate*). The relaxed, almost countrified atmosphere at the upstairs rooms above the trendy pub (of the same name) belies the precision cooking. Global inspiration but strong French strain, particularly in the sauces. *Closed Sun eve.* ⊖ *Westbourne Park.*

Luna Rossa, 190–2 Kensington Park Rd, **t** (020) 7229 0482 (*moderate*). Great Italian trattoria, with good atmosphere and service. ⊖ *Notting Hill Gate.*

Red Pepper, 8 Formosa St, W9, **t** (020) 7266 2708 (*moderate*). Really excellent pizza plus an interesting menu of fish and meat dishes in this classy, crowded place with a heated outdoor terrace. Good service. ⊖ *Warwick Avenue.*

Osteria Basilico, 29 Kensington Park Rd, W11, **t** (020) 7727 9372 (*moderate–inexpensive*). Intensely popular, hence intensely noisy restaurant with warm ochre walls. New-wave Italian dishes that are now becoming the norm, like spaghetti with fresh lobster and tomato, and linguini with spiced salami, parmesan, tomato and basil. Wooden kitchen tables and chairs, and echoey floors. Brazen staff. ⊖ *Ladbroke Grove.*

Brasserie du Marché aux Puces, 349 Portobello Road, W10, **t** (020) 8968 5828 (*inexpensive*). Inventive, café-style restaurant (the name means flea-market brasserie, as it's near Portobello market). Serves eclectic menu including an extraordinary haggis in filo pastry with quince purée. Old-fashioned but popular. *Closed Sun eve.* ⊖ *Notting Hill Gate, Ladbroke Grove.*

Casa Santana, 44 Golborne Rd, W10, **t** (020) 8968 8764 (*inexpensive*). Neighbourhood Portuguese restaurant (Madeiran to be precise) – meat stews and smoked cod – with bags of character and good food. Triumphant desserts and Madeiran beers. *Closed Mon.* ⊖ *Ladbroke Grove, Westbourne Park.*

Galicia, 323 Portobello Rd, W10, **t** (020) 8969 3539 (*inexpensive*). Galicia jostles with a rum mixture of authentic 'Gallego' locals and a trendy crowd of Notting Hill Gate fashion fiends. But the produce, the waiters and the 'feel' are uncannily real. *Closed Mon eve.* ⊖ *Ladbroke Grove.*

Geale's, 2 Farmer St, W8, **t** (020) 7727 7528 (*inexpensive*). Superior fish and chips (deep-fried in beef dripping for a touch of class). Recent new ownership has seen an expansion of the menu. Very busy. *Closed Sun lunch.* ⊖ *Notting Hill Gate.*

Kalamaras, 76–8 Inverness Mews, W2, **t** (020) 7727 9122 (*inexpensive*). Very friendly Greek basement restaurant which has been going strong since 1961. *Closed Mon–Fri lunch.* ⊖ *Bayswater, Queensway.*

Khans, 13–15 Westbourne Grove, W2, **t** (020) 7727 5420 (*inexpensive*). Hectic, helter-skelter Indian restaurant popular with students;

frantic waiters collide with waiting queues. Noise drowns intimacy and yet the main dining room preserves its charm – painted clouds waft all about you and palm trees act as columns. ⊖ *Bayswater.*

Standard Indian Restaurant, 21–3 Westbourne Grove, W11, **t** (020) 7229 0600 (*inexpensive*). First-rate tandoori restaurant with excellent pickles and friendly service. Unassuming name and room belie the high quality of the food. ⊖ *Bayswater.*

Mandola, 139–41 Westbourne Grove, W11, **t** (020) 7229 4734 (*cheap*). Delightful Sudanese restaurant which has had to expand to cope with demand. Simple wooden décor with a few African exotica. Strong Arabic overtones to the dishes: *filfilia* (mixed vegetable stew), *addas* (lentil stew dressed with caramelized garlic). Generous portions. Unlicensed. ⊖ *Notting Hill Gate.*

Rôtisserie Jules, 133A Notting Hill Gate, W11, **t** (020) 7221 3736 (*cheap*). Cheap but good. Good free-range chicken and other meats, with huge portions. Three courses for a very modest bill. Two other branches in Bute St, SW7, and 338 King's Rd, SW3. *Open all day from noon.* ⊖ *Notting Hill Gate.*

Satay House, 13 Sale Place, W2, **t** (020) 7723 6763 (*cheap*). Small, intimate shop front serving delicious Malaysian food – most of the customers appear to be Malaysian, which suggests authenticity. Strong flavours and a broad range of delicious recipes, chargrilled, baked and marinated. Photographs of Malay pop stars adorn the walls downstairs. ⊖ *Edgware Road, Paddington.*

Camden

Mango Room, 10 Kentish Town Road, NW1, **t** (020) 7482 5065 (*moderate*). Big splashes of colour announce this popular Caribbean restaurant just 20 yards from Camden Town station. Hearty cuisine (plantain, sweet potato, goat curry) is served in a consciously hip atmosphere, though the service (and occasionally the food) can be a little erratic. *Closed Mon lunch.* ⊖ *Camden Town.*

Café Corfu, 7–9 Pratt St, N1, **t** (020) 7267 8088 (*inexpensive*). Cheerfully eccentric décor – lots of candles and old posters – and excellent, crisply presented Greek food. This is widely regarded as one of the best Greek restaurants in London. The wine list is superb and there are belly-dancers at weekends. *Closed Mon.* ⊖ *Camden Town.*

Café Delancey, 3 Delancey St, NW1, **t** (020) 7387 1985 (*inexpensive*). Charming, discreet French restaurant with robust, attractively presented dishes. Caters for all types. Brasserie food: venison but also snacks and soups. Popular for brunch. *Open all day.* ⊖ *Camden Town.*

Jamon Jamon, 38 Parkway, NW1, **t** (020) 7284 0606 (*inexpensive*). Fantastic tapas in a charming, fun atmosphere: *patatas bravas*, serrano ham and prawns in garlic, all in generous helpings. ⊖ *Camden Town.*

Odette's, 130 Regent's Park Rd, NW1, **t** (020) 7586 5486 (*inexpensive*). This Primose Hill gem is cosy and romantic, twinkling in mirrors and serving modern European cooking to an appreciative clientele. *Closed Sun.* ⊖ *Chalk Farm.*

Andy's Taverna, 81A Bayham St, NW1, **t** (020) 7485 9718 (*cheap*). Highly thought-of Greek eatery with a flower-walled backyard. The menu looks standard Greek, but the ingredients are high quality and the cooking light. ⊖ *Camden Town.*

Islington

Metrogusto, 11–13 Theberton St, N1, **t** (020) 7226 9400 (*inexpensive*). Cool, simple but sophisticated modern Italian food in this relaxed, welcoming restaurant. ⊖ *Angel.*

Le Mercury, 140A Upper St, N1, **t** (020) 7354 4088 (*cheap*). Delightful French restaurant with surprisingly ambitious food at rock-bottom prices. The décor is simple, with wooden tables, candles and plain walls, and the staff are friendly. Book, or arrive early and ask for a table downstairs – upstairs they tend to forget you're there. ⊖ *Angel, Highbury and Islington.*

Smithfield/East End

Searcy's, Level 2, Barbican, Silk St, EC1, **t** (020) 7588 3008 (*expensive*). The Barbican's in-house restaurant has generally good and beautifully presented modern European cooking, and the view over the water-filled central courtyard is great, though it's not often buzzing with atmosphere. However, prices are fierce and unless you're there for a pre-theatre meal the service can be slow. *Closed Sat lunch. ⊖ Barbican, Moorgate.*

Alba, 107 Whitecross St, EC1, **t** (020) 7588 1798 (*expensive–moderate*). Quietly good Italian restaurant, specializing in polenta, risotto and other northern or Piedmontese dishes. Pink and minimalist inside. *Closed Sat eve and Sun eve. ⊖ Barbican, Moorgate.*

Quality Chop House, 94 Farringdon Rd, EC1, **t** (020) 7837 5093 (*moderate*). Superior English specialities like fishcakes, game pie and roast lamb, though a modern Mediterranean influence has crept on to the menu. All served in the highly atmospheric rooms of a former 19th-century working-class men's club. *Closed Sat lunch. ⊖ Farringdon.*

St John, 26 St John St, EC1, **t** (020) 7251 0848 (*moderate*). A converted smokehouse, still with an industrial feel to it. Hearty, meaty, ingenious British cooking with a difference: every conceivable part of the animal (trotters, oxheart, bone barrow) is presented in interesting dishes. No fussiness, crisp vegetables. *Closed Sat lunch, all day Sun. ⊖ Farringdon.*

The Peasant, 240 St John St, EC1, **t** (020) 7336 7726 (*inexpensive*). Attractive and pristine little room above a handsome Victorian pub. Inspiration for the sophisticated menu comes from around the world – from chicken *paillarde* to an excellent choice of *meze* dishes. *Closed Sat lunch and Sun. ⊖ Angel, Farringdon.*

South of the River

Le Pont de la Tour, Butlers Wharf, 36d Shad Thames, SE1, **t** (020) 7403 8403 (*luxury*). The flagship of Terence Conran's little restaurant empire at Butlers Wharf, with high-class but overpriced French food and views of the river, Tower Bridge and the City. *Closed Sat lunch. ⊖ London Bridge, Bermondsey.*

Delfina Studio Café, 50 Bermondsey St, **t** (020) 7537 0244 (*expensive*). Large, airy gallery-cum-café serving excellent and thoughtful cuisine. Dishes span the world, from spaghetti with scallops to chargrilled kangaroo. This street is becoming increasingly fashionable. Dinner booking essential. *Closed Sat and Sun. ⊖ London Bridge.*

Blue Print Café, Design Museum, Butlers Wharf, Shad Thames, SE1, **t** (020) 7378 7031 (*moderate*). French and Italian food at the Pont de la Tour's less expensive sister establishment. The conservatory emphasizes the terrific views over the river and Tower Bridge, as well as Canary Wharf. *Closed Sun eve. ⊖ London Bridge, Bermondsey.*

The Fire Station, 150 Waterloo Rd, SE1, **t** (020) 7620 2226 (*moderate*). This former fire station has been converted into a packed, vibrant pub-like eatery, just opposite the Old Vic theatre. Easy-going modern British. *⊖ Waterloo.*

RSJ Brasserie, 13a Coin St, SE1, **t** (020) 7928 4554 (*moderate*). Flamboyant, innovative French cooking, with a certain amount of global influence from Thailand and elsewhere. Extremely popular. Delightful upper rooms. *Closed Sat lunch, all day Sun. ⊖ Waterloo.*

Arancia, 52 Southwark Park Rd, SE16, **t** (020) 7394 1751 (*inexpensive*). Friendly, easy-going and surprisingly creative Italian restaurant with good vegetarian options. It's popular with the hip young City-workers who are moving into the neighbourhood in droves. *Closed Sun. ⊖ Bermondsey.*

Waterloo Bar and Kitchen, 131 Waterloo Road, **t** (020) 7928 5086 (*inexpensive*). Serious modern European food, simple but well prepared, with dreamy carpaccio and a good wine list. Small, informal setting, with wooden floors, long tables and ochre wall, behind the Old Vic. Always busy. *Closed Sat and Sun. ⊖ Waterloo.*

Richmond

Chez Lindsay, 11 Hill Rise, Surrey, **t** (020) 8948 7473 (*moderate–inexpensive*). Pretty Breton-style French restaurant on the banks of the

Thames. Delicious crêpes and galettes – the seafood fillings are particularly good. ⊖ *Richmond.*

Cafés, Teahouses and Snack Foods

Ever since the rise of the City coffee house in the 17th century, London has been addicted to the relaxed charm of café culture. These days it seems to be labouring under one of its periodic illusions that Britain enjoys a Mediterranean climate: pavement cafés, along with alfresco dining, are all the rage.

You will soon discover the new vogue for coffee, whether at one of the city's many Italian-style espresso bars or at the even newer chains offering much the same thing Pacific Northwest style: skinny wet caps and the rest.

Back indoors, you will still find a cosy kind of establishment geared towards the English ritual of afternoon tea and cakes. Tea, being the quintessential English drink, tends to be delicious; you'll be given a bewildering choice of varieties.

Soho and Covent Garden

Bar Italia, 22 Frith St, W1. The café with the best coffee in town and it knows it. The mirrored bar, complete with TV showing Italian soccer games, could have come straight from Milan or Bologna. The seating is a bit cramped, but at least there are tables on the pavement. Better to stand. *Open 24hrs Mon–Sat, Sun 7am–4am.* ⊖ *Leicester Square, Tottenham Court Road.*

Maison Bertaux, 28 Greek St, W1. Mouthwatering pastries in a slightly cramped upstairs tearoom which is always crowded. ⊖ *Leicester Square, Tottenham Court Road.*

Pâtisserie Valerie, 44 Old Compton St, W1. Excellent French cakes and coffee. *Open Mon–Fri 7.30–8, Sat 8–8.30, Sun 9–6.30.* ⊖ *Leicester Square, Tottenham Court Road.*

Mayfair

Browns Hotel, 33–4 Albermarle St, W1, **t** (020) 7518 4108. Tea served 3–5.45pm daily. Very traditional English hotel serving tea to all-comers, as long as you dress to fit the part. Set tea £23, £29, £33. ⊖ *Green Park.*

La Madeleine, 5 Vigo St, W1, **t** (020) 7734 8353. Delightful, relaxing spot serving heavenly cakes and pastries, as well as great coffee. There are some light meals available too, and very friendly staff. *Closed Sun.* ⊖ *Piccadilly Circus.*

The Ritz, Piccadilly, W1, **t** (020) 7493 8181. Reserved tea sittings at 1.30, 3.30 and 5.30 daily. The fanciest, most indulgent tea in town, served in the sumptuous Edwardian Palm Court. You'll definitely need to book. ⊖ *Green Park.*

Knightsbridge/Kensington

The Orangery, Kensington Palace, **t** (020) 7376 0239. Elegant café with a delightful summer terrace. Try the spiced apple cake. ⊖ *High St Kensington.*

Pâtisserie Valerie, 215 Brompton Rd, SW3. Branch of the Soho French pâtisserie. ⊖ *Knightsbridge, South Kensington.*

Notting Hill/Holland Park

Julie's Wine Bar, 135–7 Portland Road, W11. Multilevel and multipurpose establishment with eccentric décor that is part café, part wine bar, part restaurant. The place is at its best for afternoon tea when it is neither too expensive nor pretentious. ⊖ *Holland Park.*

Lucky Seven, 127 Westbourne Park Road, W11, **t** (020) 7727 6771. Tom Conran's latest venture, an American diner-style place that has Notting Hill trendies and stars flocking to be seen.

City/East End

Brick Lane Beigel Bake, 159 Brick Lane, E1. Round-the-clock bagels. Always crowded, even at three in the morning. *Open 24hrs.* ⊖ *Liverpool Street.*

North London

Carmelli's, 128 Golders Green Rd, NW11. The best bagels in London, in the heart of Jewish Golders Green, though you can't eat them on the premises. ⊖ *Golder's Green*.

The Coffee Cup, 74 Hampstead High St, NW3. Dazzling menu including delicious raisin toast. Good for watching the beautiful people walk by. ⊖ *Hampstead*.

Louis Pâtisserie, 32 Heath St, Hampstead, NW3. Famous Hungarian tearoom which has been a haunt of middle-European emigrés for decades. Wonderful cheesecake and cream cakes brought on a tray for you to choose from. ⊖ *Hampstead*.

Pubs and Bars

The London pub – gaudily decorated with gleaming brass, ornate mirrors and stained glass – is still an essentially Victorian establishment, at least to look at. Although some recently built pubs have carried on this tradition, others have embraced modern décor and turned themselves into more upmarket establishments, serving food and becoming known as 'gastropubs'. Licensing hours, although now much extended, are still rigorously enforced; the landlord usually rings a bell when it is time to drink up, like a fussy schoolmaster. Gone, however, are the days when the pubs closed just when you were feeling thirsty; you can now drink without interruption between 11am and 11pm every day. Many pubs in outer London still close every afternoon, however.

Beer is still the drink of choice. British beer is admittedly an acquired taste – stronger, darker and flatter than lager and served lukewarm rather than stone cold – but easy to get hooked on in time. Unfortunately, London pubs are being swamped, like everywhere else, with generic multinational lagers – Carlsberg, Heineken, Budweiser and the rest. This is far from good news for traditional local breweries, who are fighting an energetic rearguard campaign with the help of CAMRA, the Campaign for Real Ale. CAMRA's influence has been greater in country pubs and the cities of northern England than it has in London, where wine and American-style cocktails are more popular than in the rest of the country; in the capital you will nevertheless find decent bitters like Fullers London Pride and Youngs, and creamy, full-bodied ales like Theakston's, Abbot and Ruddles.

The following list is necessarily short, since few London pubs really shine above the rest. Most of them make the list because of their location – overlooking the river, maybe, or in a quiet row of Georgian houses – or because of a particular historical association. You'll notice their eccentric names, which date from a time when most drinkers were illiterate and recognized pubs only by their signs. Hence the preponderance of coats of arms (King's Arms, Queen's Arms, Freemasons' Arms, etc.) and highly pictorial appellations (Wheatsheaf, Dog and Duck, Nag's Head, Slug and Lettuce, etc.). One thing to look out for is the name of the brewer that owns the pub. If the sign says 'Free House', that means the pub is independent and generally has a better range of beers. Quite a few London pubs are venues for theatre or concerts; where the entertainment is the main attraction, you will find them in the 'Entertainment' chapter rather than here.

Long gone, however, are the days when all that London had to offer was the traditional pub. The Atlantic Bar marked the beginning of a new wave of designer bars, where style can sometimes seem more important than content. These are the places where the wannabes want to be seen and rub shoulders with Madonna or the stars of *Big Brother*. They have led a revolution in the kind of drinks on offer. Ask for a Screaming Orgasm or a Sloe Comfortable Screw and you'll get a pitying look – these days it's all about *caipirinhas* and martinis made with fresh fruit and your choice of vodka from 17 different countries. But it's a fickle business and the crowd can soon move on. Bars come and go, but we list a few that have stayed the course.

Soho/Covent Garden/ Fitzrovia

Alphabet, 61–3 Beak St, W1. Busy arty bar, good for cocktails. Basement lounge bar with DJs playing chilled-out sounds. ⊖ *Leicester Square, Piccadilly Circus*.

Atlantic Bar & Grill, 20 Glasshouse St, W1. The rich and famous have moved on, but the

Atlantic retains much of its glamour – chandeliers, marble columns and fake leopardskin still have style. ⊖ *Piccadilly Circus.*

La Casa del Habano, 100 Wardour St, W1. A cigar bar – this little place has a gentleman's club atmosphere, with leather chairs, low tables, and cigars lining one wall from which you make your selection. Tapas served too. ⊖ *Oxford Circus.*

Dog and Duck, 8 Bateman St, W1. Soho's smallest pub. Customers spill out on to the pavement in the summer, and huddle round the log fire in the winter. ⊖ *Oxford Circus, Piccadilly Circus.*

The French House, 49 Dean St, W1. Meeting-place for De Gaulle's Free French during the Second World War; now adorned with pictures of famous Frenchmen. ⊖ *Leicester Square, Tottenham Court Road.*

Fitzroy Tavern, 16 Charlotte St, W1. Dylan Thomas's main drinking haunt; see the literary mementoes on the walls downstairs. ⊖ *Goodge Street.*

Lab, 12 Old Compton St, W1. Award-winning cocktail bar attracting a style-conscious but laid-back crowd, on two floors – the basement bar is more spacious. ⊖ *Piccadilly Circus, Leicester Square.*

Lamb and Flag, 33 Rose St, WC2. One of few wooden-framed buildings left in central London, dating back to the 17th century, with low ceilings and a lively atmosphere. The pub was for a long time nicknamed the Bucket of Blood because it staged bare-knuckled fights. Now you just have to knuckle your way past the crowds at the bar. ⊖ *Covent Garden, Leicester Square.*

Mash, 19–21 Great Portland St, W1. One of the most well-known style bars, Mash has fun retro décor across three floors, including a basement lounge bar. Try its impressive cocktails or a beer from the on-site micro-brewery. ⊖ *Oxford Circus.*

Holborn/Fleet Street

Cittie of York, 22 High Holborn, WC1. The longest bar in London. Cosy, separate booths, ideal for winter lunchtimes. ⊖ *Holborn.*

Ye Olde Cheshire Cheese, Wine Office Court, 145 Fleet St, EC4. Dr Johnson's old haunt, with atmospheric beams but disappointing food. ⊖ *Blackfriars.*

Punch Tavern, 99 Fleet St, EC4. Britain's satirical magazine *Punch* was created in this small London pub in 1841, and cartoons cover the walls; there is also Punch and Judy memorabilia, ornate décor and plush furnishings. ⊖ *Blackfriars.*

The Eagle, 159 Farringdon Rd, EC1. New wave pub with less emphasis on drinking and more on food, good atmosphere and general hanging out. Gets crowded. ⊖ *Farringdon.*

East End

Ten Bells, 84 Commercial St, E1. The original Jack the Ripper pub, with oodles of memorabilia. Marred by the tourist coaches who drop in during the evening but friendly enough at lunchtime. ⊖ *Aldgate East.*

Town of Ramsgate, 62 Wapping High St, E1. The pub where the merciless 17th-century Judge Jeffreys finally got his comeuppance. Friendly East End atmosphere, with a riverside garden and view of the post where smugglers and pirates used to be condemned to hang in chains for the duration of three high tides. ⊖ *Wapping.*

Southwark/Rotherhithe/ Greenwich

Anchor Inn, 1 Bankside, SE1. Superior food and excellent river views in this ancient Bankside institution where fugitives from the Clink prison next door used to hide in cubby holes. ⊖ *London Bridge.*

The Angel, 101 Bermondsey Wall East, Rotherhithe, SE16. The pub where Captain Cook had his last drink before sailing to Australia. Notable for its ship's wheel, smugglers' trapdoor and balcony overlooking Tower Bridge and Execution Dock. ⊖ *Rotherhithe.*

George Inn, George Inn Yard, off Borough High St, SE1. The last surviving coaching inn in London, the George goes back to the 16th century, although the present buildings date from shortly after the Great Fire. It is an elegant terrace of small interconnecting wooden bars looking out on a quiet courtyard, where during the summer you can see morris dancing and Shakespeare. ⊖ *London Bridge, Borough*.

The Mayflower, 117 Rotherhithe St, SE16. Inn from which the Pilgrim Fathers set out for America, and the only place in Britain where you can buy US postage stamps. There's a long jetty from which to admire the river. Avoid the indifferent food. ⊖ *Canada Water, Rotherhithe*.

Trafalgar Tavern, Park Row, Greenwich, SE10. Famous for its Whitebait Dinners, at which cabinet ministers and senior public figures would hold informal chats over seafood from the Thames. River pollution ended the tradition in 1914, though you can still eat rather indifferent whitebait from the pub menu. Nice views. **DLR** *Cutty Sark*.

Islington/Highgate/ Hampstead

The Bull, 13 North Hill, Highgate, N6. A large tree-lined garden and patio are the most attractive features of this former drinking haunt for painters such as Hogarth and Millais. ⊖ *Archway, Highgate*.

Canonbury Tavern, 21 Canonbury Place, Islington, N1. Delightful garden pub with an unusual court for playing *pétanque*. ⊖ *Highbury and Islington*.

The Flask, 77 Highgate West Hill, N6. Friendly pub dating back to the 17th century at the top of Highgate Hill, with a garden and good food. ⊖ *Archway, Highgate*.

Freemasons Arms, 32 Downshire Hill, Hampstead, NW3. Huge garden and terrace, fountain and pitch to play the ancient game of pell-mell. Gets crowded. ⊖ *Hampstead*.

The Holly Bush, 22 Holly Mount, Hampstead, NW3. Idyllic pub with five low rooms grouped around an old wooden bar. ⊖ *Hampstead*.

King's Head, 115 Upper St, Islington, N1. Popular Islington pub, where the money is still counted according to the old pre-decimal system of pounds, shillings and pence. The pub theatre is excellent and the atmosphere is very genial. ⊖ *Angel, Highbury and Islington*.

Spaniards Inn, Spaniards Road, Hampstead Heath, NW3. Reputed as a highwayman's pub patronized by Dick Turpin and a host of scurrilous scribblers including Byron and Shelley. Wonderful garden and, of course, the expanse of Hampstead Heath just across the road. ⊖ *Hampstead*.

West London

Anglesea Arms, 15 Selwood Terrace, SW7. Good beer in this local Chelsea haunt. ⊖ *Gloucester Road, South Kensington*.

The Cow, 89 Westbourne Park Rd, W2. Busy and fashionable Irish-style pub and restaurant specializing in seafood. ⊖ *Royal Oak, Westbourne Park*.

Dukes Head, 8 Lower Richmond Rd, Putney. Fine views along the river, though you have to put up with plastic cups if you sit outside. ⊖ *Putney Bridge*.

Havelock Tavern, 57 Masbro Road, W14. Popular pub serving high-quality pub food. ⊖ *Hammersmith, Olympia*.

King's Head and Eight Bells, 50 Cheyne Walk, SW3. Enjoy the antiques displays in this 16th-century building. There are views of the Battersea peace pagoda across the river. ⊖ *Sloane Square*.

Ladbroke Arms, 54 Ladbroke Rd, Notting Hill, W11. Very popular pub with flower-lined patio. Don't bring the car as there's a police station next door and they'll nick you for drink-driving. ⊖ *Ladbroke Grove*.

Queen's Head, Brook Green (West Kensington), W6. Old coaching inn overlooking a green, with a beer garden at the back. ⊖ *Hammersmith*.

The White Cross, Water Lane, Riverside, Richmond. A pub that turns into an island at high tide. Enjoy the real fires and good food. ⊖ *Richmond*.

London: Where to Stay

13

There is only one word to describe London's hotels and that word is *nightmare*. Accommodation, although improving slowly, is on the whole shamelessly expensive and shamelessly shoddy. You can pay up to £80 for an ordinary double room with no guarantee of quality or even basic hygiene; and you can pay up to twice that without even approaching the luxury category. There is no universal rating system, and the variously sponsored star or crown systems are so unreliable as to be virtually useless.

If at all possible, try to arrange accommodation from your home country. Flight and accommodation packages cover a wide price range and can work out to your advantage. Otherwise, try the numbers below. You can usually confirm your booking by giving a credit card number. The London Tourist Board also operates a telephone credit card booking service on **t** (09068) 663344, which is open Mon–Fri 9.30–6. If you turn up in London without a room in your name and you get nowhere ringing the numbers listed below, you can line up outside a tourist office and try your luck there. Try Victoria station forecourt, Liverpool St station, or the underground concourse at Heathrow Terminals 1–3. Commission for all booking services is around £5. If you are travelling out of high season (i.e. not the summer), try haggling a bit and you might negotiate your own discount. Weekend rates are common, and if you stay for a week you might get one night free. You can further save your pennies by declining breakfast (a possible £10 saver) or by asking for a room without a bath; in the cheaper establishments, the corridor bathrooms are usually better than the *en suite* kind. The following Internet address may also be useful: *www.smoothhound.co.uk/hotels*.

Most hotels are in the West End and around, Kensington, Chelsea, Earl's Court and west London. Try to avoid streets like Sussex Gardens in Bayswater, which is something of a hotel ghetto. Finding somewhere quiet can be a problem, especially in the busy summer months. The best places to stay are in districts like Notting Hill and Holland Park, or else by the river – don't forget the newer hotels in Docklands. Bloomsbury offers some excellent bargains as well as the proximity of the British Museum.

Hotel Prices

luxury £200 and over
expensive £120–200
moderate £80–120
inexpensive under £80

Prices given in the box above are for a normal double room for one night, but – again – find out about discounts before dismissing a place as too dear. Remember that space is tight, so book as far in advance as possible, whatever the category of accommodation.

Hotels

Mayfair

Brown's, Albemarle St, W1, **t** (020) 7493 6020, *www.brownshotel.com* (*luxury*). Old-fashioned establishment, with the air of a country house and impeccable, stiff service. Attractive if smallish rooms. ⊖ *Green Park*.

Claridges, Brook St, W1, **t** (020) 7629 8860, *www.claridges.co.uk* (*luxury*). Art Deco bedrooms, black and white marbled foyer and a touch of royal class at London's most celebrated smaller luxury hotel. ⊖ *Bond St*.

Connaught, 16 Carlos Place, W1, **t** (020) 7499 7070, *www.the-connaught.co.uk* (*luxury*). Attentive service commands a troupe of loyal devotees. An air of calm exclusivity presides. Book in writing well in advance. ⊖ *Green Park, Bond St*.

Dorchester, 53 Park Lane, W1, **t** (020) 7629 8888, *www.dorchesterhotel.com* (*luxury*). Triple-glazed rooms (to foil the Park Lane traffic) and views over Hyde Park, plus a dazzling choice of fine restaurants and acres of gold and marble. ⊖ *Hyde Park Corner*.

Metropolitan, 19 Old Park Lane, W1, **t** (020) 7447 1000, *www.metropolitan.co.uk* (*luxury*). Cool hip minimalism permeates; the young staff wear DKNY and each room has its own CD player, DVD, fax, Kiehl's toiletries and a minibar stocked with all the usual plus an instamatic camera. The ultra-fashionable Nobu restaurant and Met bar are located here. ⊖ *Hyde Park Corner, Green Park*.

Ritz, Piccadilly, W1, **t** (020) 7493 8181, *www.theritzlondon.com* (*luxury*). Marble galore, gorgeous rococo carpets, plus glorious views over Green Park if you pick your room right. *Ancien régime* luxury. ⊖ *Green Park.*

West End

Hazlitt's, 6 Frith St, W1, **t** (020) 7434 1771, *www.hazlittshotel.com* (*luxury*). Small Georgian rooms with some four posters and claw-footed iron baths in the former home of essayist William Hazlitt. Palm trees and classical busts adorn the premises. ⊖ *Tottenham Court Road, Leicester Square.*

One Aldwych, 1 Aldwych, WC2, **t** (020) 7300 1000, *www.onealdwych.co.uk* (*luxury*). Contemporary chic at its most sophisticated. Opened in 1998, this has become a bolthole for the stars. ⊖ *Holborn, Charing Cross.*

Sanderson, 50 Berners St, W1, **t** (020) 7300 1400 (*luxury*). The team behind St Martin's Lane – Ian Schrager and Philippe Starck – have given a 60s office block the minimalist makeover. Look out for weekend deals. ⊖ *Tottenham Court Road, Oxford Circus.*

Savoy, Strand, WC2, **t** (020) 7836 4343, *www.the-savoy.co.uk* (*luxury*). A sleeker, more business-like luxury here. The *fin de siècle* dining room is a favourite venue for afternoon tea. Restaurants and bars and discreet good service. ⊖ *Charing Cross.*

Bryanston Court, 56–60 Great Cumberland Place, W1, **t** (020) 7262 3141, *www.bryanstonhotel.com* (*expensive*). Business-like hotel with few frills but a pleasant atmosphere and an open fire in winter. ⊖ *Marble Arch.*

Durrants, George St, W1, **t** (020) 7935 8131, *www.durrantshotel.co.uk* (*expensive*). An 18th-century coaching inn with many old-fashioned touches including silver plate covers in the restaurant. Rooms are simple, a few on the small side. ⊖ *Marble Arch.*

Blandford, 80 Chiltern St, W1, **t** (020) 7486 3103, *www.capricornhotels.co.uk* (*moderate*). Simple bed-and-breakfast-style hotel, offering decent rooms and a good morning meal, in a quiet side street. ⊖ *Baker Street.*

Concorde, 50 Great Cumberland Place, W1, **t** (020) 7402 6169, *www.bryanstonhotel.com* (*moderate*). Plain and inexpensive but light and efficient, under the same management as the Bryanston Court. With self-catering options. ⊖ *Marble Arch.*

Edward Lear, 28–30 Seymour St, W1, **t** (020) 7402 5401, *www.edlear.com* (*moderate*). Named after the nonsense-verse writer. Small hotel with a homey feel. Informal but efficient. ⊖ *Marble Arch.*

Fielding, 4 Broad Ct, Bow St, WC2, **t** (020) 7836 8305, *www.the-fielding-hotel.co.uk* (*moderate*). A pretty good deal for central London, right opposite the Opera House. Smallish rooms and a tiny reception area. ⊖ *Covent Garden, Holborn.*

Georgian House Hotel, 87 Gloucester Place, W1, **t** (020) 7834 1438, *www.georgianhouse-hotel.co.uk* (*moderate*). Spacious rooms with personality; quietly high standards and good prices. Great discounts on 'student' rooms up 3 or 4 flights of stairs. ⊖ *Baker Street.*

Hart House Hotel, 51 Gloucester Place, W1, **t** (020) 7935 2288, *www.harthouse.co.uk* (*moderate*). Superbly run hotel in a Georgian mansion overlooking Portman Square. ⊖ *Marble Arch, Baker Street.*

Parkwood, 4 Stanhope Place, W2, **t** (020) 7402 2241, *www.parkwoodhotel.com* (*inexpensive*). Family-run hotel with attractive prices. Charming Georgian mansion near Hyde Park. ⊖ *Marble Arch.*

Bloomsbury/Holborn

Charlotte Street Hotel, 25 Charlotte St, W1, **t** (020) 7806 2000, *www.charlottestreethotel.com* (*luxury*). Chic little boutique hotel which has proved a big hit with the media crowd. Rooms are stylishly decorated with a charming mix of the traditional and the contemporary – CD and DVD players in all rooms. The staff are perhaps the nicest in all London. The restaurant is a treat. ⊖ *Tottenham Court Road, Goodge Street.*

Academy, 17–21 Gower St, WC1, **t** (020) 7631 4115, *www.theetoncollection.com* (*expensive*). Enjoy the atmosphere of a Georgian town-house. Cosy library and small paved garden. An antique charm. ⊖ *Goodge Street.*

Bonnington, 92 Southampton Row, WC1, **t** (020) 7242 2828, *www.bonnington.com* (*expensive*). Renovated Edwardian establishment with bland furniture but warm management. Plenty of beds, relatively easy to book. ⊖ *Holborn.*

myhotel Bloomsbury, 11–13 Bayley St, WC1, **t** (020) 7667 6000, *www.myhotels.co.uk* (*expensive*). Designed by the Conran partnership, this is a cool, clean hotel where you are sent a questionnaire in advance asking for your pillow (feather or foam) and music (country or pop) preferences. Lots of Aveda goodies in the bathroom. Health studio, Yo Sushi bar, smart restaurant, champagne bar. ⊖ *Goodge Street, Tottenham Court Road.*

Russell, Russell Square, WC1, **t** (020) 7837 6470 (*expensive*). Extravagant Gothic Revival architecture and an atmosphere to match. A renovated ballroom. Friendly service. ⊖ *Russell Square.*

Crescent, 49–50 Cartwright Gdns, WC1, **t** (020) 7387 1515, *www.crescenthoteloflondon.com* (*moderate*). Use of the garden and tennis courts a big plus here, as is family atmosphere. Old-fashioned and good value. ⊖ *King's Cross, Euston.*

Harlingford, 61–3 Cartwright Gardens, WC1, **t** (020) 7387 1551 (*moderate*). Floral-print wallpaper adorns the simple rooms. Access to tennis courts possible. ⊖ *Euston.*

Tavistock, Tavistock Square, WC1, **t** (020) 7278 7871, *www.imperialhotels.co.uk* (*moderate*). Large rooms, a good location, Art Deco finishes but impersonal atmosphere and tour-group clientele. Views over Tavistock Square Garden a plus. ⊖ *Euston, Russell Sq.*

Arran House, 77–9 Gower St, WC1, **t** (020) 7636 2186, *www.london-hotel.co.uk* (*inexpensive*). Wonky floors and a lovely rose garden add charm to this otherwise no-frills guest house. In-house laundry and use of kitchen including microwave. ⊖ *Goodge Street.*

Avalon, 46–7 Cartwright Gardens, WC1, **t** (020) 7387 2366, *www.avalonhotel.co.uk* (*inexpensive*). No-frills cheapie in a bright, old-fashioned Georgian house in a beautiful crescent packed with similar establishments. Drying and ironing facilities. ⊖ *Euston.*

Celtic, 61–3 Guildford St, WC1, **t** (020) 6737 9258 (*inexpensive*). Simple, unexciting family-run bed and breakfast. No private bathrooms. Street rooms can be noisy. ⊖ *Russell Square.*

Elmwood, 19 Argyle Square, WC1, **t** (020) 7837 9361 (*inexpensive*). Basic, cheap, in a lovely square near the British Library. ⊖ *King's Cross.*

St Margaret's, 26 Bedford Place, WC1, **t** (020) 7636 4277 (*inexpensive*). Clean, fresh hotel with a plant-filled dining room and a wide variety of large, well-proportioned rooms. ⊖ *Russell Square, Holborn.*

Mabledon Court, 10–11 Mabledon Place, WC1, **t** (020) 7388 3866 (*inexpensive*). Clean but unexciting hotel near King's Cross with reasonable rates. ⊖ *King's Cross.*

Bayswater/Notting Hill

Byron, 36–8 Queensborough Terrace, W2, **t** (020) 7243 0987, *www.capricornhotels.co.uk* (*luxury*). Young, friendly atmosphere in this smart hotel full of sunshine and flowers. ⊖ *Queensway.*

Hempel, 31–5 Craven Hill Gardens, W2, **t** (020) 7298 9000, *www.the-hempel.co.uk* (*luxury*). Luxury hotel designed by Anoushka Hempel. Takes minimalism to its logical, most exotic extreme. Pure white blank foyer. ⊖ *Lancaster Gate, Queensway, Bayswater.*

Pembridge Court, 34 Pembridge Gardens, W2, **t** (020) 7229 9977, *www.pemct.co.uk* (*expensive*). Elegant Victorian townhouse, fastidiously deconstructed; but flourishing vegetation and a collection of Victoriana plus cat. Next to Portobello market. ⊖ *Notting Hill Gate.*

Portobello, 22 Stanley Gardens, W11, **t** (020) 7727 2777, *www.portobello-hotel.co.uk* (*expensive*). Victorian Gothic furniture conceals all mod cons including a health club. Idiosyncratic rooms. ⊖ *Holland Park.*

Ashley, 15–17 Norfolk Square, W2, **t** (020) 7723 9966/3375, *www.ashleyhotels.com* (*moderate*). Maniacally clean, quiet hotel, ideal for people looking for peace. Party animals stay away. ⊖ *Paddington.*

Delmere, 128 Sussex Gardens, W2, **t** (020) 7706 3344, *www.delmerehotels.com* (*moderate*). Smart building on an otherwise miserable street of hotels. Some tiny rooms; others are spacious and comfortable. ⊖ *Paddington.*

Gate, 6 Portobello Rd, W11, **t** (020) 7221 0707, *www.hydeparkinn.com/gatehotel* (*moderate*). Well-appointed, flower-bedecked no-nonsense hotel in plum location among the antique shops of Portobello Rd. ⊖ *Notting Hill Gate.*

Kensington Gardens, 9 Kensington Gardens Square, W2, **t** (020) 7221 7790, *www.kensingtongardenshotel.co.uk* (*moderate*). Attractive rooms, good bath facilities and a light, pleasant breakfast room make this a good mid-range choice. ⊖ *Queensway*.

Mornington, 12 Lancaster Gate, W2, **t** (020) 7262 7361, *www.mornington.com* (*moderate*). Scandinavian-run hotel with serious but professional staff. Nice library. Next to the Football Association. ⊖ *Queensway*.

Abbey House, 11 Vicarage Gate, W8, **t** (020) 7727 2594, *www.abbeyhousekensington.com* (*inexpensive*). Simple, spacious rooms in this delightful Victorian town house in a quiet square. Preserves many original features. ⊖ *High Street Kensington, Notting Hill Gate*.

Border, 14 Norfolk Square, W2, **t** (020) 7723 2968 (*inexpensive*). No-nonsense hotel with simple, cheap facilities, in a square full of other similar hotels. ⊖ *Paddington*.

Garden Court, 30–31 Kensington Gardens Square, W2, **t** (020) 7229 2553, *www.gardencourthotel.co.uk* (*inexpensive*). Simple bed and breakfast with nice views over the square at the front and gardens at the back. Well located. ⊖ *Queensway, Bayswater*.

Manor Court, 7 Clanricarde Gardens, W2, **t** (020) 7727 5407 (*inexpensive*). Simple, friendly B&B offering basic accommodation close to Kensington Palace. There are seven family rooms which are remarkably good value. ⊖ *Notting Hill Gate*.

Ravna Gora, 29 Holland Park Avenue, W11, **t** (020) 7727 7725, *www.ravnagorahotel.co.uk* (*inexpensive*). Palatial Holland Park mansion turned slightly dilapidated bed and breakfast, with a talkative Serbian owner. ⊖ *Holland Park*.

South Kensington

Aster House, 3 Sumner Place, SW7, **t** (020) 7581 5888, *www.asterhouse.com* (*expensive*). Silk-wall décor and lots of flowers all over this award-winning hotel. Light breakfast alternatives. ⊖ *South Kensington*.

Blakes, 33 Roland Gardens, SW7, **t** (020) 7370 6701, *www.blakeshotels.com* (*expensive*). Richly decorated hotel with four-poster beds and antique lacquered chests. Birdcages and carved giraffes to boot. ⊖ *South Kensington*.

Claverly, 13–14 Beaufort Gardens, SW3, **t** (020) 7589 8541 (*expensive*). Lovingly detailed and award-winning hotel, with attractive rooms and an imaginative breakfast. ⊖ *Knightsbridge*.

Five Sumner Place, 5 Sumner Place, SW7, **t** (020) 7584 7586, *www.sumnerplace.com* (*expensive*). The feel of a country home in the heart of London, with a stunning conservatory-style breakfast room. Smart but unpretentious. Quiet. ⊖ *South Kensington*.

The Gore, 190 Queen's Gate, SW7, **t** (020) 7584 6601, *www.gorehotel.co.uk* (*expensive*). Gothic and Edwardian décor, plus hundreds of old prints, make this an atmospheric stopover. ⊖ *Gloucester Road*.

Number Sixteen, 16 Sumner Place, SW7, **t** (020) 7589 5232, *www.firmdale.com* (*expensive*). Charming Victorian house with a garden and fountains, plus large reception areas and rooms with balconies. Posh B&B. ⊖ *South Kensington*.

Hotel 167, 167 Old Brompton Rd, SW5, **t** (020) 7373 0672, *www.hotel167.com* (*moderate*). Attractive Victorian corner house with young clientele. ⊖ *South Kensington*.

Knightsbridge

Carlton Tower, 2 Cadogan Place, SW1, **t** (020) 7235 1234 (*luxury*). De luxe mod cons, marble bathrooms, a stone's throw from Harrods, with a well-equipped health club, swimming pool and spacious rooms. ⊖ *Knightsbridge*.

Diplomat, 2 Chesham St, SW1, **t** (020) 7235 1544 (*expensive*). Elegant rooms and suites up and down a glass-domed stairwell. Copious buffet breakfast and just a short walk to Beauchamp Place and Harrods. ⊖ *Sloane Square, Knightsbridge*.

Victoria/Pimlico

Tophams Belgravia, 28 Ebury St, SW1, **t** (020) 7730 8147 (*expensive*). Labyrinthine corridors connect the beautifully laid out rooms in this long-established neighbourhood favourite. ⊖ *Victoria, Sloane Square*.

Windermere Hotel, 142–4 Warwick Way, SW1, **t** (020) 7834 5163, *www.windermere-hotel.co.uk* (*moderate*). Delightful little hotel with a small restaurant and bar. Quiet and unassuming. ⊖ *Victoria, Sloane Square.*

Collin House, 104 Ebury St, SW1, **t** (020) 7730 8031 (*inexpensive*). Clean, hospitable bed and breakfast behind Victoria station. Homey but fresh. ⊖ *Victoria, Sloane Square.*

Enrico, 77–9 Warwick Way, SW1, **t** (020) 7834 9538 (*inexpensive*). Basic but comfortable hotel in Pimlico. ⊖ *Victoria, Pimlico.*

Huttons Hotel, 53–7 Belgrave Rd, SW1, **t** (020) 7834 3726, *www.huttons-hotel.co.uk* (*inexpensive*). Dapper, family-run B&B which has recently been renovated. ⊖ *Victoria, Pimlico.*

Oak House, 29 Hugh St, SW1, **t** (020) 7828 6792 (*inexpensive*). Small rooms with basic catering facilities. Breakfast is in your room. No advance booking, so roll up early. ⊖ *Victoria.*

Earl's Court/Fulham

Hogarth, 35–7 Hogarth Rd, SW5, **t** (020) 7370 6831, *www.thehogarthhotel.co.uk* (*expensive*). Part of Best Western chain, a hotel with full amenities near Earl's Court Exhibition Centre. Busy but friendly. ⊖ *Earl's Court.*

Beaver, 57–9 Philbeach Gardens, SW5, **t** (020) 7373 4553, *www.beaverhotel.co.uk* (*moderate*). Simple, attractive establishment, pool table and cheap car parking. Plush lounge with polished wooden floors. Lovely street. ⊖ *Earl's Court.*

Elsewhere

Dorset Square, 39–40 Dorset Square NW1, **t** (020) 7723 7874 (*luxury*). Restored Regency building between Madame Tussaud's and Regent's Park with beautiful furniture and a strong cricket theme because of the nearby Lord's ground. ⊖ *Baker Street, Marylebone.*

Thistle Tower, St Katharine's Way E1, **t** 0870 333 9106, *www.thistlehotels.com* (*expensive*). Not a great beauty, but ideally placed next to the Tower overlooking the river. Ultra-modern fittings and every conceivable comfort. ⊖ *Tower Hill.*

La Gaffe, 107 Heath St, Hampstead NW3, **t** (020) 7435 4941, *www.lagaffe.co.uk* (*moderate*). Charming bed and breakfast above an Italian restaurant in a former shepherd's cottage. Bedrooms reached via a precipitous stairway. ⊖ *Hampstead.*

London County Hall Travel Inn, Belvedere Rd, SE1, **t** 0870 238 3300/**t** (020) 7902 1619, *www.travelinn.co.uk* (*moderate*). A chain hotel in a prime location – very reasonably priced rooms close to the river. Sadly the views are reserved for the expensive Mariott hotel round the corner. An excellent choice for families. ⊖ *Waterloo, Westminster.*

Swiss Cottage, 4 Adamson Rd NW3, **t** (020) 7722 2281 (*moderate*). Olde worlde atmosphere with antiques, reproduction furniture and even a grand piano. Good location near Hampstead and Camden. ⊖ *Swiss Cottage.*

Hampstead Village Guesthouse, 2 Kemplay Rd NW3, **t** (020) 7435 8679, *www.hampsteadguesthouse.com* (*inexpensive*). Family household just a step away from Hampstead Heath. Lots of books and pot plants, plus fridges in your rooms. ⊖ *Hampstead.*

Camden Lock Hotel, 89 Chalk Farm Rd, NW1, **t** (020) 7267 3912, *www.camdenlockhotel.co.uk*. (*inexpensive*). Small, modern hotel with very helpful and friendly staff. It's geared towards business travellers but offers excellent weekend deals. Handy for Camden Market. ⊖ *Chalk Farm.*

Bed and Breakfast

The bed and breakfast is a British (and Irish) tourist institution: you get to stay in someone's house, enjoy their company and eat a slap-up breakfast for a fraction of the cost of a hotel. Go through an agency:

Bulldog Club, 14 Dewhurst Road, W14, **t** (020) 7371 3202, *www.bulldogclub.com* (*moderate*). Will fix you up in palatial surroundings in the city or the country – at a price, of course.

Host and Guest Service, 103 Dawes Rd, SW6, **t** (020) 7385 9922, *www.host-guest.co.uk* (*inexpensive*). Agency with 3,000 homes on its books all over London. £18 per person.

Uptown Reservations, 41 Paradise Walk, SW3, **t** (020) 7351 3445,www.*uptownres.co.uk* (*moderate*). Offers homes in Knightsbridge, Chelsea and similar neighbourhoods.

Worldwide Bed and Breakfast Association, PO Box 2070, London W12 8QW, **t** (020) 8742 9123, *www. bestbandb.co.uk* (*inexpensive*). Offers rooms in upmarket private homes for £26–85.

London: Entertainment and Nightlife

14

The indispensable guide to the week's events is the listings magazine *Time Out*.

If you venture far afield, or if you have a long way to get home, you'll need to think carefully about transport. The Underground system dries up soon after midnight, and taxis can be hard to find even in central London,and charge 20% more than in the daytime. Night buses head to and from Trafalgar Square. If these aren't convenient, you may have to resort to a minicab. Don't let yourself be cajoled into taking a minicab off the street; not only is it illegal for drivers to solicit business this way, it may not be safe either. *See* pp.9–10.

Theatre

Foreign visitors will find the cast lists of plays showing in London disconcertingly familiar: it looks as though the villains and eccentrics of Hollywood have mounted a takeover. In fact, the London stage is where actors like Anthony Hopkins, Ralph Fiennes and Alan Rickman come home to roost when they are not making megabucks in the movies. England boasts no equivalent of Pirandello or Brecht – but has nevertheless turned out compelling and challenging dramas of a quality not seen in any other European city.

What to See and Where to Go

The major commercial theatre companies are concentrated in the West End, just as the main New York stages are grouped together on Broadway. Two distinct traditions are forever jostling for attention: the straight play and the musical. Shakespeare is of course a perennial favourite, along with Chekhov, Shaw and Noel Coward, but in pure terms of seat numbers the darling of the British musical, Andrew Lloyd Webber, is way ahead in the popularity ratings.

Established playwrights such as Tom Stoppard, David Hare, Harold Pinter and David Mamet are increasingly turning to the off-West End theatre companies to stage their work. The most consistent and reliable of these is the three-stage **Royal National Theatre** on the South Bank, which puts on superb versions of the classics as well as showcasing high-quality new writing. The RNT is followed closely by the **Royal Shakespeare Company**, based at venues around London, which concentrates mainly on the Bard and his contemporaries. The **Royal Court**, Sloane Square and **Lyric Hammersmith** are excellent venues for new work, while experimental shows and reworkings of established plays are the hallmark of the **Almeida** in Islington, the **Hampstead Theatre**, and the **Donmar Warehouse** in Covent Garden.

The **fringe** is always active, and occasionally you can find first-rate shows in draughty halls or upstairs rooms in pubs. If you are in London during the summer, don't forget about open-air venues like the **Globe Theatre**, **Regent's Park**, **Holland Park** and the garden of the **Royal Observatory** in Greenwich, where you can enjoy Shakespeare (particularly *A Midsummer Night's Dream*) and lively modern comedies.

A Few Addresses

There's not a lot of point recommending individual theatres, as the quality of each production cannot be guaranteed, but the following addresses – most outside the West End – should give you some pointers. The telephone numbers are for the box office.

Royal National Theatre, South Bank, **t** (020) 7452 3400, *www.nationaltheatre.org*. The National has three stages – the large amphitheatre of the Olivier, the conventional proscenium at the Lyttelton and the smaller, cosier Cottesloe. An evening here not only guarantees top-notch theatre: you can enjoy foyer concerts, browse through the bookshops and linger in the cafés with views out over the Thames. ⊖ *Waterloo*.

Barbican Arts Centre, Silk St, Barbican, **t** (020) 7638 4141, *www.barbican.org.uk*. One of Europe's largest arts centres, the Barbican presents a year-round programme of art, music, film and theatre. Although the Royal Shakespeare Company no longer uses the Barbican as its London home, it continues to perform here as well as at other London venues. Many of its productions are transfers from its base in Stratford-upon-Avon. The Barbican is also the venue for BITE, an annual festival of international theatre. ⊖ *Barbican, Moorgate*.

Royal Court, Sloane Square, **t** (020) 7565 5000. The major venue for experimental or counter-cultural writing. The Theatre

Practical Details

Most performances start at 7.30 or 8pm, with matinées usually scheduled on Wednesdays and Saturdays. By far the best way to book is through the theatre itself. At most places you can pay by credit card over the phone, then pick up the tickets just before the curtain goes up. Booking details and seating plans can be found on *www.londontheatre.co.uk*. **Ticket agents** charge stinging commissions, usually 22 per cent, although they can be a necessary evil to get into the big musicals (try Ticketmaster on **t** (020) 7344 4444, *www.ticketmaster.co.uk*, or First Call on **t** (020) 7420 0000). The Royal National Theatre offers a limited number of cheap tickets from 10am on the day of the performance, and the Society of London Theatre has a **ticket booth** in Leicester Square (*open 2.30–6.30pm, or noon–6pm on matinée days*) with half-price tickets for West End shows that night. If all else fails, you can try for **returns** in the hour before the performance starts; **students** can get a hefty discount this way.

Upstairs on the first floor is one of the better fringe venues. ⊖ *Sloane Square*.

Old Vic, Waterloo Rd, **t** 0870 060 6628, *www.oldvictheatre.com*. The former home of the National Theatre now has Hollywood actor Kevin Spacey in charge, directing and acting. ⊖ *Waterloo*.

Young Vic, 66 The Cut, **t** (020) 7928 6363, *www.youngvic.org*. Near to the Old Vic, the studio theatre presents old and new plays, sometimes quite innovative, aimed mainly at younger audiences. ⊖ *Waterloo*.

Wyndham's, Charing Cross Rd, **t** 0870 060 6633, *www.theambassadors.com*. One of the more reliable West End addresses, with serious productions. ⊖ *Leicester Square*.

Theatre Royal Haymarket, Haymarket, **t** 0870 901 3356, *www.trh.co.uk*. Unadventurous choice of plays, but impeccable production and acting standards in this early 19th-century theatre built by John Nash. Maggie Smith, Vanessa Redgrave and Ian McKellen are regulars. ⊖ *Piccadilly Circus*.

Donmar Warehouse, 41 Earlham St, Covent Garden, **t** (020) 7240 4882, *www.donmarwarehouse.com*. Excellent venue where many distinguished young directors have cut their teeth. ⊖ *Covent Garden*.

Lyric Hammersmith, King St, **t** 08700 500 511, *www.lyric.co.uk*. Hosts many regional and foreign theatre companies. Home also to the experimental Studio. ⊖ *Hammersmith*.

Hampstead Theatre, Eton Avenue, **t** (020) 7449 4200, *www.hampsteadtheatre.co.uk*. Actors and audiences often mingle in the bar after the show at this friendly neighbourhood theatre. ⊖ *Swiss Cottage*.

Theatre Royal Stratford East, Gerry Raffles Square, Stratford, **t** (020) 8534 0310, *www.stratfordeast.com*. High-quality drama in a crumbling Victorian palace in the midst of grey tower blocks. Worth the long trip out east. **DLR** *Stratford*.

King's Head, 115 Upper St, Islington, **t** (020) 7226 1916. Eccentric pub with popular theatrical tradition in a charming back room. Serves a 3-course dinner in the theatre just before the curtain rises. ⊖ *Angel*.

Almeida, Almeida St, Islington, **t** (020) 7359 4404, *www.almeida.co.uk*. A fringe theatre with a formidable reputation. Stages different productions every six or seven weeks. ⊖ *Angel, Highbury and Islington*.

The Gate, 11 Pembridge Road, Notting Hill, **t** (020) 7229 5387, *www.gatetheatre.co. uk*. Excellent pub theatre with new plays as well as ambitious reworkings of the classics. ⊖ *Notting Hill Gate*.

BAC (Battersea Arts Centre), 176 Lavender Hill, **t** (020) 7223 6557, *www.bac.org.uk*. Lively theatre venue south of the river. ⇌ *Clapham Junction*.

Shakespeare's Globe, 21 New Globe Walk, **t** (020) 7401 9919. Opened for business in 1997, this lovingly reconstructed version of Shakespeare's original London theatre puts on three or four Elizabethan productions each year, most of them by the Bard, in a season that lasts from May until September. (*See* p.32 for more on the theatre itself.) ⊖ *Southwark, London Bridge*.

Regent's Park Open Air Theatre, Inner Circle, Regent's Park, **t** 0870 601 811, *www.openairtheatre.org.uk*. Open-air theatre from May to September. Bring a blanket and umbrella. ⊖ *Baker Street, Regent's Park*.

Holland Park Theatre, Holland Park, **t** 0845 230 9769, *www.operahollandpark.com*. Open-air only from June to August, but puts on all manner of productions, mostly operas. *See* p.178. ⊖ *High Street Kensington*.

Opera and Classical Music

London has classical music coming out of its ears: two major opera companies, five world-class orchestras, lunchtime concerts, summer festival concerts, open-air concerts. London's weakness is undoubtedly in contemporary and avant-garde music; programmers tend to play very safe.

Royal Opera House, Covent Garden, **t** (020) 7304 4000, *www.royalopera.org*. Britain's leading opera venue is right up there with the Met, the Staatsoper and La Scala, but the top prices are almost as high as the top C in the Queen of the Night's bravura aria from Mozart's *Magic Flute*. Since restoration was completed in 1999, however, the building is a joy to behold. ⊖ *Covent Garden*.

London Coliseum, St Martin's Lane, **t** (020) 7632 8300, *www.eno.org*. Home to the English National Opera, which performs in English to high musical standards and with infectious enthusiasm. Much cheaper (*£3–66*). *See* p.69. ⊖ *Charing Cross*.

South Bank Centre, South Bank, Belvedere Rd, **t** (020) 7921 0600, *www.sbc.org.uk*. Three first-rate concert halls under the same roof: the Royal Festival Hall; the Queen Elizabeth Hall, which is smaller; and the Purcell Room, for chamber music and recitals. *See* p.86. ⊖ *Waterloo*.

Barbican Centre, Silk St, **t** (020) 7638 4141, *www.barbican.org.uk*. Home to the London Symphony Orchestra and English Chamber Orchestra. Excellent acoustics make up for the out-of-the-way venue. *See* p.61. ⊖ *Barbican, Moorgate*.

Royal Albert Hall, Kensington Gore, **t** (020) 7589 8212, *www.royalalberthall.com*. Hosts the Promenade concerts, or Proms, which run every year from July until early September. The Proms are an eclectic platform for music old and new. The Last Night of the Proms is a raucous affair at which the all-English orchestra plays all-English music, and the all-English audience sings along to the national anthem and 'Rule Britannia'. It's such a popular event that you can't even apply for a ticket unless you have also booked for six other concerts in the Proms season (but it *is* relayed onto a big screen in Hyde Park). *See* p.26. ⊖ *South Kensington*.

Wigmore Hall, 36 Wigmore St, **t** (020) 7935 2141, *www.wigmore-hall.org.uk*. An intimate venue with excellent acoustics that attracts solo performers. The tickets are very cheap – between £6 and *£20* – and sell out very fast. ⊖ *Bond Street, Oxford Circus*.

Sadler's Wells, Rosebery Ave, **t** (020) 7863 8000, *www.sadlers-wells.com*. Venue for all kinds of music, as well as dance and theatre; productions are usually of a high standard. ⊖ *Angel*.

St John's Smith Square, Smith Square, Westminster, **t** (020) 7222 1061, *www.sjss.org.uk*. This fine Baroque church is one of the best lunchtime concert spots in town. Other good church venues, whether for lunchtime or evening concerts, include **St James Piccadilly** (usually on Mon, Wed, Fri at 1pm); **St Martin-in-the-Fields** in Trafalgar Square (which boasts its own excellent chamber orchestra); **St Bride's Fleet St**; **St Michael's Cornhill** (organ recitals); **St Anne and St Agnes**, Gresham St; **St Giles Cripplegate**, Silk St; **St Sepulchre-without-Newgate** (mainly piano recitals on Fridays); the magnificently restored **St Helen's Bishopsgate**; and **St John's Waterloo**.

Kenwood House, Hampstead Lane, tickets on **t** 0870 333 6206. From June to September, enjoy idyllic outdoor concerts beside a lake at the top of Hampstead Heath. Highly recommended. Other open-air summer venues include Hampton Court and Marble Hill House in Twickenham (*August weekends only*). Information on concerts at Kenwood and Marble Hill can be found at *www.picnicconcerts.com*. *See* p.112. ⊖ *Hampstead, then bus 210*.

Holland Park Theatre, Holland Park, **t** (020) 7937 5464, *www.operahollandpark.com*. Open-air season, from June to August, with all manner of productions including opera and dance. ⊖ *Holland Park*.

Dance

London puts on everything from classical ballet to performance art. Covent Garden (*see above*) is home to the highly accomplished Royal Ballet, which is cheaper and much less snooty than the Royal Opera in the same building. For around £10 you can sit in on one of the Royal Ballet's eight yearly practice sessions in their newly built Clore Studio – be aware that these tickets are extremely popular, so you'll have to race to claim a seat. The English National Ballet perform at the **London Coliseum** during the Christmas season, taking their productions elsewhere throughout the rest of the year (call **t** (020) 7581 1245 or visit *www.ballet.org.uk* for further information). **Sadler's Wells** (*see* opposite) used to have its own ballet company, but it decamped to Birmingham in 1990; the theatre nevertheless puts on an eclectic dance programme that has recently included both the mime artist Lindsay Kemp and the National Ballet of Cambodia. Two other addresses worth knowing about are the **ICA** on the Mall (**t** (020) 7930 3647, *www.ica.org.uk*), arguably the most avant-garde address in town; and **The Place Theatre** (17 Duke's Rd, Bloomsbury, **t** (020) 7387 0031, *www.theplace.org.uk*), in The Place building, which is also home to the London Contemporary Dance School. Every autumn, from mid-October to early December, London stages a festival called **Dance Umbrella**. It's also worth checking out the listings for the Royal Festival Hall and the Barbican.

Jazz

Jazz came to London in the 1950s, largely thanks to the effort of the late Ronnie Scott and his excellent club in Soho, and it has gone from strength to strength ever since. Check *Time Out* for jazz concerts in pubs and foyers of the larger theatres. Note that many clubs charge a (usually nominal) membership fee. You may find it hard to book for the more popular shows at Ronnie Scott's, for example, if you are not already a member.

Ronnie Scott's, 47 Frith St, W1, **t** (020) 7439 0747, *www.ronniescotts.co.uk* (*closed Sun*). The prime jazz venue in town, with a steady flow of big names and a suitably low-key, laid-back atmosphere. Book if you have time, and get there early (around 9pm) to ensure a decent seat. Admission is £15 Mon–Thurs, £25 Fri–Sat, or more for a very big name band. 8.30pm–3am. ⊖ *Leicester Square*.

100 Club, 100 Oxford St, W1, **t** (020) 7636 0933. Lively basement venue with an eclectic mix of trad and modern jazz, as well as blues, swing and rockabilly. The Sex Pistols gave one of their first performances here in the mid-1970s. ⊖ *Tottenham Court Road*.

606 Club, 90 Lots Rd, Fulham, **t** (020) 7352 5953. Seven-nights-a-week basement club featuring many local musicians, with emphasis on contemporary jazz. Late-night restaurant licence and good modern food, (dinner obligatory for non-members). £6–8, 8.30pm–2am. ⊖ *Fulham Broadway*.

Jazz After Dark, 9 Greek St, Soho, **t** (020) 7734 0545. Jazz, Latin jazz and salsa, with a cocktail bar and restaurant (licensed to 2am, 3am at weekends). Mon–Thurs £3–4, Fri and Sat £8–10. Booking essential at weekends. ⊖ *Tottenham Court Road*.

Jazz Café, 5 Parkway, Camden, t (020) 7344 0044. Typical of the new-style jazz club, a slick venue with standing room and plush dinner-table seating (food optional). The music is first-rate. ⊖ *Camden Town*.

Pizza Express, 10 Dean St, Soho, **t** (020) 7439 8722. Be-bop to accompany your pizza; an unlikely setting, but a congenial one which boasts its own resident band as well as many prestigious visitors. 7.45pm–12am, £8–20. ⊖ *Tottenham Court Road*. Branch at **Pizza on the Park**, 11 Knightsbridge, off Hyde Park Corner, **t** (020) 7235 5273. £10–20.

Rock, Pop and World Music

With Wembley Stadium out of the picture until at least 2006 while it undergoes a multi-million-pound rejuvenation, London is turning to its smaller, more audience-friendly venues for its regular fixes of mainstream rock and pop, such as the Carling Apollo, Forum and Brixton Academy. The city also has a wide selection of venues dedicated to more esoteric and international music, such as the Africa Centre in Covent Garden. Posters and press adverts will tell you how to buy tickets. You'll probably have to go through a ticket agency (*see* box, p.177) for the bigger acts, otherwise go direct.

Wembley Arena, Empire Way, Wembley, **t** 0870 060 0870. The indoor neighbour of the stadium, with a seating capacity of 12,500. ⊖ *Wembley Park.*

Royal Albert Hall, Kensington Gore, **t** (020) 7589 8212, *www.royalalberthall.com*. The iffy acoustics and somewhat grandiose Victorian architecture are more than compensated for by intelligent programming – folk-rock and R'n'B by the likes of Bonnie Raitt, Eric Clapton, etc. ⊖ *South Kensington.*

Brixton Academy, 211 Stockwell Rd, Brixton, **t** 0905 020 3999. Much more like it. Raw, raucous music in a crumbling Art Deco setting. Sweaty but exhilarating. ⊖ *Brixton.*

Forum, 9–17 Highgate Rd, Kentish Town, **t** (020) 7344 0044. Formerly known as the Town and Country Club and arguably the best rock venue in town; an excellent blend of high-quality facilities and first-rate bands. ⊖ *Kentish Town.*

Shepherd's Bush Empire, Shepherd's Bush Green, **t** 0905 020 3999. Similar-sized venue to the Forum, with seats upstairs. Attracts big names; great atmosphere. ⊖ *Shepherd's Bush.*

Africa Centre, 38 King St, Covent Garden, **t** (020) 7836 1973. Groovy atmosphere and infectious African music most Friday nights, with occasional gigs during the week. Cheap and great fun. ⊖ *Covent Garden.*

Carling Apollo Hammersmith, Queen Caroline St, Hammersmith, **t** 0870 606 3400. A big-name venue, recently relaunched as a 5,000-capacity, all-standing venue. ⊖ *Hammersmith.*

London Arena, Limeharbour, Isle of Dogs, **t** (020) 7538 1212, *www.londonarena.co.uk*. Still gleaming from its multi-million pound refurbishment, this enormous venue hosts chart-topper concerts along with numerous other events, including ice-shows and high-profile boxing matches. **DLR** *Crossharbour.*

Comedy Clubs

Comedy has been all the rage in London since the early 1980s, and clubs have been sprouting with amazing speed all over town. Established performers mingle easily with new talent in more than 20 major venues. Sit in the front rows at your peril, as you are likely to be roped into the act and insulted or humiliated. Some of the humour is a bit parochial, revolving around British adverts and TV, but many acts are truly inspired. Usually several artists will contribute to a single evening. Look out for hilarious Boothby Graffoe, Al Murray's Pub Landlord and the political radical Mark Thomas; but going to a good club to see acts you've never heard of can be just as rewarding as following the big names.

Check out *www.chortle.co.uk*.

Comedy Store, 1a Oxendon St, **t** 0800 060 0800, *www.thecomedystore.co.uk*. Improv on Wed and Sun by the Comedy Store Players, otherwise stand-up. The most famous comedy club of them all has got a bit slick for its own good and the hefty admission fee (£13–15) reflects that. The standard remains very high, however. ⊖ *Piccadilly Circus, Leicester Square.*

Bound and Gagged, Tufnell Park Tavern, 162 Tufnell Park Road, **t** (020) 8450 4100, *www.bound andgaggedcomedy.com*. Above-pub club with unusual acts. ⊖ *Tufnell Park.*

Jongleurs: 49 Lavender Gardens, Battersea, ⇌ *Clapham Junction*; Bow Wharf, 221 Grove Rd, ⊖ *Mile End*; Camden Lock, Dingwalls Bldg, Middle Yard, Chalk Farm Rd, ⊖ *Camden Town*. All **t** 0870 787 0707, *www.jongleurs.com*. Top acts on Fri/Sat nights. Always popular, so book in advance.

Meccano Club, The Dove Regent, 65 Graham Street, Islington, N1, **t** (020) 7813 4478. This trendy bar is one of the great London clubs, always worth a visit. ⊖ *Angel.*

Hackney Empire, 291 Mare St, Hackney, **t** (020) 8510 4500, *www.hackneyempire.co.uk*. Comedy with a political edge in a newly restored and much-loved Victorian theatre which was nearly closed down recently due to lack of funding, but survived by the skin of its teeth after high-profile comedians joined a rescue campaign. ⇌ *Hackney Central.*

Downstairs at the King's Head, 2 Crouch End Hill, **t** (020) 8340 1028. Warm atmosphere encouraged by the very funny compères. *Open Thurs–Sun.* ⊖ *Finsbury Park.*

Red Rose Comedy Club, 129 Seven Sisters Rd, Finsbury Park, **t** (020) 7281 3051. Top acts at knock-down prices in a slightly iffy area. *Open Sat.* ⊖ *Finsbury Park.*

Up the Creek, 302 Creek Rd, Greenwich, **t** (020) 8858 4581, *www.up-the-creek.com*. This friendly, purpose-built comedy club is one of London's best comedy venues thanks to compère and owner Malcolm Hardee. *Open Fri–Sun*. ⊖ *Greenwich*.

Backyard Comedy Club, 231–7 Cambridge Heath Road, E2, **t** (020) 7739 3122. Excellent line-ups in this former dress factory owned and run by comedian Lee Hurst. £10–13. *Comedy nights Thurs, Fri, Sat*. ⊖ Bethnal Green.

Banana Cabaret, The Bedford, 77 Bedford Hill SW12, **t** (020) 8673 8904. Comedy on Friday and Saturday nights – very popular, so grab a seat early. £7–14. ⊖ *Balham*.

Comedy Café, 66–8 Rivington St, EC2, **t** (020) 7739 5706. Decent acts at one of the city's leading venues. *Open Wed–Sat*. ⊖ *Old Street*.

Cinema

London cinemas are a bit like the British film industry – bursting with potential, forever on the verge of a real breakthrough, but poorly looked after and often disappointing. The mainstream cinemas are on the whole unfriendly and very expensive (£7 or more for a ticket, regardless of whether the venue is a plush auditorium with THX Dolby sound or a cramped backroom with polystyrene walls). The multiplex has hit London in a big way, for example at the Warner and Empire in Leicester Square or at Whiteleys in Queensway.

On the plus side, the arthouse and repertory sector is healthy, showing subtitled foreign-language films as well as the classics of American and British cinema. Prices are lower than first-run cinemas – £5–6 is normal – and can be lower still if you pay a membership fee and return regularly. The National Film Theatre offers the broadest range, while clubs like the Everyman attract a fiercely loyal clientele.

Film censorship in general is very strict, and in some cases the British Board of Film Classification cuts out footage it finds offensive without alerting the audience. Films are graded U (family films), PG (parental guidance recommended), 12 (nobody under that age), 15 (ditto) or 18 (ditto).

Odeon Leicester Square, Leicester Square, **t** 0871 2244 007, *www.odeon.co.uk*. London's plushest venue, which premières major Hollywood productions, often with royals and film stars in tow. Even more expensive than the average mainstream cinema. ⊖ *Leicester Square*.

Warner Village West End, 3 Cranbourn Street, Leicester Square, **t** 0870 240 6020, *www.warnervillage.co.uk*. Larger-than-life models of Bugs, Daffy *et al.* greet filmgoers in this vast 9-screen complex, part of the global cinema chain. Pricey, crowded and mainstream. ⊖ *Leicester Square*.

UCI Empire Leicester Square, Leicester Square, **t** 0870 010 2030; *www.uci.co.uk*. Three screens and the latest blockbusters. UCI also has an 8-screen multiplex in Whiteleys Shopping Centre in Queensway. ⊖ *Leicester Square, Piccadilly Circus*.

Prince Charles, Leicester Place, **t** (020) 7437 8181. This former soft-porn cinema has smartened up its act and shows a constantly changing schedule of cult classics at £3–4 a seat for non-members. Surely this can't go on...take advantage while you can. ⊖ *Leicester Square*.

Curzon Mayfair, 38 Curzon St, **t** (020) 7495 0500. Cinema showing art or foreign films. ⊖ *Hyde Park Corner*. A more relaxed venue is its sister-cinema, the **Curzon Soho** at 93 Shaftesbury Ave, **t** (020) 7439 4805, ⊖ *Piccadilly Circus, Leicester Square*.

Metro, 11 Rupert St, **t** (020) 7734 1506. Two-screen cinema that shuns Hollywood fare in favour of independent productions. ⊖ *Piccadilly Circus, Leicester Square*.

Renoir, Brunswick Centre, Brunswick Square, **t** (020) 7837 8402. The most adventurous of central London's cinemas, showing lots of foreign films and the best of British and American independents. ⊖ *Russell Square*.

Screen on the Hill, 230 Haverstock Hill, Belsize Park, **t** (020) 7435 3366. Popular first-run and art cinema with excellent coffee at the bar. ⊖ *Belsize Park*. Affiliated cinemas include the rather cramped **Screen on Baker Street** (96 Baker St, **t** (020) 7486 0036; ⊖ *Baker St*) and the more commercial **Screen on the Green** (83 Upper St, Islington, **t** (020) 7226 3520; ⊖ *Angel*). Listings and booking facilities for all the Screen cinemas are at *www.screencinemas.co.uk*.

Chelsea Cinema, 206 King's Road, **t** (020) 7351 3742. A small cinema that is particularly good for mainstream movies from across Europe and beyond. ⊖ *Sloane Square*.

Gate, 87 Notting Hill Gate, **t** (020) 7727 4043. Classy west London cinema with lively Sunday matinée line-ups. First-run films and classic revivals. ⊖ *Notting Hill Gate*.

National Film Theatre, British Film Institute, South Bank, **t** (020) 7928 3232, *www.bfi.org*. The mecca of London's film junkies and main venue for the annual London Film Festival each late Oct/early Nov. Lots of old and new films always showing in rep, with special seasons, for instance on Iranian cinema. ⊖ *Waterloo*.

Everyman, Hollybush Vale, Hampstead, **t** 0870 066 4777. The oldest rep cinema in London with an excellent bar. Lots of old favourites and a dedicated, studenty audience. ⊖ *Hampstead*.

ICA Cinemathèque, Carlton House Terrace, The Mall, **t** (020) 7930 3647. The wackiest film selection in town, with the emphasis on the avant-garde, especially feminist and gay cinema. ⊖ *Charing Cross*.

Clapham Picture House, 76 Venn St, **t** (020) 7498 3323. Cheap and appealing cinema showing intelligent recent releases. A rare cinematic high spot south of the river. ⊖ *Clapham Common*.

Ciné Lumière, French Institute, 17 Queensberry Place, South Kensington, **t** (020) 7073 1350. A good place to catch up on Gabin, Godard *et compagnie*. ⊖ *South Kensington*.

Electric, 191 Portobello Road, **t** (020) 7908 9696. One of the country's oldest cinemas reopened in February 2001 after lavish refurbishment, with its original mosaic floor and wall friezes restored to their former glory. Screenings are a combination of popular and cult films, both historic and contemporary. ⊖ *Ladbroke Grove*.

Riverside Studios, Crisp Rd, **t** (020) 8237 1111, *www.riversidestudios.co.uk*. A popular rep cinema for classic revivals and world cinema. ⊖ *Hammersmith*.

IMAX cinemas, *see* p.88.

Nightclubs and Discos

From the hot and sweaty to the cool and sophisticated, London has about 150 clubs and discos providing anything from big-band swing to rap and techno. The London club scene always used to be hampered by the strict licensing laws. Now you should be able to drink alcohol until 3am at most establishments and carry on dancing until dawn or beyond. The main handicap is price: it usually costs around £10 to get into a club, and £3 or more to buy a drink. Some clubs and club bars have dress codes, which may mean no jeans or trainers.

Things change fast in clubland: the following venues are all long-lasting but opening nights and music may change. Check *Time Out* or *Metro*, the Thursday supplement to the *Evening Standard*.

Bar Rumba, 36 Shaftesbury Ave, **t** (020) 7287 2715. Lively bar and club, with some of the best dancing in town. Excellent one-nighters all through the week. *Open 10pm–at least 3am (5am Sat)*. ⊖ *Piccadilly Circus*.

Café de Paris, 3 Coventry St, **t** (020) 7734 7700. Club music all night in this 1920s ballroom. Very glamorous, with lots of red velvet and Jacuzzis, but expensive. *Open Thurs, Fri, Sat only 6–4*. ⊖ *Piccadilly Circus*.

Camden Palace, 1a Camden High St, **t** (020) 7387 0428. Huge main floor and balcony offering space for a loyal, young crowd to dance to garage and techno. *Closed Sun and Mon*. ⊖ *Mornington Crescent*.

The Cross, Goods Way Depot, off York Way, **t** (020) 7837 0828. Low brick arches add to the hot, sweaty atmosphere. Three bars and a chill-out garden. Friendly crowd. Friday night is mixed gay night. The rather out-in-the-sticks location lends a certain exclusive air to proceedings. *Fri and Sat only*. ⊖ *King's Cross*.

The End, 16a West Central St, **t** (020) 7419 9199. Classic house party tunes at this central venue. Thurs is gay night. *Open Mon and Thurs–Sat*. ⊖ *Holborn, Tottenham Court Rd*.

Fabric, 77a Charterhouse St, **t** (020) 7336 0444, *www.fabric-london.com*. One of the new breed of superclubs, based in an old warehouse in Smithfield, attracting huge crowds for an all-night party. Sunday is 'polysexual' night, with Addiction to DTPM's mix of disco, hip-hop and Latino house. ⊖ *Farringdon*.

The Fridge, Town Hall Parade, Brixton Hill, **t** (020) 7326 5100. Funky music and a packed dance floor in south London's biggest venue. *Open Fri and Sat.* ⊖ *Brixton.*

The Gardening Club, 4 The Piazza, Covent Garden, **t** (020) 7497 3154. Next to the Rock Garden, with varied music during the week. House dominates at weekends. ⊖ *Covent Garden.*

G.A.Y., London Astoria, 157 Charing Cross Rd (*Thurs, Fri, Sat*); The Mean Fiddler, 165 Charing Cross Rd (*Mon*), **t** (020) 7734 9592. Ever-popular superclub for mainly younger lovers of pop and trash, with chart-toppers on stage most Saturdays. *Open Mon and Thurs 10.30pm–4am, Fri 11pm–4am, Sat 10.30pm–5am.* ⊖ *Tottenham Court Road.*

Gossips, 69 Dean St, **t** (020) 7434 4480. Atmospheric dark cellar with wide range of music including 80s, Gothic, rock and dance. Cheapish entry. *Closed Sun.* ⊖ *Tottenham Court Road.*

Hanover Grand, 6 Hanover St, **t** (020) 7499 7977. A converted ballroom is the ideal spot for glamorous girls and boys. ⊖ *Oxford Circus.*

Heaven, Under the Arches, Craven St, **t** (020) 7930 2020. Excellent club with multiple bars, dance floors, laser shows and crazy lighting. The biggest gay club in Europe, with regular distinct gay, mixed and straight nights, but typically very cool about anyone who wants to come. ⊖ *Embankment, Charing Cross.*

Hippodrome, Cranbourn St, **t** (020) 7437 4311. Vastly popular club with a rather naff reputation, attracting a large crowd of non-Londoners. Trapeze artists and fire-eaters. *Closed Sun.* ⊖ *Leicester Square.*

Madame Jo Jo's, 8–10 Brewer St, **t** (020) 7734 3040. Alternative music including rare funk and new jazz. It's not the brash 'n' brassy gay club some assume, although it does organize drag cabaret shows on Saturday nights. ⊖ *Piccadilly Circus.*

Ministry of Sound, 103 Gaunt St, Elephant and Castle, **t** (020) 7740 8851. Expensive (£12–15), but very trendy and popular and always packed. A New York-style club with lots of garage, house music and R'n'B. Expect long queues. *Open all night Fri and Sat only.* ⊖ *Elephant and Castle.*

The Scala, 278 Pentonville Rd, **t** (020) 7833 2022. Excellent club/live music venue. Friday is gay indie night Popstarz. ⊖ *King's Cross.*

Stringfellow's, 16 Upper St Martin's Lane, **t** (020) 7240 5534. Glamour models and footballers come here, as do lots of tourists dressed up in their smartest togs for this pricey yet somewhat tawdry night spot. Decent food. They describe their dress code as 'corporate'. *Open Mon–Sat 7.30pm–3.30am.* ⊖ *Leicester Square.*

Turnmills, 63 Clerkenwell Rd, **t** (020) 7250 3409. Everything from funky jazz to house and techno at the home of Trade, London's original gay late-nighter (*Fri and Sat*). ⊖ *Farringdon.*

Gay Bars

London has one of the most vibrant gay scenes in Europe. For years Earl's Court was the focal point for gay clubs and bars, but the focus has shifted to Soho, Hampstead and Clapham. Old Compton Street in Soho is something of a gay high street, with specialist bars, shops, a travel agency, hairdressers and taxi company; media suits mingle freely with fashion queens. Past squabbles between restaurateurs and Westminster Council over tables thrust on to wobbly narrow footpaths have been resolved in an untidy but lively compromise. The tidal pink pound has seen the rise and demise of many places to be seen in; what follows is a snapshot of the current scene in Soho and beyond.

Some of London's best nightclubs, such as Heaven, The End and Turnmills, either have a strong gay element or else are completely gay. There are also plenty of gay bars and cafés. You'll find zillions of suggestions and write-ups in one of London's gay magazines, such as *Boyz*, *QX*, or the *Pink Paper*, which are all available free from gay venues. You can pick up the more glossy magazines, such as *Attitude*, *Diva*, *Gay Times*, *Axiom* and *Fable*, from most newsagents.

Admiral Duncan, 54 Old Compton St. Traditional gay pub in the heart of Soho. Bombed by a bigot in 1999, it has acquired a certain iconic status as a symbol of resistance to prejudice. *Open Mon–Sat 11–11, Sun 12–10.30.* ⊖ *Leicester Square, Piccadilly Circus.*

Bar Aquda, 13–14 Maiden Lane, **t** (020) 7557 9891. Stylish café-bar. ⊖ *Leicester Square, Covent Garden.*

BarCode, 3 Archer St, Soho. Clubby bar for muscle boys and cropped hair. The comedy club in the basement offers some gay-themed nights. *Open 12 noon–11 daily.* ⊖ *Leicester Square, Piccadilly Circus.*

The Black Cap, 171 Camden High St. Friendly local pub upstairs and late-night bar and club downstairs with regular cabaret. *Open Mon–Thurs noon–2am, Fri and Sat noon–3am, Sun noon–3pm.* ⊖ *Camden Town.*

The Box, 32 Monmouth St, Covent Garden. Café by day and lively bar by night, attracting a young, trendy crowd and some celebs. *Open Mon–Sat 11–11, Sun 12–10.30.* ⊖ *Leicester Square.*

Bromptons, 294 Old Brompton Road. One of London's oldest gay bars. Very popular and animated, with late-night opening upstairs till 2am. ⊖ *Earl's Court.*

The Candy Bar, 4 Carlisle St, **t** (020) 7494 4041, *www.candybar.easynet.co.uk*. Modern friendly bar – London's best-known and longest-running venue for lesbians and their male guests. *Open Mon–Thurs 5–11.30pm, Fri–Sat 5pm–2am, Sun 5–11pm.* ⊖ *Tottenham Court Road.*

The Edge, 11 Soho Square. Relaxed, mixed crowd in this four-floor bar. *Open Mon–Sat noon–1am, Sun 1–10.30.* ⊖ *Tottenham Court Road.*

First Out Café Bar, 52 St Giles High Street. Great veggie food served at this café-bar, the first of its type in the West End. *Open 10am–11pm. Women only on Fri eve.* ⊖ *Tottenham Court Road.*

Freedom, 60–66 Wardour St, Soho. Large café-bar serving food and cocktails to a trendy mixed crowd posing in designer gear. One of the most hetero-friendly gay spots, so you can bring your straight pals along for the ride. *Open 11am–3am.* ⊖ *Leicester Square, Piccadilly Circus.*

Friendly Society, 79 Wardour St. Basement bar with chilled music and cocktails, given an alternative look with Barbie dolls on the wall. ⊖ *Leicester Square, Piccadilly Circus.*

King William IV, 77 High Street, Hampstead. Lays claim to being Britain's oldest gay pub. It's a classy joint, with contemporary décor and a professional, moneyed crowd. ⊖ *Hampstead.*

Ku Bar, 75 Charing Cross Road, Soho. Popular with young, scene-loving crowd. *Open Mon–Sat 4–11pm, Sun 4–10.30.* ⊖ *Leicester Square.*

Kudos, 10 Adelaide St, Covent Garden. Modern café-bar with a darker cruisey basement bar. *Open Mon–Sat 10–11, Sun 12–10.30.* ⊖ *Covent Garden, Leicester Square.*

The Retro Bar, 2 George Court, off Strand, Covent Garden. Attitude-free two-storey pub for lovers of indie and retro sounds. *Open Mon–Sat 12–11, Sun 12–10.30.* ⊖ *Charing Cross.*

Rupert Street, 50 Rupert St. Modern café-bar segueing into a busy venue in the evenings for men in suits and designer labels. *Open Mon–Sat 11–11, Sun 12–10.30.* ⊖ *Piccadilly Circus.*

The Shadow Lounge, 5 Brewer St. Upmarket style bar with cocktails and DJs, attracting a fashion-conscious crowd. *Open Mon–Sat 7pm–3am.* ⊖ *Leicester Square, Piccadilly Circus.*

Two Brewers, 114 Clapham High St, SW4. Friendly-modern bar, with late-night club and nightly cabaret. *Open Mon–Thurs noon–2am, Fri–Sat noon–3am, Sun noon–midnight.* ⊖ *Clapham Common.*

Vespa Ladies' Lounge, 15 St Giles High St. Laid-back bar for lesbians and their male guests. ⊖ *Tottenham Court Road.*

Village, 81 Wardour St, Soho. Stylish bar on two floors. *Open Mon–Thurs 11–11, Fri, Sat 11–12, Sun 11– 10.30.* ⊖ *Leicester Square, Piccadilly Circus.*

The Yard, 57 Rupert Street, Soho. Good food attracting mixed stylish crowd. Outdoor courtyard a bonus. *Open Mon–Sat noon–11, Sun noon–10.30.* ⊖ *Piccadilly Circus.*

Paris: Introduction

Paris has been a wonder for nearly a thousand years, from the time when masons came to learn the magic numbers of Gothic architecture, to the present day when we come to ponder the fearful symmetry of its latest geometric tricks – a pyramid of glass, a hollow cube, a sphere of a thousand mirrors.

Modern Paris offers a bigger *embarras du choix* than ever. Squeezed into one place are the brains, mouth, piggybank and bossy-stick of a wealthy and talented nation that fondly regards itself as the most rational and sensible land on Earth; the Ville Lumière is France's collective dream, the vortex of all its vanity, its parasite and its shimmering showcase. The results are there for all to enjoy, for Emerson's statement that 'England built London for its own use, but France built Paris for the world' is true in both senses: as a monumental show-off, but a generous and cosmopolitan one.

The Pick of Paris in a Weekend

First-time visitors

Most people would want to start by visiting Paris's ancient core and essential attractions: Ile de la Cité – with Notre-Dame and the Sainte-Chapelle – the Eiffel Tower, the Louvre, Montmartre, and the Musée d'Orsay. For a taste of Paris at its best, consider one of the *quartiers*: the Marais on the right bank and St-Germain are two of the best for this. Take a boat ride along the Seine, browse at the *bouquinistes* along the *quais*, and dine at one of the classic old *bouillons* like Petit Bofinger if you're on a budget, or La Tour d'Argent or Lapérouse if you're not.

Second-time visitors

Have a look at the parts of the centre you haven't seen yet – Les Halles, the Latin Quarter or the Opéra, and the Palais Royal and the *passages*. Visit the Musée Rodin, Musée de Cluny with its Lady and the Unicorn tapestries, maybe Père-Lachaise cemetery. To really get to know the city and its history well, a trip to the Musée Carnavalet is indispensable. Go and see a dance performance at the Opéra. Eat in the Latin Quarter's brasserie Balzar or at La Coupole or one of the other classics up in Montparnasse.

Third-time visitors

Take the Métro to the Mouffetard and the Jardin des Plantes. Find an obscure museum that fits some special interest, from television to crystal to Lenin to Louis Quinze chairs. There are still more fascinating cemeteries, the Sewers and the Catacombs. See a film at Studio 28 or the Grand Rex. Dine at Jacques Cagna or Le Pied de Fouet and have a glass of Paris red at the Café Mélac.

Haven't-been-back-latelys

Take in the *Grands Projets* if you haven't seen them: the Grande Arche de La Défense, the Louvre Pyramid and glittering Louvre-Rivoli subterranean shopping

A Sentimental Dissection

'Paris Intra Muros is the same organism from top to bottom, from solid rim to rim... You could lift it whole from a plate, like a nicely fried egg,' as John Gunther noted. It covers 86.8 sq km (33.5 sq miles), being slightly larger than Manhattan (not counting the recently annexed Bois de Boulogne and Bois de Vincennes).

Paris' first centre was the corner of Rue St-Jacques and Rue Cujas, where Roman surveyors laid out their *cardo* and *decumanus*. Since then the fried egg has spread out gradually and logically. The map shows its growth like rings on a tree trunk: the medieval walls (now the Grands Boulevards); the 18th-century Farmers-General wall (the next ring of boulevards) and the Thiers fortifications of the 1840s (the *Boulevards des Maréchaux* and present city limits). Since the Revolution, the city has been divided

centre, the newly refurbished Champs-Elysées, the Institut du Monde Arabe, the Opéra de la Bastille. Have dinner at the Café Marly, listen to some jazz at the Sunset club, and see a play at the Cartoucherie.

Paris in the summer

Summer, especially August, is notoriously the time not to visit Paris, at least if you want to see the city as it usually functions, with the streets full of Parisians (instead of 75 per cent tourists) and all the shops and restaurants open. July, however, is a treat: the gardens are superb, especially the Bagatelle in the Bois de Boulogne, host to an annual international rose competiton. There are chamber music concerts in the Bagatelle's Orangerie and in Sainte-Chapelle, outdoor films, firemen's balls in the 13th and a parade down the Champs-Elysées and fireworks on Bastille Day. Take a Paris-by-bicycle tour. Dine out on the lovely terrace of Le Pré Catelan.

Nostalgic Paris

Wander through the old residential streets of Montmartre and those off Rue du Faubourg St-Antoine in the Bastille quarter. Visit the Musée Carnavalet, Musée de Montmartre, Musée de la Vie Romantique or Père-Lachaise. Dine at a classic *brasserie* like Bofinger or Le Train Bleu in the Gare de Lyon, and follow in the footsteps of Toulouse-Lautrec at Au Lapin Agile.

Impressionists' Paris

There are three major collections of Impressionists in the city where Impressionism was born: the Musée d'Orsay, the Marmottan and the Orangerie.

Medieval Paris

Paris was hopping in the Middle Ages. Visit Chartres, Notre-Dame, Sainte-Chapelle, St-Eustache, the Tour St-Jacques, the cathedral of Saint-Denis, and the fabulous medieval collections and concerts in the Musée de Cluny, as well as the smaller churches of St-Julien le Pauvre and St-Séverin. In March the churches host a festival of ancient music.

into 20 numbered *arrondissements*, spiralling outwards from the centre like a snail. Getting to know these is one of the first jobs of any new Parisian or visitor.

Paris is the biggest tourist destination in Europe; the two million play host each year to some 12 million tourists. It draws more Americans than Brits or anyone else, and it probably has more luxury hotels than any other city – also more outrageously expensive restaurants and shops. If all the flowers are grown in Provence, here they are distilled into perfume. Paris is the top.

The rest of the French don't particularly care for their capital, no matter how jealous they may be of it. In Provence they call Parisians *les envahisseurs* (the invaders). Paris' heavy-handed predominance caused the cultural and economic backwardness of most other French cities; critics still moan about the 'French desert' – everything outside the city walls. Twenty-five per cent of all the public employees in France live here.

Partly because of these, Paris is a city of strangers – only one in eight Parisians has even one Paris-born parent. In a sense Paris isn't a city, a real community, at all, but a career stage – once you can move there, you've made it. But not everyone in Paris is a well-off government or corporate employee, or a student. Among those working in the city are huge numbers of immigrants (10 per cent of the metropolitan population) who do all the city's dirty work – and, increasingly, run the small businesses. Add some 75,000 seamstresses, who help make the garment district around Rue Réaumur one of the liveliest parts of town; if they're 26 and unmarried, they are the *Catherinettes* and wear big, silly hats on St Catherine's day. And don't forget the 13,976 professional cooks – almost three times as many as there are lawyers.

For all the high-tech fireworks of its new building projects, there's still much in Paris that seems preposterously quaint: the Académie Française, for example, or the ubiquitous 'keep off the grass' signs in the parks. But there are many other relics that seem wonderfully civilized, the sort of thing we go to Paris for: the *bouquinistes* by the Seine, the flower markets, the arcades around the Palais Royal, the politeness and decorum. Every tourist goes out for a stroll on the boulevards, even if the Parisians pay little heed to them any more. The classic street furnishings – the trees, the Wallace fountains (donated by Richard Wallace, who left Paris a compensation for the art collection he removed to London) and the Morris columns for theatre posters – are symbols of Paris everyone knows.

Paris: Practical A–Z

16

Calendar of Events

Dates for nearly all the events listed below change every year. The central tourist office at 127 Avenue des Champs-Elysées provides precise dates in their annual publication *Saisons de Paris* or their monthly *Paris Sélection*.

January

1 Jan *La Grande Parade de Paris*. A New Year's Day parade from Porte St-Martin to the Madeleine via the Grands Boulevards, with floats, bands, clowns, etc.

March

Festival des Instruments Anciens. Medieval, Renaissance and Baroque music, mostly in the city's churches.

Late March *Festival du Chien* dog show, Bercy; orchid show, Bois de Vincennes.

April

Foire du Trône ancient traditional funfair, Porte Dorée, Bois de Vincennes.

Marathon International de Paris 42km race from Place de la Concorde to the Hippodrome de Vincennes.

May

1 May Trade unions march and people buy sprigs of *muguet* (lily-of-the-valley) while the National Front rallies around the statue of Joan of Arc in Place des Pyramides.

Some time in May *Salon de Montrouge*, one of Paris's more intriguing annual art shows.

June

Late May–June French Open Tennis Championships at Roland Garros.

Pentecost Dual pilgrimages by modern Catholics and traditionalist Lefèbvrites from Chartres to the Sacré-Cœur.

Mid-June International fireworks contest, in Chantilly; *Festival de Saint-Denis*, classical music concerts, through early July.

Late June St John's Eve – fireworks show at Sacré-Cœur; *Fête du Marais* – jazz and classical music and drama.

21 June *Fête de la Musique*, free concerts across town.

Late June Waiters' race – 8km circuit holding their trays, beginning and ending at the Hôtel de Ville; beginning of the *Foire de Paris* at the Porte de Versailles – the closest equivalent of the old St-Germain fair, with all kinds of new-fangled gadgets, food, wine and more.

July

Early July *Festival de Saint-Denis*, classical music; *La Villette Jazz Festival*, two-week-long, big-name jazzfest at Parc de la Villette.

13 July Firemen's feasts and balls in the *quartiers*.

14 July Bastille Day: Military parade on the Champs-Elysées; fireworks at Trocadéro; *Bastille Ball*, rollicking all-night gay party.

A few days later End of the *Tour de France* in the Champs-Elysées.

September

September *Fête de l'Humanité*, lively national Communist festival, in suburban La Courneuve; *Festival de l'Automne*, music dance and drama lasting until December.

October

October FIAC – *Foire Internationale de l'Art Contemporain* – choice selections from galleries around the world.

First Saturday Wine harvest in Montmartre – lots of good clean fun.

Mid-October *20km de Paris race*, open to all and sundry – entries in past years have numbered over 20,000.

November

November *Salon d'Automne*, major art salon in the Grand Palais.

25 November *Les Catherinettes*, women in the fashion trade who are 26 that year and single don outrageous hats made by co-workers – '*coiffer la Sainte-Catherine*'.

December

Christmas Eve Midnight Réveillon feast – Parisians eat out and gorge like geese. Billions of oysters meet their maker.

New Year's Eve Saint-Sylvestre, occasion for another ultra-rich midnight feast – in a week, Paris downs 2,000 tons of *foie gras*.

Consulates in Paris

UK: 36 Rue du Faubourg-St-Honoré, **t** 01 44 51 31 00, Ⓜ *Madeleine*.
USA: 2 Rue St-Florentin, **t** 01 43 12 22 22, Ⓜ *Concorde*.
Canada: 35 Av Montaigne, **t** 01 44 43 29 00, Ⓜ *Franklin D. Roosevelt*.

Crime and Police Business

Nothing is likely to happen to you in Paris. For most Americans and British city-dwellers, in fact, coming here will be statistically less dangerous than staying at home. Streets are safe at night. You will need to watch out for pickpockets, in the Métro, in the flea markets (where everyone deals in cash), and wherever people are standing around to watch street performers.

Report thefts to the nearest police station. If your passport is stolen, contact the police and your nearest consulate for emergency travel documents. Carry photocopies of your passport, driver's licence, etc. – it makes it easier when reporting a loss. By law, the police in France can stop anyone anywhere and demand ID. The drug situation is the same in France as anywhere in the West: soft and hard drugs are widely available, and the police only make an issue of victimless crime when it suits them. Smuggling any amount of marijuana into the country can mean a prison term, and there's not much your consulate can or will do about it.

Disabled Travellers

Travellers can contact in advance the **Comité National Français de Liaison pour la Réadaptation des Handicapés (CNRH)**, Service Publication, 236 bis Rue de Tolbiac, 75013 Paris, **t** 01 53 80 66 66, *www.handitel.org*.

The city has an (ill-informed) information office for the disabled in Place Mazas, 12e, **t** 01 43 47 76 60, and a hotel with complete facilities for travellers with disabilities: the **Résidence Internationale de Paris**, 44 Rue Louis-Lumière, 75020, **t** 01 40 31 45 45.

For public transport, only bus lines 88, 85 and 20, some of the RER stations and line 14 on the Métro are accessible. The RATP and SNCF offer a *Compagnon de Voyage* service (**t** 01 45 83 67 77; €10/hr). Call at least 24hrs in advance. **Taxis** are required by law to accept all disabled travellers, whatever the circumstances.

National **museums** offer the disabled free admission.

Detailed information is available by **Minitel**, 3614 HANDITEL (ask at your hotel or use the Minitel at any post office). *See* p.20 for useful addresses in the UK and USA.

Electricity

The voltage is 220 and plugs have small round prongs; Brits will need only an adapter, Americans a voltage converter for any radios or appliances. The BHV department store on Rue de Rivoli, Ⓜ *Louvre*, has a good selection of such items.

Health

Local hospitals are the place to go in an emergency (*urgence*). If you need an ambulance and paramedic (SAMU), dial **t** 15. Doctors take turns going on duty out of hours – pharmacies will know who to contact, or else telephone **SOS Médecins** (**t** 01 47 07 77 77), or **SOS Dentaire** (**t** 01 43 37 51 00). If it's not an emergency, the pharmacies have addresses of local doctors, or you can visit the clinic at a *Centre Hospitalier*. Pharmacists are trained to administer first aid and dispense free advice for minor problems. Pharmacies open on a rota basis but **Pharmacie Dhéry**, 84 Av des Champs-Elysées, **t** 01 45 62 02 41, and **Pharmacie Européenne**, 6 Place de Clichy, **t** 01 48 74 65 18, are open 24hrs a day.

There is a standard agreement for citizens of EU countries, entitling you to a certain amount of free medical care (75–80% of the cost, reimbursed a week to 10 days later). Fill out form **E111** before travelling, available from your local health authority (and from post offices in the UK). Non-EU travellers should check with their policies at home to see if they are covered in France, and judge whether it's advisable to take out additional insurance. However you're insured, you pay up front for everything, unless it's an emergency, when you will be billed later.

Travel insurance will cover you for delays, lost baggage,theft, etc., as well as offering 100% medical refund and emergency repatriation if necessary. Ring around for the best deal. Be sure to save all doctors' receipts, pharmacy receipts and police documents (if you're reporting a theft).

There's some consolation for concerned North Americans in knowing that France is a civilized country, and that no one will die alone outside a hospital (although the French are quite fastidious in asking about arrangements for payment).

Condoms are available in pharmacies and tobacconists and now in machines in many Métro stations.

Pharmacists who speak English and can help match foreign prescriptions are **Pharmacie Swann**, 6 Rue Castiglione, 1er, **t** 01 42 60 72 96, and **British and American Pharmacy**, 1 Rue Auber, 9e, **t** 01 47 42 49 40.

Internet

Internet access is available at:

Café Orbital, 13 Rue Médicis, **t** 01 43 25 76 77, *www.orbital.fr*. Paris's first cybercafé has Macs and PCs to choose from. Food and drink available. 5hrs costs €30.50, but you can also pay per minute. *Open Mon–Sat 10am–9pm, Sun 12–8pm.* **RER** *Luxembourg* or Ⓜ *Odéon*.

Cyberport Forum des Images, Forum des Halles (Porte St-Eustache), **t** 01 44 76 63 44. One of the nicest Internet cafés in Paris. First 30mins €5.50, subsequent 30min sessions €4.50. Free half-hour introduction to the Internet. Food and drink available. *Open Tues–Sun 1pm–9pm, Thurs till later.* Ⓜ *Châtelet-Les Halles*.

easyInternetcafé, 31–7 Bd de Sébastopol, **t** 01 40 41 09 10. Parisian outpost of the popular British Internet café. Rates start at €3; the cheapest time is the evening. *Open daily 24hrs.* Ⓜ *Châtelet-Les Halles*.

Money and Banks

On 1 January 1999 the **euro** became the official currency of France (and 10 other nations of the European Union).

The euro is divided into 100 cents. Notes come in denominations of 5, 10, 20, 50, 100, 200 and 500 euros; coins come in denominations of 1, 2, 5, 10, 20 and 50 cents, and 1 and 2 euros. At the time of writing, the euro was worth around UK£0.65, US$0.94 and C$1.47.

Traveller's cheques are the safest way of carrying money, but the wide acceptance of **credit and debit cards** and the presence of **ATMs** (*distributeurs de billets*), at banks and post offices, make using a card a convenient alternative. The types of card accepted are marked on each machine, and most give instructions in English. Check with your bank before you leave whether your debit/cash cards can be used in France. Credit card companies charge a fee for cash advances, but rates are often better than those at banks. Visa is the most readily accepted of the international credit cards; American Express is often not accepted. Smaller hotels and restaurants may not accept cards at all. Some shops and supermarkets experience difficulties reading UK-style magnetic strips.

In the event of lost or stolen credit cards, call the following emergency numbers:

American Express: **t** 01 47 77 72 00.
Barclaycard: **t** (00 44) 1604 230 230 (UK).
Diner's Club: **t** 01 49 06 17 50.
Mastercard: **t** 08 00 96 47 67.
Visa: **t** 08 00 90 11 79.

National Holidays

On French national holidays, banks, shops, museums and businesses close, but most restaurants stay open. The holidays are:

1 January New Year's Day
Easter Sunday March or April
Easter Monday March or April
1 May *Fête du Travail* (Labour Day)
8 May VE Day, Armistice 1945
Ascension Day usually end of May
Pentecost (Whitsun) and the following Monday, beginning of June
14 July Bastille Day
15 August The Assumption
1 November All Saints' Day
11 November Remembrance Day (First World War Armistice)
25 December Christmas Day

Opening Hours

Normal opening hours in Paris are from 9 or 10 in the morning to 7 or 8 in the evening, Tuesday through Saturday. Smaller boutiques often take a couple of hours off for lunch.

Note that many shops in Paris close on Sundays and Mondays, with the exception of *boulangers*, grocers and *supermarchés* (closed Sun, open Mon).

Food **markets** dwindle away at noon; most permanent street markets are open morning and afternoon, including Sunday morning but not on Mondays; markets selling clothes, art, antiques, etc., run into the afternoon.

Post Offices

The modern French post office, the *PTT* or *Bureau de Poste*, is still distinguished by a blue bird on a yellow background. Post offices are open Mon–Fri 8am–7pm, and Sat 8am–12pm. You can purchase stamps in tobacconists as well as post offices.

The **main post office**, 52 Rue du Louvre, Ⓜ *Les Halles, Louvre*, is open 24hrs for all services. The office at 71 Avenue des Champs-Elysées, Ⓜ *George V*, stays open till 7.30pm, 7pm Sat.

You can receive ***poste restante*** (general delivery) at any post office provided you give the office's address and postcode. The letter will be held for 15 days and collecting the item will cost you around 50 cents.

Telephones

Apart from bars where you can still find coin-operated *points phones*, all other public telephones in Paris have switched over to *télécartes*, which you can purchase at any tobacconist, Métro or train station, or post office for €7.50 for 50 *unités* or €15 for 120 *unités*.

All French phone numbers have 10 digits and all Paris ones begin with 01; if you're ringing from abroad, dial France's international code 33 and drop the first '0' of the number. For international calls from Paris, dial 00 followed by the country code (UK 44; USA and Canada 1; Ireland 353; Australia 61; New Zealand 64, etc.), and then the local code (minus the 0 for UK numbers) and number.

The easiest way to **reverse the charges** is to spend a few euros ringing the number you want to call and quickly give them your number in France, which is always posted in the box. Alternatively ring your national operator under the *Pays* (Country) *Direct* system; the codes for each country are to be found among the first few pages of the Yellow Pages (*Pages Jaunes*). From there you can make your reverse charge call (*appeler en p.c.v.*) or charge it to a credit card or your home phone number.

Most post offices have public **fax machines** and offer free use of a **Minitel** electronic directory (alternatively dial **t** 12, free, for a human directory enquiries operator; most speak some English). International directory assistance is **t** 00 33 12 followed by the country code. And, as anywhere else, remember that only billionaires and fools use the telephones in their hotel rooms.

Time

Paris is one hour ahead of GMT, six hours ahead of US Eastern Standard Time, and nine ahead of California. Nine hours *behind* Sydney. Except during summer (daylight-saving) time of course, which begins and ends on the same dates as Britain. The question of summer time is under review in France but in the meantime will continue unchanged.

Tipping

Almost all restaurants and cafés automatically add an extra 15% to the bill, and there's no need to leave any more unless you care to or in recognition of special service. The taxi driver will be happy with 10%, the cinema usher a few cents.

Toilets

That most fragrant and funky piece of Parisian street furniture, the sidewalk *pissoir* or *vespasienne* (named after the rough-edged Roman Emperor Vespasian, who collected urine to sell to fullers), has gone the way of the dodo, to be replaced by the ugly beige spaceship toilets of the Decaux Company. They cost 50 cents for 15 minutes of privacy, and are automatically sanitized after each user although sometimes they're out of order.

Museums (except for the Natural History) have decent facilities, and you'll have to be very unlucky to find a café that hasn't improved on a hole-in-the-floor squatter ('worthy of Central Asia' was how George Orwell described the lavatory in the restaurant where he worked). In return for such luxury, though, you're more or less obliged to buy something or be sneaky. Train stations have a charge of around 50 cents and fancier cafés with an attendant should be tipped the same – though some attendants invent their own complex rate schedules. For all that, the reek in narrow alleys and *impasses* proves that not everyone feels like paying for a pee. If you're feeling nostalgic you can visit the last rusting *vespasiennes* in Paris in Boulevard Arago, in front of La Santé prison, in the 14e, or near the Pont Mirabeau.

Tourist Information

The main office is at 127 Av des Champs-Elysées, 8e, **t** 08 92 68 31 12, near the Arc de Triomphe (*open daily 9am–8pm; low season same, but Sun 11–6*). Bilingual and obliging, the staff can help you find a hotel room, sell you a museum pass (*see* p.266), fill you in on events, and tell you about places to see in the Ile-de-France region.

Other offices are to be found at the **Gare du Nord**, near the international arrivals area, **t** 01 45 26 94 82, and the Office de Tourisme et des Congrès de Paris at the **Gare de Lyon**, **t** 08 22 68 31 12, *www.paris-touristoffice.com* (*open Mon–Sat 8–8*).

Maps: For detailed information, the Michelin *Paris-Plan 14* (the little blue book) is indispensable: brilliantly conceived, a cartographical work of art. For day trips into the outskirts of the city, Michelin's green *Environs de Paris 106* is the best. Otherwise, most stationery stores sell the useful *Plan de Paris*, a little book that details every tiny street, Métro station and attraction you could ever hope to visit.

Paris: Essential Sights

17

Arc de Triomphe

Place Charles-de-Gaulle; pedestrian tunnel at the right-hand side of the Champs-Elysées; Ⓜ *Charles de Gaulle-Etoile;* **t** *01 55 37 73 77, www.monum.fr.*

Open Oct–Mar daily 9–10.30pm; April–Sept daily 9.30–11pm; adm.

The Arc de Triomphe is not a tribute to Napoleon, although it certainly would have been if the Emperor had been around to finish it. The arch commemorates the armies of the Revolution: the heroic, improvized citizen levy that protected their new freedoms against the *anciens régimes* of the rest of Europe, and liberated other peoples.

In the 18th century, the Etoile was a rustic *rond-point* on the boundaries of the city. Napoleon did have the idea for the arch, after his victories of 1805–6; originally he wanted it in Place de la Bastille, but his sycophants convinced him that this prominent spot in the fashionable west end would be much more fitting. A life-size model was erected in 1810, during the celebrations for Napoleon's marriage to Marie-Louise of Austria. Not surprisingly, work stopped cold in 1815. Eight years later, Louis XVIII had the really contemptible idea of finishing it as a monument to his own 'triumph' – sending an army to put down a democratic revolt in Spain. But by the reign of Louis-Philippe, the 'myth of Napoleon' had already begun its strange progress. Times were dull; Frenchmen had forgotten the huge numbers of their countrymen Napoleon had sent to die for his glory. A massive effort to complete the arch was mounted in 1832, and they had it finished four years later. And four years after that, Napoleon's remains rolled under the arch, on a grey November day where the silence of the crowds was broken only by a few old veterans croaking '*Vive l'Empereur!*' Napoleon III had Baron Haussmann make the Etoile into the showcase of Paris.

It isn't just the location and the historical connotations that make this such an important landmark. It's also a rather splendid arch. Any Frenchman would recognize the group on the right side, facing the Champs-Elysées: the dramatic *Departure of the Volunteers in 1792*, also known as the *Marseillaise*. Inside is a small **museum** of the arch; from there you can climb up to the roof for a remarkable view of the Grand Axe and the pie-slice blocks around the Etoile (especially recommended after dark).

Catacombes

1 Place Denfert-Rochereau; Ⓜ *Denfert-Rochereau;* **t** *01 43 22 47 63.*

Open Tues 11–4, Wed–Sun 9–4; closed Mon and hols; adm; take a torch.

Place Denfert-Rochereau is one of the Left Bank's busiest traffic fandangos, guarded by the sphinx-like Lion de Belfort. The two pavilions with carved friezes survive from the *Barrière d'Enfer*, or 'tollgate of hell', in the Farmers-General wall. An apt name, as one of the pavilions (no.1) serves as the entrance to the Catacombes. Down, down the 90 steps of a spiral stair are pictures of the old gypsum quarries that make Paris a gruyère cheese under all her fine frippery. Next it's a tramp through damp and dreary tunnels to a toytown Fort of Port Mahon (Menorca), hollowed out of the wall by a bored caretaker once imprisoned there. Then there's a vicious blue puddle called the *source de Léthé*, inhabited by little pale-eyed creatures who dine on bone moss. Then the doorway inscribed: 'Halt! This is the empire of the dead.' But of course you don't halt at all, for beyond is the main attraction: the last earthly remains of Mirabeau, Rabelais, Madame de Pompadour and five to six million other Parisians removed here beginning in 1786 from the putrid, overflowing cemetery of the Innocents and nearly every other churchyard in Paris.

Champs-Elysées

Ⓜ *Charles de Gaulle-Etoile, George V, Franklin D. Roosevelt, Champs-Elysées-Clemenceau.*

The Avenue des Champs-Elysées was the second step in the creation of the Grand Axe, the long radian that stretches, perfectly straight, from central Paris west to La Défense. Catherine de' Medici had fixed its eastern point with her Louvre extensions and the Tuileries gardens in the 1560s. In 1616 everything west of the Louvre was royal meadows and hunting preserves; in that year Marie de' Medici ordered the first improvement, a tree-lined drive along the Seine called the *Cours la Reine*. In 1667 Louis XIV had Le Nôtre lay out a long straight promenade through the area, continuing the perspective of the Tuileries' Grande Allée. For the next few decades the Champs-Elysées was a less aristocratic promenade; all Paris came on Sundays for a bit of fresh air, and in 1709 the pleasure promenade took its present name, the 'Elysian Fields'. The upper part of the avenue, already partly built-up, saw a speculative boom in the reign of Napoleon III. The lower part, below the Rond-Point, was saved only because it served as a pleasure ground for all the late 19th-century exhibitions, a delightful bower of groves and avenues, Chinese lanterns, brightly painted pavilions, ice-cream and lemonade. There was a glassed-in Winter Garden with banana trees; dances were held there at night. Outside there were café-concerts under the trees. Parisians and visitors agreed that it was the pleasantest place in the world.

The upper Champs-Elysées, after decades of decline, has been the subject of a recent major renovation which included everything from pavement surfaces to a second row of *platanes* (plane trees) on each side. Even the car dealers, hamburger stands, banks and obscure airline offices that took over the once-fashionable street in the 1970s have cleaned themselves up. The scheme is working well; the great avenue is always packed, and it's a lively and interesting place.

Place de la Concorde

Ⓜ *Concorde.*

Without the cars the Place de la Concorde would be a treat, the most spacious square and the finest architectural ensemble in Paris. Jacques-Ange Gabriel won the competition held by Louis XV for its design by coming up with something utterly, unaccountably original. Breaking completely with the enclosed, aristocratic ethos of the other royal squares, Gabriel laid out an enormous rectangle, built up on one side only (the north), with the Seine facing opposite and the two ends entirely open, towards the parklands of the Tuileries and the Champs-Elysées.

Later generations perfected the *place*. The Pont de la Concorde over the Seine opened in 1790; under Napoleon, the Madeleine and Palais Bourbon were added to close the views and complete the brilliant architectural ensemble. A new exclamation mark along the Grand Axe, the Egyptian obelisk, appeared in 1836. But in the meantime, the *place* had changed its name six times, and seen more trouble than any square deserves. In 1782, the spot where the obelisk stands today held a guillotine, the venue for all the most important executions under the Terror; Louis and Marie were the most famous victims; Danton, Desmoulins, Charlotte Corday and finally Robespierre himself held centre stage here while Madame Defarge knitted.

The **obelisk** comes from Luxor on the Nile, *c.* 1250 BC in the time of Ramses II. It was a gift from France's ally Muhammad Ali, semi-independent Ottoman viceroy of Egypt in the 1830s, and this spot was chosen for it because any political monument would have been a sure source of controversy in the future. Accepting an obelisk is one thing; floating the 221-tonne (225-ton) block to Paris and getting it upright again a different matter. Look at the inscriptions on the base: scenes of the erection carved in intricate detail, with thanks in big gold letters to M. LEBAS, INGENIEUR, for managing the trick, 'to the applause of an immense crowd'.

On the western edge of the *place* stands a pair of winged horses to complement those on the Tuileries side. These familiar landmarks are copies of the **Marly horses**, sculpted by Coysevox's nephew, Guillaume Coustou, in the 1740s. Like their counterparts across the Place they originally came from Louis XIV's château at Marly, destroyed in the Revolution.

La Défense

Ⓜ/RER La Défense; The Grande Arche: **t** *01 49 07 27 57, www.grandearche.com.*

Open summer daily 10–8; winter daily 10–7; adm; restaurant on 35th floor, t 01 48 07 27 32; open daily for lunch also Saturday dinner.

Forty years ago this was a dismal suburban industrial area, its only feature a *rond-point*, laid out by Madame de Pompadour's brother back in 1765 when the area was still a noble park and hunting preserve. After the siege of 1870, a statue commemorating the defence of Paris was set up here: 'La Défense' gradually gave its name to the whole area. In 1955 the national government (not the Ville de Paris) decided to make a modern, American-style business district out of the vacant land, and a state development corporation called EPAD was set up. By 1960 glass towers were sprouting like toadstools, a surreal scene for older Parisians. French directors were not slow to seize on La Défense's cinematic potential. Jacques Tati's poor bewildered Monsieur Hulot was baffled by glass doors. In *The Little Theatre of Jean Renoir* there is a vignette of a modern woman who falls hopelessly in love with her electric floor polisher; the tidy corporate people of La Défense provide a sort of Greek chorus. Today, about 150,000 people work here and there are about 55,000 residents.

The **Parvis**, also called the Podium or the Dalle, is the long pedestrian mall aligned with the Grand Axe. Sorry monoliths dubbed with corporate acronyms are interspersed with a wealth of abstract sculptures and mosaics. At the eastern end, with a broad view over Paris, is the **Takis Fountain**, illuminated in the evenings with coloured lights. In the centre, near the Agam Fountain, is the original sculpture of the '**Défense**'. Since its opening in 1989, though, the star of the show has unquestionably been François Mitterrand's personal monument, the **Grande Arche**. There's a lift, running up a glass tube through the hole; take the ride through the air to the top for a panoramic view of the city.

Eiffel Tower and Trocadéro

Ⓜ Champ de Mars-Tour Eiffel, Trocadéro; ***t*** *01 44 11 23 23, www.eiffel-tower.com.*

Open Sept–May daily 9.30–11pm; June–Aug 9–midnight; stairs close 6.30; adm exp. If you arrive later in the day, count on a good hour's wait for the lift to the first (€3.70), second (€7) and third (€10.20) platforms.

The incomparable souvenir of the 1889 Fair, the Eiffel Tower was built to celebrate the Revolution's centenary and the resurrection of France after her defeat by Prussia in 1870. Derided over the last hundred years as 'a suppository', 'a giraffe', 'a criminal, sinister pencil-sharpener', it is 300m (1,000ft) of graceful iron filigree; belly-up between its four spidery paws, its 9,700 tons may look menacing, but they sit with extraordinary lightness on the soft clay of Paris, exerting as much pressure as that of a man sitting in a chair. It was erected in two years, for less than the estimated 8 million francs, welded together with 2,500,000 rivets and built without a single fatal work accident. Until surpassed in 1930 by the Chrysler Building in New York, it was the tallest structure in the world. Originally the tower was painted several tints, lightening to yellow-gold at the top, so its appearance dissolved and changed according to the time of day and weather; now, every five or six years, forty painters cover it with 7,700lb of a sombre maroon colour called *ferrubrou*.

The competition for the design of a 1,000ft tower resulted in 700 proposals. Gustave Eiffel was already famous for his daring bridges and viaducts; in 1886 he had designed the structural frame of the Statue of Liberty, defying all the nay-sayers who said her arm would surely blow off. In its day, the Tour's engineering daredevilry bent quite a few Parisians out of shape. Residents around the Champ de Mars feared it would fall on their heads. The artistic élite, led by Charles Gounod, Charles Garnier and Alexandre Dumas, signed a vitriolic petition against the profanation and dishonour of the capital; one signer, Guy de Maupassant, left Paris for good so as never to look upon its 'metallic carcass' again. But for the 1925 Exposition des Arts Décoratifs, André Citroën paid to make the Eiffel Tower the world's largest advertising sign. In 1986 sodium lamps were installed in the structure; it's usually lit up until midnight.

To reach the **Jardins du Trocadéro** opposite, cross the Pont d'Iéna, commissioned by Napoleon I after his victory at Jena in Prussia and decked out with proud imperial eagles. The main feature of the Place du Trocadéro is the superb view from the courtyard of the Palais de Chaillot across the river and south. The name Trocadéro is derived from the name of a fort near Cádiz captured by the French in 1823. The gardens stretching to the Seine were laid out for the 1878 fair and restored in 1937; today they are home to a 1900s *carrousel* and the most complacent colony of stray cats in Paris. On Bastille Day the gardens are filled with *son et lumière* followed by fireworks.

Hôtel des Invalides

Esplanade des Invalides; Ⓜ *Invalides, Latour-Maubourg, Varenne, Ecole Militaire;* **t** *01 44 42 37 72, www.invalides.org.*

This was the Plain of Grenelles in 1670, when Louis XIV's under-minister of war, Louvois, persuaded his warmongering king to provide a military hospital for old soldiers, which could also double as a monument to the military glory and triumphs of Louis himself.

The Invalides has Siamese-twin churches, back to back, originally sharing the same altar and chancel: St-Louis for the old soldiers and staff, and the Eglise-du-Dôme for royals. The façade of **St-Louis des Invalides** (*open summer daily 9.30–5.30; winter until 4.30*) closes the south end, guarded by the statue of Napoleon, 'the Little Corporal', in his old grey coat and hat. As you leave the church, the arcade to your left enshrines one of the 700 Paris taxicabs requisitioned during the night of 6 September 1914 to transport 7,000 soldiers 35km to the front and save Paris at the Battle of the Marne. It's a preview of the vast collections of the **Musée de l'Armée** (*open April–Sept daily 10–5.45; Oct–Mar 10–4.45; closed 1 some hols; adm; tickets, sold under the right arcade, are good for two consecutive days and include entry to related museums*). A large section is devoted to Napoleon, with his coat and hat, his stuffed dog and white horse, paintings of his retreat from Moscow and *Napoleon at Fontainebleau*, the Emperor like a little boy slouching in his chair. The recently rearranged top floor, under the massive joists of the roof of the Invalides, houses the **Musée des Plans-Reliefs** (*open summer daily 10–5.45; winter daily 10–4.45; closed some hols; adm*). Louis XIV began to collect these huge scale relief models of France's fortified cities and towns upon Louvois' advice in 1686. Some of these fill entire rooms; until 1927 they were considered a military secret.

Save your ticket for the **Eglise-du-Dôme**, around to the south. Designed by Hardouin-Mansart and completed in 1706, the pointy dome is so impressive that the church itself is named after it, and so prominent on the Paris skyline that it was freshly gilded for the bicentennial of the Revolution. The greatest main-chancer in history, responsible on his own estimate for the death of 1,700,000 Frenchmen, Napoleon died on 21 May 1821. His wish, inscribed over the bronze doors to the crypt – 'I wish to be buried on the banks of the Seine, in the midst of the people of France, whom I have loved so dearly' – was imprudently granted by Louis-Philippe in 1840 as a bid to gain popularity. The design of **Napoleon's tomb** in the circular crypt is by Louis Visconti.

The Louvre

Pyramide (Cour Napoléon); Ⓜ *Palais Royal-Musée du Louvre;*
t *01 40 20 51 51, www.louvre.fr.*

Open daily except Tues 9–6; Mon and Wed evenings until 9.30 (Wed eve everything is open; Mon eve Richelieu wing only). Adm lower on Sun and after 3 daily; under 18, free adm; free for everyone on first Sun of every month. At weekends or on any day in summer, come early to avoid the queues. Call for details on which rooms are closed.

'Louvre' was the name of the area long before any palaces were dreamt of. The original castle was built some time after 1190 by Philippe-Auguste. Charles V rebuilt and extended it in the 1360s. During the worst of the Hundred Years' War, 1400–30, the kings abandoned the Louvre and Paris; the first to return was François Ier, in 1527; he demolished the old castle and began what is known today as the *Vieux Louvre*, the easternmost part of the complex, in 1546. Henri IV, Louis XIII and Louis XIV all contributed in turn to the palace. The next royal resident was a reluctant Louis XVI, brought here by force from Versailles in October 1789 and installed in the Tuileries.

Republican governments kept their offices in the Tuileries after 1795; they consolidated the art collections and made them into a public museum in 1793. Napoleon moved in in 1800, and started work on the northern wing. During the next 15 years his men looted the captive nations of Europe for their finest paintings and statues, most of which ended up here.

The Louvre was 350 years in the building, and the best parts are the oldest. Start on the eastern end, on Rue de l'Amiral de Coligny. The majestic **colonnade** (begun 1668) marks the beginning of the French classical style; its architect was Claude Perrault, brother of Charles, the famous writer of fairy tales. The outer façades of the **north wing**, facing Rue de Rivoli, are contributions of Napoleon (right half, viewed from the street) and Napoleon III (left half); both lend much to the imperial dreariness of that street. As for the **south wing**, facing the Seine, the left half is the beginning of Catherine de' Medici's long extension; its completion (right half) was done under Henri IV. The Napoleons, with their symmetrical brains, naturally had to make the Louvre symmetrical too; between them they more than doubled the size of the palace, expanding the south wing and building the northern one to mirror it.

Before a *carrousel* became a merry-go-round, the word meant a knightly tournament, involving races, jousts and even singing. The **Arc du Carrousel**, like the other monument Napoleon built to himself, the Vendôme column, is a mere copy, in this case of the Arch of Septimius Severus in the Roman Forum. A sculptural ensemble is a collection of separate works by **Aristide Maillol**, a wonderful turn-of-the-20th-century Catalan-French sculptor who started his career at age 40 and believed that any subject could be most effectively represented by female nudes of heroic proportions.

In 1981, his first year in office, President Mitterrand decided to shake it up a bit with the *Projet du Grand Louvre*, a total refurbishing of the palace, museum and the adjacent Tuileries gardens. The entire north wing, which had housed the Ministry of Finance, was cleared to expand the museum space, and a giant underground car park and plush shopping mall were burrowed under the Jardin du Carrousel. And then there's the **Pyramid** – for a simple geometric bagatelle, architect I. M. Pei's 1988 entrance to the Louvre has certainly generated a lot of ink.

Once through the door and down the long curving stairway, you are in the **Hall Napoléon**, where you can buy your ticket. From here you have a choice of three entrances into the labyrinth, up escalators marked **Denon**, **Sully** and **Richelieu**, the three sections into which the Louvre has been divided: Sully is the old Louvre, Denon the south wing, Richelieu the north wing. A free, colour-coded **orientation guide** is available at the front desk.

Highlights of the Collections

Egyptian Art: The finest and most complete collection outside Egypt itself. Keep an eye out for the surprises that make the subtle Egyptians come to life – like the dog with a bell around his neck, a sort of Alsatian, with a quizzical look. The **Mastaba of Akhetep**, a complete small funeral chapel (*c.* 2300 BC) from Saqqara. Exceptional exhibits of **Coptic Art** up to the Middle Ages.

Middle Eastern Art: The various civilizations of **Mesopotamia** (*Richelieu 3, 4, ground floor*) are well represented. You may have never heard of **Mani**, a great civilization centred on the Euphrates, now in Syria, that reached its height *c.* 1800 BC, but its people were some of the Middle East's most talented artists. From **Babylon**, which destroyed Mani: a black monument carved with the **Code of Hammurabi**, the oldest known body of laws. **Medieval Islamic** ceramics and metalwork (*Richelieu entresol*) including the *Font of St Louis*, used to baptize future kings of France.

Classical Antiquity: The ***Venus de Milo*** (*Sully 12*), for whom neither date nor provenance is known, only that the villagers of Milos sold her to the French in 1820 to keep the Turks from getting her. **Roman-era copies** of Greek works. **Etruscan art**. Rome: some penetrating, naturalistic portrait busts including *Caligula, Nero, Hadrian* and *Marcus Aurelius*. The **Cour du Sphinx**: a big room assembling some of the best antique works from all periods, including the *mosaic of the Four Seasons* and a huge anthropomorphized *River Tiber*. 5th to 7th-century **early Christian art**, mostly from Syria.

Sculpture: From the Middle Ages onwards, in the *entresol* and *ground floor* of *Denon* and *Richelieu*. See especially **French Renaissance sculpture**, not only for the quality of the work but also because there's hardly any of it in the rest of Paris. Guillaume Costou's *Marly Horses* (*c.* 1740, the originals of the ones in the Place de la Concorde).

French Painting: The earliest known French easel painting, a 1350 portrait of King Jean le Bon. Georges de la Tour, greatest of the French followers of Caravaggio, with his startling contrasts of light and shadow. Watteau's *Gilles*. Delightful landscapes by Corot and the Barbizon school, forerunners of Impressionism. David's unfinished *portrait of Madame Récamier*, the famous Paris beauty. Delacroix's *Liberty Leading the People*, the Revolutionary icon painted for the revolt of 1830, where the bourgeoisie and workers fight side by side. Géricault's dramatic *Radeau de la Méduse*.

Flemish, Dutch and German Painting: Fine 15th-century altarpieces by van Eyck, van der Weyden and Memling, Hieronymous Bosch's delightful *Ship of Fools*, Joachim Patinir's gloomy *St Jerome in the Desert*, and some beautiful, meticulous works of

Quentin Metsys. From the height of the Renaissance, from Duke Federico's Palace at Urbino, 14 remarkable *Portraits of Philosophers*. Two masterpieces of light and depth by Jan Vermeer. Joyous scenes of peasant life by David Teniers and others, some odd allegories from Jan Brueghel and 15 Rembrandts. The *Life of Marie de' Medici*, over 1,000 square metres of unchained Peter Paul Rubens, recently installed in *Richelieu 2*. Rubensian buttocks fly every which way.

Italian Painting: The Grande Galerie: (*Denon 8, first floor*). The third (and least well preserved) part of the three-piece *Battle of San Romano* by Paolo Uccello, greatest and strangest of the Early Renaissance's slaves of perspective. Some fine late altarpieces by Botticelli, an eerie *Crucifixion* by Mantegna, and good works by da Messina, Baldovinetti, Piero della Francesca, Carpaccio and Perugino. Raphael's dreamlike *St Michael and the Dragon* and his portrait of the perfect Renaissance courtier, *Baldassare Castiglione*. Leonardo da Vinci's haunting *Virgin of the Rocks* and *Virgin and Child with St Anne*. The star attraction is the room itself, flooded with light.

The Salle des Etats: The Louvre's undisputed superstar, ***Mona Lisa***, 'the most famous artwork in the world', as a local guide trumpets her, smiling from behind the glass (installed after she was slashed a few years back), as the tourists with their flash machines close in like paparazzi. In the same room: Titian's smiling portrait of *François I*[er] and works by Correggio, Pontormo, del Sarto and others, and Veronese's room-sized *Wedding at Cana*, which besides Jesus and Mary includes nearly all the celebrities of the day: Emperor Charles V, François Ier and Suleiman the Magnificent sit at the table, while Titian, Tintoretto and other artists play in the band.

Late Italian and Spanish Painting: Francesco Guardi's colourful series of 12 works on *Venetian Festivals* (1763), a sweet document of the Serenissima near the end of its career. On the grand staircase, next to the *Winged Victory of Samothrace*, a detached Botticelli fresco called **Venus and the Graces**: five perfect Botticelli maidens maintaining their poise and calm amid the crowds. One El Greco *Crucifixion*; from the golden age of Spanish painting in the 1600s, at least one of each of the masters: Velázquez (*Infanta Margarita*), Ribera, and two Zurbaráns from the cycle of *St Bonaventure* – these come from Seville. Several Goyas.

Objets d'Art: Blinding jewels and heavy gold gimcracks, tapestries, Renaissance bronzes, Merovingian treasure, sardonyx vases... In the extravagantly decorated **Salle d'Apollon** (*Denon 8, first floor*): Louis XIV's crown jewels, Henri II's rock crystal chess set, Napoleon's crown and Josephine's earrings, Charlemagne's dagger, Saint Louis' ring, Louis XV's crown, and a 107.88 carat ruby in the shape of a dragon called *La Côte de Bretagne*. The rest of the collection is separate, on the first floor in *Sully 4–5* and *Richelieu 1, 2* and *3*. Don't miss it.

Madeleine and Place Vendôme

Place de la Madeleine; Ⓜ *Madeleine.*

Construction was begun in 1764, but this church was fated to see many changes before its completion. The death of the architect in 1777 occasioned a complete rethink; the new man opted for a neoclassical Greek cross plan, imitating Soufflot's Panthéon. Only a quarter finished by 1792, the revolutionary government pondered over a new use for the project – perhaps the seat of the National Assembly, the Banque de France or the National Library. But Napoleon knew what was best – a Temple of Glory, dedicated to himself and his Grand Army. The previous plans were scrapped, the foundations razed, and in 1806 architect Barthélemy Vignon came up with an imitation Greek temple. Napoleonic efficiency got the colonnades up in nine years, but once more political change intervened; after 1815 the restored Bourbons decided to make it a church after all.

After the chilly perfection of the Madeleine's exterior, the inside comes as a surprise: windowless and overdecorated, creamy and gloomy, more like a late Baroque Italian church – or ballroom. The rustic cane chairs contrast strangely with the gilded Corinthian columns and walls covered with a dozen varieties of expensive marble. The crowning touch, near the entrance, is a glass booth with a sign reading 'Priest on Duty' in five languages.

Place Vendôme

The second of Louis XIV's 'royal squares', after Place des Victoires, was laid out in 1699 by the same architect, Jules Hardouin-Mansart. The most satisfactory of all 17th-century French attempts at urban design, the square seems the utter antithesis of a building like the Opéra – but both were built to impress. Here, however, Hardouin-Mansart does it with absolute decorum. Only two streets lead into the square, which was conceived as a sort of enclosed urban parlour for the nobility. Balls were sometimes held in it, but cafés or anything else that would encourage street life or spontaneity were strictly forbidden. Originally, the square was to house embassies and academies, but the final plan proposed the present octagon of eight mansions, with uniform façades, and an equestrian statue of – guess who – in the centre. Today the square still has a not-too-discreet aroma of money about it; it is home to the Ritz Hotel, Cartier, Van Cleef & Arpels and a fleet of other jewellers.

Musée de Cluny (Musée National du Moyen Age)

*6 Place Paul-Painlevé; Ⓜ Cluny-La Sorbonne; **t** 01 453 73 78 16, www.musee-moyenage.fr. Open Wed–Mon 9.15–5.45; closed Tues and some hols; adm, free 1st Sun of the month.*

The Musée de Cluny contains one of the world's greatest collections of medieval art. In 1832 Alexandre du Sommerard rented the first floor of the mansion to hold his private museum of art from the Middle Ages. In 1844 the state purchased the collection, baths and *hôtel particulier* for a museum. Unfortunately for you, there are no boring bits to skip in this museum, but a continuous trove of the rare and the beautiful in exquisite detail to linger over all afternoon. Among the highlights: in **Salle III**, a gorgeous English leopard embroidery believed to have been the saddlecloth of Edward III; in **Salle IV**, a delightful series of six tapestries called *La Vie Seigneuriale* on the good life 500 years ago, contemporary with the Hôtel de Cluny itself; in **Salle V**, 15th-century alabasters from Nottingham. Beyond, in the Roman section of the museum, **Salle VIII** contains the museum's newest exhibit: 21 sad, solemn, erosion-scarred heads of the kings of Judea from the façade of Notre-Dame. Revolutionaries, mistaking them for French kings, had beheaded the statues in 1793; a Catholic Royalist buried them face down in a courtyard in Rue de la Chaussée-d'Antin, where they lay until their rediscovery in 1977.

The Thermes

Lofty, vast **Salle XII** is the *frigidarium* of the Roman baths. Wide-arched openings admit light; there are niches in the walls for statues and remains of drains in the floor. It is the only Roman bath in France to keep its roof – three barrel vaults linked by a groin vault in the centre, ending at the corners with capitals carved with ships' prows. In the centre are five large blocks from an altar to Jupiter, erected under Tiberius and discovered under the choir of Notre-Dame.

The Lady and the Unicorn

Upstairs, **Salle XIII** is a rotunda containing Cluny's greatest treasure: the six Aubusson tapestries of *La Dame à la Licorne*, dating from the late 15th century. Woven for Le Viste, a Lyonnese noble family, the tapestries were only rediscovered in the 19th century, rolled up and mouldering away in an obscure château in the middle of France. The lady, unicorn and lion appear in each scene, on a blue foreground and red background called *millefleurs*, strewn with a thousand flowers, birds and animals in the early Renaissance's fresh delight in nature. The first scenes appear to be allegories of the five senses, but the meaning of the sixth, where the legend on the tent reads *A mon seul désir*, will always remain a charming mystery.

Salle XIV, a long gallery of retables, painting and sculpture, contains two masterpieces: the *Pietà de Tarascon* (1450s), influenced by Italian and Flemish artists who painted in the papal entourage of Avignon, and a moving figure of *Marie Madeleine*, sculpted in Brussels *c*. 1500. Other rooms contain ivories, crowns, a rare golden rose, reliquaries, 4th-century lion heads in rock crystal, and exquisite works in gold and enamel. In **Salle XVIII**, where you can leaf through a 15th-century *Book of Hours*, the walls are hung with the first of 23 tapestries on the *Life of St Stephen* (1490). The chapel (**Salle XX**) is a flamboyant gem.

Musée d'Orsay

1 Rue de la Légion d'Honneur; Ⓜ *Solférino,* ***RER*** *Musée d'Orsay;*
t *01 40 49 48 48, www.musee-orsay.fr. Open June–Sept Tues, Wed, Fri–Sun 10–6, Thurs 10–9.45; Oct–May Tues, Wed, Fri, Sat 10–6, Thurs 10–9.45, Sun 9–6; closed Mon; adm, free first Sun of month.*

The Gare d'Orsay is a monument born on the cusp of the 19th century: a daring work of iron weighing more than the Eiffel Tower, with a nave taller than Notre-

Dame, thrown up in two years for the 1900 World Fair to serve trains from the south-west. The architect, Victor Laloux, professor of architecture at the Ecole des Beaux-Arts, was hired to make the façade a dignified foil for the Louvre across the river. The net result is pure Napoleon III rococola; unfortunately, its platforms were too short for modern trains, and the station was abandoned in 1960. It opened as a museum in 1986, nine years after the design was approved. The core exhibits came from the former Jeu-de-Paume Museum and the 19th-century rooms of the Louvre. Here under one huge roof are gathered all its combative schools of painting and sculpture from 1848 to 1910, rounded out with a magnificent array of furniture, decorative arts, architectural exhibits and photography. You could easily spend a day here, and neither thirst nor starve, thanks to the museum's restaurant and rooftop café.

Highlights of the Collections

Sculptures command the entrance: Rude's piece of Romantic hyperbole, *Le Génie de la Patrie*, from the Arc de Triomphe, followed inside the main door by a *Lion* by Barye (d. 1875), animal sculptor extraordinaire, and Rude's *Napoleon Awaking to Immortality*.

The **Salle de l'Opéra**, dedicated to Garnier's extraordinary folly, with Carpeaux's original *La Danse* pixies from the façade. A model of the Opéra (from the 1900 World Fair) is cross-sectioned so you can see all the machinery behind the scenes. The several floors of a tower called the *Pavillon Amont* offer a compendium of Second Empire and Third Republic Paris façades and architecture from Viollet-le-Duc to Frank Lloyd Wright. Best of all is a massive 1855 *View of Paris* painted by Victor Navlet from a balloon floating over the Observatoire.

The greatest works of **Gustave Courbet** (1819–77), the formulator of **Realism** and the first artist to completely buck the *salon* system – 'I have no master; my master is myself. There is not, and never has been, any painter other than myself.'

Manet's *Olympia* (1865), which made people spit venom when shown in the Salon des Refusés; not so much because of the nude but because Manet merely sketched in the bouquet of flowers – a photograph-inspired blur of movement that damned it in the eyes of critics.

Impressionist paintings before 1870, when Monet, Renoir and Bazille (who died in the Franco-Prussian War) first took their easels out of doors.

Impressionists: Manet's *Déjeuner sur l'Herbe* (1863), an updated version of Giorgione's *Concert Champêtre* in the Louvre and the key inspiration for the Impressionists with its masterly, experimental handling of paint. And a portrait by an American friend of Manet and Baudelaire, who in his delight for arty names called it *Arrangement in Grey and Black no.1*, although everyone knows it as *Whistler's Mother*.

Monet's *Régates à Argenteuil*, Pissarro's *Les Toits Rouges* and *L'Inondation à Port-Marly*, considered the masterpiece of Alfred Sisley (1839–99), who was born in Paris of English parents and concentrated on the nuances of the changing colours of water, sky and mists. Monet's steam-filled *Gare Saint-Lazare* and his *Rue Montorgueil*. Renoir's irresistible evocation of Paris's *bals dansants*, the *Moulin de la Galette* (1876).

Manet's *Sur la Plage*, as well as everyday Paris scenes in *La Serveuse de Bocks*. His interests in turn influenced Berthe Morisot (1841–95), the grande dame of

Impressionism, whose subjects from her life and that of her friends form a woman's diary in paint (*Le Berceau*).

Degas' *A la Bourse, L'Absinthe, Les Repasseuses*; his unusual compositions were inspired in part by the spontaneity of photography and Japanese prints, although unlike the other Impressionists he never painted out of doors, but from memory. The ballet and race track became special interests of Degas after 1874, affording opportunities for unusual compositions and also for the study of movement.

Late Impressionists (after 1880): Monet's series that portray the same subject at different times of day: *Les Meules* (Haystacks), five of *Les Cathédrales de Rouen* and two versions of the *Nymphéas* (Water Lilies) painted at Giverny, where representation of form is so minimal as to verge on abstract constructions of pure colour. Renoir's *Paysage Algérien, Fête Arabe à Alger*, and *Les Grandes Baigneuses*, an extraordinary work from a man paralysed by rheumatism, who had to have his brushes strapped to his wrists.

Van Gogh (1853–90): *La Guinguette, L'Arlésienne, La Chambre de Van Gogh à Arles* and the merciless *Autoportrait*, painted during his first fit of madness in Arles.

Cézanne (1839–1906): *La Maison du Pendu* and *Une Moderne Olympia*, inspired by Manet. The other Impressionists were not very impressed by him or vice versa, and after 1877 Cézanne spent most of his time in Aix, becoming a legend towards the end of his life. The Musée d'Orsay has masterpieces of his three favourite subjects: a landscape (*L'Estaque*), figures (*Femme à la Cafetière, Les Joueurs de Cartes* and *Baigneurs*) and still lifes.

Postimpressionism: Georges Seurat's *Le Cirque*. The most scientific of painters, Seurat (1859–91) set out to rescue Impressionism from the charges of frivolity by developing his distinctive pointillist style, based on the colour theories of physicists Chevreal and N. O. Rood on the optic mixing of tones and the action of colour; when viewed from a distance, each dot of colour takes on the proper relationship with the dots around it, although remaining visible as an optic vibration.

The **Salle Redon**: devoted to the works of the elusive Odilon Redon (1840–1916), master colourist and pre-Freudian painter of dreams, who belonged to no school but greatly inspired the Symbolists, Surrealists and Metaphysical painters who followed (*Portrait de Gauguin*).

The **Salle Toulouse-Lautrec**: Lautrec (1864–1901), a descendant of the counts of Toulouse, broke both legs as a child, which seriously impeded his growth. His physical afflictions may have contributed to his empathy in the penetrating portraits of 'occupationally distorted souls', especially of prostitutes, whom he drew while living amongst them. Lautrec strove to 'paint the truth, not the ideal'.

Gauguin's lush paintings from the South Seas, where he fled to escape 'diseased' civilization to rejuvenate art by becoming 'one with nature'.

Fauvism, represented by André Derain's *Le Pont de Charing Cross* (1902) in the Kaganovitch collection in the last room on this floor.

Symbolists: *The Wheel of Fortune* by Burne-Jones, who made the Pre-Raphaelites popular in France, *Summer Night* by Winslow Homer, the famous *Portrait of Proust* by

Jacques-Emile Blanche, *Le Rêve* by Puvis de Chavannes, *Nuit d'Eté* by Munch and the extraordinary, pastel-coloured *Ecole de Platon* by Jean Delville, where naked youths with Gibson girl hairdos languidly listen to philosophy under the wisteria.

Art Nouveau: dragonfly jewellery by Lalique, furniture by Guimard (*Banquette avec Vitrine*), a desk by Henry Van de Velde, glass by Tiffany and Gallé.

The **Tour Guimard**: furniture designed by architects – beautiful chairs by Guimard, Gaudí, Bugatti, Mackintosh and Frank Lloyd Wright.

Musée Rodin

77 Rue de Varenne; Ⓜ *Varenne;* ***t*** *01 44 18 61 10, www.musee-rodin.fr.*

Open April–Sept Tues–Sun 9.30–5.45, Oct–Mar Tues–Sun 09.30–4.45, gardens close at 6.45 in summer, 5 in winter; small fee to visit the gardens only.

The Hôtel Biron (1731) was built after a plan by Jacques-Ange Gabriel for Peyrenc de Moras. It is one of the most charming and best-preserved mansions in Paris from the period, fitted with distinguished façades overlooking the front courtyard and back-gardens. When Auguste Rodin moved here in 1908, he was 68; his reputation as France's greatest sculptor was in the bag, and it was agreed that he would leave the state his works after he died, 10 days after marrying his mistress of over 50 years, in 1917.

Rodin was the last of the great Romantics. He sculpted the literary subjects of the day, but with a personal vision that liberated sculpture from its stagnant rut as portraiture, public decoration or propaganda. He studied Michelangelo in Italy and came back to cause his first sensation in 1876 with *The Age of Bronze* (*L'Age d'Airain*, Room 3), so realistic that he was accused of casting a live man in bronze. In 1880 Rodin was commissioned to make a bronze door for a museum of decorative arts, resulting in *The Gates of Hell* (in the garden). Studies are scattered throughout the museum: the *Three Shadows*, Paolo Malatesta and Francesca da Rimini in *The Kiss* (Room 5) and *The Thinker* (outside), in a pose reminiscent of the Lost Soul in Michelangelo's *Last Judgement*. The famous *La Main de Dieu* (1898) in Room 4 inaugurated Rodin's departure from academic tradition in a composition purely from his imagination. Room 6 is dedicated to sculptor Camille Claudel, sister of poet Paul and Rodin's model for his *La France and L'Aurore*; here too are examples of her work before she went mad. Room 7 has portraits of society ladies and the poignant *Mother and her Dying Daughter*, the faces and hands almost engulfed, overwhelmed by the raw marble, an emotional device Rodin often employed, inspired by Michelangelo's *nonfiniti*.

Upstairs are paintings that Rodin owned and left to the state. Outside, amid the roses of the *Cour d'Honneur*, are Rodin's *Thinker* and other masterpieces, a delightful **garden** filled with studies for the *Burghers*, and a serene duck pond containing the most harrowing sculpture of all, *Ugolin and his Sons*.

Notre-Dame

Ile de la Cité; Ⓜ *Cité,* ***RER*** *St-Michel-Notre-Dame; www.catholique.paris.com.*

Open daily 8–6.45; part or all of the cathedral is closed for services (Mon–Sat 8, 8,45, 10, 11.30, 12.45, 6.30, Sun 8, 9, 12, 6.15); guided tours of the cathedral in English Wed and Thurs 12 noon; in French Mon–Fri 12 noon, Sat–Sun 2.30; free.

This site has been holy ever since Paris was Lutetia, when a temple to Jupiter stood here. In the 6th century a small church was erected; sacked by the Normans in 857, it was reconstructed but on the same scale, hardly large enough for the growing population. A proper cathedral had to wait for Maurice de Sully, who became bishop of Paris in 1160.

Cities all over France were beginning great cathedrals. Notre-Dame came along on the crest of the wave; its architecture was destined to become the consummate work of the early Gothic, the measuring stick by which all other cathedrals are judged. Because it was in Paris, the cosmopolitan centre of learning, Notre-Dame had a considerable influence in diffusing Gothic architecture throughout Europe; for over two centuries its construction site was a busy, permanent workshop, through which passed the continent's most skilled masons, sculptors, carpenters and glassmakers. Plans changed continually, as new problems came up. Henry VI of England was crowned here in 1430; seven years later Charles VII was present at a solemn Te Deum to celebrate the retaking of Paris from the English. French coronations commonly took place at Reims; the next one here would not come until 1804, the pompous apotheosis of Emperor Napoleon, brilliantly captured in the famous propaganda painting by David.

During the Revolution, the Parisians had first trashed Notre-Dame, wrecking most of its sculptures; then they decided to demolish it. A few subtle voices stood up for its 'cultural and historical value' and the cathedral was saved to become the 'Temple of Reason', where Reason's goddess, a former dancer, held forth. Little upkeep took place for centuries. The building was literally falling to bits when Victor Hugo, with his novel *Notre-Dame de Paris*, contributed immeasurably to a revival of interest in the city's medieval roots. Serious restoration work only began in the 1840s. Eugène Viollet-le-Duc, a man who spent his life trying to redeem centuries of his countrymen's ignorance and fecklessness, worked the better part of two decades on the site. His approach to restoration was not scientifically perfect, but still far ahead of its time. Viollet-le-Duc's workshops produced original sculpture, attempting to capture the spirit of what had been destroyed or damaged instead of merely copying it.

To see the **façade** as it was intended, remember that, as with the temples of ancient Greece, originally all the statues and reliefs of a Gothic church were painted in bright colours. The statuary begins at the level of the rose window: *Adam and Eve*, on either side of the rose, and the *Virgin Flanked by Angels*. Below these, running the length of the façade, is a row of 28 Kings of Judah and Israel, the ancestors of Jesus.

Below the kings are the three portals, interspersed with four framed sculptural groups: St Stephen on the left; the *Church and Synagogue* on the two centre piers, representing the 'true and false revelations'; and, on the right pier, *St Denis*. The **left portal** is dedicated to the Virgin Mary, a lovely composition *c*. 1210. The **right portal** is dedicated to St Anne, and is the earliest of the portals (mostly *c*. 1170); and the **central portal**, the largest and most impressive of the three, finished *c*. 1220, is of the Last Judgement. Such fine portals deserve **doors** to match. The hardware and hinges for those on the left and right, still in good nick today, were made by an ironsmith named Biscornet.

We can only guess what the **interior furnishings** looked like in the days before the Revolution. In the Middle Ages, when cathedrals were the great public living rooms of the cities and always open, there would have been no chairs, of course, just rushes strewn on the floor to soak up the mud from the hordes of people who passed through daily, gabbing, gambling, making business deals, eating their lunch, waiting for the rain to stop or listening to the choir practice – throughout the Middle Ages Notre-Dame was the musical centre of Europe, where much of the new polyphonic method was invented. The decorations of the altar and chapels were more colourful and artistic than anything there now. Besides the gifts of kings and nobles, the city guilds competed ardently to embellish the cathedral for centuries.

Today, we must be content with the architecture and the remnants of the stained glass, but it's more than enough. And it's big enough: 430ft long, with room for some 9,000 people, acccording to Viollet-le-Duc's calculations. The plan set the pattern for the other cathedrals of the Ile-de-France: a wide nave with four side aisles, which curve and meet around the back of the altar. The side chapels were not original, but added in the 13th century to hold all the gifts pouring in from the confraternities and guilds. Today, sadly, there is not a single noteworthy painting or statue in any of them.

Most of the chapels were remodelled to suit the tastes of the 17th and 18th centuries, or wrecked in the Revolution. But this is nothing compared with the vandalism committed in the age of the Big Louies. In the 18th century, nearly all of the stained glass was simply removed, to let in more light. To thank the Virgin for being born, the Sun King ordered the florid, carved-wood choir stalls, and a complete rebuilding of the choir, including a new altar, flanked by statues of His Majesty himself and his father. Thank God at least he spared the original choir enclosure, lined with a series of 23 beautiful **reliefs of the life of Christ**, made in *c*. 1350 by Jean Ravy and his nephew Jean le Bouteiller.

We can be even more thankful they didn't take out the three great **rose windows**. The one in the west front, heavily restored by Viollet-le-Duc, expresses the message of this cathedral's art even better than the portals: the Virgin sits in majesty at the centre, surrounded by the virtues and vices, the signs of the zodiac and the works of the months – all the things of this world. In the left transept rose, Mary is again at the centre, in the company of Old Testament prophets, judges and kings. In the right transept rose, a truly remarkable composition, she dominates the New Testament, amid the Apostles (in the square frames) and saints.

Leaving the cathedral, turn right and right again, following the northern side of the cathedral along Rue du Cloître-Notre-Dame. Originally all of the island east of Rue d'Arcole was occupied by Notre-Dame's **cloister**. At the beginning of Rue du Cloître signs beckon you to ascend the **Tours de Notre-Dame** for the Quasimodo's-eye view over Paris and a chance to eyeball the gargoyles at close quarters (*open daily 9–8; adm*). No one has ever come up with a satisfactory explanation for the hordes of fanciful beasts that inhabit medieval churches. They have no didactic religious meaning, and probably no esoteric meaning. They seem mere flights of fancy, though if you can pick these out from ground level they are disconcerting enough. There are also the bells...

Rue du Cloître continues to the little **Musée de Notre-Dame** at No.10 (*open Wed, Sat and Sun 2.30–6; adm*). This isn't a state museum, which explains its unusual opening hours. It is run by a society of friends of Notre-Dame, charming people who like to explain things to visitors and tell stories. The exhibits, mostly old prints, views, photos and plans, are quite fascinating, offering a wealth of detail on the history of the building and the quarter. The **Place du Parvis-Notre-Dame** extends in front of the cathedral. In the Middle Ages, the miracle plays and mystery plays put on by the confraternities were one of the major public entertainments. Often they were held here, where the magnificent porch of the cathedral could serve as 'Paradise', a word that over the centuries got mangled into Parvis.

Traced in the Parvis is the former route of Rue Neuve de Notre-Dame, laid out by Louis VII in the 12th century. When new, this was the widest street in Paris – all of 21ft across. If you want to see what was underneath it, go down to the **Crypte Archéologique du Parvis-Notre-Dame** (*open daily 10–6; closed some hols; combined ticket with Musée Carnavalet available;adm, free Sun 10–1*). What was begun as an underground car park in 1965 had to become a museum when the excavations revealed the 3rd-century wall of Lutetia, traces of Roman and medieval houses, 17th-century cellars, the Merovingian cathedral that preceded Notre-Dame, and foundations of the 1750 Enfants Trouvés, or foundlings hospital, where unwanted children were left on a revolving tray.

Opéra

Place de l'Opéra; Ⓜ *Opéra, Chaussée d'Antin; www,opera-de-paris.fr.*

Tours in English Sat 12.30 (get there at 12.15); museum open Mon–Sat 10–5 exc performance days; separate adm for both. Tours include the main hall on days when there is no performance; check beforehand, **t** *01 40 01 22 63, if you want to see Chagall's ceiling.*

The supreme monument of the Second Empire was conceived in 1858, after Napoleon III was leaving a slightly more intimate theatre and one of the rabble got close enough to try and assassinate him. A competition was organized for a new Opéra, and the plan chosen was the largest, submitted by a fashionable young architect named Charles Garnier. After winning the competition, Garnier still had to convince a sceptical Napoleon and Eugénie. Asked what style his work was supposed to be, the architect replied: 'It is no style. Not Greek or Roman; it is the style of Napoleon III.' That won the Emperor over immediately.

Finally open in 1875, three years after Napoleon's death, the biggest and most sumptuous theatre in the world soon passed into legend, much of it due to Gaston Leroux's novel *Le Fantôme de l'Opéra*. There were controversies, such as the one over Carpeaux's flagrant statuary outside. The artist's rivals pretended to be shocked (naked women, in Paris!) and threw bottles of ink at them. Anarchists plotted to blow the place up, and everyone whispered about the famous Opéra masked balls ('great festivals of pederasty', one writer called them). Envied and copied throughout the world, this building contributed much to the transformation of opera into the grand spectacle and social ritual it became in the *belle époque*. It may have seemed that way to François Mitterrand, when in the 1980s he decided on the overtly political gesture of sentencing opera to the proletarian Bastille. Today the behemoth sits a bit forlorn, home only to its dance company, run until a few years ago by the late Rudolf Nureyev.

The inside is impressive, awash with gold leaf, frescoes, mosaics and scores of different varieties of precious stone, from Swedish marble to Algerian onyx. The highlight of the tour may be the hall itself, with its **ceiling** (1964) painted by Marc Chagall; the nine scenes, lovely if perhaps incongruous in this setting, are inspired by some of the artist's favourite operas and ballets. The **Musée de l'Opéra** is in the Imperial Pavilion (enter from main entrance); it has a collection of memorabilia and art, including a portrait of Wagner by Renoir.

Outside, the **Place de l'Opéra** was one of the status addresses of late 19th-century Paris; it included the original **Grand Hôtel**, opened for the World Fair of 1867. To your left and right stretch the western **Grands Boulevards**: Boulevard des Italiens, Boulevard des Capucines and Boulevard de la Madeleine. A century ago these were the brightest promenades of Paris, home of all the famous cafés and restaurants. Today the glamour is gone but the streets are popular and crowded just the same; they're a good place to take in a movie – and have been since the world's first public film show was put on by the Lumière brothers at No.14, Boulevard des Capucines, on 28 December 1895.

Pompidou Centre

Place Georges-Pompidou and Rue St-Martin; Ⓜ *Hôtel de Ville, rambuteau, Châtelet;* ***RER*** *Châtelet-Les-Halles; www.centrepompidou.fr.*

Open Mon and Wed–Sun 11–10, for guided visits call ***t*** *01 44 78 12 33. Museum open 11–9, last adm 8; adm. English audioguides extra. Atelier Brancusi open Sat–Sun 1–7.*

The 'Beau Bourg' was a village, swallowed up by Paris in the Middle Ages, that has lent its name to the neighbourhood ever since. By the 1920s it had become a grey, unloved place; the government cleared a large section, meaning to relocate the flower market from the Halles. Nothing happened, leaving the void as a challenge to Paris planners until the end of the 1960s. It was the grey, unloved president, Georges Pompidou, who came up with the idea of a 'department store for culture' accessible to the widest possible public.

The design finally chosen was the most radical of all those submitted. The architects, Richard Rogers and Renzo Piano, turned traditional ideas of building upside down – or rather, inside out. To allow larger, more open spaces on the inside, and to expose what a modern structure really is, they came up with a big rectangle of girders, from which the insides are hung, a kind of invertebrate architecture, with an insect's shell instead of a skeleton. Much more provocative was the idea of putting the technological guts of the building on the outside – celebrating the essentials instead of hiding them, and painting them in bright colours keyed to help the observer understand how it all works: electrics in yellow, air-conditioning in blue, white for ventilation ducts, etc. These are best seen on the back of the building, along Rue Beaubourg.

After the Centre opened in 1977, Parisians and tourists voiced their opinion by making it overnight the most visited sight in the city, surpassing even the Eiffel Tower. The 'Plateau' in front, redesigned by Piano into an austere, sloping rectangle, became an instant happening that even Georges Pompidou might have enjoyed (from a safe distance), where Paris's old coterie of oral tricksters – sword-swallowers, cigarette-munchers and bicycle-eaters – perform amid buskers and portrait-sketchers.

Inside, you won't need a ticket for the **escalator** to the top, by far the Centre's most popular attraction. Like everything else mechanical, it runs along the outside, providing a spectacular view over Paris that changes dramatically as you ascend; for a special treat, come back and do it at twilight, when the city is illuminated.

The major permanent feature of the Centre is the **Musée National d'Art Moderne**. This superlative collection of 20th-century art takes up where the Musée d'Orsay leaves off: at the turning point of modernity in 1904, when the Fauves (Derain, Vlaminck, Matisse, Marquet) liberated colour from its age-old function of representing nature. Van Gogh had blazed a trail by using colour to express emotions. The Fauves went a step beyond, applying colour and line on a two-dimensional surface as an intellectual expression, the way a poet uses words on a piece of paper. As Van Gogh was a prophet for the Fauves, Cézanne's experiments in rendering volume with nuances of colour inspired Cubism. A prism of aftershocks fills the next rooms, especially the first abstract works, born of Wassily Kandinsky, imaginative Expressionism and the geometric fundamentals of Mondrian and his de Stijl followers. At every point the display and organization of the museum's works explores the cross-pollination between pure and applied art, setting a Mondrian canvas of flat squares and defined boundaries with sculptures composed of squares and flat planes alongside 1920s architectural models by Paul Nelson and Le Corbusier, where the same principles have been used to transform the spaces we live in.

The excellent audioguide is especially helpful on the lower floor, 'Post 1960', where the familiar images of Pop Art and new realism and displays of space-age plastic furniture give way to the explorations of artists' cautionary responses to technology in the 1960s: Robert Rauschenberg's *Oracle* and Sigmar Polke's *Pasadena*, questioning the truth of the sudden flood of media images, information and advertising pouring over an unprepared public. The art on this floor is participatory, kinetic, interactive. Also on this floor are a Graphic Art Gallery and a New Media Centre.

On other floors of the Centre are a public library (the BPI) and musical research institute (IRCAM), a gift shop with goods inspired by the modern art collections, a café, a bookshop, a restaurant, halls for temporary exhibitions, two cinemas, two concert spaces and, out on the Plateau, the **Atelier Brancusi**, a reconstruction of the Paris studio where the Romanian sculptor lived from 1925 to 1927.

Sacré-Cœur

Ⓜ *Abbesses, Anvers, Château Rouge, Lamarck-Caulaincourt;* **t** *01 53 41 89 00, www.sacre-coeur-montmartre.com.*

Basilica open daily 6.45am–11pm, dome and crypt 9am–6.30; adm.

The story goes that between 1673 and 1689 Jesus Christ appeared to a nun from the Royal Abbey of Montmartre, demanding a church to the glory of his Divine Heart 'to serve France and repair the bitterness and outrages that have wasted her'. The project was put to every regime that followed, but nothing happened until the Commune and the fall of Rome (Napoleon III had been protecting the pope from the Italians, who captured Rome in 1870).

Many Parisians regard the result with some embarrassment, and not only for its preposterous Romano-Byzantine architecture. The national vow was imposed on the city by a vote in the National Assembly in 1873, despite opposition by radicals and many Montmartrois, who claimed it would ruin the character of the Butte (as indeed it has, drawing 6 million visitors a year). In the design competition the most pompous entry, by Paul Abadie, was chosen. It drove Adolphe Willette (the designer of the Moulin-Rouge) crazy: 'It isn't possible that God, if he exists, would consent to live there,' he declared. On the day the first bit, the crypt chapel, opened, he ran in and shouted: '*Vive le diable!*' The Montmartrois have honoured him with a square at the foot of Sacré-Cœur's stairs.

For a real descent into the abyss, visit the clammy **crypt**, with its neglected chapels, broken chairs, dingy cases of relics salvaged from the Royal Abbey of Montmartre, overgrown statues of praying cardinals, and a slide show on the building of Sacré-Cœur. The view from the dome isn't that much more spectacular than the view from the parvis, but you can look vertiginously down into the interior of the basilica.

Versailles

***RER** C or train from the Gare Montparnasse or from Gare St-Lazare to Versailles-Rive Droite, followed by a 15-minute walk;* **t** *01 30 83 78 00, www.chateauversailles.com.*

The château is open May–Sept Tues–Sun 9–6.30 , Oct–April Tues–Sun 9–5.30, closed hols; adm, reduced after 3.30, free Oct–Mar 1st Sun of the month (Grands Appartements and Galeries des Glaces only); guided tours in English from 10. Grands Appartements (entrance A). Another €4 at entrance C will get you into the Apartments of Louis XIV and the Apartments of the Dauphin and Dauphine with an audioguide in English; you can also visit the Opéra Royal, a gem designed by Gabriel for Louis XV in 1768, which is all wood, painted as marble, but designed 'to resonate like a violin' (adm extra).

In summer the garden's musical fountains are turned on (all using their original plumbing); adm; gardens free Nov–Mar, guided tour adm; open summer 7–dusk, winter 8–dusk. A Passport gives access to the Château, Grand Trianon, Petit Trianon, Coach Museum and the Groves (exc during the fountain show) for €14 (€9 low season); four Saturdays between 3 July and 18 September occasion the extravagant Grandes Fêtes de Nuit, fireworks, illuminated fountains and an 'historical fresco' (book with FNAC or Spectacles Châteaux, ***t*** *08 92 70 18 92 or 01 30 83 78 96,* ***f*** *01 30 83 78 96; Versailles Tourist Office,* ***t*** *01 39 24 88 88).*

Versailles' name comes from the clods that the farmer turns over with his plough, referring to the clearing made for a royal hunting lodge. And so Versailles remained until the young Louis XIV attended the fatal bash at Fouquet's Vaux-le-Vicomte, which turned him sour with envy. He would have something perhaps not better but certainly bigger, and hired all the geniuses Fouquet had patronized to create for himself one of the world's masterpieces of megalomania – 123 acres of rooms. They are strikingly void of art; the enormous façade of the château is as monotonous as it is tasteful, so as not to upstage the principal inhabitant. The object is not to think of the building, but of Louis, and with that thought be awed. It is the shibboleth of France, the albatross around her neck.

Versailles contributed greatly to the bankruptcy of France: Louis, used to overawing his subjects, began to believe that he could bully nature as well. He ordered his engineers to divert the Loire itself to feed his fountains and, when faced with the impossible, settled on bringing the waters of the Eure through pestilent marshes to Versailles using the aqueduct of Maintenon, a ten-year project that cost nine million *livres* and the lives of hundreds of workmen before it was abandoned. Too much sacrifice and money has been concentrated here for the French to shake the albatross loose; they are a part of it.

If there's no art in Versailles, there is certainly an extraordinary amount of skilful craftsmanship. Besides its main purpose as a stage for Louis (Versailles and its gardens were open to anyone who was decently dressed and promised not to beg in the halls; anyone could watch the king attend Mass, or dine), the palace served as a giant public showroom for French products, especially from the new luxury industries cranked up by Colbert. As such it was a spectacular success, contributing greatly to the spread of French tastes and fashions throughout Europe. One thing the restorers don't care to recreate is the palace plumbing – a mere three toilets for the estimated 20,000 residents, servants and visitors. After Louis XVI and Marie-Antoinette were evicted by the Paris mob on 6 October 1789, Versailles was left empty, and there was talk of knocking it down when Louis-Philippe decided to restore it as a museum.

The **Grands Appartements** are the public rooms traditionally open to all in Louis XIV's day – although in the crowds you may feel as squeezed as toothpaste in a tube. Beyond are the **Salle de Guerre** and **Salle de Paix**, linked by the famous 241ft **Hall of**

Mirrors, currently part of a restoration programme (until 2009) but partially visible to the public. Still crowned with Lebrun's paintings of the first 17 years of Louis XIV's reign, Louis melted down the original solid silver furniture to pay his war debts. The 17 mirrors with 578 panes are post-1975 copies, put in place after a disgruntled Breton blew up the originals; facing the windows, they reflect the sunlight into the gardens, a fantastical conceit intended to remind visitors that the Sun himself dwelt within.

Beyond the Salle de Paix are the formal apartments of the queen; their current appearance required a colossal reconstruction – shreds of fabric were found and rewoven in the original designs, and Savonnerie carpets copied from old designs. The **Chambre de la Reine** was used for the public birthing of Enfants de France.

Then there are the **gardens**, last replanted by Napoleon III, with their 13 miles of box hedges to clip, and the 1,100 potted palms and oranges of the Orangerie, all planted around the 'limitless perspective' from the terrace fading into the blue horizon of the Grand Canal. Not by accident, the sun sets straight into it on St Louis' day, 25 August, in a perfect alignment with the Hall of Mirrors. On either side Le Nôtre's original garden design – more theatrical and full of surprises than any of his other creations – is slowly being restored while hundreds of trees have been sacrificed in the name of new vistas of the château, inspired by Louis XIV's guidebook to the gardens, the *Manière de Montrer les Jardins de Versailles*. In it he devised a one-way route for his visitors to take, for even at their best Le Nôtre's gardens are essentially two-dimensional; to appreciate them they must be seen from just the right angle.

Louis kept a flotilla of gondolas on his Grand Canal, to take his courtiers for rides; today the gondoliers of Venice come to visit every September for the *Fêtes Vénitiennes*. The rest of the year you can hire a boat to paddle about or a bike to pedal through the gardens, or even catch a little zoo train to a building far more interesting than the main palace, the **Grand Trianon** (*April–Oct daily 12–6.30; Nov-Mar daily 12–5; adm*). An elegant, airy Italianate palace of pink marble and porphyry with two wings linked by a peristyle, it was designed by the staff of Hardouin-Mansart in 1687 for Louis XIV. After his divorce, Napoleon brought his new Empress Marie-Louise here, who did it up quite attractively in the Empire style.

The gardens in this area were laid out by Louis XV's architect, Jacques-Ange Gabriel, who also built the rococo **Pavillon du Jardin des Français** and the refined **Petit Trianon** nearby (*open at the same times as the Grand Trianon; adm*), intended for Louis XV's meetings with Madame de Pompadour. Louis XVI gave the Petit Trianon to Marie-Antoinette, who spent much of her time here. Beyond the Petit Trianon is the **Hameau de la Reine**, the delightful operetta farmhouse built for Marie-Antoinette, where she could play shepherdess.

Nothing escaped Louis XIV's attention, and even his carrots and cabbages were planted in geometric rigidity in his immaculate vegetable garden, **Le Potager du Roi**, arranged to please all five senses (*www.potager-du-roi.fr, entrance at 6 Rue Hardy, on the left side of Place des Armes, the square in front of the château; open April–Oct daily 10–6, adm; guided tours Sat and Sun every hour 10.30–4.30; adm; book on* **t** *01 39 24 62 62*). The visit includes the adjacent **Parc Balbi**, a romantic park planted by the Comte de Provence (future Louis XVIII) for his mistress.

Paris: *Quartiers*

18

Ile de la Cité and Ile St-Louis

Ⓜ *Cité, Pont Neuf, Châtelet, St-Michel, Pont Marie, Sully-Morland.*

Paris made its début on the Ile de la Cité and, in their congenital chauvinism, the Parisians regard their river islet to this day as not only the centre of the city, but the centre of all France. Haussmann's rebuilding banished 25,000 people who lived on a hundred colourful tiny streets and, like the City of London and Wall Street, the area is deserted at night. But two of the most luminous Gothic churches ever built are reason alone for visiting, and there are other delights – shady squares and *quais*, panoramic bridges and the perfect symmetry of neighbouring Ile St-Louis, an island-village of the *haute bourgeoisie*, concocted by 17th-century speculators and architecturally little changed since. On a Sunday morning you can hear a distant echo of the old din in Place Lépine's twittering bird market.

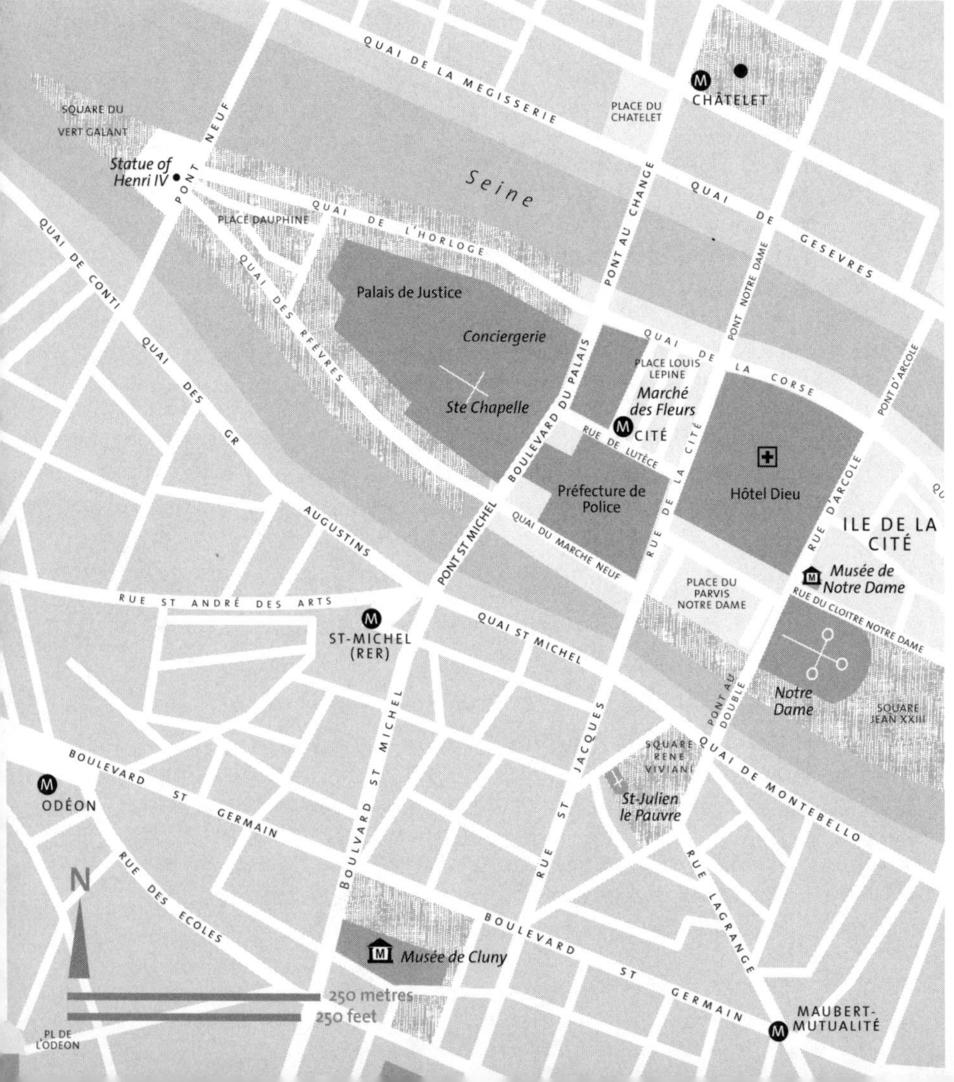

Ile de la Cité

Conciergerie

Quai de l'Horloge. Open April–Sept 9 –6, Oct–Mar 9–5; closed some hols; adm, free 1st Sun of month Oct–May; joint ticket with Ste-Chapelle; guided tours in French at 11 and 3.

To set the mood for a building known as the 'Antechamber of Death', the first of three round towers you pass along the Quai de l'Horloge is the Tour Bonbec (1250), or 'babbler', where prisoners presumed guilty were questioned. A trap door under their feet waited to pitch them into an oubliette lined with razor-sharp steel spikes; the Seine washed their mangled bodies away.

The Conciergerie wasn't always so grim. In its first, 4th-century incarnation it was the palace of Lutetia's Roman governors. Clovis requisitioned the palace *c.* AD 500, and

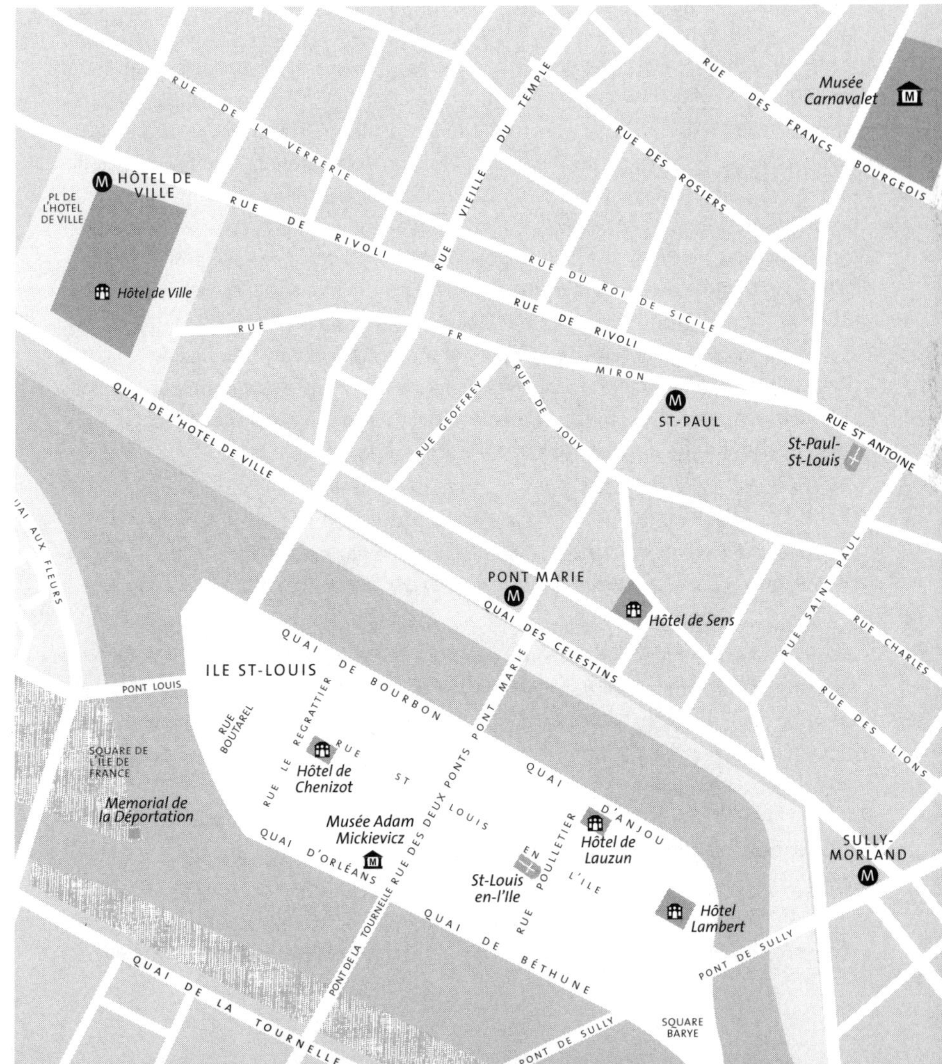

Cafés and Lunches

Taverne Henri IV, 13 Place du Pont-Neuf, **t** 01 43 54 27 90. Ancient, amiable bar in a Louis XIII building, specializing in provincial dishes and wine-tasting; where the Ile's lawyers feast on wines from Burgundy, *tartines*, *charcuterie*, boar sausage from Quercy. *Closed Sat night and Sun.*

Au Rendez-vous des Camionneurs, 72 Quai des Orfèvres, **t** 01 43 54 88 74. Delicious, French-truckers'-style cooking; lunch clientele tends to be judges, journalists and cops.

Brasserie de l'Ile Saint-Louis, 55 Quai de Bourbon, **t** 01 43 54 02 59. Has external views over the magnificent apse of Notre-Dame and a bar-view of a stuffed stork; an institution for rugby fans and lovers of old-fashioned *choucroute*.

Caveau du Palais, 19 Place Dauphine, **t** 01 43 26 04 28. Excellent quality establishment set in one of the most romantic squares of Paris. *Closed Sun in Oct–April.*

Berthillon, 31 Rue St-Louis-en-l'Ile. Queue up here for the best ice-cream and sorbet in Paris (or possibly the entire world): 70 flavours, including an absolutely luscious chocolate. *Afternoons only; closed Mon, Tues, Aug and school holidays.*

L'Ilot Vache, 35 Rue St-Louis-en-l'Ile, **t** 01 46 33 55 16. Lovely, old-fashioned and full of flowers, with an honest €33 menu that usually includes lots of seafood.

established the Frankish monarchy within its walls; in 987 Hugues Capet moved in, and it stayed in the family for 800 years. As the kings grew wealthy, their palace grew more splendid, so that by the time Richard the Lionheart came to call on Philippe-Auguste it resembled a fairy-tale miniature from the Duc de Berry's *Très Riches Heures*. In 1358, Etienne Marcel's partisans stormed the palace and assassinated the king's ministers as the Dauphin Charles V stood helplessly by. It was a lesson in the vulnerability of the royal person in Paris, and the result was the construction of the better-fortified Louvre. Abandoned by the kings, the palace evolved into Paris's seat of justice and its prison.

Architecturally, the highlight of the Conciergerie is Philippe le Bel's **Salle des Gens d'Armes** (1314), or guardroom, one of the largest Gothic halls ever built. A large percentage of the guillotine's fodder passed through the dreary **Galerie des Prisonniers**: Marie Antoinette, Danton, Desmoulins, Charlotte Corday and St-Just. All would have their collars torn and hair cut in Paris's grimmest **Salle de la Toilette** before boarding the tumbrils. Upstairs are other reconstructed cells.

Sainte-Chapelle

Cour du Mai, Palais de Justice, 4 Bd du Palais. Open April–Sept 9.30–6.30; Mar–Oct daily 10–5; closed same days as conciergerie; adm; combined ticket available.

Here, as at Notre-Dame (*see* pp.209–11), you will lose any notion you might have had about the Middle Ages being quaint and backward. Every inch declares a perfect mastery of mathematics and statistics, materials and stresses. Sainte-Chapelle has an unusual plan, somewhat like a beaver lodge: the important part, the spectacular **upper chapel**, nearly 65ft high, can only be entered from below, from a spiral staircase, and almost three-quarters of its wall area is glass. Palace servants heard Mass in the lower chapel, and the tombs belong to clerics of the 14th and 15th centuries.

Emerging from the narrow stair into the upper chapel is a startling, unforgettable experience. The other cliché in the books is that Sainte-Chapelle is a 'jewel box' for Louis' treasured relics, which is entirely apt: awash in colour and light from the tall windows, the chapel glitters like the cave of the Forty Thieves. The glass is the oldest in Paris (13th-century), though much was restored a century ago. Of all the great French glass cycles, this one makes the most complete 'picture Bible'. The atmosphere of the chapel is heightened by the lavish use of gold paint and the deep-blue ceiling painted with golden stars.

Hôtel-Dieu

Rue de la Cité.

Paris's oldest hospital, the Hôtel-Dieu was founded in AD 660 by Bishop St-Landry. Despite the very best of intentions, it was for centuries a ripe subject for horror and black humour even beyond the borders of France. Patients could count on food and spiritual comfort, but until the 18th century medical ignorance ensured that few who checked in ever checked out again.

Place Louis-Lépine

Here a **flower market** offers a haven of dewy green fragrances in the desert of offices. The orchid stalls (in the first barn, off Rue de la Cité) are definitely worth a detour, or else you can get a 10ft potted palm as a souvenir of Paris. On Sunday mornings a **bird market** takes over, a tradition dating back to the birds sold in the Middle Ages on the Pont au Change.

Pont Neuf

This is the longest and oldest bridge in Paris. By the late Middle Ages the ancient umbilical bridges tying the mother island to the banks of the Seine had become eternally jammed with traffic, and on 31 May 1578 the cornerstone for a new bridge was laid by Henri III. It was completed in 1605 and, although often restored, retains its original form. Reliefs and grotesques decorate the Pont Neuf as seen from the river, portraying the pickpockets, charlatans and tooth-extractors who harangued, amused and preyed on the passing crowds.

Square du Vert-Galant and Place Dauphine

Behind the equestrian statue of Henri IV, steps lead down to the leafy prow of the Ile de la Cité. The Vert-Galant, or 'gay old spark', was a fond nickname for Henri IV, the most Parisian of kings. The weeping willow at the tip, trailing into the river, is traditionally the first tree in Paris to burst into leaf. The square affords good views back to the Pont Neuf and its over-diligently restored carvings, and ahead to the Pont des Arts (1803), one of the first, and most elegant, iron bridges built in France. You can embark for a tour of the Seine's other bridges on a *vedette du Pont Neuf* moored at the north end of the square. In the Middle Ages, the square was the tip of a muddy islet called the Ile de Juif, a favourite place for burning Jews and witches, and used on 12 March 1314 for the execution of Jacques de Molay, the Grand Master of the Templars. Before going up in smoke, de Molay cursed his accusers, Pope Clement V and Philippe le Bel, and predicted (accurately) that they would follow him to the grave within a year. After the Templar barbecue, the Ile de Juif was joined to Ile de la Cité and made into a royal garden; in 1607 Henri IV allowed Achille de Harlay, president of the Paris *Parlement*, to convert it into a square named after the dauphin, the future Louis XIII, on condition that he make it a set architectural piece like Place des Vosges. The design, a triangle of identical houses of brick and stone with façades facing both the square and the river, has been sorely tried over the centuries: only houses Nos.14 and 16 preserve something of their original appearance. Now it is quiet, a leafy triangle in the cold stone officialdom that has usurped the Cité.

Ile St-Louis

Nearly all the houses on Ile St-Louis went up between 1627 and 1667, bestowing on the island an architectural homogeneity rare in Paris. Although it charmed the Parisians of the *Grand Siècle*, it fell out of fashion in the 18th century, and in the 19th enjoyed a Romantic revival among bohemians such as Cézanne, Daumier, Gautier and Baudelaire, who were drawn by its poetic solitude. Since the last war property prices have rocketed to the stars. The fine *hôtels particuliers* have nearly all been restored or divided into flats; bijou restaurants sprout at every corner, and during Paris's big tourist invasions its famous village atmosphere decays into the gaudy air of an ice-cream-spattered 17th-century funfair. You can do a circuit of the outside ring of streets dappled with the shadows from plane trees, and then walk the length of the bustling central Rue St-Louis-en-L'Ile in half an hour, so long as you are not seduced into every charming little shop and café.

Rue St-Louis-en-L'Ile

This has always been the island's main commercial street, with enough little village shops to keep an islander from ever really having to cross over to the mainland. But there is one striking building as well, at No.51, the **Hôtel de Chenizot** (1730). A bearded faun's head and pot-bellied chimeras enliven its doorway, one of Paris's rare rococo works. The first tiny chapel on the island, dedicated to the Virgin, was quickly deemed too dinky and common by the new islanders, and in 1664 Le Vau designed a new parish **church** (No.19), which remained unfinished until 1725. Although the clock is the only distinguishing feature of the boxy exterior, inside this is the perfect Baroque society church. At No.2, on the corner of Quai d'Anjou, is the **Hôtel Lambert**. Designed in 1641 by Le Vau for Jean-Baptiste Lambert, secretary to Louis XIII, it was given lavish interiors painted by the top decorators of the day; most of these decorations are still in place. Today Hôtel Lambert belongs to the Rothschilds, and sometimes on weekdays they leave the gate open so you can sneak a peek at the *cour d'honneur*.

At 17 Quai d'Anjou, the **Hôtel de Lauzun** was built in 1657 and sold a few years later to the Duc de Lauzun, a favourite of Louis XIV. In 1842 the hôtel was purchased by Jérôme Pichon, a bibliophile, who rented the extra rooms out to Baudelaire and Théophile Gautier, and to the Club des Haschischins, or 'hashish eaters'.

***Also see*: Notre-Dame p.209.**

***Onwards to*: Les Halles, p.223; St-Germain, p.226; the Latin Quarter, p.230; the Marais and Bastille, p.240.**

Les Halles

Ⓜ *Châtelet-Les Halles, Les Halles, Rambuteau, Etienne Marcel, Hôtel de Ville.*

This is the site of the old Paris of merchants and markets, the only *quartier* on the Right Bank with neither a royal palace nor a royal square. It was – at least until lately – the Paris of the Parisians, the place you would go to buy your turnips, pick up a strumpet or start a revolution. The streets are medieval, or older, and their names betray the gritty workaday spirit of the place: Street of the Knifesmiths, of the Goldsmiths, Goose Street. No part of Paris has seen greater changes in those 30 years and certainly not for the better. Once the Halles was a vast colourful wholesale distribution market for all Paris, and surrounded by slums. Today the Forum is instead a subterranean labyrinthine 'new town' of failing shops, the park is as full of life as a cinder cemetery and the streets are bleak un-spaces of plannerized compromise dominated by skateboarders and fast food outlets.

Les Halles

The great market, the 'Belly of Paris' as Emile Zola called it, was an 800-year-old institution before it was sacrificed in 1969. Les Halles began in the reign of Louis VI, a simple, open place. About 1183, Philippe-Auguste laid out a proper market; the people, organized in their various corporations, felt themselves representative of Paris as a whole, and they often played a hand in political affairs. Napoleon, wanting 'discipline', made the first plans for a covered market, but it was not until Napoleon III that architect Victor Baltard designed the famous, graceful green pavilions in 1851.

This Halles was in its way as much fun as its medieval predecessor. It lived by night, when the loads of meat and produce came rolling in from across France. Bars and bistrots thrived on its fringes; they stayed up all night too, giving the poets and prostitutes a place to refresh themselves. In the 1920s and through to the 1950s, Parisian toffs and English and American swells liked to end up here after a night of carousing. But markets make politicians nervous. A conspiracy grew up between the government, developers and property interests to redevelop a vast space in the very heart of Paris. Although the vast majority of Parisians were shocked by the proposed scheme, little organized opposition appeared until it was too late. By 1977 the last of Baltard's pavilions had disappeared – the same year London demolished Covent Garden.

Cafés and Lunches

L'Escargot Montorgueil, 38 Rue Montorgueil, **t** 01 42 36 83 51. Most of the décor is from the 1830s, and the big snail over the door proclaims the speciality of the house. Book. *Closed Sun and 11–21 Aug.*

Aux Tonneaux des Halles, 28 Rue Montorgueil. **t** 01 42 33 36 19. You'd think that the market porters were still alive and well and about to crowd in through the door. The genuine article, friendly, chaotic and excellent. *Closed Sun.*

Le Cochon à l'Oreille, 15 Rue Montmartre. Here is another genuine article, but be warned that space is limited and no reservations taken.

La Table des Gourmets, 14 Rue des Lombards. **t** 01 40 27 00 87. In an old vaulted cellar, light dishes for delicate souls. *Closed Sun and Aug.*

Auberge Nicolas Flamel, 51 Rue de Montmorency, **t** 01 42 71 77 78. In one of the oldest houses in Paris, refined cuisine from *maigrets* cooked with cider to seafood raviolis. *Closed Sat lunch and Sun.*

The planners did go to great lengths to make this something more than just another shopping mall. Besides the ice-cream and chain stores, there is plenty of modern art to study, as well as questionable cultural amenities, and at the **Forum des Images** (*open Wed–Sun 1–9, Tues 1–10, closed Mon; see p.302*) you can while away an afternoon watching old French television shows, movies or newsreels.

About three-quarters of the new Forum is underground, and most of the old marketplace is now the **Jardin des Halles**. One curious fragment of Catherine's palace remains: the tall column called the **Colonne de Médicis**, now standing at the south-western corner of the building on Rue de Viarmes. Inside, a spiral staircase leads to a platform where Catherine and her astrologers (including, briefly, Nostradamus) would contemplate the destinities of the dynasty and of France.

St-Eustache

The entrance to the market's own parish church is on Place du Jour. The façade, a pathetic neoclassical pudding, was added in the 1750s. St-Eustache, begun in 1532, soon became one of the most important churches in the city, second only to Notre-Dame. Richelieu, Molière and Madame de Pompadour were baptized here, and Louis XIV had his first communion. The interior shows the plan typical of great Parisian churches since Notre-Dame. The art inside, meticulously detailed at the entrance, is disappointing. Don't miss the forlorn chapel in the left aisle, near the entrance, entirely filled with Raymond Mason's 1969 work, *The Departure of the Fruits and Vegetables from the Heart of Paris*, a funny, very moving diorama of solemn, dignified market people, carrying their leeks and tomatoes into suburban exile.

Square des Innocents

The crowds of young people who have made this square their main city-centre rendezvous can be seen literally dancing on the graves of their ancestors. At one time, the entire neighbourhood was perfumed by a ripe stench of decaying corpses from the Halles' neighbour, the Cimetière des Innocents. In 1786 the cemetery was demolished, and the cleared site was converted into a market. Later it was remodelled into the present square, and the **Fontaine des Innocents** was installed at its centre. The only surviving Renaissance fountain in Paris (1549) is the work of Pierre Lescot, though the decorative reliefs are by Jean Goujon.

St-Merri

Saint Merri, or Medericus, was an abbot of Autun buried here in the early 8th century. A chapel was built over his relics, on a site then on the outskirts of the city; in the Middle Ages, with all the bankers and cloth merchants in this area, it became one of the richest parish churches of Paris. The present building was begun *c.* 1500, in somewhat the same late Flamboyant Gothic style as St-Eustache, and not completed until 1612. The last part to be finished was the bell tower, which contains a 14th-century bell called the Merri, the oldest in the city. What you see on it today are largely replacements from the 1840s, including the statues of saints and the little winged, supposedly **hermaphroditic demon** that leers over the main portal. There are frequent concerts on Sunday afternoons; after these, you can have a free guided tour (*open daily 3–7, closed Aug; free; guided tours one Sunday a month, ring* **t** *01 42 71 93 93*).

Stravinsky Fountain

Built at the same time as the Centre Pompidou (*see* pp.212–14) behind it, this broad sheet of water serves as a play pool for a collection of monsters created by that delightful sculptress from Mars, Niki de Saint-Phalle. Her colourful gadgets are each dedicated to one of Stravinsky's works; at any moment, they are likely to start spinning around. The black metal mobiles between them are the work of Jean Tinguely.

***Also see*: Pompidou Centre, p.212; Musée National des Techniques, p.271.**

***Onwards to*: Palais Royal, p.246; the Louvre, p.201.**

St-Germain

Ⓜ *St-Germain-des-Prés, Mabillon, Odéon, Cluny-La Sorbonne.*

France is one country where brainy philosophers get respect, and St-Germain is their citadel; in the postwar decades there were enough eggheads here to make omelettes, sizzling and puffing away with the latest fashionable philosophy. Since the 1960s it has cooled considerably; and in the inevitable urban cycles the haunts of the avant-garde have now been gentrified. But despite the absurd rents and surplus posers, St-Germain's essential conviviality remains intact. Its narrow streets, scarcely violated by the planners of the last two centuries, its cafés and bookshops, and the elegant Luxembourg Gardens cluttered with chairs, all invite you to debate the day away in the scholarly spirit of those first thinkers, Voltaire and Diderot, if not Camus, Sartre, Simone de Beauvoir and Foucault.

If urbanity is St-Germain's middle name, it owes much to its parent, the Benedictine abbey of St-Germain-des-Prés. The erudite monks, specialists in ancient manuscripts, set the intellectual tone of the quarter; art, food and fashion from the rest of Europe and the East were introduced into Paris through the abbey's month-long fair. Theatres prospered; the first coffee houses opened here; and actors, Protestants and foreign artists could live in independent St-Germain. In its cafés Paris's intellectuals kept the spark alive in a circle around Jean-Paul Sartre and Simone de Beauvoir, the notebook-scribbling high priest and priestess of St-Germain.

St-Germain-des-Prés

When Childebert Ier, son of Clovis, returned from the siege of Saragossa in 543, his booty included a piece of the True Cross and the tunic of St Vincent. Germanus, bishop of Paris, convinced Childebert that he should found an abbey to house the relics. When Germanus himself was canonized, the church changed its name to St-Germain. It was one of the most important Benedictine monasteries in France, and until Dagobert (d. 639) it was the burial place of the Merovingian kings. Of this early

Cafés and Lunches

Some of the more famous cafés, the Flore, Deux Magots and Brasserie Lipp, are in the text.

Polidor, 41 Rue Monsieur-le-Prince, **t** 01 43 26 95 34. A favourite of Joyce and Verlaine, and one of the few places they could still afford; good brasserie cooking and lots of it. €22 lunch menu.

Café des Beaux-Arts, 11 Rue Bonaparte, **t** 01 43 26 92 64. Arrive early to get a table at this St-Germain favourite. Lunch menu at €12.50.

Café Procope, 13 Rue de l'Ancienne-Comédie, **t** 01 43 26 99 20. Paris's oldest coffee house, restored for the Revolution's Bicentennial.

Le Petit St-Benoît, 4 Rue St-Benoît, **t** 01 42 60 27 92. Cosy and friendly, basic tasty French classics.

Mariage Frères, 19 Rue de Savoie, **t** 01 40 51 82 50. On the corner of Grands-Augustins. Paris's premier purveyors of fine tea since 1854 (400 varieties) and a *salon de thé*.

Allard, 41 Rue St-André-des-Arts, **t** 01 43 26 48 23. A *bistrot* unchanged (except for the prices) in 40 years; try the duck with olives. *Closed Sun and Aug.*

La Palette, 43 Rue de Seine, **t** 01 43 26 68 15. A charming café and terrace, but brace yourself for some of that legendary Parisian snootiness. *Open 8pm–2am, closed Sun.*

A la Cour de Rohan, in the arcade at 59–61 Rue St-André-des-Arts, **t** 01 43 25 79 67. A tranquil *salon de thé* to recharge your batteries. Light lunch (though not cheap) and delicious desserts.

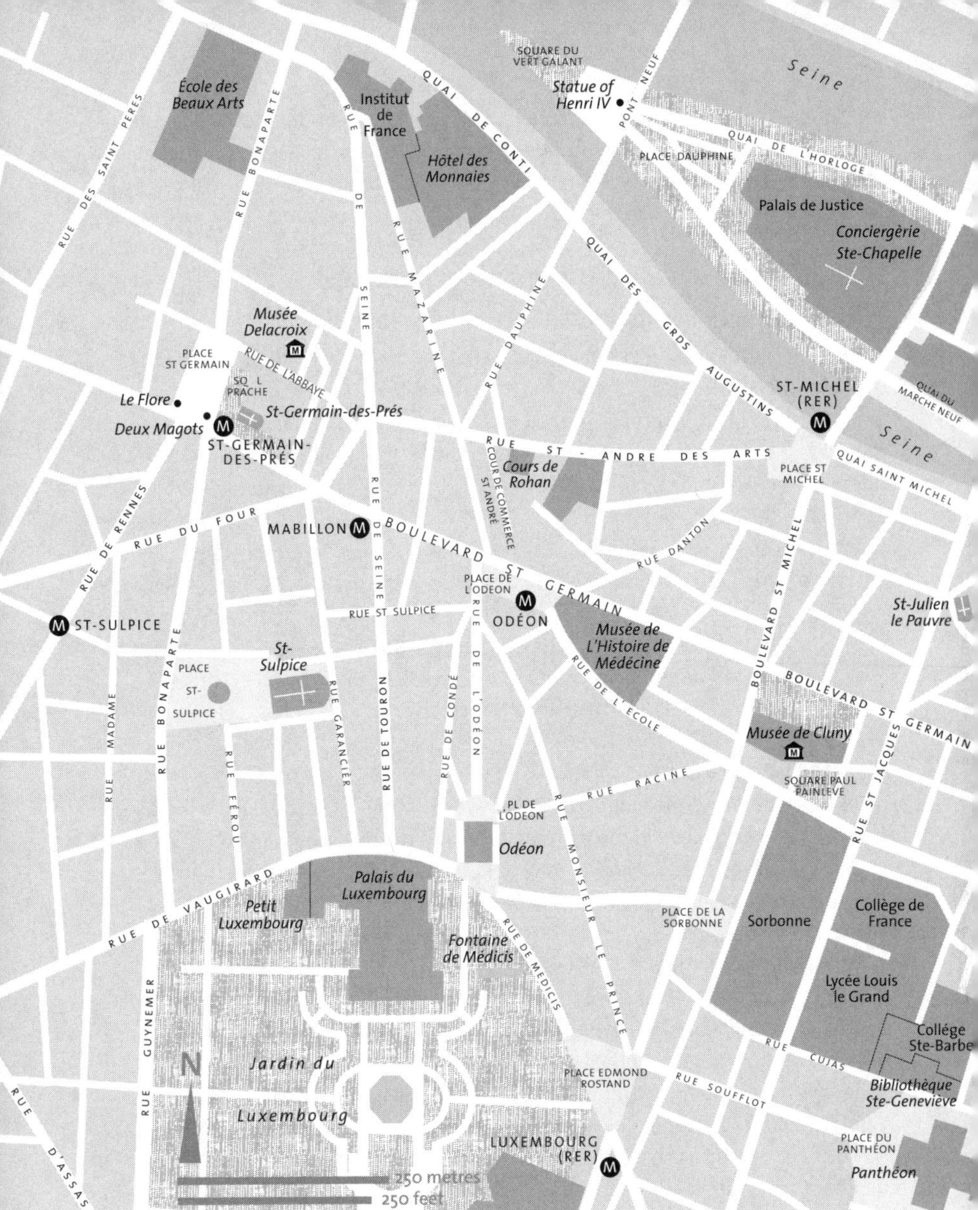

Romanesque church, little has survived: capitals, now mostly in the Musée de Cluny, and the base of the massive tower on the west front. Peter de Montreuil added a Lady Chapel, as beautiful as his Sainte-Chapelle. In 1789 St-Germain's tombs and reliquaries were destroyed, the library confiscated, while the church was converted into a saltpetre factory. In 1840 Victor Hugo led a campaign for St-Germain's restoration.

Only a damaged carved lintel survives from the original entrance, redone in the 17th century. Squint past Flandrin's colours to appreciate the proportions of the church. The marble shafts in the short columns above the arcade are from the 6th century, the only Merovingian work *in situ* in Paris.

In **Square Laurent-Prache**, at the corner of Place St-Germain-des-Prés and Rue de l'Abbaye, are fragments of architect Montreuil's Lady Chapel, chapter house (against the wall) and refectory (ruined window). Here, too, is a bronze *Head of a Woman* by Picasso (1959), a memorial to his friend, poet Guillaume Apollinaire.

Les Deux Magots, Café de Flore and Brasserie Lipp

Place St-Germain-des-Prés and Boulevard St-Germain.

Whether **Les Deux Magots** is '*le rendez-vous de l'élite intellectuelle*', according to its own menu, or the 'Two Maggots' of American teenagers, the café does offer grandstand views of St-Germain. Inside, the two statues of Chinese mandarins or *magots* date from the shop's original vocation – selling silks. The name was retained when it became a café in 1875; Mallarmé, Verlaine and Rimbaud gave it its literary seal of approval in the 1880s, and the café has distributed its own literary prize since 1933. A few doors down, its rival **the Flore** opened in 1890. It too attracted a brainy clientele: Picasso and Apollinaire would edit art magazines in the back, Sartre and Camus were regulars, only to ignore stalwartly each other's presence. On the south side of the boulevard 'Le Drugstore', a groovy hangout in the 1960s, has recently succumbed to changing tastes, although its neighbour, **Brasserie Lipp**, still packs in Paris's *Who's Who* with a *choucroute* unchanged since 1920.

Rue des Beaux-Arts

This street is one of the main axes of the slowly churning St-Germain art world. The original galleries opened in the 1920s and shocked the public by being the first to show modern and abstract works. You'll find Di Meo and Patrice Trigano, both specializing in the abstract Ecole de Paris, and Claude Bernard, with figurative works by Hockney, Bacon, Botero and others. In 1900 Oscar Wilde, aged 46 but broken by his prison term, came to die 'beyond his means' in the former Hôtel d'Allemagne (No.13).

At the end of the street is the gate into the **Ecole des Beaux-Arts** (*www.ensba.fr; courtyards open 8–8pm, otherwise admission only for exhibitions*). Exhibitions are held in the oldest buildings on this site: Queen Marguerite de Valois' Chapelle des Louanges (1606; the first dome in Paris) and a chapel (1619, with elegant doors by Goujon) built for an Augustine monastery after Marguerite's death. In 1816 this convent became the school of fine arts. The main courtyard contains a collage of architectural fragments, most notably the central façade of Henri II's Château d'Anet.

Odéon

Built by Louis XV in 1782, the neoclassical Théâtre de l'Odéon was the first public theatre in Paris designed exclusively for drama. Its austere Doric temple façade is attractively set in the semicircular Place de l'Odéon, while porticoes on either flank integrate the building into the square itself. After fires in 1807 and 1818, the theatre was faithfully reconstructed to the original design. For decades, however, the Odéon was a commercial flop. During the Revolution its troupe split, the pro-Republican actors going off to the Comédie Française and the Royalists sticking it out here until they were carted off to the slammer. In the next century the theatre had a few successes (Bizet's *L'Arlésienne*, in 1872), but it only became popular after the Second World War when Jean-Louis Barrault and Madeleine Renaud quickened its pulse with contemporary drama.

St-Sulpice

St-Sulpice's present incarnation dates from 1646; by the time the builders reached the façade in 1732, the original Baroque plan seemed old-fashioned, resulting in a competition, won by an even more antique design by a Florentine named Servandoni. Inside the grey, cavernous nave, railway clocks tick down the minutes to the next TGV to heaven. The organ is one of the most seriously overwrought in Paris; the holy water stoups are two enormous clam shells, gifts from Venice to François I. In such a setting, the lush, romantic murals by Delacroix in the first chapel on the right radiate warmth. The last chapel before the right transept contains the Hallowe'en *tomb of Curé Languet de Gergy* (1750) by Michelangelo Slodtz. The copper strip across the transept traces the Paris meridian, and if you come at the winter solstice you'll see a sunray strike the centre of the obelisk.

Musée Delacroix

6 Place Furstemberg; www.musee-delacroix.fr. Open 9.30–5, closed Tues; adm.

Serendipitous Place Furstemberg with its delicate pawlownia trees is a dainty gem of urban design that traces the ancient cloister-courtyard of the abbots' palace. In the old abbey stable is the last home of Eugène Delacroix, who moved here in 1857 to be close to St-Sulpice. Sketches, etchings and a dozen minor paintings hang in his lodgings and atelier, and there's a quiet garden that suited the old bachelor to a T. For despite the romantic, exotic pre-Impressionistic fervour of his paintings, Delacroix liked his peace and quiet.

Cour du Commerce St-André

Off Rue St-André-des-Arts is the **Carrefour de Buci**, in the 18th century one of the most fashionable crossroads of the Left Bank, and now the city's most fashionable market, particularly at weekends. When you can pull yourself away from the meticulous displays of smoked salmon and *pâtés en croûte*, backtrack a few giant steps along Rue St-André-des-Arts for a look at the cobblestoned **Cour du Commerce St-André**, opened in 1776. This is Paris's oldest *passage*, built before new iron and glass engineering techniques were to make them the marvel of the Right Bank. Midway, to your left, extend three courtyards known as the **Cour de Rohan**. In the first courtyard, the gentle Dr Joseph-Ignace Guillotin and a carpenter named Schmidt used sheep to test their decapitation machine. There's a Renaissance house covered with vines in the second courtyard, part of the *hôtel particulier* of Diane de Poitiers; the iron tripod in the corner was a once common urban sight, a *pas de mule* (horse mount).

***Also see*: Jardin du Luxembourg, p.252; Musée de la Monnaie, p.275.**
***Onwards to*: Latin Quarter, p.230; Ile de la Cité and Ile St-Louis, p.218.**

The Latin Quarter

Ⓜ *St-Michel, Cluny-La Sorbonne, Maubert-Mutualité.*

The Latin Quarter is one of Paris's great clichés. Its name was bestowed by a student named Rabelais, for Latin (with an excruciating nasal twang) was the only language permitted in the university precincts, spoken by everyone from the blackhearted judges of the Sorbonne down to their sooty kitchen scullions, until Napoleon said *non*. Napoleon's 19th-century successors tended to regard the Latin Quarter itself as an anachronism, and rubbed most of its medieval abbeys, colleges and slums off the map. But once you too have dispersed any lingering romantic or operatic notions that the Latin Quarter evokes, it can be good fun, especially at night when it becomes the headquarters for an informal United Nations of goodwill.

The Sorbonne

This area includes the ancient confines of Paris University, founded in spirit by Peter Abelard, one of the greatest thinkers of the Middle Ages. The high standards of inquiry and scholarship set by Abelard made the Left Bank a 'paradise of pleasure' for intellectuals and students from across Europe. Private citizens and religious orders built college-hostels to house the scholars and in 1180 Philippe-Auguste enclosed the whole area in his *enceinte*, walls that until the 18th century defined the University Quarter. Paris's first college, supplying room and board to poor students, was founded at the same time, and among the scores that followed was the Sorbonne, founded in 1257 by Robert de Sorbon, chaplain to St Louis. The heady freedom of thought that made Paris University great in the 13th century drew the greatest thinkers of the day. But when Philippe le Bel convinced the theological judges at the Sorbonne that they should condemn the Knights Templars in 1312, he cursed the university with a political role that compromises its independence to this day. At the trial of Joan of Arc the Sorbonne supplied the prosecutor, Pierre Cauchon, who sent the Maid to the stake.

In 1470 three Germans were invited to the Sorbonne to start the first printing press in France, beginning a renaissance of intellectual life on the Left Bank. Unfortunately the Sorbonne was too reactionary to satisfy the new thirst for knowledge. Richelieu, appointed chancellor in 1622, tried to revive the Sorbonne's flagging status with extensive rebuilding. Nothing he could do, however, halted the Latin Quarter's decline into a volatile slum. The Revolution had no qualms about closing the whole university down. Napoleon resuscitated it, but there was no going back to the old ways – if the Sorbonne was political, so were the post-Revolutionary students, who played roles in the upheavals of the 19th century, battled the Nazis in Place St-Michel, protested against the war in Algeria and in 1968 shocked the government with their uprising. But the government has accomplished its agenda anyway: the rebellious Sorbonne has been blasted into a centreless prism of 13 campuses scattered through Paris.

Enter the *cour d'honneur* at 17 Rue de la Sorbonne to see what survives from Richelieu's day: the domed **Chapelle Ste-Ursule de la Sorbonne** (1630), open only (and rarely) for temporary exhibitions. The interior decoration was destroyed when the *sans-culottes* converted it into a Temple of Reason, except for paintings in the spandrels by Philippe de Champaigne and the white marble tomb of Richelieu. If you come between lectures (or join one – they're free), take a look in the **Grand Amphithéâtre** to see the celebrated fresco of *Le Bois Sacré* by Puvis de Chavannes.

St-Julien le Pauvre

Rue St-Julien-le-Pauvre. Open 9.30–6.30; sung Mass Sun 11.

This diminutive transitional Gothic church was originally built to provide hospitality for pilgrims to Santiago de Compostela. Dating back to 587, it is one of the oldest churches in Paris. Enlarged in 1208, it became the university's assembly hall, an association that went sour when a student riot in 1524 left the church half-ruined. All members of the university were henceforth banned, and migrated up the hill to St-Etienne du Mont (*see* below), while poor St Julien was practically abandoned. In 1651 it was on the verge of collapse when the roof was lowered and the nave lopped off and it became a chapel for the Hôtel-Dieu. Behind the church is **Square René-Viviani**, whose Gothic odds and ends, melted by wind and rain, were found near Notre-Dame; the tree on concrete crutches is the oldest in Paris. It's a false acacia, called a *robinier*, after Robin the botanist who planted it in 1602.

Cafés and Lunches

Al-Dar, 8 Rue Frédéric-Sauton, **t** 01 43 25 17 15. Flashy but crowded for its delicious Middle Eastern dishes.

The Tea Caddy, 14 Rue St-Julien-le-Pauvre, **t** 01 43 54 15 56. Soft-lit tea room from the 1920s, bestowed by the Rothschilds on a favourite English governess.

Le Grenier de Notre Dame, 18 Rue de la Bûcherie, **t** 01 43 29 98 29. Simple vegetarian and macrobiotic dishes.

La Bûcherie, 41 Rue de la Bûcherie, **t** 01 43 54 78 06. Delicious classics (*coquilles St-Jacques* and wild duck) with views over Notre-Dame; fine woodwork, and an open fire in winter.

Perraudin, 157 Rue St-Jacques, **t** 01 46 33 15 75. One of the best choices in this part of Paris, a comfortable old-fashioned place with fine food and few pretensions. Tarts are a speciality. *Closed Sat and Sun.*

Chieng-Mai, 12 Rue Frédéric-Sauton (off Place Maubert), **t** 01 43 25 45 45. Lunch menus €11.50–€27.50. Paris's most authentic Thai restaurant; book.

Balzar, 49 Rue des Ecoles, **t** 01 43 54 13 67. The classic brasserie (bar/restaurant) of the quarter, with old-fashioned leather seats and lots of mirrors, packed with stars, academics and editors. Hearty food like traditional *choucroute*.

Medieval Streets

This is one of the rare corners of Paris to preserve the pre-Haussmann higgledy-piggledy. To see it all, walk straight down Rue de la Bûcherie or turn right on to Rue Lagrange then right into **Rue du Fouarre**, a mere stump of a street that in the 12th century was the very embryo of the university. Turn right at **Rue Galande**, once the start of the bustling Roman road to Lyon. Houses on Rue Galande are medieval, but have been much restored. Continue towards the river on Rue St-Julien, turning left at **Rue de la Bûcherie** for what must be the most famous English-language second-hand bookshop on the continent, **Shakespeare and Co.** (*open daily noon to midnight*). This is the namesake of Sylvia Beach's English bookshop that stood in Rue de l'Odéon between the wars. Beach's kindness and free lending library made her a den mother for many expat writers, but none owed her as much as James Joyce. After the *Ulysses* obscenity trial in 1921 precluded the publication of the book in Britain or the USA, Beach volunteered to publish it herself.

If 13th-century **Rue de la Huchette**, 'street of the little trough', seems a squeeze, take a look down the first right, **Rue du Chat-qui-Pêche** (named after a long-ago inn sign of a fishing cat). At 6ft wide it's the narrowest street in Paris, and the last really medieval one. Rue de la Huchette peters out in **Place St-Michel**, a traffic vortex laid out under Napoleon III and decorated with a striking fountain by Davioud of St Michel slaying the Dragon. It marks the beginning of the Latin Quarter's main drag, **Boulevard St-Michel**, or simply Boul' Mich, laid out in 1859. What you can't see any longer are its paving stones, which proved too convenient for slinging at the police in May 1968 and now lie under a thick coat of asphalt.

St-Séverin

Rue des Prêtres-St-Séverin. Open Mon–Sat 11–7, Sun 9–9.

Séverin was a 6th-century hermit. The original Merovingian church here was rebuilt in 1031, though its Romanesque replacement took the next 450 years to complete and evolved into Flamboyant Gothic. St-Séverin's most remarkable feature is a palm-ribbed **double ambulatory** that seems to unwind organically from the spirals of the centre column. The peaceful arcaded garden is the last charnel house in Paris. When the graveyard became too crowded, bones were dug up and embedded in the arches.

Montagne Ste-Geneviève

The crossroads of **Rue Clovis** and **Rue Descartes** is the summit of the Gallo-Roman Mont Leucotitius (Mont Lutèce), known since the Middle Ages as Montagne Ste-Geneviève, after Paris's patron saint. In 451, fresh from pillaging and deflowering 11,000 virgins in Cologne, Attila and the Huns marched towards Lutèce. Paris's Romans fled in terror, but the Parisii stuck around when Geneviève, a holy virgin living on this hill, assured them that God would spare the city. And indeed, at the last minute, the Huns veered off and sacked Orléans instead – precisely where Paris's Romans had fled to. When Clovis converted to Christianity, he built on Montagne Ste-Geneviève a **basilica** dedicated to Sts Peter and Paul. In 512 he was buried there, next to his wife Clotilde and Geneviève. Such a cult grew around the miracle-working tomb of Geneviève that the church was expanded and renamed. In 1220 Philippe-Auguste's wall around the Latin Quarter was finished – at No.3 Rue Clovis you can see a stretch of it. By the next year, so many students had moved into the quarter that a new chapel, St-Etienne, was built next to Ste-Geneviève to accommodate them. In 1802 old Ste-Geneviève was demolished to make way for Rue Clovis. Fortunately, **St-Etienne du Mont** remains, charming, asymmetrical and intact, on Place Ste-Geneviève (*open Mon 12–7.30, Tues–Fri 7.45–7.30, Sat 7.45–12 and 2.30–7.45, Sun 8.45–12.30 and 2.30–7.45; closed hols*).

Panthéon

Place du Panthéon. Open daily April–Sept 10–6.30; Oct–Mar 10–6.15; adm, free 1st Sun of the month Oct–Mar.

Old Ste-Geneviève was demolished because Louis XV, after a close call with the grim reaper in 1744, had vowed to construct a new basilica to hold the relics of Paris's patroness. Some French critics trumpet the result, by Jacques-Germain Soufflot, as 'the first example of perfect architecture', when in fact the Panthéon is a textbook case of how *not* to build, an impoverished bastard of design that has always had difficulties even standing up. It had just been completed in 1790 when the Revolution kicked off its muddled history by co-opting it as a Panthéon to honour its great and good. Even this didn't start on the right foot, when two of the first corpses, Mirabeau and Marat, were given the bum's rush in the changing political climate. Napoleon reconverted the Panthéon to a church, and the remains of two other inmates, Rousseau and Voltaire, were shunted off into an unmarked closet. Louis-Philippe thought the church was better as a pantheon, but in 1851 monks persuaded Napoleon III to reconvert the building to a church. In 1871 it became the Left-Bank HQ of the Commune; and it went back to a church again until 1885, when Victor Hugo died. Hugo was so inflated that no ordinary tomb would hold him, and his funeral inaugurated the building's current status as the pantheon of France's Great Men.

***Also see*: Musée de Cluny, p.204.**

***Onwards to*: St-Germain, p.226; Mouffetard and Jussieu, p.234; Ile de la Cité, p.218.**

Mouffetard and Jussieu

Ⓜ *Place Monge, Jussieu, Cardinal Lemoine, Censier-Daubenton, Les Gobelins.*

This *quartier*, east of the medieval walls that cradled the Latin Quarter for most of its history, offers an unusual cocktail of sights and smells that hardly seems to belong to the same city as the Eiffel Tower and Champs-Elysées – gossipy village streets, a tropical garden, a Maghrebi mosque and old geezers playing *boules* in a Roman arena.

Rue Mouffetard

Rue Mouffetard is named after the *mofette* or stench that rose from the tanners and dyers along the Bièvre. This once bucolic tributary of the Seine that rolled through woodlands and meadows became an open sewer over the centuries and was eventually covered over. The street itself is one of the most ancient in Paris, following the path of the Roman road to Lyon. Ever since then it has been lined with inns and taverns for the wayfarer; while strolling down the 'Mouff' and poking in its capillary lanes and courtyards you can pick out a number of old signs, such as the carved oak at No.69 for the Vieux Chêne, which began as a Revolutionary club. Rue du Pot-de-Fer owes its name to the Fontaine du Pot-de-Fer, one of 14 fountains donated by Marie de' Medici. In 1928, 25-year-old George Orwell moved into a seedy hotel at 6 Rue du Pot-de-Fer to live off his meagre savings while he learned the craft of writing; when he was robbed, he was reduced to washing dishes in a big hotel in the Rue de Rivoli – the source for his first published book, *Down and Out in Paris and London*.

Further south beyond Rue de l'Epée-de-Bois begins Rue Mouffetard's **market** (*closed Mon*), where shops spill out to join pavement stalls cascading with fruit and vegetables, cheeses, seafood, pâtés, sausages, bread and more, with an occasional exotic touch such as the African market in Rue de l'Arbalète.

Place de la Contrescarpe

Picturesque and piquant, the square dates only from 1852, when the 14th-century Porte Bourdelle was demolished. For the next hundred years Paris's tramps flocked here, and now, even though most of the houses have been restored (the one with the painted sign *Au Nègre Joyeux* used to be a tearoom), it still has a bohemian atmosphere, especially at weekends. Rabelais, Ronsard and du Bellay and the other Renaissance poets of the Pléiade would come to make merry at the famous Cabaret de la Pomme de Pin, at the corner of Rue Blainville (plaque at No.1). Just off the Contrescarpe, at 50 Rue Descartes, a plaque shows the original appearance of Porte Bourdelle with its drawbridge; further along, there's another 'Hemingway-was-here' plaque, and one at No.39 (now a restaurant) commemorating Paul Verlaine, who died in 1896 in a squalid hotel. In his last years, after his fiery love affair with Rimbaud ended with pistol shots and a prison term, the poet had become Paris's most famous antihero, haunting Left Bank cafés to extinguish his brain cells in absinthe.

Leading off Place de la Contrescarpe is **Rue Rollin**, a treeless street of blonde houses more Mediterranean than Parisian. A plaque at No.14 marks Descartes' address in Paris. A good Catholic, he preferred the Protestant Netherlands, and sniffed that while in France 'no one seemed to want to know anything about me except what I looked like, so I began to believe that they wanted me in France the way they might want an elephant or a panther, because it is rare, and not because it is useful.'

Grande Mosquée de Paris

Place du Puits-de-l'Ermite, **t** *01 45 35 97 33. www.mosquee-de-paris.org*
Open for visits daily except Fri 9–12 and 2–6; closed Muslim hols; adm.

Built between 1922 and 1926 in remembrance of the Muslim dead in the First World War and as a symbol of Franco-Moroccan friendship, this is nominally the central mosque for France's 4 million-plus faithful. A series of interior courtyards give on to the sumptuous prayer room, where the domes were decorated by rival teams of Moroccan artisans competing in geometric ingenuity. During Ramadan the mosque is well attended and a fair of religious items is held in the main courtyard, but at other times the place is almost deserted. Short tours of the building are available in French, on request. Behind the mosque, at Nos.39 and 41 Rue Geoffroy-St-Hilaire, there's a Turkish **hammam** (*men Tues 2–9 and Sun 10–9, women Mon, Wed, Thurs, Sat 10–9, Fri 2–9*), a delightful courtyard **café** serving mint tea and oriental pastries, a **restaurant** and an **arts and crafts shop**.

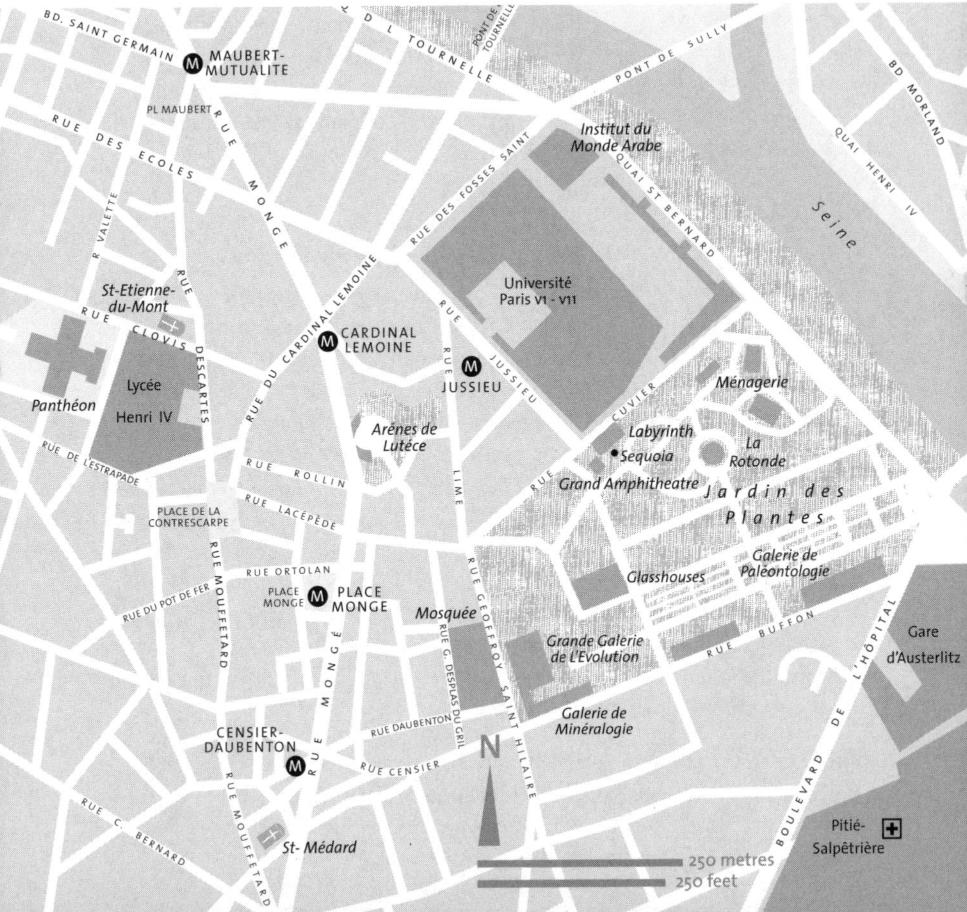

Cafés and Lunches

Café of the Grande Mosquée, 39 Rue Geoffrey-St-Hilaire. A delightful café where you can sip mint tea in a garden patio built in the style of the Alhambra. No booze.

Le Petit Navire, 14 Rue des Fossés St-Bernard, **t** 01 43 54 22 52. A popular spot with fish as the speciality.

L'Arbre à Cannelle, 14 Rue Linné. Warm and cosy tea salon with good salads, tarts, and delicious desserts.

Moissonnier, 28 Rue des Fossés-St-Bernard, **t** 01 43 29 87 65. Long-established *bistrot* serving unadulterated Lyonnais *cuisine de terroir*. Weekday lunch €23.

Gelati Alberti, 45 Rue Mouffetard. **t** 01 43 37 88 07. For delicious Italian ice-cream. *Open Tues–Sun 1–11.*

L'Époque, 81 Rue du Cardinal-Lemoine, **t** 01 46 34 15 84. Bistrot worthy of the name (*blanquette de veau, gigot d'agneau* and other hardy fare) buried among the touristy ethnics.

Le Buisson Ardent, 25 Rue Jussieu, **t** 01 43 54 93 02. Much recommended French classic with quality *à l'ancienne*. Try *confit de canard, pommes à l'ail* or *riz de veau*.

Cave la Bourgogne, 142 Rue Mouffetard. Good wine and everything else to drink, plus excellent sandwiches. Fitting termination point to a walk down the Mouff.

Arènes de Lutèce

Rue des Arènes.

The slight remains of Lutetia's Roman amphitheatre (now a garden, football pitch and *boules* court) date from the 2nd century. Originally it could seat 10,000 – half the entire population of Lutetia, which if nothing else proves that Parisians have always been inveterate theatre-goers. The amphitheatre was too convenient a quarry to survive the Dark Ages, when its stone went into fortifying the Ile de la Cité. What remained was forgotten until rediscovered in 1869, restored in 1917 and, incredibly, almost demolished in 1980 for a housing project. In the gardens that encompass the arena, don't miss the knotty beech, famous as the crookedest tree growing in Paris.

Institut du Monde Arabe

1 Rue des Fossés-St-Bernard. Open Tues–Sun 10–6, closed Mon; adm.

This coolly elegant riverside structure, completed in 1987, is nearly everyone's favourite contemporary building in Paris. The competition for the Institute's design was won in 1981 by Jean Nouvel (a Frenchman, for once), who came up with a pair of long, thin buildings, one gracefully curved to follow the line of the quay. Their walls are covered with window panels inspired by ancient Islamic geometric patterns, but equipped with photo-electric cells that activate their dilation or contraction according to the amount of sunlight – with a gentle high-tech whoosh that takes you by surprise the first time you experience it. The Institute is financed by the French government and 22 Arab countries, with the goal of introducing Islamic civilization to the public and facilitating cultural exchanges. Besides an extensive library (on the third floor, around a great spiral ramp) there are rotating exhibitions, a shop of books and crafts, and recordings and films to see in the *Espace Son et Image*.

The **museum** (*adm*), spread out on several floors, displays examples of the art and exquisite craftsmanship of the Arab world.

***Also see*: Jardin des Plantes, p.252; Manufacture Nationale des Gobelins, p.268.**
***Onwards to*: Latin Quarter, p.230; Ile de la Cité and Ile St-Louis, p.218.**

Montmartre

Ⓜ *Abbesses, Lamarck-Caulaincourt, Anvers.*

From the Eiffel Tower or the top of the Pompidou Centre, gleaming white Montmartre resembles an Italian hill town from Mars. A closer inspection reveals honky-tonk tourist Paris at its ripest, churning francs from the fantasy-nostalgia mill for the good old days of Toulouse-Lautrec, cancan girls, Renoir and Picasso. On the other hand, the area has some of Paris's last secret alleys and picturesque streets, just as pretty as they were when Utrillo painted them.

The Romans called this 423ft 'mountain' *Mons Mercurii*, after its hilltop shrine to the god of commerce, but he lost his billing in the 9th century, when the abbot of St-Denis renamed it the Hill of Martyrs, Montmartre, the *Butte Sacrée*. Montmartre became a *commune* (pop. 638) during the Revolution and was renamed Mont Marat.

The first artists, poets and composers had already moved into Montmartre with the workers, drawn by cheap rents and the quality of its air and light. The police knew the village rather as the resort of *apaches*, gangs of Parisian toughs distinguished by their wide berets and corduroy trousers; when Eric Satie began his career playing piano in a Montmartre cabaret, he came to work armed with a hammer. After the First World War the bohemians moved off to the lower rents of Montparnasse.

Place du Tertre

This was once the main square of Montmartre village. It's hard to imagine a more blatant parody of the Butte's hallowed artistic traditions: unless you come bright and early, you can scarcely see this pretty square for the easels of 200 artists.

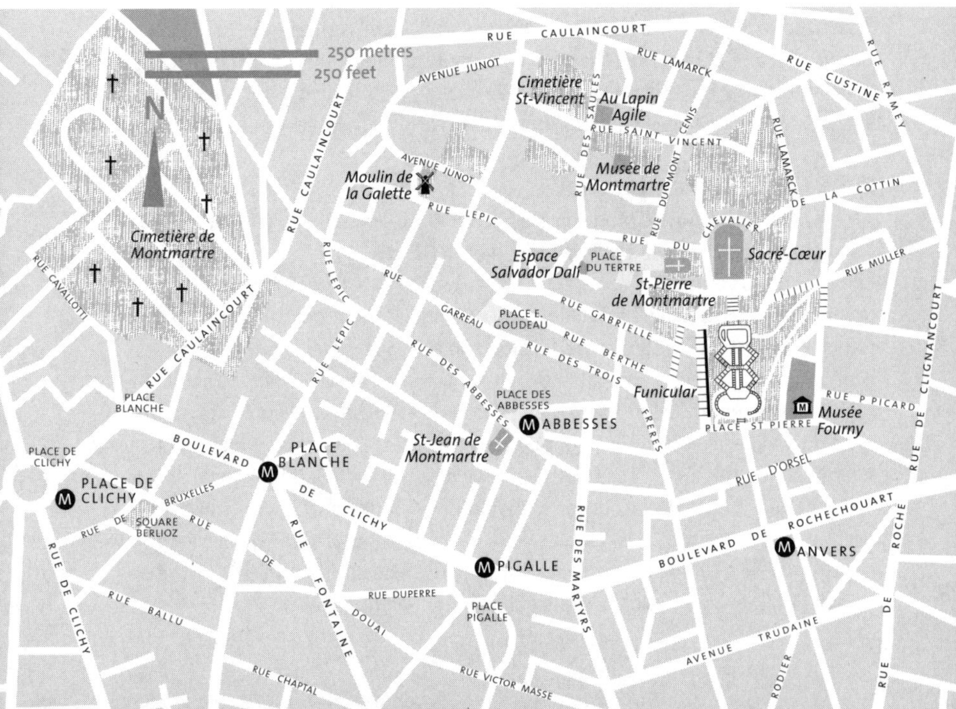

Cafés and Lunches

Chez Claude et Claudine, 94 Rue des Martyrs (a block east of Place des Abbesses). A cosy neighbourhood place, redoubtable stronghold of onion soup-and-bourguignon traditional cooking. Lunch menu €20.

Le Montagnard, 102 Rue Lepic, **t** 01 42 58 06 22. Highlights are *fondue pyrénéenne* and other mountain specialities.

L'Eté en Pente Douce, 23 Rue Muller. Ideal location for tea and patisserie on a lovely terrace with a view, east of Sacré-Cœur – but not worth staying for the full meal.

Zouave Gobichon, 8 Rue Durantin. Not North African, but the best of small bistro cooking and a bit off the tourist route. Terrific value for money.

Le Relais de La Butte, 12 Rue Ravignan. Old-fashioned, friendly and plant-filled wine bar with wines by the glass. Sit at the bar and while away the afternoon.

Beauvilliers, 52 Rue Lamarck (near the intersection with Rue Caulaincourt), **t** 01 42 54 54 42. Montmartre's gourmet restaurant and one of the finest in Paris, set in a lavish Second-Empire time capsule; good value lunch in the upper price range.

La Pomponnette, 42 Rue Lepic, **t** 01 46 06 08 36. Classic Montmartre *bistrot*, lively atmosphere and chock full of posters, watercolours and other souvenirs; delicious mackerel in white wine and home-made desserts. Menu €30. *Closed Mon*.

At the east end of the Place is **St-Pierre de Montmartre**, the Butte's oldest church, disguised with a 19th-century façade. It is the last relic of the Royal Abbey of Montmartre, which disappeared in the Revolution when the elderly, blind and deaf Mother Superior was condemned to death by Fouquier-Tinville for 'blindly and deafly plotting against the Revolution'. The tunnels underneath have so undermined it that the columns of the nave bend inwards like a German Expressionist film set.

Place des Abbesses

Part of this little square's delight is Guimard's **Métro entrance**, one of just two (the other is Porte-Dauphine) to survive with its glass roof intact. The outlandish church decorated with turquoise mosaics is one of Paris's architectural milestones, the neo-Gothic **St-Jean l'Evangéliste**, the first important building in reinforced concrete (the bricks are sham), built between 1894 and 1904 by Anatole de Baudot, a pupil of Viollet-le-Duc; step inside to see Baudot's innovative play of interlaced arches.

Rue Lepic and Avenue Junot

Here are the last two of Montmartre's 30 windmills: **Moulin du Radet** (now an Italian restaurant) and, to the left, **Moulin de la Galette**, built in 1640 and currently being restored. In the 1814 occupation (according to local legend) the miller of the Galette, his three brothers and eldest son defended their property against the Cossacks; one of the brothers was crucified on the sails of the windmill as an example. Only the eldest son survived, and converted the windmill into a *guinguette*, painted by Renoir (*The Ball at the Moulin de la Galette* 1876, Musée d'Orsay). Continue west down Rue Lepic and turn right up the first stairway passage, which climbs up to **Avenue Junot**; this 'Champs-Elysées of Montmartre' was laid out in 1910, now a rare street of peaceful Art Deco houses with gardens. Anouk Aimée lives here; No.13 is decorated with mosaics designed by Francisque Poulbot (d. 1946), the artist otherwise guilty of those cloying postcards of Montmartre urchins; at No.15 is the house of Dadaist Tristan Tzara (1926), designed by Viennese architect Adolf Loos.

Place Emile-Goudeau

This leafy, asymmetrical square with its Wallace fountain, steps and benches is the antithesis of the classic Paris square down on the 'plain' below; note the curious perspective down Rue Berthe, which, like many other streets up here, seems to lead to the end of the world. This square was the site of the famous **Bateau Lavoir** (No.13), a leaky, creaking wooden warehouse that Max Jacob named after the floating laundry concessions on the Seine. Among the 'passengers' who rented studio space in the Bateau were Braque, Gris, Van Dongen, Apollinaire and Picasso; in winter the tea in the communal pot froze every night and had to be reheated for breakfast. In 1907 Picasso painted his *Demoiselles d'Avignon*, the girls with multiple profiles. In 1970, just as the Bateau Lavoir was to be converted into a museum, it burned down and has been replaced by 25 more comfortable if less picturesque studios.

Montmartre's Vineyard

The vineyard was planted by the Montmartrois in 1886 in memory of the vines that once covered the Butte. If nothing else the harvest is an excuse for a colourful neighbourhood wine crush, which results in some 400 bottles of weedy gamay called Clos de Montmartre.

Au Lapin Agile

Rue des Saules.

It opened in 1860 as the Cabaret des Assassins, but in 1880 a painter named Gil painted the mural of a nimble rabbit avoiding the pot, a play on his name: the *lapin à Gil*. In the early days, when it was a favourite of Verlaine, Renoir and Clemenceau, customers would set the table themselves and join in singsongs, originating an informal style the French call *à la bonne franquette*. In 1903 Aristide Bruant purchased the place to save it from demolition and, thanks to the good humour of his friend Frédé, it enjoyed a second period of success. Artists could pay for their meals with paintings – as Picasso did with one of his *Harlequins*, now worth millions. Now, every evening, *animateurs* attempt to recapture that first peerless rapture.

Musée de Montmartre

12 Rue Cortot. Open Tues–Sun 11–6, closed Mon; adm.

Especially if you've already been to the tourist inferno of Place du Tertre (*see* above) you might think this is a contrived attraction; in fact it is a genuine neighbourhood museum, set up and run by the people of Montmartre. Behind a pretty courtyard full of fuchsias, so healthy they are turning into trees, you'll see prints, pictures and souvenirs that tell the real Montmartre story. There are plenty of old photos and maps of the area, some of Toulouse-Lautrec's posters, and even the original sign from the Lapin Agile.

***Also see*: Sacré-Cœur, p.214.**

***Onwards to*: Les Puces de Saint-Ouen, p.263; Opéra shopping, p.258.**

The Marais and Bastille

Ⓜ *St-Paul, Bastille.*

One of the less frantic corners of old Paris, the Marais is the aristocratic quarter *par excellence*. The main attractions are the grand *hôtels particuliers* of the 16th to 18th centuries and the museums they contain. In the area that has perhaps changed the least over the last 300 years, take time to look at details, like the 17th-century street signs carved into many old buildings or the subtle sculptural decoration.

When the Seine changed its present course, the old bed remained as low, marshy ground, especially in its eastern edge, the Marais of today. Left mostly outside the original walls of Paris, the Marais was home to several monasteries while other parts were little more than a dump for garbage and dead animals. The religious orders owned most of the land, and they undertook the slow work of reclamation. Charles V enclosed the Marais within his new wall in the 1370s, and set the tone by moving in himself, taking residence for a period at the Hôtel St-Pol near the Seine (now vanished). Nobles and important clerics followed and the old swamplands began to sprout imposing *hôtels particuliers*. What made the Marais' fortune was Henri IV's construction of the Place des Vosges in 1605. During the Revolution most of the great *hôtels particuliers* were confiscated and divided up, starting them on a career as homes for clothing makers and warehouses. They were still serving the same purpose in the 1950s and '60s, falling into ever more decay, when Parisians finally rediscovered what had become a lost world. The old working population is now long gone and the Marais has settled into a mixture of gay bars, hip boutiques and Hasidic Jews around Rue des Rosiers (with recent additions from North Africa and the Middle East).

Place des Vosges

The Place des Vosges' association with royalty began long before the Place ever appeared. The Hôtel des Tournelles, a turreted mansion built here in the 1330s, had belonged to a chancellor of France, a bishop of Paris and a pair of dukes before Charles VI purchased it in 1407. Catherine de' Medici had the palace demolished when her husband Henri II was killed there in a joust, and she seems to have had the original inspiration to replace it with Paris's first proper square. In 1605, Henri IV finally began the building of what would be known as the 'Place Royale', a centrepiece the sprawling Marais badly needed. Its architects are unknown; though the square is Italian in concept, the adaptation became something a 17th-century Frenchman could love – elegant, hierarchical and rigorously symmetrical.

After the Revolution, when all the names of *ancien régime* streets were changed, Napoleon gave it its present name in honour of the first *département* of France to pay its share of the new war taxes. Today the Place is a favourite with tourists, Parisians, groups of schoolchildren and everyone else. It's utterly pleasant under the clipped linden trees, and the statue of Louis XIII looks fondly foolish with his pencil moustache and Roman toga. The architecture, totally French and refreshingly free of any Renaissance imitation, invites contemplation. If you do so, you'll notice a lot of the 'brick' is really painted plaster; even aristocrats can cut corners.

Musée Carnavalet

23 Rue de Sévigné. Open Tues–Sun 10–5.40, closed Mon and hols; adm.

It is only fitting that this city museum of Paris should be housed in the grandest of all the *hôtels particuliers* of the Marais. Begun in 1548 for a president of the *Parlement de Paris*, the Hôtel Carnavalet was rebuilt in the *grand-siècle* style by François Mansart in 1660. *Carnavalet*, besides being the name of a former owner, also means a carnival mask; you'll notice one of these carved over the entrance. It is a reminder of how the streets of old Paris, or any other city, were an empire of symbols and pictorial allusions in the days before everyone could read. The first room of the museum is entirely devoted to the charming **shop signs** of this Paris. The rooms that follow, devoted to ancient and medieval Paris, are rather scanty. After these there's an abrupt jump to modern times, such as the faithfully reproduced **bedchamber of Marcel Proust**, where he would accept his morning *madeleine* and muse on fate and memory.

If you're nodding off after too much bourgeois plushness, the **ballroom of the Hôtel Wendel** will startle you back awake. This hotel, formerly on Avenue de New-York, gave Spanish artist José-María Sert *carte blanche* in 1924 to create a venue that would draw the avant-garde. After that comes an earlier monument of abstruse modernism, the entire **Fouquet jewellery shop** from Rue Royale, *c.* 1901. Fouquet's baubles would have been displayed to advantage in the next tableau, a **private room** from the **Café de Paris** (formerly 41 Avenue de l'Opéra), showing Art Nouveau at its sweetest.

Rue des Rosiers

Centre of a small Jewish community since the 1700s, a wave of immigration from Eastern Europe in the 1880s and '90s made it what it is today – one of the liveliest, most picturesque little streets in Paris. Recently, a number of Sephardic Jews from North Africa have moved in, adding to a scene that includes bearded Hasidim, old-fashioned *casher* (kosher) grocery shops, and famous delicatessen restaurants. There are several **synagogues**, including one around the corner at 10 Rue Pavée, designed with a stunning curvilinear façade by Hector Guimard.

Cafés and Lunches

Bofinger, 5 Rue de la Bastille, just off the Place, **t** 01 42 72 87 82. One of the prettiest brasseries in Paris and an institution for over a century; seafood platters and specialities from Alsace; wondrous choice of oysters by the dozen or half. This is a great place. 'Le Petit Bofinger', a cheaper version across the road at No.6, has an €18 menu.

La Guirlande de Julie, 25 Place des Vosges, **t** 01 48 87 94 07. A memorable lunch and a memorable setting under the arcades.

Chez Paul, 13 Rue de Charonne, 11e, **t** 01 47 00 34 57. Solid family cooking in an old Paris setting straight out of a Doisneau photo, complete with a pretty terrace.

Chez Janou, 2 Rue Roger-Verlomme, **t** 01 42 72 28 41 (north of Pl des Vosges). Friendly tiled *bistrot* from 1900 with Provençal dishes.

Jo Goldenberg, 7 Rue des Rosiers. The Marais branch of Paris's most famous delicatessen. You'll think you're in New York (the ultimate compliment for delis).

Le Loir dans la Théière, 3 Rue des Rosiers. Tea room/restaurant, mixed chairs and expectantly intellectual atmosphere. Light lunches (tarts, *pâtisseries maison*).

Chez Rami et Hanna, 54 Rue des Rosiers, 4e, **t** 01 42 74 74 99 (*cheap*). Falafel, herring, chopped liver, the whole *shtick*.

La Belle Horthense, 31 Rue Vieille du Temple. Bookshop/café in the heart of the Marais.

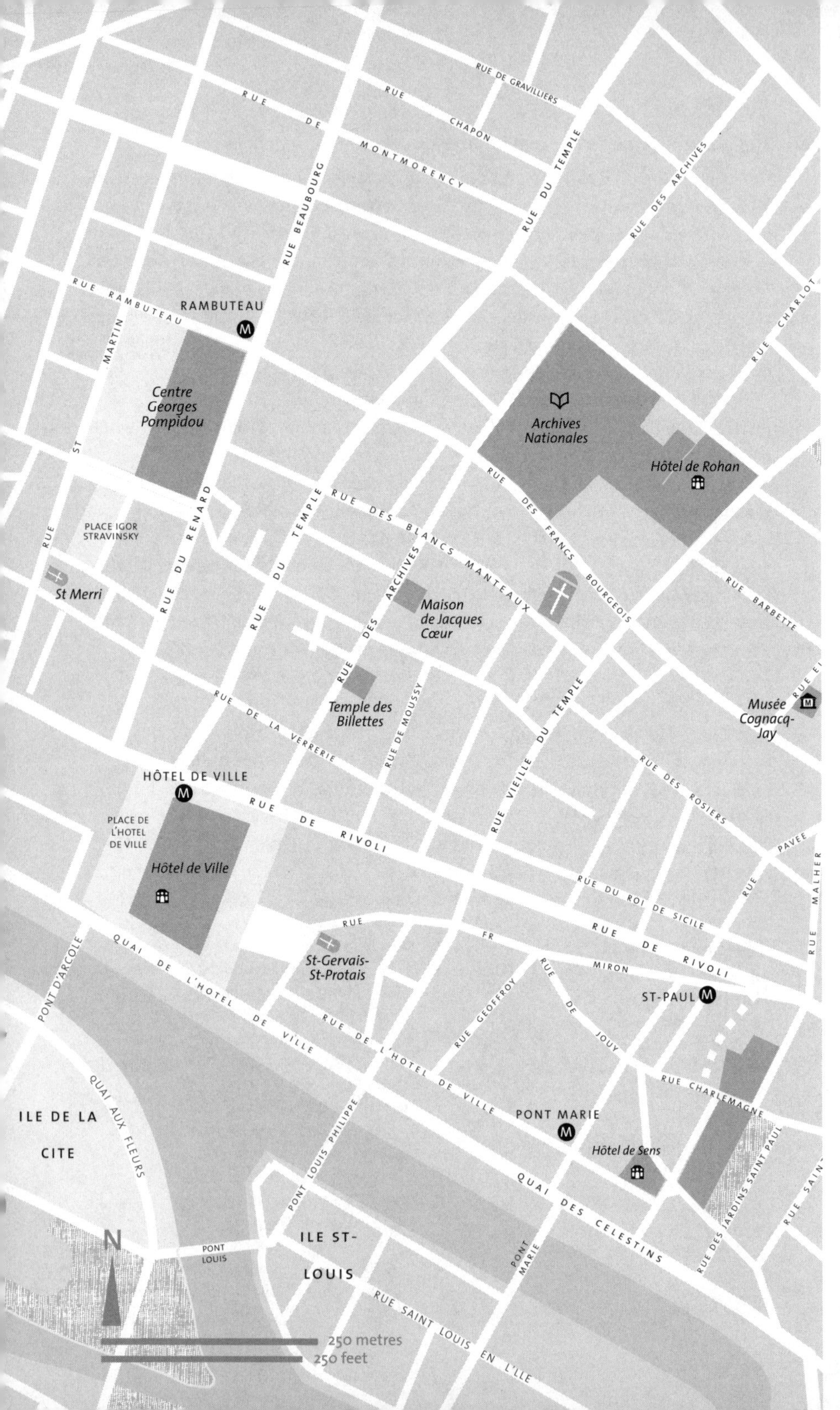

RUE DE GRAVILLIERS
RUE CHAPON
RUE DE MONTMORENCY
RUE BEAUBOURG
RUE DU TEMPLE
RUE DES ARCHIVES
RUE CHARLOT
RUE RAMBUTEAU
RAMBUTEAU
RUE ST MARTIN
Centre Georges Pompidou
Archives Nationales
Hôtel de Rohan
RUE DES FRANCS BOURGEOIS
RUE DES BLANCS MANTEAUX
RUE DU TEMPLE
RUE DU RENARD
PLACE IGOR STRAVINSKY
St Merri
RUE DES ARCHIVES
Maison de Jacques Cœur
RUE BARBETTE
Temple des Billettes
RUE DE MOUSSY
RUE DE LA VERRERIE
RUE VIEILLE DU TEMPLE
Musée Cognacq-Jay
RUE DES ROSIERS
HÔTEL DE VILLE
PLACE DE L'HOTEL DE VILLE
Hôtel de Ville
RUE DE RIVOLI
RUE PAVEE
RUE MALHER
RUE DU ROI DE SICILE
RUE FR MIRON
RUE DE RIVOLI
St-Gervais-St-Protais
QUAI DE L'HOTEL DE VILLE
PONT D'ARCOLE
RUE GEOFFROY
RUE DE JOUY
ST-PAUL
RUE DE L'HOTEL DE VILLE
RUE CHARLEMAGNE
PONT MARIE
Hôtel de Sens
RUE DES JARDINS SAINT PAUL
QUAI DES CELESTINS
ILE DE LA CITE
QUAI AUX FLEURS
PONT LOUIS PHILIPPE
PONT LOUIS
ILE ST-LOUIS
PONT MARIE
RUE SAINT LOUIS EN L'ILE
N
250 metres
250 feet

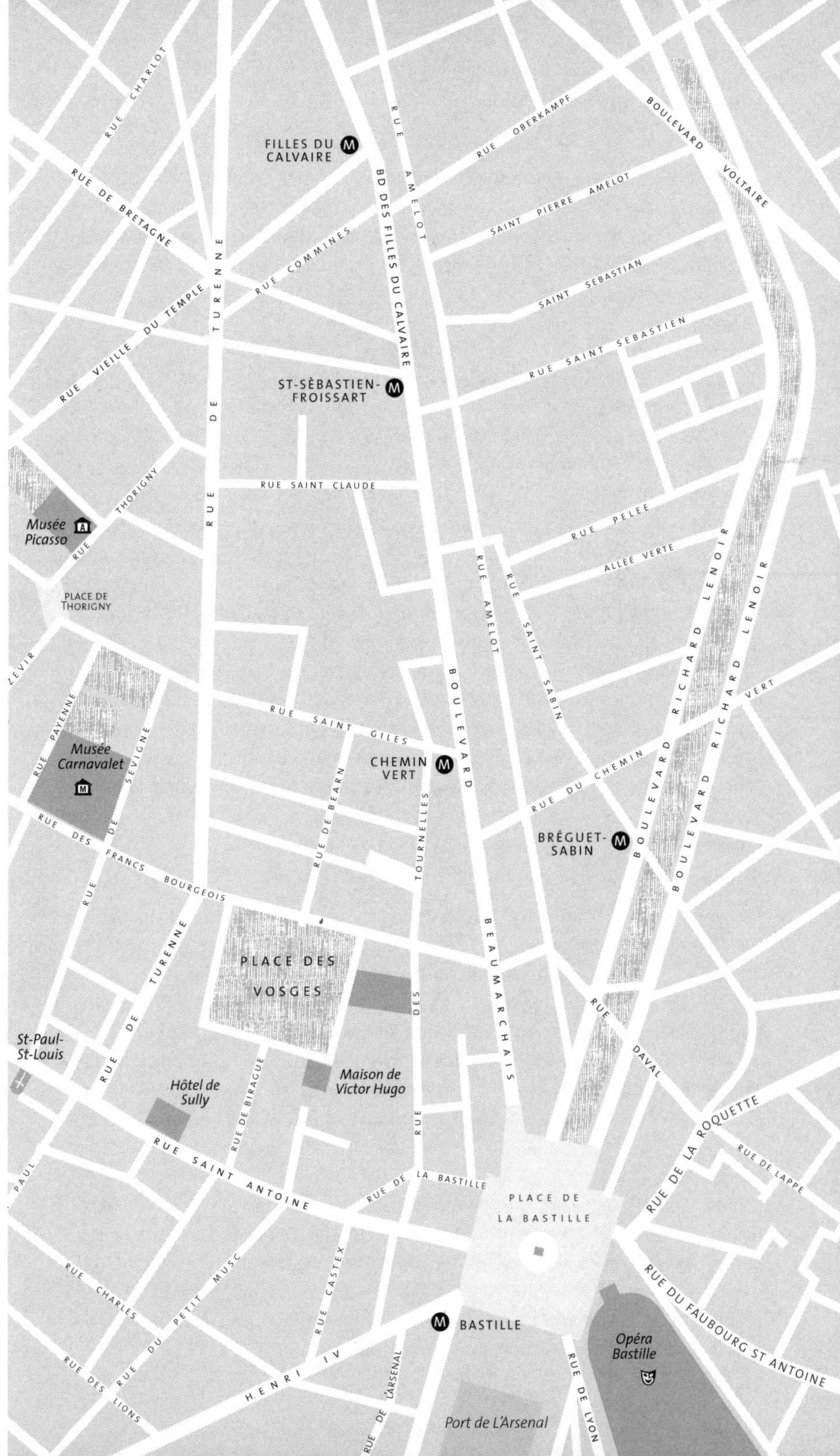

RUE CHARLOT
RUE DE BRETAGNE
RUE VIEILLE DU TEMPLE
RUE DE TURENNE
RUE COMMINES
FILLES DU CALVAIRE
BD DES FILLES DU CALVAIRE
RUE AMELOT
RUE OBERKAMPF
BOULEVARD VOLTAIRE
SAINT PIERRE AMELOT
SAINT SEBASTIAN
RUE SAINT SEBASTIEN
ST-SÈBASTIEN-FROISSART
RUE SAINT CLAUDE
RUE THORIGNY
Musée Picasso
PLACE DE THORIGNY
RUE PELEE
ALLEE VERTE
RUE SAINT SABIN
BOULEVARD RICHARD LENOIR
RUE PAYENNE
Musée Carnavalet
RUE DE SEVIGNE
RUE SAINT GILES
CHEMIN VERT
RUE DU CHEMIN VERT
RUE DE BEARN
RUE DES FRANCS BOURGEOIS
BRÉGUET-SABIN
BOULEVARD BEAUMARCHAIS
PLACE DES VOSGES
RUE DES TOURNELLES
RUE DAVAL
St-Paul-St-Louis
Hôtel de Sully
RUE DE BIRAGUE
Maison de Victor Hugo
RUE DE LA ROQUETTE
RUE DE LAPPE
RUE SAINT ANTOINE
RUE DE LA BASTILLE
PLACE DE LA BASTILLE
RUE DU FAUBOURG ST ANTOINE
RUE CHARLES
RUE DU PETIT MUSC
RUE CASTEX
BASTILLE
RUE HENRI IV
RUE DES LIONS
RUE DE L'ARSENAL
RUE DE LYON
Opéra Bastille
Port de L'Arsenal

Hôtel de Rohan

87 Rue Vieille-du-Temple. Open for special exhibitions only.

The Hôtel de Rohan is one of the last and most ambitious of all the Marais mansions. In the courtyard, over the door to the Rohans' stables, is a masterpiece of rococo sculpture, Robert le Lorrain's theatrical **Horses of Apollo** (entrance at 87 Rue Vieille-du-Temple; once inside, go through the arch to the right). The interior is one of the best preserved in Paris.

Rue des Archives

Already you will have noticed the huge neoclassical bulk of the **Archives Nationales** on your left (*www.archivesnationales.culture.gouv.fr; open Mon and Wed–Fri 10–12 and 2–5.305, Sat and Sun 2–5; closed Tues and hols; adm*). The oldest part of the complex is a turreted gateway built in the 1370s. The truly grand horseshoe-shaped courtyard facing the Rue des Francs-Bourgeois belongs to the main part of the Archives, the **Hôtel de Soubise**. The part you can visit is called the **Musée de l'Histoire de France**, which isn't for everyone, but with a little knowledge of French this collection of documents can be utterly fascinating. The best thing in the museum is a painting on the far wall: a funny 16th-century allegory of the *Ship of Faith*, piloted by the Jesuits, and rowed by priests and nuns, smiling beatifically down.

In the lower half of this street are two buildings worth a look. The **Temple des Billettes**, an 18th-century monastic church at No.22, has belonged to the Lutherans since 1812. Its cloister, simple and refined, is the only Gothic cloister left in Paris. At No.40, the 15th-century **Maison de Jacques Cœur** slept under a coat of stucco for centuries, until a chance restoration brought its brick-patterned façade to light in 1971.

Hôtel de Sens

Square de l'Ave Maria.

Strangely enough, Paris did not become an archiepiscopal see until 1623; for over a thousand years its bishops were subject to the archbishops of the little town of Sens. In the Middle Ages these influential clerics spent most of their time in the capital. One of them, *c.* 1475, built this medieval confection overlooking the Seine (today the river is two streets away). Almost completely reconstructed, it is one of the loveliest buildings in Paris. The palace is now **Bibliothèque Forney**, a remarkable institution dedicated to the old crafts and industries of France (*library open Tues–Fri 1.30–8.30, Sat 10–8.30; exhibitions Tues–Sat 1.30–8; adm; view the gardens at the back, off Rue du Figuier*).

St-Paul-St-Louis

In the late 16th century, there developed in Italy the architectural fashion that art historians used to call the 'Jesuit Style'. Combining the confident classicism of the decaying Renaissance with a sweeping bravura that would soon be perfected in the dawning Baroque, this architecture was a key part of the Jesuits' plan to forge a swanky modern image for the Counter-Reformation Church. From its opening, this church was the showcase of the new Catholicism in Paris.

The Storming of the Bastille

On the morning of the 14th July 1789, after a rousing speech by Camille Desmoulins in the Palais Royal (*see* p.246), some 600 people, including women and children, advanced across Paris to the grim fortress that had become a symbol of royal despotism. They battled all afternoon against a small garrison of Swiss Guards and retired veterans until, at about 5pm, the arrival of a detachment of revolutionary militia decided the issue. The gates were forced, the governor and many of the defenders massacred, and the last seven inmates of the Bastille were acclaimed as heroes among the crowd: the prisoners comprised four swindlers who were about to be transferred to another prison, an English idiot named Whyte, a gentleman whose family had petitioned the king to lock him up for incest and one genuine political prisoner – who had been in the Bastille since some obscure conspiracy in 1759 and didn't want to leave. The demolition commenced the following day.

Place de la Bastille

There's nothing to see of the famous fortress, of course – unless you arrive on the no.5 Métro, coming from the Gare d'Austerlitz, where some of the foundations survive around the platform. The square has been redesigned, with the outline of the fortress set into the pavement. It is the only square in town created not by kings or planners but by the people of Paris. Since they cleared the space back in 1789, the Place has been the symbolic centre of leftist politics, the setting for monster celebrations.

Today, the centrepiece of the Place de la Bastille is the 153ft **Colonne de Juillet**. The 'July column', restored for the bicentennial of the Revolution, was erected over the elephant's pedestal in honour of those who died in the 1830 revolt. On top is a figure of the 'Genius of Liberty'.

Opéra Bastille

For excellent guided tours (in French only) call **t** *01 40 01 19 70 for times and buy a ticket from the office, www.opera-de-paris.fr. Box office open daily 11–6.30 (except Sun); tickets on sale two weeks in advance,* **t** *08 92 89 90 90.*

As part of Mitterrand's notions of 'bringing culture to the people', he conjured up the startling façade of the Opéra Bastille. There used to be a small railway station here, and the buildings included a Métro pavilion that was one of the finest works of Hector Guimard. The government planners typically levelled it without a second thought when they began clearing the site for the Opéra in 1985. Uruguayan-Canadian architect Carlos Ott was chosen by President Mitterrand in 1983 as the winner of the design competition. The architectural criticism has been harsh; Ott was up against popular ideas about what an opera house should look like. On the inside, Ott did everything you could ask of an architect – the sight lines and acoustics are excellent – but the auditorium is hardly intimate: this is a stage meant for spectacle.

***Also see*: Musée Picasso, p.267; Musée Cognacq-Jay, p.268, Musée d'Art et d'Histoire du Judaïsme, p.273.**

***Onwards to*: Les Halles, p.223; Pompidou Centre, p.212.**

Palais Royal

Ⓜ *Bourse, Louvre.*

Welcome to the most unabashedly retro area of Paris. Dusty, dignified, quiet and thoroughly obsolete in a number of unimportant ways, it hasn't really been popular with Parisians or tourists or anybody else since the 1830s. But you may find it one of the most unexpected delights Paris has to offer. This *quartier* is about old books, pretty things and good architecture; in other words, the elements of civilization.

Though not a well-defined quarter like the Marais, it has assumed and thrown off various identities over the centuries: it was an area of court servants, artists and hangers-on when kings lived at the Louvre or Tuileries, and briefly Paris's tenderloin when the Palais Royal was full of bordellos. Though containing the Bourse and the Banque de France, it has been spared the fate of becoming a soulless business centre.

Palais Royal

Originally Cardinal Richelieu built this palace for himself, beginning in 1629. Naturally he willed it to the king, whose money he was playing with, long before his death in 1642. Anne of Austria and four-year-old Louis XIV moved in soon after, but left for the more defensible Louvre, and gave it to his brother Philippe, Duc d'Orléans. Much rebuilt, the Palais Royal currently houses the *Conseil d'Etat*. Next door is the **Théâtre Français**, attached to the Palais-Royal complex in 1786. Ever since, it has been the home of the Comédie-Française, founded by Louis XIV out of Molière's old troupe and some others. In the lobby, Houdon's famous statue of Voltaire is displayed.

But the real attraction is not these mournful buildings, but the sweet surprise behind them. Pass under the arch between the theatre and the palace into the **Jardins du Palais Royal**. The last descendant of the Duke of Orléans had in 1781 hit on the idea of cutting down his enormous debts by selling off part of the gardens for building lots. His architects chopped the greenery down by a third, and enclosed it with an arcaded quadrangle of terraced houses, *à la* Place des Vosges. Under the arcades, several cafés soon opened; gambling houses and bordellos thrived, quite refined, fronting as hat shops or even furniture shops. The police couldn't do a thing about it; they could not even enter the grounds without the duke's permission.

Ironically enough, this privilege helped make the Palais Royal gardens, and the cafés that proliferated around its arcades, one of the birthplaces of the Revolution. Like the Tuileries, this was one of the bastions of the *nouvellistes*, or news-mongers. You came here if you wanted to argue politics. Typically, the attack on the Bastille was spontaneously conceived here, when Camille Desmoulins jumped on to a café table and started talking, on the morning of 14 July (*see* p.245).

Fashion and vice both moved to the Grands Boulevards after 1838, when Louis-Philippe closed the gambling houses. Later, because the Dukes of Orléans were pretenders to his throne, Louis-Napoleon confiscated both the gardens and the palace. Ever since, the garden has kept well out of the mainstream of popularity. The arcades that were once packed day and night now hold only a few quietly fascinating shops, selling antiques, military models or recycled designer clothing from the 1950s.

Galeries and *Passages*

One of the oldest and prettiest of Paris's *passages*, built in 1826, the Galerie Véro-Dodat wowed the Paris crowds with its mahogany, marble and bronze decoration, as well as its use of a new technological marvel – gas lighting. Véro and Dodat were two butchers who made it big and went out of their way to impress. There are interesting shops (*see* p.260). The Galeries Vivienne and Colbert were built in the 1820s, and along with the Véro-Dodat they are the most luxurious and well-restored survivors of the genre in Paris. Light and airy, with neoclassical reliefs and mosaic floors, these arcades make a dreamy setting for their little shops and cafés (*see* p.260).

Place des Victoires

The second of Paris's 'royal' squares (after Place des Vosges), it was laid out by Hardouin-Mansart in 1685 to accommodate an equestrian statue of Louis XIV. Like its

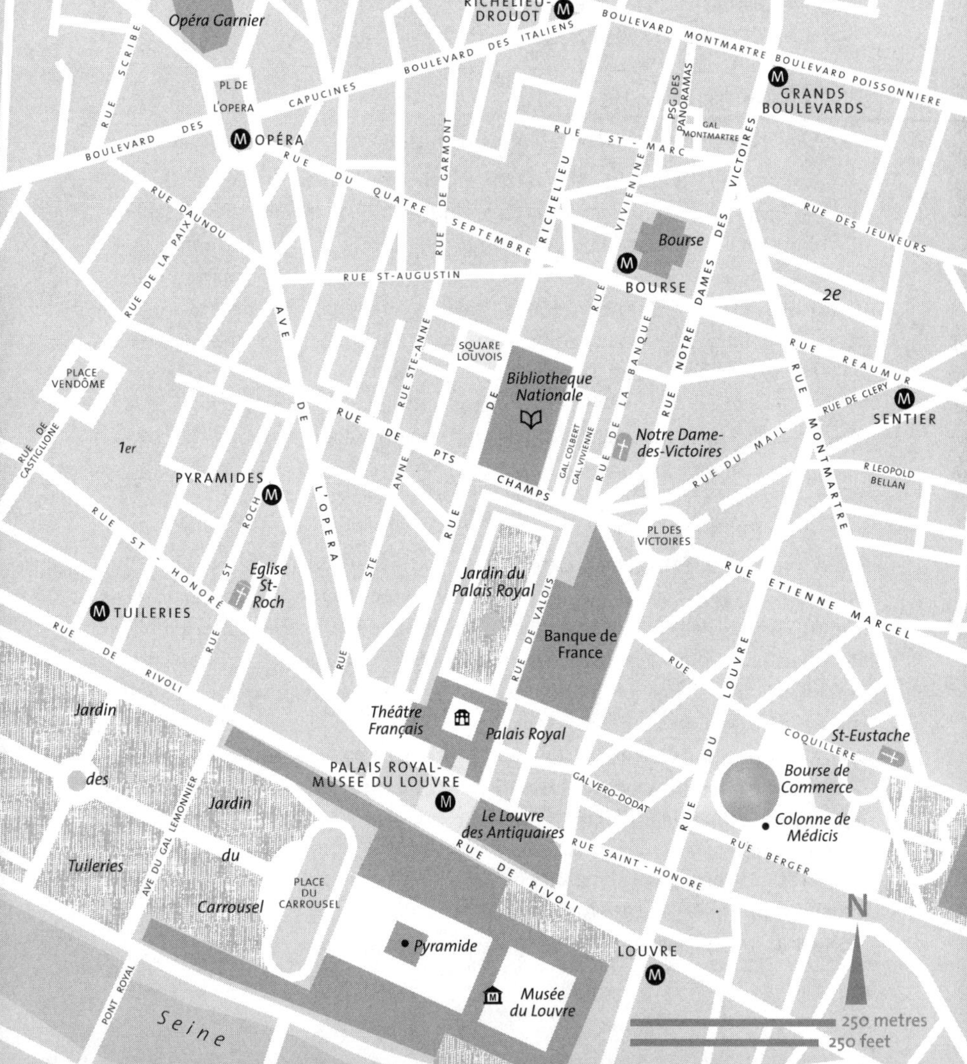

Cafés and Lunches

Le Grand Véfour, 17 Rue de Beaujolais, 1er, **t** 01 42 96 56 27. More a temple than a crass commercial enterprise, this grandest of grand old restaurants maintains a tradition in the Palais Royal that is now 200 years old. Lunch menu €75. *Closed Fri eve, Sat and Sun, and Aug.*

Palais Royal, 110 Galerie de Valois, under the arcades. Elegant surroundings, and an up-market €30 menu.

A Priori Thé, Galerie Vivienne, No.33. Come in for English tea and cheesecake; tables 'outside' under the arcade's glass roof.

Muscade, Jardin du Palais-Royal, 36 Rue de Monpensier, **t** 01 42 97 51 36. Delicious terrace dining in fair weather. *Closed Mon.*

Le Gavroche, 19 Rue St-Marc, 2e, **t** 01 42 96 89 70. The archetypal family-run *bistrot à vins* of old; authentic without even trying. Hearty country cooking and very good wines. Lunch menu €14. *Closed Sun.*

predecessor, the piazza was planned as an intimate, enclosed public space. Over the last century, the Parisians have done their best to spoil the effect. Façades were altered, and in 1883 Rue Etienne-Marcel was cut through the Place, entirely wrecking its dignified atmosphere. By the 1950s it reached a nadir of tackiness, but lately there has been a clean-up; the place now attracts high-fashion shops.

Bibliothèque Nationale

11, Quai François Mauriac, www.bnf.fr. Open Tues–Sat 10–8, Sun 12–7; adm.

A decree of 1537 inaugurated the *dépôt légal*, the requirement that anyone publishing a book must send a copy to the king – who was concerned with seeing anything that might be seditious. Louis XIV's minister, Colbert, put the library on a sound footing when he consolidated all the king's holdings in two adjacent *hôtels particuliers*. You can't use the facilities without a reader's card, but have a look inside at the old building. The main reading room has been transferred to the new site at Quai François-Mauriac; here you can see a museum of coins and medals. The exit on the opposite side of the Bibliothèque takes you to Rue de Richelieu, facing the **Square Louvois**, with a pretty fountain (1844) allegorizing the 'Four Rivers of France': the Seine, Loire, Garonne and Saône.

Eglise St-Roch

There were outbreaks of plague in France as late as the 17th century; to be on the safe side, Parisians finally decided to build a church to St Roch, the medieval plague saint from Montpellier. Finished in the 18th century, St-Roch became one of the society churches of Paris. Famous folk buried here include Diderot, Le Nôtre and Corneille. Inside, it's just another overblown and insincere church of the Age of the Louies. The best part is the frothy **Lady Chapel** behind the altar, a large circular work with a pleasing unity of equally dubious 18th-century painting, sculpture and glass. On the right, note the tomb of Amiral de Grasse, who helped make American independence possible by trapping the British at Yorktown.

Also see: **Louvre, p.201, Cabinet des Médailles et Antiques, p.266, Louvre/Rivoli shopping, pp.261, Musée des Arts Décoratifs, p.268.**

Onwards to: **Les Halles, p.223; Opéra, p.211.**

Paris: Green Spaces

19

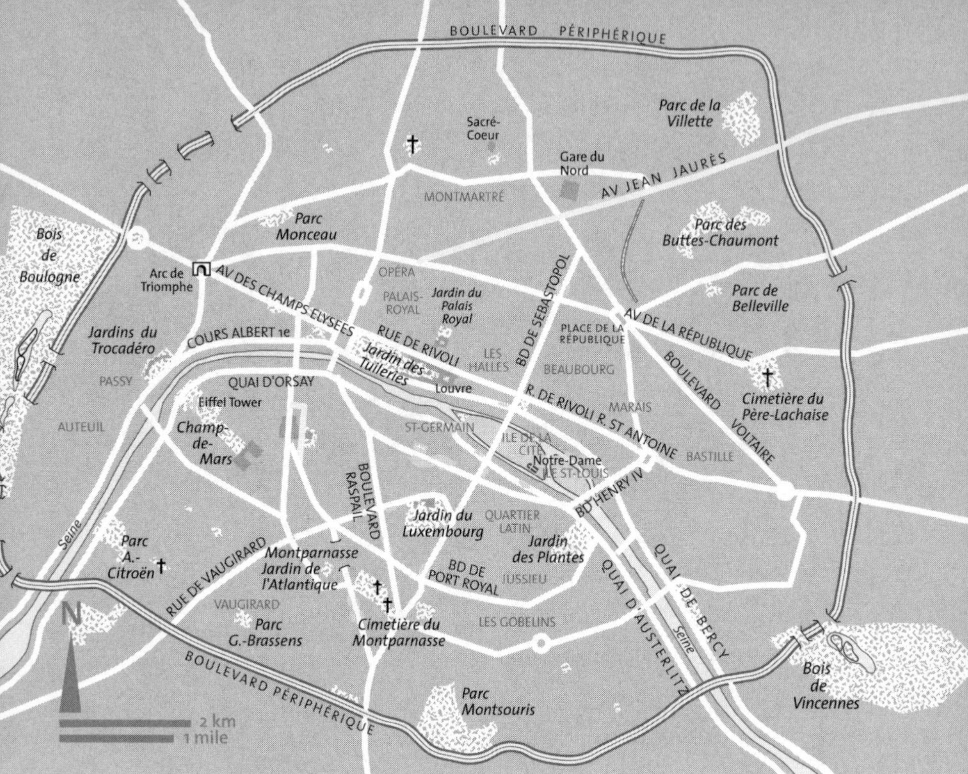

Bois de Boulogne

After the Eiffel Tower, the Bois de Boulogne was not so long ago the most visited place in Paris – the 'world capital of prostitution', no less, where every day over a million francs changed hands. It was a venerable tradition. François Ier built the Château de Boulogne here, where he installed his mistress, La Ferronnière, for whom, it is said, he died loving too fervently. Other kings installed their own loves – Diane de Poitiers and Gabrielle d'Estrées lived here. Even after the Revolution, when the château was razed, the Bois kept its reputation for love; in the 17th century its bowers were full of impetuous couples. Now all the access roads are blocked off at night, and things are considerably more staid.

The Bois owes its current appearance to Napoleon III, who spent his early years in London and gave the Bois to the city as its own Hyde Park. Roads, riding and walking paths crisscross it, but for anyone with children in tow the biggest attraction is on the Neuilly side, to the north (Ⓜ *Les Sablons*) where the **Jardin d'Acclimatation** (*www.jardinacclimatation.fr; open 10–6, till 7 in July and Aug; special activities at weekends and during school hols; adm*) has nearly every possible activity for kids – camel and canal-boat rides, playgrounds, a small zoo, a doll's house with antique toys, a *guignol* (puppet show), children's theatre, bumper cars, crafts and games.

The most scenic spots in the Bois include the **Lac Inférieur**, with its islets and emperor's kiosk (near ***RER*** *Av Henri-Martin* or Ⓜ *Ranelagh*); the **Shakespeare garden** by the open-air theatre in the **Pré Catelan**; the **Grande Cascade**, an artificial Swiss Alps waterfall just east of Longchamp; and, for garden- and rose-lovers, the sumptuous **Parc de Bagatelle** (*a 15min walk or bus 43 from Ⓜ Pont de Neuilly or take bus 244 from Ⓜ Porte Maillot or* ***RER*** *Rueil-Malmaison; open spring/summer daily 9–8, autumn daily 9–6, winter daily 9–4; adm*).

Bois de Vincennes

Ⓜ Porte Dorée for the zoo, Ⓜ Château de Vincennes for the castle.

Like the Bois de Boulogne, its matching bookend at the other end of Paris, Vincennes owes its existence to the French kings' love of hunting. They set it aside for that purpose in the 1100s, and Philippe-Auguste even built a wall around it to keep out poachers. In the 14th century the Valois kings built its castle – a real fortified castle, not just a château, for this was the time of the Hundred Years' War. As long as the nearby Marais was fashionable, so was Vincennes, but when Louis XIV left Paris in the opposite direction, for Versailles, the neglected hunting ground was turned into a public park. Besides the open spaces, the main attraction is the **zoo**, one of the largest in Europe (*open summer daily 9–6, winter 9–5.30; adm*). It offers giant pandas and a 67m (220ft) artificial mountain (which has started to collapse). Adjacent is one of the prettier parts of the park, the **Lac Daumesnil** with its islands, one blessed with a fake romantic ruin like the one in Buttes-Chaumont. Further east (*Ⓜ Château de Vincennes, then bus no.112*) is the **Parc Floral** (*open April–Sept 9.30–8, Mar and Oct daily 9.30–6, Nov– Feb daily 9.30–5; adm*): water lilies, orchids and dahlias, with rides and special entertainments.

The Castle

At the northern edge of the park; Ⓜ Château de Vincennes.

Open Oct–Mar daily 10–12 and 1.15–5; April–Sept daily 10–12 and 1–6; long and short guided tours; adm, free to under-18s.

The finest example of medieval secular architecture in Paris, this 'Versailles of the Middle Ages' shows what the French could build even in the sorrows of the 1300s. Begun under Philippe IV in 1337, it was completed in 1380. Louis was always short of prison cells – no king in French history locked up so many political prisoners – and Vincennes made a convenient calaboose. Napoleon, another ruler who liked to keep his cells full, made it a prison again while rebuilding the fortifications just in case. Unwittingly he provided Vincennes with a chance for a short but brilliant military career – the only bit of Paris that never surrendered in the Napoleonic Wars. During the First World War the trenches around the castle were used for shooting spies.

The highlight of the tour is the **donjon**, the 14th-century keep, strong and taciturn outside but a beautiful residence within, containing stained glass and excellent sculptural work. The **Salle des Gens d'Armes** is a lovely Gothic vaulted space. In the bedroom on the second floor England's King Henry V died in 1422; they parboiled him in the kitchen to keep him nice for the trip home to London. Besides these, the tour inside takes you through the **Résidence Royale**, built by Le Vau for Louis XIV, and the **Sainte-Chapelle**, almost a copy of the famous one.

Jardin du Luxembourg

RER Luxembourg.

The Jardin du Luxembourg is a welcome Left Bank oasis of greenery. Metal chairs are scattered under the trees and around a shady café and bandstand, although the scarce lawns are out of bounds. But the kids have all the fun, on an opulent carousel designed by Charles Garnier, riding pony carts and mini-cars, sailing boats in the Grand Bassin, or watching performances of *guignol* in the **Théâtre des Marionnettes** (*shows Wed at 4, Sat and Sun at 11 and 4; free;* ***t*** *01 43 26 46 47*).

Near the gate, the park remembers its foundress, Marie de' Medici, with the long pool of the **Fontaine de Médicis** (just east of the Palais du Luxembourg), a romantic rendezvous under the plane trees, dating from 1624 and adorned with 19th-century statuary of the lovers Acis and Galatea about to be ambushed by the jealous cyclops Polyphemus. They are only the first of the Luxembourg's numerous marble men and women. Marie de' Medici herself figures among the Great Women of France posing around the central basin; in the trees towards Rue Guynemer, there's a midget *Statue of Liberty* by Bertholdi, who modelled her on his monolithic mom and gradually made her bigger (as on the Ile des Cygnes) and bigger (as in New York).

Palais du Luxembourg

Jardin du Luxembourg, entrance on Rue de Vaugirard.

Interior open one or two Sundays per month for guided tours, but you have to contact Monuments Historiques for hours, ***t*** *01 44 61 20 84.*

'Twas a dark and stormy night when the newly widowed Marie de' Medici, Regent of France, ordered her coachman to drive her to the Bastille, where she brazenly pinched all the money her husband, Henri IV, had set aside in case of war. Marie used it to buy land south of Rue de Vaugirard. And in 1612, on the death of the Duke of Luxembourg, Marie added his *hôtel particulier* (now the Petit Luxembourg) to her estate. But the regent's ambitions were hardly *petit*; in fact, she dreamed of a replica of her girlhood home, Florence's enormous Pitti Palace. Architect Salomon de Brosse managed to dissuade her in favour of a more traditional French mansion, but decorated it with Florentine touches – especially the rusticated bands of stone that give it a corrugated look, and its 'ringed' Tuscan columns.

At the west end of the big Palace, at Rue de Vaugirard, delightful **Petit Luxembourg** was Paris's first public art gallery, and the **Musée du Luxembourg** (*open Tues–Thurs 10–7, Mon and Fri 10–10.30, Sat and Sun 10–9; adm*) still has temporary exhibitions.

Jardin des Plantes

Ⓜ Jussieu, Gare d'Austerlitz; www.mnhn.fr.

In 1626 doctors Jean Hérouard and Guy de La Brosse convinced their best-known patient, Louis XIII, to establish a botanical garden of medicinal plants in the capital. Some of France's most famous botanists travelled around the world to collect 2,500 species of plants and exotic trees. In 1793 the Convention created the School and Museum of Natural History, and galleries and research laboratories went up along the flanks of the gardens.

The most endearing feature of the Jardin des Plantes is a 17th-century dump that Buffon converted into a garden **labyrinth** (up on the little hill), topped by a bronze temple with a sundial called the **Gloriette de Buffon** (1786). Near the maze towers is a cedar of Lebanon, a seedling from Kew Gardens brought to Paris in 1734 by Bernard de Jussieu. And south of the Grand Amphitheatre (really a small neoclassical building near the entrance), look for one of the oddest trees, the ironbark from Iran. The tropical forest of the **Serres Tropicales** (Tropical Greenhouses) just to the south (*open 1–5, summer 1–8 at weekends, closed Tues; adm*) is sheltered in one of the world's first iron and glass pavilions, complete with mini-waterfall, stream and turtles. In front, a fence encloses the 2,600 labelled plants of the **Botanical School gardens** (*open Mon–Fri 8–11 and 1.30–5; closed Sat, Sun and hols*).

At the far west end of the formal parterres looms the impressive Zoology Building, now the centre of the Jardin des Plantes' ensemble of museums, the **Muséum National d'Histoire Naturelle**. The new centrepiece of this modernized collection is the **Grande Galerie de l'Evolution** (*36 Rue Geoffroy-St-Hilaire; open Fri–Mon and Wed 10–6, Thurs 10–10; closed Tues; adm*). After being closed for 30 years, the former zoology section is back with a vengeance – full of every sort of 'interactive exhibit' and audiovisual trick, all on the theme of evolution and the diversity of life (pull-out English translations are slotted in the benches). The long building beyond it houses the **Galerie de Minéralogie** (*open Nov–Mar 10–5, April–Oct Wed–Mon 10–5; closed Tues; adm*), displaying giant crystals from Brazil that imprison rainbows in hundreds of kilos of quartz, as well as meteorites, and the museum treasure.

Opposite the parterres, and east beyond the rose gardens, Allée de Jussieu leads to the **Ménagerie** (*open daily summer 9–6/6.30 at weekends, winter 10–5; adm*). In 1793 all wild beasts in circuses and travelling zoos were sent to the Jardin des Plantes by order of the Commune to form a public ménagerie. Larger zoo creatures are now kept at Vincennes; the Ménagerie has smaller animals, to be viewed up close – reptiles, birds of prey, foetus-like albino axolotls, insects (in the micro-zoo), deer, monkeys and a pair of bears.

Last and most surreal is the massive and eclectic brick **Galerie de Paléontologie**, overlooking Place Valhubert and the Gare d'Austerlitz (*open daily 10–5; closed Tues; adm*). The bas-reliefs of bugs, scorpions and violent battles (man v. bear, man v. crocs) that decorate the exterior reach a climax just inside the door, with a huge statue of an orang-utan strangling a man.

Jardin des Tuileries

Ⓜ *Tuileries, Concorde, Palais Royal-Musée du Louvre.*

The first gardens on this site were built at the same time as the Tuileries palace, in the 1560s. It was Catherine de' Medici's idea, following the latest fashions in landscaping from Renaissance Italy; she purchased a large tract of land behind the palace, part of which had been a rubbish dump and part a tile works – hence the name *tuileries*. Her new pleasure park, designed by Philibert de l'Orme and others, was soon the wonder of Paris; symmetrical and neat, it became the model for André Le Nôtre's work and all the classical French landscaping that followed. Contemporary accounts suggest it must have been much more beautiful, and more fun, than the present incarnation, with such features as a hedge maze, elaborate sundials, a 'grotto' lined with Sèvres porcelain and statuary and a semicircle of trees cleverly planted to create an echo effect. Louis XIV opened the park to the public and the new Tuileries became Paris's most fashionable promenade; it continued as such through the 18th century, featuring such novelties as Paris's first public toilets and first newspaper kiosk. The first gas airship took off from a spot near the octagonal pond in 1783, the same year as the Montgolfiers' pioneer hot-air balloon.

The centre of the park is shaded by avenues of chestnut trees, the *Quinconces des Marronniers*. Further up the Grande Allée (heading for the Place de la Concorde) is the **octagonal basin**, surrounded by some statues that have survived from the days when the Tuileries was a royal park: allegories of the seasons, and of French rivers, also the Nile and the Tiber. The two on winged horses, the **Chevaux Ailés** at the gates facing Place de la Concorde, are by Louis XIV's chief sculptural propagandist, Coysevox: *Mercury* and *Fame* (both copies).

Le Nôtre's plan included narrow raised terraces at the northern and southern ends, the *Terrasse des Feuillants* and the *Terrasse du Bord de l'Eau*, both favourite tracks for Parisian joggers. At the Concorde end, the terraces expand into broader plateaux supporting buildings from the time of Napoleon III. To the north is the **Jeu de Paume**, built for real tennis, the crazy medieval game where the ball bounces off walls, roofs and turrets. The building was once the Impressionists' museum in Paris; the collection has since been consolidated at the Musée d'Orsay. It now sits a bit forlorn, hosting contemporary art exhibitions (*open Wed–Sun 12–7, Sat–Sun 10–7, Tues 12–9.30; adm*). But its counterpart in the southwest corner, the **Orangerie** (*the Orangery; open daily 9.45–3.15, closed Tues*), offers an excellent permanent collection, complementary to the Musée d'Orsay, with a large lower level devoted to Monet, including one of the famous *Nymphéas* (Water Lilies).

Parc des Buttes-Chaumont

Ⓜ *Buttes Chaumont.*

A rocky haunt of outlaws in the Middle Ages, well known to François Villon, this park, now Paris's loveliest, was begun in 1867. In an age when the 'picturesque' was fully in vogue, the natural charms of the Buttes weren't quite good enough. Haussmann's designers brought in thousands of tons of rock and created the artificial cliffs that are its fame today. The centrepiece is a familiar landmark, a steep island in a lake, crowned by a small classical temple, modelled after the Temple of the Sybil in Tivoli. The climb rewards you with a seldom-seen view over Montmartre and the northern parts of Paris; before the Eiffel Tower was built this was the favourite spot for suicides.

Edith Piaf was born on the streets below, under a streetlamp, shielded behind the cloak of a kindly *gendarme* (there's a plaque at 72 Rue de Belleville).

Parc Monceau

Ⓜ *Monceau.*

As with the Palais Royal, Paris owes this rare oasis to Philippe d'Orléans (Philippe-Egalité) who had it landscaped in the 1770s – and redone a decade later, shocking Parisians by hiring a Scotsman named Blakie to turn the grounds into the city's first large English garden. History was made here in 1797, when a man named Garnerin made the world's first parachute jump: 1,000ft from one of the Montgolfiers' balloons, and he lived to tell the tale. The park is lovely and immaculately kept; it includes a large pond called the *Naumachie* near a colonnade believed to have originally stood at St-Denis, from a failed project of Catherine de' Medici to build a mausoleum for the Bourbons.

Père-Lachaise Cemetery

Ⓜ *Père Lachaise or Philippe Auguste; www.gargl.net/lachaise.*

Open daily Mon–Fri 8–6, Sat 8.30–6, Sun and hols 9–6; 6 Nov–15 Mar closes 5.30.

Père Lachaise had the best job in France. As Louis XIV's confessor, he held the keys to heaven for a king who was both superstitious and rotten to the core. It's no surprise that Lachaise got lots of presents, which he converted to real estate here in what would later be the centre of the 20e. In 1804, under Napoleon's orders, Prefect of Paris Nicholas Frochot bought the land for cemetery space. To popularize the new development, the prefect invited in a couple of celebrity corpses – Molière's and La Fontaine's.

The 'most famous cemetery in the world', and the largest in Paris, Père-Lachaise has always been a favourite place for a stroll; Balzac said he liked to come here to 'cheer himself up'. In design, it is a cross between the traditional, urban sort of French cemetery, with family mausolea in straight rows, and the modern, suburban-style model. Brongniart, the architect of the Bourse, laid it out like an English garden.

At the main entrance, you can buy a good map to all the famous stiffs. There are few signs to help you find the graves you're looking for, except rock poet Jim Morrison's; his fans have thoughtfully decorated everybody else's tombs with directions in pen.

From the entrance, Av Principale and a right down Av du Puits will take you to section 7 and the tombs of Père-Lachaise's senior residents, **Héloïse and Abelard**. In the 17th century prudish abbesses would pry their remains apart and put them in separate tombs, and romantic abbesses would reunite them. In 1792 they were moved into a double coffin.

For **Jim Morrison**, follow the crowds to section 6. The cops keep a constant eye on the place, and past sights – wild-looking Germans cooking sausages on a camp stove, naked trippers sprawled over other graves and chanting in tongues – are no longer common. Devotees today leave flowers, smokes and playing cards (face cards only), incense and small toys. There is no proof, incidentally, that Morrison is actually buried here; many people claim he isn't even dead.

Just across Av Casimir Perier is **Chopin** (sec 11). For true romantics, white roses are the token of remembrance (available at the eastern entrance). This is a favourite section for musicians, and is also the oldest and loveliest part of Père-Lachaise, with florid statuary and dead politicians around the **Rond-Point Casimir-Perier**.

South of the Rond-Point down Av des Acacias, a clique of Napoleon's marshals rests in sections 28, 29 and 39: **Cambacérès**, **Murat**, **Masséna** and **Ney**. Up Av Transversale No.1, which neatly bisects the cemetery, British admiral **Sidney Smith** (sec 43), who helped beat the French in the Napoleonic Wars, always loved Paris; you'll find him near **Corot** (sec 24), **Hugo** (sec 27), and **Molière** and **La Fontaine** (sec 25). Nearby, you can visit **Simone Signoret** (sec 44), keeping company with fellow actress **Sarah Bernhardt** (just across a path in sec 91), plus **Proust** (sec 85) and **Apollinaire** (sec 86).

From Corot, to the northwest is the cemetery **chapel**. In the sections to the north of it, along Av de la Chapelle and Av des Ailantes, you can seek out the painter **David** (sec 56), **Balzac** (sec 48), **Bizet** (sec 68) and **Delacroix** (sec 49), and the strange phallic tomb of **Félix de Beauséjour**, a judge in the Revolution.

The large structure in section 87 is the **Columbarium**, in which are kept the ashes of **Isadora Duncan**, **Max Ernst** and, for a time, **Maria Callas**. Av des Etrangers Morts pour la France runs along the north side of the Columbarium, west to a small tomb that draws as many worshippers as Morrison's, that of **Allan Kardec** (sec 44). Kardec, born Léon Rivail in 1804, was one of the fathers of 19th-century spiritualism. His followers are still numerous enough, in Paris, to keep up a near-permanent vigil around the flower-bedecked shrine. Don't fool with these people; they will come after you if you hang around too long, or if you try to photograph the tomb. But take time to read the incredible notice posted behind Kardec by the City of Paris, a calm and reasoned philosophical tract warning against the folly of adoring the remains of a mortal being.

Av des Etrangers Morts pour la France leads straight to the eastern gate. Turn right before the exit, and you'll come to section 89 and one of the grandest tombs of all, Sir Jacob Epstein's tribute to **Oscar Wilde**. As everyone knows, Oscar is here due to certain character flaws in the people and institutions of his native land. Epstein's memorial, a sort of looming Egyptian Art Deco deity, ensured that Wilde would find no peace even in the afterlife. The statue's prominent winkie became the talk of Paris. First a fig leaf was put on it, and then in 1922 an unidentified Englishwoman who apparently knew the deceased batted it off, fig leaf and all.

Press on to the far southeastern corner of the cemetery; in section 94, the fellow with the dynamo in his lap is **Théophile Gramme**, a Belgian who invented the thing in 1869. Near the wall in 94 are **Gertrude Stein** and **Alice B. Toklas** and, in 96, **Modigliani**. In the far corner is section 97; this was the last bit of free Paris in 1871, where the Versailles troops lined up the last 150 Communards against the wall (the ***Mur des Fédérés***). The wall is a place of pilgrimage for French leftists. But the most famous resident of 97 is no doubt **Edith Piaf**. For one last political martyr, there's **Victor Noir** in section 89, a brave journalist who criticized Napoleon III.

Paris: Shopping

20

People who think shopping is an art have long regarded Paris as Europe's masterpiece when it comes to consumption; throughout its history, the city has enjoyed an enviable reputation for craftsmanship, especially in luxury goods and high fashion.

Paris also invented the idea of fashion as we know it. Today you can have an *haute couture* garment hand-sewn to your measurements for several thousand euros. You can size up the current vogues, or spend a bit less, in the exalted *prêt-à-porter* (ready-to-wear) designer fashion zone in the 8e, specifically along Avenue George-V, Rue du Faubourg-St-Honoré, Rue François-1er and Avenue Montaigne. If the latest designer wear is outside your budget, there are a number of shops that sell last season's or earlier clothes and accessories, or you can tackle Paris's huge department stores.

For shoppers who prefer more intimate safaris, Paris has endless little speciality shops tucked into nearly every *arrondissement*. For the bargain-hunter there are mega-flea markets and some interesting second-hand shops.

The areas below are some of the places where shops cluster, though the list is by no means definitive. The **department stores** (Galeries Lafayette, Au Printemps, La Samaritaine, BHV, Le Bon Marché, listed in their areas below) offer a one-stop shop for those pressed for time, or you could go to one of the bigger indoor or underground **shopping centres** such as the unpleasant Forum des Halles, the much cooler Carrousel du Louvre, or the Centre Commercial Maine-Montparnasse at the foot of the Tour Montparnasse. Covered ***arcades***, mostly to the north of Palais-Royal, offer another, more civilized retail experience, and at the other end of the scale are Paris's many **markets**, from the *bouquinistes* along the Seine to the flower market in Place de la Madeleine.

VAT Refunds

Value-added tax (TVA in France) is around 20% on most goods. Non-EU citizens are entitled to a TVA refund of 12–17% on most goods if they have spent at least €180 in a single trip to one shop and have been in France for less than six months.

To get your refund, shop with your passport and ask for a *bordereau de vente à l'exportation* (export sales invoice) at the time of purchase. When you leave France, take the goods and invoice to the customs office at the point of departure and have the invoice stamped. The pink part of the invoice must then be mailed within 90 days to the shop, which will send you the refund.

Opening Hours and Sales

As a general rule, shops are open Mon–Sat 10–7; smaller shops may be closed on Monday, for lunch and during August. The big sales (*les soldes*) take place in January and July, when prices on seasonal goods are cut, often by half.

Shopping Tours

Shopping Plus, 99–103 Rue de Sèvres, **t** 01 47 53 91 17, organizes walking tours in various quarters on various themes: high fashion, antiques, gourmet food, home decoration, etc. A half-day tour for two people costs around €2.50 (there are no tours in August).

Opéra/Boulevard Haussmann

The area around the Opéra is one of Paris's liveliest shopping districts, where the managers still send hucksters out onto the street to demonstrate vegetable choppers and dab cologne on the ladies. Here are two of the biggest department stores. The lovely cupolas of grand old **Au Printemps** (1889–1911), a Paris landmark, are all that remain of a once-spectacular building now thoroughly homogenized. **Galeries Lafayette** (1900) has been more fortunate: have a look inside for the wonderful glass dome and Art Nouveau details.

Galeries Lafayette, 40 Bd Haussmann, 9e. A bit of Art Nouveau splendour has survived the current philistine management. But, better than anyone, they know what the Parisiennes like. The store puts on its own free fashion show, with selections from its various designer boutiques. Ⓜ *Chaussée d'Antin*.

Au Printemps, 64 Bd Haussmann, 9e. Squares off with the Galeries Lafayette like the Hatfields and the McCoys. On the whole Printemps is a wee bit posher, stuffier and nearer the cutting edge of fashion for women's designer clothes and accessories. Good household and linen departments, and a good view from the café on the top floor. Ⓜ *Havre-Caumartin*.

Brentano's, 37 Av de l'Opéra, 2e, **t** 01 42 61 52 50, *www.brentanos.fr*. New books and magazines in English, American interests; novels, guides, children's and art sections too. Ⓜ *Opéra*.

Franchi Chaussures, 15 Rue de la Pépinière, 8e. Men's and women's French and Italian shoes at half-price. Ⓜ *St-Augustin*.

La Cigogne, 61 Rue de l'Arcade, 8e. Delicious products and dishes from Alsace, starring tempting *tortes* and *tartes* and meaty sausages. Ⓜ *St-Lazare*.

Thierry Mugler, 49 Av de l'Opéra, 1er, *www.thierrymugler.com*. Off-the-peg fashion. Ⓜ *Opéra*.

Madeleine/Rue Royale/ Concorde

Not far from Opéra is the **Place de la Madeleine**, which surrounds the church. The area is one of Paris's gourmet paradises, with famous restaurants such as Lucas Carton, and many of the city's finest food shops, all on the north side: small places specializing in caviar (No.17) or truffles (No.19), Hédiard and the incredible **Epicerie Fauchon**. The window displays here are entirely over the top – delicacies that go for over a thousand francs a kilo. The Place also has a small but cheerful **flower market** (*daily except Mon*).

Chanel, 29 Rue Cambon,1er, *www.chanel.fr*. Probably the most famous house in Paris, now under the design wand of Karl Lagerfeld. Ⓜ *Madeleine*.

Fauchon, 26 Pl de la Madeleine, 8e. The most famous and snobbish grocery in Paris, with the best of everything you can imagine, a huge wine cellar and a self-service to try some of the goodies on the spot. Ⓜ *Madeleine*.

Ladurée, 16 Rue Royale, 8e, Ⓜ *Madeleine*; 75 Av des Champs-Elysées, Ⓜ *Franklin D. Roosevelt*, *www.laduree.fr*. Maker of heavenly chocolates.

Maison du Chocolat, 225 Rue du Faubourg St-Honoré, 8e, Ⓜ *Ternes*; 56 Rue Pierre-Charron, 8e, Ⓜ *Franklin D. Roosevelt*. Sensational variety of chocolates.

Maison de la Truffe, 19 Place de la Madeleine, 8e. Truffles and other costly delicacies from the southwest of France. Ⓜ *Madeleine*.

Chronopassion, 271 Rue St-Honoré, 1er. Paris's most extraordinary clocks and watches, astrolabes, planetary timepieces and golden cufflinks that tell the time. Ⓜ *Concorde*.

Testoni, 25 Rue Marbeuf, 8e, Ⓜ *Franklin D. Roosevelt*; also 267 Rue Royale, 8e, Ⓜ *Concorde*. Beautiful and expensive men's and women's shoes and bags from Bologna.

Institut Géographique National, 107 Rue La Boétie, 8e, *www.ign.fr*. Paris's Stanford's, with a superb collection of maps, ordnance surveys, guidebooks and everything else you need to venture off the beaten track. Ⓜ *Miromesnil*.

Artcurial, 7 Rond-Point des Champs-Elysées, 8e. Largest collection of glossy art and coffee-table books, in French and English. Ⓜ *Franklin D. Roosevelt*.

La Maroquinerie Parisienne, 30 Rue Tronchet, 9e, *www.maroquinerie-parisienne.com*. Cut-price bags and leather goods. Ⓜ *Madeleine*.

Au Nain Bleu, 408–10 Rue St-Honoré, 8e, *www.au-nain-bleu.com*. Paris's oldest and most magical toy store. Ⓜ *Concorde*.

La Maison du Miel, 24 Rue Vignon, 9e, *www.maisondumiel.com*. Charming tiled shop dating from 1908, with enough honey to sweeten the sourest disposition. Ⓜ *Madeleine*.

Rue du Faubourg-St-Honoré

Turn right off the Rue Royale for the **Rue du Faubourg-St-Honoré**, another big-name window-shopping street.

Anna Lowe, 104 Rue Faubourg-St-Honoré, 8e. One of the oldest high fashion discount houses in Paris, selling Chanel, Escada, Lacroix, YSL, etc. at 50% off. Ⓜ *Concorde*.

Saint-Laurent Rive Gauche, 38 Rue du Faubourg-St-Honoré. The new flagship of the designer's worldwide chain, and don't let anyone fool you – the latest shows have

Arcades and *Passages*

The precursors of the modern department store, the first *arcades* appeared in Paris in 1776. At first they were merely narrow shopping streets, covered up by landowners trying to boost trade by giving shoppers a place to get their feet out of the urban muck. About 1780 someone came up with the idea of covering them with glass – the beginning of the iron-and-glass revolution in architecture, the first step towards the Crystal Palace and the Louvre Pyramid. Fashionable, purpose-built *passages* became the craze in the 1820s. Paris once had 200 of them, and the idea spread to cities around the world.

Now well out of the mainstream of commerce, their charm is perfected. In any city where there are *arcades*, it's the same: they attract old-book dealers, stamp and coin shops, men who carve pipes by hand, doll hospitals and specialists in music boxes – all the fond foolishness that an angel of cities would find worthy of her protection.

One of the prettiest is the **Galerie Véro-Dodat**, 19 Rue J.-J. Rousseau, Ⓜ *Palais Royal* (*see* p.247). Today, the ornate columns and *putti* (cherubs) still glitter, though it could all use a coat or two of varnish and seems incongruous with the modern commercial world outside. There are some interesting shops, a smattering of galleries and one of Paris's eternal wonders: Robert Capia's curiosity shop at No.26. Paris's leading antique-doll expert, Capia likes everything else that is old and unusual; the stuff in the windows is fascinating, and inside it's jammed up to the ceilings.

The **Galerie Vivienne**, 4 Rue des Petits-Champs, Ⓜ *Bourse*, with its glass ceiling, together with the adjacent **Galerie Colbert**, 6 Rue Vivienne, Ⓜ *Bourse*, makes up an elegant passage complex (*see* p.247). Both have been well restored, though the Colbert has had most of the life squeezed out of it by the Bibliothèque Nationale, which has taken over most of the space for its bookshop and a deathly art gallery.

Paris's largest arcade complex is the **Passage des Panoramas**, 11 Bd Montmartre, Ⓜ *Rue Montmartre*. Robert Fulton, the American pioneer of submarines and steamboats, also invented the popular entertainment called the 'panorama', in 1796. This was a huge circular painting, illuminated from behind and plotted in exact perspective to give spectators inside the circle the impression of being in the middle of a scene from ancient history, or a famous battle. Though such static spectacles were a passing fad, big theatres were built for them in major cities, including the one here (demolished long ago), built in conjunction with one of the first of Paris's *arcades* (1800). Five distinct *arcades* intersect here (Galeries Feydeau, St-Marc, des Variétés, Montmartre and the Passage des Panoramas), to make a little self-contained city of a hundred shops. Mostly they're utilitarian establishments, with a few stamp and coin shops, printers and even a Turkish bath. Have a look in the windows of *Graveur Stern*, a print shop in business here since 1840, which loves to put its best work, along with some curiosities, on display.

On the other side of Boulevard Montmartre is another *arcade*, the **Passage Jouffroy**, 10 Bd Montmartre, Ⓜ *Rue Montmartre*. If you still haven't come to love the peculiar little world of the *passages*, this one might do the trick. A pretty play of dappled shadows lights up the faded grandeur of this busy 1846 *arcade*, which boasts its own hotel, and a wax museum. There are antique toys, oriental rugs, *Cinédoc*, a great shop for cinema books, posters and memorabilia, and an outlandish selection of antique walking sticks and canes at *Segas Gilbert*, No.36, under the stuffed moose. The **Passage Verdeau**, 6 Rue de la Grange-Batelière, Ⓜ *Richelieu-Drouot*, starts where the Jouffroy ends.

Anna Joliet, 95 Jardin du Palais Royal. The best shop in the universe for music boxes, from kid trinkets to €700 monsters in inlaid wood cases that play 12 different tunes. Ⓜ *Palais Royal-Musée du Louvre*.

A Marie Stuart, 3 Galerie Montpensier, Palais Royal, *www.a-marie-stuart.com*. Military trinkets as well as medals and decorations from around the world (comes in handy when you're invited to a diplomatic reception). Ⓜ *Palais Royal-Musée du Louvre*.

La Marelle, 21–5 Galerie Vivienne, 2e. One of the nicest *dépôt-ventes*, for women's and children's designer goods. Ⓜ *Bourse*.

Si Tu Veux, 68 Galerie Vivienne, 2e. Attractive toy shop. Ⓜ *Bourse*.

confirmed YSL as the king of Paris fashion; Catherine Deneuve and his own mom say so. Ⓜ *Concorde*.

Pierre Cardin, 59 Rue du Faubourg-St-Honoré, 8e. Classic Parisian couture. Ⓜ *Madeleine*.

Hermès, 24 Rue du Faubourg-St-Honoré, 8e. Pay a month's rent for a scarf. Ⓜ *Madeleine*.

Versace, 62 Rue du Faubourg-St-Honoré, 8e, *www.versace.com*. One of the first and most opulent 'mega-boutiques' in Paris that must be seen to be believed: Versace's fashion-as-theatre approach in a glass-domed Roman temple with changing rooms resembling ancient baths or the Paris Opéra. Clothes for men, women and children. Ⓜ *Madeleine*.

Dalloyau, 101 Rue du Faubourg-St-Honoré, 8e. Napoleon's *pâtissier*. Ⓜ *St-Philippe-du-Roule*.

Louvre/Rivoli

Rue de Rivoli is a long, busy street, lined on both sides with imposing, if not beautiful, buildings. The part to the west was begun by Napoleon, who conceived it as a personal monument, a 'triumphal way' perfect for military parades, to be bordered by arcades. The eastern end of Rue de Rivoli was only completed after 1848, beyond the Hôtel de Ville and into the Marais. Two more big department stores, **La Samaritaine** and **BHV**, are to be found along its length.

W. H. Smith, 248 Rue de Rivoli, 1er, **t** 01 44 77 88 99. Especially good for their English-language magazines; fiction, children's and travel sections. Ⓜ *Concorde*.

Galignani, 224 Rue de Rivoli, 1er, **t** 01 42 60 76 07. Cosy place founded in 1802 – the oldest English bookshop on the Continent; new titles, children's and glossy art books. Ⓜ *Tuileries*.

Louvre des Antiquaires, next to the Louvre, 1er. The poshest, biggest antiques centre and a great place for browsing. Ⓜ *Palais Royal*.

Bazar de l'Hôtel de Ville, 52 Rue de Rivoli, 4e, *www.bhv.fr*. BHV has been around since 1854 and lacks the pretensions of other department stores. A good bet for practical items not easily found: brake fluid, electric outlets and mixing bowls; and other services, like tool rental, which you'll probably manage to do without. Ⓜ *Hôtel de Ville*.

La Samaritaine, 19 Rue de la Monnaie, 1er, *www.lasamaritaine.com*. The most beautiful department store in Paris, with its Art Nouveau façade, skylight and balconies (in the old building) – though the present management thinks more like Woolworth's than Harrods. The café on its 10th-floor terrace, open April to September, has one of the most gratifying of all views over Paris, across the Pont Neuf. Ⓜ *Louvre-Rivoli*.

Unishop, 40 Rue de Rivoli, 4e (men) and 40bis Rue de Rivoli, 4e (women). High fashions, minimum 20% off the original price. Ⓜ *Hôtel de Ville*.

Gilda, 36 Rue des Bourdonnais, 1er. Huge collection of second-hand books and records in French. Ⓜ *Pont Neuf*.

Parallèles, 47 Rue St-Honoré, 1er. Media and source centre of alternative Paris, underground publications, books on music, records and more. Ⓜ *Châtelet-Les Halles*.

La Galcante, 52 Rue de l'Arbre-Sec, 1er, *www.lagalcante.com*. Old newspapers, books, magazines and posters from as far away as China; pick up the front page of a French paper on the day of your birth. Ⓜ *Louvre-Rivoli*.

Gosselin, 125 Rue St-Honoré, 1er. Voted best baguette in Paris in 1996. Ⓜ *Louvre-Rivoli*.

Philippe Model, 33 Pl du Marché-St-Honoré, 1er. Paris's top glove, hat and shoe designer. Ⓜ *Pyramides*.

Maison de l'Astronomie, 33 Rue de Rivoli, 4e, *www.maison-astronomie.net*. Everything for the astronomer in your life; also alarm clocks that keep track of the position of the moon. Ⓜ *Hôtel de Ville*.

Les Halles

Once the Halles was a vast colourful wholesale distribution market for all Paris (moved to Rungis near Orly airport) and surrounded by slums. Today the Forum is a subterranean labyrinthine 'new town' of shops and fast-food outlets. The streets around and to the north are also full of shops.

FNAC, a Paris institution – the city's biggest and fullest book chain (including some titles in English). Outlets in the Forum des Halles, Rue Pierre-Lescot, Ⓜ *Châtelet-Les-Halles*; at

136 Rue de Rennes, Ⓜ *St-Placide*; at 109 Rue Saint-Lazare, Ⓜ *St-Lazare*.

RAG, 83 Rue St-Martin, 2e. Everything from tails to kimonos, for all tastes. Ⓜ *Châtelet*.

Anthony Peto, 56 Rue Tiquetone, 2er. Superb selection of men's hats from berets to panamas. Ⓜ *Etienne Marcel*.

St-Germain-des-Prés/ St-Sulpice/Odéon

Although you'll have to save up your pocket money just to be able to afford a *café au lait*, the bustling narrow streets, legendary cafés and trendy bookshops will all invite you to explore and tempt you to spend.

La Chambre Claire, 14 Rue St-Sulpice, 6e. Grand specialist in photography; posters, manuals, books and more. Ⓜ *Odéon*.

San Francisco Book Co, 17 Rue Monsieur-le-Prince, 6e, **t** 01 43 29 15 70. Paris branch of the California-based shop with new and used books in English. Ⓜ *Odéon*.

The Village Voice, 6 Rue Princesse, 6e, **t** 01 46 33 36 47, *www.villagevoicebookshop.com*. Where Odile Hellier carries the banner of American literature in Paris, hosting scores of readings by contemporary writers; has anglophone Paris's most discriminating collections of books. Ⓜ *Mabillon*.

Marie Mercié, 23 Rue St-Sulpice, 6e. For the kind of hat you see in films and have always dreamed of on your own head. Ⓜ *St-Sulpice* or *Odéon*.

Tehen, 2 Rue Rotrou, 6e. Stylish jersey and knitwear coordinates. Ⓜ *Odéon*.

Stéphane Kélian, 13bis Rue de Grenelle, 7e, Ⓜ *Sèvres-Babylone*; also 25 Rue du Four, 6e, Ⓜ *St-Sulpice*. Perhaps the most extraordinary and certainly the most expensive women's shoes in Paris.

Madeleine Gély, 218 Bd St-Germain, 7e. Since 1834 the most imaginative cane and umbrella shop in Paris. Ⓜ *Rue du Bac*.

Barthélemy, 51 Rue de Grenelle, 7e. The *ne plus ultra* of *fromageries*: only the most refined classic French cheeses. Ⓜ *Rue du Bac*.

Debauve et Gallais, 30 Rue des Saints-Pères, 7e. Oldest and most beautiful *chocolatier* in Paris; the unusual displays (recently, chocolate passports) are worth a trip in themselves. Ⓜ *St-Germain-des-Prés*.

Poilâne, 8 Rue du Cherche-Midi, 7e, *www.poilane.fr*. Tasty sourdough country bread, the most famous in Paris; used in the best sandwiches across the city. Ⓜ *Sèvres-Babylone*.

Le Bon Marché, 35 Rue de Sèvres, 7e, *www.lebonmarche.fr*. The only department store on the Left Bank, but the grand-daddy of them all, still puts on a pretty good show of desirable stuff – its extraordinary food halls are an unrivalled gourmet cornucopia, and its prices for clothes and other goods tend to be a bit lower than its big-name rivals. Ⓜ *Sèvres-Babylone*.

L'Artisan Parfumeur, 32 Rue Bourg-Tibourg, 4e. A range of perfumes based around single flower or fruit notes, plus blends. Ⓜ *Hôtel de Ville*.

C.F.O.C., 167 Bd St-Germain, 6e. Homewares. Ⓜ *St-Germain-des-Prés*. Oriental goods.

Latin Quarter

The Latin Quarter is where Abelard taught, Villon fought, Erasmus thought and Mimi coughed. This is also the *quartier* of publishers and bookshops, and where Paris's students hang out and smoke Gauloises: the streets are lively by day and night.

The Abbey Bookshop, 29 Rue de la Parcheminerie, 5e, **t** 01 46 33 16 24, *www.abbeybookshop.com*. Genial Canadian-owned bookshop, with a good selection of new and used English and North American titles. Ⓜ *St-Michel*.

Album, 6–8 Rue Dante, 5e. Best shop for comic-book collectors. Ⓜ *Maubert-Mutualité*.

Reflet Médicis, 3 Rue Champollion, 5e. Films books, posters and stills. Ⓜ *Cluny-La Sorbonne*.

Shakespeare and Co., 37 Rue de la Bûcherie, 5e, **t** 01 43 26 96 50. Just what a bookshop should be – a convivial treasure hunt, crammed full of inexpensive second-hand and new books in English (*see* p.232). Ⓜ *St-Michel*.

Champs-Elysées

The Champs-Elysées is still *the* street to stroll down, to see and be seen, and with its recent face-lift is looking glitzier and shinier than ever. The perfect avenue to indulge in a little *lèche-vitrine* (window shopping) and take home the ultimate Parisian souvenir.

Caron, 34 Av Montaigne, 8e. Posh perfumes. Ⓜ *Franklin D. Roosevelt.*

Guerlain, 68 Av des Champs-Elysées, 8e. A beautiful shop, displaying Guerlain's famous range of perfumed seduction. Ⓜ *Franklin D. Roosevelt.*

La Maison du Chocolat, 56 Rue Pierre-Charron, 8e. Chocolates to buy, and rich hot chocolate to drink. Ⓜ *Franklin D. Roosevelt.*

Monoprix, 52 Av des Champs-Elysées, Ⓜ *Franklin D. Roosevelt.* Useful chain of supermarkets where you can pick up toiletries, make-up, underwear, clothes, shoes and accessories as well as food and freshly baked bread and pastries. *Open Mon–Sat 9am–midnight.*

Marais

The elegant streets and old palaces of the Marais are a bit more jolly than the cadaverous hulks of the Faubourg St-Germain. The most ambitious restoration effort in Paris has spruced the quarter up, ready for your inspection (*see* pp.240–45). The shops are small, exclusive and individual: antiques, jewellery, crafts, books and unusual objects that make it the perfect area for gift-hunting.

Art Dépot, 3 Rue du Pont-Louis-Philippe, 4e. Lots of fun (and packable) Art Deco pieces. Ⓜ *St-Paul.*

Markets

The **C2 organization** (**t** 01 47 05 33 22) holds street markets across Paris at weekends. Ring for details or ask at the tourist office. They are often a good place to find antiques.

Flea, Books, Flowers and Birds

Les Puces de Saint-Ouen, the mother of all flea markets. *Open Sat, Sun and Mon.* Ⓜ *Porte de Clignancourt.*

Les Puces de Montreuil, great junky flea market. *Open Sat, Sun and Mon.* Ⓜ *Porte de Montreuil.*

Les Puces de Vanves, the most humble, and potentially most exciting market for the eagle-eyed, with many amateurs. *Open Sat and Sun.* Ⓜ *Porte de Vanves.*

Marché aux Fleurs, Place de la Madeleine, 8e (*Mon–Sat*); Place des Ternes, 8e (*daily except Mon*); and Place Lépine, 4e (*Mon–Sat*). Parisians love flowers and flower markets.

Marché du Livre Ancien et d'Occasion, Rue Brancion, Parc Georges-Brassens, 15e. Second-hand book market, *Sat–Sun.* Ⓜ *Porte de Vanves.*

Marché aux Timbres. The stamp market (the same one that co-starred in *Charade* with Audrey Hepburn and Cary Grant) north of Théâtre Marigny, near the intersection of Avenues Gabriel and de Marigny, 8e. *Open Thurs, Sat and Sun.* Ⓜ *Champs-Elysées.*

Marché aux Vieux Papiers de St-Mandé, Av de Paris, 12e. One of the more obscure markets – old books, postcards and prints. *Open Wed.* Ⓜ *Porte de St-Mandé Tourelle.*

Food Markets

The permanent street markets listed below are intoxicating to visit, even if you're just picking up the ingredients for a park picnic. Most are lined with shops that spill out into the street.

These markets are open daily except Sunday afternoons and all day Monday, and some shops close for lunch off season.

The most captivating are listed below – for a complete list of all the covered markets and the 60 travelling street markets, open one or two days a week, ask at the tourist office.

Place d'Aligre, 12e. Colourful, with a strong North African presence. Ⓜ *Ledru-Rollin.*

Buci, 6e. One of the liveliest, with a good selection; best on Sunday mornings. Ⓜ *Mabillon.*

Rue Cler, 7e. The market of the aristocratic Faubourg, noted for its high quality. Ⓜ *Ecole Militaire.*

Rue de Lévis, 17e. Similar to the above, the *haute bourgeoisie* equivalent of Rue Cler. Ⓜ *Villiers.*

Montorgueil, 1er. On the street of the same name, north of Rue Etienne-Marcel, convivial and fun, a whiff of the old atmosphere of nearby Les Halles. Ⓜ *Etienne Marcel.*

Mouffetard, 5e. Lower end of Rue Mouffetard, with lots of character and characters. Ⓜ *Censier-Daubenton.*

A la Bonne Renommée, 26 Rue Vieille-du-Temple, 4e. Beautiful, richly coloured satins, silks and velvets with a folkloric touch. Ⓜ *St-Paul.*

Agnès B, 17 Rue Dieu, 10e, *www.agnesb.fr.* Fashion, cosmetics and accessories. Ⓜ *République.*

Boutique Paris Musées, 29bis Rue des Francs-Bourgeois, 4e. Rounds up items from all the museum shops in Paris. Ⓜ *St-Paul.*

Izraël, 30 Rue François-Miron, 4e. Good for exotic imports from Brazil, China, North Africa and just about everywhere else. Ⓜ *St-Paul.*

Jo Goldenberg's, 7 Rue des Rosiers, 4e. Paris's best Jewish deli and a godsend to any New Yorker living in Paris. Ⓜ *St-Paul.*

Mariage Frères, 30 Rue du Bourg-Tibourg, 4e. 400 different types of tea and tea-flavoured goodies. Ⓜ *St-Paul.*

Paris: Museums and Galleries

21

Opening Hours and Admission

Opening hours often change with the season: longer summer hours usually begin in May or June and last through September. Admission charges are €2–7. Note, however, that many museums offer reduced admissions on Sundays and after 3.30 and sliding fees for other days – one price (often free) for under-18s, another for 18–25-year-olds, another for EU citizens over 60 and a heftier charge for everyone else. If you have to pay the full whack and mean to average more than two museums or monuments a day, consider a *Carte Musées et Monuments*, valid for one day (€22), three days (€38), or five consecutive days (€52), which can save both money and time. Purchase your pass at the museums, tourist offices or in the larger Métro stations. Participating museums are marked with an asterisk* in the listing below.

Painting and Sculpture

Cabinet des Médailles et Antiques

Bibliothèque Nationale, Rue Vivienne; Ⓜ Bourse. Open Mon–Sat 1–5, Sun 12–6.

Occupying its own wing of the Bibliothèque complex is an amazing little museum that not one visitor to Paris in a thousand has heard of, let alone seen. The collection, really the treasure-trove of the kings of France, goes back at least to Philippe-Auguste in the 12th century. Nationalized during the Revolution and combined with the confiscated church treasures of St-Denis and Sainte-Chapelle, it contains the 1st-century AD *Camée de Sainte-Chapelle*, the biggest cameo ever made; the *Treasure of Berthouville*, an impressive hoard of Gallo-Roman jewellery; good collections of Greek, Roman and Etruscan jewellery. Coins, medals and commemorative medallions follow, in which the show is stolen by a fine collection from the undisputed, all-time greatest in this medium, the Renaissance Italian Pisanello.

Espace Montmartre Salvador Dalí

11 Rue Poulbot, Ⓜ Abbesses. Open daily 10–6, July–Aug daily 10–9; free.

Exhibitions on Salvador Dalí.

*Musée Antoine Bourdelle

16 Rue Antoine-Bourdelle; Ⓜ Montparnasse-Bienvenüe. Open 10–6, closed Mon; adm.

Antoine Bourdelle (1861–1929) was a student of Rodin. Even more prolific than Rodin, he left some 900 statues and studies in this curious red-brick building. Bourdelle's great obsession was Beethoven, whom he carved 62 times.

Musée d'Art Juif

42 Rue des Saules; Ⓜ Lamarck-Caulaincourt. Open Sun–Thurs 3–6; closed Aug; adm.

Museum of Jewish art over a synagogue. Here are works by Soutine, Benn, Max Libermann and Chagall (an illustrated Pentateuch), ritual items, casts of tombstones from Prague and a collection of models of fortified synagogues in Lithuania and Poland.

*Musée d'Art Moderne de la Ville de Paris

11 Av du Président Wilson, www.paris-france.org/musees; Ⓜ Alma-Marceau. Open Tues–Fri 10–6, Sat, Sun 10–7; adm.

Another relic of the 1937 Fair, the huge Palais de Tokyo, contains this museum in the east wing. There's a small permanent collection of works from Matisse onwards, as well as changing exhibitions, usually on contemporary artists. In the west wing is the innovative **Site de Création Contemporaine** (*open daily exc Mon noon–midnight*).

Musée d'Art Naïf Max Fourny

Halle St-Pierre, 2 Rue Ronsard, www.hallesaintpierre.org; Ⓜ Anvers. Open daily 10–6; closed Aug; adm.

Some 500 works by *naïf* painters from around the world.

*Musée Delacroix

6 Place Furstemberg, www.musee-delacroix.fr; Ⓜ St-Germain-des-Prés. Open 9.30–5, closed Tues; adm. See p.229.

Musée Gustave Moreau

14 Rue de la Rochefoucauld; Ⓜ St-Georges. Open 10–12.45 and 2–5.15, closed Tues; adm.

The introspective Symbolist Moreau lived here with his parents, painting his strange mythologies and mystical exotica from dead civilizations with lush jewel-like encrustations of paint which personify *fin-de-siècle* decadence, especially his *femmes fatales*.

Musée Jacquemart-André

158 Boulevard Haussmann, www.musee-jacquemart-andre.com; Ⓜ *St-Philippe-du-Roule. Open daily 10–6; adm.*

If one day you want to look at some beautiful pictures, but don't care to tackle the daunting Louvre, there's probably no better choice than this museum, assembled by Edouard André and his wife Nélie Jacquemart at the turn of the century. Nélie was a painter herself, and had a sharp eye. Works from the Italian Renaissance rival the Louvre's collection. Don't miss Tiepolo's fresco on the stairs.

*Musée du Louvre

***t** 01 40 20 51 51, www.louvre.fr;* Ⓜ *Palais Royal-Musée du Louvre. Open daily exc Tues 9–6; adm.* *See pp.201–203.*

Musée Maillol-Fondation Dina-Vierny

59 Rue de Grenelle; Ⓜ *Rue du Bac. Open daily exc Tues and hols 11–6; adm.*

Dedicated to the French-Catalan sculptor whose other works can be seen around the Arc du Carrousel by the Louvre.

Musée Marmottan

2 Rue Louis-Boilly, www.marmottan.com; Ⓜ *La Muette. Open 10–5.30; closed Mon; adm.*

This museum houses some of Monet's best works. The Marmottan family also collected medieval miniatures, tapestries and Napoleonic art and furniture, but the Monet works are the highlight: some of the *Nymphéas* ('Water Lilies'), a view of the Pont de l'Europe behind Gare St-Lazare, one of the Cathédrale de Rouen and a view of the British Houses of Parliament.

*Musée National d'Art Moderne

Pompidou Centre; Ⓜ *Châtelet-Les Halles. Closed Tues; adm.* *See p.213.*

*Musée National des Monuments Français

Palais de Chaillot; Ⓜ *Trocadéro. Open daily 10–6; free.*

Facing Place du Trocadéro are the entrances to the Palais de Chaillot's four museums. The oldest, in the east wing, is this, perhaps the most undervisited museum in Paris. Viollet-le-Duc had the idea of creating a central collection of exact, lifesize copies of France's finest architectural features, sculptures and mural paintings from the early Romanesque period to the 19th century. The result was first exhibited at the 1889 World's Fair; over the years the collection has grown to 2,000 replicas, arranged to help you study the evolution of French art and architecture.

*Musée National de l'Orangerie des Tuileries

Tuileries; Ⓜ *Concorde. Open Wed–Mon 9.45–3.15.*

In the southwest corner of the Tuileries, the Orangerie offers a collection complementary to the Musée d'Orsay, with a large lower level devoted to Monet. Many of the big-name artists of the 20th century are represented, though the works are seldom among their best: dissolving landscapes of Soutine, Cézanne still lifes and portraits, rosy Renoir *fillettes*, Paris scenes by Utrillo, and a trio of Modigliani weird sisters. Go to the Musée d'Orsay and the Musée National d'Art Moderne to see them at their best. The highlights are the luminous canvases of Monet, including one of the *Nymphéas*, and two wonderful pictures by the Douanier Rousseau.

*Musée d'Orsay

Ⓜ *Solférino. Closed Mon; adm.* *See pp.205–8.*

*Musée du Petit Palais

Ⓜ *Champs-Elysées-Clemenceau. Closed for renovation until 2005/6.*

There is a 'permanent collection' inside, but not quite a 'museum' – restorations and rearrangements have been going on for years. The present collection, when it's open again, consists of a large collection of 18th-century art and furniture, a selection of medieval art and a smattering of works from the Renaissance, including Italian majolica and Venetian glass. The main attraction is 19th-century French painting and sculpture.

*Musée Picasso

Hôtel Salé, 5 Rue de Thorigny; Ⓜ *St-Paul. Open summer 9.30–6, winter 9.30–5.30, closed Tues; adm.*

The 'Salted Palace' takes its name from its original occupant, Jean Bouiller, a collector of the hated *gabelle* (salt tax) for Louis XIV. Picasso's heirs donated most of the works here to the state in the 1970s in lieu of inheritance taxes. There are few really famous pictures, but representational works can be seen from all Picasso's diverse styles: a 'blue-period' *Self-portrait* of 1901 through the Cubist *Man with a Guitar* (1912) and beyond. This is Picasso at the top of his art, exquisite draughtsmanship and the most skilful use of colour, especially in the series of *corridas* and *minotauromachies*, employing mythological elements later seen in *Guernica*. One room of the museum contains paintings from Picasso's personal collection, including works by Corot, Matisse and Cézanne. There is also a sculpture garden of Picasso works from many periods.

*Musée Rodin

Ⓜ Varenne. Closed Mon; adm. See p.208.

Musée de la Sculpture en Plein Air

Quai St-Bernard; Ⓜ Austerlitz. Always open.

Set up in 1980, modelled after one in Tokyo; along with all the usual river activities to see are sculptures by Brancusi, César and Zadkine, among others.

*Musée Zadkine

100bis Rue d'Assas; Ⓜ Notre-Dame-des-Champs. Open Tues–Sun 10–5.40; adm, free Sun.

Ukrainian sculptor Osip Zadkine purchased this charming house in 1928; among the works displayed here in his garden and studio is a model of his masterpiece, *The Destroyed City* (1947), in Rotterdam.

Design/Decorative Arts

Fondation Le Corbusier

8–10 Square du Docteur-Blanche, www.fondationlecorbusier.asso.fr; Ⓜ Jasmin. Open Mon 1.30–6, Tues–Thurs 10.30–12.30 and 1.30–6, Fri 10–30–12.30 and 1.30–5; closed Aug; adm.

The home of the foundation, which puts on exhibitions about Le Corbusier, is the Swiss architect's best Parisian work, the adjacent La Roche and Jeanneret houses. Both look like modern additions to small art museums, but that is only because Le Corbusier has had so many followers. These are good buildings and it isn't hard to imagine how revolutionary they must have looked in 1927.

Manufacture Nationale des Gobelins

42 Av des Gobelins; Ⓜ Les Gobelins. Only open for short guided tours in French Tues– Thurs at 2.15 and 2.45; adm.

Up until the 19th century, the little river Bièvre still flowed openly, its banks lined by tanners and dyers. The most famous of the latter was a family named Gobelin, who owed their great fame and fortune to the discovery of a prized scarlet dye. Ironically, the Gobelins have gone down in history for tapestries, an art they themselves never touched. Since 1940 the three state weaving factories – the Gobelins, Beauvais and the Savonnerie – have been consolidated here at the old Gobelins site, producing as they have for the past 300 years all the tapestries, rugs and furniture covers required by the French state. Recently there has been a great deal of talk about restructuring and selling. The Gobelins remains a village enclave remote from Paris and the 20th century. It has pretty cobbled courtyards with statues of Colbert and Lebrun, its own chapel and shady gardens. Of the hundred Gobelins weavers (mostly women since the war), half still live there.

*Musée des Arts Décoratifs

107 Rue de Rivoli, www.ucad.fr; Ⓜ Palais Royal. Open Tues–Fri 11–6, Sat and Sun 10–6; closed Mon; adm.

Part of the Louvre, the museum was founded in 1877, its purpose to show the public beautiful things so that people would be more demanding about what they bought for themselves. At present parts of the museum are under renovation.

Musée Baccarat

Rue de Paradis, 10e; Ⓜ Poissonnière. Open Mon–Sat 10–6; adm.

Crystal glass and chandeliers.

*Musée Cognacq-Jay

8 Rue Elzévir; Ⓜ St-Paul. Open daily except Mon 10–5.40; free.

It's somewhat ironic that Ernest Cognacq, the thoroughly modern department store magnate who founded the Samaritaine department store, should have devoted his free time to accumulating bric-a-brac from that quaintest of centuries, the eighteenth. The collection of ladies' cosmetic boxes will leave you speechless. There is also ornate furniture and a good collection of painting.

Musée de la Mode et du Costume

10 Avenue Pierre 1er de Serbie; Ⓜ Alma-Marceau. Open daily except Mon 10–6; adm.

Municipal museum of fashion. The pseudo-Italian Renaissance Palais Galliera (1894) was built to house the 17th-century Italian art that the Duchess of Galliera meant to donate to Paris, until she changed her mind and gave it to Genoa instead. Paris did get the palace, however. Because of space and the fragility of its piece collection, the museum devotes itself entirely to two exhibitions a year.

Musée des Arts de la Mode et du Textile

Palais du Louvre, 107 Rue de Rivoli; Ⓜ Tuileries. Open Tues–Fri 11–6, Sat and Sun 10–6; adm.

Opened in 1986 under the premise that women's clothing, if sufficiently expensive, is an art that enriches all our lives.

Historical

*Musée des Antiquités Nationales

*St-Germain-en-Laye; **RER** A. Open Wed–Sun 9–5.15; adm.*

Excellent archaeological collection.

*Musée Carnavalet

Rue de Sévigné; Ⓜ St-Paul. Open Tues–Sun 10–5.40, exc Mon and hols; adm. See p.241.

Musée de l'Histoire de France

Rue des Archives; Ⓜ Rambuteau. Open Mon and Wed–Fri 10–12 and 2–5.30, Sat–Sun 10–12 and 2–5; adm. See p.244.

Musée de Montmartre

12 Rue Cortot; Ⓜ Lamarck-Caulaincourt. Open Tues–Sun 10–12.30 and 1.30–6; adm. See p.239.

*Musée National du Moyen Age – Thermes de Cluny

6 Place Paul-Painlevé; Ⓜ Cluny-La Sorbonne. Open daily exc Tues 9.15–5.45; adm, reduced price Sun. See pp.204–205.

*Musée de la Vie Romantique

16 Rue Chaptal; Ⓜ St-Georges. Open daily except Mon and hols 10–5.50; adm.

George Sand and Chopin lived opposite one another in the **Square d'Orléans**. Their time is documented here. Exhibits concentrate on George Sand: her jewels, ties, drawings and bric-a-brac.

Military

*Mémorial du Maréchal Leclerc et de la Libération de Paris–Musée Jean Moulin

Bâtiment Nord-Parc; Ⓜ Gaîté. Open Tues–Sun 10–5.40; free.

The history of the Resistance and liberation.

*Musée de l'Armée

Ⓜ Varenne. April–Sept daily 10–5.45; Oct–Mar daily 10–4.45; adm. See p.200.

*Musée de la Légion d'Honneur et des Ordres de Chevalerie

Hôtel Salm, corner of Rue de Bellechasse; Ⓜ Solférino. Closed for renovations until some time in 2005.

The Hôtel Salm is French neoclassicism at its most graceful, small in scale, with a miniature triumphal arch and Ionic colonnade around its forecourt. This is a replica (the original was burned in the Commune); there's another copy in San Francisco.

*Musée de la Marine

Palais de Chaillot, www.musee-marine.fr; Ⓜ Trocadéro. Open daily 10–5.50; closed Tues and May 1; adm.

Haughty Brits may turn a blind eye, like Nelson, but France has its own proud tradition on the sea. As you might expect, gloriously detailed ship models make up the bulk of the exhibits. Don't miss the collection of navigational instruments and compasses.

*Musée des Plans-Reliefs

Hôtel des Invalides; Ⓜ Varenne. Open daily summer 10–5.45, winter 10–4.45; closed some hols; adm. *See p.200.*

Monuments and Subterranean Paris

*Arc de Triomphe

Ⓜ Charles-de-Gaulle. Open Oct–Mar daily 9.30am–10.30pm; April–Sept 9.30am–11pm; adm. *See p.196.*

*Basilique St-Denis

Ⓜ St-Denis-Basilique. Open April –Sept Mon–Sat 10–6.30, Sun 12–6.30; Oct–Mar, closes at 5.15.

The first Gothic church anywhere, and last resting place of the kings of France.

Catacombes

Place Denfert-Rochereau; Ⓜ Denfert-Rochereau. Open Tues 11–4, Wed–Sun 9–4; closed Mon and hols; adm. *See pp.196–7.*

*Conciergerie

Quai de l'Horloge, Ile de la Cité; Ⓜ Cité. Open April–Sept 9–6, Oct–Mar 9–5; adm; joint ticket with Ste-Chapelle. *See p.219.*

*Crypte de Notre-Dame

Cathédrale Notre-Dame; Ⓜ Cité. Open daily 10–6, closed some hols; adm; combined ticket with Musée Carnavalet. *See p.211.*

Grande Arche de La Défense

Ⓜ La Défense. Open daily summer 10–8, winter 10–7; adm. *See pp.198–9.*

*Musée des Egouts de Paris

Quai d'Orsay, www.paris-france.org; Ⓜ Alma-Marceau. Open summer Sat–Wed 11–5, winter 11–4; closed Thurs and Fri, most of Jan; adm.

Although Baron Haussmann is best known for Paris's boulevards, he was personally more interested in the sewers, which he entrusted to an engineer named Belgrande. Victor Hugo, in his long digression on Paris's intestines in *Les Misérables*, gave these drains a peculiar romance to match their aroma, and ever since the World Fair of 1867 visitors have descended to the sewers, originally to be pulled along in little wagons. These were replaced by boats, which since 1972 have been replaced by a silly film, a museum and a stroll along a sewer.

*Panthéon

Place du Panthéon; Ⓜ Cardinal Lemoine. Open daily Oct–Mar 10–6.15, April–Sept 10–6.30, last ticket 5.45; adm. *See p.233.*

*Sainte Chapelle

Cour du Mai, Palais de Justice, Ile de la Cité; Ⓜ Cité. Open April–Sept 9.30–6.30, Oct–Mar 10–5; adm. *See p.220.*

*Tours de Notre-Dame

Rue du Cloître; Ⓜ Cité. Open summer daily 9.30–7.30; winter 10–5.30; adm. *See p.211.*

Science, Medicine and Technology

*Cité des Sciences et de l'Industrie – La Villette

La Villette; Ⓜ Porte de la Villette. Open Tues–Sat 10–6, Sun 10–7; adm, under 7s free – the Cité des Enfants, Techno City, exhibitions, Music City, the Argonaute, Cineaxe and the Géode require separate adm.

Now that the slaughterhouse has metamorphosed into the Cité des Sciences et de l'Industrie, a rectangle of glass and exposed girders reminiscent of the Pompidou Centre, Mitterrand's critics have had their fun with this project too. As a science museum, it duplicates the Palais de la Découverte, only it's flashier and more up to date. It has its own internal television station, a staff of costumed *animateurs* speaking 15 different languages, computerized magneto-sensitized tickets, 'infra-red headphones', and lasers, buzzing gimcracks and whirling gizmos. Bring the children to help you get through alive. There are **Planétarium** shows (with English translations) and 3-D films in the **Louis Lumière cinema**. On the ground floor, the **Cité des Enfants** is a brilliant place for children to experiment with plants, animals and computers, with expert attendants to help. There are two sections: one for ages 3–5, one for ages 5–12; Techno Cité is designed for children from age 11 up. For a different way to start a day's excursion, sail to La Villette from the Musée d'Orsay.

Musée de l'Histoire de la Médecine

Faculté de Médicine, Rue Antoine-Dubois/Rue de l'Ecole de Médecine; Ⓜ Odéon. Open summer Mon–Wed, Fri and Sat 2–5.30; guide tour on Tues at 2.30; adm.

This museum reopened on 7 January 1992 after a major restoration. That very night a fire brought down the roof. Fortunately its prizes have survived: the very first stethoscope (invented by Laënnec in 1817, just in time to hear the dying heartbeats of Madame de Staël); a 3,000-piece wooden skeleton commissioned by Napoleon; a 17th-century Japanese mannequin showing acupuncture points; and the lancet used on Louis XIV's anal fistula in 1687.

Musée Minéralogique de l'Université Pierre et Marie Curie

34 Rue Jussieu; Ⓜ Jussieu, Cluny-La Sorbonne. Open 1–6, closed Tues; adm.

Gems and minerals.

Muséum National d'Histoire Naturelle

Jardin des Plantes; Ⓜ Austerlitz. See p.253.

Musée National des Techniques

Rue Réaumur; Ⓜ Arts et Metiers. Open Tues–Sun 10–6, Thurs 10–9.30; adm.

This museum is in the former monastery of St-Martin, now the Conservatoire des Arts et Métiers, a technical and science education facility responsible for continuing education. During the Revolution, the monastery was an arms factory until the Conservatoire, a scientific laboratory and technical school, was established in 1798. Jacques Vaucanson, a maker of machines and automata, contributed his own collection to start the Musée des Techniques in 1802. In the years since it has grown into an enormous, odd and dusty hoard of gadgets and models, scientific breakthroughs and techno-dinosaurs, with more junk than any junkyard and more mad-scientist gear than the Universal Studios properties department.

Start on the ground floor, where an old painting of an 'Allegory of Science' welcomes you. This hall is a trick echo chamber: whisper into one corner, and someone else will be able to hear you clearly in the corner opposite. First comes a room with the quaint instruments of the great chemist Lavoisier. Next comes a mercilessly didactic exhibit on weights and measures through the ages, and another on railways, including some wonderful **model trains**. There are **mathematical instruments** and old **astronomical instruments**. Absolutely positively do not miss the magnificent collection of **18th-century clocks**. And don't miss the room of **automata** hidden in the far corner.

For readers of Umberto Eco's *Foucault's Pendulum*, the highlight of the museum will be the interior of St Martin's church, now stuffed full of cars, aircraft engines, pumps and some heavy bits that defy all identification, incongruously sprawling under the medieval vaulting. The mystic **pendulum** (1855) hangs from the vaulting. Léon Foucault, who also first measured the speed of light, thought up this toy, which proves the rotation of the earth by tracing a daily circle in its oscillations (the earth turns underneath it). The original experiment, conducted in 1851 under the dome of the Panthéon, had a swing wide enough to keep it going a full day.

Palais de la Découverte

Grand Palais, www.palais-decouverte.fr; Ⓜ Champs-Elysées-Clemenceau. Open Tues–Sat 9.30–6, Sun and hols 10–7; adm (more exp inc. planetarium); times for planetarium vary with the season.

The rear of the Grand Palais has been declared a palace in itself, the science museum of the 'Palace of Discovery'. Neither you nor the children will be bored, even if you can't read much French; there are lasers to play with, ant colonies, and computers to make simple programmes on. For all of you, whatever your age, the best part may be the **Eureka** rooms, up the left staircase from the entrance: hands-on games and tricks to learn about colours, optics and elementary physics. The scary stuff is kept at the back of the ground floor and mezzanine: big Van de Graaff generators that crank out a million and a half volts (but hardly any amperage; you can touch it, should you dare, making your hair stand on end), and a nuclear exhibit where the kids can make various objects radioactive.

Temporary Exhibitions

Fondation Cartier pour l'Art Contemporain

261 Bd Raspail, www.fondation.cartier.fr; Ⓜ Raspail. Open 12–8; closed Mon; adm.

International contemporary art.

Galerie Nationale du Jeu de Paume

Tuileries; Ⓜ Concorde. Open Wed–Sun 12–7, Tues 12–9.30; adm. *See p.254.*

Galeries Nationales du Grand Palais

Av Winston Churchill and Av du Général Eisenhower; Ⓜ Champs-Elysées-Clemenceau. Open for special temporary exhibitions daily 11–8, 11–10 on Wed; mornings by appt; ***t*** *01 44 13 17 17, groups* ***t*** *01 44 13 17 10; adm.*

The Grand Palais, built for the 1900 exhibition, is one of the biggest surprises in Paris, and beyond any doubt the capital's most neglected and unloved monument. The main entrance on Avenue Winston-Churchill has been barricaded for years and whatever renovations are supposed to be under way have been stalled. But you can peek through the glass doors at the grandest interior space in Paris, if not all Europe: a single glass arcade 1,100ft long with a glass dome at the centre, flanked by several levels of balconies and a magnificent grand stair.

The building itself was an allegory: 'A Monument Consecrated by the Republic to the Glory of French Art'. In 1900, for a novelty, 22 works of the major Impressionists – already a bit dated – were included in a separate room, something that would have been unthinkable in 1878 or 1889. When President Emile Loubet came to see the show, a fashionable academician named Gérôme was showing him around; at the Impressionists' room, Gérôme flung himself in front of the doorway, crying: 'Go no further, Monsieur le Président; here France is dishonoured!'

Regular world-touring exhibitions are held in the northern end of the Grand Palais.

Musée du Luxembourg

Rue de Vaugirard; ***RER*** *Luxembourg. Open Tues–Thurs 10–7, Sat–Sun 10–9 , Mon and Fri 10–10.30pm; adm.*

At the west end of the big Palace, at Rue de Vaugirard, the delightful Petit Luxembourg was Paris's first public art gallery.

Famous Homes

*Maison de Balzac

47 Rue Raynouard; Ⓜ Passy or La Muette. Open daily exc Mon and hols, 10–6; free, but adm to exhibitions.

The novelist lived in a dozen Paris houses in his lifetime, but he spent seven years here working to pay off his creditors. Rue Berton, just behind , is one of the few streets unchanged from the times when Passy was a rustic village.

*Maison de Victor Hugo

6 Place des Vosges; Ⓜ Chemin Vert. Open daily except Mon 10–5.40; free.

The master lived here between 1832 and 1848, and the place has been turned into a somewhat lugubrious shrine. Of interest, besides Hugo's charming mock-Chinese dining room, are original illustrations from his books and a good number of Hugo's own peculiar drawings.

Musée Georges Clemenceau

8 Rue B. Franklin; Ⓜ Passy. Open Tues, Thurs, Sat, Sun; closed Aug; free.

Atmospheric apartment where the 'Tiger' spent his last 37 years.

Musée Lénine

4 Rue Marie-Rose (between Rue du Père-Corentin and Rue Sarrette), ***t*** *01 43 21 89 04; Ⓜ Alésia. Open by appt; free.*

Lenin spent his last three years in Paris at this address; the museum has items relating to his stay, including his dishes and chess set (donated by Gorbachev in 1986).

Musée Pasteur

25 Rue du Dr-Roux, www.pasteur.fr; Ⓜ Pasteur. Open 2–5.30; closed Aug; adm.

The 15e is the address of the prestigious Institut Pasteur, recently in the news in the who-discovered-the-AIDS-virus controversy. It was founded by Louis Pasteur in 1888 and continues his research; his apartment, drawings, portraits, items relating to his career and to the Institute are part of the Musée Pasteur.

World Art and Ethnographic Collections

*Musée d'Art et d'Histoire du Judaïsme

71 Rue du Temple, 3e, www.mahj.org; Ⓜ Rambuteau, Hôtel de Ville. Open Mon–Fri 11–6, Sun 10–6, closed Sat; free.

Fascinating and illuminating collection of Jewish art and historical artefacts.

*Musée Cernuschi

Parc Monceau, 7 Av Velasquez; Ⓜ Villiers. Closed until mid 2005.

A small and seldom-visited museum, bequeathed (along with the house) by another turn-of-the-century collector, this one is entirely devoted to Chinese art, from a serene 5th-century seated Buddha to a T'ang dynasty spittoon. Currently closed for renovation, with a small temporary exhibition.

*Musée d'Ennery

59 Avenue Foch; Ⓜ Porte Dauphine. Closed for renovation.

Far Eastern art, puppets, masks and especially *netsukes* (carved Japanese buttons).

*Musée Guimet des Arts Asiatiques

Place d'Iéna, www.museeguimet.fr; Ⓜ Iéna. Open Wed–Sat and Mon 10–6; Sun 10–4; adm.

Founded in 1879 by an industrialist from Lyon, Emile Guimet, this is one of the world's richest collections of art from India, China, Japan, Indochina, Indonesia and central Asia. The collection of Khmer art from the 8th century to the mid-12th (the period of Angkor Wat and meditative smiles) is the best outside Cambodia. The fascinating Salle Hackin proves ancient commercial and artistic links between East and West in Hellenistic times, producing some charming, sensual works – Préparatifs du Grand Départ. On the top floor are works from Japan (a 17th-century screen showing the arrival of the Portuguese), a 3rd-century Korean crown, and a collection of Chinese ceramics from the Han dynasty to the Ming. The Panthéon next door holds Guimet's unique collection of Buddhas and figures of the Six Hierarchies from Japan and China, dating back to the 6th century. Afterwards, you can put your feet up in the peaceful Japanese garden in the back.

Musée de l'Homme

Palais de Chaillot, www.mnhn.fr; Ⓜ Trocadéro. Open Wed–Mon 9.45–5.15; closed hols; adm.

Excellent anthropology museum, opened the year after the 1937 World Fair, offering lots of dusty display cases and long explanations in French of things you never dreamed existed. The best part is the gallery of African cultural anthropology, with fascinating exhibits on the life and architecture of the rather mysterious Dogon of the Sahel (who told anthropologist Marcel Griaule lots of things he didn't know about astronomy), a facsimile of the 1858 Royal Palace façade of King Gleté of Dahomey, and brilliant art from all over the continent.

*Musée de l'Institut du Monde Arabe

1 Rue des Fossés St-Bernard, Pont de Sully; Ⓜ Jussieu. Open 10–6; closed Mon. See p.236.

*Musée National des Arts et Traditions Populaires

6 Av du Mahatma-Gandhi; Ⓜ Les Sablons. Open daily except Tues 9.30–5.15; adm.

Another good bet for older children (and especially for adults), a 1969 functionalist building housing beautiful displays of pre-industrial art and cultural artefacts from France's provinces, arranged according to the dictum of Claude Lévi-Strauss: 'All human civilization, no matter how humble, presents two major aspects: on one hand, it is in the universe, on the other, it is a universe itself.'

*Palais de la Porte Dorée

293 Av Daumesnil, www.musee-afriqueoceanie.fr; Ⓜ Porte Dorée. Wed–Mon 10–5.15; adm.

In 1931 Paris felt compelled to put on another World Fair, the first in six long years. This one was a little different: the *Exposition Coloniale* was a government effort put on to show the French how wonderful it was to be imperialists, and how much money they were earning by it. The White Man's Burden was a commonplace in France up to the 1960s, not surprising in a country that has always felt it had a *mission civilisatrice*. The one permanent building was the 'Museum of the Colonies' which after the war became the 'Museum of Overseas France'. This is one of the best collections of African and Pacific Islands art anywhere in Europe. But before the art, in the basement is an excellent **Tropical Aquarium**. On the main floor, the strangest ethnic artworks are the painted Art Deco celebrations of colonialism by the French themselves. **Oceanian art**, in two rooms on the main floor, includes everyday objects from Melanesia and some exceptional bark paintings from Australian aborigines. Upstairs, the first floor is devoted to artefacts from **Black Africa** – and not only from French colonies. The **Maghreb** – Algeria, Morocco and Tunisia – gets the second floor to itself.

One-offs

Musée Adam Mickiewicz

6 Quai d'Orléans, Ile St-Louis; Ⓜ *Pont Marie. Open Thurs 2–6; adm.*

The first floor, devoted to Chopin, has original scores and the composer's death mask, while upstairs are ephemera on the life and times of poet and patriot Adam Mickiewicz (1798–1855), founder of Polish Romanticism. He held the chair of Slavic literature at the Collège de France from 1841–44 and was the leading voice of Paris's many Polish émigrés.

Musée de l'Automobile

1 Place du Dôme, Colline de La Défense; Ⓜ *Grande Arche de La Défense. Open daily 12–7, Sat until 9; free.*

Historic collection of French cars.

Musée des Collections Historiques de la Préfecture de Police

Rue des Carmes; Ⓜ *Maubert-Mutualité. Open Mon–Fri 9–5, Sat 10–5; free.*

The Parisians, for all their fine manners, can be a rascally herd. The Fronde uprising in Louis XIV's minority revealed how many weapons were loose in the streets; although only gentlemen and soldiers on active duty were allowed to carry swords, in practice the whole city was armed to the teeth. People were openly robbed and swindled, even on the Pont Neuf, and no one disagreed when the satirist Boileau wrote in 1660: 'The darkest forest is a safe haven after Paris.'

Louis XIV reacted to this crime wave by founding the ancestor of the modern Paris police in 1667. His lieutenant was the tough but fair-minded Nicolas-Gabriel de La Reynie, who personally did much to temper the king's more inhumane commands. It was just as well, for La Reynie and his successors with their teams of sergeants and informers (*mouches*) not only policed but governed Paris, responsible for the city's security, equipment and modernization, and also its morals, religious affairs and public health. Louis himself didn't give a fig for Paris, but he would summon his lieutenants to Versailles to hear the latest gossip of dukes caught singing rude ditties or pissing out of windows, which always made Louis chuckle before he sent stern notes threatening them with the Bastille. Original documents in the museum range from his *lettres de cachet* to the criminal report on Verlaine and Rimbaud; there are police uniforms, a guillotine blade, anarchist bombs, documents on the ex-convict Vidocq, and Grandville's hilarious engraving of conspiring umbrellas called the *Cauchemar du Préfet de Police*. The biggest exhibit covers *anthropométrie* – the method invented by commissioner Alphonse Bertillon to identify crooks by photographing and measuring their noses, ears and eyes. In 1903 Bertillon obtained the first conviction in Europe using fingerprints as evidence, a mere 1,400 years after Chinese detectives did it.

Musée de la Contrefaçon

16 Rue de la Faisanderie; Ⓜ *Porte Dauphine. Open Tues–Sun 2–5.30; closed Mon; adm.*

Run by Paris's Manufacturers' Union to display the thing they hate most: counterfeits. Cartier watches, rum labels, Lacoste shirts, some pretty good and some ludicrous; but legal as long as the name is spelled differently (Channel No.5, Contreau Triple-Sec).

Musée de la Curiosité et de la Magie

11 Rue Saint-Paul, 4e, www.museedelamagie.com; Ⓜ St-Paul. Open Wed, Sat and Sun 2–7; adm.

Historical items related to magic, games and demonstrations of conjuring tricks.

Musée de la Franc-Maçonnerie

16 Rue Cadet; Ⓜ Cadet.
Open Tues–Sat 2–6; adm.

France's oldest masonic organization, an offshoot of the British original of the 18th century, tells its story in documents, pictures and memorabilia.

Musée Galerie de la Seita

Rue Surcouf; Ⓜ Invalides. Open Mon–Sat 11–7; adm.

Although Jean Nicot gave his name to nicotine in 1560, the first French cigarettes weren't made until the 19th century at the Tabacs de Gros Caillou, in a huge factory built over a farm once belonging to Beaumarchais. When the area became residential in 1905, only the administration building remained; the museum first opened for the 1937 Exposition. Exhibits cover the history of tobacco, smoking paraphernalia and the evolution of its social acceptance (Sir Walter Raleigh was enjoying a pipe when his servant, thinking he was on fire, put him out with a bucket of water).

Musée Grévin

10 Boulevard Montmartre, www.grevin.com; Ⓜ Grands Boulevards. Open Mon–Fri 10–5.30, Sat, Sun and hols 10–6; adm exp.

After surrendering an outrageous sum to get in, you notice there are no labels near any of the figures – so that, right on cue, a little man comes up and sells you a programme for another €1. But no matter: this is a blatant tourist attraction and fun – maybe even worth it. The Grévin is built inside an old theatre lobby, and the delicious 19th-century brass-and-upholstery setting quite upstages the wax dummies, which aren't that lifelike anyhow. But it's done with some wit: Woody Allen taking a spacewalk, fake museum guards giving you a real glass eye, or the lady adjusting her stocking.

On the top floor, current celebrities are portrayed doing things celebrities do: eating dinner, or staring blankly at the walls. Downstairs in the dungeon-like *galeries souterraines* is a series of tableaux from the history of France. In the inevitable cinema section, the star attraction is a soulful, white-clad Marilyn Monroe, a foot away from you, emoting on her subway grating from *The Seven Year Itch*. Maybe the admission is so high because they have such problems protecting the exhibits. Excited Frenchmen are constantly molesting dummies of politicians; voodoo worshippers stick pins in pop singers, and a few years back the Basque ETA admitted knocking off King Juan Carlos' head in a daring daylight *attentat*.

Le Grévin Forum

Forum des Halles; Ⓜ Les Halles.
Open daily 10.30–6.45, Sun 1–6.30; adm exp.

Another branch of the wax museum, specializing in Paris's *belle époque* – re-creating Les Halles and Montmartre of the 1890s.

*Musée de la Monnaie

Quai de Conti, entrance in Rue Guénégaud, www.monnaiedeparis.fr; Ⓜ Pont Neuf. Open daily except Mon 11–5.30, Sat and Sun 12–5.30; adm; free tours of the medal workshops Tues and Fri at 2.15, but go early to claim your place.

The mastodontic Hôtel des Monnaies until recently minted all the francs in France. Jean-Denis Antoine, charged by Louis XV to design the Mint, bucked every lingering rococo urge of the day in favour of clean lines and minimal decoration. The interior offers decidedly more: a fine double-curving stair by the main entrance, handsome courtyards, one with a marker indicating the Paris meridian, and the Musée de la Monnaie – not dusty cases of coins and medals, but a vivid, historical display that makes money indecently engrossing.

Although a new mint has been built near Bordeaux, the Hôtel des Monnaies still produces commemorative medals, a Renaissance art inspired by ancient Roman coins. No one familiar with the taste of Napoleon III will be surprised to see his new railways commemorated with medals of naked ladies stroking big locomotives; more recent medals are on sale in the Mint's shop.

*Musée de la Musique

Cité de la Musique, La Villette, www.cite-musique.fr; Ⓜ Porte de Pantin. Open Tues–Sat 12–6, Sun 10–6; adm.

Across the Canal de l'Ourcq from the Cité and the Géode, the southern half of the Parc de La Villette is occupied by the two new white asymmetrical buildings of the **Cité de la Musique**, designed by French architect Christian de Portzamparc: concert halls (one with hyper-acoustics designed by Pierre Boulez), the Conservatoire of dance and music, and a **Musée de la Musique** with 4,500 instruments, including Stradivarius and Guarnieri violins, and Beethoven's clavichord, all cosily gathered together in one place.

Musée de l'Opéra

Place de l'Opéra, www.opera-de-paris.fr; Ⓜ Opéra. Open daily 10–5, exc Sun and matinee days; adm. *See pp.211–12.*

Musées des Parfumeries Fragonard

9 Rue Scribe; Ⓜ Opéra. Open 9–5.30; closed Sun Oct–Mar; free.

Old, famous perfumes and bottles.

*Musée de la Poste

34 Bd de Vaugirard, www.laposte.fr/musee; Ⓜ Montparnasse-Bienvenüe. Open Mon–Sat 10–6; adm.

Just behind the Gare de Montparnasse a cream-coloured building decorated with concrete prisms holds the Musée de la Poste. Five floors offer an overview of postal history, from ancient letters on clay tablets to the modern PTT. There's a complete collection of French stamps (note the meticulous engravings on issues up to the 1960s), and memorabilia from the siege of 1870.

Musée de Radio France

116 Av du Président-Kennedy Ⓜ *Ranelagh; Open for tours only daily at 3pm; adm.*

Every Parisian knows the most imposing landmark in the 16e, on the Seine: a round aluminium and glass complex begun in 1953, it is the perfect symbol of postwar Paris – a weird, inhuman tribute to unchained technology, housing a weary, state-controlled media bureaucracy. Some of its own employees call the place 'Alphaville' after the spooky 1960s science-fiction film by Godard; the architect, Henry Bernard, had been a winner of the academics' Holy Grail, the *Prix de Rome*. The tour (*Mon–Fri 10, 11, 2.30, 3 and 4; adm; ring* **t** *01 56 40 15 16 for times of tours in English*) offers exhibits on the beginnings of French TV, going back to the first broadcast in 1931 (America didn't manage one until 1939). Before privatization, this building was also the home of ORTF, the television monopoly that acted as a shameless propaganda organ for the government in the de Gaulle years.

Musée de la Serrurerie (Musée Bricard)

1 Rue de la Poste; Ⓜ St-Paul. Open Mon–Fri 8.30–12.30 and 1.40–5.30; adm.

If you were Louis XVI, who enjoyed his hobby of locksmithing much more than any affairs of state, you would certainly stop here. The museum is housed in the 1685 Hôtel Libéral-Bruant, built by the architect of the Invalides for himself. The Bricard company, which makes (can you guess?) locks, has assembled a small collection of door and window hardware from Roman times to the present. Highlights include some fancy Renaissance door-knockers from Venice and a reproduction of an old Parisian locksmith's shop.

Musée du Vin

Rue des Eaux, www.museeduvinparis.com; Ⓜ Passy. Open daily except Mon 10–6; adm.

Didactic exhibits and wax dummies set in old quarries that were converted into wine cellars by monks in the 1400s. Ticket price includes a *dégustation* at the end.

Pavillon de l'Arsenal

21 Bd Morland, www.pavillon-arsenal.com; Ⓜ Sully-Morland. Open daily except Mon 10.30–6.30, Sun 11–7; free.

Since 1988 this has been a special exhibition dedicated to Paris, its history and the planning currently under way for its future. The exhibits, beginning with a 540-sq-ft model of the entire city that lights up to point out sites and stages in the city's development, are as high-tech and glitzy as the *grands projets* themselves; the whole thing is relentlessly educational, and does a good job of presenting the planners' doubtful case.

Paris: Children and Sports

22

Children

Theme Parks

Indulging the little rascals in (or talking them out of) **Disneyland® Resort Paris** (*32km east of Paris at Marne-la-Vallée; **RER** A4: Marne-la-Vallée/Chessy. Open daily 9–8, July–Aug 9am–11pm; **t** 0870 606 6800 (UK residents), **t** 00 33 1 60 30 60 81 (US residents), for all information, events schedules, and hotel/bungalow reservations, www.disneyland paris.com; high season adm €41, €33 for children 3–11; multi-pass available, good for two or three days*) is the first major hurdle for most parents.

Parc Astérix (*in Plailly, 38km north of Paris off the A1, linked every 30mins by Courriers Ile-de-France shuttle bus from **RER** B Charles-de-Gaulle 1; www. parcasterix.fr; open April–June and Sept–mid-Oct daily 10–6, July–Aug 9.30–7; adm €31 adults, €23 children*) is a good alternative. It may not have as many rides and attractions as Disneyland, but Parc Astérix is, at least, genuinely French. Astérix, the Roman-bashing Gaul, has long been France's most popular cartoon character and his adventures are among its most successful literary exports – translated into over 40 languages. The theme park is divided into themed areas, including a Gaulish village, a Roman city and Ancient Greece. There are also lots of hair-raising rides.

Sights and Museums

Obvious options are excursions up to the top of the **Eiffel Tower** (corny but they'll always remember it, *see* p.199) or up the Towers of **Notre-Dame** (*see* p.211) or, for cheapskates, up the free escalators of **Beaubourg/ Centre Pompidou** for the view, a hotdog and a soda pop (*see* pp.212–14). Alternatively, if your kids are at the grisly stage, a trip down the city's **catacombs** (*see* p.196) or **sewers** (*see* p.270) might be intriguing. Or take the funicular up to **Sacré-Cœur** (Métro tickets valid) for an effortless and fun alternative to climbing all those steps.

Then there's the obligatory day at the **Cité des Sciences et de l'Industrie** (*see* p.270) with its absolutely fabulous Inventorium for kids aged 3–6 and 6–12, its various *Folies*, with more kids' activities and workshops, as well as the Géode cinema, which even the most hardened teenagers enjoy.

Other kid-pleasers include the gadgetry in the **Palais de la Découverte** (*see* p.271), the ships in the **Musée de la Marine** (*see* p.269), the aeroplanes and spaceship at the **Musée de l'Air et de l'Espace at Le Bourget** (*www.mae. org; open April–Sept Tues–Sun 10–6, Oct–Mar Tues–Sun 10–5; adm; take bus 350 from Gare de l'Est or Porte de la Chapelle or bus 152 from Porte de la Villette*), the dinosaur bones in the **Galerie d'Anatomie Comparée et de Paléontologie** and the stuffed beasts in the **Grande Galerie d'Evolution** in the Jardin des Plantes (*see* p.252).

Even young children enjoy the hoaked up wax people at the **Musée Grevin** (*see* p.275), and the magic tricks at the **Musée de la Curiosité et de la Magie** (*see* p.275).

The **Centre Pompidou**, **t** 01 44 78 12 33, *www. centrepompidou.fr*, encourages creativity by offering various events and workshops for children (*see* website for programme). There is also a special afternoon, 'La Découverte des Collections', in the Galerie des Enfants (*Wed, Sat, and daily during school hols, 2–4pm*).

Activities

Incurable video game heads can easily blow all their pocket money at the **Centre Sega**, 5 Bd des Italiens, Passage des Princes, 2e, Ⓜ *Richelieu-Drouot* (*open 12 noon–8pm*).

For an extra-extra special treat for kids of any age (must reserve weeks in advance), book a day at the circus at the **Cirque de Paris**, 115 Bd Charles-de-Gaulle, Villeneuve-la-Garenne, bus 137 from Ⓜ *Porte de Clignancourt*, **t** 01 47 99 43 40 (*Nov–June: in termtime shows on Weds and Sun; in school hols daily; July–Oct circus is on the road*). The performers put children through the fundamentals of their art as they rehearse, have lunch with them, and from 3–5pm the children attend the circus itself. A day for a child ranges from €29 to €34.50 (depending on the seat for the performance), for adults €26.50–41 (performance only less expensive).

The tropical pool complex at **Aquaboulevard**, the biggest sport and leisure centre in Paris, should keep kids of all ages happy (*just outside the Périphérique at 4 Rue Louis-Armand, 15e, **t** 01 40 60 10 00; open Mon–Thurs 9am–11pm, Fri and Sat till midnight; Sun 8am–11pm;* Ⓜ *Balard*).

Parks and Gardens

A sure winner for younger kids is the **Jardin d'Acclimatation** in the Bois de Boulogne, with lots of participatory activities (*see* p.250).

Kids used to running around like banshees and kicking a ball around a field won't have it quite all their own way in Paris. Grass is still a sacred herb in the more formal parks, the **Parc Monceau**, for example, and some parts of the **Jardin du Luxembourg**; where prohibited there is usually a sign or a fence. But otherwise access is being liberalized: the **Parc des Buttes-Chaumont**, **Parc Georges-Brassens**, **Jardin du Ranelagh** and **Parc de la Villette** offer most activities for squirmy youth. But do not despair – almost every little green space shown on the Michelin map 11 has a play-ground ranging from the rudimentary to sandpits, climbing bars and slides. The larger parks will offer seasonal pony rides, a carousel, puppet shows and roller-skating rinks. Traditional ***marionnette*** (*guignol*) perform-ances are usually on Wednesdays, Saturdays and Sundays (listings in the back of *Pariscope* along with children's theatre and circuses under the heading '*Pour Les Jeunes*').

There are **zoos** at the Jardin des Plantes (*see* p.253) and the Bois de Vincennes (*see* p.251), the latter of which could be easily combined with a few hours at the delightful **Parc Floral**, a lower-key version of the Bois de Boulogne's Jardin d'Acclimatation (*Rte de la Pyramide*) or the aquarium and ethnographic exhibits at the **Palais de la Porte Dorée** (*see* p.273).

If the weather's good, you can park your 7–15-year-olds for a couple of hours in the delightful fantasy playground (especially in the Labyrinth) of the **Jardin des Halles**, 105 Rue Rambuteau (*open Tues–Thurs and Sat 10–7, Fri 2–7, Sun and bank hols 1–7; adm;* Ⓜ *Châtelet-Les Halles*).

Eating Out

If your fussy eater is suffering severe culture shock at the thought of eating real food in French restaurants (note that these are usually very good about doing children's portions), some 50 McDonald's and other fast-food clones wait to ward off starvation.

Two child-friendly chains to look out for are **Bistro Romain** and **Hippopotamus**. Both serve burgers, chips, etc., and the Hippo chain will provide games and puzzles. Other good places include the following:

Altitude 95, First Level, Eiffel Tower, Champ de Mars. Perhaps the best location in Paris, with spectacular views. There's a children's menu and they are very welcoming to families. *Open daily 12–2 and 7–9.* Ⓜ *Bir-Hakeim.*

Berthillon, 31 Rue St-Louis-en-l'Ile, Ile St-Louis. The best ice-creams and sorbets in town, and always popular. Be prepared to queue. *Open Wed–Sun 10–8.* Ⓜ *Cité.*

Terrasse de la Samaritaine, Quai du Louvre. Decent café on the roof of the department store. Good for a drink, a snack or a reason-ably priced meal. And the views. *Open daily 9.30–7, Thurs till 10pm.* Ⓜ *Pont Neuf, Châtelet.*

Le Totem, Musée de l'Homme, 17 Place du Trocadéro. Best for families during the day, when it serves snacks and drinks. The inte-rior reflects the exhibits in the museum, and there's a breathtaking view of the Eiffel Tower. *Open daily noon–2.30am.* Ⓜ *Trocadéro.*

Babysitting or Child-minding Services

Most of the places listed below charge an agency fee (*€7.70–11*) in addition to the hourly rate (*around €5.50*) that goes to the sitter. If you're out after the last Métro, you'll be expected to drive the sitter home or pay for a taxi. These are the biggest agencies, but locals are listed by *arrondissement* in the Yellow Pages (*Pages Jaunes*) under *Gardes d'enfants.*

Allô Assistance Babychou, t 01 43 13 33 23. Qualified babysitters recognized by the Préfecture. *€10 initial fee (valid 6 months) plus €5.70 per hour or €52 per day (10 hours).*

Babysitting Express, t 06 09 04 41 81. Qualified babysitters recognized by the Préfecture. *€7.70 initial fee plus €5.40 an hour.*

Le CROUS, t 01 40 51 37 52. Student organiza-tion which organizes babysitting (among other things). *€5.35 an hour; €0.75 more after 10pm.*

Kid Services, t 01 42 61 90 00. Qualified nurses will look after newborns (less than 3 months) or older babies. *Initial fee €11. Newborns €7.70 an hour, €58 a night; older babies €5.50 an hour, €30.50 a night.*

Spectator Sports

There are plenty of sports to watch (check listings in the Wednesday *Le Figaro* or the sports-only paper, *L'Equipe*) but you have to scramble for tickets for the major events in the calendar: the French Open, the last leg of the Tour de France (round the Arc de Triomphe, the third week in July), the Five Nations rugby matches, and horse races – the *Prix du Président de la République* steeplechase in April at Auteuil and the *Grand Prix de l'Arc de Triomphe* flat race, the first Sunday in October at Longchamp. Note that the racecourses close from mid-July through August, and information on all may be had by ringing **t** 01 49 10 20 30; off-track betting (even the little old ladies do it) takes place in any bar with the sign PMU. The following are the major venues:

Hippodrome d'Auteuil, Bois de Boulogne, 16e. Steeplechase (hurdle) racetrack. Ⓜ *Porte d'Auteuil.*

Hippodrome de Chantilly, in Chantilly. The prettiest racecourse in France; site of the prestigious Prix du Jockey Club (second Sunday in June) and the Prix de Diane (third Sunday in June).

Hippodrome de Longchamp, Bois de Boulogne, 16e. Flat races. Ⓜ *Porte d'Auteuil, then shuttle bus.*

Hippodrome de Vincennes, Bois de Vincennes, 12e. Trotting (harness racing). **RER** *Joinville.*

Palais Omnisport Paris-Bercy, 8 Bd de Bercy, 12e, **t** 01 43 46 12 21. A distinctive stadium with slanted walls that require the attention of a lawnmower; designed to host 22 sports from hockey to motorcross. Ⓜ *Gare de Lyon.*

Parc des Princes, 24 Rue du Commandant-Guilbaud, 16e, **t** 01 42 30 03 60, *www.paris-valdemarne.archi.fr*. Big concrete stadium, home to Paris's two soccer teams – St-Germain and Racing-Paris I – its rugby union team and other rugby events. Football information **t** 01 10 41 71 71, rugby **t** 01 53 21 15 15. Ⓜ *Porte de St-Cloud.*

Roland Garros, 2 Av Gordon-Bennett, 16e, **t** 01 47 43 48 00. Site of the prestigious French Open last week May and first week June; reserve by Feb in writing to FFT, Service Réservation, BP 333-16, 75767 Paris Cédex 16. Ⓜ *Porte d'Auteuil.*

Stade de France. Outside Paris proper, yet the city's latest sporting pride and joy, the sleek new stadium was inaugurated in style in 1998 as the French team (Les Bleus) won football's World Cup. Tickets for sporting events are sold through the organizations sponsoring them or call **t** 01 55 93 00 00. Ⓜ *St-Denis Porte de Paris.* If you can fit in a meal, there is no better brasserie for hungry sports-lovers than **Chez Serge**, on your way or your way back (on the same Métro line), every day except Sunday, 7 Boulevard Jean-Jaurès, St-Ouen. Ⓜ *Mairie de St-Ouen.*

Paris: Food and Drink

Restaurant Prices

luxury over €90
expensive €55–90
moderate €30–55
inexpensive €15–30
cheap under €15

For an average *à la carte* meal for one person, with wine and service included. Set menus will be much cheaper.

Nearly all the restaurants listed below offer set-price menus, sometimes including wine. Little adventures *à la carte* are liable to make prices double. Some expensive restaurants put on an inferior, inexpensive lunch menu just to get people in the door. On the other hand, some of the most famous places offer excellent bargain lunch menus.

For dinner, bookings are essential – weeks in advance (lunch too) for real gourmet citadels on popular dates. Brasseries tend to have lots of tables, and spare ones aren't difficult to find except at the most famous. Brasseries usually serve meals around the clock until midnight, rather like American diners, and many offer breakfast. Other restaurants open more or less from 12 with last orders at 2 and 7 until 10.30 or 11; in Paris though, the trend is towards staying open later and later. Remember that many restaurants are closed in August.

For lunch look for the *plat du jour* (the chef's special) or a *formule* (set-price little-choice menu); nearly any café will make you an omelette, *steack frites*, *poulet-frites*, a hot dog, a burger with egg, or ham and melted cheese on toast called *croque-monsieur* or *croque-madame* (same but with an egg set on top).

Restaurants: Right Bank and Islands

Ile de la Cité and Ile St-Louis

L'Orangerie, 28 Rue St-Louis-en-l'Ile, 4e, **t** 01 46 33 93 98 (*expensive*). One of the most elegant and romantic dining rooms in Paris, founded by actor Jean-Claude Brialy as an after-theatre rendezvous; *cuisine bourgeoise*. *Dinner only; book.* Ⓜ *Pont Marie.*

Brasserie de l'Ile Saint-Louis, 55 Quai de Bourbon, 4e, **t** 01 43 54 02 59 (*moderate*). For lovers of *choucroute*. *Closed all day Wed, and Thurs lunch.* Ⓜ *Pont Marie.*

Caveau du Palais, 19 Place Dauphine, 4e, **t** 01 43 26 04 28 (*moderate*). Excellent quality establishment with a terrace, set in one of the most romantic squares in Paris. *Closed Sun in Oct–April.* Ⓜ *Cité, Pont Neuf.*

L'Ilot Vache, 35 Rue St-Louis-en-l'Ile, 4e, **t** 01 46 33 55 16 (*moderate*). Lovely, old-fashioned and full of flowers, with an honest €33 menu that usually includes lots of seafood. *Evenings only.* Ⓜ *Pont Marie.*

Au Rendez-vous des Camionneurs, 72 Quai des Orfèvres, 1er, **t** 01 43 54 88 74 (*moderate–inexpensive*). Good French-truckers' style cooking. Ⓜ *Cité.*

Les Halles/Beaubourg

Benoît, 20 Rue St-Martin, 4e, **t** 01 42 72 25 76 (*luxury – €90 per head; lunch menus moderate*). Considered by many the most genuine Parisian *bistrot*, opened by current owner Michel Petit's grandfather, devoted to the most perfectly prepared dishes of *la grande cuisine bourgeoise française*. Ⓜ *Châtelet.*

Ambassade d'Auvergne, 22 Rue du Grenier-St-Lazare, 3e, **t** 01 42 72 31 22, *www.ambassade-auvergne.com* (*moderate*). Mouthwatering *cuisine de terroir* from the Auvergne (*soupe aux choux et au roquefort, Charlotte aux marrons*). Ⓜ *Rambuteau.*

Caveau François Villon, 64 Rue de l'Arbre-Sec, 1er, **t** 01 42 36 10 92 (*moderate*). A *bistrot* in a 15th-century cellar, with a strumming guitar in the evening; delicious fresh salmon with orange butter. *Closed Sun, and Mon lunch.* Ⓜ *Louvre-Rivoli.*

Chez La Vieille, 37 Rue de l'Arbre-Sec, 1er, **t** 01 42 60 15 78 (*moderate*). La Vieille may have retired, but the food is still first-rate (e.g. *pot-au-feu*); a classic French repast. *Closed evenings (except Thurs) and all day Sat and Sun.* Ⓜ *Louvre-Rivoli.*

Au Pied de Cochon, 6 Rue Coquillière, 1er, **t** 01 40 13 77 00 (*moderate*). An institution. Famous for its *pied de cochon* as well as its seafood platter. *Open 24 hours.* Ⓜ *Les Halles, Louvre.*

La Tour de Montlhéry (Chez Denise), 5 Rue des Prouvaires, 1er, **t** 01 42 36 21 82 (*moderate*). An old-fashioned *bistrot* with character and excellent cooking, full of locals not tourists, with hams hanging from the ceiling. Excellent cooking including hearty *andouillette*, tripe and *gigot d'agneau*. *Open 24hrs, closed Sat and Sun.* Ⓜ *Les Halles, Louvre-Rivoli.*

Auberge Nicolas Flamel, 51 Rue de Montmorency, 3e, **t** 01 42 71 77 78, *http://nicolasflamel.parisbistro.net* (*moderate–inexpensive; €12 lunch menus*). In one of the oldest houses in Paris, refined cooking from *maigrets* cooked with cider to seafood raviolis. *Closed Sat lunch and Sun.* Ⓜ *Rambuteau.*

Le Pharamond, 24 Rue de la Grande-Truanderie, 1er, **t** 01 40 28 45 18 (*moderate–inexpensive*). This has been here since 1832. The Belle Epoque interior is a national monument, and the recipes could be as well, especially the roast pheasant and rich *tripes à la mode de Caen*. *Closed Sun and Aug.* Ⓜ *Etienne Marcel, Les Halles.*

La Taverne de Maître Kanter, 16 Rue Coquillière, 1er, **t** 01 42 36 74 24, *www.tavernes-maitre-kanter.com* (*inexpensive; menus from €16.50*). A brasserie that never closes, with plenty of shellfish to go along with the *choucroute* and Alsatian whites. *Open 24 hours.* Ⓜ *Les Halles.*

Aux Tonneaux des Halles, 28 Rue Montorgueil, 1er, **t** 01 42 33 36 19 (*inexpensive*). You'd think that the market porters were still alive and well and about to crowd in through the door. Again, the genuine article: friendly, chaotic and excellent. *Closed Sun.* Ⓜ *Etienne Marcel.*

Les Forges, 5 Rue des Forges, 2e, **t** 01 42 36 40 83 (*cheap*). The true Sentier restaurant: owners, models and drivers all eating together. Fresh fish. *Closed Sat and Sun.* Ⓜ *Sentier.*

Marais

L'Ambroisie, 9 Place des Vosges, 4e, **t** 01 42 78 51 45 (*luxury*). Under the supreme fine touch and imagination of master chef Bernard Pacaud, one of the top gastronomic addresses in the country, in the elegant Hôtel de Luynes. *Closed Sun and Mon, Aug and two weeks in Feb.* Ⓜ *Bastille.*

Bofinger, 5 Rue de la Bastille, 4e, **t** 01 42 72 87 82 (*expensive; menus lunch €21.50, lunch and eves €30.50*). The prettiest of brasseries, and an institution for over a century. Oysters by the dozen or half; wonderful seafood specialities. A great place. Ⓜ *Bastille.*

Le Petit Bofinger, 6 Rue de la Bastille, 4e, **t** 01 42 72 05 23 (*moderate*). This cheaper version of Bofinger (*see* above), across the road, has a Mon–Sat lunch menu for €18 (*à la carte* €27), a children's menu and a non-smoking section. Ⓜ *Bastille.*

A la Biche au Bois, 45 Av Ledru-Rollin, 12e, **t** 01 43 43 34 38 (*moderate; menu €22*). An example of the best Paris has to offer in moderately priced traditional cuisine. Outdoor terrace. *Closed Sat, Sun, and Mon lunch.* Ⓜ *Gare de Lyon/Ledru-Rollin.*

Chez Julien, 1 Rue Pont Louis-Philippe, 4e, **t** 01 42 78 31 64 (*moderate; menus €28*). Well-cared-for Belle Epoque restaurant. Excellent, traditional fare. *Closed Sun.* Ⓜ *Hôtel de Ville.*

La Galoche d'Aurillac, 41 Rue de Lappe, 11e, **t** 01 47 00 77 15 (*moderate; menus €24 and €35*). On a street once lined with *bal-musettes* (there are still a couple), this surly old Auvergnat *bistrot* hung with wooden clogs and hams is more popular than ever. *Closed Sun and Mon.* Ⓜ *Bastille.*

La Guirlande de Julie, 25 Place des Vosges, 3e, **t** 01 48 87 94 07 (*moderate*). A memorable lunch and a memorable setting under the arcades; mid- to upper-price. *Closed Mon in winter.* Ⓜ *Chemin Vert, Bastille.*

Jo Goldenberg, 15 Rue des Rosiers, 4e, t 01 48 87 20 16 (*moderate–inexpensive*). The Marais branch of Paris's most famous delicatessen. You'll think you're in New York (the ultimate compliment for delis). Classic noshes to eat in or take out. Ⓜ *St-Paul.*

Chez Janou, 2 Rue Roger-Verlomme, 3e, **t** 01 42 72 28 41 (north of Pl des Vosges) (*inexpensive; €13 lunch menu*). Friendly tiled *bistrot* from 1900 with inventive dishes from Provence (*no credit cards*). Ⓜ *Chemin Vert, Bastille.*

Chez Paul, 13 Rue de Charonne, 11e, **t** 01 47 00 34 57 (*inexpensive*). Solid family cooking (*rillettes*, duckling with prunes) in an old Paris setting straight out of a Doisneau photo, complete with a pretty terrace. Ⓜ *Bastille.*

Les Philosophes, 28 Rue Vieille-du-Temple, 4e, **t** 01 48 87 49 64 (*inexpensive*). A trendy place with forthright cuisine. Sit amongst the stone walls or outside on the terrace. Ⓜ *St-Paul, Hôtel de Ville.*

Le Trumilou, 84 Quai de l'Hôtel-de-Ville, 4e, **t** 01 42 77 63 98 (*inexpensive*). A popular old Auvergnat *bistrot*, on the *quai* although a view of the Seine is blocked by a store wall. Ⓜ *Hôtel de Ville.*

Piccolo Teatro, 6 Rues des Ecouffes, 4e, **t** 01 42 72 17 (*cheap*). Not an Italian restaurant but the best vegetarian place in the area. Imaginative dishes with pretentious names. Lunch menu €8.90/14.70. Ⓜ *St-Paul.*

Chez Rami et Hanna, 54 Rue des Rosiers, 4e, **t** 01 42 74 74 99 (*cheap*). Falafel, herring, chopped liver, the whole shtick. Ⓜ *St-Paul.*

Palais Royal/Bourse

Le Grand Véfour, 17 Rue de Beaujolais, 1er, **t** 01 42 96 56 27, *www.relaischateaux.com* (*luxury; lunch menu €75*). More a temple than a crass commercial enterprise, this grandest of grand old restaurants with one of the loveliest dining rooms in Paris maintains a tradition in the Palais Royal that is now two hundred years old. *Closed Fri eve, Sat and Sun, and Aug.* Ⓜ *Palais Royal, Bourse.*

Chez Georges, 1 Rue du Mail, 2e, **t** 01 47 03 34 28 (*expensive*). This fine establishment is at the very pinnacle of the *bistrot* range. Not cheap, but the equal of many with much heftier prices. Ⓜ *Sentier.*

Il Cardinale, 34 Rue de Richelieu, 1er, **t** 01 49 27 05 22 (*moderate; lunch menu €13, dinner €20*). Friendly Italian restaurant with its own pet budgies, serving fresh pasta and other dishes. Also sells Italian products (Illy coffee and olive oil). Ⓜ *Pyramides.*

Le Gavroche, 19 Rue St-Marc, 2e, **t** 01 42 96 89 70 (*inexpensive; lunch menu €14*). The archetypal family-run *bistrot à vins* of old; authentic without even trying. Hearty country cooking from *cassoulet* to *pot-au-feu*, and very good wines. *Closed Sun.* Ⓜ *Bourse.*

L'Incroyable, 26 Rue de Richelieu, 2e, **t** 01 42 96 24 64 (*inexpensive*). Truly incredible *bistrot* in an alley off the street. *Only stays open until 9pm; closed Sun.* Ⓜ *Richelieu-Drouot.*

Opéra/Madeleine/ St-Honoré

Les Ambassadeurs, Hôtel de Crillon, 10 Place de la Concorde, 8e, **t** 01 44 71 16 16, *www.crillon.com* (*luxury*). The €62 menu is a relative bargain for highly rated cuisine in a sumptuous setting. Book well ahead. Ⓜ *Concorde.*

Drouant, 18 Place Gaillon, 2e, **t** 01 42 65 15 16, *www.drouant.com* (*luxury; lunch menu €53, dinner €104*). Since 1914 the seat of the Académie Goncourt, where it bestows France's most sought-after literary prize. Sumptuous Art Deco interior; famous for its elegant sauces, wine cellar and its *grand dessert Drouant. Closed Sat and Sun.* The **Café Drouant** has a €30 menu. *Open daily.* Ⓜ *Opéra, Quatre Septembre.*

Lucas Carton, 9 Pl de la Madeleine, 8e, **t** 01 42 65 22 90, *www.lucascarton.com* (*luxury; menu gastronomique €360, lunch menu €76*). The perfect marriage of tradition, beautiful surroundings and one of the top-rated modern chefs, Alain Senderens. *Closed Sat lunch, Sun, Mon lunch.* Ⓜ *Madeleine.*

Maxim's, 3 Rue Royale, 8e, **t** 01 42 65 27 94, *www.maxims-de-paris.com* (*luxury*). Still the most beautiful restaurant in the galaxy, with perfectly preserved Belle Epoque rooms, and the food isn't bad either. Overpriced, though. *Closed Sat lunch, Sun and Mon.* Ⓜ *Concorde.*

Goumard, 9 Rue Duphot, 1er, **t** 01 42 60 36 07, *www.goumard.fr* (*expensive; menu €40*). Near the Madeleine. A top-rated seafood restaurant since the 1890s, recently completely renovated, though the original bathrooms are a listed monument. *Closed 5–20 Aug.* Ⓜ *Madeleine.*

Brasserie Mollard, 115 Rue St-Lazare, across from the station, 8e, **t** 01 43 87 50 22 (*moderate*). Spectacular 1895 decoration: mirrors, terracotta, rare marble and ceiling mosaics. Lots of oysters and other seafood. Ⓜ *St-Lazare.*

Pierre à la Fontaine Gaillon, Place Gaillon, 2e, **t** 01 47 42 63 22 (*moderate*). Seasonal menus based on seafood in the mansion of the Duc de Lorgues; tables out on the terrace by the Fontaine d'Antin. *Closed Sat, Sun and Aug.* Ⓜ *Opéra.*

Le Poquelin, 17 Rue Molière, 1er, **t** 01 42 96 22 19 (*moderate; lunch menu €25*). Opposite Molière's birthplace and popular with actors from the Comédie Française. *Closed Sat lunch, Sun, and Mon lunch.* Ⓜ *Pyramides.*

Le Roi du Pot au Feu, 34 Rue Vignon, 9e, **t** 01 47 42 37 10 (*inexpensive*). Entirely devoted to the most humble and traditional of all French dishes, but here raised to an art form. *Closed Sun, and 15 July–15 Aug.* Ⓜ *Madeleine.*

Champs-Elysées/Passy

Taillevent, 15 Rue Lamennais, 8e, **t** 01 44 95 15 01, *www.taillevent.com* (*luxury; menus €130 and €180*). M. Vrinat is still at the top, despite all the young hot-shots. In the handsome *hôtel particulier* of the Duc de Morny; booking essential. *Closed Sat and Sun.* Ⓜ *George V.*

Copenhague, 142 Av des Champs-Elysées, 8e, **t** 01 44 13 86 26 (*luxury–expensive; menus €46, €63, €100*). Sophisticated Scandinavian cuisine. *Closed Sat and Sun.* Ⓜ *George V.*

Le Scheffer, 22 Rue Scheffer, 16e, **t** 01 47 27 81 11 (*moderate*). Neighbourhood restaurant serving good *entrecôte bordelaise* and a diet-demolishing dark *mousse au chocolat. Closed Sat and Sun in July and Aug.* Ⓜ *Trocadéro.*

Montmartre

Beauvilliers, 52 Rue Lamarck, 18e, **t** 01 42 54 54 42 (*expensive*). Montmartre's gourmet restaurant and one of the oldest in France (1787); very romantic. *Closed Sun, and Mon lunch.* Ⓜ *Lamarck-Caulaincourt.*

La Pomponnette, 42 Rue Lepic, 18e, **t** 01 46 06 08 36 (*moderate; lunch menu €17.50*). Classic Montmartre *bistrot*, lively atmosphere; delicious mackerel in white wine and home-made desserts. *Closed Sun.* Ⓜ *Blanche.*

Chez Ginette, 101 Rue Caulaincourt, near the métro, 18e, **t** 01 46 06 01 49 (*inexpensive*). Very reasonable, and plenty of fun; a complete night out. *Closed Sun and Aug.* Ⓜ *Lamarck-Caulaincourt.*

L'Afghani, 16 Rue Paul-Albert, 18e, **t** 01 42 51 08 72 (*inexpensive*). Local restaurant. Delicious starters and filling main courses: roast meats, *ashak* (Afghan raviolis) or vegetarian. *Open Mon–Sat 8–11pm.* Ⓜ *Château Rouge.*

Le Montagnard, 102 Rue Lepic, 18e, **t** 01 42 58 06 22 (*inexpensive*). Good-quality traditional country cooking in an old Montmartre grill. Highlights are fondue and other mountain specialities. Impressive attention to detail and excellent value. *Closed Tues.* Ⓜ *Abbesses.*

Le Restaurant, 32 Rue Véron (south of Rue des Abbesses), 18e, **t** 01 42 23 06 22 (*inexpensive*). A recent high-quality addition to Montmartre with dishes such as *canette rotie au miel.* Ⓜ *Abbesses.*

Rest of the Right Bank

Le Pré Catelan, Rte de Suresnes, Bois de Boulogne, **t** 01 44 14 41 14 (*luxury; lunch menu €55*). Lovely Belle Epoque restaurant immersed in garden far from the hubbub; food fit for an emperor – pressed pigeon, succulent langoustines, heavenly chocolate desserts. *Closed Sun eve exc July and Aug, Mon, and Feb.* Ⓜ *Porte Dauphine.*

Le Train Bleu, Gare de Lyon, first floor, 12e, **t** 01 43 43 09 06, *www.le-train-bleu.com* (*expensive; lunch menu €43, juinor menu €15*). After Maxim's, perhaps the most spectacular decoration in Paris; frescoes and gilt everywhere in this showpiece, built for the 1900 World Fair. Cuisine not memorable but good enough. Ⓜ *Gare de Lyon.*

L'Art des Choix, 36 Rue Condorcet, 9e, **t** 01 48 78 30 61 (*moderate; lunch menus €16 and €21*). *Confits* and *maigrets, cassoulet, cabécou* and *vin de Cahors*: all the delights of this part of southwest France famous for its *cuisine de terroir. Closed Sun and Mon.* Ⓜ *Anvers.*

Charlot Roi des Coquillages, 12 Place de Clichy, 9e, **t** 01 53 20 48 *(moderate)*. This 1930s brasserie is a true kitsch-palace, renowned for its fish. You would have to head south towards Marseilles for better seafood. It has some meat too. *Open until 1am Thurs–Sat.* Ⓜ *Place de Clichy.*

Da Mimmo, 39 Bd Magenta, 10e, **t** 01 42 06 44 47 (*inexpensive*). Arguably the best pizza in Paris. *Open Tues–Sat 12–2.30 and 7–11.30.* Ⓜ *Jacques-Bonsergent.*

Restaurants: Left Bank

Latin Quarter

La Tour d'Argent, 15 Quai de la Tournelle, 5e, **t** 01 43 54 23 31, *www.tourdargent.com* (*luxury; lunch menu €65*). Established here in the reign of Henri II in 1582 and recently brought back to splendour by a new chef. Unforgettable, romantic views of Notre-Dame, unique atmosphere and a superlative wine cellar. *Closed Mon, and Tues lunch.* Ⓜ *Maubert-Mutualité.*

Atelier de Maître Albert, 1 Rue Maître-Albert, 5e, **t** 01 46 33 13 78 (*moderate; menu €36*). Stone walls, exposed beams and an open fire create one of Paris's most medieval environments. *Closed Sun.* Ⓜ *Maubert-Mutualité.*

Balzar, 49 Rue des Ecoles, 5e, **t** 01 43 54 13 67 (*moderate*). An institution from the 1930s where stars and Sorbonne *intellectuels* rub shoulders – you might find yourself sitting next to Gwyneth Paltrow! Limited menu, but superb. Also has a cheaper brasserie. Ⓜ *Maubert-Mutualité.*

Chez Maître Paul, 12 Rue Monsieur-le-Prince, 6e, **t** 01 43 54 74 59 (*moderate*). Ordinary-looking but highly recommended, with dishes from the Franche-Comté to match – *poulette à la crème gratinée* and delicious apple or walnut desserts, washed down with wines from the Jura. *Closed Sun and Mon in July and Aug.* Ⓜ *Odéon.*

Le Vivario, 6 Rue Cochin (south of Quai de la Tournelle), 5e, **t** 01 43 25 08 19 (*moderate–inexpensive*). Authentic Corsican-Sicilian cuisine. *Closed Sat lunch, Sun, Mon lunch.* Ⓜ *Maubert-Mutualité.*

Chieng-Mai, 12 Rue Frédéric-Sauton (off Place Maubert), 5e, **t** 01 43 25 45 45 (*inexpensive; menus lunch €11.50 and €14, dinner €20 and €27*). Paris's most authentic Thai restaurant; reserve. Ⓜ *Maubert-Mutualité.*

Chez Hamadi, 12 Rue Boutebrie, 5e, **t** 01 43 54 03 30 (*cheap*). Not much to look at but good North African cuisine. Ⓜ *St-Michel.*

Panthéon/Rue Mouffetard

Au Petit Marguery, 9 Bd de Port-Royal, 13e, **t** 01 43 31 58 59 (*expensive–moderate; menus lunch €25.20, dinner €34+*). Innovative brasserie run by the Cousin brothers, who perform an aromatic magic with seasonal ingredients; black truffles in the spring, game dishes and wild mushrooms in the autumn. *Closed Aug, Sun and Mon.* Ⓜ *Les Gobelins.*

Les Délices d'Aphrodite, 4 Rue de Candolle, 5e, (opposite the church of St-Médard), **t** 01 43 31 40 39 (*moderate; menus €16 lunch, €18 dinner*). The Mavromatis family serves some of the best Greek food in Paris, in one of the most serendipitous locations. *Closed Sun.* Ⓜ *Censier-Daubenton.*

Perraudin, 157 Rue St-Jacques, 5e, **t** 01 46 33 15 75 (*inexpensive*). Comfortable old-fashioned place; one of the best choices in this *quartier*. Fresh tarts are a speciality. *Closed Sat and Sun.* ***RER*** *Luxembourg.*

Foyer des Etudiants Vietnamiens, 80 Rue Monge, 5e, **t** 01 45 35 32 54 (*cheap*). Modest establishment but the staples – soup, noodles and rice – are good and filling. *Closed Sun.* Ⓜ *Place Monge.*

St-Germain

Jacques Cagna, 14 Rue des Grands-Augustins, 6e, **t** 01 43 26 49 39, *www.jacques-cagna.com* (*luxury; lunch menu €80*). One of Paris's most gracious institutions; an unforgettable lunch menu. *Closed Sat lunch, Sun, and Mon lunch.* Ⓜ *Odéon.*

Alcazar, 62 Rue Mazarine, 6e, **t** 01 53 10 19 99, *www.alcazar.fr* (*expensive; lunch menus €16, €22, €26*). Once home to a famous transvestite cabaret bar, since 1998 a modern brasserie owned by English restaurateur, Terence Conran. Featuring classic English and French dishes: fish and chips or *plateau de fruits de mer*. The Az Bar, overlooking the restaurant, has become a pre-clubbing venue par excellence. Ⓜ *Odéon.*

Lapérouse, 51 Quai des Grands-Augustins, 6e, **t** 01 43 26 68 04 (*expensive; lunch menu €30*). Luscious Second Empire décor and alcoves for romantic rendezvous; some highly innovative dishes from the Basque chef. *Closed Sat lunch, Sun and Aug.* Ⓜ *St-Michel.*

Le Récamier, 4 Rue Récamier, 7e, **t** 01 45 48 86 58, *www.lerecamier.fr* (*expensive*). In a quiet cul-de-sac, a favourite of the Left Bank;

an Empire dining room where publishers and journalists dawdle over Chateaubriand or *bœuf bourguignon*. *Closed Sun.* Ⓜ *Sèvres-Babylone.*

Aux Charpentiers, 10 Rue Mabillon, 6e, **t** 01 43 26 30 05 (*moderate; menus €19–25*). Located in the former carpenters' guildhall (with a little museum about it), serving excellent *pot-au-feu, boudin* and other everyday French basics; economical *plats du jour.* Ⓜ *Mabillon.*

Restaurant Indonesia, 12 Rue de Vaugirard, 6e, **t** 01 43 25 70 22 (*inexpensive; menus €9, €15, €17*). A workers' co-operative and Paris's first Indonesian restaurant. *Closed Sat.* Ⓜ *Odéon.*

Eiffel Tower/Faubourg St-Germain

Le Bourdonnais, 113 Av de la Bourdonnais, 7e, **t** 01 47 05 47 96 (*luxury; lunch menus €42, €64, €86*). Beautifully prepared dishes from the fragrant Midi. Ⓜ *Ecole Militaire.*

Le Jules Verne, Eiffel Tower (private lift to 2nd floor), 15e, **t** 01 45 55 61 44 (*luxury; menus Mon–Fri lunch €51, eves and weekends €114*). Highly rated *haute cuisine* high above Paris. Ⓜ *Bir-Hakeim.*

Tan Dinh, 60 Rue de Verneuil, 7e, **t** 01 45 44 04 84 (*moderate*). Vietnamese cooking in a way Parisians like it – steamed crab pâté, lobster triangles with ginkgo nuts and much more. *Closed Sun and Aug.* Ⓜ *Solférino.*

Au Pied de Fouet, 45 Rue de Babylone, 7e, **t** 01 47 05 12 27 (*cheap*). Le Corbusier's favourite restaurant, with checked tablecloths and long queues for its tasty and very affordable meals. *Closed Sat night, Sun and Aug.* Ⓜ *Sèvres-Babylone.*

Montparnasse

Dominique, 19 Rue Bréa, 6e, **t** 01 43 27 08 80, *www/dominique-fr.com* (*expensive; lunch menus €40 and €55*). A favourite of Paris's Russians since the 1920s, with succulent chicken Kiev, *chachlick caucasien* and Russian cheesecake (*vatrouchka*). *Closed Sun and Mon.* Ⓜ *Vavin.*

La Coupole, 102 Bd du Montparnasse, 14e, **t** 01 43 20 14 20 (*expensive–moderate; menus lunch €29, eves €30.50*). The police had to control the crowds when it opened its doors in the 1920s, and it's still a sight to behold in full flight. A wide variety of dishes on the menu, and the old-fashioned dancing in the afternoons (*Sat and Sun*) can be fun. *Open until 2am daily.* Ⓜ *Vavin.*

Wine Bars

Sometimes called *bistrots à vin* or, like the English, *bars à vin*, this once-common city institution is enjoying a revival as Parisians have begun to expand their wine consciousness. There are even chains like L'Ecluse that aim to re-create the old *bistrot à vin* environment. Any old traditional *bistrot à vin* will serve something to go along with the wine: plates of sausages or pâté, onion soup, cheese, sandwiches or even three-course meals.

Right Bank

A la Cloche des Halles, 28 Rue Coquillière, 1er. Wine bar of renown; excellent choices to go with solid country snacks of cheese and *charcuterie. Closed Sat night and Sun.* Ⓜ *Châtelet.*

L'Entracte, 47 Rue Montpensier, 1er. A favourite of Diderot when it was called La Pissotte, now specializing in wines from the Loire and plates of tasty *charcuterie*; reasonable prices. *Open daily until 2am or so.* Ⓜ *Palais Royal.*

Le Rubis, 10 Rue du Marché-St-Honoré, 1er. One of the oldest and best, with a range of delicious snacks and affordable wines by the glass. Ⓜ *Pyramides.*

Willis's Wine Bar, 13 Rue des Petits-Champs, 1er. A well-regarded British wine bar in Paris, and one of the few to serve wines from around the world. *Open until 11pm, closed Sun.* Ⓜ *Pyramides.*

La Tartine, 24 Rue de Rivoli, 4e. Unchanged more or less for over 90 years, though newly fashionable. *Closed Tues and Aug.* Ⓜ *St-Paul.*

Les Vins des Pyrénées, 25 Rue Beautreillis, 4e. One of the last non-trendy wine bars *à l'ancienne* with regional food; a place of character and characters. Ⓜ *Bastille, St-Paul.*

Café Mélac, 42 Rue Léon Front, 11e. The jovial proprietor ages his Château Mélac plonk (from his drainpipe vine) in the fridge, and has even organized a co-operative of urban wine-growers, the Vignerons de Paris. *Closed Sun, Mon night.* Ⓜ *Charonne.*

Clown-Bar, 114 Rue Amelot, 11e. Old gathering place for circus folk near the Cirque d'Hiver. Fascinating décor of old circus memorabilia. *Closed Sun.* Ⓜ *Filles du Calvaire.*

Le Baron Rouge, 1 Rue Théophile-Roussel, 12e. Fill your bottle from the keg or savour a glass, accompanied by good food. *Closed Mon.* Ⓜ *Ledru-Rollin.*

Au Négociant, 27 Rue Lambert, 18e. Very affordable and affable, and a good bet for lunch. *Closed Sat and Sun.* Ⓜ *Château Rouge.*

Le Relais de la Butte, 12 Rue Ravignan, 18e. Old-fashioned, friendly and plant-filled wine bar with wines by the glass. Sit at the bar and while away the afternoon. Ⓜ *Abbesses.*

Le Baratin, 3 Rue Jouye-Rouve, 20e. Popular new *bistrot à vin*, with delicious, hearty snacks. *Open until 1am.* Ⓜ *Pyrénées.*

Islands and Left Bank

Henri IV, 13 Pl du Pont Neuf, 1er. Good snacks with a southwest flavour. *Closed Sat night and Sun.* Ⓜ *Pont Neuf.*

Cave la Bourgogne, 142 Rue Mouffetard, 5e. Good wine and everything else to drink, plus excellent sandwiches. Fitting termination point to a walk down the Mouff. *Closed Mon.* Ⓜ *Place Monge.*

Le Sancerre, 22 Avenue Rapp, 7e. Red, white, rosé: pick your Sancerre and chow down at the oyster bar. Cosy, classy atmosphere with warmth. Ⓜ *Ecole Militaire.*

Le Rallye Peret, 6 Rue Daguerre, 14e. Owned by the same family for over 80 years, with the biggest variety of bottles to choose from (especially Beaujolais). *Closed Sun, Mon and Aug.* Ⓜ *Denfert-Rochereau.*

Bars, Beer Cellars, Pubs, *Tapas*

Cafés are Parisian, bars are not, except for the old working-class watering holes that have disappeared from the city landscape. Therefore almost all the bars you will find in this city have one sort of angle or another: immigrant bars, gay bars, beer bars, music bars or whatever (for those offering entertainment, *see* p.304). Beer is trendy in this city, and more places devoted to it are opening up all the time. In recent years the institution of the happy hour has hit Paris in a big way – keep an eye out for signs in the windows, as discounts on drinks can be spectacular.

Right Bank

Le Comptoir, 14 Rue Vauvilliers, 1er. Fashionable 1950s retro; beers, cocktails and very fancy *tapas. Open until 2am, 4am weekends.* Ⓜ *Les Halles.*

Costes Bar, Hôtel Costes, 239 Rue St-Honoré, 1er. A useful address if you need a drink in the middle of the night. Small with very glamorous crowd. Ⓜ *Tuileries.*

Le Sous Bock, 49 Rue St-Honoré, 1er. Cocktails and the best imported beers; snacks of mussels and *frites* at all hours. 180 varieties of whisky. *Open until 5am.* Ⓜ *Châtelet.*

Le Baragouin, 17 Rue Tiquetonne, 2e. Lively, affordable Breton bar. *Open until 2am, closed afternoons.* Ⓜ *Les Halles.*

La Champmeslé, 4 Rue Chabanais, 2e. Very intimate, very feminine and romantic bar. *Open 6–10pm; closed Sun.* Ⓜ *Pyramides, Bourse.*

Harry's Bar, 5 Rue Daunou, 2e. Since 1911 the most famous American bar in Paris, home of the Bloody Mary and Side Car, where a big international business clientele gathers to discuss making more do-re-mi over one of 180 different brands of whisky. *Open daily until 4am.* Ⓜ *Opéra.*

La Perla, 26 Rue François-Miron, 4e. Laid-back California-Mexican, good margaritas, Mexican beers, flavoured tequilas and snacks. *Open until 2am.* Ⓜ *St-Paul.*

Le Fouquet's, 99 Av des Champs-Elysées, 8e. A Paris institution for the rich and famous. Ⓜ *George V.*

Café de l'Industrie, 16 Rue St-Sabin, 11e. A Bastille institution. Photos of actors on the walls and corners crammed full of ornaments. A peaceful place in the afternoon, but come evening its fans pile in. Ⓜ *Bastille.*

Pause Café, 41 Rue de Charonne, 11e. Popular café-bar, loved by locals and tourists alike. The service can be unreliable, but there are cheap eats. Ⓜ *Ledru-Rollin.*

China Club, 50 Rue de Charenton, 12e. In an old ice house, one of the most beautiful bars in Paris, with leather sofas and high ceilings; elegant atmosphere, Chinese snacks. *Open until 2am.* Ⓜ *Ledru-Rollin.*

Le Totem, Palais de Chaillot (Musée de l'Homme), 17 Place du Trocadéro, 16e. Popular and trendy bar and restaurant; terrace with view of the Eiffel Tower. Ⓜ *Trocadéro.*

Bar Belge, 75 Av de St-Ouen, 17e. Paris's oldest, friendliest, most extensive Belgian beer cellar, with Flemish snacks. *Open until 3am, closed Mon.* Ⓜ *Guy Moquet.*

Left Bank

Académie de la Bière, 88bis Bd de Port-Royal, 5e. German beer specialists, with over 50 different varieties, mussels and *frites. Open until 3am.* **RER** *Port-Royal.*

Le Crocodile, 5 Rue Royer-Collard, 5e. Cosy, intimate night haunt for serious cocktail aficionados, with over 120 varieties. *Open until 2am, closed Sun.* **RER** *Luxembourg.*

La Gueuze, 19 Rue Soufflot, 5e. Extremely popular café with Paris's most impressive *carte des bières* – over 400 kinds of brew from around the world. **RER** *Luxembourg.*

Polly Magoo, 11 Rue St-Jacques, 5e. Sleazy down-at-heel fun in the modern equivalent to the old haunts of Villon, practically unchanged since it opened in 1970. *Open until 4 or 5am.* Ⓜ *St-Michel.*

La Closerie des Lilas, 171 Boulevard de Montparnasse, 6e. Unchanged since Verlaine and Hemingway boozed here; cocktails at a price. *Open until 2am.* **RER** *Port-Royal.*

Le Lutétia, Hotel Lutétia, 45 Bd Raspail, 6e. The bar in the beautiful Hotel Lutétia is one of the few hotel bars worth recommending. It's not cheap, but it's classy, and you're likely to rub shoulders with stars such as Catherine Deneuve or Paolo Coelho. Ⓜ *Sèvres-Babylone.*

Le Mazet, 61 Rue St-André-des Arts, 6e. A serious beer cellar (15 kinds on tap) where you can also get a bowl of onion soup in the wee hours. Ⓜ *Odéon.*

La Mezzanine de l'Alcazar, 62 Rue Mazarine, 6e. The first-floor bar of Terence Conran's Paris restaurant has become a trendy hangout for the beautiful people (you might see Madonna). Ⓜ *Odéon.*

Pub Saint-Germain (Parrot's Tavern), 17 Rue de l'Ancienne-Comédie, 6e. A popular non-stop haven for beer connoisseurs, with over 100 varieties in bottles and 20 on tap. *Open 24hrs; ring the bell if it looks closed.* Ⓜ *Odéon.*

Café Thoumieux, 4 Rue de la Comète, 7e. Plush *tapas* bar associated with high-quality restaurant around the corner. *Open 12pm–2am.* Ⓜ *Invalides.*

Cafés, *Salons de Thé, Glaciers*

Nearly every crossroads in Paris has its café, an institution dating back to the 17th century, where people could shed their social and class distinctions and speak their minds about politics and (eventually) start revolutions.

A *salon de thé*, on the other hand, tends to be more inward-looking, concentrating on light (and often overpriced) luncheons, but usually good for a quality cup of coffee or tea and pastries.

Right Bank and Islands

Angelina, 226 Rue de Rivoli, 1er, *www.angelina.fr.* A Viennese confection, vintage 1903 (when it was called Rumpelmayer), with a special rich African chocolate and the world's best *montblanc* (chestnut cream, meringue and chantilly). Ⓜ *Tuileries.*

Café Marly, in the Louvre courtyard, facing the Pyramid, 1er. New, beautifully designed chic hangout in the old ministries vacated for the Grand Louvre project. Especially pretty at night. Ⓜ *Palais Royal-Musée du Louvre.*

A Priori Thé, 35–7 Galerie Vivienne, 2e. Take a trip back in time over a cup of English tea and cheesecake under the glass-roofed *passage.* Ⓜ *Bourse.*

La Belle Horthense, 31 Rue Vieille du Temple, Marais, 4e. Bookshop/café in the heart of the Marais. Ⓜ *St-Paul, Filles du Calvaire.*

Berthillon, 31 Rue St-Louis-en-l'Ile, Ile St-Louis, 4e. Paris's best ice-creams and sorbets with a list of flavours a mile long; you can also enjoy them sitting down in most of the island's cafés. Ⓜ *Pont Marie.*

Le Flore en l'Ile, 42 Quai d'Orléans, Ile St-Louis, 4e. Great view over Notre-Dame, great tea, great Berthillon ice cream (straight and in exotic cocktails). Ⓜ *Pont Marie*.

Le Loir dans la Théière, 3 Rue des Rosiers, 4e. Tranquil and popular tearoom in the Marais, with mixed chairs and expectantly intellectual atmosphere. It also serves light lunches (tarts and cheese dishes, *pâtisseries maison*). Ⓜ *St-Paul*.

Ma Bourgogne, 19 Pl des Vosges, 4e. Vortex of café life in the Place des Vosges. Ⓜ *St-Paul*.

Mariage Frères, 30 Rue du Bourg-Tibourg, 4e. Paris's best-known purveyors of tea; hundreds of blends to sample with a pastry. Ⓜ *St-Paul*.

Brasserie Mollard, 115 Rue St-Lazare, 8e. Beautiful Art Nouveau café-brasserie. Ⓜ *St-Lazare*.

Ladurée, 16 Rue Royale, 8e. Exquisite and precious *salon de thé*, famous for its macaroons. Bring your laciest great aunt along for tea. Ⓜ *Madeleine*. Another branch at 75 Av des Champs-Elysées, 8e. Ⓜ *Franklin D. Roosevelt*.

Baggi, 33 Rue Chaptal, 9e. The best home-made ice-cream on the Right Bank, founded in 1850 and still going strong, using 100% natural ingredients. Ⓜ *Pigalle*.

Café de la Paix, 3 Place de l'Opéra, 9e. A historic landmark; if you can't afford a ticket to the Opéra, you might just be able to manage the price of a coffee here; architect Garnier's second-best effort in the outlandish style he invented – Napoleon III. Ⓜ *Opéra*.

Left Bank and Islands

La Fourmi Ailée, 8 Rue du Fouarre, 5e. A cosy atmosphere in a former glassworks, fire in the fireplace, good salads, scones and excellent desserts. *Open 12–12*. Ⓜ *St-Michel, Maubert-Mutualité*.

Les Deux Magots, 6 Pl St-Germain-des-Prés, 6e. A hoot for all its pretensions, and usually full of tourists, but the chocolate and ice cream are compensations. Note, however, if it's crowded, you may be pressured into making a second order or leaving – inexcusable! Ⓜ *St-Germain-des-Prés*.

Café de Flore, 172 Bd St-Germain, 6e. Fabled literary café, everything just so Parisian, but full of tired vampires trying to suck out your soul with their cool, discerning eyes. So popular with tourists that they've opened their own boutique. Ⓜ *St-Germain-des-Prés*.

Le Procope, 13 Rue de l'Ancienne-Comédie, 6e. Paris's oldest, restored for the Revolution's Bicentennial. Ⓜ *Odéon*.

Le Sélect Montparnasse, 99 Bd du Montparnasse, 6e. The last place to get a feeling for what Montparnasse was all about between the wars. *Open until 2am*. Ⓜ *Vavin*.

Le Bac à Glaces, 109 Rue du Bac, 7e, *www.bacaglaces.com*. Charming tearoom and delectable home-made ice-creams and sorbets. Ⓜ *Sèvres-Babylone*.

Calabrese Glacier, 15 Rue d'Odessa, 14e. The Leonardo da Vinci of ice-cream inventions, home of the famous vanilla and cinnamon *soupe anglaise*. Ⓜ *Montparnasse*.

Paris: Where to Stay

24

There are basically three kinds of hotel in the centre of Paris: big luxury grand hotels, mainly on the Right Bank; business hotels, scattered everywhere; and small, privately owned hotels, some very fashionable and some dogged dives.

Advance bookings are essential in June, and in September and October when Paris is awash in *salons* and conventions. July and August are low season, and some expensive hotels offer discounts then. As a general rule, you'll be asked to send the first night's charge as a deposit. If you arrive without a reservation, booking services in the tourist offices will find you a room.

The categories relate to prices for an average double room. In most places each room has its own price, depending on its view, plumbing, heated towel racks, etc. This is the French way of doing things, and it's also perfectly normal to visit rooms or press the proprietor for details and negotiate. The one hitch is that there are few single rooms.

Optional continental breakfast costs from €4 at the cheapie places to €12 a head at the Ritz. Many proprietors pretend not to know it's optional, but the same cup of coffee and croissant in the bar across the street will be more fun and save you lots of money.

The annual hotel list for Paris available from the Office du Tourisme (127 Av des Champs-Elysées, 75008) indicates all hotels with facilities for the disabled, as well as the most current prices. The Office du Tourisme rates hotels from five stars to none at all. Note that these ratings reflect plumbing and other amenities (lifts, bar, room telephones, etc.) – not intangible qualities such as tranquillity, ambience or good service.

Hotel Prices

luxury over €230
expensive €100–230
moderate €60–100
inexpensive €30–60
cheap under €30
An average double room with bath/shower.

Hotels

Ile de la Cité and Ile St-Louis

Islands have a certain magic, even in urban rivers; they are also central but quiet at night.

****Jeu de Paume, 54 Rue St-Louis-en-l'Ile, 75004, **t** 01 43 26 14 18, **f** 01 40 46 02 76, *www.jeudepaumehotel.com* (*luxury–expensive*). Paris's last real-tennis venue is now the most enchanting little inn on the Seine, complete with a lovely sunny garden. Ⓜ *Pont Marie.*

***Hôtel des Deux Iles, 59 Rue St-Louis-en-l'Ile, 75004, **t** 01 43 26 13 35, **f** 01 43 29 60 25, *www.parishotels.com* (*expensive*). In an 18th-century house, smallish rooms but decorated with period pieces and Provençal fabrics. There's a late-night bar in the cellar. Ⓜ *Pont Marie.*

***Hôtel de Lutèce, 65 Rue St-Louis-en-l'Ile, 75004, **t** 01 43 26 23 52, **f** 01 43 29 60 25, *www.hoteldelutece.com* (*expensive*). Charming, tasteful and small, many rooms with beams. Lift. Ⓜ *Pont Marie.*

***Saint-Louis, 75 Rue St-Louis-en-l'Ile, 75004, **t** 01 46 34 04 80, **f** 01 46 34 02 13, *http://hotels-parishotels/com* (*expensive*). Fashionable, antique furniture, but smallish rooms (no Amex). Lift. Ⓜ *Pont Marie.*

Henri IV, 25 Place Dauphine, 75001, **t** 01 43 54 44 53 (*inexpensive*). 400 years old, frumpy flowered wallpaper, and toilets and showers down the hall, but visitors book months in advance to stay in all simplicity in this most serendipitous square (no credit cards). Ⓜ *Pont Neuf, Cité.*

Beaubourg/Les Halles

Your most likely abode on the Right Bank. Hotels in all categories, near restaurants and lively corners.

***St-Merry, 78 Rue de la Verrerie, 75004, **t** 01 42 78 14 15, **f** 01 40 29 06 82, *www.hotelmarais.com* (*luxury–expensive*). A stone's throw from the Pompidou Centre, this was once St Merri's presbytery and later a bordello. Its latest metamorphosis as a hotel stands out for the beautiful Gothic rooms (no credit cards). Ⓜ *Hôtel de Ville.*

***Hôtel de la Bretonnerie, 22 Rue Ste-Croix-de-la-Bretonnerie, 75004, **t** 01 48 87 77 63, **f** 01 42 77 26 78, *www.labretonnerie.com*, *hotel@bretonnerie.com* (*expensive*). A very popular small hotel: Louis XIII furnishings and television. Ⓜ *Hôtel de Ville*.

*****Grand Hôtel de Champaigne**, 17 Rue Jean-Lantier, 75001, **t** 01 42 36 60 00, **f** 01 45 08 43 33, *champaigne@hotelchampaigneparis.com* (*expensive*). Relatively quiet, near busy Place du Châtelet; originally decorated rooms, many with murals; fancy breakfast buffet. Ⓜ *Châtelet*.

*****Hôtel des Ducs de Bourgogne**, 19 Rue du Pont-Neuf, 75001, **t** 01 42 33 95 64, **f** 01 40 39 01 25, *www.hotel-paris-bourgogne.com* (*expensive*). Characterful hotel with simple rooms which have excellent facilities and nice bathrooms. Downstairs, there's a hat rack with vintage hats and photos of astronauts who stay here when they're visiting the French Space Centre on the same street. Ⓜ *Châtelet*.

****Hôtel du Vieux Marais**, 8 Rue du Plâtre, 75004, **t** 01 42 78 47 22, **f** 01 42 78 34 32, *www.vieuxmarais.com* (*expensive*). Most rooms with TV; all with bath or shower. Ⓜ *Hôtel de Ville*.

****Andréa**, 3 Rue Saint-Bon, 75004, **t** 01 42 78 43 93, **f** 01 44 61 28 36, *www.hotelandrearivoli.com* (*moderate*). Decent quiet choice near the Rue de Rivoli. Ⓜ *Hôtel de Ville*.

***Hôtel de la Vallée**, 84–6 Rue St-Denis, 75001, **t** 01 42 36 46 99, **f** 01 42 36 16 66, *hvallee@noos.fr* (*inexpensive*). Excellent bargain choice, between Les Halles and Beaubourg. Ⓜ *Châtelet-Les Halles*.

St-Germain

St-Germain has a high density of smart, charming hotels, but prices tend to smart in another way.

******L'Hôtel**, 13 Rue des Beaux-Arts, 75006, **t** 01 44 41 99 00, **f** 01 43 25 64 81, *www.l-hotel.com, reservation@l-hotel.com* (*luxury*). Besides seeing the last of Oscar Wilde, this is one of the most romantic hotels in Paris; the honeymoon suite is outrageously furnished with a mirrored set which once belonged to Mistinguett, the 1920s and '30s star at the Moulin-Rouge and Folies-Bergère. Ⓜ *St-Germain-des-Prés*.

******Lutétia**, 45 Bd Raspail, 75006, **t** 01 49 54 46 46, **f** 01 49 54 46 00, *www.lutetia-paris.com, lutetia-paris@lutetia-paris.com* (*luxury*). Renovated early Art Deco palace, a favourite for honeymoons since Pablo and Olga Picasso and Charles and Yvonne de Gaulle canoodled here. When it was requisitioned by the Nazis, the staff walled up the prize wine cellars, and in spite of German interrogations never gave away the secret. Ⓜ *Sèvres-Babylone*.

******Le Relais Christine**, 3 Rue Christine, 75006, **t** 01 40 51 60 80, **f** 01 40 51 60 81, *www.relais-christine.com* (*luxury*). Luxurious, colourful rooms in a 16th-century Augustinian cloister, a quiet oasis. Ⓜ *Odéon*.

******La Villa Saint-Germain**, 29 Rue Jacob, 75006, **t** 01 43 26 60 00, **f** 01 46 34 63 63, *www.villasaintgermain.com* (*luxury*). *Le dernier cri* in St-Germain, with precocious bathrooms of chrome, glass and marble and a chi-chi piano bar. Ⓜ *St-Germain-des-Prés*.

*****Hôtel de l'Abbaye**, 10 Rue Cassette, 75006, **t** 01 45 44 38 11, **f** 01 45 48 07 86, *www.hotel-abbaye.com* (*luxury–expensive*). One of the swankiest small Left Bank hotels – originally a monastery – and despite the traffic serenely quiet, especially if you get one of the bedrooms over the lovely garden courtyard. Four suites available. Ⓜ *St-Sulpice*.

*****Duc de Saint-Simon**, 14 Rue de St-Simon, 75007, **t** 01 44 39 20 20, **f** 01 45 48 68 25, *duc.de.saint.simon@wanadoo.fr* (*luxury–expensive*). In a 17th-century house in a quiet side street off Bd St-Germain, one of the most fashionable little hotels on the Left Bank, all antiques, old beams, stone walls and snob appeal, its cellars converted into a string of bars and salons. Lift. Ⓜ *Rue du Bac*.

*****Académie**, 32 Rue des Sts-Pères, 75007, **t** 01 45 49 80 00, f 01 45 44 75 24, *www.academiehotel.com, academie hotel@aol.com* (*expensive*). A converted 18th-century residence, with Louis XIV, Louis XVI and Directory repros among exposed stone walls and beams that would have shocked the original owners. Lift. Ⓜ *St-Germain-des-Prés*.

*****Hôtel d'Angleterre**, 44 Rue Jacob, 75006, **t** 01 42 60 34 72, **f** 01 42 60 16 93, *anglehotel@wanadoo.fr* (*expensive*). A former British embassy, now a hotel with character. Some rooms have vertiginously high ceilings; huge double beds. Ⓜ *St-Germain-des-Prés*.

*****Hôtel Bersoly's**, 28 Rue de Lille, 75007, **t** 01 42 60 73 79, **f** 01 49 27 05 55, *hotelbersolys@wanadoo.fr* (*expensive*). An 18th-century mansion converted into a beautiful, small hotel. Rooms are small and clean with all mod cons, including modem. Each is named after a different artist and features reproductions of their paintings. Lift. Cots and babysitting available. *Closed Aug.* Ⓜ *Rue du Bac.*

*****Crystal**, 24 Rue St-Benoît, 75006, **t** 01 45 48 85 14, **f** 01 45 49 16 45, *hotel.crystal@wanadoo.fr* (*expensive*). Just around the corner from the church of St-Germain, a charming, cosy and lovingly cared-for little hotel. Ⓜ *St-Germain-des-Prés.*

*****Hôtel Luxembourg**, 4 Rue de Vaugirard, 75006, **t** 01 43 25 35 90, **f** 01 43 25 17 18, *www.hotel-luxembourg.com, luxhotel@luxembourg.mgn.fr* (*expensive*). A small comfortable hotel by the Luxembourg gardens where Verlaine often stayed at the end of his life, at least when he was flush. No restaurant. Ⓜ *Odéon.*

*****Les Marronniers**, 21 Rue Jacob, 75006, **t** 01 43 25 30 60, **f** 01 40 46 83 56 (*expensive*). An enchanting hotel at the bottom of a courtyard, with a garden at the back, but book well in advance. Ⓜ *St-Germain-des-Prés.*

*****Hôtel de l'Université**, 22 Rue de l'Université, 75007, **t** 01 42 61 09 39, **f** 01 42 60 40 84, *www.hoteluniversite.com, hoteluniversite@wanadoo.fr* (*expensive*). In a refurbished 17th-century town house, a few minutes from St-Germain-des-Prés – 27 stylish, quiet rooms, each with a safe, bath and TV. Ⓜ *Rue du Bac, St-Germain-des-Prés.*

****Hôtel La Louisiane**, 60 Rue de Seine, 75006, **t** 01 44 32 17 17, **f** 01 44 32 17 18, *www.hotel-lalouisiane.com* (*expensive*). Set amid the colourful Rue de Buci market, a celebrated favourite of Left Bank literati. Most of the rooms are fairly plain and modern, but the friendly, good-humoured atmosphere makes all the difference. Reserve well in advance due to the slow turnaround, as some guests can't bear to leave – Simone de Beauvoir and Sartre stayed long enough to write several books. Lift. Ⓜ *St-Germain-des-Prés.*

****Hôtel du Quai Voltaire**, 19 Quai Voltaire, 75007, **t** 01 42 61 50 91, **f** 01 42 61 62 26, *www.quaivoltaire.fr* (*expensive*). A hotel since the 19th century, overlooking the Seine and the Louvre, a favourite of Baudelaire, Sibelius and Richard Wagner. **RER** *Musée d'Orsay.*

****Hôtel Saint-Germain**, 50 Rue du Four, 75006, **t** 01 45 48 91 64, **f** 01 45 48 46 22, *www.hotel-saint-germain.com* (*expensive*). Rooms pretty, cosy and homey enough for a hobbit, who would appreciate the minibar, if not the French telly – babysitting available. Ⓜ *St-Sulpice/Sèvres-Babylone.*

****Welcome**, 66 Rue de Seine, 75006, **t** 01 46 34 24 80, **f** 01 40 46 81 59 (*moderate*). Renovated, simple, soundproofed, and a warm welcome. Ⓜ *Mabillon, Odéon.*

***Saint-André des Arts**, 66 Rue St-André-des-Arts, 75006, **t** 01 43 26 96 16, **f** 01 43 29 73 34, *hsaintand@wanadoo.fr* (*moderate*). A 17th-century musketeers' barracks, lively and often noisy until late. Ⓜ *Odéon.*

***Hôtel de Nesle**, 7 Rue de Nesle, 75006, **t** 01 43 54 62 41, **f** 01 43 54 31 88 (*moderate*). Slightly dilapidated but welcoming hotel of character that hasn't accepted reservations since it was an international be-in in the 1960s. Each room is in a different style: no.9 is Egyptian. Ⓜ *Odéon, Pont Neuf.*

Latin Quarter

Very convenient, but apt to be noisy at night.

*****Melia Colbert**, 7 Rue de l'Hôtel-Colbert, 75005, **t** 01 56 81 19 00, **f** 01 56 81 19 02, *melia.colbert@solmelia.com* (*luxury*). Elegant, peaceful hotel with tearoom south of Place Maubert. Ⓜ *Maubert-Mutualité.*

*****Hôtel Dacia Luxembourg**, 41 Bd St-Michel, 75005, **t** 01 53 10 27 77, **f** 01 44 07 10 33, *www.dacia-paris-hotel.com* (*expensive*). On brash and bold Boul'Mich, very close to the Sorbonne and Jardin du Luxembourg, but soundproofed, prettily decorated rooms offer a quiet haven. Ⓜ *Sully-La Sorbonne.*

*****Hôtel des Grands Hommes**, 17 Place du Panthéon, 75005, **t** 01 46 34 19 60, **f** 01 43 26 67 32, *www.hoteldesgrandshommes.com* (*expensive*). Earned a place in French literary history when resident André Breton defined Surrealism here in the 1920s. Furnishings, however, are more in the spirit of Voltaire and Rousseau, entombed in the Panthéon just in front – there's a small garden, cable TV, baby-sitting and minibar. **RER** *Luxembourg.*

★★★**Hôtel du Panthéon**, 19 Pl du Panthéon, 75005, **t** 01 43 54 32 95, **f** 01 43 26 64 65, *hotel.pantheon@wanadoo.fr* (*expensive*). Small, elegant hotel overlooking the Panthéon. Downstairs, there's a bar and lounge, as well as a courtyard garden. Lift. Ⓜ *Cardinal Lemoine*, **RER** *Luxembourg*.

★★★**Grand Hôtel St-Michel**, 19 Rue Cujas, 75005, **t** 01 46 33 33 02, **f** 01 40 46 96 33, *grand.hotel.st.michel@wanadoo.fr* (*expensive*). Fully renovated, fairly quiet choice near the Panthéon with a garden and lift. Ⓜ *Cluny-La Sorbonne*, **RER** *Luxembourg*.

★★**Les Degrés de Notre-Dame**, 10 Rue des Grands-Degrés, 75005, **t** 01 55 42 88 88, **f** 01 40 46 95 34 (*expensive*). Ten charming rooms, many with prize views over Quasimodo's favourite perch. A quiet street, and a restaurant downstairs, serving classic French and North African dishes. All rooms with showers and WC. Ⓜ *Maubert-Mutualité*.

★★**Familia Hôtel**, 11 Rue des Ecoles, 75005, **t** 01 43 54 55 27, **f** 01 43 29 61 77, *www.hotel-paris-familia.com* (*expensive–moderate*). Comfortable, with frescoes in some rooms and great views of Notre-Dame from the top floors. Ⓜ *Cardinal Lemoine*.

★★**Les Argonautes**, 12 Rue de la Huchette, 75005, **t** 01 43 54 09 82, **f** 01 44 07 18 84 (*moderate*). Perfect for Latin Quarter night-owls and other urban creatures, on the corner of the narrowest street in Paris. Ⓜ *St-Michel*.

★★**Hôtel du Collège de France**, 7 Rue Thénard, 75005, **t** 01 43 26 78 36, **f** 01 46 34 58 29, *www.hotel-collegedefrance.com, hotel.du.college.de.france@wanadoo.fr* (*moderate*). Good-value and very popular small hotel offering spacious, spotless rooms with all mod cons. Some have views of Notre-Dame and some have their own balcony. Lovely dark red salon and breakfast room for the hotel's good breakfasts. Lift. Cots available. Ⓜ *Maubert-Mutualité*.

★★**Home Latin Hôtel**, 15–17 Rue du Sommerard, 75005, **t** 01 43 26 25 21, **f** 01 43 29 87 04, *www.homelatinhotel.com, hotel-home-latin@easynet.fr* (*moderate*). Calm, well kept and friendly. Ⓜ *Maubert-Mutualité*, *St-Michel*.

★**Esméralda**, 4 Rue St-Julien-le-Pauvre, 75005, **t** 01 43 54 19 20, **f** 01 40 51 00 68 (*moderate*). Endearing, romantic hotel in a 16th-century building with a *classé* stairway and 19th-century furnishings. Ⓜ *St-Michel*.

★**Marignan**, 13 Rue du Sommerard, 75005, **t** 01 43 54 63 81, **f** 01 43 25 16 69 (*moderate*). Friendly, informal and simple – pay showers down the hall. Ⓜ *Maubert-Mutualité*.

★**Delhy's Hôtel**, 22 Rue de l'Hirondelle, 75006, **t** 01 43 26 58 25, **f** 01 43 26 51 06, *delhys@wanadoo.fr* (*moderate*). Modest choice on a quiet lane tucked near busy Place St-Michel. Ⓜ *St-Michel*.

Mouffetard/Jardin des Plantes

Pleasant, lively at night and cheaper than St-Germain.

★★★**Hôtel des Grandes Ecoles**, 75 Rue du Cardinal-Lemoine, 75005, **t** 01 43 26 79 23, **f** 01 43 25 28 15, *www.hotel-grandes-ecoles.com, hotel.grandes.ecoles@wanadoo.fr* (*expensive*). One of the most amazing settings in Paris, a peaceful cream-coloured villa in a beautiful garden courtyard. Reserve weeks ahead. Ⓜ *Cardinal Lemoine*.

★★**Timhotel Jardin des Plantes**, 5 Rue Linné, 75005, **t** 01 47 07 06 20, **f** 01 47 07 62 74, *www.timhotel.fr* (*expensive*). The best choice in the area, with its sauna, cheerful décor, and sunbathing on 5th-floor terrace overlooking the botanical gardens. Ⓜ *Jussieu*.

★★**Hôtel Résidence Les Gobelins**, 9 Rue des Gobelins, 75013, **t** 01 47 07 26 90, **f** 01 43 31 44 05, *www.hotelgobelins.com* (*moderate*). Friendly hotel at the bottom of the price range, on a quiet street just behind the Manufacture des Gobelins and just a few minutes' walk from Rue Mouffetard. The hotel has a lovely patio with comfortable chairs as well as a pretty sitting room and light-filled breakfast room. All rooms have shower or bath, and are well equipped and quite spacious. Lift. Ⓜ *Les Gobelins*.

★**Port Royal**, 8 Bd Port Royal, 75005, **t** 01 43 31 70 06, *www.portroyalhotel.fr.st* (*moderate–inexpensive*). Family-run, simple, immaculately clean, with garden and lift. Ⓜ *Les Gobelins*.

★**Hôtel des Alliés**, 20 Rue Berthollet, 75005, **t** 01 43 31 47 52, **f** 01 45 35 13 92 (*inexpensive*). Simple place in a quiet street by the Val de Grâce. Ⓜ *Censier-Daubenton*.

★**Le Central**, 6 Rue Descartes, 75005, **t** 01 46 33 57 93 (*inexpensive*). Conveniently located, family-run haven. No en-suite bathrooms. Ⓜ *Maubert-Mutualité, Cardinal Lemoine*.

Montmartre/Place de Clichy

Note that, because of the steps, disabled access is very limited.

★★★★**Hôtel Terrass**, 12 Rue Joseph-de-Maistre, 75018, **t** 01 44 92 34 14, **f** 01 42 52 29 11, *www.terrass-hotel.com* (*luxury–expensive*). The area's most luxurious hotel, overlooking the cemetery and rest of Paris. Also a good restaurant with a terrace. Ⓜ *Place de Clichy*.

★★**Timhotel Montmartre**, 11 Rue Ravignan, 75018, **t** 01 42 55 74 79, **f** 01 42 55 71 01, *www.timhotel.fr* (*expensive*). Henry Miller knew it when it was called Paradis. It's still one of the most romantic hotels in Paris, overlooking delightful Place Emile-Goudeau. Ⓜ *Abbesses*.

★★**Prima Lepic**, 29 Rue Lepic, 75018, **t** 01 46 06 44 64, **f** 01 46 06 66 11, *www.hotel-paris-lepic.com* (*expensive–moderate*). Pleasant and pretty rooms on the slope of the Butte. Ⓜ *Abbesses, Blanche*.

★★**Eden**, 90 Rue Ordener, 75018, **t** 01 42 64 61 63, **f** 01 42 64 11 43, *www. edenhotel-montmartre.com*, *j.delasalle@free.fr* (*moderate*). Behind Sacré-Cœur, pleasant, family run, and equipped with satellite TV. Ⓜ *Jules Joffrin*.

★★**Ermitage Hôtel**, 24 Rue Lamarck, 75018, **t** 01 42 64 79 22, **f** 01 46 64 10 33 (*moderate*). A charming little white hotel under the gardens around Sacré-Cœur (no credit cards). Ⓜ *Lamarck-Caulaincourt*.

★★**Hôtel des Arts**, 5 Rue Tholozé, 75018, **t** 01 46 06 30 52, **f** 01 46 06 10 83, *www.arts-hotel-paris.com* (*moderate*). Excellent value, family-run hotel on a quiet street. Rooms are well furnished in bright colours and there are views of the Sacré-Cœur and Eiffel Tower from the 6th-floor rooms. Lift to the 5th floor. Cots available. Ⓜ *Blanche*.

★★**Régyn's Montmartre**, 18 Place des Abbesses, **t** 01 42 54 45 21, **f** 01 42 23 76 69, *www.regynsmontmartre.com* (*moderate*). A simple but good address in the heart of Montmartre, with good views over Paris. Ⓜ *Abbesses*.

Marais/Bastille

★★★**Caron**, 12 Rue Vieille-du-Temple, 75004, **t** 01 42 72 34 12, **f** 01 42 72 34 63, *www.caron-debeaumarchais. com* (*expensive*). A small, beautifully restored hotel near the Jewish quarter. The lobby sets the tone, with period fireplace and furniture. The small bedrooms and bathrooms are carefully designed for maximum comfort (bathrobes are provided) and some have balconies. A much-loved hotel with many regular visitors. Lift. Cots available. Ⓜ *Hôtel de Ville*.

★★★**Hôtel des Chevaliers**, 30 Rue de Turenne, 75003, **t** 01 42 72 73 47, **f** 01 42 72 54 10, *info@hoteldeschevaliers.com* (*expensive*). Charming hotel in the heart of the Marais, just by the Musée Picasso. Rooms are stylish, comfortable and well equipped, and breakfast is served in the vaulted cellar. Good service. Lift. Ⓜ *St-Paul*.

★★**Hôtel de la Place des Vosges**, 12 Rue de Birague, 75004, **t** 01 42 72 60 46, **f** 01 42 72 02 64, *hotel.place.des.vosges@gofornet.com* (*expensive*). Well restored, and just a few steps from the *place*. Ⓜ *Bastille*.

★★**Saint-Louis Marais**, 1 Rue Charles-V, 75004, **t** 01 48 87 87 04, **f** 01 48 87 33 26, *www.saint-louis-marais.com* (*expensive*). An 18th-century Celestine convent offering romantic if monk-sized rooms. Five floors, but no lift. Ⓜ *Sully-Morland*.

★★**Hôtel Jeanne d'Arc**, 3 Rue de Jarente, 75004, **t** 01 48 87 62 11, **f** 01 48 87 37 31, *information@hoteljeannedarc.com* (*moderate*). Ancient, cute and well run, close to the Place des Vosges; book well ahead. Ⓜ *St-Paul*.

★★**Sévigné**, 2 Rue Malher, 75004, **t** 01 42 72 76 17, **f** 01 42 78 68 26, *contact@le-sevigne.com* (*inexpensive*). Nice place right around the corner from the nosher's paradise of Rue des Rosiers. Ⓜ *St-Paul*.

Opéra/Palais Royal

Quiet at night – a desert in fact, off the main boulevards – and in daytime convenient for many sights.

★★★★**Hôtel Meurice**, 228 Rue de Rivoli, 75001, **t** 01 44 58 10 10, **f** 01 44 58 10 15, *www.meuricehotel.com, reservations@meurice hotel.com* (*luxury*). Reopened in July 2000, this is one of Paris's most opulent hotels. Even if you can't stretch to staying here, pop in for tea in the Jardin d'Hiver, the palm-filled tearoom beneath its Art Nouveau glass roof, or have a drink in the dark wood Fontainebleau bar, with soft leather armchairs and *trompe l'œil* ceiling. If you're in the money, the Belle Etoile suite on the top floor has a 360° view of Paris. Ⓜ *Tuileries*.

★★★**Brébant**, 32 Bd Poissonnière, 75009, **t** 01 47 70 25 55, **f** 01 42 46 65 70, *www.abprom hotels.com, hotel.brebant@wanadoo.fr*, (*expensive*). Smart, stylish, crisply run hotel midway between the striped suits in the Bourse and the Folies-Bergère girlie shows. Ⓜ *Grands Boulevards*.

★★**Antin-Trinité Hôtel**, 74 Rue de Provence, 75009, **t** 01 48 74 29 07, **f** 01 42 80 26 68, *www.paris-hotel-antin.com, hotel@hotel-antin-trinite.fr* (*expensive*). Perfect location for shopaholics, just by the *grands magasins* on Boulevard Haussmann. The small rooms are decorated in pretty colours and have all mod cons. Good value. Lift. Cots available. Ⓜ *Chaussée d'Antin-Lafayette*.

Hôtel Chopin, 46 Passage Jouffroy, 75009, **t** 01 47 70 58 10, **f** 01 42 47 00 70 (*moderate*). Lovely hotel located at the end of one of Paris's prettiest *passages*. Good area for shopaholics and almost next door to the recently reopened Musée Grévin. The peaceful rooms are simply decorated in bright colours, most with shower or bath. The staff are very friendly and the hotel attracts independent travellers who return time and again. Lift. Cots available. Ⓜ *Grands Boulevards*.

★★**Hôtel de la Cité Rougemont**, 4 Cité Rougemont, 75009, **t** 01 47 70 25 95, **f** 01 48 24 14 32 (*moderate*). A good mid-price bet in the area, located in a traffic-free street off Rue Bergères. Ⓜ *Grands Boulevards*.

★★**Vivienne**, 40 Rue Vivienne, 75002, **t** 01 42 33 13 26, **f** 01 40 41 98 19, *paris@hotel-vivienne.com* (*moderate*). Very basic, near the Bibliothèque and *arcades*. No en-suite bathrooms. Ⓜ *Grands Boulevards*.

★**Hôtel de Rouen**, 42 Rue Croix-des-Petits-Champs, 75001, **t** and **f** 01 42 61 38 21 (*inexpensive*). Old and comfortable, a good choice near the Palais Royal. Ⓜ *Palais Royal*.

Hôtel de Lille, 8 Rue du Pélican, 75001, **t** 01 42 33 33 42 (*inexpensive*). A rare bargain hotel between the Louvre and Palais Royal. Old and plain. Ⓜ *Palais Royal, Musée du Louvre*.

Montparnasse

A crop of big-business hotels, modern and low on charm, but a few stand out:

★★★**Lenox Montparnasse**, 15 Rue Delambre, 75014, **t** 01 43 35 34 50, **f** 01 43 20 46 64, *www.hotellenox.com, hotel@lenoxmont parnasse.com* (*expensive*). A large, elegant hotel, just off Boulevard Raspail, opposite the seven cinemas. Ⓜ *Vavin, Edgar Quinet*.

★★★**Hôtel de l'Orchidée**, 65 Rue de l'Ouest, 75014, **t** 01 43 22 70 50, **f** 01 42 79 97 46, *orchidee@escapade-paris.com* (*expensive*). Up-to-date, with a Jacuzzi, garden and sauna. Ⓜ *Gaîté, Pernety*.

★★★**La Villa des Artistes**, 9 Rue de la Grande-Chaumière, 75006, **t** 01 43 26 60 86, **f** 01 43 54 73 70, *www.villa-artistes.com, hotel@villa-artistes.com* (*expensive*). Where Samuel Beckett stayed; recent Art Deco facelift – some of Montparnasse's artists had studios across the street. Ⓜ *Vavin*.

★★**Hôtel Daguerre**, 94 Rue Daguerre, 75014, **t** 01 43 22 43 54, **f** 01 43 20 66 84, *hotel daguerre@wanadoo.fr* (*moderate*). Just by the Cimetière du Montparnasse on a partly pedestrianized street (there is access by car to the hotel). Rooms are simple, but nicely decorated; some overlook the small garden, others have views towards Montmartre and Sacré-Cœur, or their own terrace. The sitting and breakfast rooms downstairs are rather grander. Lift. Ⓜ *Gaîté*.

★★★**Delambre**, 35 Rue Delambre, 75014, **t** 01 43 20 66 31, **f** 01 45 38 91 76, *www.hotelde lambre.com, hotel@hoteldelambre.com* (*moderate*). André Breton once lived in this house, now a good-value, attractive hotel. Rooms are decorated in bright colours, with all mod cons, including modem connections. Downstairs is the charming breakfast room. Lift. Cots available. Ⓜ *Vavin*.

★★**Istria**, 29 Rue Campagne-Première, 75014, **t** 01 43 20 91 82, **f** 01 43 22 48 45 (*moderate*). A charming, kind and cosy hotel that was a favourite of Man Ray, Aragon, Marcel Duchamp, Rilke and Walter Benjamin. Lift. Ⓜ *Raspail*.

★★**Hôtel du Parc,** 6 Rue Jolivet, 75014, **t** 01 43 20 95 54, **f** 01 42 79 82 62, *www.hotelduparc-paris.com, contact@hotelduparc-paris.com* (*moderate*). A TV in each room, many over-looking sunny Square Gaston-Baty. Lift. Ⓜ *Edgar Quinet*.

★**Hôtel des Académies**, 15 Rue de la Grande-Chaumière, 75006, **t** 01 43 26 66 44, **f** 01 43 26 03 72 (*moderate*). Simple, unpretentious family hotel near the Luxembourg gardens. Ⓜ *Vavin*.

★★**Stanislas**, 5 Rue du Montparnasse 75006, **t** 01 45 48 37 05,, **f** 01 45 44 54 43 (*inexpensive*). A well-kept, agreeable hotel in crêpe alley – TV, WC, shower and phones in each room. Ⓜ *Notre-Dame-des-Champs*.

Concorde/Faubourg St-Honoré

The lap of luxury, as far as hotels go; few possibilities below the luxury threshold.

★★★★★**Hôtel de Crillon**, 10 Pl de la Concorde, 75008, **t** 01 44 71 15 00, **f** 01 44 71 15 02, *www.crillon.com* (*luxury*). Behind the classic 18th-century façade stands the last luxury hotel in Paris to remain completely in French hands. Inside are some of the most exquisite and prestigious suites in town, and rooms, if not always grand, done up in choice style with marble baths to match. Ⓜ *Concorde*.

★★★★**Intercontinental**, 3 Rue de Castiglione, 75001, **t** 01 44 77 11 11, **f** 01 44 77 14 60, *www. intercontinental.com, paris@interconti.com* (*luxury*). Built by Garnier nearly as lavishly as his Paris Opéra. Three of the seven grand imperial ballrooms have so much gilt and trimmings that they're listed as national monuments. The hotel takes up a whole city block, and encompasses 390 rooms and 62 suites. Ⓜ *Tuileries, Concorde*.

★★★★ **Hôtel Ritz**, 15 Pl Vendôme, 75001, **t** 01 43 16 30 30, **f** 01 43 16 36 68, *www.ritzparis.com, resa@ritzparis.com* (*luxury*). One of the most famous hotels in the world. Keeping abreast of the times and the demands of its contemporary clientele, today's Ritz has not only soundproof but bullet-proof glass on the ground floor, a new tiled pool and health centre, free cookery classes that perpetuate the tradition of César Ritz's partner, the legendary chef Escoffier, business services and exclusive nightclub. Ⓜ *Opéra*.

★★★**Hôtel des Tuileries**, 10 Rue St-Hyacinthe, 75001, **t** 01 42 61 04 17, **f** 01 49 27 91 56, *www.hotel-des-tuileries.com, htuileri@ aol.com* (*expensive*). A quiet 18th-century *hôtel particulier* with antiques. Ⓜ *Tuileries/ Pyramides*.

Faubourg St-Germain: Eiffel Tower/Invalides

Proust fans may want to sleep in the fabled Faubourg, but don't expect any life or spontaneity to put in your own album of remembrances.

★★★**Hôtel La Bourdonnais**, 111 Av de La-Bourdonnais, 75007, **t** 01 47 05 45 42, **f** 01 45 55 75 54, *www.hotellabourdonnais.fr* (*expensive*). Airy, elegant and comfortable, and breakfast is served in a sunlit indoor garden. Ⓜ *Ecole Militaire*.

★★★**Les Jardins d'Eiffel**, 8 Rue Amélie, 75007, **t** 01 47 05 46 21, **f** 01 45 55 28 08, *www.hotel-jardinseiffel.fr, paris@hotel jardinseiffel.com* (*expensive*). Built at the same time as the 1889 Exposition. Rooms are cosy in an old-fashioned way, and there's a sauna; book a room on the top floor for a view of Mr Eiffel's flagpole. Ⓜ *Latour-Maubourg*.

★★★**Hôtel de Londres Eiffel**, 1 Rue Augereau, 75007, **t** 01 45 51 63 02, **f** 01 47 05 28 96, *www.londres-eiffel.com, info@londres-eiffel.com* (*expensive*). Small, friendly hotel near the Eiffel Tower; some rooms on the top floors have a Tower view. Rooms are comfortable with pretty decoration, all with bath or shower. The sitting area downstairs has stylish furniture. Lift.Ⓜ *Ecole Militaire*.

★★★**Hôtel de Varenne**, 44 Rue de Bourgogne, 75007, **t** 01 45 51 45 55, **f** 01 45 51 86 63, *www.paris-hotel-varenne.com, hotelde varenne@aol.com* (*expensive*). An attractive converted town house with an interior courtyard in a peaceful corner of Paris;

comfortable rooms all with bath and TV. Ⓜ *Varenne*.

★★**La Motte Picquet**, 30 Av de la Motte-Picquet, 75007, **t** 01 47 05 09 57, **f** 01 47 05 74 36, *www.hotelmottepicquet.com* (*expensive*). A small hotel with flowers in window boxes and 18 rooms over three floors. The bedrooms are simply but pleasantly furnished, with small bathrooms, and there is a small sitting area downstairs. Good location for shopping. Lift. Babysitting available. Ⓜ *Ecole Militaire*.

★★**Hôtel de la Tulipe**, 33 Rue Malar, 75007, **t** 01 45 51 67 21, **f** 01 47 53 96 37, *www.hoteldelatulipe.com* (*expensive*). Former convent, now a charming, small hotel on two floors around a garden courtyard. The rooms have been designed in a country style with warm colours, fresh flowers and wooden beams; no.24 is the most romantic, in what was once the chapel and overlooking the courtyard. No lift. Cots available. Ⓜ *Latour-Maubourg, Invalides*.

★★**Kensington**, 79 Av de La Bourdonnais, 75007, **t** 01 47 05 74 00, **f** 01 47 05 25 81, *www.hotel-kensington.com, hk@hotel-kensington.com* (*moderate*). Pleasant and friendly, small and tidy. Ⓜ *Ecole Militaire*.

★★**Grand Hôtel Lévèque**, 29 Rue Cler, 75007, **t** 01 47 05 49 15, **f** 01 45 50 49 36, *www.hotel-leveque.com, info@hotel-leveque.com* (*moderate*). Friendly and pleasant and in the middle of Rue Cler market. Lift. Ⓜ *Ecole Militaire*.

★★**La Serre**, 24bis Rue Cler, 75007, **t** 01 47 05 52 33, **f** 01 40 62 95 66, *www.eiffeltower-hotel-paris.com, laserre@easynet.fr* (*moderate*). Old-fashioned hotel on Faubourg St-Germain's liveliest market street, and one of the cheapest in the quarter. Ⓜ *Latour-Maubourg*.

Champs-Elysées/Etoile/Passy/Auteuil

★★★★**George V**, 31 Av George-V, 75008, **t** 01 49 52 70 00, **f** 01 49 52 70 20, *par. www.fourseasons.com, reservations@fourseasons.com* (*luxury*). Recently restored Art Deco hotel minutes from the glittering shops of the Champs-Elysées, with 18th-century tapestries, a restaurant, bar and coffee lounge, health club, pool and spa, and some private terraces with fantastic views over Paris. Ⓜ *George V*.

★★★★**Plaza Athénée**, 25 Av Montaigne, 75008, **t** 01 53 67 66 67, **f** 01 53 67 66 66, *www.plaza-athenee-paris.com, reservation@ plaza-athenee-paris.com* (*luxury*). Celebrated for its voluptuous luxury and superb service – there are twice as many staff as rooms, and more money spent on fresh flowers than lights. Mata Hari was arrested in its bar, but the spies have since given way to celebrities and corporate bosses – business services, stockmarket info, ticket agencies are just some of the services offered. Ⓜ *Franklin D. Roosevelt, Alma- Marceau*.

★★★★**Raphaël**, 17 Av Kléber, 75116, **t** 01 53 64 32 00, **f** 01 53 64 32 01, *www.raphael-hotel.com, reservation@raphael-hotel.com* (*luxury*). Built in the 1920s, and like its namesake in Rome élite, intimate, splendid and artsy, plus an English bar and garden terrace with a view over Paris. Ⓜ *Kléber*.

★★★★**Vernet**, 25 Rue Vernet, 75008, **t** 01 44 31 98 76, **f** 01 44 31 85 69, *www.hotelvernet.com* (*luxury*). Just off Place Charles-de-Gaulle. Handsomely furnished and air-conditioned, each room has a marble bath with a jacuzzi. Guests have free access to the Hotel Royal Monceau's health centre and heated pool; the Vernet's Belle-Epoque restaurant, Les Elysées, has a lovely crystal roof and two Michelin stars. Ⓜ *George V, Charles de Gaulle-Etoile*.

★★★★**Hôtel de Vigny**, 9–11 Rue Balzac, 75008, **t** 01 42 99 80 80, **f** 01 42 99 80 40, *www.relaischateaux.fr/vigny* (*luxury*). Transformed in 1990 from a town house into one of Paris's most sumptuous small hotels, its bar evoking the Paris of the 1930s salons. Soundproof, marble bathrooms, library, cable TV. Ⓜ *George V*.

★★★★**Villa Maillot**, 143 Av de Malakoff, 75016, **t** 01 53 64 52 52, **f** 01 45 00 60 61, *resa@lavilla-maillot.fr* (*luxury*). Former Art Deco embassy of Sierra Leone, with many vintage 1930s furnishings. Air conditioning, minibars, cable TV, etc. Ⓜ *Porte Maillot*.

★★**Villa d'Auteuil**, 28 Rue Poussin, 75016, **t** 01 42 88 30 37, **f** 01 45 20 74 70, *www.cofrase.com/hotel/villauteuil* (*inexpensive*). Pleasant tidy rooms; ask for one over the courtyard. Ⓜ *Porte d'Auteuil*.

Youth Hostels and *Foyers*

The three top *foyers* in Paris are superb *hôtels particuliers* in the Marais, all furnished with period pieces and immaculately maintained, where you can stay up to seven days at only €30–36 per person (in a double room), with breakfast. Too good to be true? The hitch is that they are often occupied by groups and take no individual bookings; to nab a bed, come at 8am (cash only). They are run by the **Maison Internationale de la Jeunesse et des Etudiants** (MIJE), **t** 01 42 74 23 45, **f** 01 40 27 81 64 and are:

Le Fauconnier, 11 Rue du Fauconnier, 75004; Ⓜ *St-Paul.*

Hôtel de Fourcy, 6 Rue de Fourcy, 75004; Ⓜ *St-Paul.*

Hôtel Maubuisson, 12 Rue des Barres, 75004; Ⓜ *Hôtel-de-Ville.*

Short-term Rentals and Residence Hotels

If you plan to spend a week or more in Paris, a short-term let may save you money, especially if you're travelling with the family, when eating out for every meal including breakfast can be more expensive than a hotel room. Listings per *arrondissement* can be found in the *Pages Jaunes* under *Location d'appartements.*

Booking from the UK

At Home in Paris, 16 Rue Médéric, 75017, **t** 01 42 12 40 40, **f** 01 42 12 40 48, *www.at-home-in-paris.com*. Studios to six-bedroom flats. Studios €600–1,000 a month, one-bed flats €900–2,200 a month. One month minimum stay. English-speaking staff.

Citadines Apart'Hotels, **t** 08 25 33 33 32, *www.citadines.com*. A large and well-run chain of short-term flat operators, with units available in almost all parts of Paris. Prices vary widely from luxury in the 8ᵉ to cram-'em-in in the 14ᵉ.

Paris Appartements Services, 20 Rue Bachaumont, 75002, *www.paris-appartements-services.fr*, **t** 01 40 28 01 28, **f** 01 40 28 92 01. Studios (€90–150) and one-room (€134–214) apartments of character in central Paris.

Paris Séjour Réservation, France: 90 Av des Champs-Elysées, **t** 01 53 89 10 50, **f** 01 53 89 10 59; USA: 770 North La Salle Street, Suite 500 G, Chicago, Illinois 60610, t (312) 58 77 707, **f** (312) 58 79 887/800 58 27 274, *www.psrparis.com*. Flats to buy or rent. Studios €65–150 per night; one-bed flats €75–255 per night.

Booking from the US

At Home in France, P.O. Box 643, Ashland, OR 97520, **t** (541) 488 9467, **f** (541) 488 9468, *www.athomeinfrance.com*, *info@athomeinfrance.com*. Apartments for rent in Paris, from moderate to deluxe. Minimum stay 7 days.

Doorways Ltd., 900 County Line Road, Bryn Mawr, PA 19010, **t** 800 261 4460, **t** (610) 520 0806, **f** (610) 520 0807, *info@doorwaysltd.com*, *www.villavacations.com*. Apartments for rent in Paris.

New York Habitat, 307 7th Av, Suite 306, New York, NY 10001, **t** (212) 255 8018, **f** (212) 627 1416, *www.nyhabitat.com*. Five hundred apartments throughout Paris; minimum stay three days. Also offer B & B accommodation; minimum stay two nights.

Paris: Entertainment and Nightlife

25

When the last museums and shops close, the City of Light turns on the switch for a night of fun. There are several main circuits: from the Latin Quarter and across the Seine to Les Halles, the trendy new Bastille area, the Butte de Montmartre and Pigalle, St-Germain, Rue Mouffetard, Montparnasse and the Plaisance-Pernety area in the 14e. In a city as full of fashion slaves as Paris, the most *branché* ('plugged-in', literally) clubs change fairly rapidly.

Besides the plethora of posters that cover the Métro stations, cafés and Morris columns, there are weekly guides that come out on Wednesdays, when the cinemas change their programmes: very cheap *Pariscope* (including everything from art exhibitions and museum hours to wife-swapping supper clubs, and in summer an English language section written by *Time Out*, a nightlife hotline, **t** 08 36 68 88 55, and a website, *www.Pariscope.fr*), the similar *L'Officiel des Spectacles*, and *7 à Paris* (same listings as *Pariscope*, but with articles and reviews). The Wednesday *Figaro* has weekly listings; *Libération* has good pieces on art and music; the monthly *Paris Free Voice* has reviews in English.

Film

The Parisians may well be the biggest film junkies in the world, and chances are that, in one of their 320 screens, one will show that obscure flick you've been dying to see for years. Films are a common topic of conversation in the city, often bringing forth some curious and striking cultural differences. You can live in Paris for years and still not understand the city's lively appreciation for Jerry Lewis, or just what they find so alluring in Woody Allen.

Note that films dubbed in French or which were originally made in several languages and are being shown in French are labelled v.f.; if shown in English, it will say *version anglaise*; if in the original language, with French subtitles, they'll say v.o. (*version originale*). Average admission prices are €6–7; students and senior citizens are often eligible for discounts at weekday matinées. In some larger cinemas, the usherette should be tipped 50¢.

Ticket Agents

Concerts, shows, plays, sporting events, etc. may be booked through the tourist office's **Billetel** ticket counter (127 Champs-Elysées, **t** 08 92 68 36 22, Ⓜ *Charles de Gaulle-Etoile* (*open daily 9am–8pm*).

FNAC has ticket offices all over the city and a general number, **t** 01 44 09 18 00.

Virgin Megastore, 52 Champs-Elysées, **t** 01 49 53 50 00, *www.ticketnet.fr*, Ⓜ *George V*, is similar and open until midnight.

Kiosque Théâtre, near 15 Pl de la Madeleine, 8e, Ⓜ *Madeleine*; also on the Parvis de la Gare Montparnasse (*open Tues–Sat 12.30–8 and Sun 12.30–4; closed Sun in July and Aug*). Same-day, half-price theatre tickets, plus a commission; expect a queue.

A Paris institution, the **Cinémathèque** (*www.cinemathequefrancaise.com*) has one of the most extensive film libraries in the world. In the autumn of 2005 it is opening a new headquarters in a Frank Gehry building at 51 Rue de Bercy, 12e, Ⓜ *Gare de Lyon*. Check the website for opening hours.

Forum des Images, Porte St-Eustache in the Forum des Halles, **t** 01 44 76 62 00, *www.forumdesimages.net* (*open Tues–Sun 1–9pm; adm €5.50 for the day*). Films and documentaries on changing themes. Ⓜ *Châtelet-Les Halles*.

Salle Garance at the Pompidou Centre, **t** 01 42 78 37 29, *www.centrepompidou.fr* (*closed Tues; adm €4*). Subtitled films from around the world with French subtitles. Ⓜ *Châtelet, Rambuteau*.

Accattone, 20 Rue Cujas, 5e, **t** 01 46 33 86 86. Lesser-known classics from Russia and Eastern Europe and alternative films from almost everywhere else. **RER** *Luxembourg*.

Action, Grand Action, 5 Rue des Ecoles, 5e, **t** 01 43 29 44 40, Ⓜ *Cardinal Lemoine*; nearby **Action Ecoles**, 23 Rue des Ecoles, **t** 01 43 29 79 89, is smaller. A small Paris chain of cinemas specializing in retrospectives of great old films, most on fresh prints drawn from the negatives.

Dôme IMAX, 1 Place du Dôme, La Défense, **t** 08 36 67 06 06. Known as the 'Largest Wraparound Movie Theatre in the World'. Ⓜ *Grande Arche de La Défense*.

L'Escurial Panorama, 11 Bd de Port-Royal, 13e, **t** 01 47 07 28 04. Plush red-velvet movie palace, showing quality films in v.o. Ⓜ *Les Gobelins*.

L'Entrepôt, 7–9 Rue Francis-de-Pressensé, 14e, **t** 01 45 40 78 38. One of the best: three rooms showing some of the best art and third-world fare in Paris, also a bookshop, bar, satellite and cable TV. Ⓜ *Pernety*.

La Géode, 26 Av Corentin-Cariou, 19e, **t** 01 40 05 12 12, *www.lageode.fr*. Extraordinary OMNIMAX cinema of the Cité des Sciences puts on shows with fish-eye-lens cameras that make you feel as if you were in the centre of the action. Hourly showings Tues–Sun of National-Geographic-type fare for €8.75. Booking strongly suggested in advance for evening showings, same day only. Ⓜ *Porte de la Villette*.

Gaumont Kinopanorama, 60 Av de La Motte-Picquet, 15e, **t** 01 40 30 20 10. Popular, 180° cinema, 70mm film, high definition Showscan (60 images per second) and extraordinary sound (€8.25). Ⓜ *La Motte-Picquet*.

Latina, 20 Rue du Temple, 4e, **t** 01 42 78 47 86. Latin American film specialist. Bar with warm hispanic atmosphere. Ⓜ *Hôtel de Ville*.

Max Linder Panorama, 24 Bd Poissonnière, 9e, **t** 08 36 68 50 52. Most sumptuous and plush, state-of-the-art equipment; great for first-run films in v.o. Ⓜ *Grands Boulevards*.

Grand Rex, 1 Bd Poissonnière, 2e, **t** 01 42 36 83 93. Films are all dubbed into French, but the Rex is a must for lovers of old Hollywood Busby Berkeley 1930s extravaganzas with one of the biggest screens in Europe, 2,750 seats and a great ceiling. Ⓜ *Bonne Nouvelle*.

Studio 28, 10 Rue Tholozé, 18e, **t** 01 46 06 36 07. Founded in 1928, charming, family-run. Films always in v.o. Ⓜ *Abbesses*.

Studio Galande, 42 Rue Galande, 5e, **t** 01 43 26 94 08. Brave little cinema, with lots of old Fellini and Terry Gilliam, and *The Rocky Horror Picture Show* Fri and Sat nights, all in v.o. Ⓜ *St-Michel*.

Trois Luxembourgs, 67 Rue Monsieur-le-Prince, 6e, **t** 01 46 33 97 77. Very basic inside, but worth visiting for its great Dada sign, and innovative offerings on three screens. **RER** *Luxembourg*.

Quartier Latin, 9 Rue Champollion, 5e, **t** 01 43 26 84 65. Small alternative cinema. Ⓜ *Cluny-La Sorbonne*.

Opera, Classical and Contemporary Music

Paris has traditionally had an ambivalent attitude towards classical music. It is the only great European capital without a proper symphony auditorium, not to mention a great orchestra to play in it; even the productions in its lavish new opera house only seldom hit a high note of quality. Thanks to the Ministry of Culture and reforms in education that have brought music into the schools, there is more interest in music than before: there are frequent lunchtime concerts in the churches (listed in *Pariscope*), medieval music and choirs at Sainte-Chapelle and chamber music at the Orangerie at La Bagatelle.

Cité de la Musique, 221 Av Jean Jaurès, 19e, **t** 01 44 84 44 84. Two high tech venues, one home to Pierre Boulez's Ensemble Inter-Contemporain. Ⓜ *Porte de Pantin*.

Opéra de Paris Bastille, Pl de la Bastille, 12e, **t** 0892 89 90 90, *www.opera-de-paris.fr*. Opened by Mitterrand in 1990, the slugfest of controversy over its architecture, management, and obfuscating productions 'for the masses' has diminished to the occasional slap on the wrist. The acoustics, however, are great; tickets are €10–109. Ⓜ *Bastille*.

Opéra Comique, 5 Rue Favart, 2e, **t** 01 42 44 45 40, *www.opera-comique.com*. An older hall used by the Opéra Comique for a repertoire ranging from Lully to Carmen and the occasional operettas. Ⓜ *Richelieu-Drouot*.

Salle Pleyel, 252 Rue du Faubourg-St-Honoré, 8e, **t** 01 45 61 53 00. Where Chopin last played in public; recitals and orchestral performances by the Orchestre Philharmonique de Radio France. Ⓜ *Ternes*.

Théâtre des Champs-Elysées, 15 Av Montaigne, 16e, **t** 01 49 52 50 50. The Paris equivalent of Carnegie Hall, where Josephine Baker first danced in Paris, and a favourite of big-name classical performers; also some opera. Ⓜ *Franklin D. Roosevelt*.

Théâtre du Châtelet, Pl du Châtelet, 1er, **t** 01 40 28 28 40. 130-year-old theatre that saw the first season of the Ballets Russes in 1909, and since 1980 very successfully run by the City of Paris, with better opera than the Bastille. Ⓜ *Châtelet*.

Théâtre de la Ville, 2 Pl du Châtelet, 4e, **t** 01 42 74 22 77. Excellent city-run theatre: every kind of music, from piano recitals to jazz to African songs. Ⓜ *Châtelet*.

Jazz, Blues, Rock and World Music

In 1925, when La Revue Nègre opened in Paris, it set off a craze for *le jazz hot*, Sidney Bechet, Mezz Mezzrow, the Charleston and Black Bottom so overwhelming that it undermined the old *bals musette*. The French had to rewrite the rules, saying that half the members of any band had to be French nationals – a problem the Americans got round by having the French musicians just sit there, holding their instruments. By the next decade France began to catch up by producing its own jazz, led by violinist Stéphane Grappelli and the three-fingered guitarist Django Reinhardt, while continuing to welcome and support black Americans.

Still considered the jazz capital of Europe, Paris since the early 1970s has been in the forefront of another phenomenon: world music, with its African, North African, Latin, Brazilian and Caribbean zouk clubs, where many modern stars found their first audiences. Paris is also the base of Cheb Khaled, the best-known *raï* singer, whom some people call the Algerian Jim Morrison.

Check out the smaller independent magazines for their day-by-day listings. Cithea (*see below*) has stacks of these, of which the most important is ***Lylo***, a free rag published every three weeks, and generally available in bars, record shops or directly from their office at 55 Rue des Vinaigriers, 10e, and includes a special ravers' page for techno addicts. ***Nova Mag***, available in any kiosk, is also very useful for all events featuring the aforementioned music, as well as techno. **Nova 101.5 FM** broadcasts a daily listing of parties. **Radio FG** (Gay Frequency, 98.2 FM) is one of the capital's biggest and hippest radio stations, playing exclusively chemical sounds, house and techno. Radio FG often takes part in the events at Queen's and other famous clubs, and between 7.30 and 9pm they broadcast all the essential parties in Paris and checkpoints for underground raves around the city.

Major bar hot spots are around the Carrefour de l'Odéon, the Marais, Rue du Trésor, the Butte aux Cailles (behind the Place d'Italie), Place Clichy and of course Place Pigalle. Clubs are concentrated in the same areas and tend to charge admission or an exorbitant price for a first drink.

Music Bars and Clubs

Buddha Bar, Rue Boissy d'Anglas, 8e, t 01 53 05 90 00. A chic bar for chic people with a huge main dance floor. Drinks are pretty expensive; pop in and see the 20ft statue of Buddha, the biggest in town. Ⓜ *Concorde*.

La Chapelle des Lombards, 19 Rue de Lappe, 11e, **t** 01 43 57 24 24, *http://chapelle.lombards.free.fr* (*open Tues–Sun*). Some of the best, newest, affordable Caribbean and African music. Ⓜ *Bastille*.

Cithea, 112 Rue Oberkampf, 11e, **t** 01 40 21 70 95 (*open daily 10pm–6am, concert at 11pm; adm Sun–Thurs free, Fri and Sat €7.70*). Live soul, blues, jazz, funk, etc. A favourite of local musicians, but unfortunately there's not much room and it gets often overcrowded. If you can squeeze in, fun is guaranteed. Free entrance most nights. Ⓜ *Ménilmontant*.

Divan du Monde, 75 Rue des Martyrs, 18e, **t** 01 55 79 09 52 (*open daily 11.30pm–dawn; adm €8–20*). Exciting club dedicated to a wide variety of world music and dance, mostly from South America. Ⓜ *Pigalle*.

Flèche d'Or, 102bis Rue de Bagnolet, 20e, **t** 01 43 72 04 23 (*open Tues–Sun 6pm–2am*). Parisians often say they particularly like the Flèche d'Or: it is in a former train station, is charming, drinks are cheap after 9pm, food is available, and the music is always good – roots, rock, reggae and funk, with many live performers and jam sessions. During the day, you can hang around reading the papers and playing chess or cards; there are sometimes exhibitions of local artists. Don't hesitate to phone to find out what's up. Entrance might be charged but it will never be expensive. Ⓜ *Alexandre Dumas, Gambetta*.

Folie's Pigalle, 11 Place Pigalle, 9e, **t** 01 48 78 55 25 (*open Tues–Fri and Sun midnight –6am, Sat until noon, shows 8–11; adm €15–25, show €23*). An old cabaret that hasn't really changed much. The sound is mainly house and garage, with disco-funk on Mon and rap on Sun. A popular place for a nightcap. At 7am, half the population will be going to bed, while others will still be arriving. One dance floor and a large balcony (sometimes reserved for VIP nights). Ⓜ *Pigalle*.

Jazz and Blues

Le Bilboquet, 13 Rue St-Benoît, 6e, **t** 01 45 48 81 84. St-Germain club, vintage 1947, on the main drag of cool jazz in the 1950s; popular with tourists remembering golden days. Pricey; average French jazz. Doors open 10pm. Ⓜ *St-Germain-des-Prés*.

Caveau de la Huchette, 5 Rue de la Huchette, 5e, **t** 01 43 26 65 05. Since 1946 the home of traditional live jazz and bebop in a 14th-century cellar. Doors open 9.30pm. Ⓜ *St-Michel*.

Au Duc des Lombards, 42 Rue des Lombards, 1er, **t** 01 42 33 22 88. One of the best; popular, friendly, dimly lit lounge, with jazz piano, trios and crooners ranging from excellent to competent (*daily 9.30pm–3am*). Ⓜ *Châtelet*.

New Morning, 7–9 Rue des Petites-Ecuries, 10e, **t** 01 45 23 51 41. Not very cosy, but lots of room and fine acoustics. *The* place to find international jazz all-stars and first-rate world music, although it has recently opened its doors to a larger range of musicians. Ⓜ *Château d'Eau*.

Opus Jazz and Soul Club, 167 Quai de Valmy, 10e, **t** 01 40 34 70 00 (*open Tues–Sat from 7pm*). Swell bar with a mezzanine where you can easily sit and have an affordable drink while listening to funk rock. Ring them up for their programme. Entrance fee for live bands. Ⓜ *Château Landon*.

Petit Journal Montparnasse, 13 Rue du Commandant-Mouchotte, 14e, **t** 01 43 21 56 70 (*open Mon–Sat 12–3.30pm and 8pm–2am; closed July and Aug*). One of the best, with enough space for big bands from France and abroad as well. Ⓜ *Gaîté*.

Slow Club, 130 Rue de Rivoli, 1er, **t** 01 42 33 84 30 (*open Tues–Sat from 10pm*). The late Miles Davis's favourite jazz club in Paris, and a must for lovers of swing, New Orleans and traditional jazz. Ⓜ *Châtelet-Les Halles*.

Sunset, 60 Rue des Lombards, 1er, **t** 01 40 26 46 60 (*open Mon–Sat 9pm–2am; €8–22*). Jazz, fusion, bebop, in the redecorated cellar-cum-tiled Métro tunnel. Also includes **Le Sunside, t** 01 40 26 21 25 for accoustic jazz. Ⓜ *Châtelet-Les Halles*.

Major Concert Venues

Le Bataclan, 50 Bd Voltaire, 11e, **t** 01 43 14 35 35. Not really comfortable as you won't find any place to sit, but surely one of the best spots to listen to roots and reggae music. Ⓜ *Oberkampf, St-Amboise*.

La Cigale, 120 Bd de Rochechouart, 18e, **t** 01 49 25 89 99. Nicely restored vaudeville theatre with the seats removed; plenty of rock. Ⓜ *Pigalle*.

Elysée Montmartre (*see* p.306).

Olympia, 28 Bd des Capucines, 9e, **t** 01 47 42 25 49. Delightful Art Deco hall, where Piaf and other stars of music-hall performed, and still do, with the likes of Tom Waits other days. Ⓜ *Madeleine*.

Palais Omnisport Bercy, 8 Bd de Bercy, 12e, **t** 08 03 03 00 31. The biggest, with 16,000 seats, expensive, and for music obnoxious in almost every possible way, though it puts on more concerts than any other place in this list. Ⓜ *Bercy*.

Zénith, 211 Av Jean-Jaurès, 19e, **t** 01 42 08 60 00. La Villette's inflatable, pop music hall decorated with a red aeroplane about to nosedive. Ⓜ *Porte de Pantin*.

Nightclubs, Discothèques and *Bals Musette*

Unfortunately, most discos in Paris take themselves seriously and are full of uncool people posing for one another's benefit. Your appearance tends to be all-important and the bouncers at the door can be picky if you're not their type.Entrance fees and first drinks are usually €7, €10 weekends.

Alizée Club, 14 Rue de la Croix-Nivert, 15e, **t** 01 56 58 09 09 (*open Fri–Sun*). Great Caribbean sounds, with lots of reggae and ragga. Ⓜ *Cambronne-La Fourche*. **Les Bains Douches**, 17 Rue du Bourg-L'Abbé, 3e, **t** 01 48 87 01 80 (*open 11pm–6am; restaurant open until 1am; adm €15.25*). The ultimate place for beautiful people. Ⓜ *Etienne Marcel*.

Le Batofar, 11 Quai François Mauriac, 13e, **t** 01 56 29 10 00 (*open Tues–Sun*). On a boat on the Seine. Specialized in drum n' bass, jungle, sweet techno, with jazz on Mondays. Its bus will take you home. Ⓜ *Bibliothèque-F*.

La Casbah, 18–20 Rue de la Forge-Royale, 11e, **t** 01 43 71 04 39 (*open Thurs–Sat*). Re-creation of Rick's in Casablanca; Moroccan cuisine in the restaurant (book), funk, house, acid and rock on the dance floor. Ⓜ *Ledru-Rollin*.

Elysée Montmartre, 72 Bd de Rochechouart, 18e, **t** 01 44 92 45 45, *www.elyseemontmartre.com*. In a hall designed by Eiffel, the place where La Goulue first cancanned now hosts alternative and world music bands, with one of the best dance floors in Paris. It's also used for big parties organized by radio stations and clubs. Golden oldies, twist, disco, reggae every other Saturday night. Ⓜ *Anvers*.

La Java, 105 Rue du Faubourg-du-Temple, 10e, **t** 01 42 02 20 52. A grand old music hall opened in the 1920s, where Piaf got her first break; Thurs and Fri live salsa, Sat *bal musette*, Sun night Brazilian. Ⓜ *Goncourt, Belleville*.

Le Latina Café, 114, Av des Champs-Elysées, 8e, **t** 01 42 89 98 89. Dance floor in the basement – great for trendy salsa-lovers. Live concerts broadcast from here. And if you are a bit rusty, there are salsa classes on Sun nights (€7.70, including a drink). Ⓜ *Georges V*.

Stringfellow's, 27 Av des Ternes, 17e, **t** 01 47 66 45 00. Sophisto-sister disco of the one in London, with bookcases, plush sofas, and the occasional celebrity; good restaurant, and disco after 12.30am. Ⓜ *Ternes*.

Gay Music Bars and Clubs

Club 18 du Palais Royal, 18 Rue de Beaujolais, 1er, **t** 01 42 97 52 13. Lots of mirrors and techno in the basement disco, quieter upstairs in the bar and mezzanine. Ⓜ *Palais Royal, Bourse*.

L'Insolite, 33 Rue des Petits-Champs, 1er, **t** 01 40 20 98 59 (*open nightly from 11pm*). Small club playing mainly disco music apart from Fiesta Night on Sunday. Popular with over 30s. Ⓜ *Pyramides*.

Bar Duplex, 25 Rue Michel-Le-Comte, 3e, **t** 01 42 72 80 86. Friendly artsy gay and straight music bar with affordable drink prices. Ⓜ *Rambuteau*.

Le Bear's Den, 6 Rue des Lombards, 4e, **t** 01 42 71 08 20 (*open daily 4pm–2am, Happy Hour 5–8*). Where beards and moustaches are all the rage. Tea dances on Sun afternoons, square dances on Weds evenings, Nordic apperitfs on Tues afternoons. Ⓜ *Hôtel-de-Ville* or *Châtelet*.

Le Queen, 102 Av Champs-Elysées, 8e, **t** 01 53 89 08 90. The hippest and most sophisticated gay disco draws a fair mix of stylish heteros as well, as long as they look like one of the beautiful people; special Boy night on Thurs; free hetero night on Wed; disco Mon. Ⓜ *Rue Montmartre*.

Les Piétons, 8 Rue des Lombards, 4e, **t** 01 48 87 82 87. New cool music at an essentially Spanish music bar in the Marais with *tapas* and a Sunday brunch. Ⓜ *Hôtel de Ville*.

Le Vagabond, 14 Rue Thérèse, 1er, **t** 01 42 96 27 23. First gay bar-restaurant in Paris, cosy atmosphere. Ⓜ *Pyramides*.

Lesbian Clubs

La Champmeslé, 4 Rue Chabanais, 2e, **t** 01 42 96 85 20. Risqué decor and cheap drinks, and a cabaret every Thurs night (*open from 5pm till morning light, closed Sun*). Ⓜ *Pyramides*.

Chansons

Paris's own art form, first popularized by Aristide Bruant, revived in the 1950s and '60s by Jacques Brel, Georges Brassens and Juliette Greco (who's still alive and kicking) and currently being revived again for both the Parisians and tourists.

Au Lapin Agile, 22 Rue des Saules, 18e, **t** 01 46 06 85 87 (*open 9pm–2am, closed Mon; adm €24 including drink*). A valiant attempt at bringing old French traditional song back to life to busloads of Japanese tourists. Ⓜ *Lamarck-Caulaincourt*.

Cabarets, Drag and Ethnic Shows

Paris rivals Las Vegas for over the top kitsch-and-glitter-oozing, tit-and-feather spectaculars, invariably advertised as 'sophisticated', for fleecing tourists, provincials and businessmen.

Club des Poètes, 30 Rue de Bourgogne, 7e, **t** 01 47 05 06 03 (*closed Sun; dinner and show €22–30.50*). A treat for fans of French poetry, with a spectacle featuring the greats from Villon to Boris Vian. Ⓜ *Varenne*.

Crazy Horse Saloon, 12 Av George-V, 8e, **t** 01 47 23 32 32 (*shows Sun–Fri 8.30 and 11, Sat 8, 10.15, 12.15; €49–90 at the bar, dinner-spectâcle €125–65*). High temple of naked Barbie dolls with names like Bettina Uranium and Pussy Duty-Free dressed in leather straps. Ⓜ *Alma-Marceau*.

Lido, 116 Av des Champs-Elysées, 8e, **t** 01 40 76 56 10 (*dinner and show €145, show only €90 with champagne or €130 at the bar at 10 and midnight*). The best special effects perk up the act of the 60 Bluebell Girls. Ⓜ *George V*.

Michou, 80 Rue des Martyrs, 18e, **t** 01 46 06 16 04 (*dinner and show €90; show starts 8.30pm*). Reserve a place at Michou, a funny satirical drag show that draws even the celebrities to see themselves being parodied. Reserve. Ⓜ *Abbesses*.

Moulin-Rouge, 82 Bd de Clichy, 11e, **t** 01 53 09 82 82, *www.moulin-rouge.fr* (*open daily from 7pm, show at 9 and 11; adm from €87, with dinner from €140*). The most famous and the most Las-Vegasey of the lot, with its guest stars and cancanning Doriss Girls. Ⓜ *Blanche*.

Le Paradis Latin, 28 Rue du Cardinal-Lemoine, 5e, **t** 01 43 25 28 28, *www.paradis-latin.com* (*dinner-spectacle Wed–Mon at 8pm, from €109*). In an old theatre built by Eiffel, this is the one music hall-cum-cabaret with Parisian customers. Ⓜ *Cardinal Lemoine*.

Dance

There's a good range of dance to see in Paris, but little of it's home-grown, thanks to the decision of the Culture Ministry to subsidize companies out in the provinces, rather than in Paris. Many of the already listed theatres and concert halls schedule dance performances, often by visiting companies, and each week's listings seem to bring forth new studios or theatre venues.

Places especially dedicated to dance in Paris are:

Opéra de Paris-Garnier, Place de l'Opéra, 9e, **t** 0892 89 90 90, *www.opera-de-paris.fr*. Home of the Ballet de l'Opéra de Paris. The exterior has just been renovated and looks fantastic. Guided tour during the week; call for info. Ⓜ *Opéra*.

Studio Regard du Cygne, 210 Rue de Belleville, 20e, **t** 01 40 38 38 46. Devoted to innovative international companies. Ⓜ *Place des Fêtes*.

Café de la Danse, 5 Passage Louis-Philippe, 11e, **t** 01 47 00 57 59. The place to see small innovative contemporary companies. Ⓜ *Bastille*.

Theatre and Performance Arts

The first theatre in Paris was built by Cardinal Richelieu in the Palais Royal in 1641, and the trickery of the stage machines played as big a role in the performances as the music and dance. Over the last 350 years, Paris has come full circle: the blockbusters in its theatres are multimedia extravaganzas with extraordinary special effects. The only serious contemporary dramas are translations from the West End in London. Otherwise, French-speakers can still find plenty of Racine and Molière from the excellent Comédie-Française and frequent revivals of Ionesco, Anouilh, Genet and company, not to mention Paris's perennial bland boulevard comedies, inevitably about extra marital hanky-panky.

Bouffes du Nord, 37bis Bd de la Chapelle, 10e, **t** 01 46 07 34 50. Former neighbourhood music hall that has become Peter Brook's baby; now a venue for acclaimed experimental productions. Ⓜ *La Chapelle*.

Cartoucherie Théâtre du Soleil, Rte du Champ-de-Manœuvre, 12e, **t** 01 43 74 24 08. Ariane Mnouchkine's five-stage complex is home to perhaps the most thought-provoking theatre in Paris, including plays in their original language. Phone ahead to reserve at the theatres: **La Tempête**, **t** 01 43 28 36 36; **L'Epée de Bois**, **t** 01 43 08 39 74; **Le Chaudron**, **t** 01 43 28 97 04; **Aquarium**, **t** 01 43 74 99 61, Ⓜ *Château de Vincennes*, linked with a free shuttle bus.

Théâtre National de Chaillot, Pl du Trocadéro, 16e, **t** 01 47 27 81 15. Frequently the stage for lavish productions of Brecht *et al*. Ⓜ *Trocadéro*.

Comédie-Française, 2 Rue de Richelieu, 1er, **t** 01 44 58 15 15. Founded in 1680 and playing in the beautiful Salle Richelieu in the Palais Royal; excellent productions of the old classics by Molière, Beaumarchais, Marivaux and Racine, also foreign classics in translation; seats sold two weeks in advance. Ⓜ *Palais Royal*.

Comédie Italienne, 17 Rue de la Gaîté, 14e, **t** 01 43 21 22 22. The old Comédie Italienne was a rival of the Comédie-Française until Louis XIV banished them for calling Mme de Maintenon a prude and the king Monsieur de Maintenon. In a poky theatre among 'live sex' shops, the revived company puts on Goldoni, Commedia dell'Arte and Pirandello in French. Ⓜ *Edgar Quinet*.

Odéon Théâtre de l'Europe, 1 Pl Paul-Claudel, 6e, **t** 01 44 41 36 36. Shares resources with Comédie-Française, its fellow state theatre; Grande Salle is often the stage of the Théâtre Populaire National; Petit Odéon sees alternative theatre and foreign companies' productions in their own language. Ⓜ *Odéon*.

Palais-Royal, 38 Rue de Montpensier, 1er, **t** 01 42 97 59 81. Loveliest place to take in a boulevard comedy. Ⓜ *Palais Royal*.

Theâtre de la Bastille , 76 Rue de la Roquette, **t** 01 43 57 42 14. Top quality modern theatre and dance. Ⓜ *Bastille*.

Théâtre de la Huchette, 23 Rue de la Huchette, 5e, **t** 01 43 26 38 99. They've been doing Ionesco's *La Cantatrice Chauve* and *La Leçon* for 40 years. Ⓜ *St-Michel*.

Théâtre National de la Colline, 15 Rue Malte-Brun, 20e, **t** 01 44 62 52 52. Dedicated to contemporary European works. Ⓜ *Gambetta*.

Théâtre de Nesle, 8 Rue de Nesle, 6e, **t** 01 46 34 61 04. Often hosts performances of the city's English-language companies. Ⓜ *Odéon*.

Théâtre de la Porte St-Martin, 18 Bd St-Martin, 10e, **t** 01 42 08 00 32. Often sparkling, very Parisian productions and one-man shows. Ⓜ *Strasbourg-St-Denis*.

Index

Main page references are in **bold**. Page references to maps are in *italics*.

London and Paris have been indexed separately. The Paris index follows the London index.

London

Paris